P9-CDU-978

The College
Writer

A Guide to Thinking, Writing, and Researching

Second Edition

Randall VanderMey
Westmont College

Verne Meyer
Dordt College

John Van Rys
Redeemer University College

Dave Kemper

Pat Sebranek

WITHDRAWN

HOUGHTON MIFFLIN COMPANY
BOSTON   NEW YORK

Publisher: Pat Coryell
Editor in Chief: Suzanne Phelps Weir
Senior Development Editor: Judith Fifer
Assistant Editor: Anne Leung
Editorial Associate: John McHugh
Senior Project Editor: Aileen Mason
Editorial Assistant: Susan Miscio
Manufacturing Manager: Karen B. Fawcett
Senior Marketing Manager: Cindy Graff Cohen
Marketing Assistant: Kelly Kunert

Cover Design: Tammy Hintz
Illustrations: Chris Krenzke
CD: Chris Erickson, Janae Sebranek, Mark Fairweather, Steve Augustyn, Jason Reynolds, Lester Smith
Editorial: J. Robert King, Claire Ziffer, Laura Bachman, Steven E. Schend, Stephen D. Sullivan, Joyce Becker Lee, Mariellen Hanrahan, Lois Krenzke, Betsy Rasmussen, Pat Kornelis, Kim Van Es, Sarah Den Boer, Leah Zuidema
Production: Christine Rieker, Kathy Strom, April Barrons, Colleen Belmont, Ellen Leitheusser, Karl Leitheusser, Judy Kerkhoff, Ron Bachman, Jean Varley

"A Hanging" from SHOOTING AN ELEPHANT AND OTHER ESSAYS by George Orwell, copyright 1950 by the Estate of Sonia B. Orwell and renewed by Sonia Pitt-Rivers. Reprinted by permission of Harcourt, Inc.

(Other credits appear on page 680, which constitutes an extension of the copyright page.)

Copyright © 2007 by Houghton Mifflin Company. All rights reserved.

No part of this book may be reproduced or transmitted in any form or by any means, electronic or mechanical, including photocopying and recording, or by any information storage or retrieval system without the prior written permission of Houghton Mifflin Company unless such copying is expressly permitted by federal copyright law. Address inquiries to College Permissions, 222 Berkeley Street, Boston, MA 02116-3764.

Printed in the U.S.A.

Library of Congress Control Number: 2005937206

ISBN 13 (paper): 978-0-618-64205-2
ISBN 10 (paper): 0-618-64205-6

ISBN 13 (cloth): 978-0-618-64202-1
ISBN 10 (cloth): 0-618-64202-1

2 3 4 5 6 7 8 9 –DOC– 10 09 08 07 06

Preface

The first edition of *The College Writer* succeeded in its goal of providing thorough yet accessible coverage of the writing process for today's visually oriented students. The text also included a wealth of rhetorical strategies that instructors and students found accessible and helpful.

The new second edition reinforces these strengths with enhanced coverage of many important topics such as analyzing the rhetorical situation, evaluating sources, avoiding plagiarism, and developing visual literacy. The second edition also has sixteen new professional readings to better model excellent writing.

Key Features of *The College Writer*, Second Edition

- Coverage of critical thinking in Chapter 1 and throughout the text helps students learn to analyze, synthesize, and develop sound arguments.

- Tabbed sections help students quickly find pertinent topics, while the colorful design and visuals reinforce the concepts and aid retention.

- The unique at-a-glance format presents each concept in a one- or two-page spread for accessibility, while the friendly coaching tone helps students feel at ease with the material.

- Coverage of drafting, writing, revising, and proofreading is complete and thorough, with sample paragraphs and visuals that walk students through the rhetorical situation (identifying purpose, audience, and context).

- Both student and professional samples of each type of writing are included in the text, so students can select appropriate models. A new literary-analysis model shows a thorough study of a short story.

- A new model MLA paper illustrates a wide variety of research-writing practices, including the use of graphics. Expanded coverage of MLA documentation, especially for electronic sources, helps students credit their sources.

- Thorough coverage of research methods, including Internet research, helps students conduct research, document sources, and avoid plagiarism.

- The handbook section covers key points of grammar, mechanics, and punctuation, and is reinforced by exercises available to students on the text's companion website, <**www.thecollegewriter.com**>.

A thematic table of contents at the front of the book supports instructors who prefer to organize their instruction around themes, such as character and conscience, ethics and ideology, and memory and tradition.

New to This Edition

Critical viewing. The new edition of *The College Writer* now includes coverage of critical viewing in addition to existing coverage of critical reading, writing, and thinking. In today's multimedia environment, students constantly encounter images that they must learn to examine, evaluate, and utilize in their work. A new section in Chapter 1, "Critical Thinking Through Reading, Viewing, and Writing," presents strategies for viewing and evaluating images such as fine art, advertisements, and websites. Critical viewing is also integrated throughout the text in chapter features such as Guidelines and Checklists.

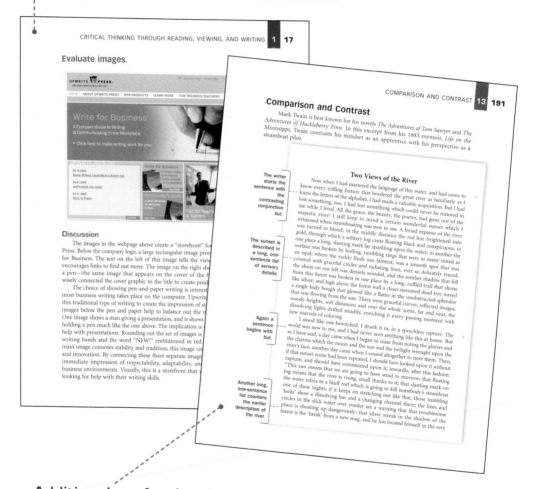

Additional professional essays. In Part II, "A Reader: Strategies and Models," sixteen professional readings have been added to the text to provide timely and well-written samples for students to model. As in the first edition, student models are presented first in each chapter, followed by two to four professional readings. (All student models from the first edition are available at <**www.thecollegewriter.com**>.)

More diversity in reading topics. Reading selections have been added to reflect both national and international perspectives and to feature topics of significant interest to students, such as Jack Shaheen's "The Media's View of Arabs," Richard Rodriguez's "None of This Is Fair," and Debra Dickerson's "Who Shot Johnny?"

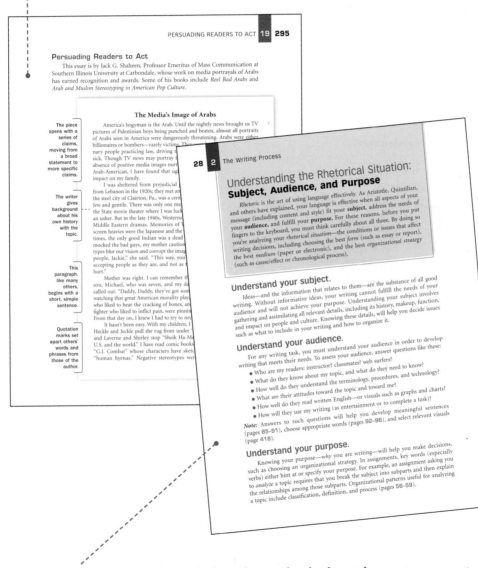

PERSUADING READERS TO ACT **19** **295**

Persuading Readers to Act

This essay is by Jack G. Shaheen, Professor Emeritus of Mass Communication at Southern Illinois University at Carbondale, whose work on media portrayals of Arabs has earned recognition and awards. Some of his books include *Reel Bad Arabs* and *Arab and Muslim Stereotyping in American Pop Culture.*

The Media's Image of Arabs

The piece opens with a series of claims, moving from a broad statement to more specific claims.

America's bogyman is the Arab. Until the nightly news brought us TV pictures of Palestinian boys being punched and beaten, almost all portraits of Arabs seen in America were dangerously threatening. Arabs were either billionaires or bombers—rarely victims. They in nary people practicing law, driving t sick. Though TV news may portray t absence of positive media images nurt Arab-American, I have found that ug impact on my family.

The writer gives background about his own history with the topic.

I was sheltered from prejudicial from Lebanon in the 1920s; they met an the steel city of Clairton, Pa., was a cent Jew and gentile. There was only one ma the State movie theater where I was luck an usher. But in the late 1940s, Westerns Middle Eastern dramas. Memories of screen heavies were the Japanese and the times, the only good Indian was a dead mocked the bad guys, my mother cautior types blur our vision and corrupt the imag people, Jackie," she said. "This way, you accepting people as they are, and not as hurt."

This paragraph, like many others, begins with a short, simple sentence.

Mother was right. I can remember th son, Michael, who was seven, and my da called out: "Daddy, Daddy they've got son watching that great American morality play who liked to hear the cracking of bones, an fighter who liked to inflict pain, were pinnin From that day on, I knew I had to try to net

Quotation marks set apart others' words and phrases from those of the author.

It hasn't been easy. With my children, I Heckle and Jeckle pull the rug from under and Laverne and Shirley stop "Sheik Ha-M U.S. and the world." I have read comic books "G.I. Combat" whose characters have sketc "human hyenas." Negative stereotypes wer

28 **2** The Writing Process

Understanding the Rhetorical Situation: Subject, Audience, and Purpose

Rhetoric is the art of using language effectively. As Aristotle, Quintilian, and others have explained, your language is effective when all aspects of your message (including content and style) fit your **subject**, address the needs of your **audience**, and fulfill your **purpose.** For these reasons, before you put fingers to the keyboard, you must think carefully about all three. By doing so you're analyzing your *rhetorical situation*—the conditions or issues that affect writing decisions, including choosing the best *form* (such as essay or report), the best *medium* (paper or electronic), and the best *organizational strategy* (such as cause/effect or chronological process).

Understand your subject.

Ideas—and the information that relates to them—are the substance of all good writing. Without informative ideas, your writing cannot fulfill the needs of your audience and will not achieve your purpose. Understanding your subject involves gathering and assimilating all relevant details, including its history, makeup, function, and impact on people and culture. Knowing these details, will help you decide issues such as what to include in your writing and how to organize it.

Understand your audience.

For any writing task, you must understand your audience in order to develop writing that meets their needs. To assess your audience, answer questions like these:

- Who are my readers: instructor? classmates? web surfers?
- What do they know about my topic, and what do they need to know?
- How well do they understand the terminology, procedures, and technology?
- What are their attitudes toward the topic and toward me?
- How well do they read written English—or visuals such as graphs and charts?
- How will they use my writing (as entertainment or to complete a task)?

Note: Answers to such questions will help you develop meaningful sentences (pages 85–91), choose appropriate words (pages 92–96), and select relevant visuals (page 418).

Understand your purpose.

Knowing your purpose—*why* you are writing—will help you make decisions, such as choosing an organizational strategy. In assignments, key words (especially verbs) either hint at or specify your purpose. For example, an assignment asking you to *analyze* a topic requires that you break the subject into subparts and then explain the relationships among those subparts. Organizational patterns useful for analyzing a topic include classification, definition, and process (pages 56–59).

Enhanced coverage of the rhetorical situation. Chapter 3 of *The College Writer* now includes more grounding in the history of rhetoric and added coverage of audience, purpose, and subject. Later chapters continue to expand on discussion of the rhetorical situation.

A separate chapter on Internet research. This revised chapter provides special guidance in conducting Internet research and evaluating and acknowledging sources found on the web, as well as avoiding Internet plagiarism in the research process.

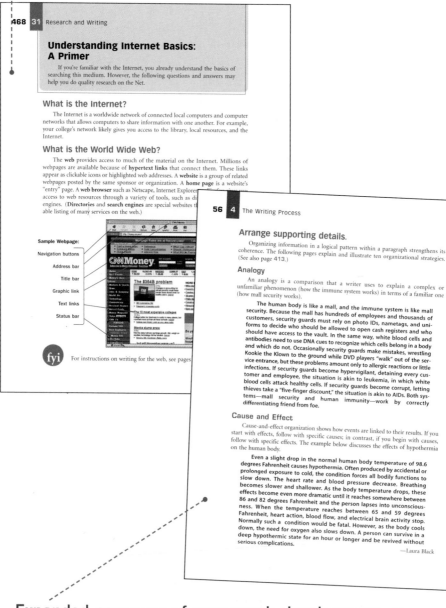

468 31 Research and Writing

Understanding Internet Basics: A Primer

If you're familiar with the Internet, you already understand the basics of searching this medium. However, the following questions and answers may help you do quality research on the Net.

What is the Internet?

The Internet is a worldwide network of connected local computers and computer networks that allows computers to share information with one another. For example, your college's network likely gives you access to the library, local resources, and the Internet.

What is the World Wide Web?

The **web** provides access to much of the material on the Internet. Millions of webpages are available because of **hypertext links** that connect them. These links appear as clickable icons or highlighted web addresses. A **website** is a group of related webpages posted by the same sponsor or organization. A **home page** is a website's "entry" page. A **web browser** such as Netscape, Internet Explorer access to web resources through a variety of tools, such as di engines. (**Directories** and **search engines** are special websites th able listing of many services on the web.)

Sample Webpage:

Navigation buttons
Address bar
Title bar
Graphic link
Text links
Status bar

For instructions on writing for the web, see pages

---

56 4 The Writing Process

Arrange supporting details.

Organizing information in a logical pattern within a paragraph strengthens its coherence. The following pages explain and illustrate ten organizational strategies. (See also page 413.)

Analogy

An analogy is a comparison that a writer uses to explain a complex or unfamiliar phenomenon (how the immune system works) in terms of a familiar one (how mall security works).

> The human body is like a mall, and the immune system is like mall security. Because the mall has hundreds of employees and thousands of customers, security guards must rely on photo IDs, nametags, and uniforms to decide who should be allowed to open cash registers and who should have access to the vault. In the same way, white blood cells and antibodies need to use DNA cues to recognize which cells belong in a body and which do not. Occasionally security guards make mistakes, wrestling Kookie the Klown to the ground while DVD players "walk" out of the service entrance, but these problems amount only to allergic reactions or little infections. If security guards become hypervigilant, detaining every customer and employee, the situation is akin to leukemia, in which white blood cells attack healthy cells. If security guards become corrupt, letting thieves take a "five-finger discount," the situation is akin to AIDs. Both systems—mall security and human immunity—work by correctly differentiating friend from foe.

Cause and Effect

Cause-and-effect organization shows how events are linked to their results. If you start with effects, follow with specific causes; in contrast, if you begin with causes, follow with specific effects. The example below discusses the effects of hypothermia on the human body.

> Even a slight drop in the normal human body temperature of 98.6 degrees Fahrenheit causes hypothermia. Often produced by accidental or prolonged exposure to cold, the condition forces all bodily functions to slow down. The heart rate and blood pressure decrease. Breathing becomes slower and shallower. As the body temperature drops, these effects become even more dramatic until it reaches somewhere between 86 and 82 degrees Fahrenheit and the person lapses into unconsciousness. When the temperature reaches between 65 and 59 degrees Fahrenheit, heart action, blood flow, and electrical brain activity stop. Normally such a condition would be fatal. However, as the body cools down, the need for oxygen also slows down. A person can survive in a deep hypothermic state for an hour or longer and be revived without serious complications.

> —Laura Black

Expanded coverage of paragraph development. The paragraph section now includes models of ten organizational strategies.

Expanded coverage of style. Included are enhanced sections on passive and active voice, strong versus weak verbs, and other stylistic weaknesses.

Revised oral presentations. This chapter has been revised to include coverage of multimedia formats for presentations.

Expanded coverage of ESL issues. The completely revised ESL chapter presents solutions to special challenges for non-native English speakers. The CD-ROM includes tutorials that help the students understand the writing process and the forms of writing.

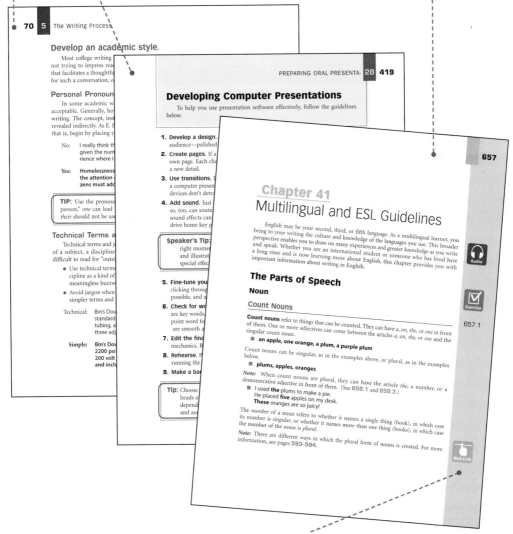

Integration of multimedia components. The multimedia components in *The College Writer*—CD-ROM, website, and practice exercises in both print and electronic form—expand on and enhance the text.

Supplements for the Student

The CD-ROM for *The College Writer* features the entire text in a searchable format, as well as audio and video tutorials, additional models, and grammar exercises.

The Online Study Center at <www.thecollegewriter.com> offers grammar exercises, writing assignments, student writing samples, annotated readings, reading-comprehension exercises, journal support, and links to other helpful sites. Icons in the text margins integrate the CD-ROM, Online Study Center, and exercises with the text.

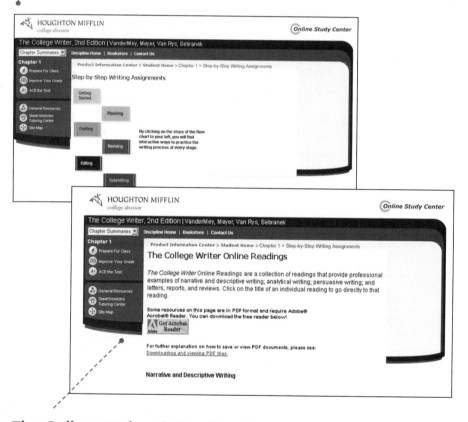

The College Writer Online Readings is an additional bank of fourteen professional readings that can be packaged with the text. Students receive a special passkey to access these supplementary readings.

An Exercise Booklet is available to be packaged with the text. It provides a number of exercises for grammar, style, punctuation, mechanics, spelling, and ESL.

SMARTHINKING™ links students to experienced writing instructors for one-on-one online tutoring during peak study hours.

Supplements for the Instructor

The *Instructor's Resource Manual*, available in print and on the Online Teaching Center, contains an overview of the course, sample syllabi, chapter summaries, and teaching suggestions.

The Online Teaching Center at <www.thecollegewriter.com> has a downloadable version of the *Instructor's Resource Manual*, assessment rubrics, learning objectives, and access to all materials in the Online Study Center.

The WriteSpace Online Writing Program is an integrated, customizable classroom-management system with a wide variety of content that can be administered as self-paced exercises or gradable exams. WriteSpace delivers exercises, diagnostic tests, assignments, and learning modules for more effective writing, as well as access to SMARTHINKING™ online tutoring.

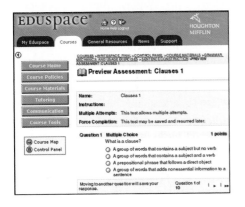

Acknowledgments

The authors wish to express their gratitude to the following people who have contributed their valuable time, energy, and ideas in the development of *The College Writer* and its supplements:

Instructors: Mary Adams, *Peru State College;* Jim Addison, *Western Carolina University;* Susan Aguila, *Palm Beach Community College;* Cathryn Amdahl, *Harrisburg Area Community College;* Edmund August, *McKendree College;* Richard Baker, *Adams State College;* Thomas G. Beverage, *Coastal Carolina Community College;* Patricia Blaine, *Paducah Community College;* Tammie Bob, *College of DuPage;* Candace Boeck, *San Diego State University;* Charley Boyd, *Genesee Community College;* Deborah Bradford, *Bridgewater State College;* Linda Brender, *Macomb Community College;* Colleen M. Burke, *Rasmussen College;* Vicki Byard, *Northeastern Illinois University;* Susan Callender, *Sinclair Community College;* Sandra Camillo, *Finger Lakes Community College;* Sandy Cavanah, *Hopkinsville Community College;* Annette Cedarholm, *Snead State Community College;* James William Chichetto, *Stonehill College;* Sandra Clark, *Anderson University;* Beth Conomos, *Erie Community College, SUNY;* Keith Coplin, *Colby Community College;* Sue Cornett, *St. Petersburg College;* Debra Cumberland, *Winona State University;* David Daniel, *Newbury College;* Sarah

Dangelantonio, *Franklin Pierce College;* Rachelle L. Darabi, *Indiana University, Purdue University Fort Wayne;* Judy C. Davidson, *University of Texas, Pan American;* Helen Deese, *University of California, Riverside;* Darren DeFrain, *Wichita State University;* Sarah Dengler, *Franklin Pierce College;* Linda Dethloff, *Prairie State College;* Steven Dolgin, *Schoolcraft College;* Carol Jean Dudley, *Eastern Illinois University;* Chris Ellery, *Angelo State University;* Ernest J. Enchelmayer, *Louisiana State University;* Anne K. Erickson, *Atlantic Cape Community College;* Kelly A. Foth, *University of Dubuque;* Julie Foust, *Utah State University;* Lyneé Lewis Gaillet, *Georgia State University;* Gregory R. Glau, *Arizona State University;* Patricia Glynn, *Middlesex Community College;* Samuel J. Goldstein, *Daytona Beach Community College;* Kim Grewe, *Wor-Wic Community College;* Loren C. Gruber, *Missouri Valley College;* Michael Hammond, *Northeastern Illinois University;* Katona Hargrave, *Troy State University;* Dick Harrington, *Piedmont Virginia Community College;* Karla Hayashi, *University of Hawaii, Hilo;* Anne Christine Helms, *Alamance Community College;* Stan Hitron, *Middlesex Community College;* Karen Holleran, *Kaplan College;* Barbara Dondiego Holmes, *University of Charleston;* Maurice Hunt, *Baylor University;* Barbara Jacobskind, *University of Massachusetts, Dartmouth;* Linda G. Johnson, *Southeast Technical Institute;* Alex M. Joncas, *Estrella Mountain Community College;* Nina B. Keery, *Massachusetts Bay Community College;* Sandra Keneda, *Rose State College;* Margo LaGattuta, *University of Michigan, Flint;* Richard Larschan, *University of Massachusetts, Dartmouth;* Dusty Maddox, *DeVry University;* Bonnie J. Marshall, *Grand Valley State University;* Daphne Matthews, *Mississippi Delta Community College;* Claudia Milstead, *Missouri Valley College;* Kate Mohler, *Mesa Community College;* Meghan Monroe, *Central Michigan University;* Ed Moritz, *Indiana University, Purdue University Fort Wayne;* Linda Morrison, *Niagara University;* Deborah Naquin, *Northern Virginia Community College;* Julie Nichols,

Okaloosa-Walton Community College; Robert H. Nordell, *Des Moines Area Community College;* Christine Pavesic, *University of Wisconsin, Waukesha;* Sherry Rankin, *Abilene Christian University;* Laura Robbins, *Portland Community College;* Matthew Roudané, *Georgia State University;* Robert E. Rubin, *Wright State University;* Nancy Ruff, *Southern Illinois University, Edwardsville;* Christine M. Ryan, *Middlesex Community College;* Larry W. Severeid, *College of Eastern Utah;* Donna K. Speeker, *Wallace State Community College;* Talbot Spivak, *Edison College;* Joyce Swofford, *Clayton College & State University;* Terry Thacker, *Coastline Community College;* Diane Thompson, *Northern Virginia Community College;* Monica Parrish Trent, *Montgomery College;* Dori Wagner, *Austin Community College;* Shonda Wilson, *Suffolk County Community College;* Frances J. Winter, *Massachusetts Bay Community College;* Kelly Wonder, *University of Wisconsin, Eau Claire;* Benjamin Worth, *Bluegrass Community and Technical College;* Deanna L. Yameen, *Quincy College.*

Students: Lindsi Bittner, *St. Petersburg College;* Danielle Brown, *Oakton Community College;* Marie Burns, *University of Tampa;* Will Buttner, *University of Tampa;* Debra Cotton, *St. Petersburg College;* Jessica de Olivera, *Northeastern Illinois University;* Petra Hickman, *St. Petersburg College;* Anne Hsiao, *Oakton Community College;* Cassie Hull, *St. Petersburg College;* Courtney Langford, *St. Petersburg College;* Sandy Lehrke, *Hillsborough Community College;* Michael Pistorio, *Oakton Community College;* Crystal Smuk, *Triton Junior College;* Marc Sordja, *St. Petersburg College;* Johnny Velez, *Hillsborough Community College;* Anthony Zalud, *Harper Community College;* Omar Zamora, *Northeastern Illinois University.*

Special Thanks: A special thanks goes to Sarah Dangelantonio and Sarah Dengler of *Franklin Pierce College* for their work on the *Instructor's Resource Manual.* Also, thanks to Mark Gallaher, Kelly McGuire, Julie Nash, Dee Seligman, and Janet Young.

Randall VanderMey • Verne Meyer • John Van Rys • Dave Kemper • Pat Sebranek

Contents

Documentation and Format Styles

IV. Handbook

Punctuation, Mechanics, Usage, and Grammar

Sentence Issues

Addressing Multilingual/ESL Issues

Thematic Table of Contents for Readings

I. A Rhetoric: College Student's Guide to Writing

CONTENTS

Reading, Thinking, Viewing, and Writing

The Writing Process

The College Essay

Chapter 1
Critical Thinking Through Reading, Viewing, and Writing

In many respects, critical thinking defines your college work. When you think critically, you examine ideas fully and logically, weigh multiple perspectives on issues, and draw reasonable conclusions. In the process, you carry on an in-depth dialogue with information and evidence.

In various courses your instructors will ask you to undertake critical thinking through reading, viewing, and writing. You might have to analyze Flannery O'Connor's short story "Good Country People," identify the comic conventions in the film *Sideways*, or analyze data gathered about the fermentation of ethanol. In all of these assignments you are being pressed to think critically, using reading, viewing, and writing—connected as they are—to make sense of things. And your training in critical thinking prepares you for work in your profession and in the public square.

Thoughtful reading and viewing, then, lie at the heart of critical thinking and feed into thoughtful writing. These natural reading-viewing-thinking-writing connections are this chapter's focus.

What's Ahead

- Critical Thinking Through Reading
- Reading Actively
- Responding to a Text
- Summarizing a Text
- Critical Thinking Through Viewing
- Interpreting an Image
- Evaluating an Image
- Critical Thinking Through Writing
- Practicing Modes of Thinking in Your Writing
- Critical Thinking Checklist and Writing Activities

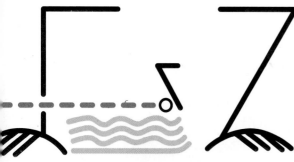

Critical Thinking Through Reading

Reading is basic to writing the way that eating is basic to cooking. Just as creating food worth tasting and digesting is at the heart of cooking, so is making words worth reading at the heart of writing. And while the cook must plan the meal around the tastes of his or her guests, the writer must always develop his or her text with awareness of readers' perspectives. To appeal to a reader, in other words, the writer has to know firsthand what good reading is.

Use a reading strategy: SQ3R.

Obviously, reading a novel, a textbook, and a webpage are all different activities. Nevertheless, all college reading assignments can be approached systematically, especially when your goal is to absorb and engage the text. One such strategy for critical reading, especially of information-rich texts, is called **SQ3R: Survey, Question, Read, Recite, and Review**. Here is how SQ3R works.

Survey

The first step in SQ3R is to preview the material. Try to spot main ideas. These will serve as reference points during the reading that follows. Perhaps you've been given questions or a study guide. Read those first. Then read the introductory and concluding paragraphs and glance at each page in between. Pay special attention to headings, chapter titles, illustrations, and boldfaced type. Also check out any graphics—charts, maps, diagrams, illustrations—that visually reinforce key points.

Benefits: Surveying serves three important purposes: (1) it gives you the big picture, (2) it stabilizes and directs your thoughts, and (3) it gets you over the starting hump.

Question

As you survey, begin to ask questions that you hope to answer as you read.

- Turn the headings and subheadings into questions. For example, if the subhead says "Methods," ask, "What methods did the researcher use?"

- Imagine a specific test question covering each major point in your reading. For example, if the reading addresses the media and the ethics of cloning, as shown on page **7**, you might imagine this test question: "What can the media do to foster productive public debate on cloning?"

- Be thorough by asking the journalist's questions: who, what, when, where, why, and how. Examples: *Who are the media? What's the popular understanding of cloning? How have the media presented cloning? Why does the author see the media's treatment of cloning as an ethical issue?*

- Look over any questions found at the end of the text or the chapter.

Benefits: Asking questions will keep you actively thinking about what is coming up and will help you to maintain an appropriate critical distance.

Read

As you encounter facts and ideas, ask these questions: What does this mean? How do the ideas relate to each other and to what I know? What's coming next?

Keep track of your answers by taking notes, annotating the text, mapping, or outlining. (See pages **6–9** for more on these active-reading techniques.) Read difficult parts slowly; reread them if necessary. Look up unfamiliar words or ideas, and use your senses to imagine the events, people, places, or things you are reading about. Imagine talking with the writer. Express agreement, lodge complaints, ask for proof—and imagine the writer's response or look for it in the text.

Benefits: Engaging actively with the text in this way will draw you deeper into the world of the writing. You'll trigger memories and make surprising connections.

Recite

After finishing a page, section, or chapter, recite the key points aloud. Answering *Who? What? When? Where? Why?* and *How?* questions is a quick way of testing yourself on how well you understand what you have read. You can also recite by listing the key points or writing a summary (see page **11**).

Benefits: Reciting tests your comprehension, drives the material deeper into your long-term memory, and helps you connect the content with what you already know.

Review

As soon as you finish reading the material, double-check the questions you posed in the "question" stage of SQ3R. Can you answer them? Glance over any notes you made as well. But don't stop there if the reading is especially important. You will remember it much better by spacing out your reviews; spend a few minutes reviewing on each of the next few days. Consider the following helpful memory techniques:

- Visualize the concepts in concrete ways. *Example:* If a text discusses media sound bites about cloning, imagine a television panel discussing the topic.

- Draw diagrams, or clusters. *Example:* See the cluster on page **34**.

- Put the material in your own words. *Example:* see the summary on page **11**.

- Teach it to someone. *Example:* For a text on cloning, explain the main points to a friend or relative—in person, on the phone, or by e-mail.

- Use acronyms or rhymes. *Example:* "*i* before *e* except after *c*."

Benefits: Research shows that reviewing within 24 hours helps considerably to move information from your short-term to your long-term memory. You will also improve your memory if you create a network of associations with the information you want to remember, if you link the memory to two or more senses, or if you reorganize the material while still retaining the substance with accuracy.

Reading Actively

Truly active reading requires more than highlighting every line in yellow or pink. Active reading is really *inter*-active, a kind of mental dialogue with the writer. Certain practical techniques will help you stay alert for active reading:

- **Pace yourself.** Read in stretches of thirty to forty-five minutes, followed by short breaks. As you read, slow down in tough spots, respond to the text, ask questions, and note your reactions.
- **Project.** Based on where you've been and where you are in the text, anticipate what will come next and why.
- **Speak the text.** Read difficult parts out loud, or take turns reading aloud with a partner.
- **Track the text.** Record your dialogue with the text through writing strategies such as note taking, annotating, mapping, and outlining (all of which are explored on the following pages).

Take thoughtful notes.

Find a note-taking system that suits you, using legal tablets, note cards, laptop software, or a palm device. Your system should allow you to distinguish clearly among facts, quotations, paraphrases, summaries, and personal remarks. It is good to include a reference number or topic word at the top of each note to help you organize your notes later.

Although effective note taking is crucial for typical reading assignments in your courses, it's especially important for any research-based writing. On pages **440–443** you'll find more instruction on note-taking systems.

Annotate the text.

Annotating involves marking up the text itself. If you own the book you're reading or you are reading a photocopy, write notes in the margins. Writing activates your thinking and records your insights. Try these techniques, shown in the sample passage on the next page:

- Write a question—or a simple "?"—next to anything that concerns or puzzles you. See if the text eventually answers your question.
- Link related passages by drawing circles, lines, or arrows, or by making notes such as "see page 36."
- Add personal observations. Keep track of your reactions without worrying about them initially. You can analyze these reactions later.
- Create a marginal index. Write key words in the margin or at the top of the page to identify important themes, names, or patterns. For books, list these key words, with page numbers, on a blank page at the end. By doing so, you'll create an index for future use.

Annotating in Action

The excerpt below is from an article written by Leigh Turner, an academic and medical professional who has studied, worked, and taught in both the United States and Canada. Written in the wake of the first successful animal cloning, of Dolly the sheep, this reading might be assigned in a communication, philosophy, biology, environmental studies, political science, or agriculture course for class discussion, a written response, a test, or a research writing. This excerpt shows how a student reader engages the text and comments on key ideas. (The full essay appears on pages **309–313**.)

What's the connection?

The Media and the Ethics of Cloning

Who is he? check

If the contemporary debate on cloning has a patron saint, surely it is Andy Warhol. Not only did Warhol assert that everyone would have 15 minutes of fame—witness the lawyers, philosophers, theologians, and bioethicists who found their expertise in hot demand on the nightly morality plays of network television following Ian Wilmut's cloning of the sheep Dolly—but he also placed "clones," multiple copies of the same phenomenon, at the heart of popular culture. Instead of multiple images of Marilyn Monroe and Campbell's soup cans, we now have cloned sheep. Regrettably, it is Warhol's capacity for hyperbole rather than his intelligence and ironic vision that permeates the current debate on cloning.

see textbook p. 375

good definition of cloning

means extreme exaggeration

It would be unfair to judge hastily written op-ed pieces, popular talk shows, and late-night radio programs by the same standards that one would apply to a sustained piece of philosophical or legal analysis. But the popular media could do more to foster thoughtful public debate on the legal, moral, political, medical, and scientific dimensions of the cloning of humans and nonhuman animals.

media needs to consider cloning thoughtfully

As did many of my colleagues at the Hastings Center, I participated in several interviews with the media following Ian Wilmut's announcement in *Nature* that he had succeeded in cloning Dolly from a mammary cell of an adult sheep. After clearly stating to one Los Angeles radio broadcaster before our interview that I was not a theologian and did not represent a religious organization, I was rather breathlessly asked during the taping what God's view on cloning is and whether cloning is "against creation." Predictably, the broadcaster didn't want to discuss how religious ethicists are contributing to the nascent public discourse about the ethics of cloning. Instead, he . . .

INSIGHT: Underlining or highlighting key words or phrases can be helpful, but don't overdo it. If you're not careful, too much highlighting or underlining becomes a means of evading rather than engaging the text. Excessive highlighting might be your brain saying "I'll learn this later." Moreover, excessive highlighting can make the text difficult to reread and hence tough to review.

Map the text.

If you are visually oriented, you may understand a text best by mapping out its important parts. One way to do so is by "clustering." Start by naming the main topic in a circle at the center of the page. Then branch out using lines and "balloons," each balloon containing a word or phrase for one major subtopic. Branch out in further layers of balloons to show even more subpoints. If you wish, add graphics, arrows, drawings—anything that helps you visualize the relationships among ideas.

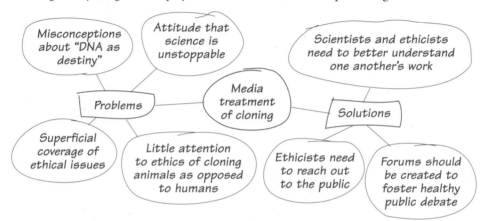

Outline the text.

Outlining is the traditional way of showing all the major parts, points, and subpoints in a text. An outline uses parallel structure to show main points and subordinate points. See pages **44–45** for more on outlines.

Sample outline for *"The Media and the Ethics of Cloning"*

1. Introduction: The debate about cloning is filled with exaggeration.
2. The mass media have confused the debate:
   - Bombarding the public with sound bites
   - Focusing on human cloning and ignoring animal cloning
   - Wrongly stressing that people are products of their genes
   - Promoting the idea that scientific "progress" can't be stopped
3. Thesis: The discussion can be improved in three ways:
   - Scientists and ethicists must learn to understand one another's work.
   - Ethicists need to improve how they communicate to the mass media.
   - Public debate about scientific topics must be expanded to forums and outreach programs.
4. Conclusion: We need more intelligent discussion so that the public is not misled by the mass media.

Responding to a Text

In a sense, when you read a text you enter into a dialogue with it. Your response expresses your turn in the dialogue. Such a response can take varied forms, from a journal entry to a blog to a discussion-group posting.

Follow these guidelines for response writing.

On the surface, responding to a text seems perfectly natural—just let it happen. But it can be a bit more complicated. A written response typically is not the same as a private diary entry but is instead shared with other readers, whether your instructor or a class. You develop your response keeping in mind your instructor's requirements and the response's role in the course. Therefore, follow these guidelines:

1. Be honest. Although you want to remain sensitive to the context in which you will share your response, be bold enough to be honest about your reaction to the text— what it makes you think, feel, and question. To that end, a response usually allows you to express yourself directly using the pronoun "I."

2. Be fluid. Let the flow of your thoughts and feelings guide you in what you write. Don't stop to worry about grammar, punctuation, mechanics, and spelling. If required, these can be quickly cleaned up before you share or submit your response.

3. Be reflective. Generally, the goal of a response is to offer thoughtful reflection as opposed to knee-jerk reaction. Show, then, that you are engaging the text's ideas, relating them to your own experience, looking both inward and outward. Avoid a shallow reaction that comes from skimming the text or misreading it.

4. Be selective. By nature, a response must limit its focus; it cannot exhaust all your reactions to the text. So zero in on one or two elements of your response, and run with those to see where they take you in your dialogue with the text.

Sample Response

Here is part of a student's response to Leigh Turner's "The Media and the Ethics of Cloning," on pages **309–313**. Note the informality and exploratory tone.

> Turner seems dead right about the treatment of cloning in the media, based on some news stories I've recently heard about food from cloned cows. The media just don't go very deep, especially on science issues, which most people find too tough to understand anyway.
>
> Like most people, I've focused on the (scary?) idea of human cloning, afraid of what it could lead to, but I'm also curious about it. Cloning animals is an issue that hasn't been on my radar screen much. Cloning animals just for the benefit of people, is that right? Would I approve of human cloning if it benefited me, if it helped someone I loved or saved my own life?

INSIGHT: A response does not simply summarize the text. See the next page to understand the difference between a response and a summary.

Evaluate the text.

Critical reading does not mean disproving the text or disapp
thoughtfully inspecting, weighing, and evaluating the writer's ı
your reading skills, learn to evaluate texts using the criteria below

1. Judge the reading's credibility. Where was it published? H
author? How current is the information? How accurate and complet
be In addition, consider the author's tone of voice, attitude, and app

Discussion Leigh Turner, the author of "The Media and the Ethı
on pages 309–313, tells us that he is a member of the Hastings Cente
research institute. How does this information build or break his credib
the article, how does he build credibility?

2. Put the reading in a larger context. How do the text's ideas match
know from other sources? What details of background, history, and socia
help you understand this text's perspective? How have things changed or rema
same since the text's publication? What allusions (references to people, events,
on) does the writer use? Why?

Discussion The topic of cloning belongs to the broader subjects of ge
research and ethics. In addition, the topic relates to debates over the nature of hu
identity, and cloning research has advanced and expanded dramatically since
article's publication. As for allusions, Turner refers to the artist Andy Warhol and t
cloning of the sheep Dolly. What else is part of this context?

3. Evaluate the reasoning and support. Is the reasoning clear and logical? Are the
examples and other supporting details appropriate and enlightening? Are inferences
(what the text implies) consistent with the tone and message? (Look especially for
hidden logic and irony that undercut what is said explicitly.)

Discussion Turner uses examples and illustrations extensively in his article. He
analyzes the problem by breaking it down, and he systematically presents a three-part
solution. Is his reasoning sound?

4. Reflect on how the reading challenges you. Which of your beliefs and values
does the reading call into question? What discomfort does it create? Does your own
perspective skew your evaluation?

Discussion The article may make us feel uncomfortable about several issues:
our lack of concern for animals, our inability to see past the media's treatment of
cloning, and the application of cloning to several areas of life (including replication
of ourselves). What other challenges does the article raise?

fyi For additional help evaluating texts, see pages 434–437. For information
on detecting logical fallacies often used in texts by writers, see pages
255–258.

Summarizing a Text

Writing a summary disciplines you by making you pull only essentials from a reading—the main points, the thread of the argument. By doing so, you not only create a brief record of the text's contents but also exercise your ability to comprehend, analyze, and synthesize information.

Use these guidelines for summary writing.

Writing a summary requires sifting out the least important points, sorting the essential ones to show their logical relationships, and putting those points in your own words. Follow these guidelines:

1. Skim first; then read closely. First, get a sense of the whole, including the main idea and strategies for support. Then read carefully, taking notes as you do.

2. Capture the text's argument. Review your notes and annotations, looking for main points and clear connections. State these briefly and clearly, in your own words. Include only what is essential, excluding most examples and details. Don't say simply that the text talks about its subject; tell *what it says* about that subject.

3. Test your summary. Aim to objectively provide the heart of the text; avoid interjecting your own opinions and presence as a writer. Similarly, don't confuse an objective summary of a text with a response to it (shown on the previous page). Finally, check your summary against the original text for accuracy and consistency.

Sample Summary

Below is a student's summary of Leigh Turner's article, "The Media and the Ethics of Cloning," on pages **309–313**. Note how the summary writer includes only main points and phrases them in terms she understands. She departs from the precise order of ideas in the original but communicates their sense accurately.

> **Popular media cover the topic of cloning inadequately. They offer unfocused and one-sided coverage, typically ignoring animal cloning, especially the ethics of cloning animals to create "pharmaceutical factories." By stressing "genetic essentialism," the idea that people are simply products of their genes, they ignore the complexity of growth. And last, the media make it sound as though the advance of cloning is unstoppable. How can this problem be resolved? First, through training, scientists and ethicists need to understand one another's work better. Second, ethicists need to be better communicators in the media, especially by publishing in journals that nonscientists can understand. Finally, public institutions need to sponsor debates so that views can be expressed at the grass roots level.**

INSIGHT: Writing formal summaries—whether as part of literature reviews or as abstracts—is an important skill, especially in the social and natural sciences. For help, go to <http://www.thecollegewriter.com>.

Critical Thinking Through Viewing

A flood of visual images—magazine covers, movie trailers, webpages, cell phones with flip-up video screens—affect the way we think. Images quicken our work, provoke ideas, and often trigger our emotions. Moreover, images included in written texts can grab viewers' attention, convey persuasive ideas, simplify complex concepts, and dramatize important points.

But images have drawbacks, too. They can distort facts, manipulate emotions, and shortcut reasoning. As a writer, you must learn to think critically through viewing—to "read" images actively; to interpret what is meant by an image, not just what is shown; and to evaluate the quality and value of an image. These challenges are addressed on the following pages.

Consider these guidelines for viewing images.

Good readers approach words and visual images as part of the same message, reading both while noting how each complements or completes the message. Use the guidelines below to become a more active viewer of images in a text. (See page **13**.)

View actively. Give the image your active attention.

- **Question the image.** Remember the journalist's questions (page **4**)? *Who* made the image? *What* does it show? *When* was it made? *Where* in the text does the image appear? *Why* was it placed there?
- **Inspect all of it.** Let your sight "touch" every part of the image, as if you were reading Braille. Hints of its meaning may lurk in the tiny details.

View with a purpose. The purpose for reading needs to be appropriate to the type of image. Is the image meant to . . .

- **arouse curiosity?** Open your imagination, but stay on guard.
- **inform?** Search for key information; note what's left out.
- **illustrate?** Relate the image to the words it illustrates; does it clarify their meaning or distort it?
- **persuade?** Critique the appeals that the image uses, looking for elements that are manipulative, clichéd, or fallacious.
- **summarize?** Look for the main points to remember.

View with a plan. Here's a viewing plan for understanding an image:

1. Survey the image. What is your general impression? What intrigues you?
2. Question the image as shown above.
3. Relate the image's parts to one another.
4. Relate the image to the surrounding text, to other images, and to the world as you know it.
5. Decide what to do with the information it offers.

View an image.

Discussion

The drawing "Stopping by Woods on a Snowy Evening" by Chris Krenzke fits perfectly with the poem it illustrates. The illustration depicts a man on a farm wagon pausing on a country lane to stare at the snow-covered pines. The overall shape of the illustration is circular, a shape that gives the piece a serene feeling. The artist repeats this circular pattern elsewhere in the composition—in the distant snowy hills, in the wagon wheels, even in the pair of milk canisters. The top of the illustration is blue-black, with faint snowflakes wafting downward. The middle section of the drawing contains subtle shades of brown, green, and gray. The lowest part of the illustration bleeds into white snow, extending the visual circle down into the page. The drawing has a clear direction, from the back of the wagon on the left toward the little village crouched on the hill in the far right, suggesting the farmer's return home.

Mr. Krenzke uses the posture of the farmer and the horse to tell the story. Both of these travelers are turned away from the viewer, both with their hearts pointed toward the snowy houses in the distance. Their heads, though, look to the woods beside the road. Simply by turning their heads in partial profile, Mr. Krenzke has paused the motion of the wagon and captured this moment of gentle reflection.

Perhaps the greatest success of this illustration, however, is its poetic nature. It captures in line, texture, and color the same serene moment that Frost captures in words. The houses and the trees all rhyme in shape, much like the wheels, the canisters, and the overall form of the illustration. This drawing does more than illustrate the poem—it transforms it into an image.

Interpreting an Image

Viewing for general understanding is simply the first step in working with an image. Interpreting means figuring out what the visual image or graphic design is really meant to do, say, or show. If the meaning were fixed, like the number of jellybeans in a jar, interpreting would be easy. But the meaning is something you have to gather for yourself by considering all the evidence.

Understand the elements of interpretation.

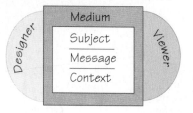

Keep in mind the following elements as you interpret an image. The **designer** of the image (for example, a cartoonist or webpage editor) uses an **image** to get some kind of **message** across to a **viewer**. The image offers a certain view of a certain **subject** in a certain **medium**. All of this is set in a certain **context**—a page of a textbook, an annual report, or a webpage. When you interpret the image, you consider each of these elements to arrive at an overall sense of meaning.

Understand the complications in interpretation.

Each of the elements in the chart above may offer special challenges to the reader:

Image: It might be strange, deceiving, very detailed, or highly technical.

Designer: He or she might be unknown or representing someone else, or it might be a team of people.

Viewer: You might be uninterested in the subject, unfamiliar with the visual "language" used by the designer, or biased toward the subject.

Subject: It might be vague, unfamiliar, complex, or disturbing.

Message: It might be mixed, implied, ironic, unwelcome, or distorted.

Context: It might be disconnected from the image, changing, or multilayered.

Medium: It might be multiple, awkward, or "the message."

INSIGHT: Like words, visuals can be clichés—trite, misleading, or worn-out expressions of concepts or ideas. For example, TV ads for weight-loss drugs commonly picture scantily clad, fit young people, incorrectly suggesting that using the drugs will produce fit, youthful bodies.

Interpret an image.

Discussion

In this black-and-white photo, the words "Beauty Shop" contrast starkly with the appearance of the building. The photo evokes the old saying, "Beauty is only skin deep," and in this case, the skin of the old building has certainly lost its beauty. Dingy stucco, peeling paint, weed-filled alleys, cracked sidewalks—these details mock the shop's name.

Designer:	Unknown photographer
Medium:	Black-and-white photograph
Subject:	A rundown beauty shop
Message:	Beauty fades
Context:	A writing handbook
Viewer:	The reader

This irony creates opposing feelings in the viewer: amusement and sadness. The viewer is amused that the beauty shop has so little beauty. However, the cracks and grime tell the viewer that the ugliness results from a battle against age and cultural changes. The further irony is that this shop once was beautiful. Perhaps it was a local gathering point, though all of that loveliness now is gone.

The photographer apparently intends to create this feeling. The black-and-white medium creates a grave appearance, and the darkened corners make the photo itself seem older than it is. The formal symmetry of the shot suggests that the photographer wants the viewer to pause, to think, and to feel just slightly haunted by the message: beauty fades.

Evaluating an Image

When you encounter an image, you must do more than understand and interpret it: You have to decide whether it is worth your time and attention. In other words, you have to evaluate it. When you have done that well, you can fairly say you have thought it through. The following questions will guide you.

Consider the purpose.

What purpose does the visual image best seem to serve?

- **Ornamentation:** Makes the page more pleasing to the eye
- **Illustration:** Supports points made in the accompanying text
- **Revelation:** Gives an inside look at something or presents new data
- **Explanation:** Uses imagery or graphics to clarify a complex subject
- **Instruction:** Guides the viewer through a complex process
- **Persuasion:** Influences feelings or beliefs
- **Entertainment:** Amuses the reader

Evaluate the quality.

Essentially, how good is the image?

- Is the image done with skill? A map, for example, should be accurately and attractively drawn, should use color effectively, and should be complete enough to serve its purpose.
- Does the image measure up to standards of quality?
  See <www.thecollegewriter.com> for design tips for a variety of visuals.
- Is it backed by authority? Does the designer have a good reputation?
  Does the publication or institution have good credentials?
- How does the image compare to other images like it? Are clearer or more accurate images available?
- What are its shortcomings? Are there gaps in its coverage? Does it twist the evidence? Does it convey clichéd or fallacious information? (See pages 255–258 for a discussion of logical fallacies.)
- Could you think of a better way to approach the image's subject? If you were to produce the visual, what might you improve?

Determine the value.

What is the image's tangible and intangible worth? Its benefits and drawbacks?

- Is the visual worth viewing? Does it enrich the document by clarifying or otherwise enhancing its message?
- Does the visual appeal to you? Listen to authorities and peers, but also consider your own perspective.

Evaluate images.

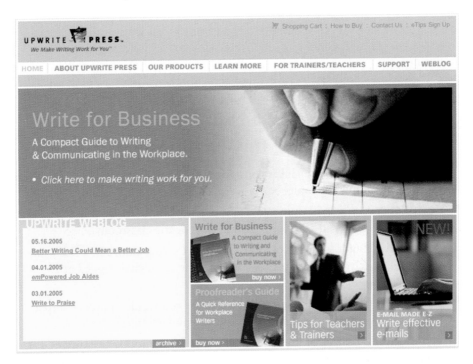

Discussion

The images in the webpage above create a "storefront" for the company Upwrite Press. Below the company logo, a large rectangular image promotes a product—*Write for Business*. The text on the left of this image tells the viewer about the book and encourages links to find out more. The image on the right shows a hand writing with a pen—the same image that appears on the cover of the book. This business has wisely connected the cover graphic to the title to create product recognition.

The choice of showing pen-and-paper writing is interesting, especially given that most business writing takes place on the computer. Upwrite Press seems to be using this traditional type of writing to create the impression of stability and tradition. The images below the pen and paper help to balance out the traditional writing model. One image shows a man giving a presentation, and it shows a hand in the foreground, holding a pen much like the one above. The implication is that *Write for Business* can help with presentations. Rounding out the set of images is an open laptop with more writing hands and the word "NEW!" emblazoned in red on the picture. While the main image connotes stability and tradition, this image connotes modern technology and innovation. By connecting these three separate images, Upwrite Press creates an immediate impression of respectability, adaptability, and applicability to different business environments. Visually, this is a storefront that would appeal to individuals looking for help with their writing skills.

Critical Thinking Through Writing

In college your writing often must show your ability to think critically about topics and issues by analyzing complex processes, synthesizing distinct concepts, weighing the value of opposing perspectives, and practicing new applications of existing principles. To hone your critical-thinking skills you need to develop sound critical-thinking habits, sharpen your reasoning skills, and distinguish inductive and deductive logic.

Develop sound critical-thinking habits.

Like everything worthwhile, improving your critical-thinking skills takes time and practice. But cultivating the habits below will pay off in sound, thoughtful writing.

1. **Be curious.** Ask "why?" Cultivate your ability to wonder; question what you see, hear, and read—both inside and outside the classroom.

2. **Be creative.** Don't settle for obvious answers. Look at things in a fresh way, asking "what-if" questions such as, "What if the earth's axis tipped at 25 degrees instead of 23.5 degrees?"

3. **Be open to new ideas.** Approach thinking as you would approach a road trip—looking for the unexpected and musing over mysteries.

4. **Value others' points of view.** Look at issues from another person's perspective and weigh that against your own. Honestly examine how the core of her or his perspective compares to the core of your perspective, and how each basis for thought might lead to different conclusions.

5. **Get involved.** Read books, journals, and newspapers. Watch documentaries. Join book clubs, film clubs, or political and social-action activities.

6. **Focus.** Sharpen your concentration, looking for details that distinguish a topic and reveal key questions related to its nature, function, and impact.

7. **Be rational.** Choose logical thinking patterns like those discussed in this chapter, and then work through the steps to deepen and develop your understanding of a topic.

8. **Make connections.** Use writing to explore how and why topics or issues are related. Use comparisons to identify and name these relationships.

9. **Tolerate ambiguity.** Respectfully analyze issues not readily resolved—and acknowledge when your position requires further research or thought.

10. **Test the evidence.** Be properly skeptical about all claims (see pages 252–254). Look for corroboration (or verification) in other sources.

11. **Develop research-based conclusions.** Focus on understanding issues, assessing their history, development, function, and impact. During the process, gather details that lead to and support a reasonable conclusion.

12. Expect results. Consider each paper a benchmark that reflects your progress in developing your thinking and writing skills. Save your papers for periodic analyses of your progress and revision of the writing.

 For more help with thinking skills such as making and supporting claims, recognizing logical fallacies, and dealing with opposition, see "Strategies for Argumentation and Persuasion," pages **247–262.**

Ask probing questions.

Every field uses questions to trigger critical thinking. For example, scientific questions generate hypotheses, sociological questions lead to studies, mathematical questions call for proofs, and literary criticism questions call for interpretations. A good question opens up a problem and guides you all the way to its solution. But not all questions are created equal. Consider the differences:

- "Rhetorical" questions aren't meant to be answered. They're asked for effect. *Example:* Who would want to be caught in an earthquake?
- Closed questions seek a limited response and can be answered with a "yes," "no," or a simple fact. *Example:* Would I feel an earthquake measuring 3.0 on the Richter scale?
- Open questions invite brainstorming and discussion. *Example:* How might a major earthquake affect this urban area?
- Theoretical questions call for organization and explanation of an entire field of knowledge. *Example:* What might cause a sudden fracturing of Earth's crust along fault lines?

To improve the critical thinking in your writing, ask better questions. The strategies below will help you think freely, respond to reading, study for a test, or collect your thoughts for an essay.

Ask open questions. Closed questions sometimes choke off thinking. Use open questions to trigger a flow of ideas.

Ask "educated" questions. Compare these questions: (A) What's wrong with television? (B) Does the 16.3 percent rise in televised acts of violence during the past three years signal a rising tolerance for violence in the viewing audience? You have a better chance of expanding the "educated" question—question B—into an essay because the question is clearer and suggests debatable issues.

Keep a question journal. Divide a blank notebook page or split a computer screen. On one side write down any questions that come to mind regarding the topic that you want to explore. On the other side write down answers and any thoughts that flow from them.

Write Q & A drafts. To write a thoughtful first draft, write quickly, then look it over. Turn the main idea into a question and write again, answering your question. For example, if your main idea is that TV viewers watch far more violence than they did ten years ago, ask *Which viewers? Why?* and *What's the result?* Go on that way until you find a key idea to serve as the main point of your next draft.

Practice inductive and deductive logic.

Questions invite thinking; reasoning responds to that challenge in an organized way. Will the organization of your thoughts be inductive or deductive? **Inductive logic** reasons from specific information toward general conclusions. **Deductive logic** reasons from general principles toward specific applications. Notice in the diagram below that inductive reasoning starts with specific details or observations (as shown at the base) and then moves "up" to broader ideas and eventually to a concluding generalization. In contrast, deduction starts with general principles at the top and works down, applying the principles to explain particular instances.

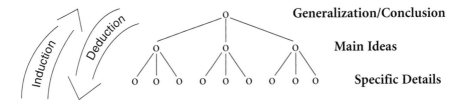

Sentences, paragraphs, and entire essays can be organized either inductively or deductively. Use induction when you want to postpone your conclusions. Use deduction for logical clarity, directness, and strength, or to apply what is already agreed on to what is still under dispute. Narrative or personal essays tend toward inductive organization, whereas analytical essays (particularly those written in the social or natural sciences) typically use both induction and deduction.

Example: Read through the paragraphs below from the student essay "If We Are What We Wear, What Are We?" by Allison Young <http://www.thecollegewriter.com>. The first paragraph works deductively, the second paragraph inductively. Note how each approach affects the message.

Deduction: generalization to specific details

The American excuse for owning multiples is that clothing styles change so rapidly. At the end of the '80s, trends in high fashion changed every two and a half months (During 95). Even for those of us who don't keep up with high fashion, styles change often enough that our clothing itself lasts much longer than the current trend. Perhaps this is one of the reasons the average American spent $997 on clothing in 1996 (U.S. Department of Commerce).

Induction: specific details to generalization

While Americans are spending a thousand dollars on clothing a year, people in Ethiopia make an average of only $96 a year, those in Bangladesh $280, and the average Filipino worker makes $1,052 (United Nations Statistics Division). I, on the other hand, made over $5,000 last year, and that job was only part-time. When an American college student can earn more money at her part-time job than three billion people each make for a living, it's time to question our culture and ask, as Alan During did, "How much is enough?"

Practicing Modes of
Thinking in Your Writing

In your various writing assignments, you will need to practice specific modes of thinking. The table below maps out these modes (from elementary to complex) and the tasks each requires. The more complex modes are then fleshed out on the following pages.

When you are asked to _____ , *be ready to* _____ .

Know
		call to mind what you have learned
define	memorize	■ Recall information
identify	name	■ List details
list	recall	■ Define key terms
match	recognize	■ Identify main points

Understand
		show what you have learned
comprehend	interpret	■ Connect related examples
connect	restate	■ Summarize important details
explain	summarize	■ Explain how something works
grasp		■ Interpret what something means

Analyze
		break down information
characterize	contrast	■ Divide a whole into its parts
classify	divide	■ Group things into categories
compare	examine	■ Analyze causes and effects
		■ Examine similarities and differences

Synthesize
		shape information into a new form
assemble	imagine	■ Bring together a body of evidence
combine	invent	■ Blend the old with the new
construct	link	■ Predict or hypothesize
formulate		■ Construct a new way of looking at something

Evaluate
		determine the worth of information
assess	measure	■ Point out a subject's strengths and weaknesses
check	monitor	■ Evaluate its clarity, accuracy, logic, value, and so on
critique	rank	
judge	rate	■ Convince others of its value/worth

Apply
		use what you have learned
anticipate	propose	■ Propose a better way of doing something
choose	select	■ Generate a plan of action
generate		■ Offer solutions to a problem

Think by using analysis.

The word *analyze* literally means "to loosen or undo." When you analyze some-thing, you break it down into parts and examine each part separately. You classify information, compare objects, trace a process, or explain causes.

As you analyze, think about the questions listed below. Note that each type of thinking answers certain kinds of questions. Remember, too, that thinking tasks often require two or more kinds of analysis that support one another.

- **Composition:** What elements does it contain? What is not part of it?
- **Categories:** How are things grouped, divided, or classified?
- **Structures:** What are the parts or elements? How are they related?
- **Comparisons/ contrasts:** How are things similar? How are they different?
- **Causes/effects:** Why did this happen? What are the results?
- **Processes:** How does it work or happen? What are the stages?

Example: Read through the passage below, from "A Fear Born of Sorrow" (pages **189–190**). Note how the writer compares and contrasts the September 11, 2001, attack on the World Trade Center with the Oklahoma City bombing in 1995, and then analyzes the causes and effects of the emotions triggered by both events.

> **The writer develops contrasts signaled by "however." While doing so, she also analyzes causes and explains effects.**
>
> The Oklahoma City bombing was grievous and alarming, but localized. The bomber was soon arrested, his motives deduced, and justice served. While lives were changed and a nation was shaken, the world community remained composed. However, the September 11 attack unsettled us more, in part because the World Trade Center stood for so much more than the Oklahoma City Federal Building did. The Twin Towers symbolized American domination of world finances: They were a major center for the Internet, a hub for international business, and an emblem of American life. The fall of the towers struck violently at the nation's psyche, and the manner in which they were destroyed—with America's own airplanes filled with passengers—has raised questions about America's security and future. Threatened to their core, Americans have demanded retaliation—but against whom? The terrorists' identity is not clear, and evidence seems elusive. In a sense, an unknown offender has injured Americans, and they beat the air in the dark. In such a case, terrorism is aptly named, for America's outcry expresses more than sorrow—it also expresses fear.

Think by using synthesis.

Synthesis is the opposite of analyzing. Where analysis breaks things down into parts, synthesis combines elements into a new whole. In your writing, when you pull together things that are normally separate, you are synthesizing. Common ways of synthesizing are predicting, inventing, redesigning, and imagining a whole new way of looking at something.

Working with synthesis involves both reason and imagination. Start by looking closely at two or more items that you want to synthesize, and then think of fresh ways they can be related. Don't be afraid to see your subjects in a new way. In other words, think "sideways" rather than straight ahead. For example, to explain how hair grows on a scalp, consider how grass might grow in a field. Then consider parallel traits, such as that both hair and grass have roots, both grow in spurts, both need cutting, and so on.

The following kinds of questions may get you started:

- **Applying:** What can I do with both? What will be the outcome?
- **Bridging:** How can I build a connection between the two?
- **Combining:** How can I connect, associate, or blend the two?
- **Conflicting:** Which is good, better, or best? What strength does each offer the other?
- **Inventing:** What parts could these two play in a drama?
- **Proposing:** What do you suggest doing with both?
- **Sequencing:** Which comes first? Is one an extension of the other?

Example: Read through the passage below, from "Hair Today, Gone Tomorrow" (pages **222–223**), in which Verne Meyer describes how hair grows. He asks readers to imagine the scalp as a field of grass.

The writer uses an analogy to introduce the process and distinguish its steps.	Imagine a field covered with two layers of soil: first a layer of clay, and on top of that a layer of rich, black dirt. Then imagine that 100,000 little holes have been poked through the black dirt and into the clay, and at the bottom of each hole lies one grass seed.
	Slowly each seed produces a stem that grows up through the clay, out of the dirt, and up toward the sky. Now and then each stem stops for awhile, rests, and then starts growing again. At any time about 90 percent of the stems are growing and the others are resting. Because the field gets shaggy, sometimes a gardener comes along and cuts the grass.
He explains the analogy.	Your skull is like that field, and your scalp (common skin) is like the two layers of soil. The top layer of the scalp is the epidermis, and the bottom layer is the dermis. About 100,000 tiny holes (called follicles) extend through the epidermis into the dermis.

Think by using evaluation.

Movies, proposals, arguments—anything can be evaluated. Evaluation measures the value or worth of things. For example, when you express your judgment about an issue or discuss the weak and strong points of what someone else has said, you are evaluating. Many kinds of writing are evaluative.

To evaluate a topic, start by learning as much about it as possible. Then consider what criteria or standards are appropriate. Next, judge how it measures up according to those criteria. You can compare the topic (such as a movie based on a book) to a standard (the movie carefully follows the book) or to something else (whether the book and movie each have their own qualities). Along the way, support your own judgment with concrete details, examples, illustrations, and comparisons.

Questions like these will help you evaluate things in writing:

- **Aspects:** What elements of the topic will you evaluate?
- **Vantage Point:** What are your experience and point of view?
- **Criteria:** On what standards will you base your judgment?
- **Assessment:** How does the topic measure up by those standards?
- **Comparison:** How does it compare to and contrast with similar things?
- **Recommendation:** Based on your evaluation, what do you advise?

Example: The paragraphs below are from a student essay in which the writer calls readers to abandon *cute* as a worn-out word. She begins evaluating, through a playful critique, the word's current use.

The writer forcefully states her claim about the word's lack of meaning. She calls *cute* a "cop-out descriptor" and backs her claim with vivid examples.

If there's one word that deserves to be hauled into a back alley and dismembered letter by letter, it's *CUTE*. Just looking at the word brings up images of pink, frilly dresses; *Veggie Tales*; and helpless puppies. And the word brings up my breakfast. But why do I want to deface pictures of babies sitting in flowers? Why do I want to smash Precious Moments figurines into smithereens? And why do I want to put big black X's over stylized hearts?

For as long as I can remember, *cute* has inspired nothing in me but contempt. It's a cop-out descriptor. Whenever I hear it, I think, "What? Can you find no better adjective? With so many options, how could you choose *cute*?" Because *cute* is used so often and so carelessly, it means so little.

"Your shirt is sooo cute!"

"They make such a cute couple!"

"What a cute idea!"

Soon we'll be calling Jesse Ventura cute, or Fidel Castro, or nuclear warfare. Just recently I heard a girl squeal about a plain-faced education prof, "Oh, Dr. O'Reilly is so cute!" Get me a bucket so I can throw up. Cutely, of course.

Think by using application.

Thinking by application defines the practical implications of something. It involves using what you know to demonstrate, show, relate, or extend ideas in view of their outcomes. For example, using what you have learned about the ecology of forest fires to examine the effects of a particular fire—that's application in action.

Applying involves moving from ideas to possible action. First, understand the information you have. Second, relate this information to a given situation. Third, select those facts and details that clarify and support the application. Fourth, test the application to see whether it has been reasonable.

When applying ideas, let questions like these guide your writing:

- **Purpose:** What is something designed to be or do?
- **Benefits:** What would this idea make clearer, better, or more complete?
- **Solutions:** What problems are solved by application of this idea?
- **Outcomes:** What results can be expected? Where could we go from there?

Example: Read the paragraphs below, from Anna Quindlen's "Uncle Sam and Aunt Samantha" (pages **306–308**). In this essay, Quindlen argues that in the United States, women— as well as men—should be eligible to be drafted for military service. In the passage below, she applies the concept of equal rights to this specific situation.

Using the word "egalitarian" to refer to a key principle, the writer points out the real inequality and argues for a change.

Parents face a series of unique new challenges in this more egalitarian world, not the least of which would be sending a daughter off to war. But parents all over this country are doing that right now, with daughters who enlisted; some have even expressed surprise that young women, in this day and age, are not required to register alongside their brothers and friends. While all involved in this debate over the years have invoked the assumed opposition of the people, even 10 years ago more than half of all Americans polled believed women should be made eligible for the draft. Besides, this is not about comfort but about fairness. My son has to register with the Selective Service this year, and if his sister does not when she turns 18, it makes a mockery not only of the standards of this household but of the standards of this nation.

She backs up her conclusion with historical context and presses readers to agree.

It is possible in Afghanistan for women to be treated like little more than fecund pack animals precisely because gender fear and ignorance and hatred have been codified and permitted to hold sway. In this country, largely because of the concerted efforts of those allied with the women's movement over a century of struggle, much of that bigotry has been beaten back, even buried. Yet in improbable places the creaky old ways surface, the ways suggesting that we women were made of finer stuff. The finer stuff was usually porcelain, decorative and on the shelf, suitable for meals and show. Happily, the finer stuff has been transmuted into the right stuff. But with rights come responsibilities, as teachers like to tell their students . . .

Critical Thinking Checklist

Use these questions as you work to improve your critical-thinking skills as they relate to reading, viewing, and writing.

_____ How can I improve my active reading skills and strategies? How can I use them to improve my writing? (See pages **4–9**.)

_____ How can I strengthen my response writing? (See page **10**.)

_____ Do I understand the characteristics of an accurate summary? (See page **11**.)

_____ What strategies should I use to be a more active, purposeful viewer of visual images? (See page **12**.)

_____ Do I effectively interpret images by analyzing the context, subject, medium, message, designer, and viewer? (See page **14–15**.)

_____ Am I able to evaluate the purpose, quality, and value of images? (See page **16**.)

_____ How can I strengthen my critical thinking habits and questioning abilities? (See pages **18–25**.)

_____ Which of the thinking modes in the chart on page **21** can I do well in my writing? Which do I need to strengthen, and how?

_____ Which of my reading, viewing, and writing habits do or do not help my critical-thinking skills?

Writing Prompt

Writing Activities

1. What thinking, reading, viewing, and writing skills are required in your field of study? Reflect on those possibilities.

2. Explore how different texts require different reading strategies. Select a novel chapter, a textbook chapter, a magazine article, and a webpage: Engage each text and take appropriate notes. Then reflect on how the different texts call for both similar and different strategies.

3. Using this chapter's guidelines on viewing, interpreting, and evaluating visual imagery, examine a visual image for its meaning. Develop a written analysis and evaluation of the image.

4. Choose a subject you know something about. Practice thinking about that subject both inductively and deductively. Then write two paragraphs—one developed through inductive reasoning, the other developed through deductive reasoning.

5. Select a sample essay from the "Strategies and Models" section. Read the piece carefully and identify where and how the writer uses different thinking modes. Do the same analysis on a recent sample of your own writing, rating your analysis, synthesis, evaluation, and application.

Chapter 2
Beginning the Writing Process

College instructors assign essays for a variety of reasons. One reason is that they want to encourage you to think and figure things out for yourself. This emphasis on clear and logical thought distinguishes college writing from writing you may have done earlier. Fortunately, writing results from a process that can be learned, practiced, and improved. Once you understand the writing process—from forming a clear sense of the assignment to submitting the final draft—you will be able to produce essays and papers that reflect your best thinking.

However, before you begin writing a paper, it's important that you understand the following points about the writing process:

- **Writing never follows a straight path.** Don't expect to move neatly through the steps in the writing process. Many times you will have to repeat a step, such as drafting a new paragraph during the editing stage.

- **Each writer works differently.** For example, some writers do extensive prewriting, while others do not. Expect to adapt writing-process guidelines to your own personality and style.

- **Each assignment presents challenges.** While a lab report may require research, a personal essay may require clustering or freewriting.

What's Ahead

- Understanding the Rhetorical Situation: Subject, Audience, and Purpose
- Understanding the Assignment
- Selecting a Subject
- Collecting Information
- Beginning the Process Checklist and Writing Activities

Understanding the Rhetorical Situation:
Subject, Audience, and Purpose

Rhetoric is the art of using language effectively. As Aristotle, Quintilian, and others have explained, your language is effective when all aspects of your message (including content and style) fit your **subject**, address the needs of your **audience,** and fulfill your **purpose.** For these reasons, before you put fingers to the keyboard, you must think carefully about all three. By doing so you're analyzing your *rhetorical situation*—the conditions or issues that affect writing decisions, including choosing the best *form* (such as essay or report), the best *medium* (paper or electronic), and the best *organizational strategy* (such as cause/effect or chronological process).

Understand your subject.

Ideas—and the information that relates to them—are the substance of all good writing. Without informative ideas, your writing cannot fulfill the needs of your audience and will not achieve your purpose. Understanding your subject involves gathering and assimilating all relevant details, including its history, makeup, function, and impact on people and culture. Knowing these details, will help you decide issues such as what to include in your writing and how to organize it.

Understand your audience.

For any writing task, you must understand your audience in order to develop writing that meets their needs. To assess your audience, answer questions like these:

- Who are my readers: instructor? classmates? web surfers?
- What do they know about my topic, and what do they need to know?
- How well do they understand the terminology, procedures, and technology?
- What are their attitudes toward the topic and toward me?
- How well do they read written English—or visuals such as graphs and charts?
- How will they use my writing (as entertainment or to complete a task)?

Note: Answers to such questions will help you develop meaningful sentences (pages **85–91**), choose appropriate words (pages **92–96**), and select relevant visuals (page **418**).

Understand your purpose.

Knowing your purpose—*why* you are writing—will help you make decisions, such as choosing an organizational strategy. In assignments, key words (especially verbs) either hint at or specify your purpose. For example, an assignment asking you to *analyze* a topic requires that you break the subject into subparts and then explain the relationships among those subparts. Organizational patterns useful for analyzing a topic include classification, definition, and process (pages **56–59**).

Understanding the Assignment

Each college instructor has a way of personalizing a writing assignment, but most assignments will spell out (1) the objective, (2) the task, (3) the formal requirements, and (4) suggested approaches and topics. Your first step, therefore, is to read the assignment carefully, noting the options and restrictions that are part of it. The suggestions below will help you do that. (Also see pages **103–107** for one writer's approach.)

Read the assignment.

Certain words in the assignment explain what main action you must perform. Here are some words that signal what you are to do:

Key Words

Analyze:	Break down a topic into subparts, showing how those parts relate.
Argue:	Defend a claim with logical arguments.
Classify:	Divide a large group into well-defined subgroups.
Compare/contrast:	Point out similarities and/or differences.
Define:	Give a clear, thoughtful definition or meaning of something.
Describe:	Show in detail what something is like.
Evaluate:	Weigh the truth, quality, or usefulness of something.
Explain:	Give reasons, list steps, or discuss the causes of something.
Interpret:	Tell in your own words what something means.
Reflect:	Share your well-considered thoughts about a subject.
Summarize:	Restate someone else's ideas very briefly in your own words.
Synthesize:	Connect facts or ideas to create something new.

Options and Restrictions

The assignment often gives you some choice of your topic or approach but may restrict your options to suit the instructor's purpose. Note the options and restrictions in the following short sample assignment:

> *Reflect on the way a natural disaster or major historical event has altered your understanding of the past, the present, or the future.*

Restrictions:	(1) you must *reflect on a change in your understanding,*
	(2) the disaster must be *natural,*
	(3) the historical event must be *major*
Options:	(1) you may choose *any natural disaster or historical event;*
	(2) you may focus on the *past, present, or future;*
	(3) you may examine *any kind of alteration*

Relate the assignment . . .

to the goals of the course.

1. How much value does the instructor give the assignment? (The value is often expressed as a percentage of the course grade.)

2. What benefit does your instructor want you to receive?
- Strengthen your comprehension?
- Improve your research skills?
- Deepen your ability to explain, prove, or persuade?
- Expand your style?
- Increase your creativity?

3. How will this assignment contribute to your overall performance in the course? What course goals (often listed in the syllabus) does it address?

to other assignments.

4. Does it build on previous assignments?

5. Does it prepare you for the next assignment?

to your own interests.

6. Does it connect with a topic that already interests you?

7. Does it connect with work in your other courses?

8. Does it connect with the work you may do in your chosen field?

9. Does it connect with life outside school?

Reflect on the assignment.

1. First impulses: How did you feel when you first read the assignment?

2. Approaches: What's the usual approach for an assignment like this? What's a better way of tackling it?

3. Quality of performance: What would it take to produce an excellent piece of writing?

4. Benefits: What are the benefits to your education? to you personally? to the class? to society?

5. Key traits: Reflect further on four key features of any writing assignment.

Purpose: What is the overall purpose of the assignment—to inform, to explain, to analyze, to entertain? What is the desired outcome?

Audience: Should you address your instructor? your classmates? a general reader? How much does the reader already know about the topic? What type of language should you use?

Form: What are the specific requirements concerning length, format, and due date?

Assessment: How will the assignment be evaluated? How can you be sure that you are completing the assignment correctly?

Selecting a Subject

For some assignments, finding a suitable subject (or topic) may require little thinking on your part. If, for example, an instructor asks you to summarize an article in a professional journal, you know what you will write about—the article in question. But suppose the instructor asks you to analyze a feature of popular culture in terms of its impact on society. You won't be sure of a specific writing topic until you explore the possibilities. Keep the following points in mind when you conduct a topic search. Your topic must . . .

- meet the requirements of the assignment
- be limited in scope
- seem reasonable (that is, be within your means to research)
- genuinely interest you

Limit the subject area.

Many of your writing assignments may relate to general subject areas you are currently studying. Your task, then, is to select a specific topic related to the general area of study—a topic limited enough that you can treat it with some depth in the length allowed for the assignment. The following examples show the difference between general subjects and limited topics:

> *General Subject Area:* Popular culture
> **Limited Topic: The Simpsons TV show**
>
> *General Subject Area:* Energy sources
> **Limited Topic: Using wind power**

Conduct your search.

Finding a writing idea that meets the requirements of the assignment should not be difficult, if you know how and where to look. Follow these steps:

1. Check your class notes and handouts for ideas related to the assignment.

2. Search the Internet. Type in a keyword or phrase (the general subject stated in the assignment) and see what you can find. You could also follow a subject tree to narrow a subject. (See page **471**.)

3. Consult indexes, guides, and other library references. *The Readers' Guide to Periodical Literature,* for example, lists current articles published on specific topics and where to find them. (See pages **460–465**.)

4. Discuss the assignment with your instructor or an information specialist.

5. Use one or more of the prewriting strategies described on the following pages to generate possible writing ideas.

Explore for possible topics.

You can generate possible writing ideas by using the following strategies. These same strategies can be used when you've chosen a topic and want to develop it further.

Journal Writing

Write in a journal on a regular basis. Reflect on your personal feelings, develop your thoughts, and record the happenings of each day. Periodically go back and underline ideas that you would like to explore in writing assignments. In the following journal writing samples, the writer came up with an idea for a writing assignment about the societal impacts of popular culture.

> I read a really disturbing news story this morning. I've been thinking about it all day. In California a little girl was killed when she was struck by a car driven by a man distracted by a billboard ad for lingerie featuring a scantily clothed woman. Not only is it a horrifying thing to happen, but it also seems to me all too symbolic of the way that sexually charged images in the media are putting children, and especially girls, in danger. That reminds me of another news story I read this week about preteen girls wanting to wear the kinds of revealing outfits that they see in music videos, TV shows, and magazines aimed at teenagers. <u>Too many of today's media images give young people the impression that sexuality should begin at an early age.</u> This is definitely a dangerous message.

Freewriting

Write nonstop for ten minutes or longer to discover possible writing ideas. Use a key concept related to the assignment as a starting point. You'll soon discover potential writing ideas that might otherwise have never entered your mind. Note in the following example that the writer doesn't stop writing even when he can't think of anything to say. *Note also that he doesn't stop to correct typos and other mistakes.*

> Popular culture. What does that include? Television obviously but thats a pretty boring subject. What else? Movies, pop music, video games. Is there a connection between playing violent video games and acting out violent behavior? Most video players I know would say no but sometimes news reports suggest a connection. Is this something I'd want to write about? Not really. What then? Maybe I could think about this a different way and focus on the positive effects of playing video games. They release tension for one thing and they can really be challenging. Other benefits? They help to kill time, that's for sure, but maybe that's not such a good thing. I would definitely read more if it weren't for video games, tv, etc. Maybe I could write about how all the electronic entertainment that surrounds us today is creating a generation of nonreaders. Or maybe I could focus on whether people aren't getting much physical exercise because of the time they spend with electronic media. Maybe both. At least I have some possibilities to work with.

Freewriting

QUICK GUIDE

Freewriting is the writing you do without having a specific outcome in mind. You simply write down whatever pops into your head as you explore your topic. Freewriting can serve as a starting point for your writing, or it can be combined with any of the other prewriting strategies to help you select, explore, focus, or organize your writing. If you get stuck at any point during the composing process, you can return to freewriting as a way of generating new ideas.

REMINDERS

- **Freewriting helps you get your thoughts down on paper.** (Thoughts are constantly passing through your mind.)
- **Freewriting helps you develop and organize these thoughts.**
- **Freewriting helps you make sense out of things** that you may be studying or researching.
- **Freewriting may seem awkward at times,** but just stick with it.

THE PROCESS

- **Write nonstop and record whatever comes into your mind.** Follow your thoughts instead of trying to direct them.
- **If you have a particular topic or assignment to complete, use it as a starting point.** Otherwise, begin with anything that comes to mind.
- **Don't stop to judge, edit, or correct your writing;** that will come later.
- **Keep writing** even when you think you have exhausted all of your ideas. Switch to another angle or voice, but keep writing.
- **Watch for a promising writing idea to emerge.** Learn to recognize the beginnings of a good idea, and then expand that idea by recording as many specific details as possible.

THE RESULT

- **Review your writing and underline the ideas you like.** These ideas will often serve as the basis for future writings.
- **Determine exactly what you need to write about.** Once you've figured out what you are required to do, you may then decide to do a second freewriting exercise.
- **Listen to and read the freewriting of others;** learn from your peers.

Listing

Freely list ideas as they come to mind, beginning with a key concept related to the assignment. (Brainstorming—listing ideas in conjunction with members of a group—is often an effective way to extend your lists.) The following is an example of a student's list of ideas for possible topics on the subject of news reporting:

Aspect of popular culture: News reporting

Sensationalism
Sound bites rather than in-depth analysis
Focus on the negative
Shock radio
Shouting matches pretending to be debates
Press leaks that damage national security, etc.
Lack of observation of people's privacy
Bias
Contradictory health news confusing to readers
Little focus on "unappealing" issues like poverty
Celebration of "celebrity"

Clustering

To begin the clustering process, write a key word or phrase related to the assignment in the center of your paper. Circle it, and then cluster ideas around it. Circle each idea as you record it, and draw a line connecting it to the closest related idea. Keep going until you run out of ideas and connections. The following is a student's cluster on the subject of sports:

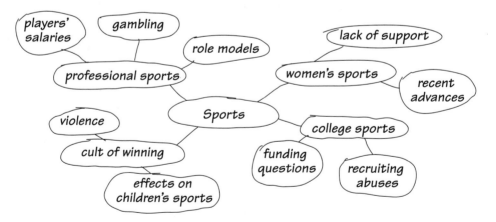

> **TIP:** After four or five minutes of listing or clustering, scan your work for an idea to explore in a freewriting. A writing idea should begin to emerge during this freewriting session. (See pages **32–33**.)

Collecting Information

Writer and instructor Donald Murray says that "writers write with information. If there is no information, there will be no effective writing." How true! Before you can develop a thoughtful piece of writing, you must gain a thorough understanding of your topic; to do so, you must carry out the necessary reading, reflecting, and researching. Writing becomes a satisfying experience once you can speak with authority about your topic. Use the following guidelines when you start collecting information. (Also see the Research Guide in this book.)

- Determine what you already know about your topic. (Use the strategies below this bulleted list.)
- Consider listing questions you would like to answer during your research. (See page **36**.)
- Identify and explore possible sources of information. (See page **37**.)
- Carry out your research following a logical plan. (See page **44**.)

Find out what you already know.

Use one or more of the following strategies to determine what you already know about a writing topic.

Focused Freewriting ■ At this point, you can focus your freewriting by (1) exploring your limited topic from different angles or (2) approaching your freewriting as if it were a quick draft of the actual paper. A quick version will tell you how much you know about your topic and what you need to find out.

Clustering ■ Try clustering with your topic serving as the nucleus word. Your clustering should focus on what you already know. (See page **34**.)

Five W's of Writing ■ Answer the five W's—*Who? What? When? Where?* and *Why?*—to identify basic information on your subject. Add *How?* to the list for better coverage.

Directed Writing ■ Write whatever comes to mind about your topic, using one of the modes listed below. (Repeat the process as often as you need to, selecting a different mode each time.)

Describe it: What do you see, hear, feel, smell, and taste?

Compare it: What is it similar to? What is it different from?

Associate it: What connections between this topic and others come to mind?

Analyze it: What parts does it have? How do they work together?

Argue it: What do you like about the topic? What you do not like about it? What are its strengths and weaknesses?

Apply it: What can you do with it? How can you use it?

Ask questions.

To guide your collecting and researching, you may find it helpful to list questions about your topic that you would like to answer. Alternatively, you can refer to the questions below. These questions address problems, policies, and concepts. Most topics will fall under one of these categories. Use those questions that seem helpful as a guide to your research.

	Description	Function	History	Value
P R O B L E M S	What is the problem? What type of problem is it? What are its parts? What are the signs of the problem?	Who or what is affected by it? What new problems might it cause in the future?	What is the current status of the problem? What or who caused it? What or who contributed to it?	What is its significance? Why? Why is it more (or less) important than other problems? What does it symbolize or illustrate?
P O L I C I E S	What is the policy? How broad is it? What are its parts? What are its most important features?	What is the policy designed to do? What is needed to make it work? What are or will be its effects?	What brought about this policy? What are the alternatives?	Is the policy workable? What are its advantages and disadvantages? Is it practical? Is it a good policy? Why or why not?
C O N C E P T S	What is the concept? What are its parts? What is its main feature? Who or what is it related to?	Who has been influenced by this concept? Why is it important? How does it work?	When did it originate? How has it changed over the years? How might it change in the future?	What practical value does it have? Why is it superior (or inferior) to similar concepts? What is its social worth?

Identify possible sources.

Finding meaningful sources is one of the most important steps you will take as you prepare to write. Listed below are tips that will help you identify good sources:

1. **Give yourself enough time.** Finding good sources of information may be time-consuming. Books and periodicals you need may be checked out, your computer service may be down, and so on.

2. **Be aware of the limits of your resources.** Print material may be out-of-date. Online information may be more current, but it may not always be reliable. (See pages **434–437** for ways to help you evaluate information.)

3. **Use your existing resources to find additional sources of information.** Pay attention to books, articles, and individuals mentioned in reliable initial sources of information.

4. **Ask for help.** The specialists in your school library can help you find information that is reliable and relevant. These people are trained to find information; don't hesitate to ask for their help. (See pages **457–459.**)

5. **Bookmark useful websites.** Include reference works and academic resources related to your major.

Explore different sources of information.

Of course, books and websites are not the only possible sources of information. Primary sources such as interviews, observations, and surveys may lead you to a more thorough and meaningful understanding of a topic. (See pages **451–456.**)

Primary Sources	Secondary Sources
Interviews	Articles
Observations	Reference book entries
Participation	Books
Surveys	Websites

Carry out your research.

As you conduct your research, try to use a variety of reliable sources. It's also a good idea to choose an efficient note-taking method before you start. You will want to take good notes on the information you find and record all the publishing information necessary for citing your sources. (See pages **440–443.**)

Reserve a special part of a notebook to question, evaluate, and reflect on your research as it develops. The record of your thoughts and actions created during this process will mean a great deal to you—as much as or more than the actual information you uncover. Reflection helps you make sense of new ideas, refocus your thinking, and evaluate your progress.

Beginning the Process Checklist

Use this checklist as a guide to help you plan your writing.

The Situation and Assignment   *I know the . . .*

_____ subject and form—essay, narrative, or research paper.

_____ audience—who they are, what they know, and what they need.

_____ purpose of the writing—to inform, explain, analyze, or persuade.

_____ main action (key words), restrictions, and options.

_____ connection to personal and course goals.

_____ requirements for length, format, and documentation.

_____ assessment method that will be used.

The Topic   *I have . . .*

_____ explored possible topics through journal writing, freewriting, listing, clustering, or dialogue.

_____ chosen a limited topic that fits the assignment and spurs my interest.

_____ recorded what I already know and what I need to learn.

_____ developed a workable research plan.

_____ collected information about the topic.

Writing Prompt

Writing Activities

1. Reread one of your recent essays. How does the writing show that you thoroughly understood your *subject*, met the needs of your *audience*, and achieved your writing *purpose*?

2. Review the wording of a recent writing assignment. What are the key words, restrictions, and options? What does the description tell you about the purpose, audience, form, and assessment of the writing? What strategies from this chapter would you use to get started?

3. Below is a list of general subject areas. Select one that interests you and do the following: Using the strategies on pages **31–34**, brainstorm possible topics. Then select one of these topics. Finally, using the strategies on pages **35–37**, explore what you know about that topic and what you need to learn.

- **Arts/music**
- **Health/medicine**
- **Environment**
- **Housing**
- **Exercise**
- **Work/occupation**

Chapter 3
Planning

Planning of almost any type requires careful thinking. When you plan an essay, you have two basic thinking objectives: (1) establish a thesis or focus for your writing, and (2) organize the supporting information. The amount of organization time required depends on the type of writing. For narratives, very little organizing may be required. For most academic essays, however, you will need to identify the method of development—comparison, cause/effect, classification—that best supports your thesis, and then organize your details accordingly. (See pages **42–43**.) At this point, your goal is to establish the general structure of your writing.

Writer and instructor Ken Macrorie offers this important insight about planning: "Good writing is formed partly through plan and partly through accident." In other words, too much early planning can get in the way. Writing at its best is a process of discovery. You never know what new insights or ideas will spring to mind until you put pen to paper or fingers to keyboard.

What's Ahead

- Taking Inventory of Your Thoughts
- Forming Your Thesis Statement
- Using Methods of Development
- Developing a Plan or an Outline
  – Types of Graphic Organizers
- Planning Checklist and Writing Activities

Taking Inventory of Your Thoughts

Suppose you've done some searching, and you've succeeded in discovering some interesting information and perspectives about your subject. Now may be a good time to see how well your findings match up with your topic.

Re-examine your topic.

After considering the following questions, you should be able to decide whether to move ahead with your planning or reconsider your topic.

Subject:

- How much do I already know about this topic?
- Do I need to know more? Is additional information available? Where?
- Have I tried any of the collecting strategies? (See page **35**.)
- What help would I need to find information, schedule an interview with a source, and so on?

Audience:

- How much does my audience already know about this subject?
- How can I get my audience interested in my idea?
- How can I help them understand related technical terms and concepts?

Purpose:

- What are the specific requirements of this assignment?
- Do I have enough time to do a good job with this topic?
- Am I writing to inform, to explain, to analyze, or to persuade?
- How important is this assignment, and how will it be assessed?

Continue the process.

Assess whether you need additional information. If you think you do, go back to researching.

Research ■ If you need to know more about your topic, continue collecting your own thoughts and/or investigating other sources of information. Remember that it is important to investigate secondary *and* primary sources of information. (See pages **450–465**.)

Review ■ If you are ready to move ahead, carefully review your initial notes. As you read through this material, circle or underline ideas that seem important enough to include in your writing. Then look for ways in which these ideas connect or relate. The activities on the following pages will help you focus your thoughts for writing.

Web Link

Forming Your Thesis Statement

After you have completed enough research and collecting, you may begin to develop a more focused interest in your topic. If all goes well, this narrowed focus will give rise to a thesis for your writing. A thesis statement identifies your central idea. It usually highlights a special condition or feature of the topic, expresses a specific feeling, or takes a stand.

State your thesis in a sentence that effectively expresses what you want to explore or explain in your essay. Sometimes a thesis statement develops early and easily; at other times, the true focus of your writing emerges only after you've written your first draft.

Find a focus.

A general subject area is typically built into your writing assignments. Your task, then, is to find a limited writing topic and examine it from a particular angle or perspective. (You will use this focus to form your thesis statement.)

FOCUSING A TOPIC

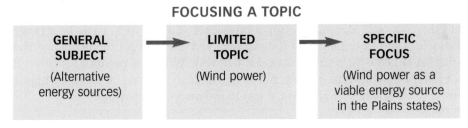

GENERAL SUBJECT	LIMITED TOPIC	SPECIFIC FOCUS
(Alternative energy sources)	(Wind power)	(Wind power as a viable energy source in the Plains states)

State your thesis.

You can use the following formula to write a thesis statement for your essay. A thesis statement sets the tone and direction for your writing. Keep in mind that at this point you're writing a *working thesis statement*—a statement in progress, so to speak. You may change it as your thinking on the topic evolves.

> **A manageable or limited topic** (wind power)
> + **a specific focus** (provides a viable energy source in the Plains states)
> = **an effective thesis statement**

THESIS STATEMENT: Wind power provides a viable energy source in the Plains states.

Thesis Checklist

1. Does the thesis statement reflect a limited topic?
2. Does it clearly state the specific idea you plan to develop?
3. Is the thesis supported by the information you have gathered?
4. Does the thesis suggest a pattern of organization for your essay?

Using Methods of Development

An organizing pattern for your essay may be built into your assignment. For example, you may be asked to develop an argument or to write a process paper. When a pattern is not apparent, one may still evolve naturally during the research and information-collecting steps. If this doesn't happen, take a careful look at your thesis statement.

Let your thesis guide you.

An effective thesis will often suggest an organizing pattern. Notice how the thesis statements below provide direction and shape for the writing to follow. (Also see page **107**.)

Thesis (Focus) for a Personal Narrative

What began as a simple prank ended up having serious consequences for all of us who were involved.

Discussion This statement identifies the focus of a personal narrative. It suggests that the essay will recount a personal experience and will most likely be arranged chronologically, beginning with the planning and execution of the prank and then going on to relate the consequences that followed. Writers of personal narratives do not always state a thesis directly, but they will generally have in mind an implied theme or main idea that governs the way they develop their writing.

Thesis for a Descriptive Essay

Although it was no more than an overgrown lot, as children we imagined the property next to my boyhood home to be a forest full of danger and adventure.

Discussion This statement indicates that the writer will describe a special place from childhood. This description might be organized spatially, moving from the edges of the wooded lot to its interior. A description may be organized thematically, in this case by describing the specific features of the lot through the adventures the children imagined having there.

Thesis for a Cause and Effect Essay

We can accept that some stress is inescapable, but for our own health and for the well-being of others, we have to do more: We have to understand what stress is—both its causes and its effects.

Discussion This thesis indicates that the writer is developing a cause and effect essay. Essays following this pattern usually begin with one or more causes followed by an explanation of the effects, or they begin with a primary effect followed by an explanation of the causes. To develop the thesis above, the writer will follow the first route, exploring the causes of stress before examining its effects.

Thesis for an Essay of Comparison

Bigger in Native Son *and Alan in* Equus *are both entering adulthood and have come to realize that they are controlled by work, religion, and the media.*

Discussion   Comparisons are patterned in two ways: Either you discuss one of the subjects completely and then the other (whole versus whole), or you discuss both subjects at the same time (point by point). The writer of this thesis is comparing two literary characters point by point.

Thesis for an Essay of Classification

There are four main perspectives, or approaches, that you can use to converse about literature.

Discussion   The writer is writing an essay of classification. Essays following this pattern identify the main parts or categories of a topic and then examine each one. In this thesis, the writer identifies four ways to discuss literature, and he examines each one in turn. (See pages **208–209** for this essay.)

Thesis for a Process Essay

When a cell begins to function abnormally, it can initiate a process that results in cancer.

Discussion   As indicated in this thesis, the writer of this essay will explain how cancer cells multiply and affect the body. Process essays, such as this one, are organized chronologically. Each step is examined in turn to help readers understand the complete process. (See pages **219–220** for this essay.)

Thesis for an Essay of Definition

My memories, like the things I enjoy, can be described in only one way: eclectic, *a word I find endlessly fascinating.*

Discussion   This essay provides an interesting personal definition of the word *eclectic*. This particular essay of definition is generally organized around explanation and analysis. The writer explains what the word means and analyzes her personal interpretation of the term.

Thesis for an Essay Proposing a Solution

The best solution to controlling deer populations is to stay as close to nature's ways as possible, and game management by hunting meets this criterion.

Discussion   The writer of this thesis is developing a problem/solution essay. Essays following this pattern usually begin with a discussion of the problem and its causes and then examine possible solutions. In this essay, the writer presents a problem's history, causes, and effects. He then identifies and dismisses some solutions before arguing for one solution in particular.

Developing a Plan or an Outline

After writing a working thesis and reviewing the methods of development (pages 42–43), you should be ready to organize the information you have collected. A simple listing of main points may work for you, or you may need to outline the information or use a graphic organizer.

- **Basic list:** a brief listing of main points
- **Topic outline:** a more formal arrangement, including main points and essential details (See below.)
- **Sentence outline:** a formal arrangement, including main points and essential details, written as complete sentences (See page 45.)
- **Graphic organizer:** an arrangement of main points and essential details in an appropriate chart or diagram (See pages 45–47.)

Choose an organization method.

If you have a good deal of information to sort and arrange, you may want to use a topic or sentence outline for your planning.

Topic Outline

In a topic outline you state each main point and essential detail as a word or phrase. Before you start constructing your outline, write your working thesis statement at the top of your paper to help keep you focused on the subject. (Do not attempt to outline your opening and closing paragraphs unless you are specifically asked to do so.)

Sample Topic Outline

Thesis: There are four main perspectives, or approaches, that you can use to converse about literature.

  I. Text-centered approaches
    A. Also called formalist criticism
    B. Emphasis on structure of text and rules of genre
    C. Importance placed on key literary elements
 II. Audience-centered approaches
    A. Also called rhetorical or reader-response criticism
    B. Emphasis on interaction between reader and text
III. Author-centered approaches
    A. Emphasis on writer's life
    B. Importance placed on historical perspective
    C. Connections made between texts
 IV. Ideological approaches
    A. Psychological analysis of text
    B. Myth or archetype criticism
    C. Moral criticism
    D. Sociological analysis

Sentence Outline

The sample outline below uses complete sentences to explain the main points and essential details that will be covered in the main part of the essay.

Sample Sentence Outline

Thesis: There are four main perspectives, or approaches, that you can use to converse about literature.

I. A text-centered approach focuses on the literary piece itself.
   A. This approach is often called formalist criticism.
   B. This method of criticism examines text structure and the rules of the genre.
   C. A formalist critic determines how key literary elements reinforce meaning.
II. An audience-centered approach focuses on the "transaction" between text and reader.
   A. This approach is often called rhetorical or reader-response criticism.
   B. A rhetorical critic sees the text as an activity that is different for each reader.
III. An author-centered approach focuses on the origin of a text.
   A. An author-centered critic examines the writer's life.
   B. This method of criticism may include a historical look at a text.
   C. Connections may be made between the text and related works.
IV. The ideological approach applies ideas outside of literature.
   A. Some critics apply psychological theories to a literary work.
   B. Myth or archetype criticism applies anthropology and classical studies to a text.
   C. Moral criticism explores the moral dilemmas in literature.
   D. Sociological approaches include Marxist, feminist, and minority criticism.

Graphic Organizers

If you are a visual person, you might prefer a graphic organizer when it comes to arranging your ideas for an essay or report. Graphic organizers can help you map out ideas and illustrate relationships among them. Here is a graphic organizer—a line diagram—that was used to organize the ideas for the essay. (Also see pages **46–47**.)

Sample Graphic Organizer

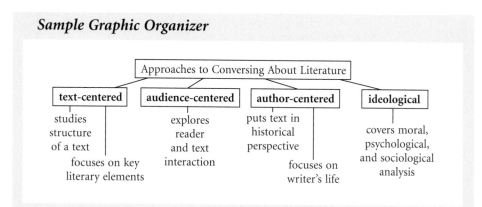

Types of Graphic Organizers

The following organizers are related to some of the methods of development discussed on pages **42–43**. Each will help you collect and organize your information. Adapt the organizers as necessary to fit your particular needs or personal style.

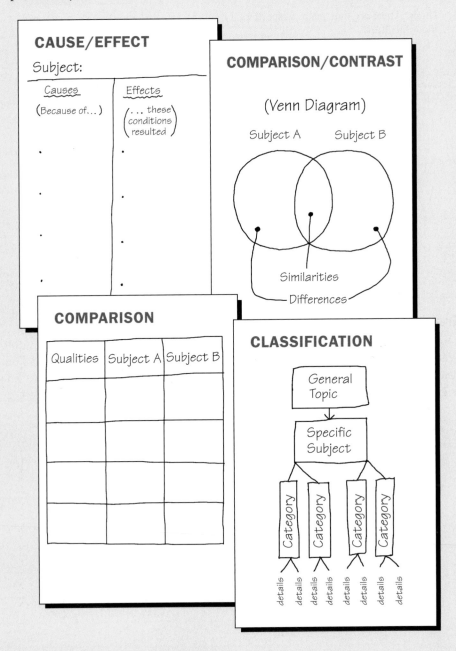

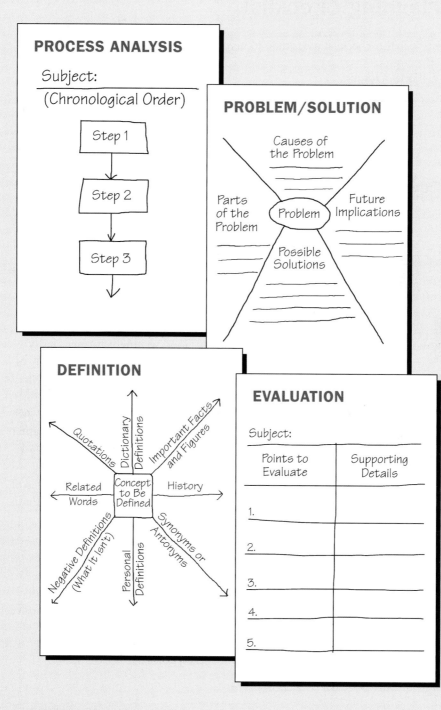

PROCESS ANALYSIS

Subject: _____

(Chronological Order)

Step 1

↓

Step 2

↓

Step 3

↓

PROBLEM/SOLUTION

Causes of
the Problem

Parts
of the
Problem

Problem

Future
Implications

Possible
Solutions

DEFINITION

Quotations

Dictionary
Definitions

Important Facts
and Figures

Related
Words

Concept
to Be
Defined

History

Negative Definitions
(What It Isn't)

Personal
Definitions

Synonyms or
Antonyms

EVALUATION

Subject: _____

Points to Evaluate	Supporting Details
1.	
2.	
3.	
4.	
5.	

Planning Checklist

Use this checklist as a guide to help you plan your writing.

Thesis *I have . . .*

_____ reviewed information I've collected up to this point.

_____ identified a specific focus or feature of my topic to develop.

_____ stated a focus in a working thesis statement.

_____ tested the thesis to make sure it is supportable.

Development *I have . . .*

_____ identified a pattern of organization to develop my thesis.

_____ organized my support in a list, outline, or graphic organizer.

_____ prepared to write the first draft.

Writing Activities

1. Author Ken Macrorie claims that "Good writing is formed partly through plan and partly through accident." Do you agree? Why or why not? Relate Macrorie's idea to your own writing experiences. How carefully do you plan? How much do you leave to accident?

2. A number of organizational patterns are discussed on pages 42–43. Choose one of these patterns and select a model essay from Chapters 10–20 that follows the pattern. Read the essay, note the thesis, and explain how the writer develops it.

3. Listed below are general subject areas. Do the following for three of these subjects: (1) identify a limited topic, (2) write a working thesis statement, and (3) identify a pattern of organization you could use to develop the thesis.

- **Afghanistan**
- **Agriculture**
- **Careers**
- **Communications**
- **Community**

- **Education**
- **Entertainment**
- **Exercise**
- **Family**
- **Freedom**

- **Iraq**
- **Medicine**
- **Natural Resources**
- **Olympics**
- **U.S. Courts**

Chapter 4
Drafting

Video

The early twentieth-century French novelist Anatole France is reported to have said that one of his first drafts could have been written by any schoolboy, his next draft by a bright upper-level student, his third draft by a superior graduate, his fourth draft by a seasoned professional, and his final draft "only by Anatole France." Even if that report is exaggerated, the point is well taken: The first draft is not the one that will distinguish you as a writer. It's a way of getting material together, starting out, connecting your ideas. A first draft gives you something to work with—verbal wet clay—that will later, through revising and editing, result in a polished piece of writing.

This section provides information and advice about drafting a college-level essay. Our special focus is on the sorts of "moves" that may occur at each major stage of the draft. If you know in advance what moves to make, you'll be in a better position to develop a thoughtful and complete draft.

What's Ahead

- Writing Your First Draft
- Opening Your Draft
- Developing the Middle
- Ending Your Draft
- Drafting Checklist and Writing Activities

Writing Your First Draft

The American novelist Kurt Vonnegut once laughingly divided writers into two categories: swoopers and bashers. Swoopers write seventeen drafts at high speed before they're done; bashers won't move to sentence number two until they have polished sentence number one. When you draft your next paper, you'll strike a better balance between carelessness and care if you focus on the essentials: audience, purpose, and subject.

Reconsider your audience.

Review who your readers are, including their knowledge of and attitude toward your topic. Then get ready to talk with them, person to person.

Reconsider your purpose.

Briefly review (1) what you want your writing to do (your task), (2) what you want it to say (your thesis), and (3) how you want to say it (list of ideas or outline).

Focus on your subject.

As you develop your first draft, these strategies can help you keep your subject in focus.

- Use your outline or writing plan as a general guide. Try to develop your main points, but allow new ideas to emerge naturally.

- Write freely without being too concerned about neatness and correctness. Concentrate on developing your ideas, not on producing a final copy.

- Include as much detail as possible, continuing until you reach a logical stopping point.

- Use your writing plan or any charts, lists, or diagrams you've produced, but don't feel absolutely bound by them.

- Complete your first draft in one or two sittings.

- Use the most natural voice you can so that the writing will flow smoothly. If your voice is too formal during drafting, you'll be tempted to stop and edit your words.

- Quote sources accurately by using your word processor's copy and paste features or by handwriting quotations carefully.

INSIGHT: If you have trouble getting started, think of your writing as half of a conversation with a reader you invent. Talk to your silent partner. Think about what you've already said and let that help you decide what you should say next.

Basic Essay Structure: Major Moves

The following chart lists the main writing moves that occur during the development of a piece of writing. Use it as a general guide for all of your drafting. Remember to keep your purpose and audience in mind throughout the drafting process.

Opening

Engage your reader.
Stimulate and direct the reader's attention.

Establish your direction.
Identify the topic and put it in perspective.

Get to the point.
Narrow your focus and state your thesis.

Middle

Advance your thesis.
Provide background information and cover your main points.

Test your ideas.
Raise questions and consider alternatives.

Support your main points.
Add substance and build interest.

Build a coherent structure.
Start new paragraphs and arrange the support.

Use different levels of detail.
Clarify and complete each main point.

Ending

Reassert the main point.
Remind the reader of the purpose and rephrase the thesis.

Urge the reader.
Gain the reader's acceptance and look ahead.

Opening Your Draft

The opening paragraph is one of the most important elements in any composition. It should accomplish at least three essential things: (1) engage the reader; (2) establish your direction, tone, and level of language; and (3) introduce your line of thought.

Advice: The conventional way of approaching the first paragraph is to view it as a kind of "funnel" that draws a reader in and narrows to a main point. Often, the final sentence explicitly states your thesis.

Cautions: **1.** Don't feel bound by the conventional pattern, which may sound stale if not handled well.

2. Don't let the importance of the first paragraph paralyze you. Relax and write.

The information on the next two pages will help you develop your opening. You can refer to the sample essays in the handbook for ideas.

Engage your reader.

Your reader will be preoccupied with other thoughts until you seize, stimulate, and direct his or her attention. Here are some effective ways to "hook" the reader:

- Mention little-known facts about the topic.
- Pose a challenging question.
- Offer a thought-provoking quotation.
- Tell a brief, illuminating story.
- Introduce your angle or focus on the topic.

Establish your direction.

The direction of your line of thought should become clear in the opening part of your writing. Here are some moves you might make to set the right course:

Identify the topic (issue) ■ Show a problem, a need, or an opportunity.

Deepen the issue ■ Connect the topic, showing its importance.

Acknowledge other views ■ Tell what others say or think about the topic.

Web Link

INSIGHT: Your opening affects the direction and line of thinking of your entire piece of writing. If you don't like the first or second attempt, keep trying. You'll know when you hit the right version because it will help you visualize the rest of your draft.

Get to the point.

You may choose to state your main point up front, or you may wait until later to introduce your thesis. Sometimes your thesis may simply be implied. In any case, the opening should at least establish a "curve" toward the central issue or thesis of your paper. Here are three ways to get to the point:

Narrow your focus ■ Point to what interests you about the topic.

Raise a question ■ You can answer the question in the rest of the essay.

State your thesis ■ If appropriate, craft a sentence that boils down your meaning. You can use the thesis sentence as a "map" for the organization of the rest of the essay. (See pages **41–43**, **104–107**, and **426–427**.)

Weak Opening

Although the opening below introduces the topic, the writing lacks interesting details and establishes no clear focus for the essay.

> I would like to tell you about the TV show *The Simpsons*. It's about this weird family of five people who look kind of strange and act even stranger. In fact, the characters aren't even real—they're just cartoons.

Strong Opening

In the essay opener below, the writer uses his first paragraph to get his readers' attention and describe his subject. He uses the second paragraph to raise a question that leads him to a statement of his thesis (underlined).

> The Simpsons, stars of the TV show by the same name, are a typical American family, or at least a parody of one. Homer, Marge, Bart, Lisa, and Maggie Simpson live in Springfield, U.S.A. Homer, the father, is a boorish, obese oaf who works in a nuclear power plant. Marge is an overprotective, nagging mother with an outrageous blue hairdo. Ten-year-old Bart is an obnoxious, "spiky-haired demon." Lisa is eight and a prodigy on the tenor saxophone and in class. The infant Maggie never speaks but only sucks on her pacifier.
>
> What is the attraction of this yellow-skinned family that stars on a show in which all of the characters have pronounced overbites and only four fingers on each hand? I contend that we see a little bit of ourselves in everything they do. <u>The world of Springfield is a parody of our own world, and Americans can't get enough of it.</u>

Web Link

Developing the Middle

The middle of an essay is where you do the "heavy lifting." In this part you develop the main points that support your thesis statement.

Advice: As you write, you will likely make choices that were unforeseen when you began. Use "scratch outlines" (temporary jottings) along the way to show where your new ideas may take you.

Cautions: **1.** Writing that lacks effective detail gives only a vague image of the writer's intent.

2. Writing that wanders loses its hold on the essay's purpose.

For both of these reasons, always keep your thesis in mind when you develop the main part of your writing. Refer to the guidelines on the next two pages for help. You can refer to the sample essays in this book for ideas.

Advance your thesis.

If you stated a thesis in the opening, you can advance it in the middle paragraphs by covering your main points and supporting them in these ways.

> *Explain:* Provide important facts, details, and examples.
>
> *Narrate:* Share a brief story or re-create an experience to illustrate an idea.
>
> *Describe:* Tell in detail how someone appears or how something works.
>
> *Define:* Identify or clarify the meaning of a specific term or idea.
>
> *Analyze:* Examine the parts of something to better understand the whole.
>
> *Compare:* Provide examples to show how two things are alike or different.
>
> *Argue:* Use logic and evidence to prove that something is true.
>
> *Reflect:* Express your thoughts or feelings about something.
>
> *Cite authorities:* Add expert analysis or personal commentary.

Test your ideas.

When you write a first draft, you're testing your initial thinking about your topic. You're determining whether your thesis is valid and whether you have enough compelling information to support it. Here are ways to test your line of thinking as you write:

Raise questions. ■ Try to anticipate your readers' questions.

Consider alternatives. ■ Look at your ideas from different angles; weigh various options; reevaluate your thesis.

Answer objections. ■ Directly or indirectly deal with possible problems that a skeptical reader might point out.

Build a coherent structure.

Design paragraphs as units of thought that develop and advance your thesis clearly and logically. For example, look at the brief essay below, noting how each body paragraph presents ideas with supporting details that build on and deepen the main idea.

The writer introduces the topic, suggests his organizational pattern (comparison), and states his thesis.

Making a transition into his discussion, the writer starts with a basic explanation of how the two types of lightbulbs function differently; details show how.

The writer shifts his attention to weaknesses of compact bulbs.

Using "On the other hand" as a transition, he next explains the strengths of compacts.

He acknowledges that compacts cost more, but he then justifies the cost.

The writer rephrases his thesis as a challenge.

Seeing the Light

All lightbulbs make light, so they're all the same, right? Not quite. You have many choices regarding how to light up your life. Two types of bulbs are the traditional incandescent and the newer, more compact fluorescent. <u>By checking out how they're different, you can better choose which one to buy.</u>

While either incandescent or compact fluorescent bulbs can help you read or find the bathroom at night, each bulb makes light differently. In an incandescent bulb, electricity heats up a tungsten filament (thin wire) to 450 degrees, causing it to glow with a warm, yellow light. A compact fluorescent is a glass tube filled with mercury vapor and argon gas. Electricity causes the mercury to give off ultraviolet radiation. That radiation then causes phosphors coating the inside of the tube to give off light.

Both types of bulbs come in many shapes, sizes, and brightnesses, but compacts have some restrictions. Because of their odd shape, compacts may not fit in a lamp well. Compacts also may not work well in very cold temperatures, and they can't be used with a dimmer switch.

On the other hand, while compact fluorescents are less flexible than incandescents, compacts are four times more efficient. For example, a 15-watt compact produces as many lumens of light as a 60-watt incandescent! Why? Incandescents turn only about 5 percent of electricity into light and give off the other 95 percent as heat.

But are compacts less expensive than incandescents? In the short run, no. A compact costs about $15 while an incandescent costs only a dollar. However, because compacts burn less electricity—and last 7 to 10 times longer—in the long run, compacts are less expensive.

Now that you're no longer in the dark about light-bulbs, take a look at the lamp you're using to read this essay. Think about the watts (electricity used), lumens (light produced), efficiency, purchase price, and lamplife. Then decide how to light up your life in the future.

Arrange supporting details.

Organizing information in a logical pattern within a paragraph strengthens its coherence. The following pages explain and illustrate ten organizational strategies. (See also page **413**.)

Analogy

An analogy is a comparison that a writer uses to explain a complex or unfamiliar phenomenon (how the immune system works) in terms of a familiar one (how mall security works).

> **The human body is like a mall, and the immune system is like mall security. Because the mall has hundreds of employees and thousands of customers, security guards must rely on photo IDs, nametags, and uniforms to decide who should be allowed to open cash registers and who should have access to the vault. In the same way, white blood cells and antibodies need to use DNA cues to recognize which cells belong in a body and which do not. Occasionally security guards make mistakes, wrestling Kookie the Klown to the ground while DVD players "walk" out of the service entrance, but these problems amount only to allergic reactions or little infections. If security guards become hypervigilant, detaining every customer and employee, the situation is akin to leukemia, in which white blood cells attack healthy cells. If security guards become corrupt, letting thieves take a "five-finger discount," the situation is akin to AIDs. Both systems—mall security and human immunity—work by correctly differentiating friend from foe.**

Cause and Effect

Cause-and-effect organization shows how events are linked to their results. If you start with effects, follow with specific causes; in contrast, if you begin with causes, follow with specific effects. The example below discusses the effects of hypothermia on the human body.

> **Even a slight drop in the normal human body temperature of 98.6 degrees Fahrenheit causes hypothermia. Often produced by accidental or prolonged exposure to cold, the condition forces all bodily functions to slow down. The heart rate and blood pressure decrease. Breathing becomes slower and shallower. As the body temperature drops, these effects become even more dramatic until it reaches somewhere between 86 and 82 degrees Fahrenheit and the person lapses into unconsciousness. When the temperature reaches between 65 and 59 degrees Fahrenheit, heart action, blood flow, and electrical brain activity stop. Normally such a condition would be fatal. However, as the body cools down, the need for oxygen also slows down. A person can survive in a deep hypothermic state for an hour or longer and be revived without serious complications.**
> —Laura Black

Chronological Order

Chronological (time) order helps you tell a story or present steps in a process. For example, the following paragraph describes how cement is made. Notice how the writer explains every step and uses transitional words to lead readers through the process.

> The production of cement is a complicated process. The raw materials that go into cement consist of about 60 percent lime, 25 percent silica, and 5 percent alumina. The remaining 10 percent is a varying combination of gypsum and iron oxide (because the amount of gypsum determines the drying time of the cement). First, this mixture is ground up into very fine particles and fed into a kiln. Cement kilns, the largest pieces of moving machinery used by any industry, are colossal steel cylinders lined with firebricks. They can be 25 feet in diameter and up to 750 feet long. The kiln is built at a slant and turns slowly as the cement mix makes its way down from the top end. A flame at the bottom heats the kiln to temperatures of up to 3,000 degrees Fahrenheit. When the melted cement compound emerges from the kiln, it cools into little marble-like balls called clinker. Finally, the clinker is ground to a consistency finer than flour and packaged as cement.
>
> —Kevin Maas

Classification

When classifying a subject, place the subject in its appropriate category and then show how this subject is different from other subjects in the same category. In the following paragraph, a student writer uses classification to describe the theory of temperament.

> Medieval doctors believed that "four temperaments rule man kind wholly." According to this theory, each person has a distinctive temperament or personality (sanguine, phlegmatic, melancholy, or choleric) based on the balance of four elements in the body, a balance peculiar to the individual. The theory was built on Galen and Hippocrates' notion of "humors," that the body contains blood, phlegm, black bile, and yellow bile—four fluids that maintain the balance within the body. The sanguine person was dominated by blood, associated with fire: blood was hot and moist, and the person was fat and prone to laughter. The phlegmatic person was dominated by phlegm (associated with earth) and was squarish and slothful—a sleepy type. The melancholy person was dominated by cold, black bile (connected with the element of water) and as a result was pensive, peevish, and solitary. The choleric person was dominated by hot, yellow bile (air) and thus was inclined to anger.
>
> —Jessica Radsma

Compare-Contrast

To compare and contrast, show how two or more subjects are similar and different. See models on pages 189–199.

Climax

Climax is a method in which you first present details and then provide a general climactic statement or conclusion drawn from the details.

> **The cockroach is unhonored and unsung. It walks about with downcast eyes. Its head hangs dejectedly between its knees. It lives on modest fare and in humble circumstances. It is drab-colored and inconspicuous. But don't let that Uriah Heep exterior fool you. For there you have Superbug, himself!**

—Edwin Way Teale, *The Lost Woods*

Definition

A definition provides the denotation (dictionary meaning) and connotation (feeling) of a given term. It often provides examples, gives anecdotes, and offers negative definitions—what the thing is *not*. In the paragraph below, the writer begins his definition by posing a question.

> **First of all, what is the grotesque—in visual art and in literature? A term originally applied to Roman cave art that distorted the normal, the grotesque presents the body and mind so that they appear abnormal— different from the bodies and minds that we think belong in our world. Both spiritual and physical, bizarre and familiar, ugly and alluring, the grotesque shocks us, and we respond with laughter and fear. We laugh because the grotesque seems bizarre enough to belong only outside our world; we fear because it feels familiar enough to be part of it. Seeing the grotesque version of life as it is portrayed in art stretches our vision of reality. As Bernard McElroy argues, "The grotesque transforms the world from what we 'know' it to be to what we fear it might be. It distorts and exaggerates the surface of reality in order to tell a qualitative truth about it."**

—John Van Rys

Illustration

An illustration supports a general idea with specific reasons, facts, and details.

> **As the years passed, my obsession grew. Every fiber and cell of my body was obsessed with the number on the scale and how much fat I could pinch on my thigh. No matter how thin I was, I thought I could never be thin enough. I fought my sisters for control of the TV and VCR to do my exercise programs and videos. The cupboards were stacked with cans of diet mixes, the refrigerator full of diet drinks. Hidden in my underwear drawer were stacks of diet pills that I popped along with my vitamins. At my worst, I would quietly excuse myself from family activities to turn on the bathroom faucet full blast and vomit into the toilet. Every day I stood in front of the mirror, a ritual not unlike brushing my teeth, and scrutinized my body. My face, arms, stomach, buttocks, hips, and thighs could never be small enough.**

—Paula Treick

Narration

In the paragraph below, the writer uses narration and chronological order to relate an anecdote—a short, illustrative story.

> When I was six or seven years old, growing up in Pittsburgh, I used to take a precious penny of my own and hide it for someone else to find. It was a curious compulsion; sadly, I've never been seized by it since. For some reason I always "hid" the penny along the same stretch of sidewalk up the street. I would cradle it at the roots of a sycamore, say, or in a hole left by a chipped-off piece of sidewalk. Then I would take a piece of chalk, and, starting at either end of the block, draw huge arrows leading up to the penny from both directions. After I learned to write I labeled the arrows: surprise ahead or money this way. I was greatly excited, during all this arrow-drawing, at the thought of the first lucky passer-by who would receive in this way, regardless of merit, a free gift from the universe. But I never lurked about. I would go straight home and not give the matter another thought, until, some months later, I would be gripped again by the impulse to hide another penny.
>
> —Annie Dillard, *Pilgrim at Tinker Creek*

Process

In the paragraph that follows, a student writer describes the process of entering the "tube," or "green room," while surfing.

> At this point you are slightly ahead of the barreling part of the wave, and you need to "stall," or slow yourself, to get into the tube. There are three methods of stalling used in different situations. If you are slightly ahead of the tube, you can drag your inside hand along the water to stall. If you are a couple of feet in front of the barrel, apply all your weight onto your back foot and sink the tail of the board into the water. This is known as a "tail stall" for obvious reasons, and its purpose is to decrease your board speed. If you are moving faster than the wave is breaking, you need to do what is called a "wrap-around." To accomplish this maneuver, lean back away from the wave while applying pressure on the tail. This shifts your forward momentum away from the wave and slows you down. When the wave comes, turn toward the wave and place yourself in the barrel.
>
> —Luke Sunukjian, "Entering the Green Room"

TIP: Choose an organizational pattern that most clearly advances your thesis for your specific audience. For example, in order to explain anorexia to readers unfamiliar with the condition, Paula Treick illustrates its effects (see page 58).

Web Link

Ending Your Draft

Closing paragraphs can be important for tying up loose ends, clarifying key points, or signing off with the reader. In a sense, the entire essay is a preparation for an effective ending; the ending helps the reader look back over the essay with new understanding and appreciation. Many endings leave the reader with fresh food for thought.

Advice: Because the ending can be so important, draft a variety of possible endings. Choose the one that flows best from a sense of the whole.

Cautions: **1.** If your thesis is weak or unclear, you will have a difficult time writing a satisfactory ending. To strengthen the ending, strengthen the thesis.

2. You may have heard this formula for writing an essay: "Say what you're going to say, say it, then say what you've just said." Remember, though, if you need to "say what you've just said," say it in new words.

The information on the next two pages will help you develop your ending. You can refer to the sample essays elsewhere in this book for ideas.

Reassert the main point.

If an essay is complicated, the reader may need reclarification at the end. Show that you are fulfilling the promises you made in the beginning.

Remind the reader ■ Recall what you first set out to do; check off the key points you've covered; or answer any questions left unanswered.

Rephrase the thesis ■ Restate your thesis in light of the most important support you've given. Deepen and expand your original thesis.

Urge the reader.

Your reader may still be reluctant to accept your ideas or argument. The ending is your last chance to gain the reader's acceptance. Here are some possible strategies:

Show the implications ■ Follow further possibilities raised by your train of thought; be reasonable and convincing.

Look ahead ■ Suggest other possible connections.

List the benefits ■ Show the reader the benefits of accepting or applying the things you've said.

INSIGHT: When your writing comes to an effective stopping point, conclude the essay. Don't tack on another idea.

Complete and unify your message.

Your final paragraphs are your last opportunity to refocus, unify, and otherwise reinforce your message. Draft the closing carefully, not merely to finish the essay but to further advance your purpose and thesis.

Weak Ending

The ending below does not focus on and show commitment to the essay's main idea. Rather than reinforcing this idea, the writing leads off in a new direction.

> So the bottom line is that Mom's photo showed how much I liked my little stream. Of course I have lots of other good childhood memories as well, like the times Dad would read to me before bedtime. I loved those books. How about you? Do you have good childhood memories?

Strong Endings

Below are final paragraphs from two essays in this book. Listen to their tone, watch how they reconsider the essay's ideas, and note how they offer further food for thought. (The first example is a revision of the weak paragraph above.)

> Sometimes, I want to go back there, back into that photo. I want to step into a time when life seemed safe, and a tiny stream gave us all that we needed. In that picture, our smiles last, our hearts are calm, and we hear only quiet voices, forest sounds, and my bubbling stream. Bitter words are silenced and tears held back by the click and whir of a camera.
>
> I've been thinking about making the journey again past the hunter's fort, under the stand of cedars, through the muck and mire, and over the rocky rise. But it's been a long summer, and the small seasonal stream running out of the overflow of the pond has probably dried up. (See the full essay on 157–158.)

> On September 11, 2001, America, along with its Western allies, lost its aura of invincibility. As the whole world watched, the towers fell, and we stumbled in shock and pain. Moreover, as time passes, America may fail to identify its enemy and to understand the attack. If this happens, the oppressed people of the world—to some extent victims of Western culture—will take notice.
>
> It is now one week since the towers fell, and the world still grieves. However, mingled with this grief is the fear that we may be mourning not only for the lives lost, but also for our lost way of life. (See the full essay on 189–190.)

INSIGHT: Think about your document's opening and closing as a type of contract that you make with your reader. Whereas the opening explains what you *intend to do*, the closing reviews and confirms what you *have done*.

Drafting Checklist

Use this checklist as a guide when you develop a first draft for an essay. (To see drafting in action, turn to pages **108–115**.)

Opening

The opening of my paper . . .

_____ engages the reader.

_____ establishes a focus.

_____ states a main point.

Middle

The middle of my paper . . .

_____ advances my thesis.

_____ develops and tests my ideas.

_____ has a clear, logical order.

_____ includes needed supporting details.

Ending

The closing of my paper . . .

_____ reasserts the main point.

_____ emphasizes the topic's relevance.

_____ completes and unifies the message.

Writing Activities

1. Study the chart on page **51**. Based on other material you have read or written, add another writing move for each of the three main parts of the essay: opening, middle, and ending. Name the move, explain it, and tell what types of writing it might appear in.

2. Read the final paragraphs of any three essays included in this book. Write a brief analysis of each ending based on the information presented on pages **60–61**.

3. Imagine that you are a journalist asked to write an article about a wedding, a funeral, or another significant event you have experienced. Choose one and sketch out a plan for your article, including the main writing moves you would use. More specifically, explain what type of information you would include at each stage of your writing.

Chapter 5
Revising

Video

Revising takes courage. Once you have your first draft on paper, the piece may feel finished. The temptation then is to be satisfied with a quick "spell check" before turning in the paper. A word to the wise: Avoid this temptation.

Good writing almost always requires revising and, in some cases, substantial rework. During this step in the writing process, you make changes in the content of your first draft until it says exactly what you mean. To get started, assess the overall quality of the ideas, organization, and voice in your writing. Then be prepared to tinker with your writing until it effectively carries your message. It's also a good idea to share your draft with your instructor, a peer, or a tutor. All writers benefit from sincere, constructive advice during the revision process. This chapter will introduce you to valuable revising guidelines and strategies to use in all of your writing.

What's Ahead

- Addressing Whole-Paper Issues
- Revising Your First Draft
- Revising for Ideas and Organization
- Revising for Voice and Style
- Addressing Paragraph Issues
- Revising Collaboratively
- Using the Writing Center
- Revising Checklist and Writing Activities

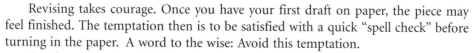

Addressing Whole-Paper Issues

When revising, first look at the big picture. Take it all in. Determine whether the content is interesting, informative, and worth sharing. Note any gaps or soft spots in your line of thinking. Ask yourself how you can improve what you have done so far. The information that follows will help you address whole-paper issues such as these.

Revisit your purpose and audience.

Remember why you are writing—your purpose. Are you sharing information, recalling an experience, explaining a process, or arguing a point? Does your writing achieve that purpose? Also, consider your readers. How much do they know about the subject? What else do they need to know?

Consider your overall approach.

Sometimes it's better to start fresh if your writing contains stretches of uninspired ideas. Consider a fresh start if your first draft shows one of these problems:

The topic is worn-out. ■ An essay titled "Lead Poisoning" may not sound very interesting. Unless you can approach it with a new twist ("Get the Lead Out!"), consider cutting your losses and finding a fresh topic.

The approach is stale. ■ If you've been writing primarily to get a good grade, finish the assignment, or sound cool, start again. Try writing to learn something, prompt real thinking in readers, or touch a chord.

Your voice is predictable or fake. ■ Avoid the bland "A good time was had by all" or the phony academic "When one studies this significant problem in considerable depth . . . " Be real. Be honest.

The draft sounds boring. ■ Maybe it's boring because you pay an equal amount of attention to everything and hence stress nothing. Try condensing less important material and expanding what's important.

The essay is formulaic. ■ That is, it follows the "five-paragraph" format. This handy organizing frame may prevent you from doing justice to your topic and thinking. If your draft is dragged down by rigid adherence to a formula, try a more original approach.

> **TIP:** To energize your writing, try these strategies:
> - Freewrite to find a new angle or approach to the topic.
> - Review your research notes for additional interesting details.
> - List and respond to arguments opposed to your thesis.

Revising Your First Draft

Revising helps you turn your first draft into a more complete, thoughtful piece of writing. The following information will help you do that.

Prepare to revise.

Once you've finished a first draft, set it aside (ideally for a few days) until you can look at the draft objectively and make needed changes. If you drafted on paper, photocopy the draft. If you drafted on a computer, print your paper (double-spaced). Then make changes with a good pencil or colored pen. If you prefer revising on the computer, consider using your software editing program. In all cases, save your first draft for reference.

Think globally.

When revising, focus on the big picture—the overall strength of the ideas, organization, and voice.

Ideas ■ Check your thesis, focus, or theme. Has your thinking on your topic changed? Also think about your readers' most pressing questions concerning this topic. Have you answered these questions? Finally, consider your reasoning and support. Are both complete and sound?

Organization ■ Check the overall design of your writing, making sure that ideas move smoothly and logically from one point to the next. Does your essay build effectively? Do you shift directions cleanly? Fix structural problems in one of these ways:

- Reorder material to improve the sequence.
- Cut information that doesn't support the thesis.
- Add details where the draft is thin.
- Rewrite parts that seem unclear.
- Improve links between points by using transitions.

Voice ■ Voice is your personal presence on the page, your tone and your attitude that others hear when reading your work. In other words, voice is the between-the-lines message your readers get (whether you want them to or not). When revising, make sure that the tone of your message matches your purpose, whether it is serious, playful, or satiric.

INSIGHT: Don't pay undue attention to spelling, grammar, and punctuation at this early stage in the process. Otherwise, you may become distracted from the task at hand: improving the content of your writing. Editing and proofreading come later.

Revising for Ideas and Organization

As you review your draft for content, make sure that all of the ideas are fully developed and the organization is clear.

Examine your ideas.

Review the ideas in your writing, making sure that each point is logical, complete, and clear. To test the logic in your writing, see pages **255–258**.

Complete Thinking

Have you answered readers' basic questions? Have you supported the thesis? The original passage below is too general; the revision is clearly more complete.

Original Passage (Too general)

As soon as you receive a minor cut, the body's healing process begins to work. Blood from tiny vessels fills the wound and begins to clot. In less than 24 hours, a scab forms.

Revised Version (More specific)

As soon as you receive a minor cut, the body's healing process begins to work. In a simple wound, the first and second layers of skin are severed along with tiny blood vessels called capillaries. As these vessels bleed into the wound, minute structures called platelets help stop the bleeding by sticking to the edges of the cut and to one another, forming a plug. The platelets then release chemicals that react with certain proteins in the blood to form a clot. The blood clot, with its fiber network, begins to join the edges of the wound together. As the clot dries out, a scab forms, usually in less than 24 hours.

Clear Thesis

Make sure that your writing centers on one main issue or thesis. Although this next original passage lacks a thesis, the revision has a clear one.

Original Passage (Lacks a thesis)

Teen magazines are popular with young girls. These magazines contain a lot of how-to articles about self-image, fashion, and boy-girl relationships. Girls read them to get advice on how to act and how to look. There are many magazines from which to choose, and girls who don't really know what they want are the most eager readers.

Revised Version (Identifies a specific thesis statement)

Adolescent girls often see teen magazines as handbooks on how to be teenagers. These magazines influence the ways they act and the ways they look. For girls who are unsure of themselves, these magazines can exert an enormous amount of influence. <u>Unfortunately, the advice these magazines give about self-image, fashion, and boys may do more harm than good.</u>

Examine your organization.

Good writing has structure. It leads readers logically and clearly from one point to the next. When revising for organization, consider four areas: the overall plan, the opening, the flow of ideas, and the closing.

Overall Plan

Look closely at the sequence of ideas or events that you share. Does that sequence advance your thesis? Do the points build effectively? Are there gaps in the support or points that stray from your original purpose? If you find such problems, consider the following actions:

- Refine the focus or emphasis by rearranging material within the text.
- Fill in the gaps with new material. Go back to your planning notes.
- Delete material that wanders away from your purpose.
- Use an additional (or different) method of organization. For example, if you are comparing two subjects, add depth to your analysis by contrasting them as well. If you are describing a complex subject, show the subject more clearly and fully by distinguishing and classifying its parts. (See pages 56–59 for more on organizational methods.)

INSIGHT: What is the best method of organization for your essay? The writing you are doing will usually determine the choice. As you know, a personal narrative is often organized by time. Typically, however, you combine and customize methods to develop a writing idea. For example, within a comparison essay you may do some describing or classifying. See pages 42–43 and 104 for more on the common methods of development.

Opening Ideas

Reread your opening paragraph(s). Is the opening organized effectively? Does it engage readers, establish a direction for your writing, and express your thesis or focus? The original opening shown below doesn't build to a compelling thesis statement. In contrast, the revised version engages the reader and leads up to the thesis statement.

Original Opening (Lacks interest and direction)

The lack of student motivation is a common subject in the news. Educators want to know how to get students to learn. Today's higher standards mean that students will be expected to learn even more. Another problem in urban areas is that large numbers of students are dropping out. How to interest students is a challenge.

Revised Version (Effectively leads readers into the essay)

How can we motivate students to learn? How can we get them to meet today's rising standards of excellence? How can we, in fact, keep students in school long enough to learn? The answer to these problems is quite simple. Give them money. Pay students to study and learn and stay in school.

Flow of Ideas

Look closely at the beginnings and endings of each paragraph. Have you connected your thoughts clearly? (See page **77** for a list of transition words.) The original opening words of the paragraph sequence below, from an essay of description, offer no links for readers. The revised versions use strong transitions indicating spatial organization (order by location).

Original First Words in the Four Middle Paragraphs

There was a huge, steep hill . . .
Buffalo Creek ran . . .
A dense "jungle" covering . . .
Within walking distance from my house . . .

Revised Version (Words and phrases connect ideas)

Behind the house, there was a huge, steep hill . . .
Across the road from the house, Buffalo Creek ran . . .
On the far side of the creek bank was a dense "jungle" covering . . .
Up the road, within walking distance from my house . . .

INSIGHT: Review "Supporting Your Claims" (pages **252–254**) and use those strategies to strengthen weak or unconvincing passages.

Closing Ideas

Reread your closing paragraph(s). Do you offer an effective summary, reassert your main point in a fresh way, and provide readers with food for thought as they leave your writing? Or is your ending abrupt, repetitive, or directionless? The original ending below is uninspiring; it adds little to the main part of the writing. The revision summarizes the main points in the essay and then urges the reader to think again about the overall point of writing.

Original Ending (Sketchy and flat)

Native Son deals with a young man's struggle against racism. It shows the effects of prejudice. Everyone should read this book.

Revised Version (Effectively ends the writing)

Native Son deals with a young man's struggle in a racist society, but also with so much more. It shows how prejudice affects people, how it closes in on them, and what some people will do to find a way out. Anyone who wants to better understand racism in the United States should read this book.

TIP: To generate fresh ideas for your closing, freewrite answers to questions like these: Why is the topic important to me? What should my readers have learned? What evidence or appeal (pages **252–254**) will help readers remember my message and act on it?

Web Link

Revising for Voice and Style

Generally, readers more fully trust writing that speaks in an informed voice and a clear, natural style. To develop an informed voice, make sure that your details are correct and complete; to develop a clear style, make sure that your writing is well organized and unpretentious. Check the issues below. (For a definition of voice, see page **65**.)

Check the level of commitment.

Consider how and to what degree your writing shows that you care about the topic and reader. For example, note how the original passage below lacks a personal voice, revealing nothing about the writer's connection to—or interest in—the topic. In contrast, the revision shows that the writer cares about the topic.

Original Passage (Lacks voice)

Cemeteries can teach us a lot about history. They make history seem more real. There is an old grave of a Revolutionary War veteran in the Union Grove Cemetery. . . .

Revised Version (Personal, sincere voice)

I've always had a special feeling for cemeteries. It's hard to explain any further than that, except to say history never seems quite as real as it does when I walk among many old gravestones. One day I discovered the grave of a Revolutionary War veteran. . . .

Check the intensity of your writing.

All writing—including academic writing—is enriched by an appropriate level of intensity, or even passion. In the original passage below, the writer's concern for the topic is unclear because the piece sounds neutral. In contrast, the revised version exudes energy.

Original Version (Lacks feeling and energy)

Motz blames Barbie dolls for all the problems that women face today. Instead, one should look to romance novels, fashion magazines, and parental training for causes of these societal problems.

Revised Version (Expresses real feelings)

In other words, Motz uses Barbie as a scapegoat for problems that have complex causes. However, a girl's interest in romance is no more Barbie's fault than the fault of books like *On the Shores of Silver Lake*. Fashion magazines targeted at adolescents are the cause of far more anorexia than is Barbie. And mothers who encourage daughters to find security in men teach female dependency, but Barbie doesn't.

INSIGHT: To develop your personal writing voice, begin each writing assignment by freely recording your thoughts and feelings about the topic.

Develop an academic style.

Most college writing requires an academic style. Such a style isn't stuffy; you're not trying to impress readers with ten-dollar words. Rather, you are using language that facilitates a thoughtful, engaged discussion of the topic. To choose the best words for such a conversation, consider the issues that follow.

Personal Pronouns

In some academic writing, such as reading responses, personal pronouns are acceptable. Generally, however, avoid using *I, we,* and *you* in traditional academic writing. The concept, instead, is to focus on the topic itself and let your attitude be revealed indirectly. As E. B. White puts it, "to achieve style, begin by affecting none— that is, begin by placing yourself in the background."

No: I really think that the problem of the homeless in Chicago is serious, given the number of people who are dying, as I know from my experience where I grew up.

Yes: **Homelessness in Chicago often leads to death. This fact demands the attention of more than lawmakers and social workers; all citizens must address the problems of their suffering neighbors.**

> **TIP:** Use the pronoun *one* carefully in academic prose. When it means "a person," *one* can lead to a stilted style if overused. In addition, the pronoun *their* should not be used with *one,* because it is a singular noun.

Technical Terms and Jargon

Technical terms and jargon—"insider" words—can be the specialized vocabulary of a subject, a discipline, a profession, or a social group. As such, jargon can be difficult to read for "outsiders." Follow these guidelines:

- Use technical terms to communicate with people within the profession or discipline as a kind of shorthand. Be careful that such jargon doesn't devolve into meaningless buzzwords and catchphrases.
- Avoid jargon when writing for readers outside the profession or discipline. Use simpler terms and define technical terms that must be used.

Technical: Bin's Douser power washer delivers 2200 psi p.r., runs off standard a.c. lines, comes with 100 ft. h.d. synthetic-rubber tubing, and features variable pulsation options through three adjustable s.s. tips.

Simple: **Bin's Douser power washer has a pressure rating of 2200 psi (pounds per square inch), runs off a common 200 volt electrical circuit, comes with 100 feet of hose, and includes three nozzles.**

Level of Formality

Most academic writing (especially research papers, literary analyses, lab reports, and argumentative essays) should meet the standards of formal English. **Formal English** is characterized by a serious tone; careful attention to word choice; longer and more complex sentences reflecting complex thinking; strict adherence to traditional conventions of grammar, mechanics, and punctuation; and avoidance of contractions.

> **Formal English, modeled in this sentence, is worded correctly and carefully so that it can withstand repeated readings without seeming tiresome, sloppy, or cute.**

You may write other papers (personal essays, commentaries, journals, and reviews) in which informal English is appropriate. **Informal English** is characterized by a personal tone, the occasional use of popular expressions, shorter sentences with slightly looser syntax, contractions, and personal references (I, we, you), but it still adheres to basic conventions.

> **Informal English sounds like one person talking to another person (in a somewhat relaxed setting). It's the type of language you are reading now. It sounds comfortable and real, not too jazzy or breezy.**

> **TIP:** In academic writing, generally avoid slang—words considered outside standard English because they are faddish, familiar to few people, and sometimes insulting.

Unnecessary Qualifiers

Using qualifiers (such as *mostly, often, likely, tends to*) is an appropriate strategy for developing defendable claims in argumentative writing. (See pages **250–251**.) However, when you "overqualify" your ideas or add intensifiers (*really, truly*), the result is insecurity—the impression that you lack confidence in your ideas. The cure? Say what you mean, and mean what you say.

Insecure: **I totally and completely agree with the new security measures at sporting events, but that's only my opinion.**

Secure: **I agree with the new security measures at sporting events.**

 Each academic discipline has its own vocabulary and its own vocabulary resources. Such resources might be called dictionaries, glossaries, or handbooks. Check your library for the vocabulary resources in your discipline. Use them regularly to deepen your grasp of that vocabulary.

Know when to use the passive voice.

Most verbs can be in either the active or the passive voice. When a verb is active, the sentence's subject performs the action. When the verb is passive, the subject is acted upon.

Active: If you *can't attend* the meeting, *notify* Richard by Thursday.

Passive: If a meeting *can't be attended* by you, Richard *must be notified* by Thursday.

Weaknesses of Passive Voice: The passive voice tends to be wordy and sluggish because the verb's action is directed backward, not ahead. In addition, passive constructions tend to be impersonal, making people disappear.

Passive: The sound system *can* now *be used* to listen in on sessions in the therapy room. Parents *can be helped* by having constructive one-on-one communication methods with children modeled by therapists.

Active: Parents *can* now *use* the sound system to listen in on sessions in the therapy room. Therapists *can help* parents by modeling constructive one-on-one communication methods with children.

Strengths of Passive Voice: Using the passive voice isn't wrong. In fact, the passive voice has some important uses: (1) when you need to be tactful (say, in a bad-news letter), (2) if you wish to stress the object or person acted upon, and (3) if the actual actor is understood, unknown, or unimportant.

Active: Our engineers determined that you *bent* the bar at the midpoint.

Passive: Our engineers determined that the bar *had been bent* at the midpoint. (tactful)

Active: Congratulations! We *have approved* your scholarship for $2,500.

Passive: Congratulations! Your scholarship for $2,500 *has been approved.* (emphasis on receiver; actor understood)

TIP: Avoid using the passive voice unethically to hide responsibility. For example, an instructor who says "Your assignments could not be graded because of scheduling difficulties" might be trying to evade the truth: "I did not finish grading your assignments because I was watching *Mystery.*"

Addressing Paragraph Issues

While drafting, you may have constructed paragraphs that are loosely held together, poorly developed, or unclear. When you revise, take a close look at your paragraphs for focus, unity, and coherence (pages **74–76**).

Remember the basics.

A paragraph should be a concise unit of thought. Revise a paragraph until it . . .

- is organized around a controlling idea—often stated in a topic sentence.
- consists of supporting sentences that develop the controlling idea.
- concludes with a sentence that summarizes the main point and prepares readers for the next paragraph or main point.
- serves a specific function in a piece of writing—opening, supporting, developing, illustrating, countering, describing, or closing.

Sample Paragraph

Topic sentence ----- Tumor cells can hurt the body in a number of ways. First, a tumor can grow so big that it takes up space needed by other organs. Second, some cells may detach from the original tumor and spread throughout the body, creating new tumors elsewhere. This happens with lymphatic cancer—a cancer that's hard to control because it spreads so quickly. A third way that **Supporting sentences** tumor cells can hurt the body is by doing work not called for in their DNA. For example, a gland cell's DNA code may tell the cell to produce a necessary hormone in the endocrine system. However, if cancer damages or distorts that code, sick cells may produce more of the hormone than the **Closing sentence** --- body can use—or even tolerate (Braun 4). Cancer cells seem to have minds of their own, and this is why cancer is such a serious disease.

Keep the purpose in mind.

Use these questions to evaluate the purpose and function of each paragraph:

- What function does the paragraph fulfill? How does it add to your line of reasoning or the development of your thesis?
- Would the paragraph work better if it were divided in two—or combined with another paragraph?
- Does the paragraph flow smoothly from the previous paragraph, and does it lead effectively into the next one?

Check for unity.

A unified paragraph is one in which all the details help to develop a single main topic or achieve a single main effect. Test for unity by following these guidelines.

Topic Sentence

Very often the topic of a paragraph is stated in a single sentence called a "topic sentence." Check whether your paragraph needs a topic sentence. If it has one, determine whether it is clear, specific, and well focused. Here is a formula for writing good topic sentences:

> *Formula:* A topic sentence = a limited topic + a specific feeling or thought about it.
>
> *Example:* **The fear that Americans feel** (limited topic) **comes partly from the uncertainty related to this attack** (a specific thought)**.**

Placement of the Topic Sentence

Normally the topic sentence is the first sentence in the paragraph. However, it can appear elsewhere in a paragraph.

- **Middle Placement:** Place a topic sentence in the middle when you want to build up to and then lead away from the key idea.

  During the making of *Apocalypse Now,* **Eleanor Coppola created a documentary about the filming called** *Hearts of Darkness: A Filmmaker's Apocalypse.* **In the first film, the insane Colonel Kurtz has disappeared into the Cambodian jungle. As Captain Willard searches for Kurtz, the screen fills with horror. However, as** *Hearts of Darkness* **relates, the horror portrayed in the fictional movie was being lived out by the production company.** **For example, in the documentary, actor Larry Fishburne shockingly says, "War is fun. . . . Vietnam must have been so much fun." Then toward the end of the filming, actor Martin Sheen suffered a heart attack. When an assistant informed investors, the director exploded, "He's not dead unless I say he's dead."**

- **End Placement:** Place a topic sentence at the end when you want to build to a climax, as in a passage of narration or persuasion.

  When sportsmen stop to reflect on why they find fishing so enjoyable most realize that what they love is the feel of a fish on the end of the line, not necessarily the weight of the fillets in their coolers. Fishing has undergone a slow evolution over the last century. While fishing used to be a way of putting food on the table, most of today's fishermen do so only for the relaxation that it provides. The barbed hook was invented to increase the quantity of fish a man could land in order to better feed his family. This need no longer exists, so barbed hooks are no longer necessary.

Supporting Sentences

All the sentences in the body of a paragraph should support the topic sentence. The closing sentence, for instance, will often summarize the paragraph's main point or emphasize a key detail. If any sentences shift the focus away from the topic, revise the paragraph in one of the following ways:

- Delete the material from the paragraph.
- Rewrite the material so that it clearly supports the topic sentence.
- Create a separate paragraph out of the material.
- Revise the topic sentence so that it relates more closely to the support.

Consistent Focus

Examine the following paragraph about fishing hooks. The original topic sentence focuses on the point that some anglers prefer smooth hooks. However, the writer leaves this initial idea unfinished and turns to the issue of the cost of new hooks. In the revised version, unity is restored: the first paragraph completes the point about anglers who prefer smooth hooks; the second paragraph addresses the issue of replacement costs.

Original (Lacks unity)

According to some anglers who do use smooth hooks, their lures perform better than barbed lures as long as they maintain a constant tension on the line. Smooth hooks can bite deeper than barbed hooks, actually providing a stronger hold on the fish. Some people have argued that replacing all of the barbed hooks in their tackle would be a costly operation.

Revised Version (Unified)

According to some anglers who do use smooth hooks, their lures perform better than barbed lures as long as they maintain a constant tension on the line. Smooth hooks can bite deeper than barbed hooks, actually providing a stronger hold on the fish. These anglers testify that switching from barbed hooks has not noticeably reduced the number of fish that they are able to land. In their experience, and in my own, enjoyment of the sport is actually heightened by adding another challenge to playing the fish (maintaining line tension).

Some people have argued that replacing all of the barbed hooks in their tackle would be a costly operation. While this is certainly a concern, barbed hooks do not necessarily require replacement. With a simple set of pliers, the barbs on most conventional hooks can be bent down, providing a cost-free method of modifying one's existing tackle. . . .

 Paragraphs that contain unrelated ideas lack unity and are hard to follow. As you review each paragraph for unity, ask yourself these questions: Is the topic of the paragraph clear? Does each sentence relate to the topic? Are the sentences organized in the best possible order?

Check for coherence.

When a paragraph is coherent, the parts stay together. A coherent paragraph flows smoothly because each sentence is connected to others by patterns in the language such as repetition and transitions. To strengthen the coherence in your paragraphs, check for the issues discussed below.

Effective Repetition

To achieve coherence in your paragraphs, consider using repetition—repeating words or synonyms where necessary to remind readers of what you have already said. You can also use parallelism—repeating phrase or sentence structures to show the relationships among ideas. At the same time, you will add a unifying rhythm to your writing.

Ineffective: **The floor was littered with discarded soda cans, newspapers that were crumpled, and wrinkled clothes.**

Effective: **The floor was littered with discarded soda cans, crumpled newspapers, and wrinkled clothes.** (Three parallel phrases are used.)

Ineffective: **Reading the book was enjoyable; to write the critique was difficult.**

Effective: **Reading the book was enjoyable; writing the critique was difficult.** (Two similar structures are repeated.)

Clear Transitions

Linking words and phrases like "next," "on the other hand," and "in addition" connect ideas by showing the relationship among them. There are transitions that show location and time, compare and contrast things, emphasize a point, conclude or summarize, and add or clarify information. (See page **77** for a list of linking words and phrases.) Note the use of transitions in the following examples:

The paradox of Scotland is that violence had long been the norm in this now-peaceful land. In fact, the country was born, bred, and came of age in war. (The transition is used to emphasize a point.)

The production of cement is a complicated process. First, the mixture of lime, silica, alumina, and gypsum is ground into very fine particles. (The transition is used to show time or order.)

INSIGHT: Another way to achieve coherence in your paragraphs is to use pronouns effectively. A pronoun forms a link to the noun it replaces and ties that noun (idea) to the ideas that follow. As always, don't overuse pronouns or rely too heavily on them in establishing coherence in your paragraphs.

Transitions and Linking Words

The words and phrases below can help you tie together words, phrases, sentences, and paragraphs.

■ **Words used to SHOW LOCATION:**

above	behind	down	on top of
across	below	in back of	onto
against	beneath	in front of	outside
along	beside	inside	over
among	between	into	throughout
around	beyond	near	to the right
away from	by	off	under

■ **Words used to SHOW TIME:**

about	during	next	till
after	finally	next week	today
afterward	first	second	tomorrow
as soon as	immediately	soon	until
at	later	then	when
before	meanwhile	third	yesterday

■ **Words used to COMPARE THINGS (show similarities):**

also	in the same way	likewise
as	like	similarly

■ **Words used to CONTRAST THINGS (show differences):**

although	even though	on the other hand	still
but	however	otherwise	yet

■ **Words used to EMPHASIZE A POINT:**

again	for this reason	particularly	to repeat
even	in fact	to emphasize	truly

■ **Words used to CONCLUDE or SUMMARIZE:**

all in all	finally	in summary	therefore
as a result	in conclusion	last	to sum up

■ **Words used to ADD INFORMATION:**

additionally	and	equally important	in addition
again	another	finally	likewise
along with	as well	for example	next
also	besides	for instance	second

■ **Words used to CLARIFY:**

for instance	in other words	put another way	that is

Note: Use transitions to link, expand, or intensify an idea, but don't add elements carelessly, creating run-on or rambling sentences (pages **651–652**).

Check for completeness.

The sentences in a paragraph should support and expand on the main point. If your paragraph does not seem complete, you will need to add information.

Supporting Details

If some of your paragraphs are incomplete, they may lack details. There are numerous kinds of details, including the following:

facts	anecdotes	analyses	paraphrases
statistics	quotations	explanations	comparisons
examples	definitions	summaries	analogies

Add details based on the type of writing you are engaged in.

Describing ■ Add details that help readers see, smell, taste, touch, or hear it.

Narrating ■ Add details that help readers understand the events and actions.

Explaining ■ Add details that help readers understand what it means, how it works, or what it does.

Persuading ■ Add details that strengthen the logic of your argument.

Specific Details

The original paragraph below fails to answer fully the question posed by the topic sentence. In the revised paragraph, the writer uses an anecdote to answer the question.

Original (Lacks completeness)

So what is stress? Actually, the physiological characteristics of stress are some of the body's potentially good self-defense mechanisms. People experience stress when they are in danger. In fact, stress can be healthy.

Revised Version (Full development)

So what is stress? Actually, the physiological characteristics of stress are some of the body's potentially good self-defense mechanisms. Take, for example, a man who is crossing a busy intersection when he spots an oncoming car. Immediately his brain releases a flood of adrenaline into his bloodstream. As a result, his muscles contract, his eyes dilate, his heart pounds faster, his breathing quickens, and his blood clots more readily. Each one of these responses helps the man leap out of the car's path. His muscles contract to give him exceptional strength. His eyes dilate so that he can see more clearly. His heart pumps more blood and his lungs exchange more air—both to increase his metabolism. If the man were injured, his blood would clot faster, insuring a smaller amount of blood loss. In this situation and many more like it, stress symptoms are good (Curtis 25–26).

INSIGHT: If a paragraph is getting long, divide it at a natural stopping point. The topic sentence can then function as the thesis for that part of your essay or paper.

Revising Collaboratively

Every writer can benefit from feedback from an interested audience, especially one that offers constructive and honest advice during a writing project. Members of an existing writing group already know how valuable it is for writers to share their work. Others might want to start a writing group to experience the benefits. Your group might collaborate online or in person. In either case, the information on the next two pages will help you get started.

Web Link

Know your role.

Writers and reviewers should know their roles and fulfill their responsibilities during revising sessions. Essentially, the writer should briefly introduce the draft and solicit honest responses. Reviewers should make constructive comments in response to the writing.

Provide appropriate feedback.

Feedback can take many forms, including the three approaches described here.

Basic Description ■ In this simple response, the reviewer listens or reads attentively and then simply describes what he or she hears or sees happening in the piece. The reviewer offers no criticism of the writing.

> *Ineffective:* "That was interesting. The piece was informative."
>
> *Effective:* "First, the essay introduced the challenge of your birth defect and how you have had to cope with it. Then in the next part you . . ."

Summary Evaluation ■ Here the reviewer reads or listens to the piece and then provides a specific evaluation of the draft.

> *Ineffective:* "Gee, I really liked it!" or "It was boring."
>
> *Effective:* "Your story at the beginning really pulled me in, and the middle explained the issue strongly, but the ending felt a bit flat."

Thorough Critique ■ The reviewer assesses the ideas, organization, and voice in the writing. Feedback should be detailed and constructive. Such a critique may also be completed with the aid of a review sheet or checklist. As a reviewer, be prepared to share specific responses, suggestions, and questions. But also be sure to focus your comments on the writing, rather than the writer.

> *Ineffective:* "You really need to fix that opening! What were you thinking?"
>
> *Effective:* "Let's look closely at the opening. Could you rewrite the first sentence so it grabs the reader's attention? Also, I'm somewhat confused about the thesis statement. Could you rephrase it so it states your position more clearly?"

Respond according to a plan.

Using a specific plan or scheme like the following will help you give clear, helpful, and complete feedback.

OAQS Method Use this simple four-step scheme—observe, appreciate, question, and suggest—to respond to your peers' writing.

1. **Observe** means to notice what another person's essay is designed to do and say something about its design or purpose. For example, you might say, "Even though you are writing about your boyfriend, it appears that you are trying to get a message across to your parents."

2. **Appreciate** means to praise something in the writing that impresses or pleases you. You can find something to appreciate in any piece of writing. For example, you might say, "You make a very convincing point" or "With your description, I can actually see his broken tooth."

3. **Question** means to ask whatever you want to know after you've read the essay. You might ask for background information, a definition, an interpretation, or an explanation. For example, you might say, "Can you tell us what happened when you got to the emergency room?"

4. **Suggest** means to give helpful advice about possible changes. For example, you might say, "With a little more physical detail—especially more sounds and smells—your third paragraph could be the highlight of the whole essay. What do you think?"

Asking the Writer Questions

Reviewers should ask the following types of questions while reviewing a piece of writing:

To help writers reflect on their purpose and audience . . .
   Why are you writing this?
   Who will read this, and what do they need to know?
To help writers focus their thoughts . . .
   What message are you trying to get across?
   Do you have more than one main point?
   What are the most important examples?
To help writers think about their information . . .
   What do you know about the subject?
   Does this part say enough?
   Does your writing cover all of the basics (*Who? What? Where? When? Why?* and *How?*)?
To help writers with their openings and closings . . .
   What are you trying to say in the opening?
   How else could you start your writing?
   How do you want your readers to feel at the end?

Web Link

Using the Writing Center

A college writing center or lab is a place where trained adviser will help you develop and strengthen a piece of writing. You can expect the writing center adviser to do certain things; other things only you can do. For quick reference, refer to the chart below.

ADVISER'S JOB	YOUR JOB
Make you feel at home	Be respectful
Discuss your needs	Be ready to work
Help you choose a topic	Decide on a topic
Discuss your purpose and audience	Know your purpose and audience
Help you generate ideas	Embrace the best ideas
Help you develop your logic	Consider other points of view; stretch your own perspective
Help you understand how to research your material	Do the research
Read your draft	Share your writing
Identify problems in organization, logic, expression, and format	Recognize and fix problems
Teach ways to correct weaknesses	Learn important principles
Help you with grammar, usage, diction, vocabulary, and mechanics	Correct all errors

TIPS for getting the most out of the writing center

- Visit the center at least several days before your paper is due.
- Take your assignment sheet with you to each advising session.
- Read your work aloud, slowly.
- Expect to rethink your writing from scratch.
- Do not defend your wording—if it needs defense, it needs revision.
- Ask questions. (No question is "too dumb.")
- Request clarification of anything you don't understand.
- Ask for examples or illustrations of important points.
- Write down all practical suggestions.
- Ask the adviser to summarize his or her remarks.
- Rewrite as soon as possible after—or even during—the advising session.
- Return to the writing center for a response to your revisions.

Revising Checklist

Use this checklist as a guide when you revise your writing. Remember to think globally first; then focus your attention on different parts. (To see revising in action, turn to pages 110–113.)

Ideas

_____ My writing has a clear thesis, focus, or theme.
_____ I have fully developed and supported that thesis with relevant, accurate details.

Organization

_____ My writing follows a clear pattern of organization that advances the main idea.
_____ I have added, cut, reordered, and rewritten material as needed.
_____ All of the paragraphs are unified, coherent, and complete.

Voice

_____ The tone is matched to the assignment, the reader, and the purpose.
_____ The style is clear, genuine, and appropriately academic.
_____ My voice sounds energetic and interested.

Writing Activities

1. Pull out a paper that you wrote recently but may not have revised thoroughly before submitting. Using the revising strategies in this chapter, improve the piece.

2. Beginnings and endings often pose the biggest challenges for writers. Review the opening and closing paragraphs of one of your essays. Then come up with fresh and different approaches for those paragraphs using the information on pages 67–68 as a guide.

3. Find a middle paragraph in one of your essays that doesn't effectively advance your thesis. Revise that paragraph using the information on pages 73–78 as a guide.

4. For your current writing assignment, ask a peer to provide detailed feedback using the information in this chapter as a guide. Then take a fresh copy of your paper to the writing center and work through your draft with an adviser. Revise the draft as needed.

Chapter 6
Editing and Proofreading

There comes a point in any writing project (like a fast-approaching due date) when you must prepare your writing for submission. At that time you must edit and proofread your revised writing so that it speaks clearly and accurately. When you edit, look first for words, phrases, and sentences that sound awkward, uninteresting, or unclear. When you proofread, check your writing for spelling, mechanics, usage, and grammar errors.

Before you begin, make sure you have the proper tools: handbook, dictionary, thesaurus, computer spell checker, and so on. Also, ask one of your writing peers to help you edit your work. Then prepare your final draft, following the guidelines established by your instructor, and proofread it for errors.

The guidelines and strategies given in this chapter will help you edit your writing for style and clarity and proofread it for errors.

What's Ahead

- Editing Your Revised Draft
- Combining Sentences
- Expanding Sentences
- Checking for Sentence Style
- Avoiding Imprecise, Misleading, and Biased Words
- Proofreading Your Writing
- Editing and Proofreading Checklist and Writing Activities

Editing Your Revised Draft

When you have thoroughly revised your writing you need to edit it, so as to make it clear and concise enough to present to readers. Use the editing guidelines below to check your revised draft.

Review the overall style of your writing.

1. Read your revised writing aloud. Better yet, have a writing peer read it aloud to you. Highlight any awkward areas where your writing doesn't read smoothly and naturally.

2. Check it against three key stylistic reminders.

Be purposeful. ■ Does your writing sound as if you wrote it with a clear goal in mind?

Be clear. ■ Are the ideas expressed concisely and directly?

Be sincere. ■ Does the writing sound authentic and honest?

3. Examine your sentences. Check them for clarity, conciseness, and variety. Replace sentences that are wordy or rambling; combine or expand sentences that are short and choppy. Also, vary the beginnings of your sentences and avoid sentence patterns that are too predictable. (See pages **85–91**.)

Consider word choice.

4. Avoid redundancy. Be alert for words or phrases that are used together but mean nearly the same thing.

repeat again   **red in color**   **refer back**

5. Watch for repetition. When used appropriately, repetition can add rhythm and coherence to your writing. When used ineffectively, however, it can be a real distraction.

> **The man** looked as if he were in his late seventies. **The man** was dressed in an old suit. I soon realized that **the man** was homeless. . . .

6. Look for general nouns, verbs, and modifiers. Specific words are much more effective than general ones. (See page **92**.)

> **The girl moved on the bench.** (general)
> **Rosie slid quietly to the end of the park bench.** (specific)

7. Avoid highly technical terms. Check for jargon or technical terms that are not well known or adequately explained. (See page **93**.)

> As the **capillaries** bleed, **platelets** work with **fibrinogens** to form a clot.

8. Use fair language. Replace words or phrases that are biased or demeaning. (See pages **94–96**.)

Combining Sentences

Effective sentences often contain several basic ideas that work together to show relationships and make connections. Here are five basic ideas followed by seven examples of how they can be combined into effective sentences.

1. The longest and largest construction project in history was the Great Wall of China.
2. The project took 1,700 years to complete.
3. The Great Wall of China is 1,400 miles long.
4. It is between 18 and 30 feet high.
5. It is up to 32 feet wide.

Edit short, simplistic sentences.

Combine your short, simplistic sentences into longer, more detailed sentences. Sentence combining is generally carried out in the following ways:

- Use a **series** to combine three or more similar ideas.

  The Great Wall of China is **1,400 miles long,** between **18 and 30 feet high,** and up to **32 feet wide.**

- Use a **relative pronoun** (*who, whose, that, which*) to introduce subordinate (less important) ideas.

  The Great Wall of China, **which is 1,400 miles long and between 18 and 30** feet high, took 1,700 years to complete.

- Use an **introductory phrase** or **clause**.

  Having taken 1,700 years to complete, the Great Wall of China was the longest construction project in history.

- Use a **semicolon** (and a conjunctive adverb if appropriate).

  The Great Wall took 1,700 years to complete; it is 1,400 miles long and up to 30 feet high and 32 feet wide.

- Repeat a **key word** or phrase to emphasize an idea.

  The Great Wall of China was the longest construction **project** in history, a **project** that took 1,700 years to complete.

- Use **correlative conjunctions** (*either, or; not only, but also*) to compare or contrast two ideas in a sentence.

  The Great Wall of China is **not only** up to 30 feet high and 32 feet wide, **but also** 1,400 miles long.

- Use an **appositive** (a word or phrase that renames) to emphasize an idea.

  The Great Wall of China—**the largest construction project in history**—is 1,400 miles long, 32 feet wide, and up to 30 feet high.

Expanding Sentences

Expand sentences when you edit so as to connect related ideas and make room for new information. Length has no value in and of itself: The best sentence is still the shortest one that says all it has to say. An expanded sentence, however, is capable of saying more—and saying it more expressively.

Use cumulative sentences.

Modern writers often use an expressive sentence form called the cumulative sentence. A cumulative sentence is made of a general "base clause" that is expanded by adding modifying words, phrases, or clauses. In such a sentence details are added before and after the main clause, creating an image-rich thought. Here's an example of a cumulative sentence, with the base clause or main idea in boldface:

> In preparation for her Spanish exam, **Julie was studying** at the kitchen table, completely focused, memorizing a list of vocabulary words.

Discussion Notice how each new modifier adds to the richness of the final sentence. Also notice that each of these modifying phrases is set off by a comma. Here's another sample sentence:

> With his hands on his face, **Tony was laughing** half-heartedly, looking puzzled and embarrassed.

Discussion Such a cumulative sentence provides a way to write description that is rich in detail, without rambling. Notice how each modifier changes the flow or rhythm of the sentence.

Expand with details.

Here are seven basic ways to expand a main idea:

1. with **adjectives and adverbs**: *half-heartedly, once again*
2. with **prepositional phrases**: *with his hands on his face*
3. with **absolute phrases**: *his head tilted to one side*
4. with **participial (-*ing* or -*ed*) phrases**: *looking puzzled*
5. with **infinitive phrases**: *to hide his embarrassment*
6. with **subordinate clauses**: *while his friend talks*
7. with **relative clauses**: *who isn't laughing at all*

INSIGHT: To edit sentences for more expressive style, it is best to (1) know your grammar and punctuation (especially commas), (2) practice tightening, combining, and expanding sentences using the guidelines in this chapter, and (3) read carefully, looking for models of well-constructed sentences.

Checking for Sentence Style

Writer E. B. White advised young writers to "approach sentence style by way of simplicity, plainness, orderliness, and sincerity." That's good advice from a writer steeped in style. It's also important to know what to look for when editing your sentences. The information on this page and the following four pages will help you edit your sentences for style and correctness.

Avoid these sentence problems.

Always check for and correct the following types of sentence problems. Turn to the pages listed below for guidelines and examples when attempting to fix problems in your sentences.

Short, Choppy Sentences ■ Combine or expand any short, choppy sentences; use the examples and guidelines on page **85**.

Flat, Predictable Sentences ■ Rewrite any sentences that sound predictable and uninteresting by varying their structures and expanding them with modifying words, phrases, and clauses. (See pages **88–90**.)

Incorrect Sentences ■ Look carefully for fragments, run-ons, and comma splices and correct them accordingly. (See pages **651–652**.)

Unclear Sentences ■ Edit any sentences that contain unclear wording, misplaced modifiers, dangling modifiers, or incomplete comparisons. (See pages **653–654**.)

Unacceptable Sentences ■ Change sentences that include nonstandard language, double negatives, or unparallel construction. (See page **655**.)

Unnatural Sentences ■ Rewrite sentences that contain jargon, clichés, or flowery language. (See page **93**.)

Review your writing for sentence variety.

Use the following strategy to review your writing for variety in terms of sentence beginnings, lengths, and types.

- In one column on a piece of paper, list the opening words in each of your sentences. Then decide if you need to vary some of your sentence beginnings.

- In another column, identify the number of words in each sentence. Then decide if you need to change the lengths of some of your sentences.

- In a third column, list the kinds of sentences used (exclamatory, declarative, interrogative, and so on). Then, based on your analysis, use the instructions on the next two pages to edit your sentences as needed.

Vary sentence structures.

To energize your sentences, vary their structures using one or more of the methods shown on this page and the next.

1. **Vary sentence openings.** Move a modifying word, phrase, or clause to the front of the sentence to stress that modifier. However, avoid creating dangling or misplaced modifiers. (See page **653**.)

    The Norm: We apologize for the inconvenience this may have caused you.

    Variation: For the inconvenience this may have caused you, we apologize.

2. **Vary sentence lengths.** Short sentences (ten words or fewer) are ideal for making points crisply. Medium sentences (ten to twenty words) should carry the bulk of your information. When well crafted, occasional long sentences (more than twenty words) can develop and expand your ideas.

    Short: Welcome back to Magnolia Suites!

    Medium: Unfortunately, your confirmed room was unavailable last night when you arrived. For the inconvenience this may have caused you, we apologize.

    Long: Because several guests did not depart as scheduled, we were forced to provide you with accommodations elsewhere; however, for your trouble, we were happy to cover the cost of last night's lodging.

3. **Vary sentence kinds.** The most common sentence is declarative—it states a point. For variety, try exclamatory, imperative, interrogative, and conditional statements.

    Exclamatory: Our goal is providing you with outstanding service!

    Declarative: To that end, we have upgraded your room at no expense.

    Imperative: Please accept, as well, this box of chocolates as a gift to sweeten your stay.

    Interrogative: Do you need further assistance?

    Conditional: If you do, we are ready to fulfill your requests.

INSIGHT: In creative writing (stories, novels, plays), writers occasionally use fragments to vary the rhythm of their prose, emphasize a point, or create dialogue. Avoid fragments in academic or business writing.

4. **Vary sentence arrangements.** Where do you want to place the main point of your sentence? You make that choice by arranging sentence parts into loose, periodic, balanced, or cumulative patterns. Each pattern creates a specific effect.

Loose Sentence:
> **The Travel Center offers an attractive flight-reservation plan for students,** one that allows you to collect bonus miles and receive $150,000 in life insurance per flight.

Analysis: This pattern is direct. It states the main point immediately (bold), and then tacks on extra information.

Periodic Sentence:
> Although this plan requires that you join the Travel Center's Student-Flight Club and pay the $10 admission fee, **you will save money in the long run!**

Analysis: This pattern postpones the main point (bold) until the end. The sentence builds to the point, creating an indirect, dramatic effect.

Balanced Sentence:
> **Joining the club in your freshman year will save you money over your entire college career;** in addition, **accruing bonus miles over four years will earn you a free trip to Europe!**

Analysis: This pattern gives equal weight to complementary or contrasting points (bold); the balance is often signaled by a comma and a conjunction (*and, but*) or by a semicolon. Often a conjunctive adverb (*however, nevertheless*) or a transitional phrase (*in addition, even so*) will follow the semicolon to further clarify the relationship.

Cumulative Sentence:
> Because the club membership is in your name, **you can retain its benefits** as long as you are a student, even if you transfer to a different college or go on to graduate school.

Analysis: This pattern puts the main idea (bold) in the middle of the sentence, surrounding it with modifying words, phrases, and clauses.

5. **Use positive repetition.** Although you should avoid needless repetition, you might use emphatic repetition to repeat a key word to stress a point.

Repetitive Sentence:
> Each year, more than a million young people who read poorly leave high school unable to read well, functionally illiterate.

Emphatic Sentence:
> Each year, more than a million young people leave high school functionally illiterate, *so* **illiterate** that they can't read daily newspapers, job ads, or safety instructions.

Use parallel structure.

Coordinated sentence elements should be parallel—that is, they should be written in the same grammatical forms. Parallel structures save words, clarify relationships, and present the information in the correct sequence. (See page **650.4**.) Follow these guidelines:

1. **For words, phrases, or clauses in a series,** keep elements consistent.

   Not parallel: I have tutored students in Biology 101, also Chemistry 102, not to mention my familiarity with *Physics 200*.

   Parallel: I have tutored students in *Biology 101, Chemistry 102, and Physics 200*.

   Not parallel: I have volunteered as a hospital receptionist, have been a hospice volunteer, and as an emergency medical technician.

   Parallel: I have done volunteer work *as a hospital receptionist, a hospice counselor, and an emergency medical technician.*

2. **Use both parts of correlative conjunctions** *(either, or; neither, nor; not only, but also; as, so; whether, so; both, and)* so that both segments of the sentence are balanced (see pages **635.3, 635.5**).

   Not parallel: *Not only* did Blake College turn 20 this year. Its enrollment grew by 16 percent.

   Parallel: *Not only* did Blake College turn 20 this year, *but* its enrollment *also* grew by 16 percent.

3. **Place a modifier correctly** so that it clearly indicates the word or words to which it refers.

   Confusing: MADD promotes *severely* punishing and eliminating drunk driving because this offense leads to a *great number* of deaths and sorrow.

   Parallel: MADD promotes eliminating and *severely* punishing drunk driving because this offense leads to *many* deaths and *untold* sorrow.

4. **Place contrasting details in parallel structures** (words, phrases, or clauses) to stress a contrast.

   Weak Contrast: The average child watches 24 hours of television a week and reads for 36 minutes.

   Strong Contrast: Each week, the average child *watches television for 24 hours but reads for only about half an hour.*

Avoid weak constructions.

Avoid constructions (like those below) that weaken your writing.

Nominal Constructions

The nominal construction is both sluggish and wordy. Avoid it by changing the noun form of a verb (*description* or *instructions*) to a verb (*describe* or *instruct*). At the same time, delete the weak verb that preceded the noun.

Nominal Constructions (noun form underlined):	Strong Verbs
Tim gave a <u>description</u> . . .	Tim *described* . . .
Lydia provided <u>instructions</u> . . .	Lydia *instructed* . . .

Sluggish: John *had a discussion* with the tutors regarding the incident. They gave him their *confirmation* that similar developments had occurred before, but they had not *provided submissions* of their reports.

Energetic: John *discussed* the incident with the tutors. They *confirmed* that similar problems had developed before, but they hadn't *submitted* their reports.

Expletives

Expletives such as "it is" and "there is" are fillers that serve no purpose in most sentences—except to make them wordy and unnatural.

Sluggish: *It is* likely that Nathan will attend the Communication Department's Honors Banquet. *There is* a journalism scholarship that he might win.

Energetic: Nathan will likely attend the Communication Department's Honors Banquet and might win a journalism scholarship.

Negative Constructions

Sentences constructed upon the negatives *no, not, neither/nor* can be wordy and difficult to understand. It's simpler to state what *is* the case.

Negative: During my four years on the newspaper staff, I *have not been* behind in making significant contributions. My editorial skills *have* certainly *not deteriorated*, as I *have never failed* to tackle challenging assignments.

Positive: During my four years on the newspaper staff, I *have made* significant contributions. My editorial skills have steadily *developed* as I *have tackled* difficult assignments.

Web Link

Avoiding Imprecise, Misleading, and Biased Words

As you edit your writing, check your choice of words carefully. The information on the next five pages will help you edit for word choice.

Substitute specific words.

Replace vague nouns and verbs with words that generate clarity and energy.

Specific Nouns

Make it a habit to use specific nouns for subjects. General nouns *(woman, school)* give the reader a vague, uninteresting picture. More specific nouns *(actress, university)* give the reader a better picture. Finally, very specific nouns *(Meryl Streep, Notre Dame)* are the type that can make your writing clear and colorful.

General to Specific Nouns

Person	Place	Thing	Idea
woman	school	book	theory
actor	university	novel	scientific theory
Meryl Streep	Notre Dame	*Pride and Prejudice*	relativity

Vivid Verbs

Like nouns, verbs can be too general to create a vivid word picture. For example, the verb *looked* does not say the same thing as *stared, glared, glanced,* or *peeked.*

- Whenever possible, use a verb that is strong enough to stand alone without the help of an adverb.

  Verb and adverb: John fell down in the student lounge.
  Vivid verb: John collapsed in the student lounge.

- Avoid overusing the "be" verbs *(is, are, was, were)* and helping verbs. Often a main verb can be made from another word in the same sentence.

  A "be" verb: Cole is someone who follows international news.
  A stronger verb: Cole follows international news.

- Use active rather than passive verbs. (Use passive verbs only if you want to downplay who is performing the action in a sentence. See page 72.)

  Passive verb: Another provocative essay was submitted by Kim.
  Active verb: Kim submitted another provocative essay.

- Use verbs that show rather than tell.

  A verb that tells: Dr. Lewis is very thorough.
  A verb that shows: Dr. Lewis prepares detailed, interactive lectures.

Replace jargon and clichés.

Replace language that is overly technical or difficult to understand. Also replace overused, worn-out words.

Understandable Language

Jargon is language used in a certain profession or by a particular group of people. It may be acceptable to use if your audience is that group of people, but to most ears jargon will sound technical and unnatural.

Jargon: The bottom line is that our output is not within our game plan.
Clear: **Production is not on schedule.**

Jargon: I'm having conceptual difficulty with these academic queries.
Clear: **I don't understand these review questions.**

Jargon: Pursuant to our conversation, I have forwarded you a remittance attached herewith.
Clear: **As we discussed, I am mailing you the check.**

Fresh and Original Writing

Clichés are overused words or phrases. They give the reader no fresh view and no concrete picture. Because clichés spring quickly to mind (for both the writer and the reader), they are easy to write and often slip by.

an axe to grind	**piece of cake**
as good as dead	**planting the seed**
beat around the bush	**rearing its ugly head**
between a rock and a hard place	**stick your neck out**
burning bridges	**throwing your weight around**
easy as pie	**up a creek**

Purpose and Voice

There are other aspects of your writing that may also be tired and overworked. Be alert to the two types of clichés described below.

Clichés of Purpose

- Sentimental papers gushing about an ideal friend or family member, or droning on about a moving experience
- Overused topics with recycled information and predictable examples

Clichés of Voice

- Writing that assumes a false sense of authority: "I have determined that there are three basic types of newspapers. My preference is for the third."
- Writing that speaks with little or no sense of authority: "I flipped when I saw *The Lord of the Rings.*"

Change biased words.

When depicting individuals or groups according to their differences, you must use language that implies equal value and respect for all people.

Words Referring to Ethnicity

Acceptable General Terms	*Acceptable Specific Terms*
American Indians, Native Americans	**Cherokee people, Inuit people,** and so forth
Asian Americans (not *Orientals*)	**Chinese Americans, Japanese Americans,** and so forth
Latinos, Latinas, Hispanics	**Mexican Americans, Cuban Americans,** and so forth

African Americans, blacks
"African American" has come into wide acceptance, though the term "black" is preferred by some individuals.

Anglo Americans (English ancestry), **European Americans**
Use these terms to avoid the notion that "American," used alone, means "white."

Additional References

Not Recommended	*Preferred*
Eurasian, mulatto	**person of mixed ancestry**
nonwhite	**person of color**
Caucasian	**white**
American (to mean U.S. citizen)	**U.S. citizen**

Words Referring to Age

Age Group	*Acceptable Terms*
up to age 13 or 14	**boys, girls**
between 13 and 19	**youth, young people, young men, young women**
late teens and 20's	**young adults, young women, young men**
30's to age 60	**adults, men, women**
60 and older	**older adults, older people** (not *elderly*)
65 and older	**seniors** (*senior citizens* also acceptable)

INSIGHT: Whenever you write about a person with a disability, impairment, or other special condition, give the person and your readers the utmost respect. Nothing is more distracting to a reader than an insensitive or outdated reference.

Words Referring to Disabilities or Impairments

In the recent past, some writers were choosing alternatives to the term *disabled*, including *physically challenged, exceptional,* or *special.* However, it is not generally held that these new terms are precise enough to serve those who live with disabilities. Of course, degrading labels like *crippled, invalid,* and *maimed,* as well as overly negative terminology, must be avoided.

Not Recommended	*Preferred*
handicapped	**disabled**
birth defect	**congenital disability**
stutter, stammer, lisp	**speech impairment**
an AIDS victim	**person with AIDS**
suffering from cancer	**person who has cancer**
mechanical foot	**prosthetic foot**
false teeth	**dentures**

Words Referring to Conditions

People with various disabilities and conditions have sometimes been referred to as though they *were* their condition (*quadriplegics, depressives, epileptics*) instead of people who simply happen to have a particular disability. As much as possible, remember to refer to the person first, the disability second.

Not Recommended	*Preferred*
the disabled	**people with disabilities**
cripple	**person who has difficulty walking**
the retarded	**people with a developmental disability**
dyslexics	**students with dyslexia**
neurotics	**patients with neuroses**
subjects, cases	**participants, patients**
quadriplegics	**people who are quadriplegic**
a wheelchair user	**people who use wheelchairs**

Additional Terms

Make sure you understand the following terms that address specific impairments:

hearing impairment = partial hearing loss, hard of hearing
(not *deaf,* which is total loss of hearing)

visual impairment = partially sighted
(not *blind,* which is total loss of vision)

communicative disorder = speech, hearing, and learning disabilities affecting communication.

Words Referring to Gender

- Use parallel language for both sexes:

  The **men** and the **women** rebuilt the school together.

  Hank and **Marie**

  Mr. Robert Gumble, Mrs. Joy Gumble

  Note: The courtesy titles *Mr., Ms., Mrs.,* and *Miss* ought to be used according to the person's preference.

- Use nonsexist alternatives to words with masculine connotations:

  humanity (not *mankind*)   **synthetic** (not *man-made*)

  artisan (not *craftsman*)

- Do not use masculine-only or feminine-only pronouns *(he, she, his, her)* when you want to refer to a human being in general:

  A politician can kiss privacy good-bye when he runs for office.
  (not recommended)

  Instead, use *he or she*, change the sentence to plural, or eliminate the pronoun:

  A politician can kiss privacy good-bye when he or she runs for office.

  Politicians can kiss privacy good-bye when they run for office.

  A politician can kiss privacy good-bye when running for office.

- Do not use gender-specific references in the salutation of a business letter when you don't know the person's name:

  Dear Sir: **Dear Gentlemen:** (neither is recommended)

  Instead, address a position:

  Dear Personnel Officer:

  Dear Members of the Economic Committee:

Occupational Issues

Not Recommended	Preferred
chairman	chair, presiding officer, moderator
salesman	sales representative, salesperson
mailman	mail carrier, postal worker, letter carrier
insurance man	insurance agent
fireman	firefighter
businessman	executive, manager, businessperson
congressman	member of Congress, representative, senator
steward, stewardess	flight attendant
policeman, policewoman	police officer

Web Link

Proofreading Your Writing

The following guidelines will help you check your revised writing for spelling, mechanics, usage, grammar, and form. Also refer to the Handbook in this book for additional help. (See pages **573–679**.)

Review punctuation and mechanics.

1. **Check for proper use of commas** before coordinating conjunctions in compound sentences, after introductory clauses and long introductory phrases, between items in a series, and so on. (See pages **571–575**.)
2. **Look for apostrophes** in contractions, plurals, and possessive nouns. (See pages **587–588**.)
3. **Examine quotation marks** in quoted information, titles, or dialogue. (See pages **582–583**.)
4. **Watch for proper use of capital letters** for first words in written conversation and for proper names of people, places, and things. (See pages **589–592**.)

Look for usage and grammar errors.

1. **Look for misuse of any commonly mixed words:** *there/their/they're; accept/except.* (See pages **607–618**.)
2. **Check for verb use.** Subjects and verbs should agree in number: singular subjects go with singular verbs; plural subjects go with plural verbs. Verb tenses should be consistent throughout. (See pages **627–628**.)
3. **Review for pronoun/antecedent agreement problems.** A pronoun and its antecedent must agree in number. (See page **649**.)

Check for spelling errors.

1. **Use a spell checker.** Your spell checker will catch most errors.
2. **Check each spelling you are unsure of.** Especially check those proper names and other special words your spell checker won't know.
3. **Consult your Handbook.** Use the list of commonly misspelled words in the Handbook (pages **601–605**), as well as an up-to-date dictionary.

Check the writing for form and presentation.

1. **Note the title.** A title should be appropriate and lead into the writing.
2. **Examine any quoted or cited material.** Are all sources of information properly presented and documented? (See pages **499–524** and **541–555**.)
3. **Look over the finished copy of your writing.** Does it meet the requirements for a final manuscript? (See page **120**.)

Editing and Proofreading Checklist

Use this checklist as a guide when you edit and proofread your writing. Edit your writing only after you have revised it. To see editing and proofreading in action, turn to pages 114–115.

Sentence Structure

_____ Sentences are clear, complete, and correct.

_____ They flow smoothly and have varied lengths, beginnings, kinds (exclamatory, declarative), and arrangements (loose, periodic).

Word Choice

_____ The writing is free of vague words, jargon, and clichés.

_____ The language is unbiased and fair.

Correctness

_____ Spelling, punctuation, and mechanics are correct.

_____ Verb tenses are correct.

_____ Subjects agree with their verbs; pronouns agree with their antecedents.

_____ Research documentation is punctuated correctly.

_____ Formatting and design follow assigned instructions.

Writing Prompt

Writing Activities

1. Choose a writing assignment that you have recently completed. Edit the sentences in this writing for style and correctness using pages 85–91 as a guide. Then use pages 92–96 in this chapter to edit the piece of writing for vague words, jargon, clichés, and biased language.

2. Choose one or two editing or proofreading topics that are discussed in this chapter that you find challenging. Then select another piece of your writing and check it for those problems.

3. Combine some of the following ideas into longer, more mature sentences. Write at least four sentences, using page 85 as a guide.

- **Dogs can be difficult to train.**
- **The necessary supplies include a leash and treats.**
- **Patience is also a necessity.**
- **Dogs like to please their owners.**
- **Training is not a chore for dogs.**
- **A well-trained dog is a pleasure to its owner and to others.**

Chapter 7
Submitting Writing and Creating Portfolios

Video

Submitting a final paper is the driving force behind writing. It explains why you may have spent so much time planning, drafting, and revising an essay or a paper in the first place—to share a finished piece of writing that effectively expresses your thoughts and feelings. Often, the most immediate and important form of submitting is sharing a finished piece of writing with your instructor and writing peers. It can also be the most helpful. As writer Tom Liner states, "You learn ways to improve your writing by seeing its effect on others."

You can also submit a piece of writing to a newspaper, journal, or website—or simply place it in your writing portfolio. This chapter will help you prepare your writing for virtually any audience or publication.

What's Ahead

- Formatting Your Writing
- Submitting Writing and Creating Portfolios
- Submissions and Portfolio Checklist and Writing Activities

Formatting Your Writing

A good page design makes your writing clear and easy to follow. Keep that in mind when you produce a final copy of your writing.

Strive for clarity in page design.

Examine the following design elements, making sure that each is appropriate and clear in your project and in your writing.

Format and Documentation

Keep the design clear and uncluttered. ■ Aim for a sharp, polished look in all your assigned writing.

Use the designated documentation form. ■ Follow all the requirements outlined in the MLA (pages **495–536**) or APA (pages **537–566**) style guides.

Typography

Use an easy-to-read serif font for the main text. ■ *Serif* type, like this, has "tails" at the tops and bottoms of the letters. For most types of writing, use a 10- or 12-point type size.

Consider using a sans serif font for the title and headings. ■ Sans serif type, like this, does not have "tails." Use larger, perhaps 18-point, type for your title and 14-point type for any headings. You can also use boldface for headings if they seem to get lost on the page.

Because most people find a sans serif font easier to read on screen, consider a sans serif font for the body and a serif font for the titles and headings in any writing you publish online.

Spacing

Follow all requirements for indents and margins. ■ This usually means indenting the first line of each paragraph five spaces, maintaining a one-inch margin around each page, and double-spacing throughout the paper.

Avoid widows and orphans. ■ Avoid leaving headings, hyphenated words, or single lines of new paragraphs alone at the bottom of a page. Also avoid single words at the bottom of a page or carried over to the top of a new page.

Graphic Devices

Create bulleted or numbered lists to highlight important points. ■ However, be selective; your writing should not include too many lists.

Include charts or other graphics. ■ Graphics should not be so small that they get lost on the page, nor so large that they overpower the page.

Submitting Writing and Creating Portfolios

Once you have formatted and proofread your final draft, you should be ready to share your writing. For college assignments, you will often simply turn in your paper to your instructor. However, you should also think about sharing your writing with other audiences, including those who will want to see your writing portfolio.

Consider potential audiences.

You could receive helpful feedback by doing the following:

- Share your writing with peers or family members.
- Submit your work to a local publication or an online journal.
- Post your writing on an appropriate website, including your own.
- Turn in your writing to your instructor.

Select appropriate submission methods.

There are two basic methods for submitting your work.

- **Paper Submission:** Print an error-free copy on quality paper.
- **Electronic Submission:** If allowed, send your writing as an e-mail attachment.

Use a writing portfolio.

There are two basic types of writing portfolios: (1) a *working portfolio* in which you store documents at various stages of development, and (2) a *showcase portfolio* with which you share appropriate finished work. For example, you could submit a portfolio to complete course requirements or to apply for a scholarship, graduate program, or job. The documents below are commonly included in a showcase portfolio.

- A table of contents listing the pieces included in your portfolio.
- An opening essay or letter detailing the story behind your portfolio (how you compiled it and why it features the qualities expected by the intended reader).
- A specified number of—and types of—finished pieces.
- A cover sheet attached to each piece of writing, discussing the reason for its selection, the amount of work that went into it, and so on.
- Evaluation sheets or checklists charting the progress or experience you want to show related to issues of interest to the reader.

Submissions and Portfolio Checklist

Use the checklist below to review details regarding submitting, publishing, and portfolios.

_____ The submission method (such as an essay given to instructor or posted on a website) is appropriate for my assignment, program, and career goals.

_____ The publishing process and method test and develop my skills as a writer and scholar.

_____ The document's format (paper or electronic; font and typeface; form and documentation; layout and graphics) conforms to all of the publisher's guidelines.

_____ My portfolio documents address the types of topics and show the level of scholarship expected by my readers.

_____ The voice and style of my portfolio documents are appropriate for the kinds of writing done in the program or job for which I am applying.

_____ The portfolio includes an engaging essay or cover letter that clearly explains the portfolio's design, purpose, and focus.

Writing Activities

1. Choose one of your recent writing assignments and use the instructions on page 100 to assess the quality of your formatting and page design. Edit and redesign the paper as needed.

2. For the class in which you are using this book, begin two working portfolios: (1) an electronic portfolio on your computer, and (2) a paper portfolio in a sturdy folder or binder. In the electronic portfolio, store all drafts of your assignments, as well as all related electronic correspondence with your instructor. In your paper portfolio, store all printed drafts of your work, including copies that show your instructor's notations and grades.

Chapter 8
One Writer's Process

An essay is an attempt to understand a topic more deeply and clearly. That's one of the reasons this basic form of writing is essential in many college courses. It's a tool for both discovering and communicating.

How do you move from an assignment to a finished, polished essay? The best advice is take matters one step at a time, from understanding the assignment to submitting the final draft. Don't try to churn out the essay the night before it's due.

This chapter shows up-close how student writer Angela Franco followed the writing process outlined in Chapters 2 through 7.

What's Ahead

- Angela's Assignment and Response
- Angela's Planning
- Angela's First Draft
- Angela's First Revision
- Angela's Second Revision
- Angela's Edited Draft
- Angela's Proofread Draft
- Angela's Finished Essay
- Writing Activities
- Effective Writing Checklist

Video

Audio

Angela's Assignment and Response

In this chapter you will follow student Angela Franco as she writes an assigned essay for her Environmental Policies class. Start by carefully reading the assignment and discussion below, noting how she thinks through the assignment's purpose, audience, form, and assessment method.

Angela examined the assignment.

Angela carefully read her assignment and responded with the notes below.

"Explain in a two- to three-page essay how a recent environmental issue is relevant to the world community. Using *The College Writer* as your guide, document sources in APA form, but omit the title page and abstract. You may seek revising help from a classmate or from the writing center."

Subject

- *The subject is a recent environmental issue.*

Purpose

- *My purpose is to explain how the issue is relevant to all people. That means I must show how this issue affects my audience— both positively and negatively.*

Audience

- *My audience will be people like me—neighbors, classmates, and community members.*
- *I'll need to keep in mind what they already know and what they need to know.*

Form

- *I need to write a two- to three-page essay—that sounds formal.*
- *I'll need to include a thesis statement, as well as references to my sources.*

Assessment

- *I'll use the guidelines and checklists in the handbook to evaluate and revise my writing.*
- *I'll get editing feedback from Jeanie and from the writing center.*

> **TIP:** For each step in the writing process, choose strategies that fit your writing situation. For example, a personal essay in English class might require significant time getting started, whereas a lab report in chemistry class might require little or none.

Angela explored and narrowed her assignment.

Angela explored her assignment and narrowed its focus by clustering and freewriting.

Angela's Cluster

When she considered environmental issues, Angela first thought of water pollution as a possible topic for her essay. After writing the phrase in the center of her page, she drew from memories, experiences, and readings to list related ideas and details. Notice how she used three different-colored inks to distinguish the topic (blue) from ideas (red) and details (green).

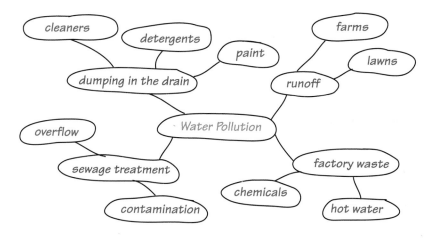

Angela's Freewriting

Angela decided to freewrite about the water pollution caused a few years earlier by improper sewage treatment in a small Canadian town.

I remember reading an article about problems in a small Canadian town. People actually died. The water they drank was contaminated. This is becoming a problem in developed countries like ours. I thought for a long time this was a problem only in developing countries. So who is responsible for sewage treatment? Who guarantees the safety of our drinking water? How does water get contaminated? Are there solutions for every kind of contamination: mercury, PCBs, sewage?

Angela's Narrowed Assignment

Based on her freewriting, Angela rephrased her assignment to narrow its focus.

Explain in a two- to three-page essay how a recent water pollution problem in a small Canadian town is relevant to the world community.

Angela's Planning

Angela reviewed her narrowed assignment and reassessed her topic.

Narrowed Writing Assignment: *Explain in a two- to three-page essay how a recent water-pollution problem in a small Canadian town is relevant to the world community.*

Angela focused her topic.

To focus her topic, Angela answered the journalistic questions (five Ws and H).

Topic: Water pollution in a small Canadian town

Who? - *Farm operators, wastewater officials, Walkerton residents*

What? - *Water supply contaminated*

   - *Spread bacteria (E. coli)*

   - *Caused disease*

   - *Clean, fresh water depleted*

Where? - *Walkerton, Ontario*

When? - *May 2000*

Why? - *Improper regulation; human error*

How? - *Groundwater from irrigation, untreated sewage, and runoff*

Angela researched the topic.

Angela then did some research to check her information and collect more details for her paper. She recorded all the essential data on each source and then listed the specific details related to her topic. Here's one source:

Nikiforuk, Andrew. "When Water Kills." Maclean's. 12 June 2000: 18–21.

   - *Factory farms hold as many as 25,000 cattle*

   - *Manure contains things like heavy metals (from mineral-rich feed), nutrients, and pathogens (E. coli)*

   - *8,000 hogs can produce as much waste as 240,000 people*

   - *Six rural Ontario counties had high E. coli 0157 levels in 1990 and 1995*

> **TIP:** During your research, take time to create or copy visuals (charts, graphs, or photos) that clarify details about which you're writing. If you copy an item, be sure to correctly record the source as well. To create your own graphic, gather the data that you want to present, and then choose the type of graphic (table, pie graph, bar graph) that best displays your point.

Angela decided how to organize her writing.

With a focus selected, Angela used the three guidelines below to choose the best organizational pattern for her writing.

Guidelines

1. Review your assignment and record your response.

ASSIGNMENT: Explain in a two- to three-page essay how a recent environmental issue is relevant to the world community.

RESPONSE: *My assignment clearly states that I need to explain my topic, so I have a general idea of how my paper will be organized.*

2. Decide upon your thesis statement and think about your essay's possible content and organization.

THESIS STATEMENT: The water pollution incident in Walkerton, Ontario, had a devastating effect that every town should learn from.

REFLECTION: *After reading my thesis statement, it's obvious that I'm going to be writing about a problem and its causes.*

3. Choose an overall method and reflect on its potential effectiveness.

REFLECTION: *Looking at the list of methods, I see that I can use cause/effect or problem/solution. After making two quick lists of my main points using both approaches, I decided to use a problem/ solution approach. I will still talk about causes and effects in my essay—they just won't be front and center.*

With problem/solution, I need to first present the problem clearly so that readers can fully understand it and see why it's important. Then I need to explore solutions to the problem—maybe what they did in Walkerton and what we all need to do to make water safe.

TIP: Many essays you write will be organized according to one basic method or approach. However, within that basic structure you may want to include other methods. For example, while developing a comparison essay you may do some describing or classifying. In other words, you should choose methods of development that (1) help you understand the topic and (2) help your readers understand your message.

Audio

Angela's First Draft

After composing her opening, middle, and closing paragraphs, Angela put together her first draft. She then added a working title.

Video

The writer uses a series of images to get the reader's attention.

The thesis statement (boldfaced) introduces the subject.

Video

The writer describes the cause of the problem.

Water Woes

It's a hot day. Several people just finished mowing their
lawns. A group of bicyclists—more than 3,000—have been
passing through your picturesque town all afternoon. Dozens of
Little Leaguers are batting, running, and sweating. What do all
these people have in common? They all drinks lots of tap water,
especially on hot summer days. They also take for granted that
the water is clean and safe. But in reality, the water they drink
could be contaminated and pose a serious health risk. **That's
just what happened in Walkerton, Ontario, where a water
pollution incident had a devastating effect that every town can
learn from.**

What happened in Walkerton Ontario? Heavy rains fell
on May 12. It wasn't until May 21 that the townspeople were
advised to boil their drinking water. The rains washed cattle
manure into the town well. The manure contained E coli, a type
of bacteria. E coli is harmless to cattle. It can make people sick.
Seven days after the heavy rains, people began calling public
health officials. The warning came too late. Two people had
already died.

Once Walkerton's problem was identified, the solutions were
known. The government acted quickly to help the community
and to clean the water supply. One Canadian newspaper
reported that a $100,000 emergency fund was set up to help
families with expenses. Bottled water for drinking and
containers of bleach for sanitizing and cleaning were donated
by local businesses.

So what messed up Walkerton? Basically, people screwed

1

2

3

4

up! According to one news story, a flaw in the water treatment system allowed the bacteria-infested water to enter the well. The manure washed into the well, but the chlorine should have killed the deadly bacteria. In Walkerton, the PUC group fell asleep at the wheel.

The writer covers the solutions that were used to resolve the problem.

At last, the Provincial Clean Water Agency restored the main water and sewage systems by flushing out all of the town's pipes and wells. The ban on drinking Walkerton's water was finally lifted seven months after the water became contaminated.

5

The concluding paragraph stresses the importance of public awareness.

Could any good come from Walkerton's tragedy? Does it have a silver lining? It is possible that more people are aware that water may be contaminated. Today people are beginning to take responsibility for the purity of the water they and their families drink. In the end, more and more people will know about the dangers of contaminated water—without learning it the hard way.

6

Video

Angela kept a working bibliography.

As she researched her topic, Angela kept a working bibliography—a list of resources she thought might offer information helpful to her essay. During the writing process, she deleted some resources, added others, and edited the document that became the references page on **119**.

Working References

Wickens, Barbara. "Tragedy in Walkerton." *Maclean*'s. 5
    June 2000: 34–36.

Phone interview with Alex Johnson, Walkerton Police
    Department, 23 September 2005.

Blackwell, Thomas. "Walkerton Doctor Defends Response."
    The Edmonton Journal. 9 January 2001.
    http://edmontonjournal.com.

Angela's First Revision

Video

Audio

After finishing the first draft, Angela set it aside. When she was ready to revise it, she looked carefully at global issues—ideas, organization, and voice. She wrote notes to herself to help keep her thoughts together.

Angela's comments

Water Woes

an unusually   Saturday afternoon

It's a hot ~~day.~~ Several people just finished mowing their

I need to give my opening more energy.

lawns. A group of bicyclists ~~more than 3,000 have been~~ *pedal up the street*

~~passing through your picturesque town all afternoon.~~ Dozens of

Little Leaguers are batting, running, and sweating. What do all

these people have in common? They all drink lots of tap water,

especially on hot summer days. They also take for granted that

the water is clean and safe. But in reality, the water they drink

Does my thesis still fit the paper?— Yes.

could be contaminated and pose a serious health risk. That's just

what happened in Walkerton, Ontario, where a water pollution

incident had a devastating effect that every town can learn from.

What happened in Walkerton, Ontario? Heavy rains fell on

May 12. [It wasn't until May 21 that the townspeople were

advised to boil their drinking water.] The rains washed cattle

Using time sequence, put this paragraph in better order.

manure into the town well. The manure contained E coli, a type

of bacteria. E coli is harmless to cattle. It can make people sick.

Seven days after the heavy rains, people began calling public

health officials. The warning came too late. Two people had

already died.

Once Walkerton's problem was identified, the solutions were

known. The government acted quickly to help the community

and to clean the water supply. One Canadian newspaper

Move this paragraph— it interrupts the discussion of causes.

reported that a $100,000 emergency fund was set up to help

families with expenses. Bottled water for drinking and

containers of bleach for sanitizing and cleaning were donated

by local businesses.

1

2

3

My voice here is too informal.

went wrong in

So what ~~messed up~~ Walkerton? Human error was a critical factor. ~~Basically, people screwed~~ 4
First,
~~up!~~ According to one news story, a flaw in the water treatment
Even after
system allowed the bacteria-infested water to enter the well. The
manure washed into the well, ~~but~~ the chlorine should have killed

Explain "fell asleep."

Move paragraph three here and combine.

the deadly bacteria. In Walkerton, the ~~PUC group fell asleep at the wheel.~~

In addition,
~~At last~~ the Provincial Clean Water Agency restored the 5
main water and sewage systems by flushing out all of the
town's pipes and wells. The ban on drinking Walkerton's water
was finally lifted seven months after the water became
contaminated.

Cut the clichés.

Could any good come from Walkerton's tragedy? ~~Does it~~ 6
~~have a silver lining?~~ It is possible that more people are aware
that water may be contaminated. Today people are beginning to
take responsibility for the purity of the water they and their
families drink. In the end, more and more people will know
about the dangers of contaminated water—without learning it
the hard way.

Public Utilities Commission was responsible for overseeing
the testing and treating of the town's water, but they
failed to monitor it properly. Apparently, shortcuts were
taken when tracking the water's chlorine level, and as a
result, some of the water samples were mislabeled. There
was also a significant delay between the time that the
contamination was identified and the time it was reported.

Video

Angela's Second Revision

Next, Angela asked a peer to review her work. His comments are in the margin. Angela used them to make additional changes, including writing a new opening and closing.

Reviewer's comments	Angela's changes

Water Woes

WARNING: City tap water is polluted with animal waste. Using the water for drinking, cooking, or bathing could cause sickness or death. [1]

Could you make the opening more relevant and urgent?

   According to the Seirra Club, run-off pollutants from farm cites are [2] *steadily seeping into our streams, lakes, reservoirs and wells. Because much of our drinking water comes from these resources, warnings like the one above are already posted in a number of U.S. and Canadian communities, and many more postings will be needed (Sierra Club, 2005). As the Seirra Club argues, the pollution and related warnings are serious, and failure to take them seriously could be deadly. For*

Could you clarify your focus on the topic?

- - - *example, a few years ago the citizens of Walkerton Ontario learned that the water that they believed to be clean was actually poisoned.*

   The events   *began*
~~What happened~~ in Walkerton, ~~Ontario? Heavy rains fell~~ [3]
   , 2000, when heavy rains
on May 12/ ~~The rains~~ washed cattle manure into the town well. The manure contained E coli, a type of bacteria. E coli is harmless to cattle. It can make people sick. Seven days after

Add the year and other specific details.

                   to complain of nausea and diarrhea⊙
the heavy rains, people began calling public health officials, It wasn't until May 21 that the townspeople were advised to boil their drinking water. The warning came too late. Two people had
, and more than 2,000 were ill (Wickens, 2001)⊙
already died.
      Several factors contributed to the terrible tragedy in Walkerton,
~~So what went wrong in Walkerton? Human error was a~~ [4]
including human error.   *The Edmonton Journal*
~~critical factor.~~ First, according to ~~one news story~~, a flaw in the

Add your sources.

water treatment system allowed the bacteria-infested water to
(Blackwell, 2001)⊙
enter the well. Even after the manure washed into the well, the chlorine should have killed the deadly bacteria. In Walkerton, the Public Utilities Commission was responsible for overseeing

the testing and treating of the town's water, but it failed to monitor it properly. Apparently, shortcuts were taken when tracking the water's chlorine level, and as a result, some of the water samples were mislabeled. There was also a significant delay between the time that the contamination was identified and the time it was reported.

Use active voice.

Once Walkerton's problem was identified, the ~~solutions were known.~~ The government acted quickly to help the community and ~~to clean the water supply.~~ One Canadian newspaper *The Edmonton Journal* reported a $100,000 emergency fund was set up to help families with expenses. *Local businesses donated* Bottled water for drinking and containers of bleach for basic sanitizing and cleaning ~~were donated by local businesses.~~ In addition, the Provincial Clean Water Agency restored the main water and sewage systems by flushing out all of the town's pipes and wells. The ban on drinking Walkerton's water was finally lifted seven months after the water became contaminated.

Consider adding details—maybe an entire paragraph—calling readers to action, and stating your thesis clearly.

As the Sierra Club warned and the citizens of Walkerton learned, water purity is a life-and-death issue. Fortunately, both the United States and Canada have been addressing the problem. For example, since 2001, more states and provinces are tightening their clean-water standards, more communities have begun monitoring their water quality, and more individuals have been using water-filtration systems, bottled water, or boiled tap water. However, a tragedy like that in Walkerton could happen again. To avoid such horror, all of us must get involved by demanding clean tap water in our communities and by promoting the polices and procedures needed to achieve that goal.

Angela's Edited Draft

When Angela began editing, she read each of her sentences aloud to check for clarity and smoothness. **The first page of Angela's edited copy is shown below.**

The writer revises the title.

in Walkerton
Water Woes∧

> *Warning: City tap water is polluted with animal waste. Using the water for drinking, cooking, or bathing could cause sickness or death.*

According to the Seirra Club, run-off pollutants from farm

1

cites are steadily seeping into our streams, lakes, reservoirs∧ and

wells. Because much of our drinking water comes from these

resources, warnings like the one above are already posted in a

number of U.S. and Canadian communities, and many more

She qualifies her statement, replacing "will" with "might"

might   in the future
postings ~~will~~ be needed∧ (Sierra Club, 2005). As the Seirra Club

argues, the pollution and related warnings are serious, and

failure to take them seriously could be deadly. For example, a

few years ago the citizens of Walkerton Ontario learned that the

tragically
water that they believed to be clean was ∧~~actually~~ poisoned.

The events in Walkerton began on May 12, 2000, when heavy

2

rains washed cattle manure into the town well. The manure

She rewrites and combines several choppy sentences.

commonly called   While E coli
contained ~~E. coli. a~~ bacteria∧ ∧E coli∧ is harmless to cattle.∧ It can

make people sick. Seven days after the heavy rains, people began

calling public health officials to complain of nausea and diarrhea.

It wasn't until May 21 that the townspeople were advised to boil

their drinking water. The warning came too late. Two people had

already died, and more than 2,000 were ill (Wickens, 2001).

Several factors contributed to the ~~terrible~~ tragedy in

3

Angela deletes unnecessary words.

Walkerton, including human error. First, according to *The*

Edmonton Journal, a flaw in the water treatment system allowed

the ~~bacteria~~-infested water to enter the well (Blackwell, 2001).

Even after the manure washed into the well, the chlorine . . .

Video

Angela's Proofread Draft

Angela reviewed her edited copy for punctuation, agreement issues, and spelling. **The first page of Angela's proofread essay is shown below.**

Water Woes in Walkerton

Warning: City tap water is polluted with animal waste. Using the water for drinking, cooking, or bathing could cause sickness or death.

The writer corrects an error that the spell checker did not pick up.

She corrects spelling errors.

She adds a comma between the city and province.

According to the Sierra Club, run-off pollutants from farm sites are steadily seeping into our streams, lakes, reservoirs, and wells. Because much of our drinking water comes from these resources, warnings like the one above are already posted in a number of U.S. and Canadian communities, and many more postings might be needed in the future (Sierra Club, 2005). As the Sierra Club argues, the pollution and related warnings are serious, and failure to take them seriously could be deadly. For example, a few years ago the citizens of Walkerton, Ontario, learned that the water that they believed to be clean was tragically poisoned.   1

She adds periods and italicizes "E. coli" to show that it is a scientific term.

The events in Walkerton began on May 12, 2000, when heavy rains washed cattle manure into the town well. The manure contained bacteria commonly called *E. coli* While *E. coli* is harmless to cattle, it can make people sick. Seven days after the heavy rains, people began calling public health officials to complain of nausea and diarrhea. It wasn't until May 21 that the townspeople were advised to boil their drinking water. The warning came too late. Two people had already died, and more than 2,000 were ill (Wickens, 2000).   2

She adds a word for clarity.

Several factors contributed to the tragedy in Walkerton, including human error. First, according to *The Edmonton Journal,* a flaw in the water treatment system allowed the infested water to enter Walkerton's well (Blackwell, 2001). Even after the manure washed ~~into the well~~ *into Walkerton's well*, the chlorine should have . . .   3

Angela's Finished Essay

After proofreading and formatting her essay, Angela added a heading and page numbers. She also added more documentation and a references page at the end. As assigned, she omitted the title page and abstract.

Clean Water Is Everyone's Business 1

Complete details are supplied in the heading.

Angela Franco

Professor Kim Van Es

English 101

October 12, 2005

Clean Water Is Everyone's Business

The title is changed. The warning is emphasized with red print.

> Warning: City tap water is polluted with animal waste. Using the water for drinking, cooking, or bathing could cause sickness or death.

An appropriate font and type size are used.

According to the Sierra Club, run-off pollutants from farm sites are steadily seeping into our streams, lakes, reservoirs, and wells. Because much of our drinking water comes from these resources, warnings like the one above are already posted in a number of U.S. and Canadian communities, and many more postings might be needed in the future (Sierra Club, 2005). As the Sierra Club argues, the pollution and related warnings are serious, and failure to take them seriously could be deadly. For example, a few years ago the citizens of Walkerton, Ontario, learned that the water that they believed to be clean was tragically poisoned.

The events in Walkerton began on May 12, 2000, when heavy rains washed cattle manure into the town well. The

Clean Water Is Everyone's Business 2

Title and page number are used on each page.

manure contained the bacteria commonly called *E. coli.* While *E. coli* is harmless to cattle, it can make people sick. Seven days after the heavy rains, people began calling public health officials to complain of nausea and diarrhea. It wasn't until May 21 that the townspeople were advised to boil their drinking water. The warning came too late. Two people had already died, and more than 2,000 were ill (Wickens, 2001).

Several factors contributed to the tragedy in Walkerton, including human error. First, according to *The Edmonton Journal,* a flaw in the water treatment system allowed the infested water to enter Walkerton's well (Blackwell, 2001). Even after the manure washed into Walkerton's well, the chlorine should have killed the deadly bacteria. In Walkerton, the Public Utilities Commission was responsible for overseeing the testing and treating of the town's water, but they failed to monitor it properly ("Walkerton's water-safety," 2000). Apparently, shortcuts were taken when tracking the water's chlorine level, and as a result, some of the water samples were mislabeled. There was also a significant delay between the time that the contamination was identified and the time it was reported.

Once Walkerton's problem was identified, the government acted quickly to help the community. In its December 7, 2000, edition, *The Edmonton Journal* reported that a $100,000 emergency fund was set up to help families with expenses. Local businesses donated bottled water for drinking and containers of bleach for basic sanitizing and cleaning. In addition, the

The writer continues to give credit throughout the essay.

Clean Water Is Everyone's Business 3

Provincial Clean Water Agency restored the main water and sewage systems by flushing out all of the town's pipes and wells. Seven months after the water became contaminated, the ban on drinking Walkerton's water was finally lifted.

As the Sierra Club warns and the citizens of Walkerton learned, water purity is a life-and-death issue. Fortunately, both the United States and Canada have been addressing the problem. For example, since 2001, more states and provinces are tightening their clean-water standards, more communities are monitoring their water quality, and more individuals are using water-filtration sytems, bottled water, or boiled tap water. However, a tragedy like that in Walkerton could happen again. To avoid such horror, all of us must get involved by demanding clean tap water in our communities and by promoting the policies and procedures needed to achieve that goal.

5

The writer restates her thesis in the last sentence.

Clean Water Is Everyone's Business 4

References

Blackwell, T. (2001, January 9). Walkerton doctor defends

    response. *The Edmonton Journal.* Retrieved April 7, 2005,

    from <http://edmontonjournal.com>.

Sierra Club. (n.d.) Water sentinels: Keeping it clean around the

    U.S.A. Retrieved April 5, 2005, from <http://

    sierraclub.org/watersentinels/>.

Walkerton's water-safety tests falsified regularly, utility

    official admits. (2000, December 7). *The Edmonton

    Journal.* Retrieved April 2, 2005, from <http://

    edmontonjournal.com>.

Wickens, B. (2000, June 5). Tragedy in Walkerton. *Maclean's*,

    113(23): 34–36.

Sources used are listed correctly, in alphabetical order.

Writing Prompt

Writing Activities

1. Review Angela's writing process. How does it compare with your own writing process on a recent assignment?

2. Reread the new opening and closing that Angela drafts in her second revision (112–113), and consider how they strengthen her essay. Then analyze the opening and closing of one of your own recent essays and revise both as needed.

3. Review the peer-editing instructions in "Revising Collaboratively" (pages 79–80). Then reread the reviewer's comments in the margins of Angela's second revision (pages 112–113). Do the comments reflect the instructions? Explain.

Effective Writing Checklist

Whatever form your writing takes—essay, report, narrative, or research paper—it should demonstrate the following traits. Check your finished work using these traits or standards as a guide.

Stimulating Ideas

The writing . . .

_____ Presents interesting and important information.

_____ Maintains a clear focus or purpose—centered on a thesis, theme, concern, or question.

_____ Develops the focus with sufficient detail.

_____ Holds the reader's attention (and answers his or her questions).

Logical Organization

_____ Includes a clear beginning, middle, and ending.

_____ Contains specific details, arranged in the best order.

_____ Uses transitions to link sentences and paragraphs.

Engaging Voice

_____ Speaks in a sincere, natural way that fits the writing situation.

_____ Shows that the writer really cares about the subject.

Appropriate Word Choice

_____ Contains specific, clear words.

_____ Uses an appropriate level of language.

Overall Fluency

_____ Flows smoothly from sentence to sentence.

_____ Displays varied sentence beginnings and lengths.

_____ Follows a style that fits the situation.

Correct, Accurate Copy

_____ Adheres to the rules of grammar, spelling, and punctuation.

_____ Follows established documentation guidelines.

_____ Exhibits a polished, professional design.

II. A Reader: Strategies and Models

Strategies & Models

CONTENTS

Writing Across the Curriculum

Chapter 9
Forms of College Writing

In college, professors in nearly all departments give writing assignments. Why? Because they know that writing helps you in two ways: (1) to learn course content and (2) to learn how to carry on a written dialogue with others in your field. In other words, writing will help you learn course material today, but it will also help you use that information in subsequent college courses and in the workplace.

The purpose of this chapter is to show you three important things about writing across the curriculum:

- How a college curriculum and faculty are organized
- What kinds of writing you can expect to do in your courses
- How writing and thinking skills required in one class are linked to writing and thinking skills required in another class

To accomplish these tasks, the chapter begins by showing the big picture: The three divisions into which most college curricula are divided, and the academic departments that constitute each division. The chapter then presents more specific information about academic departments, including the topics students study, the forms of writing teachers assign, and the traits of those forms.

What's Ahead

- Three Curricular Divisions
- Types of Writing in Each Division
- Traits of Writing Across the Curriculum

Three Curricular Divisions

Based on each department's area of study and focus, the college curriculum is generally divided into three groups: humanities, social sciences, and natural and applied sciences. These groups are then subdivided into specific departments, such as biology, chemistry, and physics. Below you will find an explanation of each division, along with its more common departments.

Humanities

Scholars within this division study human culture, both past and present. They examine topics such as the history of civilization, cultural institutions and trends, religious beliefs and practices, languages and their use, and artwork and performance skills. Some departments in this division include the following:

• Archeology	• Ethnic Studies	• Modern Languages	• Theater Arts
• Asian Studies	• Film Studies	• Music	• Theology
• Dance	• Graphic Design	• Philosophy	• Visual Art
• English	• History	• Religion	• Women's Studies

Social Sciences

Scholars in this division study human behavior and societies using research strategies **adapted from the natural sciences.** For example, a researcher may develop a hypothesis regarding a topic or phenomenon, and then devise an experiment to test that hypothesis. Students study economic systems, correctional programs, and personality disorders. Departments in this division include the following:

• Anthropology	• Economics	• Geophysics	• Psychology
• Business	• Education	• Government	• Social Work
• Communication	• Genetics	• Health & Phys. Ed.	• Sociology
• Criminology	• Geography	• Political Science	• Urban Planning

Natural and Applied Sciences

The natural sciences (such as biology, zoology, and chemistry) focus on specific aspects of nature, such as animal life, plant life, and molecular structures. In contrast, the applied sciences (such as mathematics, computer science, and engineering) consider how to use science-based information to understand concepts and develop artifacts. Here are some of the departments in this division:

• Agriculture	• Biology	• Environment	• Physics
• Agronomy	• Botany	• Forestry	• Physiology
• Anatomy	• Chemistry	• Mathematics	• Public Health
• Architecture	• Computer Science	• Nutrition	• Space Science
• Astronomy	• Engineering	• Oceanography	• Zoology

Types of Writing in Each Division

Listed below are the types of writing commonly assigned in the three academic divisions. Often instructors in different divisions will assign the same type of essay—but with a different purpose, audience, or focus. When an assigned form differs from the one shown in the book, adapt the guidelines in the book to the form stated in the assignment.

Humanities

Application Writing (387–398)
Cause and Effect (175–186)
Classification (203–216)
Comparison and Contrast (187–202)
Definition (231–244)
Describing a Process (217–230)
Description and Reflection (155–172)
Essay Test (375–386)
Interview Report (333–340)
Literary Analysis (357–374)

Narration and Description (131–154)
Oral Presentations (411–420)
Observation Report (319–332)
Personal Essay (131–172)
Persuading Readers to Act (283–300)
Proposing a Solution (301–316)
Research Paper (423–492)
Taking a Position (263–282)
Test Taking (375–386)
Web Writing (399–410)

Social Sciences

Abstracts, Summaries (538, 540, 557)
Application Writing (387–398)
Cause and Effect (175–186)
Classification (203–216)
Comparison and Contrast (187–202)
Definition (231–244)
Describing a Process (217–230)
Description and Reflection (155–172)
Experiment Report (341–354)

Interview Report (333–340)
Literary Analysis (357–374)
Oral Presentations (411–420)
Personal Essay (131–172)
Persuading Readers to Act (283–300)
Proposing a Solution (301–316)
Research Report (423–492)
Taking a Position (263–282)
Web Writing (399–410)

Natural and Applied Sciences

Abstracts/Summaries (538, 540, 557)
Application Writing (387–398)
Cause and Effect (175–186)
Classification (203–216)
Comparison and Contrast (187–202)
Definition (231–244)
Describing a Process (217–230)
Experiment Report (341–354)
Field Report (341–354)

Interview Report (333–340)
Lab Report (341–354)
Personal Essay (131–172)
Persuading Readers to Act (283–300)
Proposing a Solution (301–316)
Research Paper (423–492)
Test Taking (375–386)
Web Writing (399–410)

Traits of Writing Across the Curriculum

Listed below are the more common writing tasks in each of the three divisions, along with seven traits that distinguish good writing for each task.

Humanities

Idea: **Personal writing:** Explores the writer's ideas, experiences, and feelings

Organization: Usually chronological

Voice: Engaging, fits the story, honest, direct

Word Choice: Words are precise and fit the writer's topic, purpose, audience, and characters

Sentences: Appropriate for dialogue and description; others use varied forms

Correctness: Documentation (where necessary) follows MLA or CMS style

Design: Designed as an essay with proper formatting and typeface

---

Idea: **Analyze a work of art:** Describes the work and analyzes its parts and how they function

Organization: Appropriate for the work and the writer's focus

Voice: Objective appraisal and analysis, supported by evidence

Sentences: Varied in length and structure, with clear transitions

Word Choice: Appropriate for the art form; technical terms explained

Correctness: Documentation follows MLA or CMS style

Design: Designed as an essay with proper formatting and typeface

---

Idea: **Argue a point:** Persuades reader regarding the point's meaning, importance, and truth

Organization: Order fits the topic and purpose: cause/effect, compare/contrast, and so on

Voice: Informed, impartial, inviting

Word Choice: Precise, with scholarly terms used in the discipline

Sentences: Tend to be longer; complexity fits the topic and audience

Correctness: Documentation follows MLA or CMS style

Design: Designed as an essay with proper formatting and typeface

---

Idea: **Analyze a phenomenon:** Explains its meaning in relation to its historical, social, and/or natural context (e.g., Marxism)

Organization: Often combines cause/effect, compare/contrast, and examples

Voice: Scholarly, fair, informed, balanced

Word Choice: Precise, often including scholarly terms used in the discipline

Sentences: Tend to be longer; complexity fits the topic and audience

Correctness: Documentation follows MLA or CMS style

Design: Designed as an essay with proper formatting and typeface

Social Sciences

Idea: **Case study:** Describes and analyzes the topic, identifies methodology, gives results

Organization: Gives overview, presents steps chronologically, analyzes outcome

Voice: Impartial reporting; respectful, thoughtful analysis

Word Choice: Precise statistics and discipline-related terms

Sentences: Medium-length sentences with clear transitions

Correctness: Documentation follows APA or CMS style

Design: Formatted as a report for easy reading and in accordance with the discipline's or department's style guide

---

Idea: **Literature review:** Summarizes and evaluates journal articles (usually research based) on a topic

Organization: Each article discussed separately followed by conclusions

Voice: Unbiased reporting, formal tone, logical analysis

Word Choice: Includes precise technical terms and statistics

Sentences: Shorter sentences and paragraphs with clear transitions

Correctness: Documentation follows APA or CMS style

Design: Formatted as a report for easy reading and in accordance with the discipline's or department's style guide

---

Idea: **Analyze a policy or project:** Analyzes the topic, its history, and its effects

Organization: Analysis often uses cause/effect, classification, and compare/contrast

Voice: Impartial, informed, concerned, thoughtful

Word Choice: Includes precise technical terms and statistics

Sentences: Sentences are varied in length and structure, with clear transitions

Correctness: Documentation follows APA or CMS style

Design: Formatted as a report for easy reading and in accordance with the discipline's or department's style guide

---

Idea: **Describe a process:** Describes materials, steps in the process, and the importance of the process

Organization: Usually states topic and outcome, gives steps chronologically

Voice: Objective, yet concerned about effectiveness and safety

Word Choice: Precise, often including technical terms

Sentences: Description of a process—sentences tend to be short, direct

Correctness: Documentation follows APA or CMS style

Design: Formatted as a report for easy reading and in accordance with the discipline's or department's style guide; or as workplace instructions with numbered steps and graphics

Natural and Applied Sciences

Idea: **Lab or experiment report:** Includes clear data, logical analysis, unbiased reporting
Organization: States issues and hypothesis, methods with procedure, results with data, discusses results
Word Choice: Precise, often including scientific and technical terms
Sentences: Medium length, logical, passive voice only when needed
Voice: Interested, curious, impartial, logical, meticulous
Correctness: Documentation and format follow CSE or APA style
Design: Formatted as a report in accordance with the discipline's style guide; graphics (such as tables, charts) are clear

---

Idea: **Field report:** includes clear data and unbiased reporting
Organization: States focus and issues, methods with procedure, results with data, discusses results
Voice: Interested, curious, logical, meticulous
Word Choice: Precise, often including scientific and technical terms
Sentences: Medium length, logical, passive voice only when needed
Correctness: Documentation and format follow CSE or APA style
Design: Formatted as a report in accordance with the discipline's style guide; graphics (such as tables, photos) are strong

---

Idea: **Literature review:** Summarizes and compares journal articles (usually research based)
Organization: Each article discussed separately, followed by conclusions
Voice: Equitable reporting, formal tone, logical, clear analysis
Word Choice: Includes technical scientific words and concepts; first person rarely used
Sentences: Shorter sentences and paragraphs with clear transitions
Correctness: Documentation and format follow CSE or APA style
Design: Formatted as a report with proper spacing and typeface

---

Idea: **Explain a process:** Describes each step in a process
Organization: Usually states topic, gives steps chronologically, closes
Voice: Impartial, concerned about effectiveness and safety
Word Choice: Precise, often including scientific and technical terms
Sentences: Description of a process—sentences vary depending on the form; instructions—short, direct
Correctness: Description follows CSE or APA style
Design: Formatted as an essay or workplace instructions

Research and Documentation Websites

MLA Modern Language Association <**www.mla.org**>
APA American Psychological Association <**www.apa.org**>
CMS Chicago Manual of Style <**www.press.uchicago.edu**>
CSE Council of Science Editors <**councilscienceeditors.org**>

NOTE: CSE has replaced CBE (*Council of Biology Editors*)

Narrative, Descriptive, and Reflective Writing

Chapters 10 and 11 offer instruction in writing personal essays, pieces that focus on experience, especially the writer's experience—whether of places, people, or events—with the goal of vividly sharing that experience with readers. To that end, personal essays tend to be informal in voice and style, freely using personal pronouns such as "I" and "we." Note, too, that such writing depends on strategies of narration, description, and reflection. While virtually all personal essays blend the three techniques, Chapter 10 focuses on the combination of narration and description, and Chapter 11 focuses on the combination of description and reflection.

As with all forms of writing, you should develop your personal essays using whatever strategies fit your writing situation: your subject, audience, and purpose. For examples, watch how the authors of the essays in Chapters 10 and 11 use not only the strategies narration, description, and reflection (commonly associated with personal writing), but also the strategies cause/effect, compare/contrast, and definition (often associated with analytical writing).

CONTENTS

Narrative, Descriptive, and Reflective Writing

Chapter 10
Narration and Description

A personal narrative is a story—a story that mirrors you and your experiences. In it, you may tell about a time when you were afraid, lost something (or someone), found joy, learned a tough lesson, or discovered some secret. Whatever the topic, your story should help readers see, hear, touch, and taste those details that make your experience come alive. To do that, you must carefully describe key aspects of the experience.

As you prepare to share your story with others, get ready to relive it yourself—to reexperience all that you felt, thought, or sensed during the original event. But get ready also to learn something new about the event, about others, and even about yourself. That's what writing a personal narrative can do.

What's Ahead

- Overview: Writing Narration and Description
  - Student Models
  - Professional Models
- Guidelines
- Writing Checklist and Activities

Web Link

Overview
Writing Narration and Description

Writer's Goal

Your goal is to write a personal narrative about something significant that has happened to you. Write in a way that allows your readers to vividly relive the experience and to learn something about you and about themselves.

Keys for Success

Be passionate. ■ Choose an experience from your life, anchored in your memory, that still makes you feel happy, angry, humble, afraid, or some other strong emotion.

Include characters. ■ Make the people in your narrative come to life. Let your story unfold through their actions and words. Above all, show how you—and these other people—react to the experience.

Create memorable descriptions. ■ Choose details that create pictures in your readers' minds. First, use your senses to trigger the readers' senses. What did you see? What did you hear? Next, choose strong nouns and active verbs. Finally, show—don't tell.

Topics to Consider

Memorable experiences can be categorized in a number of ways. Understanding these categories may help you identify possible subjects for your narratives. *Remember:* Your personal narratives should show something significant about you and about human nature in general.

- **Initiation:** Think of a time when you had to prove yourself, test your abilities, or "grow up." Share this "test" with your readers.

- **Loss:** Explore a time when you lost someone or something that was important to you.

- **Run-In:** Consider an unavoidable confrontation with another person. How did you react to the situation? What did you learn about yourself?

- **Arrival:** Recall when you were the new kid on the block or in school. How did the experience change your life? Or remember a time when someone new arrived in your life. How did this person affect you?

- **Occasion:** Focus on a revealing get-together, celebration, holiday, party, or vacation experience. What did you learn from the experience?

Next Step Read the model essays and perform the activities that follow. As you read, think of "defining experiences" in your life. How did each shape you? Would your readers find something of value for themselves in your experiences? Would they sense the importance of your experience?

Personal Narrative

A common personal narrative is the anecdote—a short, direct story that adds spark to your writing while introducing a topic or illustrating an idea. Below and on the following page are three anecdotes taken from essays in this book or the book's companion website.

Anecdote introducing a topic:

The story gets our attention and shows some causes and effects of stress.

It was 8:00 a.m.; her husband, Lance, had left for work without filling the tank on the Mazda; and her daughter, Gina, had gotten on the school bus without her show-and-tell bunny. "Great!" thought Jan, "now I have to get gas at Demler's, stop by Gina's school, and drop Alex off at day care—all before my 9:30 class!" Quickly she grabbed the diaper bag, picked up the baby, and headed for the door. At 9:35, with her heart pounding and hands sweating, she scrambled into the classroom, found an open seat, and was hurriedly pulling out her psych notes when the prof asked, "So . . . precisely what does Jung mean by 'collective unconscious'—Jan?"

The transition links the anecdote and the thesis.

"Uh . . . what was the question?" she responded.

Does the scene sound familiar—too much work, too little time, and too much stress?

From "Life-Threatening Stress"

See <www.thecollegewriter.com>

Anecdote illustrating a point:

The transition tells why the anecdote is used.

Steve is a good example. When he entered the nursing home just six months ago, he was experiencing the early stages of dementia. Today, however, his illness is much more advanced. The stress of moving into this new environment and leaving his wife at home alone affected Steve deeply. When he first arrived, Steve often cried and begged to be taken home. "I'll give you $20—please just take me home," he'd plead.

The quote and description show how a dementia patient feels.

Painfully, I would explain, "Steve, this is your home." After some time, the situation got so bad that he would not sleep or eat. He was depressed, and he cried often, thinking that no one cared about him. Eventually, Steve was given stronger drugs to help with the depression. For a few months, the medication seemed to work—he laughed at jokes and occasionally told one himself. But then Steve's dementia returned. Soon he was asking his same sad questions: "Where am I?" and "Do you know what I'm doing here?"

The transition shifts the focus.

So what is the best "medication" for people with dementia?

From "Understanding Dementia," page **236**

Anecdote illustrating character traits:

The writer reflects on how she and other relatives feel about the person who shot her nephew.

Oddly, we feel little curiosity or specific anger toward the man who shot him. We have to remind ourselves to check in with the police. Even so, it feels pro forma, like sending in those $2 rebate forms that come with new pantyhose: You know your request will fall into a deep, dark hole somewhere, but still, it's your duty to try. We push for an arrest because we owe it to Johnny and to ourselves as citizens. We don't think about it otherwise—our low expectations are too ingrained. A Harvard aunt notwithstanding, for people like Johnny, Marvin Gaye was right that only three things are sure: taxes, death, and trouble. At least it wasn't the second.

1

She creates a transition with the opening sentence. She then relays a story showing that even though she has not met the shooter, she understands who he is and what he does.

We rarely wonder about or discuss the brother who shot him because we already know everything about him. When the call came, my first thought was the same one I'd had when I'd heard about Rosa Parks's beating: A brother did it. A non-job-having, middle-of-the-day malt-liquor-drinking, crotch-clutching, loud-talking brother with many neglected children born of many forgotten women. He lives in his mother's basement with furniture rented at an astronomical interest rate, the exact amount of which he does not know. He has a car phone, an $80 monthly cable bill, and every possible phone feature but no savings. He steals Social Security numbers from unsuspecting relatives and assumes their identities to acquire large TV sets for which he will never pay. On the slim chance that he is brought to justice, he will have a colorful criminal history and no coherent explanation to offer for his act. His family will raucously defend him and cry cover-up. Some liberal lawyer just like me will help him plea-bargain his way to yet another short stay in a prison pesthouse that will serve only to add another layer to the brother's sociopathology and formless, mindless nihilism. We know him. We've known and feared him all our lives.

2

From "Who Shot Johnny?," page **167**

Reading for Better Writing

1. Check the essay from which each anecdote is taken and explain why the story does or does not accomplish its task.

2. How does each transitional sentence link the story to the rest of the essay?

3. Find the introductory anecdotes on pages **165** and **235**, and explain why each is effective.

Narration and Description

In this essay, student writer Jacqui Nyangi Owitti recalls an important personal experience in her life that taught her the pain of loss.

Mzee Owitti

The opening sets the scene and gives background information.

I am about 12 years old. We are en route from Nairobi, the capital city, to the rural area of Kisumu on the eastern shores of Lake Victoria in western Kenya, where my grandparents live. My five brothers and I are traveling with Mum on the overnight train. I am not particularly sad, though I know what has happened. I base my reactions on my mother's, and since she appears to be handling the whole thing well, I am determined to do the same. You see, my grandfather has died. My dad's dad.

We reach the town of my ancestry just as dawn lazily turns into early morning. We buy snacks and hire a car for the last leg of the journey. We then meander through a bewildering maze of mud huts, sisal scrub, and sandy clay grassland, until we come within sight of my grandfather's land, the place where my father grew up.

The narrator describes what she sees and how she feels.

The first thing I notice is a crude "tent" made by sticking four poles in the ground, crisscrossing the top with long branches, and covering that with thatch. Despite the early hour, the place is filled with dignitaries, guests, and people like my mother's parents, who have traveled far to honor our family. I am struck by the stillness and all-pervading silence. Everything seems frozen. Time itself seems to mourn, and even the wind is still. The car stops a short distance from the property, and we sit motionless and quiet.

Verbs in present tense describe the action.

I turn to my mother, questioning. But she has drawn a handkerchief from somewhere and is climbing out of the car. Almost as an actor on the stage, she releases a sound I have never heard before. It is a moan, a scream, and a sob that is deep-throated, guttural, and high-pitched all at the same time. This sudden transformation from a calm, chipper person to a stricken stranger strikes in me a fear that I will long remember. Holding her handkerchief to her face, she breaks into a shuffling run. I sit in the car petrified, watching the drama unfold.

Out of seemingly nowhere, wailing answers my mother's cry. Other women appear at a run, heading for my mother, hands fluttering from the tops of their heads, to their waists, to their feet. Their heads are thrown back and from side to side in restless anguish. Their bodies are half-bent forward, and their feet are in constant motion even though no distance is covered. My aunts and close female relatives weep, letting loose high-pitched ululating moaning in support of my mother.

The last sentence explains the women's actions.

As the wife of the first child and only son, she commands a high place, and she must not grieve alone.

In the confusion, one lady is knocked down, and she seems to rock with her legs separated in a way that in other circumstances would be inappropriate and humiliating. Oddly, the people in the tent, mostly male,

1

2

3

4

5

6

appear to have seen and heard nothing. They continue silent and still. The whole scene seems unreal. Seeing my fear and confusion, the driver talks soothingly, explaining what is going on.

A paragraph describes one segment of the ceremony.

The wailing and mourning continue intermittently for a couple of days. Then the time comes for my grandfather to be taken from the mortuary in Kisumu to his final resting place. We all travel to the mortuary. He is dressed in his best suit and then taken to church, where his soul is committed to God. Afterward, the procession starts for home. On the way we are met by the other mourners, who, according to tradition, will accompany the hearse on foot, driving along the cows that are a symbol of wealth in life and a testament to a good life, respectability, and honor in death. Being city kids unable to jog for an hour with the mourners and cows, we ride in a car.

A transition word indicates a shift.

Finally, we are back at the homestead. My grandfather is put in the house where he spent the latter part of his life. The crying and mourning are now nearly at a feverish pitch, and the sense of loss is palpable. However, before people may enter the house to pay their last respects, one—they call him "Ratego"—must lead the way to say his good-byes. Suddenly, there is a commotion, and I stare in disbelief as a big bull, taller than my tall-for-my-age twelve-year-old height and wider than the doorway, is led toward my grandfather's house. Long, thick horns stick out of the colossal head. The body, pungent with an ammonia-laced, grassy smell, is a mosaic of black and brown—an odorous, pulsing mountain.

Precise words tell what the narrator sees and smells.

The bull's wild, staring eyes seem fixed on me. An old, barefoot man, dressed in a worn, too-short jacket and dusty black pants, leads this bull with a frayed rope. He waves his rod, yelling and leaping in syncopation with the bull's snorting and pawing. Dust puffs dance around their feet. The bull is a symbol of high honor for my grandfather, and only the largest bull in the land can embody this deep respect. Although I do not fully comprehend its significance, I know that it is the biggest animal I have ever seen. I step back as people try to get the bull into the house to pay its respects to my grandfather. After much yelling, shoving, and cries of pain from those whose feet the bull steps on, the effort is abandoned. Ratego is much too big.

The narrative approaches its climax.

As the bull is led away into the *boma*, people enter the room that has been emptied of furniture. I squeeze through the heaving, weeping mass, almost suffocating in the process. The room is surprisingly cool and dim, unlike the hot and bright sun outside. I approach curiously and cautiously, not knowing what to expect. At last I stand before the casket and look at my grandfather. He does not look dead. In fact, he is smiling! He looks like the person I remember, who always had a smile and an unshared secret lurking in the depths of his eyes.

A flashback adds depth to the present.

I peer into his face, recalling a time when I was four and he caught me doing something that deserved a reprimand. I had thought no one had seen me. However, my grandfather, on one of his rare visits to the city, had seen. Standing in front of his casket, I again hear him laugh. I remember how his kind, brown eyes had twinkled, and his white mustache, white teeth, and rich bitter-chocolate face had broken into an all-knowing, but-you-can-trust-me smile. I remember how the deep love that radiated from him assured me that I was his no matter what. And I remember how I had responded to his love by laughing happily and then skipping away, his answering laugh reverberating in my ears.

The narrator describes a pivotal point in the story.

That is my grandfather. Death cannot possibly touch him! Then I look closer and realize that the white streak breaking up his face is not the white teeth I remember. It is, instead, cotton stuffed into his mouth, as white as his teeth had been, making a mockery of my memories. At that moment, my granddaddy dies.

The last sentence offers a powerful image.

Until this point the whole has been a drama played out before my stunned, wide-eyed gaze. Rich in ancestry and tradition, its very nature and continuity are a celebration of life rather than death, fostering in me a keen sense of identity and a strong desire to keep the ancestral torch burning brightly, fiercely, and with pride. Now, however, Grandpa is dead. It is now that I cry. I am grieving. My granddaddy is gone, and the weighted arrow of sorrow pierces home. The pain is personal, unrelenting, and merciless. I stare at him and cannot tear myself away. I weep, saying over and over that he is smiling, he is smiling. My heartbreak and tears echo the refrain. He is smiling—a radiant, unforgettable smile. ∎

11

12

13

Reading for Better Writing

1. The writer uses verbs in the present tense to tell her story. How does this choice affect (a) the clarity of the plot, (b) the tension in the episode about the bull, and (c) your empathy with the narrator in the closing?

2. Choose a paragraph containing a particularly vivid description. How do the word choice, sentence structure, and punctuation affect your ability to sense the action?

3. In a conversation with an editor of this book, Jacqui Nyangi Owitti described her love for her grandfather and her pride in her heritage. Does the story reflect that love and pride? Explain.

Narration and Description

James C. Schaap is a writer and college professor. In this essay he describes the place he took his writing students on a particularly memorable day. The essay was first published in the *Des Moines Register*.

That Morning on the Prairie

The writer introduces the setting.

On some beautiful early fall days out here on the emerald cusp of the Great Plains, it's hard to believe that we are where we are. Warm southern breezes swing up from Texas, the sun smiles with a gentleness not seen since June, and the spacious sky reigns over everything in azure glory. *1*

Early on exactly that kind of fall morning, I like to take my writing classes to a ghost town, Highland, Iowa, ten miles west and two south, as they say out here on the square-cut prairie. Likely as not, Highland fell victim to a century-old phenomenon in the Upper Midwest: 100 years ago, land was cut into 160-acre chunks, most had homesteads, and small towns thrived. Today, when the portions are ten times bigger, fewer people live out here, and many towns have died out. *2*

He details the location.

What's left of Highland is a stand of pines circled around no more than twenty gravestones, and an old carved sign with hand-drawn figures detailing what was home for some people—a couple of Protestant churches, a couple of horse barns, and a blacksmith shop, little else. The town of Highland once flourished atop this swell of land at the confluence of a pair of nondescript gravel roads that still float out in four distinct directions like dusky ribbons over undulating prairie. But mostly, today, it's gone. *3*

He explains why he takes students to Highland— and how they respond.

I like to take my students to Highland because what's not there never fails to silence them. Maybe it's the emaciated cemetery; maybe it's the south wind's low moan through that stand of pines, a sound you don't hear often on the plains; maybe it's some variant of culture shock—they stumble sleepily out of their cubicle dorm rooms and wake up suddenly in a place with no walls. *4*

I'm lying. I know why they fall into psychic shock. It's the sheer immensity of the land that unfurls before them, the horizon only seemingly there where earth weaves effortlessly into sky; it's the vastness of rolling landscape William Cullen Bryant once claimed looked like an ocean stopped in time. It seems as if there's nothing here, and everything, and that's what stuns them into silence. That September morning, on those gravel roads, no cars passed. We were alone—20 of us, all alone and vulnerable on a high-ground swath of prairie once called Highland, surrounded by nothing but startling openness. *5*

The topic sentence indicates a transition.

That's where I was—and that's where they were—on September 11, 2001. We left for Highland about the same time Mohamed Atta and his friends were commandeering American Airlines Flight 11 into the north *6* tower of the World Trade Center, so we knew absolutely nothing about what had happened until we returned. While the rest of the world watched in horror, my students, notebooks and pens in hand, looked over a landscape so immense only God could live there—and were silent.

They found it hard to leave, but then no one can stay on retreat forever, so when we returned we heard the horrible news. All over campus and all over town, TVs blared.

I like to think that maybe on our campus that morning my students were best prepared for the horror everyone felt—prepared, not by having been warned, but by having been awed.

Every year it's a joy for me to sit at Highland with a new group of students, all of us trying to define and describe the beauty of what seems characterless prairie. But this year our being there on the morning of September 11 was more than a joy—it was also a kind of blessing. ∎

The writer reflects on the trip's impact on students.

Writing Prompt

Reading for Better Writing

1. In the first three paragraphs of his essay, the writer describes Highland. Cite passages that do or do not help you see the setting. What mood or feeling does the description evoke?

2. James C. Schaap, himself a writer, takes his students to Highland, where he asks them to use the setting as a writing prompt. What could students learn from the experience? Why?

3. Schaap concludes the essay by saying that his students' presence in Highland on September 11 was "a kind of blessing." What does he mean?

4. What do you think the writer is trying to say in the last several lines?

Narration and Description

Eric Arthur Blair, better known as George Orwell, was a British author who wrote political and cultural commentary in the 1930s and 1940s. Some of his best-known works include the novels *Animal Farm* and *1984* and essays such as this one.

A Hanging

The writer starts in the middle of the scene so that we have to keep reading to learn what is happening.

It was in Burma, a sodden morning of the rains. A sickly light, like yellow tinfoil, was slanting over the high walls into the jail yard. We were waiting outside the condemned cells, a row of sheds fronted with double bars, like small animal cages. Each cell measured about ten feet by ten and was quite bare within except for a plank bed and a pot for drinking water. In some of them brown, silent men were squatting at the inner bars, with their blankets draped round them. These were the condemned men, due to be hanged within the next week or two. [1]

The word *caressing* is an unexpected choice to describe the handling of the prisoner.

One prisoner had been brought out of his cell. He was a Hindu, a puny wisp of a man, with a shaven head and vague liquid eyes. He had a thick sprouting mustache, absurdly too big for his body, rather like the mustache of a comic man on the films. Six tall Indian warders were guarding him and getting him ready for the gallows. Two of them stood by with rifles and fixed bayonets, while the others handcuffed him, passed a chain through his handcuffs and fixed it to their belts, and lashed his arms tight to his sides. They crowded very close about him, with their hands always on him in a careful, caressing grip, as though all the while feeling him to make sure he was there. It was like men handling a fish which is still alive and may jump back into the water. But he stood quite unresisting, yielding his arms limply to the ropes, as though he hardly noticed what was happening. [2]

Eight o'clock struck and a bugle call, desolately thin in the wet air, floated from the distant barracks. The superintendent of the jail, who was standing apart from the rest of us, moodily prodding the gravel with his stick, raised his head at the sound. He was an army doctor, with a grey toothbrush mustache and a gruff voice. "For God's sake, hurry up, Francis," he said irritably. "The man ought to have been dead by this time. Aren't you ready yet?" [3]

The writer offers few details about the characters and event, building our curiosity.

Francis, the head jailer, a fat Dravidian in a white drill suit and gold spectacles, waved his black hand. "Yes sir, yes sir," he bubbled. "All iss satisfactorily prepared. The hangman iss waiting. We shall proceed." [4]

"Well, quick march, then. The prisoners can't get their breakfast till this job's over." [5]

We set out for the gallows. Two warders marched on either side of the prisoner, with their rifles at the slope; two others marched close against him, gripping him by arm and shoulder, as though at once pushing and [6] supporting him. The rest of us, magistrates and the like, followed behind. Suddenly, when we had gone ten yards, the procession stopped short without any order or warning. A dreadful thing had happened—a dog, come goodness knows whence, had appeared in the yard. It came bounding among us with a loud volley of barks and leapt round us wagging its whole body, wild with glee at finding so many human beings together. It was a large woolly dog, half Airedale, half pariah. For a moment it pranced around us, and then, before anyone could stop it, it had made a dash for the prisoner, and jumping up tried to lick his face. Everybody stood aghast, too taken aback even to grab the dog.

> The quotation enlivens the scene.

"Who let that bloody brute in here?" said the superintendent angrily. "Catch it, someone!" *7*

A warder detached from the escort, charged clumsily after the dog, but *8* it danced and gambolled just out of his reach, taking everything as part of the game. A young Eurasion jailer picked up a handful of gravel and tried to stone the dog away, but it dodged the stones and came after us again. Its yaps echoed from the jail walls. The prisoner, in the grasp of the two warders, looked on incuriously, as though this was another formality of the hanging. It was several minutes before someone man-

> The writer offers a specific detail.

aged to catch the dog. Then we put my handkerchief through its collar and moved off once more, with the dog still straining and whimpering.

> *This man was not dying, he was alive . . .*

It was about forty yards to the gallows. *9* I watched the bare brown back of the prisoner marching in front of me. He walked clumsily with his bound arms, but quite steadily, with that bobbing gait of the Indian who never straightens his knees. At each step his muscles slid neatly into place, the lock of hair on his scalp danced up and down, his feet printed themselves on the wet gravel. And once, in spite of the men who gripped him by each shoulder, he stepped lightly aside to avoid a puddle on the path.

> Multiple details show that the man "was alive just as we are alive."

It is curious; but till that moment I had never realized what it means to *10* destroy a healthy, conscious man. When I saw the prisoner step aside to avoid the puddle, I saw the mystery, the unspeakable wrongness, of cutting a life short when it is in full tide. This man was not dying, he was alive just as we are alive. All the organs of this body were working—bowels digesting food, skin renewing itself, nails growing, tissues forming—all toiling away in solemn foolery. His nails would still be growing when he stood on the drop, when he was falling through the air with a tenth-of-a-second to live. His eyes saw the yellow gravel and the grey walls, and his brain still remembered, foresaw, reasoned—even about puddles. He and we were a party of men walking together, seeing, hearing, feeling, understanding the same world; and in two minutes, with a sudden snap, one of us would be gone— one mind less, one world less.

Details help us to picture the scene.

The gallows stood in a small yard, separate from the main grounds of the prison, and overgrown with tall prickly weeds. It was a brick erection like three sides of a shed, with planking on top, and above that two beams and a crossbar with the rope dangling. The hangman, a greyhaired convict in the white uniform of the prison, was waiting beside his machine. He greeted us with a servile crouch as we entered. At a word from Francis the two warders, gripping the prisoner more closely than ever, half led, half pushed him to the gallows and helped him clumsily up the ladder. Then the hangman climbed up and fixed the rope around the prisoner's neck.

Details about sounds and sights help us imagine the scene.

We stood waiting, five yards away. The warders had formed in a rough circle round the gallows. And then, when the noose was fixed, the prisoner began crying out to his god. It was a high, reiterated cry of "Ram! Ram! Ram! Ram!" not urgent and fearful like a prayer or cry for help, but steady, rhythmical, almost like the tolling of a bell. The dog answered the sound with a whine. The hangman, still standing on the gallows, produced a small cotton bag like a flour bag and drew it down over the prisoner's face. But the sound, muffled by the cloth, still persisted, over and over again: "Ram! Ram! Ram! Ram!"

The writer contrasts the superintendent's musings about the prisoner's vitality with the spectators' desire that the man die quickly so order can be restored.

The hangman climbed down and stood ready, holding the lever. Minutes seemed to pass. The steady, muffled crying from the prisoner went on and on, "Ram! Ram! Ram!" never faltering for an instant. The superintendent, his head on his chest, was slowly poking the ground with his stick; perhaps he was counting the cries, allowing the prisoner a fixed number—fifty, perhaps, or a hundred. Everyone had changed colour. The Indians had gone grey like bad coffee, and one or two of the bayonets were wavering. We looked at the lashed, hooded man on the drop, and listened to his cries—each cry another second of life; the same thought was in all our minds; oh, kill him quickly, get it over, stop that abominable noise!

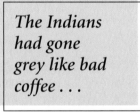

The Indians had gone grey like bad coffee . . .

Suddenly the superintendent made up his mind. Throwing up his head he made a swift motion with his stick. "Chalo!" he shouted almost fiercely.

There was a clanking noise, and then dead silence. The prisoner had vanished, and the rope was twisting on itself. I let go of the dog, and it galloped immediately to the back of the gallows; but when it got there it stopped short, barked, and then retreated into a corner of the yard, where it stood among the weeds, looking timorously out at us. We went round the gallows to inspect the prisoner's body. He was dangling with his toes pointed straight downwards, very slowly revolving, as dead as a stone.

"He's all right" is an unexpected, ironic remark.

The superintendent reached out with his stick and poked the bare brown body; it oscillated slightly. "*He's* all right," said the superintendent.

11

12

13

14

15

16

He backed out from under the gallows, and blew out a deep breath. The moody look had gone out of his face quite suddenly. He glanced at this wrist-watch. "Eight minutes past eight. Well, that's all for this morning, thank God."

The warders unfixed bayonets and marched away. The dog, sobered and conscious of having misbehaved itself, slipped after them. We walked out of the gallows yard, past the condemned cells with their waiting prisoners, into the big central yard of the prison. The convicts, under the command of warders armed with lathis, were already receiving their breakfast. They squatted in long rows, each man holding a tin pannikin, while two warders with buckets marched around ladling out rice; it seemed quite a homely, jolly scene, after the hanging. An enormous relief had come upon us now that the job was done. One felt an impulse to sing, to break into a run, to snigger. All at once everyone began chattering gaily. ◼

> **The closing describes an orderly, upbeat scene.**

17

Reading for Better Writing

1. Orwell's title, "A Hanging," summarizes the plot and forecasts the closing. Would the climax of the piece shift if the hanging were a surprise? How and why?

2. What effect does the writer create by beginning the essay in the middle of the action, without explaining what led up to the hanging?

3. We anticipate that a hanging will take place, so the event itself is no surprise. However, some characters' actions do surprise us. Cite examples and explain their effects.

4. What do we learn about the narrator by what is—and is not—included in his retelling of events? For example, how do you respond to his summary of the hanging as "a job" and "a relief"? Why do you think the prisoner "vanishes" from the narrative after the hanging?

5. Throughout the piece, the narrator carefully describes the setting while offering few details about characters' emotional responses to the hanging. Why?

Narration and Description

Bel Kaufman is known as the author of *Up the Down Staircase* and as a scholar and a teacher. In this piece she explores what happens when an academic couple encounters a bully in the park.

Sunday in the Park

The writer first describes the couple's background and interests.

It was still warm in the late-afternoon sun, and the city noises came muffled through the trees in the park. She put her book down on the bench, removed her sunglasses, and sighed contentedly. Morton was reading the *Times Magazine* section, one arm flung around her shoulder; their three-year-old son, Larry, was playing in the sandbox; a faint breeze fanned her hair softly against her cheek. It was five-thirty of a Sunday afternoon, and the small playground, tucked away in a corner of the park, was all but deserted. The swings and seesaws stood motionless and abandoned, the slides were empty, and only in the sandbox two little boys squatted diligently side by side. *How good this is*, she thought, and almost smiled at her sense of well-being. They must go out in the sun more often; Morton was so city-pale, cooped up all week inside the gray factorylike university. She squeezed his arm affectionately and glanced at Larry, delighting in the pointed little face frowning in concentration over the tunnel he was digging. The other boy suddenly stood up and with a quick, deliberate swing of his chubby arm threw a spadeful of sand at Larry. It just missed his head. Larry continued digging; the boy remained standing, shovel raised, stolid and impassive.

We learn the woman's thoughts through a third-person narrator (with a perspective of limited "omniscience" or awareness).

"No, no, little boy." She shook her finger at him, her eyes searching for the child's mother or nurse. "We mustn't throw sand. It may get in someone's eyes and hurt. We must play nicely in the nice sandbox." The boy

The writer shifts her focus to physical traits.

looked at her in unblinking expectancy. He was about Larry's age but perhaps ten pounds heavier, a husky little boy with none of Larry's quickness and sensitivity in his face. Where was his mother? The only other people left in the playground were two women and a little girl on roller skates leaving now through the gate, and a man on a bench a few feet away. He was a big man, and he seemed to be taking up the whole bench as he held the Sunday comics close to his face. She supposed he was the child's father. He did not look up from his comics, but spat once deftly out of the corner of his mouth. She turned her eyes away.

At that moment, as swiftly as before, the fat little boy threw another spadeful of sand at Larry. This time some of it landed on his hair and forehead. Larry looked up at his mother, his mouth tentative; her expression would tell him whether to cry or not.

Her first instinct was to rush to her son, brush the sand out of his hair, and punish the other child, but she controlled it. She always said that she wanted Larry to learn to fight his own battles.

"Don't *do* that, little boy," she said sharply, leaning forward on the bench. "You mustn't throw sand!" 5

The man on the bench moved his mouth as if to spit again, but instead he spoke. He did not look at her, but at the boy only. 6

"You go right ahead, Joe," he said loudly. "Throw all you want. This here is a *public* sandbox." 7

She felt a sudden weakness in her knees as she glanced at Morton. He had become aware of what was happening. He put his *Times* down carefully on his lap and turned his fine, lean face toward the man, smiling the shy, apologetic smile he might have offered a student in pointing out an error in his thinking. When he spoke to the man, it was with his usual reasonableness. 8

The writer describes the action, helping us picture the scene.

"You're quite right," he said pleasantly, "but just because this is a public place. . . ." 9

Morton's tone and word choice contrast with those of the other man.

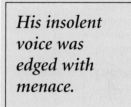

His insolent voice was edged with menace.

The man lowered his funnies and looked at Morton. He looked at him from head to foot, slowly and deliberately. "Yeah?" His insolent voice was edged with menace. "My kid's got just as good right here as yours, and if he feels like throwing sand, he'll throw it, and if you don't like it, you can take your kid the hell out of here." 10

The children were listening, their eyes and mouths wide open, their spades forgotten in small fists. She noticed the muscle in Morton's jaw tighten. He was rarely angry; he seldom lost his temper. She was suffused with a tenderness for her husband and an impotent rage against the man for involving him in a situation so alien and so distasteful to him. 11

"Now, just a minute," Morton said courteously, "you must realize. . . ." 12

"Aw, shut up," said the man. 13

Her heart began to pound. Morton half rose; the *Times* slid to the ground. Slowly the other man stood up. He took a couple of steps toward Morton, then stopped. He flexed his great arms, waiting. She pressed her trembling knees together. Would there be violence, fighting? How dreadful, how incredible. . . . She must do something, stop them, call for help. She wanted to put her hand on her husband's sleeve, to pull him down, but for some reason she didn't. 14

For the second time, the woman resists the impulse to act.

Morton adjusted his glasses. He was very pale. "This is ridiculous," he said unevenly. "I must ask you. . . ." 15

"Oh, yeah?" said the man. He stood with his legs spread apart, rocking a little, looking at Morton with utter scorn. "You and who else?" 16

For a moment the two men looked at each other nakedly. Then Morton turned his back on the man and said quietly, "Come on, let's get out of here." He walked awkwardly, almost limping with self-consciousness, to the sandbox. He stooped and lifted Larry and his shovel out. 17

At once Larry came to life; his face lost its rapt expression and he   18
began to kick and cry. "I don't *want* to go home, I want to play better,
I don't want any supper, I don't *like* supper. . . ." It became a chant as they
walked, pulling their child between them, his feet dragging on the ground.
In order to get to the exit gate they had to pass the bench where the man
sat sprawling again. She was careful not to look at him. With all the
dignity she could summon, she pulled Larry's sandy, perspiring little hand,
while Morton pulled the other. Slowly and with head high she walked with
her husband and child out of the
playground.

Her first feeling was one of relief   19
that a fight had been avoided, that no one
was hurt. Yet beneath it there was a layer
of something else, something heavy and
inescapable. She sensed that it was more
than just an unpleasant incident, more
than defeat of reason by force. She felt
dimly it had something to do with her
and Morton, something acutely personal, familiar, and important.

> The writer contrasts a second, unnamed feeling with the first feeling of relief.

> *Yet beneath it there was a layer of something else . . .*

Suddenly Morton spoke. "It wouldn't have proved anything."   20

"What?" she asked.   21

"A fight. It wouldn't have proved anything beyond the fact that he's   22
bigger than I am."

"Of course," she said.   23

"The only possible outcome," he continued reasonably, "would have   24
been—what? My glasses broken, perhaps a tooth or two replaced, a couple
of days' work missed—and for what? For justice? For truth?"

"Of course," she repeated. She quickened her step. She wanted only to   25
get home and to busy herself with her familiar tasks; perhaps then the
feeling, glued like heavy plaster on her heart, would be gone. *Of all the
stupid, despicable bullies*, she thought, pulling harder on Larry's hand. The
child was still crying. Always before she had felt a tender pity for his
defenseless little body, the frail arms, the narrow shoulders with sharp,
winglike shoulder blades, the thin legs, unsure, but now her mouth
tightened in resentment.

> Here the writer contrasts the woman's previous feelings for Larry with her current actions and feelings.

"Stop crying," she said sharply. "I'm ashamed of you!" She felt as if all   26
three of them were tracking mud along the street. The child cried louder.

If there had been an issue involved, she thought, *if there had been   27
something to fight for. . . . But what else could he possibly have done?
Allow himself to be beaten? Attempt to educate the man? Call a policeman?
"Officer, there's a man in the park who won't stop his child from throwing
sand on mine. . . ."* The whole thing was as silly as that, and not worth
thinking about.

> The writer's italicized "thought shots" tell us what she is thinking.

"Can't you keep him quiet, for Pete's sake?" Morton asked irritably. 28

"What do you suppose I've been trying to do?" she said. Larry pulled 29
back, dragging his feet.

"If you can't discipline this child, I will," Morton snapped, making 30
a move toward the boy.

But her voice stopped him. She was shocked to hear it, thin and cold 31
and penetrating with contempt. "Indeed?" she heard herself say. "You and
who else?" ■

Reading for Better Writing

1. Reread the first paragraph. How does Kaufman's description make
the setting seem first idyllic and then suddenly menacing?

2. Why isn't the woman given a name?

3. Notice that Morton is reading the *Times* whereas the other man is
reading the "funnies." What does Kaufman suggest about each man
by noting what he is reading?

4. How might the overall effect of the essay differ if it were told from
Morton's perspective?

5. Notice the use of contrast and repetition in this piece: repeated
references to the contrasting newspapers; repeated contrasts between
the way the woman had previously felt and the way she feels now;
repetitive physical contrasts between Morton and the man, or Larry and
the boy; and repetitive contrasts in the tone and diction of Morton
and the man. In what ways does this contrast and repetition accentuate
the significance of the woman's final question?

Narration and Description

The following passage is from "Northing," a chapter in Annie Dillard's *Pilgrim at Tinker Creek*. In it, the author vividly describes monarch butterflies and their migration.

Northing

The writer introduces the subject.

A few days later the monarchs hit. I saw one, and then another, and then others all day long, before I consciously understood that I was witnessing a migration, and it wasn't until another two weeks had passed that I realized the enormity of what I had seen.

She describes how the monarchs hatched.

Each of these butterflies, the fruit of two or three broods of this summer, had hatched successfully from one of those emerald cases that Teale's caterpillar had been about to form when the parasitic larvae snapped it limp, eating their way out of its side. They had hatched, many of them, just before a thunderstorm, when winds lifted the silver leaves of trees and birds sought the shelter of shrubbery, uttering cries. They were butterflies, going south to the Gulf states or farther, and some of them had come from Hudson's Bay.

She describes how they flew.

Monarchs were everywhere. They skittered and bobbed, rested in the air, lolled on the dust—but with none of their usual insouciance. They had but one unwearying thought: South. I watched from my study window: three, four . . . eighteen, nineteen, one every few seconds, and some in tandem. They came fanning straight toward my window from the northwest, and from the northeast, materializing from behind the tips of high hemlocks, where Polaris hangs by night. They appeared as Indian horsemen appear in movies: first dotted, then massed, silent, at the rim of a hill.

Using color, shape, texture, motion, and comparisons, she describes their bodies.

Each monarch butterfly had a brittle black body and deep orange wings limned and looped in black bands. A monarch at rest looks like a fleck of tiger, stilled and wide-eyed. A monarch in flight looks like an autumn leaf with a will, vitalized and cast upon the air from which it seems to suck some thin sugar of energy, some leaf-life or sap. As each one climbed up the air outside my window, I could see the more delicate, ventral surfaces of its wings, and I had a sense of bunched legs and straining thorax, but I could never focus well into the flapping and jerking before it vaulted up past the window and out of sight over my head.

An anecdote deepens the description.

I walked out and saw a monarch do a wonderful thing: it climbed a hill without twitching a muscle. I was standing at the bridge over Tinker Creek, at the southern foot of a very steep hill. The monarch beat its way beside me over the bridge at eye level, and then, flailing its wings exhaustedly, ascended straight up in the air. It rose vertically to the enormous height of a bankside sycamore's crown. Then, fixing its wings at a precise angle, it glided up the steep road, losing altitude extremely slowly, climbing by checking its fall, until it came to rest at a puddle in front of the house at the top of the hill.

I followed. It panted, skirmished briefly westward, and then, returning to the puddle, began its assault on the house. It struggled almost straight up the air next to the two-story brick wall, and then scaled the roof. Wasting no effort, it followed the roof's own slope, from a distance of two inches. Puff, and it was out of sight. I wondered how many more hills and houses it would have to climb before it could rest. From the force of its will it would seem it could flutter through the walls.

The writer describes their flight patterns and provides scientific background.

Monarchs are "tough and powerful, as butterflies go." They fly over Lake Superior without resting; in fact, observers there have discovered a curious thing. Instead of flying directly south, the monarchs crossing high over the water take an inexplicable turn toward the east. Then when they reach an invisible point, they all veer south again. Each successive swarm repeats this mysterious dogleg movement, year after year. Entomologists actually think that the butterflies might be "remembering" the position of a long-gone, looming glacier. In another book I read that geologists think that Lake Superior marks the site of the highest mountain that ever existed on this continent. I don't know. I'd like to see it. Or I'd like to be it, to feel when to turn. At night on land migrating monarchs slumber on certain trees, hung in festoons with wings folded together, thick on the trees and shaggy as bearskin.

She speculates about their taste.

Monarchs have always been assumed to taste terribly bitter, because of the acrid milkweed on which the caterpillars feed. You always run into monarchs and viceroys when you read about mimicry: viceroys look enough like monarchs that keen-eyed birds who have tasted monarchs once will avoid the viceroys as well. New studies indicate that milkweed-fed monarchs are not so much evil-tasting as literally nauseating, since milkweed contains "heart poisons similar to digitalis" that make the bird ill. Personally, I like an experiment performed by an entomologist with real spirit. He had heard all his life, as I have, that monarchs taste unforgettably bitter, so he tried some. "To conduct what was in fact a field experiment the doctor first went South, and he ate a number of monarchs in the field. . . . The monarch butterfly, Dr. Urquhart learned, has no more flavor than dried toast." Dried toast? It was hard for me, throughout the monarch migration, in the middle of all that beauty and real splendor, to fight down the thought that what I was really seeing in the air was a vast fluttering tea tray for shut-ins.

> *He had heard all his life, as I have, that monarchs taste unforgettably bitter, so he tried some.*

6

7

8

She describes a specific butterfly's movement, appearance, and grip.

It is easy to coax a dying or exhausted butterfly onto your finger. I saw *9* a monarch walking across a gas station lot; it was walking south. I placed my index finger in its path, and it clambered aboard and let me lift it to my face. Its wings were faded but unmarked by hazard; a veneer of velvet caught the light and hinted at the frailest depth of lapped scales. It was a male; his legs clutching my finger were short and atrophied; they clasped my finger with a spread fragility, a fineness as of some low note of emotion or pure strain of spirit, scarcely perceived. And I knew that those feet were actually tasting me, sipping with sensitive organs the vapor of my finger's skin: butterflies taste with their feet. All the time he held me, he opened and closed his glorious wings, senselessly, as if sighing.

She describes its surprising odor.

The closing of his wings fanned an almost imperceptible redolence *10* at my face, and I leaned closer. I could barely scent a sweetness, I could almost name it . . . fireflies, sparklers—honeysuckle. He smelled like honey-suckle; I couldn't believe it. I knew that many male butterflies exuded distinctive odors from special scent glands, but I thought that only labora-tory instruments could detect those odors compounded of many, many butterflies. I had read a list of the improbable scents of butterflies: sandalwood, chocolate, heliotrope, sweet pea. Now this live creature here on my finger had an odor that even I could sense—this flap actually smelled, this chip that actually took its temperature from the air like any envelope or hammer, this programmed wisp of spread horn. And he smelled of honeysuckle. Why not caribou hoof or Labrador tea, tundra lichen or dwarf willow, the brine of Hudson's Bay or the vapor of rivers milky with fine-ground glacial silt? This honeysuckle was an odor already only half-remembered, as breath of the summer past, the Lucas cliffs and overgrown fence by Tinker Creek, a drugged sweetness that had almost cloyed on those moisture-laden nights, now refined to a wary trickle in the air, a distillation pure and rare, scarcely known and mostly lost, and head-ing south.

I walked him across the gas station lot and lowered him into a field. He *11* took to the air, pulsing and gliding; he lighted on sassafras, and I lost him.

The writer describes the monarch's wings.

For weeks I found paired monarch wings, bodiless, on the grass or on *12* the road. I collected one such wing and freed it of its scales; first I rubbed it between my fingers, and then I stroked it gently with the tip of an infant's silver spoon. What I had at the end of this delicate labor is lying here on this study desk: a kind of resilient scaffolding, like the webbing over a hot-air balloon, black veins stretching the merest something across the nothingness it plies. The integument itself is perfectly transparent; through it I can read the smallest print. It is as thin as the skin peeled from sunburn, and as tough as a parchment of fleeced buffalo hide. The butterflies that were eaten here in the valley, leaving us their wings, were, however, few: most lived to follow the valley south.

She shares how the migration affected her.

The migration lasted in full force for five days. For those five days I was *13* inundated, drained. The air was alive and unwinding. Time itself was a scroll unraveled, curved and still quivering on a table or altar stone. The monarchs clattered in the air, burnished like throngs of pennies, here's one, and here's one, and more, and more. They flapped and floundered; they thrust, splitting the air like the keels of canoes, quickened and fleet. It looked as though the leaves of the autumn forest had taken flight, and were pouring down the valley like a waterfall, like a tidal wave, all the leaves

She describes the monarchs' departure and her reaction.

of hardwoods from here to Hudson's Bay. It was as if the season's color were draining away like lifeblood, as if the year were molting and shedding. The year was rolling down, and a vital curve had been reached, the lift that gives way to headlong rush. And when the monarchs had passed and were gone, the skies were vacant, the air poised. The dark night into which the year was plunging was not a sleep but an awakening, a new and necessary austerity, the sparer climate for which I longed. The shed trees were brittle and still, the creek light and cold, and my spirit holding its breath. ▪

Writing Prompt

Reading for Better Writing

1. Review the first paragraph, in which Annie Dillard introduces her topic by saying, "It wasn't until another two weeks had passed that I realized the enormity of what I had seen." What does she mean by "enormity"? Why is the migration meaningful to the writer? What dominant impression does it create?

2. List the monarchs' traits that Dillard describes. Choose one or two passages that you find particularly effective, and explain why.

3. Throughout the description, Dillard uses comparisons—similes and metaphors. Examine the comparisons in two paragraphs: What do these comparisons contribute to the description of the butterflies?

4. Describe the writer's voice and attitude toward her subject. Cite passages to support your answer.

5. Trace the organization of this description. Comment on the effectiveness of the order.

6. Summarize the closing paragraph and explain how it is effective.

Guidelines
Writing Narration and Description

1. **Select a topic.** Think about your own experiences. Sort through the stories you recall and choose one that is important enough to share with others. Think of a way to approach this experience in a personal narrative.

    TIP: If you can't think of an interesting story off the top of your head, try writing in response to the following statement: *Remember a time when you first discovered that the world was (a) stranger, (b) more wonderful, or (c) more complex than you had thought as a child.* Think about how that experience prepared you to be who you are today.

2. **Narrow your focus.** Once you have chosen an experience to write about, begin to narrow your topic by focusing on a specific moment or outcome. The following questions can help you find a clear focus:
    - What is the key moment—the significant point or climax— in the story?
    - What led up to this key moment? What resulted from it?
    - What was really going on?
    - How did others experience the event?
    - What has time taught you about this experience?
    - What would you have changed?

3. **Determine your purpose and audience.** After you have a specific focus, decide why you are telling your story and who might read the story. Personal narratives can serve one of many purposes and appeal to many audiences. Consider these purposes:
    - To entertain
    - To celebrate
    - To remind
    - To warn
    - To illustrate
    - To gain sympathy

4. **Gather details.** Gather material that will serve your purpose. Try sorting through photo albums, home videos, and letters. Interview someone who shared your experience or saw you through it. Consult your journal or diary.

5. **Collaborate.** Tell somebody your story; then ask for comments and questions. Based on the feedback you receive, create a basic writing plan. Your plan can be anything from a simple list to a detailed outline.

6. **Write your first draft**. As you write, keep in mind your specific focus and your overall purpose for telling this story. Use the following strategies as you create your first draft:

Set the stage. ■ Show where things happened and exactly what it was like there. Describe the atmosphere, the people, and the events by using precise details that appeal to the five senses. If appropriate, use comparisons and metaphors to make the descriptions hit home.

Include dialogue. ■ Recall and create conversations between the people in your story to infuse your narrative with a sense of reality.

TIP: Use dialogue to enhance a key scene or to explain the relationship between people. But be selective—don't let dialogue dribble on for its own sake.

Build the plot. ■ Arouse and sustain interest by establishing conflict, building suspense, highlighting the main point, and showing the outcome.

Express your feelings. ■ It may help to include both past and present thoughts and feelings—those you had during the experience and those you have now, looking back on the past.

Use transitions. ■ Words like *as, before, meanwhile,* and *later* show where your story is leading. (See page **77**.)

Select verbs carefully. ■ Verbs affect the movement and voice of your story. Choose strong, active verbs, and make sure tenses accurately reflect time sequences and relationships.

7. **Share your story.** Show your draft to someone. What main point does this reader see in your story? What suggestions or questions does the reader have?

8. **Revise your writing.** Carefully review and revise your writing. Remember that your goal is to recreate an interesting incident or event for your readers. Ask yourself the following questions:
   - Does the writing focus on a specific incident or event?
   - Does the writing contain effective details, descriptions, and dialogue?
   - Does the narrative effectively state or imply a theme, thesis, or point of significance?
   - Does the writing sound sincere and natural?
   - Will readers appreciate the way the story is told?

9. **Edit and proofread.** (See the checklist on page **98**.)

10. **Prepare your final copy.** Use an appropriate type font and size. Leave the right margin ragged (uneven). Place photographs or drawings close to the text they illustrate. Print your final copy on quality paper.

Writing Checklist

Use these six traits to check the quality of your writing; then revise as needed:

_____ The **ideas** focus on a specific experience or event and present an engaging picture of the action and people involved.

_____ The **organization** pattern adds to the clarity of the piece and includes a clear beginning that pulls readers in.

_____ The **voice** shows that the writer is truly interested in the subject by speaking knowledgeably and enthusiastically.

_____ The **words** _show_ instead of _tell about_; they appeal to the senses and evoke pictures in the reader's mind.

_____ The **sentences** are clear, varied in structure, and smooth.

_____ The **copy** is correct, is clean, and follows assigned guidelines for format. Photographs and drawings are clear and well-placed.

Writing Activities

1. Review "Mzee Owitti" and "Sunday in the Park," observing how the writers help you share their experiences by presenting vivid details in an open, honest way. List a few of your own experiences that you would like to explore and share. Then choose one that would be an appropriate subject for a personal narrative. Write the narrative, perhaps using some of the same organizational strategies employed in these models.

2. Review the ways in which Bel Kaufman uses dialogue, physical description, and personal objects/possessions to contrast two characters in "Sunday in the Park." Draft or revise a narrative in which you shape characters through distinctive dialogue, physical description, and personal possessions.

3. Review "A Hanging" and "Sunday in the Park," noting how the authors of both essays portray certain characters in a negative light without making direct comments to that effect. Draft or revise a portrayal of a person in which you show (rather than tell) your feelings about the individual.

4. In ten years, how will your life differ from the way it is today? Write a personal narrative from the future, describing one of the events that led to your (future) position in life. Remember to include characters and their reactions to the experience.

Chapter 11
Description and Reflection

It is human nature to reflect. On this score, eighteenth-century poet Robert Burns thought mice luckier than people. In his poem "To a Mouse," Burns noted that mice worry only about the present, whereas humans worry about past, present, and future woes. Whether or not reflecting on the past is unique to humans, we do know that this trait brings joy, regret, and a thousand variations of those feelings to humans both young and old.

A personal reflection is often written to draw wisdom from past experiences. Accordingly, you may want to explore an earlier time in your life and reflect on why you felt as you did when you suffered a stinging setback or won a glorious victory.

In this chapter, you'll find topics to consider, model essays, and guidelines that will help you describe and reflect on a memorable experience. In the process, you will likely gain insight not only into your past experience, but also into its links to your present and future.

What's Ahead

- Overview: Writing Description and Reflection
  - Student Model
  - Professional Models
- Guidelines
- Writing Checklist and Activities

Overview
Writing Description and Reflection

Writer's Goal

Your goal is to write an essay in which you carefully describe one or more past experiences and reflect on their importance in your life.

Keys for Success

Recall precise details. ■ To understand and appreciate your reflections, readers first have to grasp exactly what you experienced. For that reason, you must describe those key details (sights, smells, tastes) that make the experience memorable to you—and worth reflecting on. Often you will find these details in the hardly-noticed-at-the-time part of your memory.

Probe the topic. ■ The mind-searching aspect of writing this essay happens while asking *so-why* questions: *So why does this picture still make me smile?* or *Why does his comment still hurt?* or *Why did I do that when I knew better—or did I know better?* Your answers will help explain why this memory is important to you.

Reveal what you find. ■ Your readers need to experience what you experienced, so don't hide what's embarrassing, or painful, or still unclear. Show them the details clearly, explain your insights honestly, and then trust readers to respond with sensitivity, appreciation, and respect.

Topics to Consider

The most promising topics are experiences that gave you insights into yourself, and possibly into others as well. Often such an experience will have led you or others to change patterns of thinking, feeling, or behavior. To identify such topics, consider the categories below and then list whatever experiences come to mind:

- Times when you felt *secure, hopeful, distraught, appreciated, confident, frightened, exploited,* or *misunderstood.*

- Times when you made a decision about *lifestyles, careers, education, politics, religion, leaving home,* or *getting an education.*

- Events that tested your *will, patience, self-concept,* or *goals.*

- Events that changed or confirmed your assessment of a *person, group, institution, religious belief, political conviction,* or *philosophical worldview.*

Next Step Read the model essays and perform the activities that follow. As you read, note how the writers help you grasp *what* they experienced and *why* their experiences are important.

Description and Reflection

Nicole Suurdt is a student from Ontario, Canada. In this essay, she describes a time and place that she loved as a child and yearns for as an adult.

The Stream in the Ravine

Behind my childhood home is a small ravine, and through it runs the seasonal overflow of a little pond deep within the woods. It's a noisy stream, just narrow enough for an eight-year-old to take one stretching step across and reach the other side with dry shoes. And when I was eight, this stream was everything to me.

The writer introduces the topic and then gives background information.

You see, for most of my childhood, I lived on a small hobby farm in Ontario, Canada, where rolling pasture and croplands surrounded my home. The pasture fenced in Scottish Highland cattle with terrifying horns, unbroken horses with skittish hooves, and one half-blind, unpredictable donkey. These creatures separated me from the woods just beyond the pasture. But when I was little, it wasn't simply my fear of these fitful animals that penned me in on my side of the fence—it was a fear of what lay beyond the shadowy barrier of maples and pines.

Description of the visits builds tension.

It's not that I'd never been to the woods before. I had, twice. The first time, my brother took me in search of the tallest tree in the forest and got us lost for a couple of hours. My second visit was a dark winter journey. Dad dragged the family into the woods late one night in search of a missing cow. We found her half-devoured body lying in bloodstained snow, packed down by wolves' paws.

A transition signals a shift in the action.

But eventually, curiosity overpowered my fears. One spring day when I was eight, armed with a staff, I skirted the pasture and headed for the forest. I approached the fence that my dad had put up to ward off the woods. Quickly I scaled the fence, but then stood some time holding on to its boards, figuring that if a wolf came along, I could scramble back to the other side. However, after five minutes passed and no wolf appeared, I calmed down, let go of the fence, and stepped into the forest—lured on by the sound of chipmunks, birds, wind through trees, and snapping twigs.

Drawn forward, I discovered rocky burrows of unknown creatures. I chased chipmunks. I sang. I passed a hunter's fort perched high in a pine, deserted after last fall's deer-hunting season. I passed under an archway of tall cedars. I waded through the muck and mire surrounding a small swamp and plodded my mud-caked shoes up a small rise, thick with the faded, crumbled leaves of last year's fall. One particular sound kept pulling me forward—the gurgle of running water.

The writer describes the stream and shares its personal importance.

Standing at the peak of the rise, with brown leaves stuck to my muddy sneakers, I found the source. Below me, within its shallow bed, ran a tiny stream, little more than a trickle, really. But to me it was a beautiful, rushing brook, my own source of clear, cold water protected by oak, maple, and pine sentries. That day I spent hours scooping decaying leaves out of my stream's bed and sitting by her side to watch the water spill over the rocks and roots. She was my own discovery, my own territory, my own secret place. From that day on, the little stream past the hunter's fort, under the cedar archway, through the muck and the mire, and over the rocky rise became my quiet, private place.

The picture shows the father, the daughter, and their bridge.

But I never could keep a secret for long. During dinner one Sunday, I 7 told my parents about my stream. I figured that it needed a bridge, something only Dad could help me build. And so, that afternoon, I led Mom and Dad over the fence, into the woods, and up to my secret stream. Together, we built a bridge using the fallen branches lying about. Mom took a picture of Dad and me sitting on our homemade, lopsided bridge, the water washing over the toes of the big rubber boots that she had insisted we wear.

My parents separated eight years after that picture was taken, and I 8 haven't gone back to my stream since, though I think of it often. Somewhere, tucked away in Mom's photo albums, is the picture of a little girl in her dreamland, her dad beside her, his big feet hanging near her small ones. Her mom stands in the water just a few feet away behind the camera lens.

The writer yearns for life as shown in the photo.

Sometimes, I want to go back there, back into that photo. I want to step 9 into a time when life seemed safe, and a tiny stream gave us all that we needed. In that picture, our smiles last, our hearts are calm, and we hear only quiet voices, forest sounds, and my bubbling stream. Bitter words are silenced and tears held back by the click and whir of a camera.

I've been thinking about making the journey again past the hunter's 10 fort, under the stand of cedars, through the muck and mire, and over the rocky rise. But it's been a long summer, and the small, seasonal stream running out of the overflow of the pond has probably dried up. ■

Writing Prompt

Reading for Better Writing

1. Three times in the essay, the writer mentions four sites (hunter's fort, cedar archway, muck and mire, rocky rise) along her route. What do the references to these sites contribute to the description?

2. How does the writer organize her description? Identify the strategies used and discuss their effectiveness.

3. Review the references to the photograph taken by the mother, and describe what the photo shows. What does the writer mean when she says, "Sometimes, I want to go back there, back into that photo"?

4. Reread the opening and closing paragraphs, comparing how the writer describes the stream in each paragraph. Are the details and voices of the two passages different? Give examples.

Description and Reflection

Mary Seymour reflects on her experiences with bipolar disorder, which is sometimes called manic depression. This piece was published in *Newsweek* in 2002.

Call Me Crazy, But I Have to Be Myself

The writer labels herself "mentally ill."

1 Nearly every day, without thinking, I say things like "So-and-so is driving me crazy" or "That's nuts!" Sometimes I catch myself and realize that I'm not being sensitive toward people with mental illness. Then I remember I'm one of the mentally ill. If I can't throw those words around, who can?

2 Being a functional member of society and having a mental disorder is an intricate balancing act. Every morning I send my son to junior high school, put on professional garb and drive off to my job as alumni-magazine editor at a prep school, where I've worked for six years. Only a few people at work know I'm manic-depressive, or bipolar, as it's sometimes called.

An example illustrates the extent of the illness.

3 Sometimes I'm not sure myself what I am. I blend in easily with "normal" people. You'd never know that seven years ago, fueled by the stress of a failing marriage and fanned by the genetic inheritance of a manic-depressive grandfather, I had a psychotic break. To look at me, you'd never guess I once ran naked through my yard or shuffled down the hallways of a psychiatric ward. To hear me, you'd never guess God channeled messages to me through my computer. After my breakdown at 36, I was diagnosed as bipolar, a condition marked by moods that swing between elation and despair.

More examples show the difficulties the writer faces.

4 It took a second, less-severe psychotic episode in 1997, followed by a period of deep depression, to convince me I truly was bipolar. Admitting I had a disorder that I'd have to manage for life was the hardest thing I've ever done. Since then, a combination of therapy, visits to a psychiatrist, medication, and inner calibration have helped me find an even keel. Now I manage my moods with the vigilance of a mother hen, nudging them back to center whenever they wander too far. Eating wisely, sleeping well, and exercising regularly keep me balanced from day to day. Ironically, my disorder has taught me to be healthier and happier than I was before.

5 Most of the time, I feel lucky to blend in with the crowd. Things that most people grumble about—paying bills, maintaining a car, working 9 to 5—strike me as incredible privileges. I'll never forget gazing through the barred windows of the psychiatric ward into the parking lot, watching people come and go effortlessly, wondering if I'd ever be like them again. There's nothing like a stint in a locked ward to make one grateful for the freedoms and burdens of full citizenship.

6 Yet sometimes I feel like an impostor. Sometimes I wish I could sit at

From *Newsweek*, July 29, 2002. © 2002 Newsweek, Inc. All rights reserved. Reprinted by permission.

Each sentence begins with a similar phrase that reveals the writer's feelings.

the lunch table and talk about lithium and Celexa instead of "Will & Grace." While everyone talks about her fitness routine, I want to brag how it took five orderlies to hold me down and shoot me full of sedatives when I was admitted to the hospital, and how for a brief moment I knew the answers to every infinite mystery of the blazingly bright universe. I yearn for people to know me—the real me—in all my complexity, but I'm afraid it would scare the bejesus out of them.

Every now and then, I feel like I'm truly being myself. Like the time the school chaplain, in whom I'd confided my past, asked me to help counsel a severely bipolar student. This young woman had tried to commit suicide, had been hospitalized many times and sometimes locked herself in her dorm room to keep the "voices" from overwhelming her. I walked and talked with her, sharing stories about medication and psychosis. I hoped to show by example that manic-depression did not necessarily mean a diminished life. At commencement, I watched her proudly accept her diploma; despite ongoing struggles with her illness, she's continuing her education.

An extended example illustrates the point.

I'm able to be fully myself with my closest friends, all of whom have similar schisms between private and public selves. We didn't set out to befriend each other—we just all speak the same language, of hardship and spiritual discovery and psychological awareness.

What I yearn for most is to integrate both sides of myself. I want to be part of the normal world but I also want to own my identity as bipolar. I want people to know what I've been through so I can help those traveling a similar path. Fear has kept me from telling my story: fear of being stigmatized, of making people uncomfortable, of being reduced to a label. But hiding the truth has become more uncomfortable than letting it out. It's time for me to own up to who I am, complicated psychiatric history and all. Call me crazy, but I think it's the right thing to do. ■

The final line echoes the title.

7

8

9

Writing Prompt

Reading for Better Writing

1. What purpose does Seymour identify for writing the essay? What other purposes might be served by publishing this piece for *Newsweek*'s readers?

2. The writer starts with one category label for herself ("mentally ill") and then quickly adds another ("functional member of society"). How does the second label redefine the first?

3. Description is used to support many other kinds of writing, including the types of analytical and persuasive writing outlined here in *The College Writer*. In what other chapters could this essay have been included, and how do you know?

4. Review the section of this book on "Editing and Proofreading" (pages 83–98), especially the portion on biased words. Why does Seymour use the phrase "call me crazy"? Is her use of the word biased or insulting? Explain.

Description and Reflection

In the following essay, author Richard Rodriguez reflects on his experiences with affirmative action and how these experiences caused him guilt and confusion.

None of This Is Fair

The writer introduces a problem in his experience.

My plan to become a professor of English—my ambition during long years in college at Stanford, then in graduate school at Columbia and Berkeley—was complicated by feelings of embarrassment and guilt. So many times I would see other Mexican Americans and know we were alike only in race. And yet, simply because our race was the same, I was, during the last years of my schooling, the beneficiary of their situation. Affirmative-action programs had made it all possible. The disadvantages of others permitted my promotion: the absence of many Mexican Americans from academic life allowed my designation as a "minority student."

He summarizes his experiences and his struggle.

For me, opportunities had been extravagant. There were fellowships, summer research grants, and teaching assistantships. After only two years in graduate school, I was offered teaching jobs by several colleges. Invitations to Washington conferences arrived, and I had the chance to travel abroad as a "Mexican American representative." The benefits were often, however, too gaudy to please. In three published essays, in conversations with teachers, in letters to politicians, and at conferences, I worried about the issue of affirmative action. Often I proposed contradictory opinions. Though consistent was the admission that—because of an early, excellent education—I was no longer a principal victim of racism or any other social oppression. I said that, but still I continued to indicate on applications for financial aid that I was a Hispanic American. It didn't really occur to me to say anything else, or to leave the question unanswered.

Thus I complied with and encouraged the odd bureaucratic logic of affirmative action. I let government officials treat the disadvantaged condition of many Mexican Americans with my advancement. Each fall my presence was noted by Health, Education, and Welfare Department statisticians. As I pursued advanced literary studies and learned the skill of reading Spenser and Wordsworth and Emerson, I would hear myself numbered among the culturally disadvantaged. Still, silent, I didn't object.

Recalling feelings of guilt, he reflects on the irony of his situation.

But the irony cut deep. And guilt would not be evaded by averting my glance when I confronted a face like my own in a crowd. By late 1975, nearing the completion of my graduate studies at Berkeley, I was so wary of the benefits of affirmative action that I feared my inevitable success as an applicant for a teaching position. The months of fall—traditionally that time of academic job-searching—passed without my applying to a single school. When one of my professors chanced to learn this in late November,

The writer summarizes an encounter.

he was astonished, then furious. He yelled at me: Did I think that because I was a minority student jobs would just come looking for me? What was I thinking? Did I realize that he and several other faculty members had already written letters on my behalf? Was I going to start acting like some other minority students he had known? They struggled for success and then, when it was almost within reach, grew strangely afraid and let it pass. Was that it? Was I determined to fail?

I did not respond to his questions. I didn't want to admit to him, and thus to myself, the reason I delayed. 5

He narrows the focus to his job-search experience.

I merely agreed to write to several schools. (In my letter I wrote: "I cannot claim to represent disadvantaged Mexican Americans. The very fact that I am in a position to apply for this job should make that clear.") After two or three days, there were telegrams and phone calls, invitations to interviews, then airplane trips. A blur of faces and the murmur of their soft questions. And, over someone's shoulder, the sight of campus buildings shadowing pictures I had seen years before when I leafed through Ivy League catalogues with great expectations. At the end of each visit, interviewers would smile and wonder if I had any questions. A few times I quietly wondered what advantage my race had given me over other applicants. But that was an impossible question for them to answer without embarrassing me. Quickly, several persons insisted that my ethnic identity had given me no more than a "foot in the door"; at most, I had a "slight edge" over other applicants. "We just looked at your dossier with extra care and we liked what we saw. There was never any question of having to alter our standards. You can be certain of that." 6

In the early part of January, offers arrived on stiffly elegant stationery. Most schools promised terms appropriate for any new assistant professor. A few made matters worse—and almost more tempting—by offering more: the use of university housing; an unusually large starting salary; a reduced teaching schedule. As the stack of letters mounted, my hesitation increased. I started calling department chairmen to ask for another week, then ten more days—"more time to reach a decision"—to avoid the decision I would need to make. 7

As the search proceeds, the pressure and tension mount for the writer.

At school, meantime, some students hadn't received a single job offer. One man, probably the best student in the department, did not even get a request for his dossier. He and I met outside a classroom one day, and he asked about my opportunities. He seemed happy for me. Faculty members beamed. They said they had expected it. "After all, not many schools are going to pass up getting a Chicano with a Ph.D. in Renaissance literature," somebody said, laughing. Friends wanted to know which of the offers I was going to accept. But I couldn't make up my mind. February came and I was running out of time and excuses. (One chairman guessed my delay was a bargaining ploy and increased his offer with each of my calls.) I had to promise a decision by the 10th—the 12th at the very latest. 8

On the 18th of February, late in the afternoon, I was in the office I 9
shared with several other teaching assistants. Another graduate student was
sitting across the room at his desk. When I got up to leave, he looked over
to say in an uneventful voice that he had some big news. He had finally
decided to accept a position at a faraway university. It was not a job he
especially wanted, he admitted. He felt trapped, and depressed, since his job
would separate him from his young daughter.

> **The writer details an especially important encounter.**

I tried to encourage him by remarking that he was lucky at least to have 10
found a job. So many others hadn't been able to get anything. But before I
finished speaking, I realized that I had said the wrong thing. And I anticipated his next question.

"What are your plans?" he wanted to know. "Is it true you've gotten an 11
offer from Yale?"

I said that it was. "Only, I still haven't made up my mind." 12

He stared at me as I put on my jacket. And smiling, then unsmiling, he 13
asked if I knew that he, too, had written to Yale. In his case, however, no
one had bothered to acknowledge his letter with even a postcard. What did
I think of that?

> **Narration and quotation build the episode's intensity.**

He gave me no time to answer. 14

"Damn!" he said sharply, and his chair rasped the floor as he pushed 15
himself back. Suddenly, it was to me that he was complaining. "It's just not
right, Richard. None of this is fair. You've done some good work, but so
have I. I'll bet our records are just about equal. But when we look for jobs
this year, it's a different story. You get all the breaks."

To evade his criticism, I wanted to side with him. I was about to admit 16
the injustice of affirmative action. But he went on, his voice hard with accu-
sation. "It's all very simple this year. You're a Chicano. And I am a Jew.
That's the only real difference between us."

> **The narrative leads to a crisis of conscience.**

His words stung me: there was nothing he was telling me that I 17
didn't know. I admitted everything already. But to hear someone else say
these things, and in such an accusing tone, was suddenly hard to take. In a
deceptively calm voice, I responded that he had simplified the whole issue.
The phrases came like bubbles to the tip of my tongue: "new blood"; "the
importance of cultural diversity"; "the goal of racial integration." These
were all the arguments I proposed several years ago—and had long since
abandoned. Of course, the offers were unjustifiable. I knew that. All I
was saying amounted to a frantic self-defense. I tried to find an end to a
sentence. My voice faltered to a stop.

"Yeah, sure," he said. "I've heard all that before. Nothing you say really 18
changes the fact that affirmative action is unfair. You see that, don't you?
There isn't any way for me to compete with you. Once there were quotas to
keep my parents out of certain schools; now there are quotas to get you in,
and the effect on me is the same as it was for them."

I listened to every word he spoke. But my mind was really on some- *19*
thing else. I knew at that moment that I would reject all of the offers. I
stood there silently surprised by what an easy conclusion it was. Having
prepared for so many years to teach, having trained myself to do nothing
else, I had hesitated out of practical fear. But now that it was made, the
decision came with relief. I immediately knew I had made the right choice.

My colleague continued talking, and I realized that he was simply right. *20*
Affirmative-action programs are unfair to white students. But as I listened
to him assert his rights, I thought of the seriously disadvantaged. How different they were from white, middle-class students who come armed with
the testimony of their grades and aptitude scores and self-confidence to
complain about the unequal treatment they now receive. I listen to them. I

> **The writer broadens the discussion.**

do not want to be careless about what they say. Their rights are important
to protect. But inevitably when I hear them or their lawyers, I think about
the most seriously disadvantaged, not simply Mexican Americans, but all
those who do not ever imagine themselves going to college or becoming
doctors: white, black, brown. Always poor. Silent. They are not plaintiffs
before the court or against the misdirection of affirmative action. They lack
the confidence (my confidence!) to assure their right to a good education.
They lack the confidence and skills that a good primary and secondary education provides and that are prerequisites for informed public life. They

> **He closes with a strong image.**

remain silent.

- - - - - - The debate drones on and surrounds them in stillness. They are dis- *21*
tant, faraway figures like the boys I have seen peering down from freeway
overpasses in some other part of town. ■

Reading for Better Writing

1. The writer shares several experiences that took place over several years.
   Trace these experiences. Describe the methods he uses to present them,
   and explain why he uses these methods.

2. He says that his life differed from the lives of those for whom
   affirmative action was intended. How does he support that point?

3. The writer relates a key exchange with a Jewish classmate. Why are this
   classmate and his story especially important to the writer?

4. What role does reflection play in the essay? How does the writer weave
   his past and present thoughts and feelings into his experiences?

Description and Reflection

Debra Dickerson's recent books include the memoir *An American Story* and *The End of Blackness: Returning the Souls of Black Folk to Their Rightful Owners*. Her essay below describes the July 27, 1995, shooting of her nephew and appeared in *The New Republic* on January 1, 1996.

Who Shot Johnny?

The writer builds our expectations about what kind of person she is by listing some of her activities and views on life.

Given my level of political awareness, it was inevitable that I would come to view the everyday events of my life through the prism of politics and the national discourse. I read *The Washington Post, The New Republic, The New Yorker, Harper's, The Atlantic Monthly, The Nation, National Review, Black Enterprise,* and *Essence* and wrote a weekly column for the Harvard Law School *Record* during my three years just ended there. I do this because I know that those of us who are not well-fed white guys in suits must not yield the debate to them, however well-intentioned or well-informed they may be. Accordingly, I am unrepentant and vocal about having gained admittance to Harvard through affirmative action; I am a feminist, stoic about my marriage chances as a well-educated, thirty-six-year-old black woman who won't pretend to need help taking care of herself. My strength flags, though, in the face of the latest role assigned to my family in the national drama. On July 27, 1995, my sixteen-year-old nephew was shot and paralyzed.

The word *though* suggests an important contrast to the earlier depiction.

Talking with friends in front of his house, Johnny saw a car he thought he recognized. He waved boisterously—his trademark—throwing both arms in the air in a full-bodied, hip-hop Y. When he got no response, he and his friends sauntered down the walk to join a group loitering in front of an apartment building. The car followed. The driver got out, brandished a revolver, and fired into the air. Everyone scattered. Then he took aim and shot my running nephew in the back.

> *He lay in the road, trying to understand what had happened to him . . .*

Johnny never lost consciousness. He lay in the road, trying to understand what had happened to him, why he couldn't get up. Emotionlessly, he told the story again and again on demand, remaining apologetically firm against all demands to divulge the missing details that would make sense of the shooting but obviously cast him in a bad light. Being black, male, and shot, he must apparently be involved with gangs or drugs. Probably both. Witnesses corroborate his version of events.

Nearly six months have passed since that phone call in the night and my nightmarish headlong drive from Boston to Charlotte. After twenty hours behind the wheel, I arrived haggard enough to reduce my mother to fresh tears and to find my nephew reassuring well-wishers with an eerie sang-froid.

I take the day shift in his hospital room; his mother and grandmother, 5 a clerk and cafeteria worker, respectively, alternate nights there on a cot. They don their uniforms the next day, gaunt after hours spent listening to Johnny moan in his sleep. How often must his subconscious replay those events and curse its host for saying hello without permission, for being carefree and young while a would-be murderer hefted the weight of his uselessness and failure like Jacob Marley's chains? How often must he watch himself lying stubbornly immobile on the pavement of his nightmares while the sound of running feet syncopate his attacker's taunts?

> **Rhetorical questions emphasize the writer's helplessness in fixing the problem.**

I spend these days beating him at gin rummy and Scrabble, holding a 6 basin while he coughs up phlegm and crying in the corridor while he catheterizes himself. There are children here much worse off than he. I should be grateful. The doctors can't, or won't, say whether he'll walk again.

I am at once repulsed and fascinated by the bullet, which remains 7 lodged in his spine (having done all the damage it can do, the doctors say). The wound is undramatic—small, neat, and perfectly centered—an impossibly pink pit surrounded by an otherwise undisturbed expanse of mahogany. Johnny has asked me several times to describe it but politely declines to look in the mirror I hold for him.

> *I am at once repulsed and fascinated by the bullet.*

Here on the pediatric rehab ward, Johnny speaks little, never cries, 8 never complains, works diligently to become independent. He does whatever he is told; if two hours remain until the next pain pill, he waits quietly. Eyes bloodshot, hands gripping the bed rails. During the week of his intravenous feeding, when he was tormented by the primal need to masticate, he never asked for food. He just listened while we counted down the days for him and planned his favorite meals. Now required to dress himself unassisted, he does so without demur, rolling himself back and forth valiantly on the bed and shivering afterward, exhausted. He "ma'am"s and "sir"s everyone politely. Before his "accident," a simple request to take out the trash could provoke a firestorm of teenage attitude. We, the women who have raised him, have changed as well; we've finally come to appreciate those boxer-baring, oversized pants we used to hate—it would be much more difficult to fit properly sized pants over his diaper.

> **The writer illustrates her nephew's changed attitude.**

He spends a lot of time tethered to rap music still loud enough to break 9 my concentration as I read my many magazines. I hear him try to soundlessly mouth the obligatory "mothafuckers" overlaying the funereal dirge of the music tracks. I do not normally tolerate disrespectful music in my or my mother's presence, but if it distracts him now . . .

> **The ellipsis encourages us to finish the idea ourselves.**

"Johnny," I ask later, "do you still like gangster rap?" During the long *10* pause I hear him think loudly, *I'm paralyzed Auntie, not stupid.* "I mostly just listen to hip-hop," he says evasively into his *Sports Illustrated.*

Miserable though it is, time passes quickly here. We always seem to be *11* jerking awake in our chairs just in time for the next pill, his every-other-night bowel program, the doctor's rounds. Harvard feels a galaxy away—the world revolves around Family Members Living with Spinal Cord Injury class, Johnny's urine output, and strategizing with my sister to find affordable, accessible housing. There is always another long-distance uncle in need of an update, another church member wanting to pray with us, or Johnny's little brother in need of some attention.

> Comparing the situation with an ordinary event helps to convey the writer's feelings.

We Dickerson women are so constant a presence the ward nurses and cleaning staff call us by name and join us for cafeteria meals and cigarette breaks. At Johnny's birthday pizza party, they crack jokes and make fun of each other's husbands (there are no men here). I pass slices around and try not to think, *Seventeen with a bullet.*

> *Oddly, we feel little curiosity or specific anger toward the man who shot him.*

12

Oddly, we feel little curiosity or specific *13* anger toward the man who shot him. We have to remind ourselves to check in with the police. Even so, it feels pro forma, like sending in those $2 rebate forms that come with new pantyhose: you know your request will fall into a deep, dark hole somewhere, but still, it's your duty to try. We push for an arrest because we owe it to Johnny and to ourselves as citizens. We don't think about it otherwise—our low expectations are too ingrained. A Harvard aunt notwithstanding, for people like Johnny, Marvin Gaye was right that only three things are sure: taxes, death, and trouble. At least it wasn't the second.

> The writer creates a composite of the unknown gunman, assigning the traits and actions of many men who have affected her in similar negative ways to the personality she imagines.

We rarely wonder about or discuss the brother who shot him because *14* we already know everything about him. When the call came, my first thought was the same one I'd had when I'd heard about Rosa Parks's beating: a brother did it. A non-job-having, middle-of-the-day malt-liquor-drinking, crotch-clutching, loud-talking brother with many neglected children born of many forgotten women. He lives in his mother's basement with furniture rented at an astronomical interest rate, the exact amount of which he does not know. He has a car phone, an $80 monthly cable bill, and every possible phone feature but no savings. He steals Social Security numbers from unsuspecting relatives and assumes their identities to acquire large TV sets for which he will never pay. On the slim chance that he is brought to justice, he will have a colorful criminal history and no coherent explanation to offer for his act. His family will raucously defend him and cry cover-up. Some liberal lawyer just like me will help him plea-bargain his way to yet another short stay in a prison pesthouse that will serve only to add another layer to the brother's sociopathology and formless, mindless nihilism. We know him. We've known and feared him all our lives.

As a teenager, he called, "Hey, baby, gimme somma that boodie!" at us from car windows. Indignant at our lack of response, he followed up with, "Fuck you, then, 'ho!" He called me a "white-boy-lovin' nigger bitch oreo" for being in the gifted program and loving it. At twenty-seven, he got my seventeen-year-old sister pregnant with Johnny and lost interest without ever informing her that he was married. He snatched my widowed mother's purse as she waited in predawn darkness for the bus to work and then broke into our house while she soldered on an assembly line. He chased all the small entrepreneurs from our neighborhood with his violent thievery and put bars on our windows. He kept us from sitting on our own front porch after dark and laid the foundation for our periodic bouts of self-hating anger and racial embarrassment. He made our neighborhood a ghetto. He is the poster fool behind the maddening community knowledge that there are still some black mothers who raise their daughters but merely love their sons. He and his cancerous carbon copies eclipse the vast majority of us who are not sociopaths and render us invisible. He is the Siamese twin who has died but cannot be separated from his living, vibrant sibling; which of us must attract more notice? We despise and disown this anomalous loser, but for many he *is* black America. We know him, we know that he is outside the fold, and we know that he will only get worse. What we didn't know is that, because of him, my little sister would one day be the latest hysterical black mother wailing over a fallen child on TV.

Alone, lying in the road bleeding and paralyzed but hideously conscious, Johnny had lain helpless as he watched his would-be murderer come to stand over him and offer this prophecy: "Betch'ou won't be doin' nomo' wavin', mothafucker."

Fuck you, asshole. He's fine from the waist up. You just can't do anything right, can you? ■

15

16

17

> The description of the gunman continues with personal connotations and a parallel sentence structure.

> *He and his cancerous carbon copies eclipse the vast majority of us who are not sociopaths and render us invisible.*

Reading for Better Writing

1. The title of this piece could be understood in at least two ways: As a question about the identity of the actual person who shot Johnny, or as a question about which groups of people are responsible for Johnny's shooting. How do you understand the title, and why?

2. Dickerson uses the first full paragraph and scattered references throughout the essay to portray herself as a black woman who is highly educated and independent. Why might she have chosen this strategy? How might the essay be received differently if these passages were excluded?

3. Review paragraphs 14 and 15 in which Dickerson bundles together the traits of many "brother[s]" whom she "despise[s] and disown[s]" into one composite character. Note how she describes the character in a series of parallel clauses, each beginning with "He" followed by a verb. How do the tone and content of these sentences relay the writer's assessment of and attitude toward the character?

4. In paragraph 16, Dickerson describes her nephew lying helplessly in the road, looking up at the "would-be murderer." She concludes the paragraph by quoting him. What does the quotation suggest about the individual's personality, attitude, and understanding of what he has done? How does the quotation link this individual to the composite character described in paragraphs 14 and 15?

5. A writer's word choice must fit his or her subject, audience, and purpose. Explain how Dickerson's quotation in paragraph 16 and expletives in paragraph 17 do or do not fit her subject, audience, and purpose.

6. Given Dickerson's characterization of the gunman, it seems unlikely that he would have read this piece in *The New Republic* (where it was first published), a magazine that has the self-proclaimed mission "to provide its readers with an intelligent, stimulating and rigorous examination of American politics, foreign policy and culture." Why, then, might the writer directly address a second person ("you") in the final paragraph? Why does she open the paragraph with expletives? What might it mean for the addressed "you" to get things right? Finally, in what ways might Dickerson hope that this paragraph would impact *The New Republic*'s audience?

Guidelines
Writing Description and Reflection

1. **Select a topic.** Choose an experience or experiences that influenced you in some key way—either confirming what you thought or planned at that time or changing those thoughts or plans. (Revisit the "Topics to Consider" on page **156** for additional ideas.)

   TIP: If you can't think of any experiences, try listing topics in response to the following statement: *Reflect on times when you first discovered that the world was one of the following—strange, wonderful, complex, frightening, boring, small, uncaring, like you, unlike you, full, or empty.* How did these experiences affect who you are today?

2. **Get the big picture.** Once you have chosen one or more experiences to write about, gather your thoughts by reflecting on the questions below through brainstorming or by freewriting.
   - What are the key moments—the pivotal points—in your experiences?
   - What led to those key moments? Why? What resulted from them?
   - What was going on from your perspective?
   - How did others experience the events?
   - What did you learn from these experiences?
   - Did these experiences end as you had hoped? Why or why not?
   - What themes, conflicts, and insights arose from these experiences?
   - How do your feelings now differ from your feelings then?

   TIP: To find out more details about the event or people involved, sort through photo albums and home videos to trigger memories; talk to someone who shared your experiences or saw you through them; or consult your journal, diary, old letters, and saved e-mail.

3. **Get organized.**
   - Review your brainstorming or freewriting, and highlight key details, quotations, or episodes that you want to include in your writing.
   - Draft a brief outline that shows where key information fits into the big picture.
   - List the main events in chronological order, or use a cluster to help you gather details related to your experiences.

   TIP: To help you decide which details to include and how to organize your information, consider what your audience needs to understand and appreciate your story.

4. **Write the first draft**. Review your outline and rough out the first draft in one sitting. Then test your reflection for its significance. Does it answer these questions: What happened? How did the experience affect you? How do you feel about it now?

5. **Review and revise.** After drafting the essay, take a break. Then read your document again for accuracy and completeness. Look first at the entire piece. Does it say what you wanted to say? Does it include any gaps or weak spots? Check your outline to make sure all key details are covered and in the right sequence. (See the checklist on page **82**.)

6. **Test your reflection.** Review what you say about the experiences:
   - Does the tone—whether sarcastic, humorous, regretful, or meditative—fit the content of the reflection?
   - Have you established a viewpoint, and is the reflection built on this point of view?
   - Will the intended readers appreciate the treatment of the subject?

7. **Get feedback**. Ask a classmate or someone in the writing center to read your paper, looking for the following:
   - An opening that pulls the reader into the reflection
   - Experiences that are portrayed clearly and vividly
   - An explanation of how you've changed that is woven naturally into the experiences
   - Transitions that connect paragraphs effectively
   - A conclusion that restates the point of the reflection clearly and succinctly

8. **Edit and proofread your essay**. Once you have revised the content, organization, and voice of your personal reflection, polish it. Carefully check your choice of words; the clarity of your sentences; and your grammar, usage, and mechanics.

9. **Publish your writing by doing one or more of the following**:
   - Share your essay with friends and family.
   - Publish it in a journal or on a website.
   - Make copies of your writing, read it to a class of high school students, and discuss their responses.
   - Place a copy in your professional portfolio.
   - Submit a copy to your instructor.

Writing Checklist

Use these six traits to check the quality of your writing; then revise as needed:

____ The **ideas** (the topic being reflected on) provide the reader with an interesting look at your experience.

____ The **organization** pattern effectively blends narration and reflection.

____ The **voice** is reflective, and characters and events are treated respectfully.

____ The **words** are precise and clear; descriptions help the reader experience what you experienced.

____ The **sentences** are smooth and natural.

____ The **copy** is correct and in a format appropriate for your assignment.

Writing Prompt

Writing Activities

1. Writing reflectively requires sharing personal thoughts and feelings about experiences and events—a task that can be difficult to do effectively. Review Mary Seymour's piece, "Call Me Crazy," noting the places where she uses phrases similar to "I think" and "I feel," along with an example or comparison to make her perspective clear to her readers. Draft or revise a reflection in which you use these strategies to clarify your own point of view.

2. In "None of This Is Fair," the writer reflects on his individual relationship to his community. When have you learned a lesson about what it means to be a part of *or* outside a community? When did you learn about unfair advantage and disadvantage? Write a personal-reflection essay based on these experiences.

3. Review the portions of "Who Shot Johnny?" in which Debra Dickerson creates a composite character assigned the traits and actions of many people who have affected her in similar ways. Draft a character sketch of your own in which you create one character who brings together the associated traits and behaviors of many individuals who have affected you in a collective manner.

Analytical Writing

Chapters 12 through 16 introduce the traditional modes of analytical writing: cause-effect, comparison-contrast, classification, process, and definition. All of these modes are analytical in the sense that they involve mentally "breaking down" a topic in order to reveal structures and logical relationships. Often called expository writing, such modes seek to clearly explain to readers the logical workings of a given topic—from adrenaline to dog food to dementia.

Note, however, that virtually any piece of analytical writing blends these distinctive modes. For example, you might use compare-contrast as the primary organizational strategy for an entire essay, but you also might use another mode (such as definition) to organize a specific paragraph within that essay. In all of your writing, you should choose the writing strategy that best fits your subject, audience, and purpose.

CONTENTS
Analytical Writing

Chapter 12
Cause and Effect

Now, why did that happen? We ask this question every day at home, in college, and on the job. But why do we ask, "Why?"

We ask it to understand and cope with things that happen in our lives. For example, knowing why our car overheated will help us avoid that problem in the future. Knowing what causes a disease such as diabetes—or knowing its effects—helps us understand and control the condition. In other words, cause and effect reasoning helps us deal with everyday issues.

In a cause and effect essay, the writer develops the thesis through cause and effect reasoning. That is, he or she analyzes and explains the causes, the effects, or both the causes and the effects of a phenomenon.

Are you ready to write—to analyze and explain the causes and/or effects of one of life's "happenings"? This chapter will help you do so.

What's Ahead

- Overview: Writing a Cause and Effect Essay
  - Student Model
  - Professional Models
- Guidelines
- Writing Checklist and Activities

Overview
Web Link
Writing a Cause and Effect Essay

Writer's Goal

Your goal is to analyze and explain the causes, the effects, or both the causes and the effects of some phenomenon (fact, occurrence, or circumstance).

Keys for Success

Know your readers. ■ Consider what your readers know and think about your subject. Are they aware of the cause/effect connection associated with it? Do they accept it? Why or why not? If they deny that the connection exists or is relevant, what arguments support their position? Are these arguments strong?

Think logically. ■ Linking cause to effect, or vice versa, requires clear, logical thinking supported by strong evidence. To practice this kind of reasoning, (1) research the topic for evidence connecting a specific cause and/or effect to a specific phenomenon, (2) draft a working thesis stating that connection, and (3) explain the connection in language that your readers will understand.

Test your thinking. ■ Check your main points for clarity, your supporting points for relevance, and your overall argument for logic. Use the list of logical fallacies to identify common weaknesses. (See pages 255–258, especially "False Cause" on page 257.)

Topics to Consider

Choose a topic that you care about. Begin by thinking about categories such as those listed below. Then brainstorm a list of phenomena related to each category. From this list, choose a topic and prove its causes, its effects, or both.

- **Family life:** adult children living with parents, increasing number of stay-at-home dads, families choosing to simplify their lifestyles, more people squeezed by needs of children and parents, older women having babies
- **Politics:** decreasing number of student voters, increasing support for oil exploration, increased interest in third-party politics, tension between political action groups
- **Society:** nursing shortage, security concerns, nursing-care facilities, immigrant-advocacy groups, shifting ethnic balances
- **Environment:** common water pollutants, new water-purification technology, effects of a community's recycling program
- **Workplace:** decreasing power of unions, more businesses providing child-care services, need for on-the-job training in technology

Next Step Read the model essays and do the activities that follow. As you read, note how the writers develop their theses using cause and effect reasoning.

Cause and Effect

Sarah Hanley is a college student living on a U.S. military base in Germany. In this essay, she uses both research and her military experience to identify the causes and effects of adrenaline highs.

Adrenaline Junkies

The writer introduces the topic by asking a series of questions.	What do you picture when you hear the phrase "adrenaline junkie"? Evel Knievel soaring through the air on a motorcycle? Tom Cruise rappelling down the side of a mountain? An excited retiree stuffing quarters in a slot machine? Actually, all three qualify as adrenaline junkies if they do the activities to get their adrenaline highs. But what, exactly, is an adrenaline high, what causes it, what are its effects, and are the effects positive? *1*
She describes the causes and effects of an adrenaline high.	Adrenaline (also called epinephrine) is a hormone linked to the two adrenal glands located on top of the kidneys. Each gland has two parts: the outer portion called the cortex, and the inner portion called the medulla. When a person experiences an unusual exertion or a crisis situation, his or her brain triggers the medullas, which release little packets of adrenaline into the bloodstream (Nathan). The rush of adrenaline in the blood leads to increased blood pressure, heart rate, sugar metabolism, oxygen intake, and muscle strength. All these phenomena cause an adrenaline high: feeling highly alert and very energetic (Scheuller 2). *2*

However, while all healthy people experience adrenaline highs, different people need different levels of stimuli to trigger the highs. The level of stimulus that a person needs depends on the amount of protein in his or her medullas. In other words, the medullas release adrenaline through channels containing a certain protein. If the channels contain a large amount of the protein, they release adrenaline more easily than channels containing less protein. Therefore, a person with a higher level of protein in the channels of his or her medullas experiences an adrenaline release more easily than someone with a lower level of the protein (Scheuller 4). *3*

She uses an illustration to clarify a point. To illustrate this difference, we'll call the people with a higher level of protein (and a more easily stimulated output of adrenaline) Type N, for nervous; the others we'll call Type C, for calm. Because Type N people release adrenaline more easily than Type C people do, Type Ns require a lesser stimulus to trigger an adrenaline release. For example, a Type N person may get an adrenaline high from finishing his research paper on time, whereas a Type C person will get a similar buzz only when she parachutes from a plane at 10,000 feet! *4*

While different people get their adrenaline highs differently, any person's highs can be channeled for healthy or harmful effects. For example, the Type N person who gets a rush from finishing the research project could do good work as a research technician in a science lab. As long as he avoids becoming a workaholic, seeking the highs won't threaten his health, and the *5* work may contribute to the overall welfare of society. Similarly, the Type C person who gets her highs by jumping out of airplanes could do good work as a fire-fighter or a brain surgeon. As long as she gets periodic relief from the tension, the highs won't hurt her health, and the work could help her community.

An introductory phrase signals a shift in focus.

On the other hand, pursuing the wrong type of adrenaline high, or seeking too many highs, can be destructive. Examples of this kind of behavior include compulsive gambling, drug use, careless risk taking in sports, and win-at-all-cost business practices. Destructive pursuits have many high-cost results including bankruptcy, broken relationships, physical injury, drug addiction, and death (Lyons 3). 6

The writer concludes by reviewing her main points.

Because adrenaline highs can lead to positive results, maybe we waste time worrying about becoming adrenaline junkies. Instead, we should ask ourselves how to pursue those highs positively. In other words, the proteins, hormones, and chemical processes that produce adrenaline highs are, themselves, very good—and they can be used for good. In fact, someday we may figure out how to bottle the stuff and put it on the market! ■ 7

> *Note:* The Works Cited page is not shown. For sample pages, see MLA (pages **495–536**) and APA (pages **537–566**).

Writing Prompt

Reading for Better Writing

1. Name two or more ways that the opening paragraph engages you and effectively introduces the topic and thesis.

2. Paragraphs three and four explain how different people need different levels of stimulus to trigger adrenaline highs. Is this explanation clear and believable? Why or why not?

3. In one sentence, summarize the writer's explanation of the causes and effects of an adrenaline high. Explain why you do or do not find this interpretation convincing.

4. The writer concludes the essay with a playful sentence suggesting that someday adrenaline may be bottled and sold. Explain why you think the sentence is or is not an effective closing.

Cause and Effect

Christy Haubegger is the founder of *Latina* magazine. This essay was originally published in the July 12, 1999, issue of *Newsweek* magazine.

The Legacy of Generation Ñ

About 20 years ago, some mainstream observers declared the 1980s the *1* "decade of the Hispanic." The Latino population was nearing 15 million! (It's since doubled.) However, our decade was postponed—a managerial oversight, no doubt—and eventually rescheduled for the '90s. What happens to a decade deferred? It earns compounded interest and becomes the next hundred years. The United States of the 21st century will be undeniably ours. Again.

> A metaphor helps to make the writer's point.

It's Manifest *Destino*. After all, Latinos are true Americans, some of the *2* original residents of the *Américas*. Spanish was the first European language spoken on this continent. Which is why we live in places like *Los Angeles, Colorado* and *Florida* rather than The Angels, Colored and Flowered. Now my generation is about to put a Latin stamp on the rest of the culture—and that will ultimately be the Ñ legacy.

> The writer lists examples that illustrate her claim.

We are not only numerous, we are also growing at a rate seven times *3* that of the general population. Conservative political ads notwithstanding, this growth is driven by natural increase (births over deaths) rather than immigration. At 30, I may be the oldest childless Latina in the United States. More important, however, while our preceding generation felt pressure to assimilate, America has now generously agreed to meet us in the middle. Just as we become more American, America is simultaneously becoming more Latino.

> Examples from pop culture connect with readers and help to make the writer's ideas memorable.

This quiet *revolución* can perhaps be traced back to the bloodless coup *4* of 1992, when salsa outsold ketchup for the first time. Having toppled the leadership in the condiment category, we set our sights even higher. Fairly soon, there was a congresswoman named Sanchez representing Orange County, a taco-shilling Chihuahua became a national icon, and now everyone is *loca* for Ricky Martin.

We are just getting started. Our geographic concentration and reputa- *5* tion for family values are making us every politician's dream constituency. How long can New Hampshire, with just four Electoral College votes—and probably an equal number of Hispanic residents—continue to get so much attention from presidential candidates? Advertisers will also soon be begging for our attention. With a median age of 26 (eight years younger than the general market), Latinos hardly exist outside their coveted 18–34 demographic. Remember, we may only be 11 percent of the country, but we buy 16 percent of the lipliner.

From *Newsweek*, July 12, 1999. © 1999 Newsweek, Inc. All rights reserved. Reprinted by permission.

> The writer transitions to the anticipated effects of the population growth she has described.

The media will change as well, especially television, where we now appear to be rapidly approaching extinction. Of the 26 new comedies and dramas appearing this fall [1999] on the four major networks, not one has a Latino in a leading role. The Screen Actors Guild released employment statistics for 1998 showing that the percentage of roles going to Hispanic actors actually declined from the previous year. But, pretty soon, the cast of "Friends" will need to find some *amigos*. Seeing as they live in New York City, and there's almost 2 million of us in the metropolitan area, this shouldn't prove too difficult.

6

> Shifting to future tense ("will") marks these statements as predictions.

Face it: this is going to be a bilingual country. Back in 1849, the California Constitution was written in both Spanish and English, and we're headed that way again. If our children speak two languages instead of just one, how can that not be a benefit to us all? The re-Latinization of this country will pay off in other ways as well. I, for one, look forward to that pivotal moment in our history when all American men finally know how to dance. Latin music will no longer be found in record stores under foreign and romance will bloom again. Our children will ask us what it was like to dance without a partner.

7

"American food" will mean low-fat enchiladas and hamburgers served with rice and beans. As a result, the American standard of beauty will necessarily expand to include a female size 12, and anorexia will be found only in medical-history books. Finally, just in time for the baby boomers' senescence, living with extended family will become hip again. "Simpsons" fans of the next decade will see Grandpa moving back home. We'll all go back to church together.

8

> The paragraph begins with the word *dawn* and ends with *mañana* and *morning*.

At the dawn of a new millennium, America knows Latinos as entertainers and athletes. But, someday very soon, all American children can dream of growing up to be writers like Sandra Cisneros, astronauts like Ellen Ochoa, or judges like Jose Cabranes of the Second Circuit Court of Appeals. To put a Latin spin on a famous Anglo phrase: It is truly *mañana* in America. For those of you who don't know it (yet), that word doesn't just mean tomorrow; *mañana* also means morning. ■

9

Reading for Better Writing

1. In one sentence, summarize the cause(s) and effect(s) of the changes described in this essay.

2. Writers must make their claims using words that convey an appropriate level of certainty. Is Haubegger's use of "will" (versus "may") appropriate in paragraphs seven and eight? Why?

3. The last paragraph emphasizes the writer's main point. What is her point, and do you agree? Why?

4. The writer published this essay in 1999. Cite examples showing that the changes she described are continuing.

Cause and Effect

Anna Quindlen's 1992 *New York Times* column "Public and Private" won the Pulitzer Prize for commentary. She now writes a regular column for *Newsweek* magazine, where the piece below was originally published in 2001.

Our Tired, Our Poor, Our Kids

The title includes an allusion to a well-known phrase from the Statue of Liberty.

Six people live here, in a room the size of the master bedroom in a modest suburban house. Trundles, bunk beds, dressers side by side stacked with toys, clothes, boxes, in tidy claustrophobic clutter. One woman, five children. The baby was born in a shelter. The older kids can't wait to get out of this one. Everyone gets up at 6 a.m., the little ones to go to day care, the others to school. Their mother goes out to look for an apartment when she's not going to drug-treatment meetings. "For what they pay for me to stay in a shelter I could have lived in the Hamptons," Sharanda says.

The writer describes the problem and cites statistics showing its breadth.

Here is the parallel universe that has flourished while the more fortunate were rewarding themselves for the stock split with SUVs and home additions. There is a boom market in homelessness. But these are not the men on the streets of San Francisco holding out cardboard signs to the tourists. They are children, hundreds of thousands of them, twice as likely to repeat a grade or be hospitalized and four times as likely to go

> *They are children, hundreds of thousands of them . . .*

hungry as the kids with a roof over their heads. Twenty years ago New York City provided emergency shelter for just under a thousand families a day; last month it had to find spaces for 10,000 children on a given night. Not since the Great Depression have this many babies, toddlers and kids had no place like home.

Quotations from primary sources personalize the statistics.

Three mothers sit in the living room of a temporary residence called Casa Rita in the Bronx and speak of this in the argot of poverty. "The landlord don't call back when they hear you got EARP," says Rosie, EARP being the Emergency Assistance Rehousing Program. "You get priority for Section 8 if you're in a shelter," says Edna, which means federal housing programs will put you higher on the list. Edna has four kids, three in foster care; she arrived at Casa Rita, she says, "with two bags and a baby." Rosie has three, they share a bathroom down the hall with two other families. Sharanda's five range in age from thirteen to just over a year. Her eldest was put in the wrong grade when he changed schools. "He's humiliated, living here," his mother says.

All three women are anxious to move on, although they appreciate this place, where they can get shelter, get sober and keep their kids at the same time. They remember the Emergency Assistance Unit, the city office that is the gateway to the system, where hundreds of families sit every day surrounded by their bags, where children sleep on benches until they are shuffled off dull-eyed for one night in a shelter or a motel, only to return as supplicants again the next day.

In another world middle-class Americans have embraced new-home starts, the stock market and the Gap. But in the world of these displaced families, problems ignored or fumbled or unforeseen during this great period of prosperity have dovetailed into an enormous subculture of children who think that only rich people have their own bedrooms. Twenty years ago, when the story of the homeless in America became a staple of news reporting, the solution was presented as a simple one: affordable housing. That's still true, now more than ever. Two years ago the National Low Income Housing Coalition calculated that the hourly income necessary to afford the average two-bedroom apartment was around $12. That's more than twice the minimum wage.

The result is that in many cities police officers and teachers cannot afford to live where they work, that in Las Vegas old motels provide housing for casino employees, that in shelters now there is a contingent of working poor who get up off their cots and go off to their jobs. The result is that if you are evicted for falling behind on your rent, if there is a bureaucratic foul-up in your welfare check or the factory in which you work shuts down, the chances of finding another place to live are very small indeed. You're one understanding relative, one paycheck, one second chance from the street. And so are your kids.

> *[P]olice officers and teachers cannot afford to live where they work . . .*

So-called welfare reform, which emphasizes cutbacks and make-work, has played a part in all this. A study done in San Diego in 1998 found that a third of homeless families had recently had benefits terminated or reduced, and that most said that was how they had wound up on the street. Drugs, alcohol and domestic abuse also land mothers with kids in the shelter system or lead them to hand their children over to relatives or foster homes. Today the average homeless woman is younger than ever before, may have been in foster care or in shelters herself and so considers a chaotic childhood the norm. Many never finished high school, and have never held a job.

Ralph Nunez, who runs the organization Homes for the Homeless, says that all this calls for new attitudes. "People don't like to hear it, but shelters are going to be the low-income housing of the future," he says. "So how do

---

The conjunction *but* emphasizes the contrast between the first two sentences and settings.

The word *result* is a clue to cause/effect organization.

The writer includes quotes from sources with expertise on the topic.

5

6

7

8

we enrich the experience and use the system to provide job training and education?" Bonnie Stone of Women in Need, which has eight other residences along with Casa Rita, says, "We're pouring everything we've got into the nine months most of them are here—nutrition, treatment, budgeting. By the time they leave, they have a subsidized apartment, day care and, hopefully, some life skills they didn't have before."

The writer addresses the audience directly: *you.*

But these organizations are rafts in a rising river of need that has roared 9 through this country without most of us ever even knowing. So now you know. There are hundreds of thousands of little nomads in America, sleeping in the back of cars, on floors in welfare offices or in shelters five to a room. What would it mean, to spend your childhood drifting from one strange bed to another, waking in the morning to try to figure out where you'd landed today, without those things that confer security and happiness: a familiar picture on the wall, a certain slant of light through a curtained window? "Give me your tired, your poor," it says on the base of the Statue of Liberty, to welcome foreigners. Oh, but they are already here, the small refugees from the ruin of the American dream, even if you cannot see them. ■

The quotation recalls the title phrase.

Writing Prompt

Reading for Better Writing

1. In one sentence, state the cause/effect relationship that Quindlen outlines in "Our Tired, Our Poor, Our Kids."

2. In writing, an *allusion* is an indirect reference to another text. What allusions can you identify in this piece? Why does the writer use allusions in this essay?

3. Use a pencil or sticky notes to distinguish portions of the essay where Quindlen addresses the cause(s) and the effect(s) of the problem. What is the approximate ratio of space given to each? How are the cause and effect sections arranged? How do these factors affect the essay's message?

4. Notice that Quindlen occasionally begins sentences with conjunctions such as *but* or *and*. Where, and why? Where might this strategy work in your writing?

Guidelines
Writing a Cause and Effect Essay

1. **Select a topic.** Look again at the list of facts, occurrences, or circumstances mentioned under "Topics to Consider" on page **176**. Expand the list by jotting down additional items for each category, or listing new categories along with related items. From this finished list, choose a topic and prove its causes, its effects, or both.

   TIP: If your professor approves, you could write an essay contradicting the logic in another writer's cause and effect essay. For an example, see "An Apology for the Life of Ms. Barbie D. Doll" on pages **265–266**.

2. **Narrow and research the topic.** Write down or type your topic. Below it, brainstorm a list of related causes and effects in two columns. Next, do preliminary research to expand the list and distinguish primary causes and effects from secondary ones. Revise your topic as needed to address only primary causes and/or effects that research links to a specific phenomenon.

Cause/Effect Topic: _____	
_____	
_____	
Causes	**Effects**
(Because of)	(this results)
1. _____	1. _____
2. _____	2. _____
3. _____	3. _____
4. _____	4. _____

3. **Draft and test your thesis.** Based on your preliminary research, draft a working thesis (you may revise it later) that introduces the topic, along with the causes and/or effects you intend to discuss. Limit your argument to only those points you can prove.

4. **Gather and analyze information.** Research your topic, looking for clear evidence that links specific causes to specific effects. At the same time, avoid arguments mistaking a coincidence for a cause/effect relationship. Use the list of logical fallacies (see pages **255–258**) to weed out common errors in logic. For example, finding chemical pollutants in a stream running beside a chemical plant does not "prove" that the plant caused the pollutants.

5. **Get organized.** Develop an outline that lays out your thesis and argument in a clear pattern. Under each main point asserting a cause/effect connection, list details from your research that support the connection.

   Thesis: _____

Point #1	*Point #2*	*Point #3*
• Supporting details	• Supporting details	• Supporting details
• Supporting details	• Supporting details	• Supporting details
• Supporting details	• Supporting details	• Supporting details

6. Use your outline to draft the essay. Try to rough out the essay's overall argument before you attempt to revise it. As you write, show how each specific cause led to each specific effect, citing examples as needed. To show those cause/effect relationships, use transitional words like the following:

• accordingly	• for this purpose	• since	• therefore
• as a result	• for this reason	• so	• thus
• because	• hence	• such as	• to illustrate
• consequently	• just as	• thereby	• whereas

7. Revise the essay. Whether your essay presents causes, effects, or both, use the checklist below to trace and refine your argument.

____ The thesis and introduction clearly identify the causes and/or effects.

____ All major causes and/or effects are addressed.

____ Statements regarding the causes and/or effects are sufficiently limited and focused.

____ Supporting details are researched, relevant, and strong.

____ Links between causes and effects are clear and logical.

____ The conclusion restates the main argument and unifies the essay.

8. Get feedback. Ask a peer reviewer or someone from the college's writing center to read your essay for the following:

- An engaging opening
- A clear and logical thesis
- Clear and convincing reasoning that links specific causes to specific effects
- A closing that wraps up the argument, leaving no loose ends

9. Edit the essay for clarity and correctness. Check for the following:

- Precise, appropriate word choice
- Complete, smooth sentences
- Clear transitions between paragraphs
- Correct names, dates, and supporting details
- Correct mechanics, usage, and grammar

10. Publish your essay. Share your writing with others as follows:

- Submit it to your instructor.
- Post it on the class's or department's website.
- Submit the essay for presentation at an appropriate conference.
- Send it as a service to relevant nonprofit agencies.
- Share the essay with family and friends.

Writing Checklist

Use these six traits to check the quality of your writing, then revise as needed:

____ The **ideas** explain the causes and/or effects of the topic in a clear, well-reasoned argument supported by credible information.

____ The **organization** helps the reader understand the cause/effect relationship. The links between the main points and the supporting points are clear.

____ The **voice** is informed, polite, and professional.

____ The **words** are precise and clear. Technical or scientific terms are defined. Causes are linked to effects with transitional words and phrases such as *therefore, as a result,* and *for this reason.*

____ The **sentences** are clear, varied in structure, and smooth.

____ The **copy** is correct, is clean, and follows assigned guidelines for format.

Writing Prompt

Writing Activities

1. In "Adrenaline Junkies" the writer describes a form of addiction: adrenaline highs. List other addictions, choose one, and write an essay proving its causes and/or effects.

2. Draft an essay in which you make or support a claim. Experiment with different levels of certainty appropriate for your topic, audience, and purpose.

3. One way to instill coherence in an essay is to make direct or indirect connections between the opening and closing of the piece. Review Anna Quindlen's "Our Tired, Our Poor, Our Kids," noting the connections between the title and the concluding paragraph. Revise one of your essays by linking the language and ideas of the opening and closing sections.

4. Choose a phenomenon that is related to your program or major and discussed in the news media. Write an essay that analyzes and explains either its causes, its effects, or both. Consider submitting the essay to your adviser, asking for feedback, and then polishing the piece for inclusion in your professional portfolio.

Chapter 13
Comparison and Contrast

In his plays, William Shakespeare creates characters, families, and even plot lines that mirror each other. As a result, we see Hamlet in relation to Laertes and the Montagues in relation to the Capulets. In the process, we do precisely what the writer wants us to do—we compare and contrast the subjects. The result is clarity and insight: by thinking about both subjects, we understand each one more clearly.

In this chapter, four writers use compare and contrast organization: one to analyze the attack on the World Trade Center, another to explain two views of a river, a third to assess two patterns of dress for Iranian women, and a fourth to describe ethnic groups. Elsewhere in this book, you will find writers working in the natural sciences, the social sciences, and the humanities—all comparing and contrasting two or more subjects with the goal of helping their readers understand the topics.

What's the point? Comparing and contrasting is a writing-and-thinking strategy used across the curriculum and in the workplace. You are about to write an essay using this strategy. What you learn in the process will help you succeed both in other courses and in your post-college career.

What's Ahead

- Overview: Writing a
  Comparison and Contrast Essay
  – Student Model
  – Professional Models
- Guidelines
- Writing Checklist and Activities

Overview
Writing a Comparison and Contrast Essay

Writer's Goal

Your goal is to write an essay that (1) sets two or more subjects side by side, (2) shows the reader how they are similar and/or different, and (3) draws conclusions or makes some point based on what you have shown.

Keys for Success

Think about your readers. ■ What do they know about the subject? What should they know? Why should they care? Answering these questions will help you understand both your readers and your purpose for writing.

Know your purpose. ■ What do you want your essay to do? Inform? Explain? Persuade? Some combination of these? Knowing your purpose will help you decide what to include (and not include) in the essay, how to organize it, and how to help readers use the information.

Be logical. ■ Comparing and contrasting is a logical process that helps you understand your subjects more fully and explain them more clearly. Begin by determining the basis of your comparison: How are the subjects related? Then decide whether to compare, to contrast, or both. When *comparing* subjects, show how they are similar. When *contrasting* them, show how they are different. When *comparing* and *contrasting* subjects, show how they are both similar and different. To choose which of the three patterns to follow, think about your purpose. Which pattern will help your essay accomplish what you want it to?

Topics to Consider

Choose subjects that are related in some important way. To get started, think about pairs of objects, events, places, processes, people, ideas, beliefs, and so on. For more inspiration, read the four models in this chapter and scan the models listed below. Each of these essays uses compare/contrast strategies. List topics similar to those in the models.

- "Three Family Cancers," pages 205–207
- "Four Ways to Talk About Literature," pages 208–209
- "No Wonder They Call Me a Bitch," pages 210–213

Next Step Read the model essays and perform the activities that follow. As you read, note whether the writer compares, contrasts, or both. Also note the pattern used to organize the essay: subject by subject, trait by trait, and so on.

Comparison and Contrast

One week after the attack on the World Trade Center, when the causes and consequences were still unclear, Canadian student Anita Brinkman wrote this editorial. To make her point, she compares the attack to other significant tragedies.

A Fear Born of Sorrow

The writer cites statistics that introduce her topic.

More than 100 people were killed in the tragic bombing of the Oklahoma Federal Building in 1995. About 6,000 die in Africa each day of AIDS. Between 8,000 and 10,000 people worldwide die of starvation daily. Tragedies occur all around us, and we accept them out of necessity as a part of life. But sometimes the horror of a tragedy affects us in a new way: It overwhelms a nation and stuns the international community. This is what happened last week when two hijacked passenger planes hit the twin towers of the World Trade Center, and their resulting collapse killed thousands of people from several countries. News of the tragedy flashed around the globe. Everywhere, it seemed, people in uncomprehending horror listened to reports on their radios or watched endless replays on their televisions. Several countries declared days of mourning and scheduled services of remembrance. Now, one week after the attack, tokens of grief and letters of condolence still flood U.S. embassies and government offices worldwide. But why is the outpouring of grief so much deeper for this tragedy than for others? Why isn't the attack considered just a large-scale repeat of the Oklahoma City bombing? Could it be that our grief is more than sorrow, and that our loss is much more than what lies in the rubble? *1*

She states her thesis as a question.

Two parallel events are compared and contrasted.

The Oklahoma City bombing was grievous and alarming, but localized. The bomber was soon arrested, his motives deduced, and justice served. While lives were changed and a nation was shaken, the world community remained composed. However, the September 11 attack unsettled us more, in part because the World Trade Center stood for so much more than the Oklahoma Federal Building did. The twin towers symbolized American domination of world finances: They were a major center for the Internet, a hub for international business, and an emblem of American life. The fall of the towers struck violently at the nation's psyche, and the manner in which they were destroyed—with America's own airplanes filled with many American passengers—has raised questions about America's security and future. Threatened to their core, Americans have demanded retaliation—but against whom? The terrorists' identity is not clear, and evidence seems elusive. In a sense, an unknown offender has injured Americans, who beat the air in the dark. In such a case, terrorism is aptly named, for America's outcry expresses more than sorrow—it also expresses fear. *2*

The word "fear" links this paragraph with the previous one.

The fear that Americans feel comes partly from the uncertainty related to this attack. The attackers demonstrated technical and planning skills that *3* surprised Americans, making them question their safety and fear future attacks. Air travel, long considered safe, now includes security measures like armed guards, luggage searches, and bomb-sniffing dogs—all strategies to achieve safety. As Americans struggle to find answers in the shattered peace, nations are forming alliances, war seems imminent, and the whole world waits anxiously to see where it all will lead.

The writer contrasts the Sept. 11 and Pearl Harbor attacks.

Fear and uncertainty are new to Americans living today because   4
America has not been attacked in this way since Britain ruled her as a colony. While the bombing of Pearl Harbor awoke many to the fact that America could be targeted, the Japanese bombers hit Hawaii—then a U.S. territory, not a state and not the mainland. Following World War II, many in the world community again thought of America as the invulnerable Land of Opportunity. However, this belief is now shattered, and many citizens of the global village fear that what was lost last week includes more than what lies in the rubble.

She shows how the events differ.

On September 11, 2001, America, along with its Western allies, lost its   5
aura of invincibility. As the whole world watched, the towers fell, and we stumbled in shock and pain. Moreover, as time passes, America may fail to identify its enemy and to understand the attack. If this happens, the oppressed people of the world—to some extent victims of Western culture—will take notice.

She restates her thesis.

It is now one week since the towers fell, and the world still grieves.   6
However, mingled with this grief is the fear that we may be mourning not only for the lives lost, but also for our lost way of life. ■

Writing Prompt

Reading for Better Writing

1. Review the title and explain how it does or does not forecast the essay's main idea.

2. The writer compares and contrasts the September 11 attack with the Oklahoma City and Pearl Harbor attacks. What does she conclude from each comparison? Explain why you do or do not agree with her.

3. Review the essay's final paragraph and explain why it is or is not an effective closing.

Comparison and Contrast

Mark Twain is best known for his novels *The Adventures of Tom Sawyer* and *The Adventures of Huckleberry Finn.* In this excerpt from his 1883 memoir, *Life on the Mississippi,* Twain contrasts his mindset as an apprentice with his perspective as a steamboat pilot.

Two Views of the River

The writer starts the sentence with the contrasting conjunction *but*.

Now when I had mastered the language of this water, and had come to know every trifling feature that bordered the great river as familiarly as I knew the letters of the alphabet, I had made a valuable acquisition. But I had lost something, too. I had lost something which could never be restored to me while I lived. All the grace, the beauty, the poetry, had gone out of the majestic river! I still keep in mind a certain wonderful sunset which I witnessed when steamboating was new to me. A broad expanse of the river was turned to blood; in the middle distance the red hue brightened into gold, through which a solitary log came floating black and conspicuous; in one place a long, slanting mark lay sparkling upon the water; in another the surface was broken by boiling, tumbling rings that were as many-tinted as an opal; where the ruddy flush was faintest, was a smooth spot that was covered with graceful circles and radiating lines, ever so delicately traced; the shore on our left was densely wooded, and the somber shadow that fell from this forest was broken in one place by a long, ruffled trail that shone like silver; and high above the forest wall a clean-stemmed dead tree waved a single leafy bough that glowed like a flame in the unobstructed splendor that was flowing from the sun. There were graceful curves, reflected images, woody heights, soft distances; and over the whole scene, far and near, the dissolving lights drifted steadily, enriching it every passing moment with new marvels of coloring. *1*

The sunset is described in a long, one-sentence list of sensory details.

I stood like one bewitched. I drank it in, in a speechless rapture. The world was new to me, and I had never seen anything like this at home. But as I have said, a day came when I began to cease from noting the glories and the charms which the moon and the sun and the twilight wrought upon the river's face; another day came when I ceased altogether to note them. Then, if that sunset scene had been repeated, I should have looked upon it without rapture, and should have commented upon it, inwardly, after this fashion: "This sun means that we are going to have wind tomorrow; that floating log means that the river is rising, small thanks to it; that slanting mark on the water refers to a bluff reef which is going to kill somebody's steamboat one of these nights, if it keeps on stretching out like that, those tumbling 'boils' show a dissolving bar and a changing channel there; the lines and circles in the slick water over yonder are a warning that that troublesome place is shoaling up dangerously; that silver streak in the shadow of the forest is the 'break' from a new snag, and he has located himself in the very *2*

Again a sentence begins with *but*.

Another long, one-sentence list counters the earlier description of the river.

best place he could have found to fish for steamboats; that tall dead tree, with a single living branch, is not going to last long, and then how is a body ever going to get through this blind place at night without the friendly old landmark?"

> **The paragraph ends with a series of interrelated questions.**

No, the romance and beauty were all gone from the river. All the value   *3* any feature of it had for me now was the amount of usefulness it could furnish toward compassing the safe piloting of a steamboat. Since those days, I have pitied doctors from my heart. What does the lovely flush in a beauty's cheek mean to a doctor but a "break" that ripples above some deadly disease? Are not all her visible charms sown thick with what are to him the signs and symbols of hidden decay? Does he ever see her beauty at all, or doesn't he simply view her professionally, and comment upon her unwholesome condition all to himself? And doesn't he sometimes wonder whether he has gained most or lost most by learning his trade? ■

Reading for Better Writing

1. The purpose for comparing and contrasting two things is to make a point. What two specific things is Twain comparing and contrasting, and what is the point he is making? How do you know?

2. Twain first describes one way of looking at the river, then another. How else might he have organized the ideas in this passage? Make an argument for the organizational pattern that you think is most effective.

3. At two points in the passage, Twain begins sentences with the conjunction *but*. Why doesn't he simply combine these sentences with those that precede them?

4. Find examples of short, average, and long sentences in this passage. Where are they located, and why does Twain vary his sentence length in this way?

5. This passage ends with a series of rhetorical questions—questions that are intended to provoke thought but not an expressed answer. What clues suggest that Twain is expecting thought rather than actual answers? Why might he use this strategy?

Comparison and Contrast

Gelareh Asayesh grew up in Iran before moving to Florida. She writes about her experiences in *Saffron Sky: A Life Between Iran and America*. The article below first appeared in *The New York Times* in November 2001.

Shrouded in Contradiction

Two contrasting scenes appear in the first sentence.

I grew up wearing the miniskirt to school, the veil to the mosque. In the Tehran of my childhood, women in bright sundresses shared the sidewalk with women swathed in black. The tension between the two ways of life was palpable. As a schoolgirl, I often cringed when my bare legs got leering or contemptuous glances. Yet, at times, I long for the days when I could walk the streets of my country with the wind in my hair. When clothes were clothes. In today's Iran, whatever I wear sends a message. If it's a chador, it embarrasses my Westernized relatives. If it's a skimpy scarf, I risk being accused of stepping on the blood of the martyrs who died in the war with Iraq. Each time I return to Tehran, I wait until the last possible moment, when my plane lands on the tarmaç, to don the scarf and long jacket that many Iranian women wear in lieu of a veil. To wear *hijab*—Islamic covering—is to in'
I hate it. Sometimes I value it.

> *As a schoolgirl, I often cringed when my bare legs got leering or contemptuous*

Most of the time, I don't even notice i'
pantyhose to work. It ruins my hair, but'
where I live. For many women, the veil i
It's simply what they wear, as their mo'
dry your face with after your ablutio'
to hide when he's feeling shy. Even f'
a hint of rebellion, *hijab* is just no'

Notice the one-sentence paragraph.

Except when it is.

"Sister, what kind of get-u'
asks me one summer day on th'
a gondola up a mountain, wl'
of sea and forest. Women
gleaming with sweat. Won'
jackets with pants, their '

...ng with vistas
...the heat, faces
...s wear knee-length
sheer scarves.

None have been more daring than I. I've wound my scarf into a turban, leaving my neck bare to the breeze. The woman in black is a government employee paid to police public morals. "Fix your scarf at once!" she snaps. [5]

"But I'm hot," I say. [6]

"You're hot?" she exclaims. "Don't you think we all are?" [7]

I start unwinding my makeshift turban. "The men aren't hot," I mutter. [8]

Her companion looks at me in shocked reproach. "Sister, this isn't about men and women," she says, shaking her head. "This is about Islam." [9]

I want to argue. I feel like a child. Defiant, but powerless. Burning with injustice, but also with a hint of shame. I do as I am told, feeling acutely conscious of the bare skin I am covering. In policing my sexuality, these women have made me more aware of it. [10]

The veil masks erotic freedom, but its advocates believe *hijab* transcends the erotic—or expands it. In the West, we think of passion as a fever of the body, not the soul. In the East, Sufi poets used earthly passion as a metaphor; the beloved they celebrated was God. Where I come from, people are more likely to find delirious passion in the mosque than in the bedroom. [11]

> *The veil masks erotic freedom, but its advocates believe "hijab" transcends the erotic—or expands it.* [12]

There are times when I feel a hint of this passion. A few years after my encounter on the Caspian, I go to the wake of a family friend. Sitting in a mosque in Mashhad, I grip a slippery black veil with one hand and a prayer book with the other. In the center of the hall, there's a stack of Koranic texts decorated with green-and-black calligraphy, a vase of white gladioluses and a large photograph of the dearly departed. Along the walls, women wait quietly.

From the men's side of the mosque, the mullah's voice rises in lament. His voice is deep and plaintive, oddly compelling. I bow my head, sequestered in my veil while at my side a community of women pray and weep with increasing abandon. I remember from girlhood this sense of being exquisitely alone in the company of others. Sometimes I have cried as well, free to weep without having to offer an explanation. Perhaps they are right, those mystics who believe that physical love is an obstacle to spiritual love; those architects of mosques who abstained from images of earthly life, decorating their work with geometric shapes that they believed freed the soul to slip from its worldly moorings. I do not aspire to such lofty sentiments. All I know is that such moments of passionate abandon, within the circle of invisibility created by the veil, offer an emotional catharsis every bit as potent as any sexual release. [13]

Contradictory feelings are pushed together in a compact list.

The writer offers definitions of *passion* from three different locations.

The writer uses terms of limited certainty, such as *perhaps* and *all I know*.

The final line summarizes the contradictions described in the passage.

Outside, the rain pours from a sullen sky. I make my farewells and walk 14 toward the car, where my driver waits. My veil is wicking muddy water from the sidewalk. I gather up the wet and grimy folds with distaste, longing to be home, where I can cast off this curtain of cloth that gives with one hand, takes away with the other. ■

Reading for Better Writing

1. Sometimes writers use comparison/contrast organization to take a position on an issue—in some cases to show that one side is better than the other, but in others, to show the difficulty of choosing one side over the other. What do you think is Asayesh's position on *hijab*, and why?

2. Find Asayesh's one-sentence paragraph (paragraph 3). Why might the writer have constructed the paragraph in this way? How would this excerpt differ if that sentence had been part of either the preceding or the following paragraph?

3. What contrasts are listed in paragraph 4? How does the writer use punctuation to mark the contrasts?

4. Why does Asayesh use words that indicate limited certainty, such as *perhaps* and *all I know*?

5. In what ways are the opening and closing sentences alike? How are these similarities significant for readers?

Comparison and Contrast

Author Gary Soto describes falling in love against his family's advice with a woman who is not Mexican. In doing so, he draws a number of comparisons.

The title forecasts a comparison.

An anecdote introduces the topic.

The writer subtly compares his grandmother's and mother's responses.

Like Mexicans

My grandmother gave me bad advice and good advice when I was in my early teens. For the bad advice, she said that I should become a barber because they made good money and listened to the radio all day. "Honey, they don't work como burros," she would say every time I visited her. She made the sound of donkeys braying. "Like that, Honey!" For good advice, she said that I should marry a Mexican girl. "No Okies, hijo"—she would say—"Look, my son. He marry one and they fight every day about I don't know what and I don't know what." For her, everyone who wasn't Mexican, black, or Asian was an Okie. The French were Okies, the Italians in suits were Okies. When I asked about Jews, whom I had read about, she asked for a picture. I rode home on my bicycle and returned with a calendar depicting the important races of the world. "Pues si, son Okies también!" she said, nodding her head. She waved the calendar away and we went to the living room, where she lectured me on the virtues of the Mexican girl: first, she could cook and, second, she acted like a woman, not a man, in her husband's home. She said she would tell me about a third when I got a little older.

I asked my mother about it—becoming a barber and marrying Mexican. She was in the kitchen. Steam curled from a pot of boiling beans, the radio was on, looking as squat as a loaf of bread. "Well, if you want to be a barber—they say they make good money." She slapped a round steak with a knife, her glasses slipping down with each strike. She stopped and looked up. "If you find a good Mexican girl, marry her, of course." She returned to slapping the meat, and I went to the backyard where my brother and David King were sitting on the lawn feeling the insides of their cheeks.

"This is what girls feel like," my brother said, rubbing the inside of his cheek. David put three fingers inside his mouth and scratched. I ignored them and climbed the back fence to see my best friend, Scott, a second-generation Okie. I had called him, and his mother pointed to the side of the house where his bedroom was, a small aluminum trailer, the kind you gawk at when they're flipped over on the freeway, wheels spinning in the air. I went around to find Scott pitching horseshoes.

I picked up a set of rusty ones and joined him. While we played, we talked about school and friends and record albums. The horseshoes scuffed up dirt, sometimes ringing the iron that threw out a meager shadow like a sundial. After three argued-over games we pulled two oranges apiece from

1

2

3

4

his tree and started down the alley still talking school and friends and record albums. We pulled more oranges from the alley and talked about who we would marry. "No offense, Scott," I said with an orange slice in my mouth, "but I would never marry an Okie." We walked in step, almost touching, with a sled of shadows dragging behind us. "No offense, Gary," Scott said, "but I would *never* marry a Mexican." I looked at him: a fang of orange slice showed from his munching mouth. I didn't think anything of it. He had his girl and I had mine. But our seventh-grade vision was the same: to marry, get jobs, buy cars and maybe a house if we had money left over.

We talked about our future lives until, to our surprise, we were on the downtown mall, two miles from home. We bought a bag of popcorn at Penneys and sat on a bench near the fountain watching Mexican and Okie girls pass. "That one's mine," I pointed with my chin when a girl with eyebrows arched into black rainbows ambled by. "She's cute," Scott said about a girl with yellow hair and mouthful of gum. We dreamed aloud, our chins busy pointing out girls. We agreed that we couldn't wait to become men and lift them onto our laps.

5

But signals a surprise, a difference.

But the woman I married was not Mexican but Japanese. It was a surprise to me. For years, I went about wide-eyed in my search for the brown girl in a white dress at a dance. I searched the playground at the baseball diamond. When the girls raced for grounders, their hair bounced like something that couldn't be caught. When they sat together in the lunchroom, heads pressed together, I knew they were talking about us Mexican guys. I saw them and dreamed them. I threw my face into my pillow, making up sentences that were as good as in the movies.

6

> *For years, I went about wide-eyed in my search for the brown girl in a white dress at a dance.*

7

But when I was twenty, I fell in love with this other girl who worried my mother, who had my grandmother asking once again to see the calendar of the Important Races of the World. I told her I had thrown it away many years before. I took a much-glanced-at snapshot from my wallet. We looked at it together, in silence. Then Grandma reclined in her chair, lit a cigarette, and said, "Es pretty." She blew and asked with all her worry pushed up to her forehead: "Chinese?"

The writer contrasts his original fantasies with reality.

I was in love and there was no looking back. She was the one. I told my mother, who was slapping hamburger into patties. "Well, sure, if you want to marry her," she said. But the more I talked, the more concerned she became. Later I began to worry. Was it all a mistake? "Marry a Mexican girl," I heard my mother say in my mind. I heard it at breakfast. I heard it over math problems, between Western Civilization and cultural geography. But then one afternoon while I was hitchhiking home from school, it struck

8

me like a baseball in the back: my mother wanted me to marry someone of my own social class—a poor girl. I considered my fiancee, Carolyn, and she didn't look poor, though I knew she came from a family of farm workers and pull-yourself-up-by-your-bootstraps ranchers. I asked my brother who was marrying Mexican poor that fall, if I should marry a poor girl. He screamed "Yeah" above this terrible guitar playing in his bedroom. I considered my sister, who had married Mexican. Cousins were dating Mexicans. Uncles were remarrying poor women. I asked Scott, who was still my best friend, and he said, "She's too good for you, so you better not."

> *He discovers that his family's basis for comparison is class, not race.*

I worried about it until Carolyn took me home to meet her parents. We drove in their Plymouth until the houses gave way to farms and ranches and finally her house fifty feet from the highway. We pulled into the drive; I panicked and begged Carolyn to make a U-turn and go back so we could talk

> *She pinched my cheek, calling me a "silly boy."* 9

about it over a soda. She pinched my cheek, calling me a "silly boy." I felt better, though, when I got out of the car and saw the house: the chipped paint, a cracked window, boards for a walk to the back door. There were rusting cars near the barn. A tractor with a net of spiderwebs under a mulberry. A field. A bale of barbed wire like children's scribbling leaning against an empty chicken coop. Carolyn took my hand and pulled me to my future mother-in-law, who was coming out to greet us.

> *He describes Carolyn's home and parents, stressing similarities with Mexicans.*

We had lunch: sandwiches, potato chips, and iced tea. Carolyn and her 10 mother talked mostly about neighbors and the congregation at the Japanese Methodist Church in West Fresno. Her father, who was in khaki work clothes, excused himself with a wave that was almost a salute and went outside. I heard a truck start, a dog bark, and then the truck rattle away.

Carolyn's mother offered another sandwich, but I declined with a shake 11 of my head and a smile. I looked around when I could, when I was not saying over and over that I was a college student, hinting that I could take care of her daughter. I shifted my chair. I saw newspapers piled in corners, dusty cereal boxes and vinegar bottles in corners. The wallpaper was bubbled from rain that had come in from a bad roof. Dust. Dust lay on lamp shades and windowsills. These people are just like Mexicans, I thought. Poor people.

> *He describes a kitten.*

Carolyn's mother asked me through Carolyn if I would like a sushi. 12 A plate of black and white things was held in front of me. I took one, wide-eyed, and turned it over like a foreign coin. I was biting into one when I saw a kitten crawl up the window screen over the sink. I chewed and the kitten opened its mouth of terror as she crawled higher, wanting to paw the leftovers from our plates. I looked at Carolyn, who said that the cat was just showing off. I looked up in time to see it fall. It crawled up, then fell again.

He again
focuses on
a cat and
begins his
comparison.

The writer
compares
Japanese
and Mexican
people by
comparing
their cats.

We talked for an hour and had apple pie and coffee, slowly. Finally, we   *13*
got up with Carolyn taking my hand. Slightly embarrassed, I tried to pull
away, but her grip held me. I let her have her way as she led me down the
hallway with her mother right behind me. When I opened the door, I was
startled by a kitten clinging to the screen door, its mouth screaming "cat
food, dog biscuits, *sushi. . . .*" I opened the door and the kitten, still holding
on, whined in the language of hungry animals. When I got into Carolyn's
car, I looked back: the cat was still clinging. I asked Carolyn if it were
possibly hungry, but she said the cat was being silly. She started the car,
waved to her mother, and bounced over the rain-poked drive, patting my
thigh for being her lover baby. Carolyn waved again. I looked back, waving,
then gawking at a window screen where there were now three kittens
clawing and screaming to get in. Like Mexicans, I thought. I remembered
the Molinas and how the cats clung to their screens—cats they shot down
with squirt guns. On the highway, I felt happy, pleased by it all. I patted
Carolyn's thigh. Her people were like Mexicans, only different. ■

Writing
Prompt

Reading for Better Writing

1. Briefly explain what the title, "Like Mexicans," signifies.

2. List the items the writer either directly or indirectly compares
(for example, two kitchens, two mothers). Do these comparisons
add to or detract from the essay's main point? Explain your answer.

3. Explain how the essay is organized. Is the organization effective?
Why or why not?

4. The writer describes cats three times. How is the climbing of cats
on screens related to his main point?

Guidelines
Writing a Comparison and Contrast Essay

1. **Select a topic.** List subjects that are similar and/or different in ways that you find interesting, perplexing, disgusting, infuriating, charming, or informing. Then choose two subjects whose comparison and/or contrast gives the reader some insight into who or what they are. For example, you could explain how two chemicals that appear to be similar are actually different—and how that difference makes one more explosive, poisonous, or edible.

2. **Get the big picture.** Using a computer or a paper and pen, create three columns as shown below. Brainstorm a list of traits under each heading. (Also see the Venn diagram on page **46**.)

    Traits of Subject #1   *Shared Traits*   *Traits of Subject #2*

3. **Gather information.** Review your list of traits, highlighting those that could provide insight into one or both subjects. Research the subjects, using hands-on analysis when possible. Consider writing your research notes in the three-column format shown above.

4. **Draft a working thesis.** Review your expanded list of traits and eliminate those that now seem unimportant. Write a sentence stating the core of what you learned about the subjects and whether you are comparing, contrasting, or both. If you're stuck, try completing the sentence below. (Switch around the terms "similar" and "different" if you wish to stress similarities.)

    While _____ and _____ seem similar, they are different in several ways, and the differences are important because _____ .

5. **Get organized.** Decide how to organize your essay. Generally, *subject by subject* works best for short, simple comparisons. *Trait by trait* works best for longer, more complex comparisons.

Subject by Subject:	Trait by Trait:
Introduction	Introduction
Subject #1	Trait A
• Trait A	• Subject #1
• Trait B	• Subject #2
• Trait C	Trait B
Subject #2	• Subject #1
• Trait A	• Subject #2
• Trait B	Trait C
• Trait C	• Subject #1
	• Subject #2

6. Draft the essay. Review your outline and write your first draft in one sitting if possible. Check your outline for details and integrate them into the text.

Subject-by-subject pattern:
- **Opening**—get readers' attention and introduce the two subjects and thesis.
- **Middle**—describe one "package" of traits representing the first subject and a parallel set of traits representing the second subject.
- **Conclusion**—point out similarities and/or differences, point out their significance, and restate your main point.

Trait-by-trait pattern:
- **Opening**—get readers' attention and introduce the two subjects and thesis.
- **Middle**—compare and/or contrast the two subjects trait by trait (include transitions that help readers look back and forth between the two subjects).
- **Conclusion**—summarize the key relationships, note their significance, and restate your main point.

7. Revise the essay. Check the essay for the following:
- Balanced comparisons and contrasts of comparable traits
- Complete and thoughtful treatment of each subject
- Genuine and objective voice
- Clear, smooth sentences with varied structure
- Title and introduction that spark interest
- Thoughtful, unifying conclusion

8. Get feedback. Ask a classmate or someone in the writing center to read your paper, looking for the following:
- A clear, interesting thesis
- An engaging and informative introduction
- A middle that compares and/or contrasts significant, parallel traits
- Ideas that offer insight into the subject
- A conclusion that restates the main point and unifies the essay

9. Edit your essay. Look for the following:
- Transitions that signal comparisons and link paragraphs: *on the other hand, in contrast, similarly, also, both, even though, in the same way*
- Correct quotations and documentation
- Correct spelling, punctuation, usage, and grammar

10. Publish your essay. Share your writing with others:
- Submit it to your instructor.
- Share it with other students or publish it on a website.

Writing Checklist

Use these six traits to check the quality of your writing, then revise as needed:

___ The **ideas** (points made or conclusions drawn from comparing and contrasting) provide insight into who or what both subjects are and why they are important. The basis for comparison is clear.

___ The **organization** pattern (subject by subject, trait by trait) helps readers grasp the similarities and differences between the subjects.

___ The **voice** is informed, involved, and genuine.

___ The **words** are precise and clear. Technical or scientific terms are defined. Links between subjects are communicated with transitions such as these:
- Although
- Either one
- In contrast
- Neither
- As a result
- For this reason
- In the same way
- On the other hand
- Both
- However
- Likewise
- Therefore

___ The **sentences** are clear, well-reasoned, varied in structure, and smooth.

___ The copy is **correct**, clean, and properly formatted. Graphics such as photos or drawings are clear and well-placed.

Writing Activities

Writing Prompt

1. In "A Fear Born of Sorrow," the writer analyzes the effects of the September 11 attacks by comparing and contrasting them with other historical attacks. Identify key people or events in the news this week. Choose a current events topic and explain its significance by comparing and/or contrasting it with one or more parallel topics from history.

2. Review the way in which Mark Twain makes a point in "Two Views of the River" by comparing and contrasting two perspectives of the Mississippi River. Revise or draft a passage of your own in which you use comparison and contrast to emphasize a point.

3. Review Gelareh Asayesh's article "Shrouded in Contradiction," noting how she uses comparison/contrast strategies in order to take a position. Draft or revise an essay in which you use comparison/contrast to develop or support a position.

4. In "Like Mexicans," Gary Soto compares two ethnic groups who are part of his family. List related pairs that are part of your life (siblings, uncles, homes, family conflicts, educational experiences, teachers, neighbors, and so on). Choose a topic that you and your readers would find interesting. Write an essay in which you compare and/or contrast the subjects to gain insight into your life.

Chapter 14
Classification

Classification is an organizational strategy that helps writers make sense of large or complex sets of things. A writer who is using this strategy looks at a topic and then breaks it into components that can be sorted into clearly distinguishable subgroups. For example, if writing about the types of residents who live in assisted-care facilities, a nursing student might classify possible residents according to various physical and/or mental limitations.

By sorting the residents in this way, the writer can discuss them as individuals, as representatives of a subgroup, or as members of the group as a whole. By using an additional strategy such as compare/contrast, he or she can show both similarities and differences between one subgroup and another, or between individuals within a subgroup. By using classification, the writer helps readers understand both individual components of the topic and relationships among the components.

For help as you write a classification essay, read the instructions and models in this chapter.

What's Ahead

- Overview: Writing a Classification Essay
  - Student Model
  - Professional Models
- Guidelines
- Writing Checklist and Activities

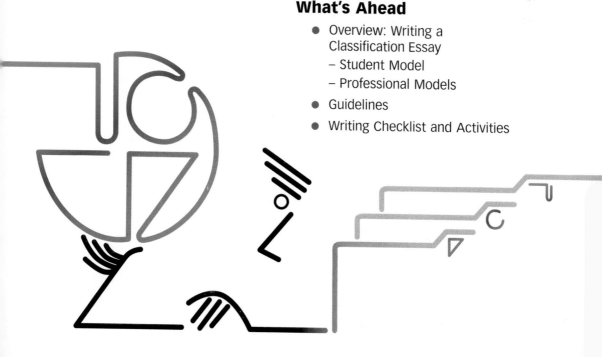

Web Link

Overview
Writing a Classification Essay

Writer's Goal

Your goal is to divide a group of people, places, things, or concepts into subgroups, and then to write an essay that helps readers understand each component, the subgroups, and the topic as a whole.

Keys for Success

Choose classification criteria that fit the topic. ■ Use classification criteria to distinguish one subgroup from another. For example, to explain her family's experience with cancer, student writer Kim Brouwer examines three types of cancer (*type* is a basis for classification). Because cancer is a complex illness, grouping by type fits her subject (see "Three Family Cancers," pages **205–207**).

Choose classification criteria that fit your purpose. ■ Use criteria that help you achieve your goal. For example, Ann Hodgman wants to assess the quality of dog-food products (her purpose). To achieve this goal, she measures their color, texture, taste, smell, and nutritional value—suitable criteria for assessing levels of quality (see "No Wonder They Call . . ." pages **210–213**).

Follow classification principles. ■ Sort items into subgroups according to the following principles:

- **Consistency:** Use the same criteria in the same way when deciding which individual items to place in which subgroups. For example, Hodgman measures the quality of all dog-food products with the same criteria: color, taste, and so on.
- **Exclusivity:** Establish distinct subgroups so that each one differs from the others. For example, in "Three Family Cancers," the writer explains three distinct—or exclusive—types of cancer. Although the three types share some traits, each type is distinct.

Topics to Consider

To choose a topic, start by writing a half-dozen general headings like the academic headings below; then list two or three related topics under each heading. Finally, pick a topic that can best be explained by breaking it into subgroups.

Engineering	Biology	Social Work	Education
• Machines	• Whales	• Child welfare	• Learning styles
• Bridges	• Fruits	• Organizations	• Testing methods

Next Step Read the model essays and do the activities that follow. As you read, note how the classification strategy helps writers address complex topics.

Classification

In the essay below, Kim Brouwer reports on her family's experience with cancer. To do so, she distinguishes three types of cancer, each of which caused the death of one of her grandparents.

Three Family Cancers

> The writer introduces the topic with an anecdote.

One day back in fourth grade, my teacher said, "Use your imagination and make an invention—something new and useful." I grumped all the way home from school. An invention? For what, I thought. What could I invent that we could use? "What about a cure for cancer?" Mom asked. *1*

A few weeks earlier my family had learned that Grandpa DeRonde had cancer, so I went to work imagining my very own miracle cure. I drew a picture of a medicine bottle, similar to a bottle of cough syrup, with a drop of liquid coming out of it. I called my masterpiece, "The Cure for Cancer." *2*

> She gives her criterion for classifying ("different forms") and identifies subgroups.

I can remember those school days pretty well, but I can't say the same for three of my grandparents—Grandma and Grandpa DeRonde and Grandpa Vernooy. Before I could grow up and get to know them, their lives were invaded, taken over, and destroyed by different forms of cancer—multiple myeloma, prostate cancer, and lung cancer. Now, years later, I am a college freshman, faced with another assignment that gives me a chance to think about cancer: What is it, and what causes it? And what were these illnesses like for my grandparents? To get some answers, I checked out some research on cancer and talked with my mother. *3*

> She explains what all forms of cancer have in common.

Cancer, as my family learned firsthand, is a serious killer. In fact, it's the second leading cause of death in the United States. Each year, the disease kills about 500,000 Americans, and doctors discover more than one million new cases (Microsoft Encarta). Cancer is so powerful because it's not one illness, but rather many diseases attacking many parts of the body. All cancers are basically body cells gone crazy—cells that develop abnormally. These cells then clone themselves using an enzyme called telomerase. As they multiply like creatures in a sci-fi horror movie, the cells build into tumors, which are tissues that can "invade and destroy other tissues" (Microsoft Encarta). *4*

> The writer categorizes carcinogens.

Researchers aren't exactly sure what triggers these cancerous growths, but they think that 80 percent of cancers happen because people come into regular contact with carcinogens—cancer-causing agents. Carcinogens are classified into three groups: chemicals, radiation, and viruses (Compton's). People can be exposed to these carcinogens in many ways and situations. One study showed that 5 percent of cancers could be traced to environmental pollution, including carcinogens in the workplace. *5*

Radiation, for example, devastated the population of Chernobyl, Russia, after the nuclear power plant meltdown. But carcinogens don't cause cancer overnight—even from exposure in a terrible accident. The cancer may take 30 to 40 years to develop (Compton's).

She describes the first subgroup.

I don't know what carcinogens attacked my Grandma DeRonde, but I do know the result: She developed multiple myeloma. For a multiple-myeloma patient, the average period of survival is 20 months to 10 years (Madden 108). When I talked with my mother, she said that my family doesn't really know when Grandma came down with multiple myeloma, but she lived for two years after learning that she had it. For two years, she suffered through radiation and chemotherapy treatments, and life seemed measured by the spaces between appointments to check her white blood cell count.   6

She gives distinguishing details.

What causes multiple myeloma remains a mystery, though its effects are well known. This cancer involves a malignant growth of cells in the bone marrow that makes holes in the skeleton. The holes develop mostly in the ribs, vertebrae, and pelvis. Because the holes make the bones brittle, the victim cannot do simple things like driving and cooking. In the end, patients fracture bones and die from infection and pneumonia (Madden 108). It was this weakening of the bones, along with the chemotherapy treatments, that made my grandmother suffer.   7

She describes the second subgroup.

My Grandpa DeRonde was diagnosed with prostate cancer several years after my grandma died. The doctors began radiation therapy right away, and my family was hopeful because the cancer was caught in its early stages. At first, the cancer seemed to go into remission, but cancer cells were actually invading other sites in his body. Because the cancer spread, the doctors couldn't treat all of it through radiation or surgery. Grandpa lived for only two years after learning he was ill, and during that time he had many chemotherapy treatments and spent a lot of time in the hospital. On his death certificate, the doctor wrote that Grandpa died of cardiac arrest and carcinoma of the lung, with metastasis.   8

Like multiple myeloma, prostate cancer is a powerful killer. Even though many technological changes help doctors catch this cancer at an early stage, the number of deaths per year is still going up. Prostate cancer is the second most common cancer in the United States, and experts believe that it can be found in about 25 million men over the age of 50 (Fintor).   9

Prostate cancer is a tumor (called a carcinoma) lining the inside of the prostate gland. Many factors trigger this form of cancer: age, diet, environmental conditions, or maybe just having a cancer-prone family ("Prostate Cancer Trends" 183). A survey of more than 51,000 American men showed that eating a lot of fat, found mostly in red meat, can lead to advanced prostate cancer. On the other hand, researchers concluded that   10 fats from vegetables, fish, and many dairy products are probably not linked to the growth of a carcinoma (Cowley 77).

She describes the third subgroup.

My second grandfather died from a different carcinoma—lung cancer. *11* Doctors found a tumor in the lower lobe of Grandpa Vernooy's right lung, recommended surgery, and removed the lung. The next winter, he weakened, got pneumonia, and died. His doctors believed that his smoking habit caused the cancer. Smoking, in fact, remains the most important factor in developing lung cancer ("Family Ties" 109). The truth is that cigarette smoking causes almost half of all cancer cases, even though only one out of ten smokers actually comes down with this disease (Compton's).

She cites distinguishing details.

One study concluded that genetics may play a role in whether a person *12* develops lung cancer. Research suggests that if a person is missing positive genes called tumor-suppressor genes, it's bad news. If these genes weren't inherited, or if smoking destroyed them, then cancer-related genes are free to do their damage (Edwards 358). Another study identified a special gene that is inherited from one or both parents and that metabolizes chemicals from cigarette smoke. In this case, if the gene is there, the cancer risk goes up, especially for smokers ("Family Ties" 109).

She closes by reviewing the subgroups and reflecting on the opening anecdote.

I still wish I could cure cancer with a magic miracle liquid in a *13* medicine bottle. But today I understand that cancer is a complicated disease. My grandparents died from three types of the disease—multiple myeloma, prostate cancer, and lung cancer. If it hadn't been for cancerous tumors taking over their bodies, my grandparents might still be alive, and I'd have many more memories of them. Maybe I'd even be sharing with them stories about my first year at college. On the other hand, perhaps this paper is a cure of a different type—while it can't change what happened, it can help me understand it. ■

Note: The Works Cited page is not shown. For sample pages, see MLA (pages **534–535**) and APA (page **564**).

Writing Prompt

Reading for Better Writing

1. The writer opens and closes the essay with a personal anecdote. Explain why this story does or does not strengthen the essay.

2. For each subgroup (type of cancer), the writer uses a grandparent as an example. Explain how her use of examples does or does not help clarify the subject.

3. Where in the essay does the writer compare and contrast different forms of cancer? Is the comparison and contrast effective? Why or why not?

4. Writing about a scientific topic like cancer nearly always requires technical terminology. Cite two such terms used in this essay, and explain how the writer clarifies each term's meaning.

Classification

In this essay John Van Rys, a college professor, classifies four basic approaches to literary criticism. His essay is intended to help college freshmen interpret literature.

Four Ways to Talk About Literature

The writer introduces the topic and criterion for creating four subgroups.

Have you ever been in a conversation where you suddenly felt lost—out of the loop? Perhaps you feel that way in your literature class. You may think a poem or short story means one thing, and then your instructor suddenly pulls out the "hidden meaning." Joining the conversation about literature—in class or in an essay—may indeed seem daunting, but you can do it if you know what to look for and what to talk about. There are four main perspectives, or approaches, that you can use to converse about literature.

He describes the first subgroup and gives an example.

Text-centered approaches focus on the literary piece itself. Often called *formalist criticism,* such approaches claim that the structure of a work and the rules of its genre are crucial to its meaning. The formalist critic determines how various elements (plot, character, language, and so on) reinforce the meaning and unify the work. For example, the formalist may ask the following questions concerning Robert Browning's poem "My Last Duchess": How do the main elements in the poem—irony, symbolism, and verse form—help develop the main theme (deception)? How does Browning use the dramatic monologue genre in this poem?

He describes the second subgroup and gives an example.

Audience-centered approaches focus on the "transaction" between text and reader—the dynamic way the reader interacts with the text. Often called *rhetorical* or *reader-response criticism,* these approaches see the text not as an object to be analyzed, but as an activity that is different for each reader. A reader-response critic might ask these questions of "My Last Duchess": How does the reader become aware of the duke's true nature if it's never actually stated? Do men and women read the poem differently? Who were Browning's original readers?

He describes the third subgroup and gives examples.

Author-centered approaches focus on the origins of a text (the writer and the historical background). For example, an author-centered study examines the writer's life—showing connections, contrasts, and conflicts between his or her life and the writing. Broader historical studies explore social and intellectual currents, showing links between an author's work and the ideas, events, and institutions of that period. Finally, the literary historian may make connections between the text in question and earlier and later literary works. The author-centered critic might ask these questions of "My Last Duchess": What were Browning's views of marriage, men and women, art, class, and wealth? As an institution, what was marriage like in Victorian England (Browning's era) or Renaissance Italy (the duke's era)? Who was the historical Duke of Ferrara?

He describes the fourth approach and gives examples of each subgroup in it.

The fourth approach to criticism applies ideas outside of literature to literary works. Because literature mirrors life, argue these critics, disciplines that explore human life can help us understand literature. Some critics, for example, apply psychological theories to literary works by exploring dreams, symbolic meanings, and motivation. Myth or archetype criticism uses insights from psychology, cultural anthropology, and classical studies to explore a text's universal appeal. Moral criticism, rooted in religious studies and ethics, explores the moral dilemmas literary works raise. Marxist, feminist, and minority criticism are, broadly speaking, sociological approaches to interpretation. While the Marxist examines the themes of class struggle, economic power, and social justice in texts, the feminist critic explores the just and unjust treatment of women as well as the effect of gender on language, reading, and the literary canon. The critic interested in race and ethnic identity explores similar issues, with the focus shifted to a specific cultural group.

5

He cites sample questions.

Such ideological criticism might ask a wide variety of questions about "My Last Duchess": What does the poem reveal about the duke's psychological state and his personality? How does the reference to Neptune deepen the poem? What does the poem suggest about the nature of evil and injustice? In what ways are the duke's motives class-based and economic? How does the poem present the duke's power and the duchess's weakness? What is the status of women in this society?

6

The closing presents qualities shared by all four approaches.

If you look at the variety of questions critics might ask about "My Last Duchess," you see both the diversity of critical approaches and the common ground between them. In fact, interpretive methods actually share important characteristics: (1) a close attention to literary elements such as character, plot, symbolism, and metaphor; (2) a desire not to distort the work; and (3) a sincere concern for increasing interest and understanding in a text. In actual practice, critics may develop a hybrid approach to criticism, one that matches their individual questions and concerns about a text. Now that you're familiar with some of the questions defining literary criticism, exercise your own curiosity (and join the ongoing literary dialogue) by discussing a text that genuinely interests you. ■

7

Writing Prompt

Reading for Better Writing

1. Explain how the writer introduces the subject and attempts to engage the reader. Is this strategy effective? Why or why not?

2. The writer uses one poem to illustrate how each of the four critical approaches works. Explain why this strategy is or is not effective.

3. Review the last paragraph and explain why it does or does not unify the essay.

Classification

This piece was first printed in *Spy* magazine, which ceased publication in 1998. In its time, the magazine was known for pieces that were both humorous and research based. Ann Hodgman was a food editor for *Spy*.

No Wonder They Call Me a Bitch

The writer previews the questions answered in the essay.

I've always wondered about dog food. Is a Gaines-burger really like a hamburger? Can you fry it? Does dog food "cheese" taste like real cheese? Does Gravy Train actually make gravy in the dog's bowl, or is that brown liquid just dissolved crumbs? And exactly what *are* by-products? 1

Having spent the better part of a week eating dog food, I'm sorry to say that I now know the answers to these questions. While my dachshund, Shortie, watched in agonies of yearning, I gagged my way through can after can of stinky, white-flecked mush and bag after bag of stinky, fat-drenched nuggets. And now I understand exactly why Shortie's breath is so bad. 2

Of course, Gaines-burgers are neither mush nor nuggets. They are, rather, a miracle of beauty and packaging—or at least that's what I thought when I was little. I used to beg my mother to get them for our dogs, but she always said they were too expensive. When I finally bought a box of cheese-flavored Gaines-burgers—after 20 years of longing—I felt deliciously wicked. 3

The writer includes quotes from printed texts.

"Dogs love real beef," the back of the box proclaimed proudly. "That's why Gaines-burgers is the only beef burger for dogs with real beef and no meat by-products!" The copy was accurate: meat by-products did not appear in the list of ingredients. Poultry by-products did, though—right there next to preserved animal fat. 4

Quotes from interviews are also included.

One Purina spokesman told me that poultry by-products consist of necks, intestines, undeveloped eggs and other "carcass remnants," but not feathers, heads or feet. When I told him I'd been eating dog food, he said, "Oh, you're kidding! Oh no!" (I came to share his alarm when, weeks later, a second Purina spokesman said that Gaines-burgers *do* contain poultry heads and feet—but *not* undeveloped eggs). 5

Up close my Gaines-burger didn't much resemble chopped beef. Rather, it looked—and felt—like a single long, extruded piece of redness that had been chopped into segments and formed into a patty. You could make one at home if you had a Play-Doh Fun Factory. 6

The writer includes descriptions based on careful observation.

I turned on the skillet. While I waited for it to heat up I pulled out a shred of cheese-colored material and palpated it. Again, like Play-Doh, it was quite malleable. I made a little cheese bird out of it; then I counted to three and ate the bird. 7

There was a horrifying rush of cheddar taste, followed immediately by the dull tang of soybean flour—the main ingredient in Gaines-burgers. Next I tried a piece of red extrusion. The main difference between the meat- 8 flavored and cheese-flavored extrusions is one of texture. The "cheese" chews like fresh Play-Doh, whereas the "meat" chews like Play-Doh that's been sitting out on a rug for a couple of hours.

The transition sentence connects discussion of two categories.

Frying only turned the Gaines-burger black. There was no melting, no sizzling, no warm meat smells. A cherished childhood illusion was gone. I flipped the patty into the sink, where it immediately began leaking rivulets of red dye.

As alarming as the Gaines-burgers were, their soy meal began to seem like an old friend when the time came to try some *canned* dog foods. I decided to try the Cycle foods first. When I opened them, I thought about how rarely I use can openers these days, and I was suddenly visited by a long-forgotten sensation of can-opener distaste. *This* is the kind of unsavory place can openers spend their time when you're not watching! Every time you open a can of, say, Italian plum tomatoes, you infect them with invisible particles of by-product.

I had been expecting to see the usual homogeneous scrapple inside, but each can of Cycle was packed with smooth, round, oily nuggets. As if someone at Gaines had been tipped off that a human would be tasting the stuff, the four Cycles really were different from one another. Cycle-1, for puppies, is wet and soyish, Cycle-2, for adults, glistens nastily with fat, but it's passably edible—a lot like some canned Swedish meatballs I once got in a care package at college. Cycle-3, the "lite" one, for fatties, had no specific flavor, it just tasted like dog food. But at least it didn't make me fat.

The writer describes the same features for each product within the canned-food category.

Cycle-4, for senior dogs, had the smallest nuggets. Maybe old dogs can't open their mouths as wide. This kind was far sweeter than the other three Cycles—almost like baked beans. It was also the only one to contain "dried beef digest," a mysterious substance that the Purina spokesman defined as "enzymes" and my dictionary defined as "the products of digestion."

Next on the menu was a can of Kal-Kan Pedigree with Chunky Chicken. Chunky chicken? There were chunks in the can, certainly—big, purplish-brown chunks. I forked one chunk out (by now I was becoming more callous) and found that while it had no discernible chicken flavor, it wasn't bad except for its texture—like meat loaf with ground-up chicken bones.

In the world of canned dog food, a smooth consistency is a sign of low quality—lots of cereal. A lumpy, frightening, bloody, stringy horror is a sign of high quality—lots of meat. Nowhere in the world of wet dog foods was this demonstrated better than in the fanciest I tried—Kal Kan's Pedigree Select Dinners. These came not in a can but in a tiny foil packet with a picture of an imperious Yorkie. When I pulled open the container, juice spurted all over my hand, and the first chunk I speared was trailing a long gray vein. I shrieked and went instead for a plain chunk, which I was able to swallow only after taking a break to read some suddenly fascinating office equipment catalogs. Once again, though, it tasted no more alarming than, say, canned hash.

Still, how pleasant it was to turn to *dry* dog food! Gravy Train was the first I tried, and I'm happy to report that it really does make a "thick, rich, real beef gravy" when you mix it with water. Thick and rich, anyway. Except for a lingering rancid-fat flavor, the gravy wasn't beefy, but since it tasted primarily like tap water, it wasn't nauseating either.   15

My poor dachshund just gets plain old Purina Dog Chow, but Purina also makes a dry food called Butcher's Blend that comes in Beef, Bacon & Chicken flavor. Here we see dog food's arcane semiotics at its best: a red triangle with a *T* stamped into it is supposed to suggest beef; a tan curl, chicken; and a brown *S*, a piece of bacon. Only dogs understand these messages. But Butcher's Blend does have an endearing slogan: "Great Meaty Tastes—without bothering the Butcher!" *You know, I wanted go buy some meat, but I just couldn't bring myself to bother the butcher. . . .*   16

Purina O.N.E. ("Optimum Nutritional Effectiveness") is targeted at people who are unlikely ever to worry about bothering a tradesperson. "We chose chicken as a primary ingredient in Purina O.N.E. for several reasonings," the long, long essay on the back of the bag announces. Chief among these reasonings, I'd guess, is the fact that chicken appeals to people who are—you know—*like us*. Although our dogs do nothing but spend 18-hour days alone in the apartment, we still want them to be *premium* dogs. We want them to cut down on red meat, too. We also want dog food that comes in a bag with an attractive design, a subtle typeface and no kitschy pictures of slobbering golden retrievers.   17

Besides that, we want a list of the Nutritional Benefits of our dog food—and we get it on O.N.E. One thing I especially like about this list is its constant references to a dog's "hair coat," as in "Beef tallow is good for the dog's skin and hair coat." (On the other hand, beef tallow merely provides palatability, while the dried beef digest in Cycle provides palatability *enhancement*.)   18

I hate to say it, but O.N.E. was pretty palatable. Maybe that's because it has about 100 percent more fat than, say, Butcher's Blend. Or maybe I'd been duped by the packaging; that's been known to happen before.   19

As with people food, dog snacks taste much better than dog meals. They're better-looking, too. Take Milk-Bone Flavor Snacks. The loving-hands-at-home prose describing each flavor is colorful; the writers practically choke on their own exuberance. Of bacon they say, "It's so good, your dog will think it's hot off the frying pan." Of liver: "The only taste your dog wants more than liver—is even more liver!" Of poultry: "All those farm fresh flavors deliciously mixed in one biscuit. Your dog will bark with delight!" And of vegetable: "Gardens of taste! Specially blended to give your dog that vegetable flavor he wants—but can rarely get!"   20

The phrase *turn to* marks a transition to another category.

Italics are used here to indicate unspoken thoughts.

The writer mentions both dog meals and snacks in the same sentence to signal her transition to another category.

Well, I may be a sucker, but advertising *this* emphatic just doesn't convince me. I lined up all seven flavors of Milk-Bone Flavor Snacks on the floor. Unless my dog's palate is a lot more sensitive than mine—and considering that she steals dirty diapers out of the trash and eats them, I'm loath to think it is—she doesn't detect any more difference in the seven flavors than I did when I tried them. 21

I much preferred Bonz, the hard-baked, bone-shaped snack stuffed with simulated marrow. I liked the bone part, that is; it tasted almost exactly like the cornmeal it was made of. The mock-marrow inside was a bit more problematic: in addition to looking like the sludge that collects in the treads of my running shoes, it was bursting with tiny hairs. 22

I'm sure you have a few dog food questions of your own. To save us time, I've answered them in advance. 23

> The question-and-answer format deals with this information quickly.

Q. *Are those little cans of Mighty Dog actually branded with the sizzling word* **BEEF**, *the way they show in the commercials?* 24

A. You should know by now that that kind of thing never happens. 25

Q. *Does chicken-flavored dog food taste like chicken-flavored cat food?* 26

A. To my surprise, chicken cat food was actually a little better—more chickeny. It tasted like inferior canned pâté. 27

Q. *Was there any dog food that you just couldn't bring yourself to try?* 28

A. Alas, it was a can of Mighty Dog called Prime Entree with Bone Marrow. The meat was dark, dark brown, and it was surrounded by gelatin that was almost black. I knew I would die if I tasted it, so I put it outside for the raccoons. ■ 29

Writing Prompt

Reading for Better Writing

1. Why does Hodgman claim to taste-test dog food and then report on her findings in writing, and how do you know? Can you think of other texts written for similar purposes?

2. What criteria does Hodgman use to divide her subject into categories? Where and how does she indicate that she is shifting her discussion from one category to the next?

3. The title grabs our attention with the word *bitch*, a word rarely used in titles. Does the word use serve additional purposes?

4. This piece is based on primary-source research. Review Chapter 30, "Conducting Primary and Library Research," especially the portion on conducting primary research. What other research strategies could the author have used to explore her topic? Which would be most effective for her *Spy* audience? How would she need to change her tactics if her audience were a scientific journal? A magazine for dog enthusiasts?

Guidelines
Writing a Classification Essay

1. **Select a topic.** Review the list of headings and topics that you developed in response to "Topics to Consider" on page **204**. Choose a topic that you find interesting and can explain well using classification strategies. If you need more choices, develop a new list of headings and topics.

2. **Look at the big picture.** Conduct preliminary research to get an overview of your topic. Review your purpose (to explain, persuade, inform, and so on), and consider which classification criteria will help you divide the subject into distinct, understandable subgroups.

3. **Choose and test your criterion.** Choose a criterion for creating subgroups. Make sure it produces subgroups that are consistent (all members fit the criterion), exclusive (subgroups are distinct—no member of the group fits into more than one subgroup), and complete (each member fits into a subgroup with no member left over).

   TIP: To better visualize how you are dividing your topic and classifying its members, take a few minutes to fill out a graphic organizer like the one shown below. (Also see the graphic organizer on page **46**.)

4. **Gather and organize information.** Gather information from library and web resources, as well as interviews. To take notes and organize your information, consider using a classification grid like the one shown below. Set up the grid by listing the classification criteria down the left column and listing the subgroups in the top row of the columns. Then fill in the grid with appropriate details. (The following grid lists the classification criterion and subgroups used in "Four Ways to Talk About Literature," pages **208–209**.)

Classification Criteria	Subgroup #1	Subgroup #2	Subgroup #3	Subgroup #4
	Text-centered approach	*Audience-centered approach*	*Author-centered approach*	*Ideas outside literature*
Focus of the critical approach	• Trait #1 • Trait #2 • Trait #3	• Trait #1 • Trait #2 • Trait #3	• Trait #1 • Trait #2 • Trait #3	• Trait #1 • Trait #2 • Trait #3

   Note: If you do not use a grid similar to this one, construct an outline to help organize your thoughts.

5. **Draft a thesis.** Draft a working thesis (you can revise it later as needed) that states your topic and main point. Include language introducing your criteria for classifying subgroups.

6. **Draft the essay.** Write your first draft, using either the organizational pattern in the classification grid or an outline.

   Opening: Get the readers' attention, introduce the subject and thesis, and give your criteria for dividing the subject into subgroups.

   Middle: Develop the thesis by discussing each subgroup, explaining its traits, and showing how it is distinct from the other subgroups. For example, in the middle section of "Four Ways to Talk About Literature," the writer first shows the unique focus of each of the four approaches to literary criticism, and then illustrates each approach by applying it to the same poem, "My Last Duchess."

   Closing: While the opening and middle of the essay separate the subject into components and subgroups, the closing brings the components and subgroups back together. For example, in "Four Ways to Talk About Literature," the writer closes by identifying three characteristics that the four subgroups have in common (see page 208–209).

7. **Get feedback.** Ask a classmate or someone from the writing center to read your essay, looking for the following:

   - An engaging opening that introduces the subject, thesis, and criteria for classification
   - A well-organized middle that distinguishes subgroups, shows why each subgroup is unique, and includes adequate details
   - A clear closing that reaches some sort of conclusion

8. **Revise the essay.** Check the essay for the following:

   - Subgroups that are consistent, exclusive, and complete
   - Organization that helps the reader understand the subject
   - Appropriate examples that clarify the nature and function of each subgroup
   - A unifying conclusion

9. **Edit the essay.** Check for the following:

   - An informed, reader-friendly voice
   - Clear, complete sentences
   - Unified paragraphs linked with appropriate transitions
   - Correct usage, grammar, punctuation, and spelling

10. **Publish the essay.** Share your writing by doing the following:

    - Offer copies to classmates and friends.
    - Publish it in a journal or on a website.
    - Place a copy in your professional portfolio.

Writing Checklist

Use these six traits to check the quality of your writing, then revise as needed:

____ The **ideas** in the classification criteria are logical and clear. The criteria result in subgroups that are consistent, exclusive, and complete.

____ The **organization** of the essay helps the reader understand the components, the subgroups, and the subject as a whole. Paragraphs form cohesive units of thought.

____ The **voice** is informed, courteous, and professional.

____ The **words** are precise, descriptive, and appropriate for the subject. Terms used in classifications are employed in the same way throughout the essay.

____ The **sentences** are complete, varied, and easy to read. Appropriate transitions link sentences and paragraphs.

____ The finished copy is **correct** and follows documentation and formatting rules.

Writing Prompt

Writing Activities

1. Kim Brouwer wrote "Three Family Cancers" to better understand a series of painful experiences in her family's life. List painful (or pleasant) experiences in your family's life, and select a topic that you can clarify by classifying. Write an essay using classification strategies that explain the topic.

2. "Four Ways to Talk About Literature" examines four approaches to reading and understanding a piece of literature. Identify a similar group of approaches to analysis or problem solving in your program or major. Write an essay in which you break your topic into subgroups, sort the subgroups, and explain the topic to the reader.

3. Review the ways in which Ann Hodgman incorporates primary-source research into her essay, "No Wonder They Call Me a Bitch." Employ this strategy in your draft or revision of an essay.

4. Develop a list of social, economic, or political topics in the news. Choose one, research it, classify its components, and then write an essay that explains the topic.

Chapter 15
Process Writing

Process writing is practical writing that answers the kinds of questions we face every day at home, in college, or on the job: "How do I remove these ugly stains?" or "How does cancer spread?" or "How do I install this software?" Writing that answers these types of questions analyzes the process in which we're interested, breaks it down into steps, and shows how the process works.

The three basic forms of process writing include *describing* a process, *explaining* a process, and giving *instructions*. This chapter distinguishes among these forms and shows how to write each. In addition, the chapter includes models of how writers have used the forms to accomplish their writing goals.

Study this chapter for tips that will help you choose a topic, break it into steps, and explain it clearly in writing.

What's Ahead

- Overview: Writing About a Process
  - Student Model
  - Professional Models
- Guidelines
- Writing Checklist and Activities

Overview
Writing About a Process

Writer's Goal

Your goal is to analyze a process, break it into specific steps, and write about it using one of the following forms: a *description* of a process, an *explanation* of the process, or *instructions* on how to carry out the process.

Keys for Success

Think logically. ■ To write one of these forms, you must study the process until you understand it, and then write clearly about it. In other words, you must know—and show—how each step leads *logically* to the next, and how all the steps together complete the process.

Know your purpose and your audience. ■ Decide what your writing should do and choose the form that fits your purpose and audience:

● To inform a broad audience how something happens naturally, *describe* the process in an essay that tells how the process unfolds: e.g., how cancer cells multiply (pages **219–220**) or how hair grows (pages **222–223**).

● To help readers who want to know how something is done or made, *explain* the process in an essay that tells how someone would complete each step: e.g., how to deal with campus racism (pages **224–227**).

● To help readers who wish to perform the process themselves, provide how-to information in brief, clear *instructions*: e.g., how to download photos onto your computer (page **221**).

Note: While descriptions and explanations are usually formatted as essays, instructions are formatted somewhat differently. Instructions include a summary of the process, a list of materials and tools, and a numbered list of steps organized chronologically and stated using clear, imperative verbs.

Consider *all* of your readers. ■ Regardless of the form that you choose, make your writing accessible to all of your readers by addressing the reader who knows the least about your topic. Include all the information that this person needs to have, and use language that everyone can understand.

Topics to Consider

● A course-related process
● A process in the news
● A process that keeps you healthy
● A process that helps you get a job
● A process that you've mastered
● A process in your planned occupation

Next Step Read the model essays and perform the activities that follow. As you read, observe how each writer approaches the task of explaining, describing, or instructing.

Process: Description

Student writer Kerri Mertz wrote this essay to help nonscientists understand how cancer cells multiply and affect the body.

Audio

Wayward Cells

The writer uses the title and an analogy to introduce the topic.

Imagine a room containing a large group of people all working hard toward the same goal. Each person knows his or her job, does it carefully, and cooperates with other group members. Together, they function efficiently and smoothly—like a well-oiled machine.

Then something goes wrong. One guy suddenly drops his task, steps into another person's workstation, grabs the material that she's working with, and begins something very different—he uses the material to make little reproductions of himself, thousands of them. These look-alikes imitate him—grabbing material and making reproductions of themselves. Soon the bunch gets so big that they spill into other people's workstations, getting in their way, and interrupting their work. As the number of look-alikes grows, the work group's activity slows, stutters, and finally stops.

She uses a simile to explain the analogy.

A human body is like this room, and the body's cells are like these workers. If the body is healthy, each cell has a necessary job and does it correctly. For example, right now red blood cells are running throughout your body carrying oxygen to each body part. Other cells are digesting that steak sandwich that you had for lunch, and others are patching up that cut on your left hand. Each cell knows what to do because its genetic code—or DNA—tells it what to do. When a cell begins to function abnormally, it can initiate a process that results in cancer.

She describes the first step in the process and cites a potential cause.

The problem starts when one cell "forgets" what it should do. Scientists call this "undifferentiating"—meaning that the cell loses its identity within the body (Pierce 75). Just like the guy in the group who decided to do his own thing, the cell forgets its job. Why this happens is somewhat unclear. The problem could be caused by a defect in the cell's DNA code or by something in the environment, such as cigarette smoke or asbestos (German 21). Causes from inside the body are called genetic, whereas causes from outside the body are called carcinogens, meaning "any substance that causes cancer" (Neufeldt and Sparks 90). In either case, an undifferentiated cell can disrupt the function of healthy cells in two ways: by not doing its job as specified in its DNA and by not reproducing at the rate noted in its DNA.

She describes the next step and its result.

Most healthy cells reproduce rather quickly, but their reproduction rate is controlled. For example, your blood cells completely die off and replace themselves within a matter of weeks, but existing cells make only as many new cells as the body needs. The DNA codes in healthy cells tell them how many new cells to produce. However, cancer cells don't have this control, so they reproduce quickly with no stopping point, a characteristic called "autonomy" (Braun 3). What's more, all their "offspring" have the same qualities as their messed-up parent, and the resulting overpopulation produces growths called tumors.

| She describes the third step— how tumors damage the body.

Tumor cells can hurt the body in a number of ways. First, a tumor can grow so big that it takes up space needed by other organs. Second, some cells may detach from the original tumor and spread throughout the body, creating new tumors elsewhere. This happens with lymphatic cancer—a cancer that's hard to control because it spreads so quickly. A third way that tumor cells can hurt the body is by doing work not called for in their DNA. For example, a gland cell's DNA code may tell the cell to produce a necessary hormone in the endocrine system. However, if cancer damages or distorts that code, sick cells may produce more of the hormone than the body can use—or even tolerate (Braun 4). Cancer cells seem to have minds of their own, and this is why cancer is such a serious disease.

6

| A transition signals a shift in focus from the illness to treatments.

Fortunately, there is hope. Scientific research is already helping doctors do amazing things for people suffering with cancer. One treatment that has been used for some time is chemotherapy, or the use of chemicals to kill off all fast-growing cells, including cancer cells. (Unfortunately, chemotherapy can't distinguish between healthy and unhealthy cells, so it may cause negative side effects such as damaging fast-growing hair follicles, resulting in hair loss.) Another common treatment is radiation, or the use of light rays to kill cancer cells. One of the newest and most promising treatments is gene therapy—an effort to identify and treat chromosomes that carry a "wrong code" in their DNA. A treatment like gene therapy is promising because it treats the cause of cancer, not just the effect. Year by year, research is helping doctors better understand what cancer is and how to treat it.

7

| The writer reuses the analogy to review main points.

Much of life involves dealing with problems like wayward workers, broken machines, or dysfunctional organizations. Dealing with wayward cells is just another problem. While the problem is painful and deadly, there is hope. Medical specialists and other scientists are making progress, and some day they will help us win our battle against wayward cells. ■

8

> *Note:* The Works Cited page is not shown. For sample pages, see MLA (pages **534–535**) and APA (page **564**).

Reading for Better Writing

1. Review the opening four-paragraph analogy used to introduce and describe the process. Explain why the analogy is or is not effective.

2. Review the three steps cited by the writer, and note the transitions used to lead into and out of each step. Are the transitions effective?

3. Review the guidelines on page **228** to identify and list traits of a *description* of a process. Explain why this essay does or does not exemplify these traits.

Process: Instructions

These instructions, like those for many technical devices, include both written and visual elements.

Opening
Use a descriptive title. Note or list materials needed.

Downloading Photographs from the MC-150 Digital Camera

Note: MC-150 software must be loaded on your computer to download photographs from the camera.

Middle
Give steps and photos in chronological order.

Add graphics (such as the arrow) to create a quick visual cue.

Boldface words that need special attention.

To show an object's size, use a reference (such as the fingers).

Use only well-focused photographs.

1. Turn your computer on.

2. Plug the camera's USB cable into your computer.

3. Turn the camera's mode dial to the **data transfer setting** (Figure 1).

4. Open the camera's flash-card door and plug the other end of the USB cable into the **camera port** (Figure 2).

Figure 1: Data Transfer Setting

5. Select USB transfer from the camera screen menu. The MC-150 software will then launch on your computer.

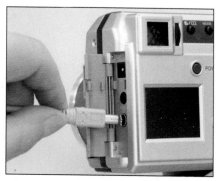

6. Follow the instructions on the computer screen to download all of your photos or specific photos.

Figure 2: Camera Port

Closing
Note common problems that are easily solved.

7. When your download is complete, turn the camera off and unplug the USB cable from the camera and the computer.

Note: If MC-150 software doesn't launch, disconnect the camera (step 7), and then restart the computer and continue on from step 2. ∎

Process: Description

Verne Meyer, an educator and a contributing editor to *The College Writer*, wrote this description of a process to help nonscientists understand how hair grows.

Hair Today, Gone Tomorrow

The writer uses an analogy to introduce the process and distinguish its steps.

Imagine a field of grass covered with two layers of soil: first a layer of clay, and on top of that a layer of rich, black dirt. Then imagine that 100,000 little holes have been poked through the black dirt and into the clay, and at the bottom of each hole lies one grass seed. [1]

Slowly each seed produces a stem that grows up through the clay, out of the dirt, and up toward the sky. Now and then every stem stops for a while, rests, and then starts growing again. At any time about 90 percent of the stems are growing and the others are resting. Because the field gets shaggy, sometimes a gardener comes along and cuts the grass. [2]

He explains the analogy.

Your skull is like that field of grass, and your scalp (common skin) is like the two layers of soil. The top layer of the scalp is the epidermis, and the bottom layer is the dermis. About 100,000 tiny holes (called follicles) extend through the epidermis into the dermis. [3]

An illustration shows parts of a hair stem.

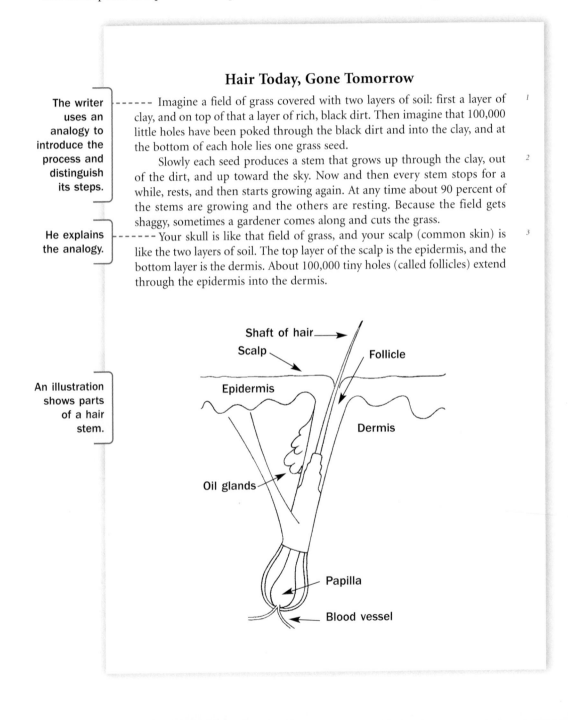

Shaft of hair
Scalp
Follicle
Epidermis
Dermis
Oil glands
Papilla
Blood vessel

The writer explains steps analogous to those in the illustration.

At the base of each follicle lies a seed-like thing called a papilla. At the bottom of the papilla, a small blood vessel drops like a root into the dermis. This vessel carries food through the dermis into the papilla, which works like a little factory using the food to build hair cells. As the papilla makes cells, a hair strand grows up through the dermis past an oil gland. The oil gland greases the strand with a coating that keeps the hair soft and moist.

4

When the strand reaches the top of the dermis, it continues up through the epidermis into the open air above. Now and then the papilla stops making new cells, rests awhile, and then goes back to work again.

5

Most of the hairs on your scalp grow about one-half inch each month. If a strand stays healthy, doesn't break off, and no barber snips it, the hair will grow about 25 inches in four years. At that point hair strands turn brittle and fall out. Every day between 25 and 250 hairs fall out of your follicles, but nearly every follicle grows a new one.

6

He closes with a brief summary and humor.

Around the clock, day after day, this process goes on . . . unless your papillas decide to retire. In that case you reach the stage in your life—let's call it "maturity"—that others call "baldness." ■

7

Writing Prompt

Reading for Better Writing

1. The writer uses an analogy to describe the process of how hair grows. List elements of the analogy, along with corresponding elements of the process. Then explain why the analogy is or is not effective.

2. The writer uses an illustration to show parts of a hair stem. Study the illustration and explain why it does or does not help clarify the message.

3. Review the introduction to the essay, noting the author's purpose for writing. Then describe his voice and explain why it does or does not help achieve his purpose.

Process: Explanation

Nikki Giovanni is an acclaimed poet and essayist; you can learn more about her work by visiting her webpage at <http://nikki-giovanni.com/index.shtml>. In this piece, first published in *Essence* in 1991, Giovanni advises African American students on how to succeed in colleges where the majority of students are white.

Campus Racism 101

The title reminds us of the names of college courses.

There is a bumper sticker that reads: *TOO BAD IGNORANCE ISN'T PAINFUL*. I like that. But ignorance is. We just seldom attribute the pain to it or even recognize it when we see it. Like the postcard on my corkboard. It shows a young man in a very hip jacket smoking a cigarette. In the background is a high school with the American flag waving. The caption says: "Too cool for school. Yet too stupid for the real world." Out of the mouth of the young man is a bubble enclosing the words "Maybe I'll start a band." There could be a postcard showing a jock in a uniform saying, "I don't need school. I'm going to the NFL or NBA." Or one showing a young man or woman studying and a group of young people saying, "So you want to be white." Or something equally demeaning. We need to quit it.

> *Where can you go and what can you do that frees you from interacting with the white American mentality?*

The writer raises a question and then provides a list of answers.

I am a professor of English at Virginia Tech. I've been here for four years, though for only two years with academic rank. I am tenured, which means I have a teaching position for life, a rarity on a predominantly white campus. Whether from malice or ignorance, people who think I should be at a predominantly Black institution will ask, "Why are you at Tech?" Because it's here. And so are Black students. But even if Black students weren't here, it's painfully obvious that this nation and this world cannot allow white students to go through higher education without interacting with Blacks in authoritative positions. It is equally clear that predominantly Black colleges cannot accommodate the numbers of Black students who want and need an education.

The series of questions contributes to a conversational tone.

Is it difficult to attend a predominantly white college? Compared with what? Being passed over for promotion because you lack credentials? Being turned down for jobs because you are not college-educated? Joining the armed forces or going to jail because you cannot find an alternative to the streets? Let's have a little perspective here. Where can you go and what can you do that frees you from interacting with the white American mentality? You're going to interact; the only question is, will you be in some control of yourself and your actions, or will you be controlled by others? I'm going to recommend self-control.

Repeated use of *you* also adds to the conversational feel.

What's the difference between prison and college? They both prescribe your behavior for a given period of time. They both allow you to read books and develop your writing. They both give you time alone to think and time with your peers to talk about issues. But four years of prison doesn't give you a passport to greater opportunities. Most likely that time only gives you greater knowledge of how to get back in. Four years of college gives you an opportunity not only to lift yourself but to serve your people effectively. What's the difference when you are called nigger in college from when you are called nigger in prison? In college you can, though I admit with effort, follow procedures to have those students who called you nigger kicked out or suspended. You can bring issues to public attention without risking your life. But mostly, college is and always has been the future. We, neither less nor more than other people, need knowledge. There are discomforts attached to attending predominantly white colleges, though no more so than living in a racist world. Here are some rules to follow that may help:

4

After a paragraph addressed to *you*, the writer shifts to *we*.

Go to class. No matter how you feel. No matter how you think the professor feels about you. It's important to have a consistent presence in the classroom. If nothing else, the professor will know you care enough and are serious enough to be there.

5

Each rule is discussed in a new paragraph and is marked with italics.

Meet your professors. Extend your hand (give a firm handshake) and tell them your name. Ask them what you need to do to make an A. You may never make an A, but you have put them on notice that you are serious about getting good grades.

6

Do assignments on time. Typed or computer-generated. You have the syllabus. Follow it, and turn those papers in. If for some reason you can't complete an assignment on time, let your professor know before it is due and work out a new due date—then meet it.

7

Go back to see your professor. Tell him or her your name again. If an assignment received less than an A, ask why, and find out what you need to do to improve the next assignment.

8

Yes, your professor is busy. So are you. So are your parents who are working to pay or help with your tuition. Ask early what you need to do if you feel you are starting to get into academic trouble. Do not wait until you are failing.

9

The writer anticipates arguments and counters them.

Understand that there will be professors who do not like you; there may even be professors who are racist or sexist or both. You must discriminate among your professors to see who will give you the help you need. You may not simply say, "They are all against me." They aren't. They mostly don't care. Since you are the one who wants to be educated, find the people who want to help.

10

Don't defeat yourself. Cultivate your friends. Know your enemies. You cannot undo hundreds of years of prejudicial thinking. Think for yourself and speak up. Raise your hand in class. Say what you believe no matter how awkward you may think it sounds. You will improve in your articulation and confidence. 11

> *Cultivate your friends. Know your enemies.* 12

Imperative statements begin with verbs, while supporting explanations begin with *you.*

Participate in some campus activity. Join the newspaper staff. Run for office. Join a dorm council. Do something that involves you on campus. You are going to be there for four years, so let your presence be known, if not felt.

You will inevitably run into some white classmates who are troubling because they often say stupid things, ask stupid questions—and expect an answer. Here are some comebacks to some of the most common inquiries and comments: 13

The question-and-answer format deals efficiently with a large number of problem situations.

Q: What's it like to grow up in a ghetto? 14

A: I don't know. 15

Q (from the teacher): Can you give us the Black perspective on Toni Morrison, Huck Finn, slavery, Martin Luther King, Jr., and others? 16

A: I can give you my perspective. (Do not take the burden of 22 million people on your shoulders. Remind everyone that you are an individual, and don't speak for the race or any other individual within it.) 17

Q: Why do all the Black people sit together in the dining hall? 18

A: Why do all the white students sit together? 19

Q: Why should there be an African-American studies course? 20

A: Because white Americans have not adequately studied the contributions of Africans and African-Americans. Both Black and white students need to know our total common history. 21

Question-answer sets are grouped in one set; comment-comeback sets in another.

Q: Why are there so many scholarships for "minority" students? 22

A: Because they wouldn't give my great-grandparents their forty acres and the mule. 23

Q: How can whites understand Black history, culture, literature, and so forth? 24

A: The same way we understand white history, culture, literature, and so forth. That is why we're in school: to learn. 25

Q: Should whites take African-American studies courses? 26

A: Of course. We take white-studies courses, though the universities don't call them that. 27

The comebacks flip the intent of language from the original comments.

Comment: When I see groups of Black people on campus, it's really intimidating. 28

Comeback: I understand what you mean. I'm frightened when I see white students congregating. 29

Comment: It's not fair. It's easier for you guys to get into college than for other people. *30*

Comeback: If it's so easy, why aren't there more of us? *31*

Comment: It's not our fault that America is the way it is. *32*

Comeback: It's not our fault, either, but both of us have a responsibility to make changes. *33*

It's really very simple. Educational progress is a national concern; education is a private one. Your job is not to educate white people; it is to obtain an education. If you take the racial world on your shoulders, you will not get the job done. Deal with yourself as an individual worthy of respect, and make everyone else deal with you the same way. College is a little like playing grown-up. Practice what you want to be. You have been telling your parents you are grown. Now is your chance to act like it. ■ *34*

> The final line uses the positive word *chance.*

Reading for Better Writing

1. Summarize Giovanni's key points. What details suggest that this essay was highly relevant when it was first published in 1991? Why might textbook and anthology editors continue to republish this essay several years later?

2. *Essence* magazine (in which this essay was first published) has been described by its editors as the "preeminent lifestyle magazine for today's African American woman." How does the *Essence* audience differ from the target audience for texts such as *The College Writer*? In what ways does Giovanni's essay speak to multiple audiences? In what ways might the piece have relevance for you and your campus?

3. Comment on Giovanni's title: Why might she have chosen it? How effective is it, and why?

4. Describe the tone of the essay. How does the writer achieve this tone, and what is the effect for you as a reader? Imagine the piece with a tone that contrasts starkly with the existing feel. How might this change the effect of the piece, and when/where might such a tone be appropriate?

5. The writer gives direct instructions to readers through the final two-thirds of the essay. Why isn't the last line an imperative or command?

Guidelines
Writing About a Process

1. **Select a topic.** Choose a topic from the list that you generated under "Topics to Consider" on page **218**. If you're stuck, review your notes and textbooks to generate more course-related topics.

2. **Review the process.** Use your knowledge of the topic to fill out an organizer like the one on the right. List the subject at the top, each of the steps in chronological order, and the outcome at the bottom. Review the organizer to find issues you need to research.

   Process Analysis
   Subject:
   - Step #1
   - Step #2
   - Step #3
   Outcome:

3. **Research as needed.** Find information that spells out the process: what it is, what steps are required, what order the steps should follow, how to do the steps, what outcome the process should produce, and what safety precautions are needed. If possible, observe the process in action or perform it yourself. Carefully record correct names, materials, tools, and safety or legal issues.

4. **Organize information.** After conducting your research, revise the organizer by adding or reordering steps as needed. Then develop an outline, including steps listed in the organizer, as well as supporting details from your research.

5. **Draft the document.** Write the document using the guidelines below.

Describing a Process	Explaining a Process	Writing Instructions
Opening: Introduce the topic, stating its importance and giving an overview of the steps.	**Opening:** Introduce the topic and give an overview of the process.	**Opening:** Name the process in the title; summarize the process and list any materials and tools needed.
Middle: Describe each step clearly (usually in separate paragraphs), and link steps with transitions like *first, second, next, finally,* and *while.* Describe the outcome and its importance.	**Middle:** Explain what each step involves and how to do it (typically using a separate paragraph for each). Use transitions such as *first, second,* and *next* to link the steps. Explain the outcome.	**Middle:** Present each step in a separate—usually one- or two-sentence—paragraph. Number the steps and state each clearly, using commands directed to the reader.
Closing: Describe the process as a whole and restate key points.	**Closing:** Explain follow-up activity and restate key points.	**Closing:** In a short paragraph, explain any follow-up action.

6. Revise the writing. Check for the following and revise as needed:
- A clear opening that identifies the process
- Steps that are stated clearly and in the correct order
    For explanations and instructions:
    - Clear details explaining how to perform each step
    - A closing that includes necessary follow-up activity
    For instructions:
    - Clear and correct safety cautions in boldface type

7. Test the writing. Read the writing for organization and completeness. For *explanations* and *instructions*, perform the process yourself using the writing as a guide. For each step, do only *what* you're told to do and *how* you're told to do it. Note where the writing is incomplete, out of order, and/or lacking adequate safety precautions. Revise as needed.

8. Get feedback. Ask a classmate who is unfamiliar with the process to read the writing for clarity, completeness, and correctness. For *instructions*, have the person use the writing as a guide to perform the process, noting where details are incomplete or unclear, and noting where word choice is either imprecise or too technical. Use the feedback to guide further revision.

9. Edit the writing by looking for the following:
- Word choice appropriate for your least-informed reader
- Clear transitions between steps
- Consistent verb tense in all steps
- For *instructions*—verbs that give clear commands
- Correct, consistent terminology
- Informed, respectful voice
- Proper format (particularly for *instructions*—adequate white space)

10. Publish the essay. Share your writing with others:
- Offer it to instructors or students working with the process.
- Offer explanations and instructions to people on campus or at non-profit agencies who can use the writing to do their work.
- Post the writing on a suitable website.

INSIGHT: The *mood* of a verb (see **629.2**) indicates the tone or attitude with which a statement is made. For instructions, writers use the imperative mood (or command form) to communicate a firm, direct, and informed tone.

Writing Checklist

Use these six traits to check your essay, then revise as needed:

_____ The **ideas** describe or explain the process clearly and completely.

_____ The **organization** sequence helps clarify the process. In explanations and instructions, the organization is chronological and helps the reader work through the process.

_____ The **voice** matches the writer's purpose. Cautions regarding safety or legal issues sound serious but are not alarming.

_____ The **words** are precise, and technical terms are defined.

_____ The **sentences** are smooth, varied in structure, and engaging. In instructions, sentences are shaped as clear, brief, no-nonsense commands.

_____ The material is **correct** and formatted properly as an essay or set of instructions.

Writing Prompt

Writing Activities

1. Review the topics that you listed under "Topics to Consider" on page **218**. Choose a topic and write about it, letting the writing take any one of these forms: *description, explanation,* or *instructions.*

2. Review the "Wayward Cells" and "Hair Today, Gone Tomorrow" models. List similar scientific or technical processes that interest you. Choose one and write about it as a *description.*

3. Review the process instructions titled "Downloading Photographs from the MC-150 Digital Camera," considering how the written and visual elements on the page work together. Draft or revise a piece in which visual elements are essential to effectively communicate your ideas. Integrate relevant, high-quality visuals (photos, illustrations, diagrams) that will help readers to better understand your ideas.

4. Review Nikki Giovanni's essay, "Campus Racism 101," watching for places where she uses the understood "you" and begins directive statements with verbs. Draft or edit a set of instructions, starting each new directive with a verb and separating each step into a new paragraph, bullet, or numbered line.

5. Using Giovanni's "Campus Racism 101" as a model, write a process essay based on your own experience in which you give advice about how to succeed in a difficult situation.

Chapter 16
Definition

Whether you're writing a persuasive essay, a lab report, or a project proposal, defining key terms helps you distinguish the boundaries of your subject.

In most writing situations, you will include short definitions of terms consisting of one or two sentences or one or two paragraphs. Although this chapter includes information that will enable you to write such brief definitions, its main purpose is to help you write longer, essay-length pieces sometimes called *extended definitions.*

When you write an extended definition, study this chapter, which will guide you through every step in the writing process—from choosing the term to refining the definition. When reading the model essays, look closely at the strategies that each writer uses "to peel the onion"—that is, to unfold and examine each layer of a word's meaning until finally reaching the core.

What's Ahead

- Overview: Writing a Definition Essay
  - – Student Models
  - – Professional Models
- Guidelines
- Writing Checklist and Activities

Web Link

Overview
Writing a Definition Essay

Writer's Goal

Your goal is to choose a word or phrase that interests you, explore what it means (and doesn't mean), and write an essay that helps readers better understand that term.

Keys for Success

Know your purpose. ■ Decide what you want your writing to do: entertain, inform, explain, persuade readers to act, or a combination of these.

Choose appropriate writing strategies. ■ Select strategies that help you accomplish your purpose. For example, the writers whose essays are included in this chapter make the following choices:

- To explore a personal experience with what it is to be *gullible*, Mary Beth Bruins examines a dictionary definition, an encyclopedia explanation, the word's etymology (or history), and quotations from three professional writers.

- To show readers how to treat patients with *dementia*, Sarah Anne Morelos defines the term using anecdotes and details gathered through research.

- To entertain and instruct people listening to his radio program, David Schelhaas examines the word *deft* by first sharing a personal anecdote, and then comparing and contrasting the definitions and etymologies of *deft* and *daft*.

- To describe her mother and herself, Cynthia Ozick offers two distinct definitions of *excellence*, each clarified with precise, colorful details.

Present fresh information. ■ Choose details that help readers understand the word's denotations (literal meanings), as well as its connotations (associated meanings). For example, one denotation of *cute* is *attractive*. Depending on the context, however, associations with this word may be positive or negative.

Topics to Consider

Beneath headings like the following, list words that you'd like to explore.

Words that are related to an art or sport:	Words that are (or should be) in the news:	Words that are over- used, unused, or abused:	Words that make you chuckle, frown, or fret:	Words that do— or do not— describe you:

Next Step Read the model essays and notice the writing strategies these writers use; think about how you might use them in your own essays.

Definition

In this essay, student writer Mary Beth Bruins describes how she earned the nickname "Gullible" and what the name means to most people—specifically, what it means to her. Notice the variety of sources the writer uses to fully define and illustrate the meaning of the word.

The Gullible Family

The writer uses the title and an anecdote to introduce the topic.

The other day, my friend Loris fell for the oldest trick in the book: "Hey, somebody wrote 'gullible' on the ceiling!" Shortly after mocking "Gullible Loris" for looking up, I swallowed the news that Wal-Mart sells popcorn that pops into the shapes of cartoon characters. And so, as "Gullible Mary," I decided to explore what our name means, and who else belongs to the Gullible family. What I learned is that our family includes both people and birds, related to each other by our willingness to "swallow."   1

She gives an example and the word's Germanic root.

A gullible person will swallow an idea or argument without questioning its truth. Similarly, the *gull* (a long-winged, web-footed bird) will swallow just about anything thrown to it. In fact, the word *gullible* comes from *gull*, and this word can be traced back to the Germanic word *gwel* (to swallow). Both *gull* and *gwel* are linked to the modern word *gulp*, which means,

> *"Hey, somebody wrote 'gullible' on the ceiling!"*

"to swallow greedily or rapidly in large amounts." It's not surprising then that Loris and I, sisters in the Gullible family, both eagerly gulped (like gulls) the false statements thrown to us.   2

She cites details from an encyclopedia.

Swallowing things so quickly isn't too bright, and *gull* (when referring to a bird or a person) implies that the swallower is immature and foolish. For example, *gull* refers to an "unfledged" fowl, which the *Grolier Encyclopedia* describes as either "an immature bird still lacking flight feathers" or something that is "inexperienced, immature, or untried." These words describe someone who is fooled easily, and that's why *gull*, when referring to a human, means "dupe" or "simpleton." In fact, since 1550, *gullet*, which means "throat," has also meant "fooled."   3

She quotes two writers.

To illustrate this usage, the *Oxford English Dictionary* quotes two authors who use *gull* as a verb meaning *to fool.* "Nothing is so easy as to *gull* the public, if you only set up a prodigy," writes Washington Irving. William Dean Howells uses the word similarly when he writes, "You are perfectly safe to go on and *gull* imbeciles to the end of time, for all I care."   4

> **She closes with a playful, positive spin.**

Both of these authors are pretty critical of gullible people, but does *gullible* have only negative connotations? Is there no hope for Gullibles like Loris and me? C. O. Sylvester Marson's comments about *gullible* may give us some comfort. He links *gullible* to "credulous, confiding, and easily deceived." At first, these adjectives also sound negative, but *credulous* does mean "to follow implicitly." And the word *credit* comes from the Latin word *credo* (meaning "I believe"). So what's bad about that? In other words, isn't *wanting to believe* other people a good thing? Why shouldn't Loris and I be proud of at least that aspect of our gull blood? We want to be positive—and we don't want to be cynics! ■

5

Writing Prompt

Reading for Better Writing

1. The writer tells anecdotes about herself and Loris. Find each anecdotal reference and explain how it does or does not help define *gullible*.

2. Review each paragraph and explain whether and how it strengthens the definition.

3. Describe the writer's voice and explain why it does or does not fit the topic.

4. The writer uses "family" as a metaphor for a group that includes both birds and people. Explain why this metaphor is or is not effective.

Definition

Based on research and her experience as a nursing home employee, student writer Sarah Anne Morelos defines a class (or group) of illnesses known as dementia.

Understanding Dementia

The writer uses the title and an anecdote to introduce the topic.

"Hello, Jenny! It's Sarah . . . I'm going to clean your room." Saying her name assured her that I knew who she was and that I was friendly. As I made her bed, I asked, "How are you doing this morning, Jenny?" [1]

"Oh, I'm good," she said. Then, after a pause, she added, "My husband, Charlie, died in this room, you know." [2]

I looked in her face and saw the familiar tears. "I'm so sorry, Jenny," I answered. Then I held her hand and listened to the same details of Charlie's death that I had heard every week for the past year. Suddenly Jenny stopped her story, looked up, and asked, "Who are you?" She didn't even remember my entering her room. [3]

Jenny has dementia, a disease that affects many people over eighty years old. When I first started work as a nursing-home housekeeper, the patients experiencing this illness frightened me. I didn't understand their words or behavior. Now that I understand more about the patients and their illness, I am better able to respond to them in a helpful way. [4]

> "You took it! You rotten thief!" she screamed.

She defines the word and distinguishes the class (dementia) from illnesses within that class.

It is now estimated that more than half of the nursing-home residents in the United States have dementia. But what, exactly, is this disease? Dementia is a broad term that refers to a number of health problems, including Alzheimer's disease, brain tumors, arteriosclerosis, and hardening of arteries to the heart. The outward symptoms of dementia are often disturbing, as this disease affects both the language skills and the behavior of the patient. [5]

She describes symptoms.

The most common and noticeable symptom is memory loss. Patients in the early stages of dementia first experience short-term memory loss; as the illness advances, they also experience long-term memory loss. For example, Jenny demonstrated short-term loss. While she could remember countless details about Charlie's death, an event that had happened ten years earlier, she could not remember my name—or even that I had entered the room. Another sign of memory loss is repetitiveness: Patients like Jenny retell their stories over and over. [6]

She uses another anecdote.

In addition to forgetting information and repeating stories, people with dementia may express strange beliefs or fears. At one point, a resident named Wilma accused me of stealing from her. "You took it! You rotten thief!" she screamed. [7]

"What are you missing, Wilma?" I asked. She started to tell me, but then couldn't remember. Soon she had forgotten the episode altogether, although she was still flustered and very angry. This irrationality may be caused by bouts of schizophrenia.   *8*

Another symptom of dementia is diminished language skills. While adults with healthy minds easily recall thousands of vocabulary words, patients with dementia struggle to name even the most common things and most familiar people in their lives. For example, a woman in the middle stages of the illness may recognize her son, but not be able to recall his name. However, as the illness advances, she will lose the ability to recognize his face as well.   *9*

For each symptom, the writer provides examples and/or anecdotes.

Patients with dementia also show behavioral changes. One common change is forgetting how to do simple tasks like washing dishes. Another change is forgetting to do basic things like shutting off the stove. Other behavioral changes signal a shift in personality. For example, fifteen years ago, Wilma was my friendly next-door neighbor who occasionally brought my family cookies. Today, Wilma is one of the dementia patients whom I take care of. As a neighbor, she was mild-mannered, but as a patient she gets very angry with anyone who enters her room. "Get out of here!" she yells with arms flailing. "You're not allowed in here!"   *10*

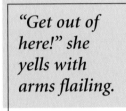

"Get out of here!" she yells with arms flailing.

Not surprisingly, dementia can also leave people unable to care for themselves. They may have trouble dressing, bathing, or even using the bathroom. This level of neediness causes two problems. First, the individual cannot do the activity, and second, he or she often suffers from related depression.   *11*

A question signals a transition.

What's the solution to dementia? Sadly, there is no cure. While nursing home staff can help patients with activities, and medication helps them cope with depression, nothing can stop the illness. Both the disease and its symptoms get worse.   *12*

The writer gives another example.

Steve is a good example. When he entered the nursing home just six months ago, he was experiencing the early stages of dementia. Today, however, his illness is much more advanced. The stress of moving into this new environment and leaving his wife at home alone affected Steve deeply. When he first arrived, Steve often cried and begged to be taken home. "I'll give you $20—please just take me home," he'd plead.   *13*

Painfully, I would explain, "Steve, this is your home." After some time, the situation got so bad that he would not sleep or eat. He was depressed, and he cried often, thinking that no one cared about him. Eventually, Steve   *14* was given stronger drugs to help with the depression. For a few months, the medication seemed to work—he laughed at jokes and occasionally told one himself. But then Steve's dementia advanced again. Soon he was asking his same sad questions: "Where am I?" and "Do you know what I'm doing here?"

So what is the best "medication" for people with dementia? While no treatment can stop the illness, understanding the disease and its symptoms is the key to helping people cope. Doctors who understand the science of dementia can prescribe medicine. However, all of us who understand the heartbreaking symptoms and effects of the disease can provide another, possibly more effective treatment. We can respond to the victim of dementia with patience, kindness, and love. ■

She closes by encouraging readers to show understanding and kindness.

15

Reading for Better Writing

1. Describe how the writer introduces the topic, and explain why the introduction is or is not effective.

2. Describe how the writer distinguishes the class (dementia) from specific illnesses within that class. How are illnesses within the class defined and explained?

3. The writer extends her definition by focusing largely on the symptoms of the disease. Examine her strategies for doing so, and explain whether you find them effective.

4. Review how the writer closes with an appeal to readers. Is the closing fitting? Why or why not?

Definition

Professor David Schelhaas delivered the following definition on his weekly radio program, *What's the Good Word?*

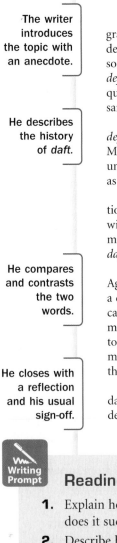

The writer introduces the topic with an anecdote.

He describes the history of *daft*.

He compares and contrasts the two words.

He closes with a reflection and his usual sign-off.

Deft or Daft

The other day, my wife, watching our son-in-law with his large hands gracefully tie the shoelaces of his little daughter, remarked, "You really are deft." Ever the cynic, I remarked, "He's not only deft, he's daft." I talk that sort of nonsense frequently, but as I said this, I began to wonder. What if *deft* and *daft* come from the same root and once meant the same thing? A quick trip to the dictionary showed that, indeed, they did once mean the same thing (though my wife thought me daft when I first suggested it). 1

Let me see if I can explain the original meaning and also how *daft* and *deft* came to part company. *Daft* originally meant mild or gentle. The Middle English *dafte* comes from the Old English *gadaefte,* which has as its underlying sense *fit* or *suitable.* Quite likely, mild or gentle people were seen as behaving in a way that was fit and suitable. 2

Gradually, however, the mild, gentle meaning descended in connotation to mean crazy or foolish. First, animals were described as daft—that is, without reason—and eventually people also. The word *silly,* which once meant happy or blessed, slid down the same slope. So that explains where *daft* got its present meaning. 3

But how does *deft,* meaning skillful or dexterous, fit into the picture? Again, if we start with the Old English meaning of *fit* or *suitable,* we can see a connection to skillful. In fact, the root of *gadaefte,* which is *dhabh,* to fit, carries with it the sense of a joiner or an artisan, someone who skillfully made the ends or corners of a cupboard or piece of furniture fit neatly together. From *fit* to *skillful* to *dexterous.* Thus we see how one root word meaning *fit* or *suitable* went in two different directions—one meaning crazy, the other meaning skillful. 4

These days it is usually considered much better to be deft than to be daft. But don't be too sure. It is good to remind ourselves that one person's deftness might very well appear as daftness to another. 5

This is David Schelhaas asking, "What's the Good Word?" ■ 6

Writing Prompt

Reading for Better Writing

1. Explain how the opening attempts to engage the reader. In what ways does it succeed?

2. Describe how the writer shows that the meanings of the words have changed. Is his explanation clear? Why or why not?

3. Describe the writer's tone and explain why it is or is not effective for a radio program.

Definition

Cynthia Ozick is an American writer known for her fiction, poetry, and essays on Jewish-American life. In 2005 she was nominated for the Man Booker International Prize for lifetime achievement in literature.

> The title indicates what term will be defined.

> The mother's standards for work are contrasted with those of a cousin, an uncle, and the writer.

> The words describing the mother have positive connotations: *splashy, satisfying, originality, panache, bountiful,* and so on.

On *Excellence*

In my Depression childhood, whenever I had a new dress, my cousin Sarah would get suspicious. The nicer the dress was, and especially the more expensive it looked, the more suspicious she would get. Finally she would lift the hem and check the seams. This was to see if the dress had been bought or if my mother had sewed it. Sarah could always tell. My mother's sewing had elegant outsides, but there was something catch-as-catch-can about the insides. Sarah's sewing, by contrast, was as impeccably finished inside as out; not one stray thread dangled.

My uncle Jake built meticulous grandfather clocks out of rosewood; he was a perfectionist and sent to England for the clockworks. My mother built serviceable radiator covers and a serviceable cabinet, with hinged doors, for the pantry. She built a pair of bookcases for the living room. Once, after I was grown and in a house of my own, she fixed the sewer pipe. She painted ceilings, and also landscapes; she reupholstered chairs. One summer she planted a whole yard of tall corn. She thought herself capable of doing anything, and did everything she imagined. But nothing was perfect. There was always some clear flaw, never visible head-on. You had to look underneath where the seams were. The corn thrived, though not in rows. The stalks elbowed one another like gossips in a dense little village.

"Miss Brrrrooooobaker," my mother used to mock, rolling her Russian *r*'s, whenever I crossed a *t* she had left uncrossed, or corrected a word she had misspelled, or became impatient with a *v* that had tangled itself up in a *w* in her speech. ("Vvventriloquist," I would say. "Vventriloquist," she would obediently repeat. And the next time it would come out "wiolinist.") Miss Brubaker was my high school English teacher, and my mother invoked her name as an emblem of raging finical obsession. "Miss Brrrrooooobaker," my mother's voice hoots at me down the years, as I go on casting and recasting sentences in a tiny handwriting on monomaniacally uniform paper. The loops of my mother's handwriting—it was the Palmer Method—were as big as hoops, spilling generous splashy ebullience. She could pull off, at five minutes' notice, a satisfying dinner for ten concocted out of nothing more than originality and panache. But the napkin would be folded a little off-center, and the spoon might be on the wrong side of the knife. She was an optimist who ignored trifles; for her, God was not in the details but in the intent. And all these culinary and agricultural efflorescences were extracurricular, accomplished in the crevices and niches of a fourteen-hour business day. When she scribbled out her family memoirs, in heaps of dog-eared notebooks or on the backs of old bills or on the margins of last year's calendar, I would resist typing them; in the speed of the chase she often omitted words like "the," "and," "will." The same flashing and bountiful hand fashioned and fired ceramic pots, and painted brilliant autumn views and vases of imaginary flowers and ferns, and decorated ordinary Woolworth platters with lavish enameled gardens. But bits of the painted petals would chip away.

A colon sets apart a word to be defined.

Lavish: my mother was as lavish as nature. She woke early and   4
saturated the hours with work and inventiveness, and read late into the night. She was all profusion, abundance, fabrication. Angry at her children, she would run after us whirling the cord of the electric iron, like a lasso or a whip; but she never caught us. When, in the seventh grade, I was afraid of failing the Music Appreciation final exam because I could not tell the difference between "To a Wild Rose" and "Barcarolle," she got the idea of sending me to school with a gauze sling rigged up on my writing arm, and an explanatory note that was purest fiction. But the sling kept slipping off. My mother gave advice like mad—she boiled over with so much passion for the predicaments of strangers that they turned into permanent cronies. She told intimate stories about people I had never heard of.

The mother's lavishness is defined through comparison and examples.

Despite the gargantuan Palmer loops (or possibly because of them), I   5
have always known that my mother's was a life of—intricately abashing word!—excellence: insofar as excellence means ripe generosity. She burgeoned, she proliferated; she was endlessly leafy and flowering. She wore red hats and called herself a gypsy. In her girlhood she marched with the suffragettes and for Margaret Sanger and called herself a Red. She made me laugh, she was so varied: like a tree on which lemons, pomegranates, and prickly pears absurdly all hang together. She had the comedy of prodigality.

After portraying her mother in detail, the writer finally uses and defines the title word: *excellence*.

My own way is a thousand times more confined. I am a pinched   6
perfectionist, the ultimate fruition of Miss Brubaker; I attend to crabbed minutiae and am self-trammeled through taking pains. I am a kind of human snail, locked in and condemned by my own nature. The ancients believed that the moist track left by the snail as it crept was the snail's own essence, depleting its body little by little; the farther the snail toiled, the smaller it became, until it finally rubbed itself out. That is how perfectionists are. Say to us "Excellence," and we will show you how we use up our substance and wear ourselves away, while making scarcely any progress at all. The fact that I am an exacting perfectionist in a narrow strait only, and nowhere else, is hardly to the point, since nothing matters to me so much as a comely and muscular sentence. It is my narrow strait, this snail's road: the track of the sentence I am writing now; and when I have eked out the wet substance, ink or blood, that is its mark, I will begin the next sentence. Only in reading out sentences am I perfectionist; but then there is nothing else I know how to do, or take much interest in. I miter every pair of abutting sentences as scrupulously as Uncle Jake fitted one strip of rosewood against

The writer explains how excellence differs from perfectionism.

Three parallel clauses state the same idea three different ways in one sentence.

another. My mother's worldly and bountiful hand has escaped me. The sentence I am writing is my cabin and my shell, compact, self-sufficient. It is the burnished horizon—a merciless planet where flawlessness is the single standard, where even the inmost seams, however hidden from a laxer eye, must meet perfection. Here "excellence" is not strewn casually from a tipped cornucopia, here disorder does not account for charm, here trifles rule like tyrants.

The writer builds her description with a list.

I measure my life in sentences, and my sentences are superior to my mother's, pressed out, line by line, like the lustrous ooze on the underside of the snail, the snail's secret open seam, its wound, leaking attar. My mother was too mettlesome to feel the force of a comma. She scorned minutiae. She measured her life according to what poured from the horn of plenty, which was her ample, cascading, elastic, susceptible, inexact heart. My narrower heart rides between the tiny horns of the snail, dwindling as it goes.

The final sentence is another list.

And out of this thinnest thread, this ink-wet line of words, must rise a visionary fog, a mist, a smoke, forging cities, histories, sorrows, quagmires, entanglements, lives of sinners, even the life of my furnace-hearted mother: so much wilderness, waywardness, plentitude on the head of the precise and impeccable snail, between the horns. ■

Reading for Better Writing

1. What words and phrases does Ozick use to define *excellence*? How does contrasting her mother's life with her own allow Ozick to further define *excellence*? What point(s) is she making about *excellence*?

2. One way to write a definition is to use words and phrases that have similar meanings to the word you wish to define. What other techniques does Ozick use to define *excellence*? What additional strategies could be used to define a term?

3. Writing a good definition is challenging because it requires the use of precise words to shed light on the meaning of another word that has its own precise meaning(s). Find instances where Ozick lists one term or idea after another to build precision into a definition. How would her meaning change if she had used only one word from the list?

4. Find examples of words that have especially positive or negative connotations. How do these connotations help Ozick to make her main point(s)?

Guidelines
Writing a Definition Essay

1. **Select a topic.** Review the words that you listed under "Topics to Consider" on page 232, and choose one that you want to explore. If you're stuck, list words similar to those defined in the five models.

   TIP: The best topics are abstract nouns (*totalitarianism, individualism,* or *terrorism*), complex terms (*code blue, dementia, spousal abuse,* or *Italian opera*), or adjectives connected to a personal experience (like the words defined in the models—*gullible, excellence, deft* and *daft*).

2. **Identify what you know.** To discern what you already know about the topic, write freely about the word, letting your writing go where it chooses. Explore both your personal and your academic connections with the word.

3. **Gather information.** To find information about the word's history, usage, and grammatical form, use such strategies as the following:
   - Consult a general dictionary, including an unabridged dictionary; list both denotative (literal) and connotative (associated) meanings for the word.
   - Consult specialized dictionaries that define words from specific disciplines or occupations: music, literature, law, medicine, and so on.
   - When appropriate, interview experts on your topic or poll students about the topic.
   - Check reference books such as *Bartlett's Famous Quotations* to see how famous speakers and writers have used the word.
   - Research the word's etymology and usage by consulting appropriate web sources such as <dictionary.com>, <m-w.com>, or <xrefer.com>.
   - Do a general search on the web to see where the word pops up in titles of songs, books, or films; company names, products, and ads; nonprofit organizations' names, campaigns, and programs; and topics in the news.
   - List synonyms (words meaning the same—or nearly the same) and antonyms (words meaning the opposite).

4. **Compress what you know.** Based on your freewriting and research, try writing a formal, one-sentence definition that satisfies the following equation:

   Equation: **Term = larger class + distinguishing characteristics**

   Examples: **Swedish pimple** = fishing lure + silver surface, tubular body, three hooks

   melodrama = stage play + flat characters, contrived plot, moralistic theme

   Alzheimer's = dementia + increasing loss of memory, hygiene, social skills

5. **Get organized.** To organize the information that you have, and to identify details that you may want to add, fill out a graphic organizer like the one on page **47**.

   TIP: Although you can draft your essay directly from the organizer, you may save time by writing a traditional outline that lists your main points, subpoints, and supporting details.

6. **Draft the essay.** Review your outline as needed to write the first draft.

   Opening: Get the reader's attention and introduce the term. If you are organizing the essay from general to specific, consider using an anecdote, illustration, or quotation to set the context for what follows. If you are organizing it from specific to general, consider including an interesting detail from the word's history or usage. Wherever you use a dictionary definition, do so with a new slant and avoid the dusty phrase "According to Webster . . . "

   Middle: Show your reader precisely what the word does or does not mean. Build the definition in unified paragraphs, each of which addresses distinct aspects of the word: common definitions, etymology, usage by professional writers, and so on. Link paragraphs so that the essay unfolds the word's meaning one layer after another.

   Closing: Review your main point and close your essay. (You might, for example, conclude by encouraging readers to use—or not use—the word.)

7. **Get feedback.** Ask a classmate or someone from the college's writing center to read your essay for the following:

   - **Engaging opening**—Does the introduction identify the word and set the context for what follows?
   - **Clarity**—Is each facet of the definition clear, showing precisely what the word does and does not mean?
   - **Continuity**—Is each paragraph unified, and is each one linked to the paragraphs that precede and follow it? Is the essay focused and unified?
   - **Completeness**—Is the definition complete, telling the reader all that he or she needs to know in order to understand and use the word?
   - **Fitting closing**—Does the conclusion wrap up the message and refocus on the word's core meaning?

8. **Revise and edit the essay.** Use the feedback to revise the essay. If necessary, do additional research to find information to answer your reader's questions. Edit the essay by looking for clear sentences; correct quotations; specific, appropriate words; and correct grammar, spelling, usage, and punctuation.

9. **Publish the essay.** Share your writing with interested readers, including friends, family, and classmates. Submit the essay to your instructor.

Writing Checklist

Use these six traits to check your essay, then revise as needed:

_____ The **ideas** in the definition clearly distinguish what the word does and does not mean. Supporting details help to strengthen main points where needed.

_____ The **organizational** pattern is logical and appropriate for the definition's content. Paragraphs are unified and ordered to build a clear pattern of thought.

_____ The **voice** is informed, engaging, and courteous.

_____ The **words** are precise and appropriate, and complex or technical terms are defined. Transitional words and phrases link paragraphs smoothly and logically.

_____ The **sentences** are complete, clear, varied in structure, and readable.

_____ The **copy** is formatted correctly and includes no errors in spelling, punctuation, or grammar.

Writing Prompt

Writing Activities

1. Review "The Gullible Family" and think about similar situations when you and your friends played with a particular word or phrase. Choose one of the words you used, research its meaning, and write an essay that defines the word.

2. Review "Understanding Dementia" and choose a similarly complex health or social condition. Research the topic and write an essay defining it.

3. Review "Deft or Daft" and choose a pair of words that similarly mirror each other's meaning. Research the words, and write an essay comparing and contrasting their etymologies and meanings.

4. Review "On *Excellence*" by Cynthia Ozick, concentrating on the way Ozick uses lists of words, phrases, and ideas to build precise definitions. Experiment with this strategy for definition in an essay that you draft or revise.

5. Write an essay defining a word or phrase that is understood by people in a particular field of study but not by "outsiders." Write for the audience of outsiders.

Persuasive Writing

"Convince me!" is the reader's cry that lies behind all persuasive writing. Whether you are taking a position on an issue (Chapter 18), persuading readers to take action (Chapter 19), or proposing a solution to a vexing problem (Chapter 20), you are arguing a point in order to persuade readers to accept your claims, with the result that they change their own thinking and perhaps even their behavior and actions. In other words, even though each of these forms has a distinctive rhetorical emphasis, all three rely on foundational strategies for argumentation and persuasion (Chapter 17): from making and supporting claims effectively to avoiding logical fallacies.

Carefully study the four chapters in this section, noting the strategies discussed in each. Then, when you're writing a persuasive essay, use those strategies that best address your writing situation: your subject, audience, and purpose.

CONTENTS

Persuasive Writing

Chapter 17
Strategies for Argumentation and Persuasion

"I wasn't convinced." "I just didn't buy it." Maybe you've said something similar while watching a political debate, viewing a TV ad, or discussing an issue in class or at work. You simply didn't find the argument logical, believable, or persuasive.

In a sense, college is a place where big issues get argued out. Your courses aim to strengthen your reasoning abilities so that you can construct persuasive arguments. Your goal as a persuasive writer is to reason effectively with your readers or listeners and to motivate them to believe, change, or act.

This chapter is a resource on reasoning. It explains the foundations of argumentation and persuasion and introduces three related forms—taking a position, persuading readers to act, and proposing a solution. The three chapters following explain and model these forms in detail.

What's Ahead

- Building Persuasive Arguments
- Preparing Your Argument
- Making and Qualifying Claims
- Supporting Your Claims
- Identifying Logical Fallacies
- Engaging the Opposition
- Using Appropriate Appeals
- Writing Activities

Web Link

Building Persuasive Arguments

What is an argument?

Formally, an *argument* is a series of statements arranged in a logical sequence, supported with sound evidence, and expressed powerfully so as to sway your reader or listener. Arguments appear in a variety of places:

- A research paper about e-mail surveillance by the FBI
- An analysis of *Beloved* (the novel) or *The Lord of the Rings* (the film)
- A debate about the ethics of transferring copyrighted music over the Internet

How do you build a persuasive argument?

Step 1: Prepare your argument.

- **Identify your audience and purpose.** Who is your audience and what is your goal? Do you want to take a position, persuade readers to act, or offer a solution?
- **Generate ideas and gather solid evidence.** You can't base an argument on opinions. Find accurate, pertinent information about the issue and uncover all viewpoints on it.
- **Develop a line of reasoning.** To be effective, you need to link your ideas in a clear, logical sequence.

Step 2: Make and qualify your claim.

- **Draw reasonable conclusions from the evidence.** State your claim (a debatable issue) as the central point for which you will argue. For example, you might assert that something is true, has value, or should be done.
- **Add qualifiers.** Words such as "typically" and "sometimes" soften your claim, making it more reasonable and acceptable.

Step 3: Support your claim.

- **Support each point** in your claim with solid evidence.
- **Identify logical fallacies.** Test your thinking for errors in logic. (See pages 255–258.)

Step 4: Engage the opposition.

- **Make concessions,** if needed, by granting points to the opposition.
- **Develop rebuttals** that expose the weaknesses of the opposition's position, whenever possible.
- **Use appropriate appeals**—emotional "tugs" that ethically and logically help readers see your argument as convincing.

Preparing Your Argument

An argument is a reason or chain of reasons used to support a claim. To use argumentation well, you need to know how to draw logical conclusions from sound evidence. Preparing an effective argument involves a number of specific steps, starting with those discussed below.

Consider the situation.

- **Clearly identify your purpose and audience.** This step is essential for all writing, but especially true when building an argument. (See page **28**.)
- **Consider a range of ideas** to broaden your understanding of the issue and to help focus your thinking on a particular viewpoint. (See page **40**.)
- **Gather sound evidence** to support your viewpoint. (See pages **252–254**.)

Develop a line of reasoning.

In argumentative writing, it's crucial that you develop a clear line of reasoning. Each point you make should clearly support your argument. This line of reasoning might develop naturally as you study the issue, or you may need to adopt a more formal approach. Use either of the following outlines as a guide to structuring your argument.

Outline 1: **Present your supporting arguments, then address counterarguments, and conclude with the strongest argument.**

    Introduction: question, concern, or claim
      1. Strong argument-supporting claim
        • Discussion and support
      2. Other argument-supporting claims
        • Discussion of and support for each argument
      3. Objections, concerns, and counterarguments
        • Discussion, concessions, answers, and rebuttals
      4. Strongest argument-supporting claim
        • Discussion and support
    Conclusion: argument consolidated—claim reinforced

Outline 2: **Address the arguments and counterarguments point by point.**

    Introduction: question, concern, or claim
      1. Strong argument-supporting claim
        • Discussion and support
        • Counterarguments, concessions, and rebuttals
      2. Other argument-supporting claims
        • For each argument, discussion and support
        • For each argument, counterarguments, concessions, and rebuttals
      3. Strongest argument-supporting claim
        • Discussion and support
        • Counterarguments, concessions, and rebuttals
    Conclusion: argument consolidated—claim reinforced

Making and Qualifying Claims

An argument centers on a claim—a debatable statement. That claim is the thesis, or key point you wish to explain and defend so well that readers agree with it. A strong claim has the following traits:

- **It's clearly arguable**—it can be vigorously debated.
- **It's defendable**—it can be supported with sufficient arguments and evidence.
- **It's responsible**—it takes an ethically sound position.
- **It's understandable**—it uses clear terms and defines key words.
- **It's interesting**—it is challenging and worth discussing, not bland and easily accepted.

Distinguish claims from facts and opinions.

A claim is a conclusion drawn from logical thought and reliable evidence. A fact, in contrast, is a statement that can be checked for accuracy. An opinion is a personally held taste or attitude. A claim can be debated, but a fact or opinion cannot.

> **Fact:** *The Fellowship of the Ring* is the first book in J. R. R. Tolkien's trilogy *The Lord of the Rings*.
>
> **Opinion:** I liked the movie almost as much as the book.
>
> **Claim:** While the film version of *The Fellowship of the Ring* does not completely follow the novel's plot, it does faithfully capture the spirit of Tolkien's novel.

Distinguish three types of claims.

Truth, value, and policy—these types of claims are made in an argument. The differences among them are important because each type has a distinct goal.

Claims of truth state that something is or is not the case. As a writer, you want readers to accept your claim as trustworthy.

> ■ **The Arctic ice cap will begin to disappear as early as 2050.**
> **The cholesterol in eggs is not as dangerous as previously feared.**
>
> **Comment:** Avoid statements that are (1) obviously true or (2) impossible to prove. Also, truth claims must be argued carefully because accepting them (or not) can have serious consequences.
>
> **Sample Essay:** "An Apology for the Life of Ms. Barbie D. Doll," pages 265–266.

Claims of value state that something does or does not have worth. As a writer, you want readers to accept your judgment.

■ **Volunteer reading tutors provide a valuable service.**
Many music videos fail to present positive images of women.

Comment: Claims of value must be supported by referring to a known standard or by establishing an agreed-upon standard. To avoid a bias, base your judgments on the known standard, not on your feelings.

Sample Essay: "Apostles of Hatred Find It Easy to Spread Their Message," pages 269–270

Claims of policy state that something ought or ought not be done. As a writer, you want readers to approve your course of action.

■ **Special taxes should be placed on gas-guzzling SUVs.**
The developer should not be allowed to fill in the pond where the endangered tiger salamander lives.

Comment: Policy claims focus on action. To arrive at them, you must often first establish certain truths and values; thus, an argument over policy may include truth and value claims.

Sample Essay: "Pornography," pages 271–276

Develop a supportable claim.

An effective claim balances confidence with common sense. Follow these tips:

Avoid all-or-nothing, extreme claims. Propositions using words that are overly positive or negative—such as *all, best, never,* and *worst*—may be difficult to support. Statements that leave no room for exceptions are easy to attack.

Extreme Claim: All people charged even once for DUI should never be allowed to drive again.

Make a truly meaningful claim. Avoid claims that are obvious, trivial, or unsupportable. None is worth the energy needed to argue the point.

Obvious Claim: College athletes sometimes receive special treatment.
Trivial Claim: The College Rec Center is a good place to get fit.
Unsupportable Claim: Athletics are irrelevant to college life.

Use qualifiers to temper your claims. Qualifiers are words or phrases that make claims more reasonable. Notice the difference between these two claims:

Unqualified: Star athletes take far too many academic shortcuts.
Qualified: Some star athletes take improper academic shortcuts.

Note: The "qualified" claim is easier to defend because it narrows the focus and leaves room for exceptions. Use qualifier words like these:

• almost	• many	• often	• tends to
• frequently	• maybe	• probably	• typically
• likely	• might	• some	• usually

Supporting Your Claims

A claim stands or falls on its support. It's not the popular strength of your claim that matters, but rather the strength of your reasoning and evidence. To develop strong support, consider how to select and use evidence.

Gather evidence.

Several types of evidence can support claims. To make good choices, review each type, as well as its strengths and weaknesses.

Observations and anecdotes share what people (including you) have seen, heard, smelled, touched, tasted, and experienced. Such evidence offers an "eyewitness" perspective shaped by the observer's viewpoint, which can be powerful but may also prove narrow and subjective.

- **Most of us have closets full of clothes: jeans, sweaters, khakis, T-shirts, and shoes for every occasion.**

Statistics offer concrete numbers about a topic. Numbers don't "speak for themselves," however. They need to be interpreted and compared properly—not slanted or taken out of context. They also need to be up-to-date, relevant, and accurate.

- **Pennsylvania spends $30 million annually in deer-related costs. Wisconsin has an estimated annual loss of $37 million for crop damage alone.**

Tests and experiments provide hard data developed through the scientific method, data that must nevertheless be carefully studied and properly interpreted.

- **According to the two scientists, the rats with unlimited access to the functional running wheel ran each day and gradually increased the amount of running; in addition, they started to eat less.**

Graphics provide information in visual form—from simple tables to more complex charts, maps, drawings, and photographs. When poorly done, however, graphics can distort the truth. See the line graph in the experiment report on page **347** and the drawing in "Hair Today, Gone Tomorrow" on page **222**.

Analogies compare two things, creating clarity by drawing parallels. However, every analogy breaks down if pushed too far.

- **It is obvious today that America has defaulted on this promissory note insofar as her citizens of color are concerned. Instead of honoring this sacred obligation, America has given the Negro people a bad check; a check which has come back marked "insufficient funds." But we refuse to believe that the bank of justice is bankrupt.**

—Martin Luther King, Jr.

Expert testimony offers insights from an authority on the topic. Such testimony always has limits: Experts don't know it all, and they work from distinct perspectives, which means that they can disagree.

- **One specialist opposed to drilling is David Klein, a professor at the Institute of Arctic Biology at the University of Alaska–Fairbanks. Klein argues that if the oil industry opens up the ANWR for drilling, the number of caribou will likely decrease because the calving locations will change.**

Illustrations, examples, and demonstrations support general claims with specific instances, making such statements seem concrete and observable. Of course, an example may not be your best support if it isn't familiar.

- **Think about how differently one can frame Rosa Parks' historic action. In prevailing myth, Parks—a holy innocent—acts almost on whim. . . . The real story is more empowering: It suggests that change is the product of deliberate, incremental action.**

Analyses examine parts of a topic through thought patterns—cause/effect, compare/contrast, classification, process, or definition. Such analysis helps make sense of a topic's complexity, but muddles the topic when poorly done.

- **A girl's interest in romance is no more Barbie's fault than the fault of books like *On the Shores of Silver Lake*. Fashion magazines targeted at adolescents are the cause of far more anorexia cases than is Barbie.**

Predictions offer insights into possible outcomes or consequences by forecasting what might happen under certain conditions. Like weather forecasting, predicting can be tricky. To be plausible, a prediction must be rooted in a logical analysis of present facts.

- **While agroterrorist diseases would have little direct effect on people's health, they would be devastating to the agricultural economy, in part because of the many different diseases that could be used in an attack.**

Use evidence.

Finding evidence is one thing; using it well is another. To marshal evidence in support of your claim, follow three guidelines:

1. **Go for quality and variety, not just quantity.** More evidence is not necessarily better. Instead, support your points with sound evidence in different forms. Quality evidence is . . .
   - *accurate:* correct and verifiable in each detail.
   - *complete:* filled with pertinent facts.
   - *concrete:* filled with specifics.
   - *relevant:* clearly related to the claim.
   - *current:* reliably up-to-date.
   - *authoritative:* backed by expertise, training, and knowledge.
   - *appealing:* able to influence readers.

2. Use inductive and deductive patterns of logic. Depending on your purpose, use inductive or deductive reasoning. (See page 20.)

Induction: Inductive reasoning works from the particular toward general conclusions. In a persuasive essay using induction, look at facts first, find a pattern in them, and then lead the reader to your conclusion.

For example, in "To Drill or Not to Drill," Rebecca Pasok first details specific threats to the environment before arriving at her claim that drilling for oil in an Alaskan wilderness refuge is not our best option. (See pages 285–287.)

Deduction: Deductive reasoning—the opposite of inductive reasoning—starts from accepted truths and applies them to a new situation so as to reach a conclusion about it. For deduction to be sound, be sure the starting principles or facts are true, the new situation is accurately described, and the application is logical.

For example, Martin Luther King opened his 1963 "I have a Dream" speech by noting that more than one hundred years earlier, the Emancipation Proclamation promised African Americans justice and freedom. He then described the continuing unjust treatment of African Americans, deducing that the promises in the Proclamation remained unfulfilled. (See pages 291–294.)

3. Reason using valid warrants. To make sense, claims and evidence must have a logical connection. That connection is called the *warrant*—the often unspoken thinking used to relate the evidence to the claim. If warrants are good, arguments hold water; if warrants are faulty, then arguments break down. In other words, beware of faulty assumptions.

Check the short argument outlined below. Which of the warrants seem reasonable and strong, and which seem weak? Where does the argument fail?

Evidence: **If current trends in water usage continue, the reservoir will be empty in two years.**

Claim: **Therefore, Emeryville should immediately shut down its public swimming pools.**

Unstated Warrants or Assumptions:
- It is not good for the reservoir to be empty.
- The swimming pools draw significant amounts of water from the reservoir.
- Emptying the pools would help raise the level of the reservoir.
- No other action would better prevent the reservoir from emptying.
- It is worse to have an empty reservoir than an empty swimming pool.

INSIGHT: Because an argument is no stronger than its warrants, you must make sure that your evidence clearly and logically supports your claims.

Identifying Logical Fallacies

Fallacies are false arguments—that is, bits of fuzzy, dishonest, or incomplete thinking. They may crop up in your own thinking, in your opposition's thinking, or in such public "arguments" as ads, political appeals, and talk shows. Because fallacies may sway an unsuspecting audience, they are dangerously persuasive. By learning to recognize fallacies, however, you may identify them in opposing arguments and eliminate them from your own writing. In this section, logical fallacies are grouped according to how they falsify an argument.

Distorting the Issue

The following fallacies falsify an argument by twisting the issue out of a logical framework.

Bare Assertion The most basic way to distort an issue is to deny that it exists. This fallacy claims, "That's just how it is."

■ **The private ownership of handguns is a constitutional right.**
(*Objection:* The claim shuts off discussion of the U.S. Constitution or the reasons for regulation.)

Begging the Question Also known as circular reasoning, this fallacy arises from assuming in the basis of your argument the very point you need to prove.

■ **We don't need a useless film series when every third student owns a DVD player or VCR.** (*Objection:* There may be uses for a public film series that private video viewing can't provide. The word "useless" begs the question.)

Oversimplification This fallacy reduces complexity to simplicity. Beware of phrases like "It's a simple question of." Serious issues are rarely simple.

■ **Capital punishment is a simple question of protecting society.**

Either/Or Thinking Also known as black-and-white thinking, this fallacy reduces all options to two extremes. Frequently, it derives from a clear bias.

■ **Either this community develops light-rail transportation or the community will not grow in the future.** (*Objection:* The claim ignores the possibility that growth may occur through other means.)

Complex Question Sometimes by phrasing a question a certain way, a person ignores or covers up a more basic question.

■ **Why can't we bring down the prices that corrupt gas stations are charging?** (*Objection:* This question ignores a more basic question—"Are gas stations really corrupt?")

Straw Man In this fallacy, the writer argues against a claim that is easily refuted. Typically, such a claim exaggerates or misrepresents the opponents' actual arguments.

■ **Those who oppose euthanasia must believe that the terminally ill deserve to suffer.**

Sabotaging the Argument

These fallacies falsify the argument by twisting it. They destroy reason and replace it with something hollow or misleading.

Red Herring This strange term comes from the practice of dragging a stinky fish across a trail to throw tracking dogs off the scent. When a person puts forth a volatile idea that pulls readers away from the real issue, readers become distracted. Suppose the argument addresses drilling for oil in the Arctic National Wildlife Refuge (ANWR) of Alaska, and the writer begins with this statement:

- **In 1989, the infamous oil spill of the *Exxon Valdez* led to massive animal deaths and enormous environmental degradation of the coastline.**
  (*Objection:* Introducing this notorious oil spill distracts from the real issue—how oil drilling will impact the ANWR.)

Misuse of Humor Jokes, satire, and irony can lighten the mood and highlight a truth; when humor distracts or mocks, however, it undercuts the argument. What effect would the mocking tone of this statement have in an argument about tanning beds in health clubs?

- **People who use tanning beds will just turn into wrinkled old prunes or leathery sun-dried tomatoes!**

Appeal to Pity This fallacy engages in a misleading tug on the heartstrings. Instead of using a measured emotional appeal, it seeks to manipulate the audience into agreement.

- **Affirmative action policies ruined this young man's life. Because of them, he was denied admission to Centerville College.**

Use of Threats A simple but unethical way of sabotaging an argument is to threaten opponents. More often than not, a threat is merely implied: "If you don't accept my argument, you'll regret it."

- **If we don't immediately start drilling for oil in the ANWR, you will soon face hour-long lines at gas stations from New York to California.**

Bandwagon Mentality Someone implies that a claim cannot be true because a majority of people are opposed to it, or it must be true because a majority support it. (History shows that people in the minority have often had the better argument.) At its worst, such an appeal manipulates people's desire to belong or be accepted.

- **It's obvious to intelligent people that cockroaches live only in the apartments of dirty people.** (*Objection:* Based on popular opinion, the claim appeals to a kind of prejudice and ignores scientific evidence about cockroaches.)

Appeal to Popular Sentiment This fallacy consists of associating your position with something popularly loved: the American flag, baseball, apple pie. Appeals to popular sentiment sidestep thought to play on feelings.

- **Anyone who has seen *Bambi* could never condone hunting deer.**

Drawing Faulty Conclusions from the Evidence

This group of fallacies falsifies the argument by short-circuiting proper logic in favor of assumptions or faulty thinking.

Appeal to Ignorance This fallacy suggests that because no one has proved a particular claim, it must be false; or, because no one has disproved a claim, it must be true. Appeals to ignorance unfairly shift the burden of proof onto someone else.

- **Flying saucers are real. No scientific explanation has ruled them out.**

Hasty or Broad Generalization Such a claim is based on too little evidence or allows no exceptions. In jumping to a conclusion, the writer may use intensifiers such as *all, every,* or *never.*

- **Today's voters spend too little time reading and too much time being taken in by 30-second sound bites.** (*Objection:* Quite a few voters may, in fact, spend too little time reading about the issues, but it is unfair to suggest that this is true of everyone.)

False Cause This well-known fallacy confuses sequence with causation: If *A* comes before *B*, *A* must have caused *B*. However, *A* may be one of several causes, or *A* and *B* may be only loosely related, or the connection between *A* and *B* may be entirely coincidental.

- **Since that new school opened, drug use among young people has skyrocketed. Better that the school had never been built.**

Slippery Slope This fallacy argues that a single step will start an unstoppable chain of events. While such a slide may occur, the prediction lacks real evidence.

- **If we legalize marijuana, it's only a matter of time before hard drugs follow and America becomes a nation of junkies and addicts.**

Misusing Evidence

These fallacies falsify the argument by abusing or distorting the evidence.

Impressing with Numbers In this case, the writer drowns readers in statistics and numbers that overwhelm them into agreement. In addition, the numbers haven't been properly interpreted.

- **At 35 ppm, CO levels factory-wide are only 10 ppm above the OSHA recommendation, which is 25 ppm. Clearly, that 10 ppm is insignificant in the big picture, and the occasional readings in some areas of between 40 and 80 ppm are aberrations that can safely be ignored.** (*Objection:* The 10 ppm may be significant, and higher readings may indicate real danger.)

Half-Truths A half-truth contains part of but not the whole truth. Because it leaves out "the rest of the story," it is both true and false simultaneously.

- **The new welfare bill is good because it will get people off the public dole.** (*Objection:* This may be true, but the bill may also cause undue suffering for some truly needy individuals.)

Unreliable Testimonial An appeal to authority has force only if the authority is qualified in the proper field. If he or she is not, the testimony is irrelevant. Note that fame is not the same thing as authority.

- **On her talk show, Alberta Magnus recently claimed that most pork sold in the United States is tainted.** (*Objection:* Although Magnus may be an articulate talk show host, she is not an expert on food safety.)

Attack Against the Person This fallacy directs attention to a person's character, lifestyle, or beliefs rather than to the issue.

- **Would you accept the opinion of a candidate who experimented with drugs in college?**

Hypothesis Contrary to Fact This fallacy relies on "if only" thinking. It bases the claim on an assumption of what would have happened if something else had, or had not, happened. Being pure speculation, such a claim cannot be tested.

- **If only multiculturalists hadn't pushed through affirmative action, the U.S. would be a united nation.**

False Analogy Sometimes a person will argue that *X* is good (or bad) because it is like *Y*. Such an analogy may be valid, but it weakens the argument if the grounds for the comparison are vague or unrelated.

- **Don't bother voting in this election; it's a stinking quagmire.** (*Objection:* Comparing the election to a "stinking quagmire" is unclear and exaggerated.)

Misusing Language

Essentially, all logical fallacies misuse language. However, three fallacies falsify the argument, especially by the misleading use of words.

Obfuscation This fallacy involves using fuzzy terms like *throughput* and *downlink* to muddy the issue. These words may make simple ideas sound more profound than they really are, or they may make false ideas sound true.

- **Through the fully functional developmental process of a streamlined target refractory system, the U.S. military will successfully reprioritize its data throughputs.** (*Objection:* What does this sentence mean?)

Ambiguity Ambiguous statements can be interpreted in two or more opposite ways. Although ambiguity can result from unintentional careless thinking, writers sometimes use ambiguity to obscure a position.

- **Many women need to work to support their children through school, but they would be better off at home.** (*Objection:* Does *they* refer to *children* or *women*? What does *better off* mean? These words and phrases can be interpreted in opposite ways.)

Slanted Language By choosing words with strong positive or negative connotations, a writer can draw readers away from the true logic of the argument. Here is an example of three synonyms for the word *stubborn* that the philosopher Bertrand Russell once used to illustrate the bias in slanted language:

- **I am firm. You are obstinate. He is pigheaded.**

Engaging the Opposition

Think of an argument as an intelligent, lively dialogue with readers. Anticipate their questions, concerns, objections, and counterarguments. Then follow these guidelines.

Make concessions.

By offering concessions—recognizing points scored by the other side—you acknowledge your argument's limits and the truth of other positions. Paradoxically, such concessions strengthen your overall argument by making it seem more credible. Concede your points graciously, using words such as the following:

Admittedly	Granted	I agree that	I cannot argue with
It is true that	You're right	I accept	No doubt
Of course	I concede that	Perhaps	Certainly it's the case

■ **Granted, Barbie's physical appearance isn't realistic. As Motz explains . . .**

Develop rebuttals.

Even when you concede a point, you can often answer that objection by rebutting it. A good rebuttal is a small, tactful argument aimed at a weak spot in the opposing argument. Try these strategies:

1. Point out the counterargument's limits by putting the opposing point in a larger context. Show that the counterargument leaves something important out of the picture.

2. Tell the other side of the story. Offer an opposing interpretation of the evidence, or counter with stronger, more reliable, more convincing evidence.

3. Address logical fallacies in the counterargument. Check for faulty reasoning or emotional manipulation. For example, if the counterargument forces the issue into an either/or straightjacket, show that other options exist.

■ **Granted, Barbie's physical appearance isn't realistic. As Motz explains . . . I say, so what? While the only "real" version of Barbie's body would be a long-limbed 13-year-old with breast implants, who cares? Arguing that Barbie's bod isn't realistic and that the lack of realism hurts girls' self-esteem is weak logic. Children have had dolls for ages. For example . . .**

Consolidate your claim.

After making concessions and rebutting objections, you may need to regroup. Restate your claim so carefully that the weight of your whole argument can rest on it.

■ **Playing with Barbies need not be an unimaginative, antisocial activity that promotes conformity, materialism, and superficial ideals.**

Using Appropriate Appeals

For your argument to be persuasive, it must not only be logical, but also "feel right." It must treat readers as real people by appealing to their common sense, hopes, pride, and notion of right and wrong. How do you appeal to all these concerns? Do the following: (1) build credibility, (2) make logical appeals, and (3) focus on readers' needs.

Build credibility.

A persuasive argument is credible—so trustworthy that readers can change their minds painlessly. To build credibility, observe these rules:

Be thoroughly honest. ■ Demonstrate integrity toward the topic—don't falsify data, spin evidence, or ignore facts. Document your sources and cite them wherever appropriate.

Make realistic claims, projections, and promises. ■ Avoid emotionally charged statements, pie-in-the-sky forecasts, and undeliverable deals.

Develop and maintain trust. ■ From your first word to your last, develop trust—in your attitude toward the topic, your treatment of readers, and your respect for opposing viewpoints.

Make logical appeals.

Arguments stand or fall on their logical strength, but your readers' acceptance of those arguments is often affected more by the emotional appeal of your ideas and evidence. To avoid overly emotional appeals, follow these guidelines:

Engage readers positively. ■ Appeal to their better natures—to their sense of honor, justice, social commitment, altruism, and enlightened self-interest. Avoid appeals geared toward ignorance, prejudice, selfishness, or fear.

Use a fitting tone ■ Use a tone that is appropriate for the topic, purpose, situation, and audience.

Aim to motivate, not manipulate, readers. ■ While you do want them to accept your viewpoint, it's not a win-at-all-costs situation. Avoid bullying, guilt-tripping, and exaggerated tugs on heartstrings.

Don't trash-talk the opposition. ■ Show tact, respect, and understanding. Focus on issues, not personalities.

Use arguments and evidence that readers can understand and appreciate. ■ If readers find your thinking too complex, too simple, or too strange, you've lost them.

INSIGHT: Remember the adage: The best argument is so clear and convincing that it sounds like an explanation.

Focus on readers' needs.

Instead of playing on readers' emotions, connect your argument with readers' needs and values. Follow these guidelines:

Know your real readers. ■ Who are they—peers, professors, or fellow citizens? What are their allegiances, their worries, their dreams?

Picture readers as resistant. ■ Accept that your readers, including those inclined to agree with you, need convincing. Think of them as alert, cautious, and demanding—but also interested.

Use appeals that match needs and values. ■ Your argument may support or challenge readers' needs and values. To understand those needs, study the table below, which is based loosely on the thinking of psychologist Abraham Maslow. Maslow's hierarchy ranks people's needs on a scale from the most basic to the most complex. The table begins at the bottom with *having necessities* (a basic need) and ends at the top with *helping others* (a more complex need). For example, if you're writing to argue for more affordable housing for the elderly, you'd argue differently to legislators (whose focus is on *helping others*) than to the elderly who need the housing (whose focus is on *having necessities*). Follow these guidelines:

- Use appeals that match the foremost needs and values of your readers.
- If appropriate, constructively challenge those needs and values.
- Whenever possible, phrase your appeals in positive terms.
- After analyzing your readers' needs, choose a persuasive theme for your argument—a positive benefit, advantage, or outcome that readers can expect if they accept your claim. Use this theme to help readers to care about your claims.

Reader needs . . .	Use persuasive appeals to . . .
To make the world better by • *Helping others*	values and social obligations
To achieve by • *Being good at something* • *Getting recognition*	self-fulfillment, status appreciation
To belong by • *Being part of a group*	group identity, acceptance
To survive by • *Avoiding threats* • *Having necessities*	safety, security physical needs

Writing Activities

1. Select an essay from Chapters 18–20, "Taking a Position," "Persuading Readers to Act," or "Proposing a Solution." Read the essay carefully. Then describe and evaluate the argumentative strategies used by the writer, answering the specific questions below:

■ *What is the main claim the writer makes? Is it a claim of truth, value, or policy?*

■ *Is the claim arguable—that is, is it supportable, appropriately qualified, and effectively phrased?*

■ *What arguments does the writer develop in support of the claim? Are these arguments logical?*

■ *What types of evidence does the writer provide to support his or her discussion? Is the evidence valid, sufficient, and accurate?*

■ *Does the writer effectively address questions, alternatives, objections, and counterarguments?*

2. Examine the essay that you read for the first activity for its persuasive strategies. Answer the following questions:

■ *Describe the writer's tone. Does it effectively engage readers? Why or why not?*

■ *Does the argument seem credible and authoritative? Explain.*

■ *Identify ways that the writer connects with readers' needs and values. How does he or she develop a persuasive theme that appeals to those needs and stresses reader benefits?*

3. Examine an ad in a newspaper or magazine, on TV, or on the Internet. What kind of persuasive appeals (pages **255–258** and **260–261**) does the ad use? Are they used effectively and appropriately? Explain.

4. Find a letter to the editor on a current controversial issue. Examine the strengths and weaknesses of the writer's argument, and construct your own argument on this issue in the form of a letter to the same editor.

5. What are some of the key academic journals in your field of study? With help from a librarian or instructor in your discipline, find a quality article in a respected journal. Read the article and then answer these questions: What forms of reasoning, appeals, and evidence does the author use? What forms does he or she avoid?

Chapter 18
Taking a Position

Sometimes you just have to take a stand. An issue comes up that hits you where you live, gets your blood flowing, or challenges your thinking. In response, you say, "Okay, this is what I believe, and this is why I believe it."

Writing a position paper gives you the opportunity to take a stand. It's a chance, in other words, to refine what you think and feel, to clarify and deepen your perspective on an issue that you find meaningful—from scientific experiments on animals to regulating pornography. The list of debate-worthy issues is endless. In fact, each discipline in college has its own controversial issues that press scholars and students to test one another's positions.

Because a position paper articulates what you profess to believe about an issue, such writing requires commitment. Use the position paper, then, as an opportunity to take a stand, to debate those who hold different positions, and to explore what you are willing to risk.

What's Ahead

- Overview: Taking a Position
  - Student Models
  - Professional Models
- Guidelines
- Writing Checklist and Activities

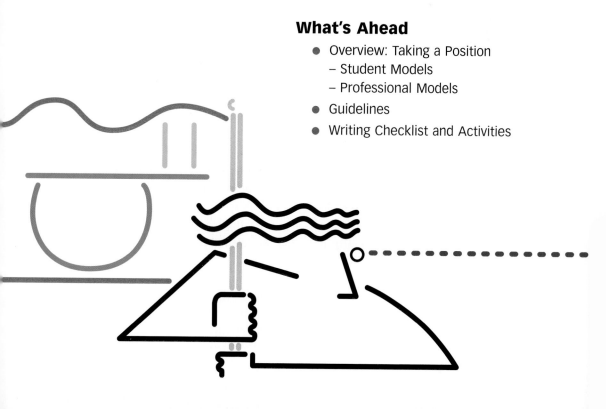

Overview
Taking a Position

Writer's Goal

Your goal is to take a stand on a controversial issue. Aim to explain what you believe and why you believe it. Be thoughtful but bold, encouraging readers to respect and even adopt your position.

Keys for Success

Explore all positions. ■ Before settling firmly on a position, study the pluses and minuses of all possible stands that could be taken on the issue.

Go beyond pure opinion. ■ Opinions and positions are different. Whereas an opinion may be uninformed and inherited, you *think* your way into a position. A position carries weight because of tested reasoning and reliable evidence. It shows mature thinking—thinking that is lively and concrete, not clichéd.

Take a measured stance. ■ Instead of taking a defend-at-all-costs approach, be reasonable. Concede points to your opponents, and address objections to your view. If necessary, soften your stance with qualifiers. Let the evidence weigh in favor of your position—not verbal aggression, bluster, or the fever of your feelings.

Topics to Consider

What topics work well for a position paper? Debatable ones, of course—ideas about which thoughtful people can reasonably disagree.

- **Current Affairs:** Explore recent trends, new laws, major changes, and emerging controversies discussed in the news media, journals, or online discussion groups.

- **Burning Issues:** What issues related to family, work, education, recreation, technology, the environment, or popular culture do you care about? Which issue do you want to confront?

- **Dividing Lines:** What dividing lines characterize the communities to which you belong—what issues set people against one another? Religion, gender, money, class, sports? Think about these broad subjects, and then identify a focused issue in one of them.

- **Fresh Fare:** Sometimes an unexpected topic, like barbed versus smooth fishing hooks, offers the most potential. Avoid tired issues unless you can revive them with a fresh perspective.

Next Step Read the model essays and perform the activities that follow. As you read, think of similar issues on which you could take a stand. What position would you take, and how would you defend it?

Taking a Position

Rita Isakson is an English major who read an article in which the writer asserted that Barbie dolls harm young girls' development. In this essay, Isakson uses logic and her own experience to build a counterargument.

An Apology for the Life of Ms. Barbie D. Doll

The writer states her opponent's arguments and disagrees with them.

Barbie's boobs and spacious mansion helped cause the decay of today's youth, supposed experts say. For example, in her article, "'I Want to Be a Barbie Doll When I Grow Up': The Cultural Significance of the Barbie Doll," Marilyn Ferris Motz argues the following: Barbie dolls encourage young girls to be conformists focused on "leisure activities, personal appearance, popularity, and the consumption of materials" (125). Barbie's skinny waist, huge bosom, and narrow hips entice girls into poor diets and eating disorders. Barbie-play trains girls to depend on Ken-figures (or other males) to achieve self-worth. Barbie's all-American-girl values teach conformity; and Barbie's racy cars, plush houses, and chic outfits cause materialism (128–132). But I don't buy Motz's "reasons." They sound fake—like the theories of somebody who lacks first-hand experience. I had Barbie dolls—twelve of them, in fact, and the Barbie Mansion and Soda Shop to boot—but I don't consider myself an anorexic, dependent, conforming, materialistic girl, at least no more than I would be had I foregone the Barbie experience. *1*

Her tone is forceful and playful, but thoughtful.

She concedes a point but rebuts the argument.

Granted, Barbie's physical appearance isn't realistic. As Motz explains, "If Barbie stood five feet nine inches tall, her bust measurement would be 33 inches, her waist a meager 18 inches, and her hips only 28 1/2 inches" (128). In addition, Motz says, "Barbie's arms are extremely thin and her hands disproportionately small. Her legs are much too long . . ." (128–129). I say, so what? While the only "real" version of Barbie's body would be a long-limbed 13-year-old with breast implants, who cares? Arguing that Barbie's unrealistic bod hurts girls' self-esteem is weak logic. Children have had dolls for ages. For example, in Pompeii, the preserved remains of a 3,000-year-old doll are displayed. That doll has an egghead, and a body that looks like a thick, shapeless rock. If Barbie's proportions hurt modern girls' self-esteem, I pity antiquity's girls, who had these lumps for models! *2*

Her own experience adds support.

Motz says that the average age of girls who play with Barbie is six, and that girls this age imitate the doll's values, like her preoccupation with appearance (127). However, while I was about six when I played with Barbie, I didn't imitate her. At age seven, I had a bowl haircut that was constantly snarled because I wouldn't take time to brush it. I didn't care about my own appearance, while fixing Barbie's was fun. I didn't fuss over my own hair and weight until I was in high school, and fashion mags were scripture. In other words, Motz's theory—that girls' preoccupation with Barbie's appearance leads to later preoccupation with their own—simply doesn't reflect my experience. Nor does her theory reflect the experiences of many other girls, including my two roommates. *3*

The writer rebuts each point in turn, often quoting directly from the article.

In response to Motz's idea that Barbies make girls dependent on males, I say, "Phooey." I played with Barbies until every last cow came home, and I am now a happy single girl. In fact, I have often been single, free from all romantic attachments. True, I've had boyfriends, but I never felt compelled to sacrifice my needs or identity to keep a boyfriend. And I am not an exception to Motz's rule! I know many girls whose primary concerns are their friends, family, and/or schoolwork. Admittedly, there is probably an equal number of girls who live only for their beaus; however, their behavior doesn't prove that Barbie causes female dependency. For example, my own interest in boys was prompted most by "good" TV shows and books—like Laura Ingalls Wilder's *On the Shores of Silver Lake*. It was stories like these—about teenage girls in love—that encouraged me to crave romance.

4

She summarizes her disagreement and offers alternative explanations.

In other words, Motz uses Barbie as a scapegoat for problems that have complex causes. For example, a girl's interest in romance is no more Barbie's fault than the fault of books like *On the Shores of Silver Lake*. Fashion magazines targeted at adolescents are the cause of far more anorexia cases than is Barbie. Mothers who encourage daughters to find security in men teach female dependency, but Barbie doesn't. In fact, Motz herself points out that when "the Barbie doll was created, many parents hailed the doll as a model of wholesome teenage behavior and appearance" (130). I would add that today many parents still hail Barbie as a model for wholesome behavior. But it is more the manner in which parents give toys to their children—the parents' ideas and instructions about how to play—that determine whether Barbie-play is good or bad.

5

Speaking directly to the opposition, the writer shares an anecdote and restates her counterclaim.

To Motz and similar "experts," I say this: Some of my finest childhood memories are of my best friend, Solara, coming over to my house with her pink carry-on suitcase stuffed with Barbies and their accoutrements. For hours we would play with them, giving haircuts, filling mixing bowls to make swimming pools, and creating small "campfires" so Barbie could make s'mores. Sometimes we dressed her in store-bought clothes, and sometimes we designed clothing for her. Other times we turned Barbie into the heroines in our books, and she helped us act out the plots. Playing with Barbies need not be an unimaginative, antisocial activity that promotes conformity, materialism, and superficial ideals. I played with Barbies and I'm fine. Take that, Motz! ■

6

Writing Prompt

Reading for Better Writing

1. The word *apology* can mean *defense,* as well as a statement of regret for wrongdoing. Is the use of the word fitting in the title? Why or why not?

2. This essay is a counterargument that relies heavily on logic and personal experience for support. How does the writer treat the original source? How do concessions and rebuttals function in the argument?

Taking a Position

In this article, student Meg Greenfield explains her position on a highly emotional issue: animal rights. As you will see, she places herself in a philosophically vulnerable position, a position that she believes many of her readers will share.

In Defense of the Animals

The writer states her position immediately, forcefully, and simply.

I might as well come right out with it. Contrary to some of my most cherished prejudices, the animal-rights people have begun to get to me. I think that in some part of what they say, they are right.

I never thought it would come to this. As distinct from the old-style animal rescue, protection, and shelter organizations, the more aggressive newcomers . . . have earned a reputation in the world I live in as fanatics and just plain kooks. And even with my own recently (relatively) raised consciousness, there remains a good deal in both their critique and their prescription for the virtuous life that I reject, being not just a practicing carnivore, a wearer of shoe leather, and so forth, but also a supporter of certain indisputably agonizing procedures visited upon innocent animals in the furtherance of human welfare, especially experiments undertaken to improve human health.

She shares her difficulty at taking this stand.

So, viewed from the pure position, I am probably only marginally better than the worst of my kind, if that: I don't buy the complete "speciesist" analysis or even the fundamental language of animal "rights" and continue to find a large part of what is done in the name of that cause harmful and extreme. But I also think, patronizing as it must sound, that zealots are required early on in any movement if it is to succeed in altering the sensibility of the leaden masses, such as me. Eventually they get your attention. And eventually you at least feel obliged to weigh their arguments and think about whether there may not be something there.

While criticizing the extremes of a movement, she concedes its force.

It is true that this end has often been achieved—as in my case—by means of vivid, cringe-inducing photographs, not by an appeal to reason or values so much as by an assault on squeamishness. From the famous 1970s photo of the newly skinned baby seal to the videos of animals being raised in the most dark, miserable, stunting environment as they are readied for their life's sole fulfillment as frozen patties and cutlets, these sights have had their effect. . . .

The word *our* draws readers into the debate.

The objection to our being confronted with these dramatic, disturbing pictures is first that they tend to provoke a misplaced, uncritical, and highly emotional concern for animal life at the direct expense of a more suitable concern for human suffering. What goes into the animals' account, the reasoning goes, necessarily comes out of ours. But I think it is possible to remain stalwart in our view that the human claim comes first, and in your acceptance of the use of animals for human betterment, and still to believe

She refines and expands her position statement.

that there are some human interests that should not take precedence. For we have become far too self-indulgent, hardened, careless, and cruel in the pain we routinely inflict upon these creatures for the most frivolous, unworthy purposes. And I also think that the more justifiable purposes, such as medical research, are shamelessly used as cover for other activities that are wanton.

She clarifies a key point with an example.

For instance, not all of the painful and crippling experimentation that is undertaken in the lab is being conducted for the sake of medical knowledge or other purposes related to basic human well-being and health. Much of it is being conducted for the sake of super-refinements in the cosmetic and other frill industries, the noble goal being to contrive yet another fragrance or hair tint or commercially competitive variation on all the daft, fizzy, multicolored "personal care" products for the medicine cabinet and dressing table, a firmer-holding hair spray, that sort of thing. . . .

This strikes me as decadent. My problem is that it also causes me to reach a position that is, on its face, philosophically vulnerable, if not absurd—the muddled, middling, inconsistent place where finally you are saying it's all right to kill them for some purposes, but not to hurt them gratuitously in doing it or to make them suffer horribly for one's own trivial whims.

Acknowledging her muddled position, the writer defends it vigorously and ends positively.

I would feel more humiliated to have fetched up on this exposed rock, if I didn't suspect I had so much company. When you see pictures of people laboriously trying to clean the Exxon gunk off sea otters even knowing that they will be able to help out only a very few, you see this same outlook in action. And I think it can be defended. For to me the biggest cop-out is the one that says that if you don't buy the whole absolutist, extreme position it is pointless and even hypocritical to concern yourself with lesser mercies and ameliorations. The pressure of the animal-protection groups has already had some impact in improving the way various creatures are treated by researchers, trainers, and food producers. There is much more in this vein to be done. We are talking about rejecting wanton, pointless cruelty here. The position may be philosophically absurd, but the outcome is the right one. ■

6

7

8

Writing Prompt

Reading for Better Writing

1. If Greenfield is actually defending animal rights, why does she spend so much time criticizing the animal-rights movement?

2. Describe Greenfield's tone. Is it effective for this topic and this audience? Why or why not?

3. After stating her position in the opening, how does Greenfield proceed to explain, clarify, and expand that stand? Note where she explicitly restates her position and look closely at her concluding paragraph.

Taking a Position

Pulitzer-winning political commentator Leonard Pitts, Jr., writes a syndicated column for the *Miami Herald*. This column was published in March 2005, shortly after news sources reported that a teen from Minnesota's Red Lake Reservation had posted messages to a neo-Nazi website before killing himself and nine others.

Apostles of Hatred Find It Easy to Spread Their Message

I just visited the website that fascinated Jeff Weise, the 16-year-old who shot up his high school last week on the Red Lake Reservation in Minnesota. There, I learned that the tribes of humanity must be separated or risk destruction by assimilation. That Jews are a "fanatical religious-ethnic" group conspiring to control communications media. And that for all the dubious talk about a "Holocaust," you never hear about the good things Adolf Hitler did.

I also read the posts that Weise left on the site's bulletin board. I was particularly interested in the one asking if the group would accept him, given that he was a Chippewa Indian. Weise was friendless, his father was dead, his mother in a nursing home, so there was something poignant and needy in the asking.

In all, I spent half an hour on nazi.org. It gave me a headache.

Used to be easier to laugh this stuff off. Once, when I was in college, a man in a "White Power" T-shirt came into the bookstore where I worked. My friend Cathy, who was white, promptly plopped herself in my lap, pecked me on the cheek and asked loudly when I might be "home" for dinner.

Mr. White Power glared at us, then beat a quick retreat.

Thirty years later, it's harder to respond to the apostles of organized hatred. Not just because the Internet gives them a reach no guy in a T-shirt could match but because many have refined their message, made it slicker, given it a patina of reason.

The people behind nazi.org, for instance, would want you to know they don't consider themselves white supremacists. To the contrary, they are open to anyone—black, Asian, Indian—who believes blacks, Asians and Indians should confine themselves to their own countries—and that Jews are "vicious," "parasitic," "liars" and "hypocrites."

I won't subject you to a treatise on why these people are abhorrent. If you don't already know, you need more help than anyone can give you in a few inches of newsprint. No, I am only here to note the sad incongruity of an American Indian boy asking admission to their ranks.

Perhaps when you heard that, you concluded that it spoke to the self-hatred that is sometimes inculcated among minority communities. But Weise's complaint wasn't that he hated Indians but, rather, that too many of his people were not "Indian" enough, that their culture was diluted by

---

Sidebar annotations:

The phrase "I learned" introduces the ideas posted on the website.

The writer notes that his friend is white and implies that he is black.

The writer justifies giving attention to only one side of the issue.

A clarification is offered.

Paragraph numbers in margin: 1, 2, 3, 4, 5, 6, 7, 8, 9, 10

exposure to others. He was especially offended by those Native youth who are fans of hip-hop. He saw them as more black than Native.

11   It's a painful reminder that building a society where different cultures are welcomed and interaction valued is a difficult task. Some of us see it as the onerous burden of a politically correct era, others, as a clear and present danger to the status quo. The latter intuit, correctly, that when one culture is exposed to another, both are likely to be changed.

> The words *us* and *we* show the writer identifying with his readers.

12   The difference between those people and the rest of us is that we aren't scared of change. We recognize that while change is a challenge, it is also a condition of life. The trick—difficult, to be sure, but also rewarding—is to hold on to what is good, yet incorporate what is new.

13   For some people, that's an accomplishment beyond achieving or even attempting.

> The writer explains how quotes from the opposing view can be used to support his own claim.

14   We don't know what role Weise's Nazi beliefs played in his decision to kill nine people before taking his own life. But it seems obvious he needed what the Nazis provided—the illusion that culture can be made orderly and change put on hold.

15   Yet what did his Nazi friends have to say after the massacre? That they would not "wring hands" over a "tragedy," the last word in quotes to indicate that it wasn't tragic at all. Makes you sorrow for the boy even in the midst of your anger at him.

16   Weise wanted so badly to belong to something. Obviously, he never did. ∎

Reading for Better Writing

1. On what issue is Pitts taking a position, and what is his view? In what ways is the topic controversial (or not), and how might this affect the ways in which various readers might respond to the piece?

2. In paragraph two, Pitts states that he "learned" a number of things from the website. What do you think he means by his use of the word "learned," and why?

3. Writers are often encouraged to explore multiple views of an issue before taking a position. Why doesn't Pitts offer a detailed explanation about why he finds the nazi.org website "abhorrent"? What do you think about this choice?

4. Where does Pitts quote from the website in question, and why?

Taking a Position

Canadian author Margaret Atwood is well known for her ability to address feminist concerns in wide range of genres. Her novels *The Handmaid's Tale* and *The Blind Assassin* (a winner of the 2000 Booker Prize) are especially well known. This essay was first published in 1983.

> The topic is clearly stated in the title.

Pornography

When I was in Finland a few years ago for an international writers' conference, I had occasion to say a few paragraphs in public on the subject of pornography. The context was a discussion of political repression, and I was suggesting the possibility of a link between the two. The immediate result was that a male journalist took several large bites out of me. Prudery and pornography are two halves of the same coin, said he, and I was clearly a prude. What could you expect from an Anglo-Canadian? Afterward, a couple of pleasant Scandinavian men asked me what I had been so worked up about. All "pornography" means, they said, is graphic depictions of whores, and what was the harm in that?

> The writer summarizes another person's comments about her to introduce and clarify her position.

Not until then did it strike me that the male journalist and I had two entirely different things in mind. By "pornography," he meant naked bodies and sex. I, on the other hand, had recently been doing the research for my novel *Bodily Harm*, and was still in a state of shock from some of the material I had seen, including the Ontario Board of Film Censors' "outtakes." By "pornography," I meant women getting their nipples snipped off with garden shears, having meat hooks stuck into their vaginas, being disemboweled; little girls being raped; men (yes, there are some men) being smashed to a pulp and forcibly sodomized. The cutting edge of pornography, as far as I could see, was no longer simple old copulation, hanging from the chandelier or otherwise: it was death, messy, explicit and highly sadistic. I explained this to the nice Scandinavian men. "Oh, but that's just the United States," they said. "Everyone knows they're sick." In their country, they said, violent "pornography" of that kind was not permitted on television or in movies; indeed, excessive violence of any kind was not permitted. They had drawn a clear line between erotica, which earlier studies had shown did not incite men to more aggressive and brutal behavior toward women, and violence, which later studies indicated did.

> She distinguishes between two terms: *erotica* and *violence*.

Some time after that I was in Saskatchewan, where, because of the scenes in *Bodily Harm*, I found myself on an open-line radio show answering questions about "pornography." Almost no one who phoned in was in favor of it, but again they weren't talking about the same stuff I was, because they hadn't seen it. Some of them were all set to stamp out bathing suits and negligees, and, if possible, any depictions of the female body whatsoever. God, it was implied, did not approve of female bodies, and sex of any kind, including that practiced by bumblebees, should be shoved back into the dark, where it belonged. I had more than a suspicion that *Lady*

1

2

3

Chatterley's Lover, Margaret Laurance's *The Diviners,* and indeed most books by most serious modern authors would have ended up as confetti if left in the hands of these callers.

For me, these two experiences illustrate the two poles of the emotionally heated debate that is now thundering around this issue. They also underline the desirability and even the necessity of defining the terms. "Pornography" is now one of those catchalls, like "Marxism" and "feminism," that have become so broad they can mean almost anything, ranging from certain verses in the Bible, ads for skin lotion and sex texts for children to the contents of *Penthouse,* Naughty '90s postcards and films with titles containing the word *Nazi* that show vicious scenes of torture and killing. It's easy to say that sensible people can tell the difference. Unfortunately, opinions on what constitutes a sensible person vary.

> *"Pornography" is now one of those catchalls . . .*

But even sensible people tend to lose their cool when they start talking about this subject. They soon stop talking and start yelling, and the name-calling begins. Those in favor of censorship (which may include groups not noticeably in agreement on other issues, such as some feminists and religious fundamentalists) accuse the others of exploiting women through the use of degrading images, contributing to the corruption of children, and adding to the general climate of violence and threat in which both women and children live in this society; or, though they may not give much of a hoot about actual women and children, they invoke moral standards and God's supposed aversion to "filth," "smut" and deviated *perversion,* which may mean ankles.

The camp in favor of total "freedom of expression" often comes out howling as loud as the Romans would have if told they could no longer have innocent fun watching the lions eat up Christians. It too may include segments of the population who are not natural bedfellows: those who proclaim their God-given right to freedom, including the freedom to tote guns, drive when drunk, drool over chicken porn and get off on videotapes of women being raped and beaten, may be waving the same anticensorship banner as responsible liberals who fear the return of Mrs. Grundy, or gay groups for whom sexual emancipation involves the concept of "sexual theater." *Whatever turns you on* is a handy motto, as is *A man's home is his castle* (and if it includes a dungeon with beautiful maidens strung up in chains and bleeding from every pore, that's his business).

Meanwhile, theoreticians theorize and speculators speculate. Is today's pornography yet another indication of the hatred of the body, the deep mind–body split, which is supposed to pervade Western Christian society? Is it a backlash against the women's movement by men who are threatened

4

5

6

7

The writer acknowledges a range of views about how to define pornography.

A list illustrates a range of arguments that are made for censoring pornography.

Another list points to a range of people who may make arguments against censoring pornography.

Yet another list represents the questions that people raise about the causes and effects of pornography.

by uppity female behavior in real life, so like to fantasize about women done up like outsize parcels, being turned into hamburger, kneeling at their feet in slavelike adoration or sucking off guns? Is it a sign of collective impotence, of a generation of men who can't relate to real women at all but have to make do with bits of celluloid and paper? Is the current flood just a result of smart marketing and aggressive promotion by the money men in what has now become a multibillion-dollar industry? If they were selling movies about men getting their testicles stuck full of knitting needles by women with swastikas on their sleeves, would they do as well, or is this penchant somehow peculiarly male? If so, why? Is pornography a power trip rather than a sex

> *Is pornography a power trip rather than a sex one?*

one? Some say that those ropes, chains, muzzles and other restraining devices are an argument for the immense power female sexuality still wields in the male imagination: you don't put these things on dogs unless you're afraid of them. Others, more literary, wonder about the shift from the 19th-century Magic Woman or Femme Fatale image to the lollipoplicker, airhead or turkey-carcass treatment of women in porn today. The

The writer labels two camps: proporners and anitporners.

proporners don't care much about theory: they merely demand product. The antiporners don't care about it in the final analysis either: there's dirt on the street, and they want it cleaned up, now.

She cites an impasse.

It seems to me that this conversation, with its *You're-a-prude/You're-a-pervert* dialectic, will never get anywhere as long as we continue to think of this material as just "entertainment." Possibly we're deluded by the packaging, the format: magazine, book, movie, theatrical presentation. We're used to thinking of these things as part of the "entertainment industry," and we're used to thinking of ourselves as free adult people who ought to be able to see any kind of "entertainment" we want to. That was what the First Choice pay-TV debate was all about. After all, it's only entertainment, right? Entertainment means fun, and only a killjoy would be antifun. What's the harm? 8

The writer identifies a key point.

This is obviously the central question: *What's the harm?* If there isn't any real harm to any real people, then the antiporners can tsk-tsk and/or throw up as much as they like, but they can't rightfully expect more legal controls or sanctions. However, the no-harm position is far from being proven. 9

(For instance, there's a clear-cut case for banning—as the federal government has proposed—movies, photos and videos that depict children engaging in sex with adults: real children are used to make the movies, and hardly anybody thinks this ethical. The possibilities for coercion are too great.) 10

A transition
sentence
predicts the
organization
of ideas that
will follow.

– – – – – To shift the viewpoint, I'd like to suggest three other models for looking *11*
at "pornography"—and here I mean the violent kind.

Those who find the idea of regulating pornographic materials *12*
repugnant because they think it's Fascist or Communist or otherwise not in
accordance with the principles of an open
democratic society should consider that
Canada has made it illegal to disseminate
material that may lead to hatred toward
any group because of race or religion. I
suggest that if pornography of the violent
kind depicted these acts being done
predominantly to Chinese, to blacks, to
Catholics, it would be off the market
immediately, under the present laws. Why
is hate literature illegal? Because whoever
made the law thought that such material
might incite real people to do real awful things to other real people. The
human brain is to a certain extent a computer: garbage in, garbage out. We
only hear about the extreme cases (like that of American multimurderer Ted
Bundy) in which pornography has contributed to the death and/or
mutilation of women and/or men. Although pornography is not the only
factor involved in the creation of such deviance, it certainly has upped the
ante by suggesting both a variety of techniques and the social acceptability
of such actions. Nobody knows yet what effect this stuff is having on the
less psychotic.

The nature
and effects
of porn are
compared to
those of hate
crimes.

> *The human
> brain is to a
> certain extent
> a computer:
> garbage in,
> garbage out.*

Studies have shown that a large part of the market for all kinds of porn, *13*
soft and hard, is drawn from the 16-to-21-year-old population of young
men. Boys used to learn about sex on the street, or (in Italy, according to
Fellini movies) from friendly whores, or, in more genteel surroundings,
from girls, their parents, or, once upon a time, in school, more or less. Now
porn has been added, and sex education in the schools is rapidly being
phased out. The buck has been passed, and boys are being taught that all
women secretly like to be raped and that real men get high on scooping out
women's digestive tracts.

References
to studies
lend
scientific
authority
to the
argument.

Boys learn their concept of masculinity from other men: is this what *14*
most men want them to be learning? If word gets around that rapists are
"normal" and even admirable men, will boys feel that in order to be normal,
admirable and masculine they will have to be rapists? Human beings are
enormously flexible, and how they turn out depends a lot on how they're
educated, by the society in which they're immersed as well as by their
teachers. In a society that advertises and glorifies rape or even implicitly
condones it, more women get raped. It becomes socially acceptable. And at
a time when men and the traditional male role have taken a lot of flak and
men are confused and casting around for an acceptable way of being male
(and, in some cases, not getting much comfort from women on that score),
this must be at times a pleasing thought.

Two models
are identified
with labels.

A
comparison
to regulated
substances
helps
support an
argument for
regulating
pornography.

It would be naïve to think of violent pornography as just harmless entertainment. It's also an educational tool and a powerful propaganda device. What happens when boy educated on porn meets girl brought up on Harlequin romances? The clash of expectations can be heard around the block. She wants him to get down on his knees with a ring, he wants her to get down on all fours with a ring in her nose. Can this marriage be saved? 15

Pornography has certain things in common with such addictive substances as alcohol and drugs: for some, though by no means for all, it induces chemical changes in the body, which the user finds exciting and pleasurable. It also appears to attract a "hard core" of habitual users and a penumbra of those who use it occasionally but aren't dependent on it in any way. There are also significant numbers of men who aren't much interested in it, not because they're undersexed but because real life is satisfying their needs, which may not require as many appliances as those of users. 16

For the "hard core," pornography may function as alcohol does for the alcoholic: tolerance develops, and a little is no longer enough. This may account for the short viewing time and fast turnover in porn theatres. Mary Brown, chairwoman of the Ontario Board of Film Censors, estimates that for every one mainstream movie requesting entrance to Ontario, there is one porno flick. Not only the quantity consumed but the quality of explicitness must escalate, which may account for the growing violence: once the big deal was breasts, then it was genitals, then copulation, then that was no longer enough and the hard users had to have more. The ultimate kick is death, and after that, as the Marquis de Sade so boringly demonstrated, multiple death. 17

> *The ultimate kick is death, and after that . . . multiple death.*

After outlin-
ing three
alternate
models, the
writer
reviews
her main
question.

She
proposes a
direction for
further study.

The existence of alcoholism has not led us to ban social drinking. On the other hand, we do have laws about drinking and driving, excessive drunkenness and other abuses of alcohol that may result in injury or death to others. 18

This leads us back to the key question: what's the harm? Nobody knows, but this society should find out fast, before the saturation point is reached. The Scandinavian studies that showed a connection between depictions of sexual violence and increased impulse toward it on the part of male viewers would be a starting point, but many more questions remain to be raised as well as answered. What, for instance, is the crucial difference between men who are users and men who are not? Does using affect a man's relationship with actual women, and, if so, adversely? Is there a clear line between erotica and violent pornography, or are they on an escalating continuum? Is this a "men versus women" issue, with all men secretly siding with the proporners and all women secretly siding against? (I think not; there *are* lots of men who don't think that running their true love through 19 the Cuisinart is the best way they can think of to spend a Saturday night, and they're just as nauseated by films of someone else doing it as women are.) Is pornography merely an expression of the sexual confusion of this age or an active contributor to it?

> **The limits of the two extreme views are reviewed.**

Nobody wants to go back to the age of official repression, when even [20] piano legs were referred to as "limbs" and had to wear pantaloons to be decent. Neither do we want to end up in George Orwell's *1984*, in which pornography is turned out by the State to keep the proles in a state of torpor, sex itself is considered dirty and the approved practice it only for reproduction. But Rome under the emperors isn't such a good model either.

> **The writer states an ideal as well as a position grounded in reality.**

If all men and women respected each other, if sex were considered [21] joyful and life-enhancing instead of a wallow in germ-filled glop, if everyone were in love all the time, if, in other words, many people's lives were more satisfactory for them than they appear to be now, pornography might just go away on its own. But since this is obviously not happening, we as a society are going to have to make some informed and responsible decisions about how to deal with it. ■

Reading for Better Writing

1. What views on pornography does Atwood examine before detailing her own view?

2. Skilled writers often "make a space" for their arguments by demonstrating the limits or shortcomings of others' ideas and then showing how their own ideas fill the gaps. How (and where) does Atwood do this?

3. Atwood proposes three alternate models for thinking about pornography. What are they? How could the piece be edited to include signal words to make these three models more readily apparent?

4. Besides stating her opinion, what does the writer do to support her position?

5. In what ways does (or doesn't) Atwood succeed in taking a measured stance that may appeal to readers on both sides of the debate?

Taking a Position

Writer Linda Chavez's essay, which was published in 1994, argues against the "advance of multiculturalism" in the United States. Chavez speaks confidently and assertively throughout the essay—conceding little to the opposition.

Demystifying Multiculturalism

> **The writer portrays the current trends, questions these trends, and raises the alarm.**

Multiculturalism is on the advance, everywhere from President 1
Clinton's cabinet to corporate boardrooms to public-school classrooms. If you believe the multiculturalists' propaganda, whites are on the verge of becoming a minority in the United States. The multiculturalists predict that this demographic shift will fundamentally change American culture—indeed destroy the very idea that America has a single, unified culture. They aren't taking any chances, however. They have enlisted the help of government, corporate leaders, the media, and the education establishment in waging a cultural revolution. But has America truly become a multicultural nation? And if not, will those who capitulate to these demands create a self-fulfilling prophecy?

> **The essay presents arguments for multiculturalism, along with counterarguments.**

At the heart of the argument is the assumption that the white popula- 2
tion is rapidly declining in relation to the nonwhite population. A 1987 Hudson Institute report helped catapult this claim to national prominence. The study, *Workforce 2000,* estimated that by the turn of the century only 15 percent of new workers would be white males. The figure was widely interpreted to mean that whites were about to become a minority in the workplace—and in the country.

> **Statistics support the writer's claims.**

In fact, white males will still constitute about 45 percent—a plurality— 3
of the workforce in the year 2000. The proportion of white men in the workforce *is* declining—it was nearly 51 percent in 1980—but primarily because the proportion of white women is growing. They will make up 39 percent of the workforce within 10 years, according to government projections, up from 36 percent in 1980. Together, white men and women will account for 84 percent of all workers by 2000—hardly a minority share. . . .

Multiculturalists insist on treating race and ethnicity as if they were 4
synonymous with culture. They presume that skin color and national origin, which are immutable traits, determine values, mores, language, and other cultural attributes, which, of course, are learned. In the multiculturalists' world view, African Americans, Puerto Ricans, or Chinese Americans living in New York City have more in common with persons of their ancestral group living in Lagos or San Juan or Hong Kong than they do with other New Yorkers who are white. Culture becomes a fixed entity, transmitted, as it were, in the genes, rather than through experience. . . .

The writer questions the opposition's logic.

Such convictions lead multiculturalists to conclude that "[T]here is no common American culture." The logic is simple, but wrongheaded: Since Americans (or more often, their forebears) hail from many different places, each of which has its own specific culture, the argument goes, America must be multicultural. And it is becoming more so every day as new immigrants bring their cultures with them.

Indeed, multiculturalists hope to ride the immigrant wave to greater power and influence. They have certainly done so in education. Some 2.3 million children who cannot speak English well now attend public schools, an increase of 1 million in the last seven years. Multicultural advocates cite the presence of such children to demand bilingual education and other multicultural services. The Los Angeles Unified School District alone currently offers instruction in Spanish, Armenian, Korean, Cantonese, Tagalog, Japanese, and Russian. Federal and state governments now spend literally billions of dollars on these programs.

She probes opposing arguments and exposes ironies.

Ironically, the multiculturalists' emphasis on education undercuts their argument that culture is inextricable from race or national origin. They are acutely aware of just how fragile cultural identification is; why else are they so adamant about reinforcing it? Multiculturalists insist on teaching immigrant children in their native language, instructing them in the history and customs of their native land, and imbuing them with reverence for their ancestral heroes, lest these youngsters be seduced by American culture.

She analyzes multicultural proponents.

The impetus for multiculturalism is not coming from immigrants, but from their more affluent and assimilated native-born counterparts. The proponents are most often the elite—the best educated and most successful members of their respective racial and ethnic groups. College campuses, where the most radical displays of multiculturalism take place, are fertile recruiting grounds. Last May, for example, a group of Mexican American students at UCLA, frustrated that the university would not elevate the school's 23-year-old Chicano studies program to full department status, stormed the faculty center, breaking windows and furniture and causing half a million dollars in damage. The same month, a group of Asian American students at UC–Irvine went on a hunger strike to pressure administrators into hiring more professors of Asian American studies. These were not immigrants or even, by and large, disadvantaged students, but middle-class beneficiaries of their parents' or grandparents' successful assimilation into the American mainstream.

She uses statistics to describe those who support multicultural policies.

Whatever their newfound victim status, these students look amazingly like other Americans on most indices. For example, the median family income of Mexican American students at Berkeley in 1989 was $32,500, slightly above the national median for all Americans that year, $32,191; and 17 percent of those students came from families that earned more than $75,000 a year, even though they were admitted to the university under affirmative-action programs (presumably because they suffered some educational disadvantage attributed to their ethnicity).

> A critical point about the source of multi-culturalism is saved for the end.

Multiculturalism is not a grassroots movement. It was created, nurtured, and expanded through government policy. Without the expenditure of vast sums of public money, it would wither away and die. That is not to say that ethnic communities would disappear from the American scene or that groups would not retain some attachment to their ancestral roots. American assimilation has always entailed some give-and-take, and American culture has been enriched by what individual groups brought to it. The distinguishing characteristic of American culture is its ability to incorporate so many disparate groups, creating a new whole from the many parts. Lately, we have nearly reversed course, treating each group, new and old, as if what is most important is to preserve its separate identity and space.

10

> The writer presses readers to question policies and closes with a provocative question.

It is easy to blame the ideologues and radicals who are pushing the "disuniting of America," to use Arthur Schlesinger's phrase, but the real culprits are those who provide multiculturalists with the money and the access to press their cause. Without the acquiescence of policy makers and ordinary citizens, multiculturalism would be no threat. Unfortunately, most major institutions have little stomach for resisting the multicultural impulse—and many seem eager to comply with whatever demands the multiculturalists make. Americans should have learned by now that policy matters. We have only to look at the failure of our welfare and crime policies to know that providing perverse incentives can change the way individuals behave—for the worse. Who is to say that if we pour enough money into dividing Americans, we won't succeed? ■

11

Writing Prompt

Reading for Better Writing

1. In a nutshell, what is Chavez arguing against, and why?

2. How would you describe her attitudes toward the topic, her readers, and her opposition?

3. Trace the writer's argument in outline form. How effectively does Chavez use counterarguments? Does she put forward her own argument, or does she simply imply it?

Guidelines
Taking a Position

Note: For in-depth help on developing persuasive arguments, see pages **248–261**.

1. **Select and narrow a topic.** Through reading, viewing, or surfing the Internet, explore current issues on which people can take different, well-reasoned positions. Select an issue that you care about, and carve that topic down to size by considering a specific angle on it.

2. **Take stock.** Before you dig into your topic, assess your starting point. What is your current position on the topic? Why? What evidence do you have?

3. **Get inside the issue.** To take a defensible position, study the issue carefully. The following strategies will help you measure and develop what you know:
   - Investigate all possible positions on the issue. Through brainstorming and research, think through all arguments and issues on all sides.
   - Consider doing firsthand research that will help you speak with authority and passion.
   - Write your position at the top of a page. Below it, set up "Pro" and "Con" columns. List arguments in each column.
   - Develop a line of reasoning supporting your position. Then test that reasoning for two things:
   First, no logical fallacies, such as broad generalization, either/or thinking, oversimplification, or slanted language. (See pages **255–258**.)
   Second, an effective range of support: statistics, observations, expert testimony, comparisons, experiences, and analysis. (See pages **252–254**.)

4. **Refine your position.** By now, you may have sharpened or radically changed your starting position. Before you organize and draft your essay, clarify your position. If it helps, use this formula:
   I believe this to be true about _____ :
   _____ .

5. **Organize your development and support.** Now you've committed yourself to a position. Before drafting, review these organizational options:
   - **Traditional Pattern:** Introduce the issue, state your position, support it, address and refute opposition, and restate your position.
   - **Blatant Confession:** Place your position statement in the first sentence —boldly displayed for your reader to chew on.
   - **Delayed Gratification:** In the first part of your essay, explore the various positions available on the topic; compare and contrast them, and then defend your position.

- **Changed Mind**: If your research changed your mind on the topic, build that shift into the essay itself. Readers may respond well to such honesty.
- **Winning Over**: If your readers may strongly oppose your position, then focus on that opposition. Defend your position by anticipating and answering each question, concern, and objection.

6. **Write your first draft**. If helpful, set aside your notes and get your position and support down on paper. If you prefer, work closely from your outline. Here are some possible strategies:

   Opening: Seize the reader's imagination. Raise concern for the issue with a dramatic story, a pointed example, a vivid picture, a thought-provoking question, or a personal confession. Supply background information that readers need to understand the issue.

   Development: Deepen, clarify, and support your position statement, using solid logic and reliable support. A clear, well-reasoned defense will help readers accept your position.

   Closing: End on a lively, thoughtful note that stresses your commitment. If appropriate, make a direct or indirect plea to readers to adopt your position.

   Title: Choose a bold title that offers a choice or stresses a stand.

7. **Share your position**. At this point, feedback from a peer or a tutor in the writing center might help. Does your reviewer accept your position? Why or why not?

8. **Revise your writing**. Consider your reviewer's comments and review the draft yourself. Cut, change, and/or add material with the following questions in mind:

   - Is the position clearly stated? Is it effectively qualified and refined?
   - Have you shown how your stand affects yourself and others?
   - Are the reasoning and support sound and complete?
   - Does the essay show awareness of questions, concerns, and other positions?
   - Do the ideas flow smoothly?
   - Is the tone confident and sincere, not bullying, cocky, or apologetic?

9. **Edit and proofread**. See pages 97–98 for guidelines, but check especially that your writing is free of slogans, clichés, platitudes, insults, and mystifying jargon. Make your language lively, concrete, and energetic.

10. **Prepare and publish your final essay**. Submit your position paper according to your instructor's requirements. In addition, seek a forum for your position—with peers in a discussion group, with relatives, or online.

Writing Checklist

Use these six traits to check your essay, then revise as needed:

_____ The **ideas** establish and defend a stand on a debatable issue. The essay provides sound reasoning and support that help the reader understand and appreciate the position.

_____ The **organization** includes an engaging opening that raises the issue, a carefully sequenced development and defense of the position, and a reflective closing.

_____ The **voice** is thoughtful, measured, committed, convincing, and knowledgeable. The feelings expressed are appropriately strong.

_____ The **words** used are precise, concrete, and lively. Jargon, clichés, platitudes, and insults are avoided.

_____ The **sentences** flow smoothly. Their lengths are varied: Short sentences make snappy points and longer sentences develop thoughtful points.

_____ The **copy** follows rules of grammar, format, and documentation.

Writing
Prompt

Writing Activities

1. Reflect on hot topics in your major—check textbooks, talk to professors or experts, and review journals in the field. Then take a position on a controversial issue.

2. Review the column "Apostles of Hatred," noting how Leonard Pitts includes quotations that oppose his view and then presents counterarguments that support his own claim. Apply this strategy as you draft or revise a position statement on a controversial issue that is relevant to your coursework.

3. Review Margaret Atwood's essay "Pornography," paying special attention to the way that she "makes a space" for her argument by demonstrating the limits or shortcomings of others' ideas and then "fills the gaps" with her own. Draft or revise a position statement in which you use these same strategies.

4. One difficulty of taking a position on a popular hot topic is that most readers will likely already have a firmly established position on the issue. Draft or revise a position statement that attempts to appeal to two well-established sides of a popular debate by taking a measured stance that both groups might find reasonable.

Chapter 19
Persuading Readers to Act

Audio

Persuasion is a challenging task, requiring that you convince readers to believe you, rethink their own perspectives, and take a concrete step. In the end, you want them to change their minds and their actions.

In an essay persuading readers to act, you seek to change readers' opinions on a debatable, complex, and timely issue about which you care deeply, such as wise energy policies or the problem of racism. In addition, your essay presses for the next logical step—motivating readers to act. You achieve that goal with sound logic, reliable support, and fitting appeals. In a sense, you say to readers, "Come, let us reason together."

What do you feel strongly about, and what actions do you want to influence? This chapter will help you write in a way that stirs people to action.

What's Ahead

- Overview: Persuading Readers to Act
  - Student Model
  - Professional Models
- Guidelines
- Writing Checklist and Activities

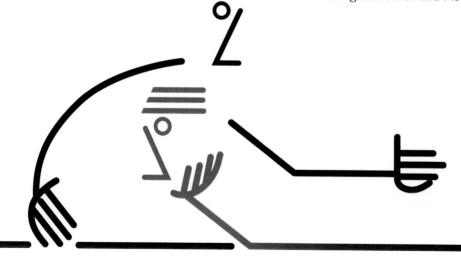

Overview
Persuading Readers to Act

Writer's Goal

Your goal is to urge individual readers to change their behavior or to take action on an issue. To accomplish this goal, you need to change the minds of those who disagree with you, and give encouragement to those who do agree with you.

Keys for Success

Know your audience. ■ When you seek to persuade, you assume that your reader will have some opposition or resistance to your viewpoint. To motivate resistant readers to act, you must know who they are—whether they are peers, professors, the college community, or your nation. Consider their knowledge of and attitudes toward the topic so that you can address their concerns.

Promote your cause—not a quarrel. ■ Your goal is to motivate your readers to act, not to manipulate them so that you win an argument. Study the topic from all sides. Bottom line: Know your subject.

Be reasonable. ■ Make logical claims about your topic, testing them to make sure that they can be supported with sufficient evidence. Review your thinking to identify any logical fallacies as well. Moreover, fine-tune the essay's voice until it is passionate, thoughtful, and sincere.

Topics to Consider

Choose a debate-worthy, timely issue that you care about. Consider topics in these categories:

- **Personal experiences:** What personal experiences have raised questions or concerns for you?
- **Personal ideas:** What issues often occupy your mind? What do you stew about or fear? What makes you say, "Something should be done"?
- **Community concerns:** Think about the different "communities" to which you belong—family, college, race, ethnic group, or gender. What issues concern each group, and why?
- **National or international affairs:** What national or global issues are discussed in your circle of friends, your college community, or the news?
- **"No comment" topics:** Consider issues about which you don't have an opinion. Would you like to develop a strong stance on one of those topics?

Next Step Read the model essays and perform the activities that follow. As you read, think of parallel issues that interest you. Why do these issues intrigue you? How could you communicate that interest to readers and challenge them to take action?

Persuading Readers to Act

Rebecca Pasok is an environmental studies major who wrote this ecological essay to persuade readers to support lifestyle choices and energy policies that do not require drilling for oil in the Arctic National Wildlife Refuge.

To Drill or Not to Drill

The opening provides background information before raising the controversial position.

Known as "America's Last Frontier," the Arctic National Wildlife Refuge (ANWR) is located in the northeast corner of Alaska, right along the Beaufort Sea. President Dwight D. Eisenhower established the refuge in 1960, and today its 19 million acres make it one of the biggest refuges in the United States and home to a wide variety of wildlife such as eagles, wolves, moose, grizzly bears, polar bears, and caribou. During the last few years, however, the security of that home has been threatened by those who want to use one section of the ANWR to drill for oil. That section—named Area 1002—encompasses 1.5 million acres of pristine land near the coast.

The writer starts with a strong argument against drilling but then maps out why others support it.

One of the strongest arguments against oil drilling anywhere in the refuge is that the environmental impact of drilling conflicts with the very purpose of the ANWR. The primary mandate for the ANWR, as laid out by the U.S. Fish and Wildlife Service that administers the refuge, is "to protect the wildlife and habitats of the area for the benefit of people now and in the future." The question then is whether drilling for oil supports, or is in conflict with, this mandate. President George W. Bush and others argue that oil drilling does not conflict with the mandate because new oil-drilling techniques cause only minimal damage to the environment. These techniques include drilling fewer wells, placing wells closer together, and building pipelines above ground so as not to disturb the animals (McCarthy).

Some environmental experts support the argument that the new techniques will not hurt wildlife. While these individuals acknowledge that some land disturbance will result, they argue that animals such as caribou will not suffer. One expert taking this position is Pat Valkenberg, a research coordinator with the Alaska Department of Fish and Game; he maintains that the caribou population is thriving and should continue to thrive. To support this point, Valkenberg notes that between 1997 and 2000, the caribou population actually grew from 19,700 to 27,128 (*Petroleum News*).

She counters the position with expert testimony for the other side.

Other experts challenge those statistics with information about the caribou's birthing patterns. These experts point to herds like the porcupine caribou that live in the ANWR and move along the coast of the Beaufort Sea in the United States and also into Canada. A majority of the females in this herd wear radio collars that have been tracked to Area 1002 during calving season. Experts who argue against drilling note that the calves born on ANWR's coastal plain have a greater chance of surviving than those that are born in the foothills, where many of their predators live (*U.S. Fish and Wildlife*). This difference in survival ratios, argue antidrilling experts, may not be accounted for in the statistics used by prodrilling advocates like Valkenberg.

One specialist opposed to drilling is David Klein, a professor at the Institute of Arctic Biology at the University of Alaska–Fairbanks. Klein argues that if the oil industry opens up the ANWR for drilling, the number of caribou will likely decrease because the calving locations would change. He points out that oil-industry work in the Prudhoe oil field (also in Alaska) has already split up the Central Arctic herd of caribou, so it is likely that drilling in Area 1002 will similarly affect the porcupine herd (McCarthy).

The writer strongly states her thesis—that she agrees with opponents of drilling.

But caribou are not the only wildlife that would be affected by drilling in Area 1002. Musk oxen, polar bears, and grizzly bears could be driven out of the refuge and possibly into regions where people live, thereby threatening both the animals' and people's safety. Clearly, the bottom line in this debate is that drilling in Area 1002 will destroy at least some of the ecological integrity that makes ANWR a natural treasure. Environmentalists say that "just as there is no way to be half-pregnant, there is no 'sensitive' way to drill in a wilderness" (McCarthy). They are right.

By looking at effects on people, the writer expands her opposition.

However, oil drilling in ANWR will hurt more than the environment and wildlife; the drilling also will hurt at least one of the two Inuit tribes living in Alaska—the Inupiat Eskimos and the Gwich'in Indians. The Inupiat is the larger group, and they favor drilling. Money generated by the oil industry, say the Inupiat, will help them improve a variety of tribal services such as education and health care. On the other hand, the Gwich'in tribe depends on the porcupine caribou for food. As a result, if oil drilling displaces such animals, the people will suffer. Not only do they need the caribou to survive, but they also need them to retain the tribe's dignity and way of life. In other words, while oil drilling in ANWR may give some residents more money, others clearly will pay a price.

A question serves as a transition to a key counter-argument.

So if oil drilling in ANWR would have so many negative effects, what is driving the argument for drilling? Unfortunately, nothing more than a shortsighted, ill-informed effort to satisfy America's excessive appetite for oil: To continue using too much, we want to produce more. But is drilling in the ANWR the answer to our consumption problem?

At best, getting more oil from Alaska is a shortsighted solution: ANWR's reserves are simply too small to provide a long-term solution. A 1998 study by the U.S. Geological Survey concluded that the total amount of accessible oil in the ANWR is 5.7 to 16 billion barrels, with an expected amount of 10.4 billion barrels (*Arctic Power*). While these figures are considered the official estimate, the National Resources Defense Council (a group of lawyers, scientists, and environmentalists) disagrees. It estimates the accessible amount to be 3.2 billion barrels—a resource the United States would use up in just six months! In the meantime, using the ANWR oil would do nothing to ease our dependence on Middle Eastern countries for oil. There has to be a better choice.

The writer redirects the discussion to the root of the problem.

And there is. The question is not whether drilling should take place in the ANWR, but how to provide energy for everyone, now and in the future. A poll taken by *The Christian Science Monitor* shows that voters believe that the best option for Americans is to develop new technologies (Dillan). Finding new energy sources, they say, is more important than finding new oil reserves.

10

There are two main problems with relying primarily on oil for our energy: Oil supplies are limited, and oil use pollutes. Democratic Representative Rosa DeLauro of Connecticut made this point well when she said the following:

11

A closing quotation focuses and supports the writer's objections; the quotation is indented ten spaces.

We need a serious energy policy in the United States. Drilling in the Arctic National Wildlife Refuge is not the solution. We should look to increase domestic production while balancing our desire for a cleaner environment. We must also look at ways to reduce our dependency on fossil fuels themselves, a smart and necessary step that will lead to a cleaner environment. (qtd. in Urban)

12

While reducing our use of fossil fuels will not be easy, it is possible if we do two things: (1) develop energy-saving technologies, and (2) make lifestyle choices that conserve energy. Unlike the short-term (and short-sighted) solution of drilling in the ANWR, these strategies will help save the environment. In addition, the strategies will help people both now and in the future. ■

13

Note: The Works Cited page is not shown. For sample pages, see MLA (pages **534–535**) and APA (page **564**).

Writing Prompt

Reading for Better Writing

1. The writer describes both positions on drilling before stating her opposition explicitly. Is this strategy effective?

2. The writer uses the testimony of experts extensively. Why?

3. What does the writer do to acknowledge, concede points to, and refute support for drilling?

4. Review pages **252–254** about types of support. Then trace the types of evidence provided in this essay. Evaluate the quality and completeness of the evidence.

5. Does the last paragraph offer an effective closing to the writer's argument? Why or why not?

Persuading Readers to Act

Paul Rogat Loeb is a freelance writer and university lecturer trained in social research. In this excerpt from his 1999 book, *Soul of a Citizen*, Loeb argues that ordinary people can bring about social change.

Soul of a Citizen: Living with Conviction in a Cynical Time

Loeb starts with a positive general claim, but he raises a related problem and a question.

Most Americans are thoughtful, caring, generous. We try to do our best by family and friends. We'll even stop to help a fellow driver stranded by a roadside breakdown or give spare change to a stranger. But increasingly, a wall separates each of us from the world outside, and from others who have taken refuge in their own private sanctuaries. How can we renew the public participation that's the very soul of democratic citizenship? [1]

Noting concerns, he concedes problems through powerful contrasts. He then offers readers an alternative vision.

To be sure, the issues we face are complex. It's hard to comprehend the moral implications of a world in which Nike pays Michael Jordan millions to appear in its ads while workers at its foreign shoe factories toil away for pennies a day. The 500 richest people on the planet now control more wealth than the poorest three billion, half the human population. Is it possible even to grasp this extraordinary imbalance? And, more important, how do we begin to redress it? [2]

Certainly we need to decide for ourselves whether particular causes are wise or foolish. But we also need to believe that our individual involvement is worthwhile, that what we might do in the public sphere will not be in vain. The challenge is as much psychological as political. As the Ethiopian proverb says, "He who conceals his disease cannot be cured." [3]

We need to understand our cultural diseases—callousness, short-sightedness, denial—and learn what it will take to heal our society and our souls. How did so many of us become convinced that we can do nothing to affect the future our children and grandchildren will inherit? And how have others managed to work powerfully for change? [4]

Key questions introduce a story that illustrates his argument.

Pete Knutson is one of my oldest friends. During 25 years as a commercial fisherman in Washington and Alaska, he has been forced to respond to the steady degradation of salmon spawning grounds. He could have accepted this as fate and focused on getting a maximum share of the dwindling fish populations. Instead, he gradually built an alliance between Washington fishermen, environmentalists, and Native American tribes, and persuaded them to demand that this habitat be preserved and restored. [5]

Cooperation didn't come easily. Washington's fisherman are historically individualistic and politically mistrustful. But with their new allies, they pushed for cleaner spawning streams, preservation of the Endangered Species Act, and increased water flow over regional dams to help boost salmon runs. Fearing that these measures would raise electricity costs or restrict development opportunities, aluminum companies and other large [6] industrial interests bankrolled a statewide referendum, Initiative 640, to regulate fishing nets in a way that would eliminate small family operations.

At first, those who opposed 640 thought they had no chance of success: They were outspent, outstaffed, outfunded. Similar initiatives backed by similar corporate interests had already passed in Florida, Louisiana, and Texas. But the opponents refused to give up. Pete and his co-workers enlisted major environmental groups to campaign against the initiative. They worked with the media to explain the larger issues at stake and focus public attention on the measure's powerful financial backers. On election day in November 1995, Initiative 640 was defeated. White fishermen, Native American activists, and Friends of the Earth staffers threw their arms around each other in victory. "I'm really proud of you, Dad," Pete's twelve-year-old son kept repeating. Pete was stunned.

We often think of social involvement as noble but impractical. Yet it can serve enlightened self-interest and the interests of others simultaneously, giving us a sense of connection and purpose nearly impossible to find in private life. "It takes energy to act," says Pete. "But it's more draining to bury your anger, convince yourself you're powerless, and swallow whatever's handed to you."

We often don't know where to start. Most of us would like to see people treated more justly and the earth accorded the respect it deserves, but we mistrust our own ability to make a difference. The magnitude of the issues at hand has led too many of us to conclude that social involvement isn't worth the cost.

Such resignation isn't innate or inevitable. It's what psychologists call learned helplessness, a systematic way of ignoring the ills we see and leaving them for others to handle. We find it unsettling even to think about crises as profound as the extinction of species, depletion of the ozone layer, destruction of the rainforests, and desperate urban poverty. We're taught to doubt our voices, to feel that we lack either the time to learn about and articulate the issues or the standing to speak out and be heard. To get socially involved, we believe, requires almost saintlike judgment, confidence, and character—standards we can never meet. Our impulses toward involvement are dampened by a culture that demands idealism, enshrines cynicism, and makes us feel naïve for caring about our fellow human beings or the planet we inhabit.

A few years ago, on Martin Luther King Day, I was interviewed on CNN along with Rosa Parks. "Rosa Parks was the woman who wouldn't go to the back of the bus," said the host. "That set in motion the yearlong bus boycott in Montgomery. It earned Rosa Parks the title of 'mother of the civil rights movement.'"

The host's description—the standard rendition of the story— stripped the boycott of its context. Before refusing to give up her seat to a white person, Parks had spent 12 years helping to lead the local National Association for the Advancement of Colored People (NAACP) chapter. The summer before, she had attended a 10-day training session at the

The example shows that successful action is possible.

He analyzes the anecdote, using a quotation for support and insight.

Anticipating objections, the writer defines a key concept. He then uses a second, well-known example for support.

Highlander Center, Tennessee's labor and civil rights organizing school, where she'd met older activists and discussed the Supreme Court decision banning "separate but equal" schools. Parks had become familiar with previous challenges to segregation: another Montgomery bus boycott, 50 years earlier; a bus boycott in Baton Rouge two years before Parks was arrested; and an NAACP dilemma the previous spring, when a young Montgomery woman had also refused to move to the back of the bus. The NAACP had considered a legal challenge but decided the unmarried, pregnant woman would be a poor symbol for a campaign.

> **Loeb describes the complexity of true social action.**

In short, Parks didn't make a spur-of-the-moment decision. She was part of a movement for change at a time when success was far from certain. This in no way diminishes her historical importance, but it reminds us that this powerful act might never have taken place without the humble, frustrating work that preceded it. *13*

We elevate a few people to hero status—especially during times of armed conflict—but most of us know next to nothing of the battles ordinary men and women fought to preserve freedom, expand democracy, and create a more just society. Many have remarked on America's historical amnesia, but its implications are hard to appreciate without recognizing how much identity dissolves in the absence of memory. We lose the mechanisms that grassroots social movements have used successfully to shift public sentiment and challenge entrenched institutional power. Equally lost are the means by which participants eventually managed to prevail. *14*

> **He contrasts familiar and anonymous heroism. He explains the costs of inaction.**

Think about how differently one can frame Rosa Parks' historic action. In prevailing myth, Parks—a holy innocent—acts almost on a whim, in isolation. The lesson seems to be that if any of us suddenly got the urge to do something heroic, that would be great. Of course, most of us wait our entire lives for the ideal moment. *15*

> **Ending positively, the writer challenges readers.**

The real story is more empowering: It suggests that change is the product of deliberate, incremental action. When we join together to shape a better world, sometimes our struggles will fail or bear only modest fruits. Other times they will trigger miraculous outpourings of courage and heart. We can never know beforehand what the consequences of our actions will be. ■ *16*

Writing Prompt

Reading for Better Writing

1. What is the writer arguing for and against? What does he want readers to do? Look at the question in the opening paragraph. What answer does Loeb present?

2. What efforts does Loeb make to address readers' questions, concerns, and opposing arguments? Are these efforts successful? Explain.

3. Consider the examples Loeb offers: Pete Knutson and Rosa Parks. Do these examples work as support for the writer's claims? Why or why not?

4. Broadly speaking, what is the author's view of life, and how does that perspective come through in the essay?

Persuading Readers to Act

Dr. Martin Luther King, Jr., was a leader in the civil rights movement during the 1950s and 1960s. On August 28, 1963, he delivered this persuasive speech to a crowd of 250,000 people gathered at the Lincoln Memorial in Washington.

I Have a Dream

King starts with a tragic contrast.

Five score years ago, a great American, in whose symbolic shadow we stand, signed the Emancipation Proclamation. This momentous decree came as a great beacon light of hope to millions of Negro slaves who had been seared in the flames of withering injustice. It came as a joyous daybreak to end the long night of captivity.

1

He uses figurative language to describe the present situation.

But one hundred years later, we must face the tragic fact that the Negro is still not free. One hundred years later, the life of the Negro is still sadly crippled by the manacles of segregation and the chains of discrimination. One hundred years later, the Negro lives on a lonely island of poverty in the midst of a vast ocean of material prosperity. One hundred years later, the Negro is still languishing in the corners of American society and finds himself an exile in his own land. So we have come here today to dramatize an appalling condition.

2

An analogy clarifies the problem.

In a sense we have come to our nation's Capitol to cash a check. When the architects of our republic wrote the magnificent words of the Constitution and the Declaration of Independence, they were signing a promissory note to which every American was to fall heir. This note was a promise that all men would be guaranteed the unalienable rights of life, liberty, and the pursuit of happiness.

3

It is obvious today that America has defaulted on this promissory note insofar as her citizens of color are concerned. Instead of honoring this sacred obligation, America has given the Negro people a bad check; a check which has come back marked "insufficient funds." But we refuse to believe that the bank of justice is bankrupt. We refuse to believe that there are insufficient funds in the great vaults of opportunity of this nation. So we

4

Repeated words and phrases create urgency.

have come to cash this check—a check that will give us upon demand the riches of freedom and the security of justice. We have also come to this hallowed spot to remind America of the fierce urgency of *now*. This is no time to engage in the luxury of cooling off or to take the tranquilizing drug of gradualism. *Now* is the time to make real the promises of Democracy. *Now* is the time to rise from the dark and desolate valley of segregation to the sunlit path of racial justice. *Now* is the time to open the doors of opportunity to all of God's children. *Now* is the time to lift our nation from the quicksands of racial injustice to the solid rock of brotherhood.

It would be fatal for the nation to overlook the urgency of the moment and to underestimate the determination of the Negro. This sweltering summer of the Negro's legitimate discontent will not pass until there is an

5

invigorating autumn of freedom and equality. 1963 is not an end, but a beginning. Those who hope that the Negro needed to blow off steam and will now be content will have a rude awakening if the nation returns to business as usual. There will be neither rest nor tranquility in America until the Negro is granted his citizenship rights. The whirlwinds of revolt will continue to shake the foundations of our nation until the bright day of justice emerges.

King addresses specific audiences in turn.

But there is something I must say to my people who stand on the warm threshold which leads into the palace of justice. In the process of gaining our rightful place we must not be guilty of wrongful deeds. Let us not seek to satisfy our thirst for freedom by drinking from the cup of bitterness and hatred. We must forever conduct our struggle on the high plane of dignity and discipline. We must not allow our creative protest to degenerate into physical violence. Again and again we must rise to the majestic heights of meeting physical force with soul force. The marvelous new militancy which has engulfed the Negro community must not lead us to a distrust of all white people, for many of our white brothers, as evidenced by their presence here today, have come to realize that their destiny is tied up with our destiny and their freedom is inextricably bound to our freedom. We cannot walk alone.

6

He responds to the arguments of opponents.

And as we talk, we must make the pledge that we shall march ahead. We cannot turn back. There are those who are asking the devotees of civil rights, "When will you be satisfied?" We can never be satisfied as long as the Negro is the victim of the unspeakable horrors of police brutality. We can never be satisfied as long as our bodies, heaving with the fatigue of travel, cannot gain lodging in the motels of the highways and the hotels of the cities. We cannot be satisfied as long as the Negro's basic mobility is from a smaller ghetto to a larger one. We can never be satisfied as long as a Negro in Mississippi cannot vote and a Negro in New York believes he has nothing for which to vote. No, no, we are not satisfied, and we will not be satisfied until justice rolls down like waters and righteousness like a mighty stream.

7

Appropriate emotional appeals are used in the context of suffering.

I am not unmindful that some of you have come here out of great trials and tribulations. Some of you have come fresh from narrow jail cells. Some of you have come from areas where your quest for freedom left you battered by the storms of persecution and staggered by the winds of police brutality. You have been the veterans of creative suffering. Continue to work with the faith that unearned suffering is redemptive.

8

Go back to Mississippi, go back to Alabama, go back to South Carolina, go back to Georgia, go back to Louisiana, go back to the slums and ghettos of our northern cities, knowing that somehow this situation can and will be changed. Let us not wallow in the valley of despair.

9

I say to you today, my friends, that in spite of the difficulties and frustrations of the moment I still have a dream. It is a dream deeply rooted in the American dream.

10

I have a dream that one day this nation will rise up and live out the true meaning of its creed: "We hold these truths to be self-evident; that all men are created equal." 11

I have a dream that one day on the red hills of Georgia the sons of former slaves and the sons of former slaveowners will be able to sit down together at the table of brotherhood. 12

The repetition of key phrases becomes a persuasive refrain.

I have a dream that the state of Mississippi, a desert state sweltering with the heat of injustice and oppression, will be transformed into an oasis of freedom and justice. 13

I have a dream that my four little children will one day live in a nation where they will not be judged by the color of their skin but by the content of their character. 14

I have a dream today. 15

I have a dream that the state of Alabama, whose governor's lips are presently dripping with the words of interposition and nullification, will be transformed into a situation where little black boys and black girls will be able to join hands with little white boys and girls and walk together as sisters and brothers. 16

I have a dream today. 17

King's vision offers hope and motivates readers to change society.

I have a dream that one day every valley shall be exalted, every hill and mountain shall be made low, the rough places will be made plain, and the crooked places will be made straight, and the glory of the Lord shall be revealed, and all flesh shall see it together. 18

This is our hope. This is the faith with which I return to the South. With this faith we will be able to hew out of the mountain of despair a stone of hope. With this faith we will be able to transform the jangling discords of our nation into a beautiful symphony of brotherhood. With this faith we will be able to work together, to pray together, to struggle together, to go to jail together, to stand up for freedom together, knowing that we will be free one day. 19

This will be the day when all God's children will be able to sing with new meaning. 20

He appeals to ideals and to humanity's better nature, ending with a vision of a just society.

My country 'tis of thee 21
Sweet land of liberty,
   Of thee I sing,
Land where my fathers died,
Land of the pilgrims' pride,
From every mountainside
   Let freedom ring.

And if America is to be a great nation this must become true. So let freedom ring from the prodigious hilltops of New Hampshire. Let freedom ring from the mighty mountains of New York. Let freedom ring from the heightening Alleghenies of Pennsylvania! 22

Let freedom ring from the snow-capped Rockies of Colorado!   23

Let freedom ring from the curvaceous peaks of California!   24

But not only that; let freedom ring from Stone Mountain of Georgia!   25

Let freedom ring from Lookout Mountain of Tennessee!   26

Let freedom ring from every hill and molehill of Mississippi! From   27
every mountainside, let freedom ring.

When we let freedom ring, when we let it ring from every village and   28
every hamlet, from every state and every city, we will be able to speed up
that day when all of God's children, black men and white men, Jews and
Gentiles, Protestants and Catholics, will be able to join hands and sing in
the words of the old Negro spiritual, "Free at last! Free at last! Thank God
almighty, we are free at last!" ■

The closing urges readers to work for a better future.

Writing Prompt

Reading for Better Writing

1. King is actually speaking to several audiences at the same time. Who are these different audiences? How does King address each?

2. For what specific changes does King call? What does he want his listeners to do?

3. Explore the writer's style. How does he use religious imagery, comparisons, and analogies? How does repetition function as a persuasive technique?

4. In a sense, King's speech addresses a gap between reality and an ideal. How does he present this gap?

Persuading Readers to Act

This essay is by Jack G. Shaheen, Professor Emeritus of Mass Communication at Southern Illinois University at Carbondale, whose work on media portrayals of Arabs has earned recognition and awards. Some of his books include *Reel Bad Arabs* and *Arab and Muslim Stereotyping in American Pop Culture.*

The Media's Image of Arabs

The piece opens with a series of claims, moving from a broad statement to more specific claims.

America's bogyman is the Arab. Until the nightly news brought us TV pictures of Palestinian boys being punched and beaten, almost all portraits of Arabs seen in America were dangerously threatening. Arabs were either billionaires or bombers—rarely victims. They were hardly ever seen as ordinary people practicing law, driving taxis, singing lullabies or healing the sick. Though TV news may portray them more sympathetically now, the absence of positive media images nurtures suspicion and stereotype. As an Arab-American, I have found that ugly caricatures have had an enduring impact on my family.

The writer gives background about his own history with the topic.

I was sheltered from prejudicial portraits at first. My parents came from Lebanon in the 1920s; they met and married in America. Our home in the steel city of Clairton, Pa., was a center for ethnic sharing—black, white, Jew and gentile. There was only one major source of media images then, at the State movie theater where I was lucky enough to get a part-time job as an usher. But in the late 1940s, Westerns and war movies were popular, not Middle Eastern dramas. Memories of World War II were fresh, and the screen heavies were the Japanese and the Germans. True to the cliché of the times, the only good Indian was a dead Indian. But when I mimicked or mocked the bad guys, my mother cautioned me. She explained that stereotypes blur our vision and corrupt the imagination. "Have compassion for all people, Jackie," she said. "This way, you'll learn to experience the joy of accepting people as they are, and not as they appear in films. Stereotypes hurt."

This paragraph, like many others, begins with a short, simple sentence.

Mother was right. I can remember the Saturday afternoon when my son, Michael, who was seven, and my daughter, Michele, six, suddenly called out: "Daddy, Daddy, they've got some bad Arabs on TV." They were watching that great American morality play, TV wrestling. Akbar the Great, who liked to hear the cracking of bones, and Abdullah the Butcher, a dirty fighter who liked to inflict pain, were pinning their foes with "camel locks." From that day on, I knew I had to try to neutralize the media caricatures.

Quotation marks set apart others' words and phrases from those of the author.

It hasn't been easy. With my children, I have watched animated heroes Heckle and Jeckle pull the rug from under "Ali Boo-Boo, the Desert Rat," and Laverne and Shirley stop "Sheik Ha-Mean-Ie" from conquering "the U.S. and the world." I have read comic books like the "Fantastic Four" and "G.I. Combat" whose characters have sketched Arabs as "lowlifes" and "human hyenas." Negative stereotypes were everywhere. A dictionary informed my youngsters that an Arab is a "vagabond, drifter, hobo and vagrant." Whatever happened, my wife wondered, to Aladdin's good genie?

To a child, the world is simple: good versus evil. But my children and others with Arab roots grew up without ever having seen a humane Arab on the silver screen, someone to pattern their lives after. Is it easier for a camel to go through the eye of a needle than for a screen Arab to appear as a genuine human being?

Hollywood producers must have an instant Ali Baba kit that contains scimitars, veils, sunglasses and such Arab clothing as *chadors* and *kufiyahs.* In the mythical "Ay-rabland," oil wells, tents, mosques, goats and shepherds prevail. Between the sand dunes, the camera focuses on a mock-up of a palace from "Arabian Nights"—or a military air base. Recent movies suggest that Americans are at war with Arabs, forgetting the fact that out of 21 Arab nations, America is friendly with 19 of them. And in "Wanted Dead or Alive," a movie that starred Gene Simmons, the leader of the rock group Kiss, the war comes home when an Arab terrorist comes to the United States dressed as a rabbi and, among other things, conspires with Arab-Americans to poison the people of Los Angeles. The movie was released last year.

The Arab remains American culture's favorite whipping boy. In his memoirs, Terrel Bell, Ronald Reagan's first secretary of education, writes about an "apparent bias among mid-level, right-wing staffers at the White House" who dismissed Arabs as "sand niggers." Sadly, the racial slurs continue. At a recent teacher's conference, I met a woman from Sioux Falls, S.D., who told me about the persistence of discrimination. She was in the process of adopting a baby when an agency staffer warned her that the infant had a problem. When she asked whether the child was mentally ill, or physically handicapped, there was silence. Finally, the worker said: "The baby is Jordanian."

To me, the Arab demon of today is much like the Jewish demon of yesterday. We deplore the false portrait of Jews as a swarthy menace. Yet a similar portrait has been accepted and transferred to another group of Semites—the Arabs. Print and broadcast journalists have started to challenge this stereotype. They are now revealing more humane images of Palestinian Arabs, a people who traditionally suffered from the myth that Palestinian equals terrorist. Others could follow that lead and retire the stereotypical Arab to a media Valhalla.

It would be a step in the right direction if movie and TV producers developed characters modeled after real-life Arab-Americans. We could then see a White House correspondent like Helen Thomas, whose father

> *To me, the Arab demon of today is much like the Jewish demon of yesterday.*

Margin annotations:

The writer makes claims related to his main thesis and then supports them with examples drawn from public and personal sources.

The writer compares the present situation with the past.

The writer states the actions that he wishes to persuade various groups to take.

came from Lebanon, in "The Golden Girls," a heart surgeon patterned after Dr. Michael DeBakey on "St. Elsewhere," or a Syrian-American playing tournament chess like Yasser Seirawan, the Seattle grandmaster.

10

Politicians, too, should speak out against the cardboard caricatures. They should refer to Arabs as friends, not just as moderates. And religious leaders could state that Islam, like Christianity and Judaism, maintains that all mankind is one family in the care of God. When all imagemakers rightfully begin to treat Arabs and all other minorities with respect and dignity, we may begin to unlearn our prejudices. ■

Reading for Better Writing

1. Shaheen's essay was first published in 1988. To what extent is his argument still relevant? Give current examples that show how media images of Arabs have or have not changed.

2. Review the section in Chapter 17 about "Making and Qualifying Claims" (pages 250–251). Make notes in the margins of Shaheen's essay, labeling facts, opinions, and claims. For each claim that you identify, label the type of claim that is being made (for example, claims of truth, value, or policy). Look over your margin notes. What observations can you make about Shaheen's essay, and why are they significant?

3. Review the section in Chapter 17 titled "Supporting Your Claims" (pages 252–254). What different kinds of evidence does Shaheen use to support his claims? Which types of evidence do you think are most or least effective in this piece? Why?

4. How might the meaning of paragraph 4 in this essay be changed if the author had omitted the quotation marks?

5. Part of Shaheen's style in this essay is to open many of his paragraphs with short, simple sentences. How does he vary the sentence length and structure throughout the remainder of each of these paragraphs? What is the effect of this variation for readers?

Guidelines
Persuading Readers to Act

Note: For in-depth help on developing persuasive arguments, see pages **248–261**.

1. **Select a topic.** List issues about which you feel passionately, issues where you see a need for change. (See "Topics to Consider" on page **284**.) Then choose a topic that meets these criteria: The topic is debatable, significant, current, and manageable.

Not Debatable	*Debatable*
Statistics on spending practices	The injustice of consumerism
The existence of racism	Solutions to racism

2. **Choose and analyze your audience.** Think about who your readers are. Make a list of words and phrases describing their perspectives on the issue.

3. **Narrow your focus and determine your purpose.** Consider what you can achieve within the assignment's constraints. Should you focus on one aspect of the issue or all of it? What patterns of thinking and behavior can you try to change? With these readers, what actions can you call for?

4. **Generate ideas and support.** Use prewriting strategies like those below to develop your thinking and gather support:
   - Set up "opposing viewpoints" columns. In one column, take one side; in the other column, take the other side.
   - Construct a dialogue between two people—yourself and someone who doesn't support your position.
   - Talk to others about the issue. How do peers, friends, coworkers, and relatives respond to your ideas?
   - Research the issue to find current, reliable sources from a variety of perspectives. Consider interviewing an expert.
   - Consider what outcome or results you want.

5. **Organize your thinking.** Get your thoughts in order so that you can step confidently into your first draft. Consider the following strategies:
   - Make a sharp claim about the issue, a claim that points toward action. Try this basic pattern:
     On the issue of _____ , *I believe* _____ .
     Therefore, we must change _____ .
   - Review the evidence, and develop your line of reasoning by generating an outline or using a graphic organizer.

> *Simple Outline:* **Introduction: claim**
> Supporting point 1
> Supporting point 2
> Supporting point 3
> **Conclusion: call to action**

6. Write your first draft. As you write, remember your persuasive goal and your specific readers. Here are some possible strategies:

Opening: Gain the readers' attention, raise the issue, help the readers care about it, and state your claim.

Development: Follow your outline but feel free to explore new ideas that arise. Decide where to place your most persuasive supporting argument: first or last. Anticipate readers' questions and objections, and use appropriate logical and emotional appeals to overcome their resistance.

Closing: Do one or more of the following: Restate your claim, summarize your support, encourage readers to take the action you want.

Title: Develop a thoughtful, energetic working title that stresses a vision or change. (For ideas, scan the titles of the sample essays in this chapter.)

7. Share your essay. Try out your thinking and persuasive appeals with a reader. Does he or she find your argument convincing? Why or why not?

8. Revise your writing. Think about your reviewer's comments, and then ask these questions of your draft:
- Does your argument flow effectively? Consider shuffling points to make the sequence more persuasive. Add transitions if necessary.
- Is the evidence credible and persuasive? Does your logic have gaps? Do you need to qualify some points and strengthen others?
- Do images, examples, and analogies help readers understand and identify with your cause? Do these elements urge readers to act?
- Is the voice fitting—energetic but controlled, confident but reasonable? Will your tone persuade readers or start a quarrel?

9. Edit and proofread. See pages 97–98 for guidelines, but check especially for appropriate word choice and clear sentences. Avoid clichés and jargon.

10. Prepare and publish your final essay. Submit your essay according to your instructor's format and documentation requirements. If appropriate, "publish" your essay and solicit feedback from your audience—perhaps on a website, in the school newspaper, or with an appropriate discussion group.

Writing Checklist

Use these six traits to check the quality of your essay; then revise as needed:

_____ The **ideas** in your essay prompt readers to change their thinking and behavior. The essay has a clear opinion statement, effective reasoning, good support, and a clear call to action.

_____ The **organization** is logical and includes an engaging opening that raises the issue, a clearly sequenced argument, and a convincing conclusion focused on change and action.

_____ The **voice** is thoughtful, caring, and convincing.

_____ The **words** are precise, concrete, and easily understood (or defined as needed). The language is free of clichés and glib phrases.

_____ The **sentences** flow smoothly, with effective transitions and logical connections.

_____ The copy follows **correct** format, documentation, and rules of writing.

Writing Activities

1. The four essays in this chapter address significant social issues. List other significant social issues, choose one, and then write an essay that persuades readers to do something related to the issue.

2. If you are a natural sciences major, consider debatable issues that are central to studying and applying the sciences—environmental, medical, biotechnical, and agricultural issues, for example. If you are a social science or humanities major, do the same brainstorming in your area.

3. Which college, community, or state policies should be strengthened or changed? Select an issue, write a persuasive essay, and submit your work as an editorial to a news publication.

4. Consider the workplace. What issues have come up in your job? Contemplate issues such as pay equity, equal opportunity, management policies, and unsafe work conditions. Then write a persuasive report to a decision maker or to fellow employees.

5. Review the section in Chapter 17 titled "Supporting Your Claims" (252–254). Consider a persuasive piece that you are drafting or revising. Which kinds of evidence would be most effective for the situation, purpose, audience, and mode of your piece? Discuss or write about your reasons for choosing these kinds of evidence, and then work to incorporate them into your persuasive piece.

Chapter 20
Proposing a Solution

Proposals are prescriptions for change. As such, they challenge readers to care about a problem, accept a solution, and act on it. A strong proposal offers a logical, practical, and creative argument that leads toward positive change, whether it's defending against terrorism, requiring both men and women to register for the military draft, or adding to the debate on cloning.

Proposal writers argue for such remedies in all areas of life. In your college courses, you'll be challenged to map out solutions to many difficult problems. In your community, you may participate in policy making and civic development. In the workplace, you may write proposals that justify expenditures, sell products, or troubleshoot problems. In each situation, you'll be challenged to clearly explain the problem, offer a solution, and argue for adopting that solution.

This chapter will walk you through the challenge of writing such proposals, from selecting a problem to submitting your plan.

Note: Some problem-solution writing can be primarily explanatory, rather than persuasive.

What's Ahead

- Overview: Proposing a Solution
  - Student Model
  - Professional Models
- Guidelines
- Writing Checklist and Activities

Overview
Proposing a Solution

Writer's Goal

Your goal is to argue for a positive change, convincing readers to accept and contribute to that change. To accomplish this goal, aim to describe a problem, analyze its causes and effects, argue for one solution among several options, defend that solution against objections, and prove the solution both feasible and desirable.

Keys for Success

Show passion for change. ■ Proposal writing requires a willingness to challenge the status quo and a mind that is open to creative possibilities. Dare to ask, "What's really wrong here, and how can we fix it?"

Avoid cosmetic solutions. ■ Whatever solution you choose, base it on a concrete and personal understanding of the problem and a bold exploration of all possible solutions. Choose the best solution only after weighing each option against sensible criteria for solving the problem, comparing and contrasting its strengths and weaknesses. Consider especially how well solutions attack root causes, bring about real benefits, and prove workable.

Know your readers. ■ Who can bring about the change you envision—specific decision makers (the city council, college administrators, a department manager) or a broader community affected by the problem? What are their allegiances and alliances? Knowing your readers will help you speak convincingly to them, build a spirit of teamwork, and persuasively challenge readers to change.

Conduct quality research. ■ Your proposal will stand or fall on the quality of both your reasoning and its support. To build that quality, conduct primary research (observations and interviews, for example), but also check journals, books, and Internet sources to understand the problem, explore possible solutions, and garner support for the solution you choose.

Problems to Consider

- **People problems:** Consider generations—your own or a relative's. What problems does this generation face?
- **College problems:** List the top ten problems faced by college students. In your major, what problems are experts trying to solve?
- **Social problems:** What problems do our communities and country face? Where do you see suffering, injustice, waste, or harm?
- **Workplace problems:** What challenges do you encounter at work?

Next Step Read the model essays and perform the activities that follow. As you read, consider the problems presented and the solutions offered. What similar problems do you care about?

Proposing a Solution

In this essay, student writer Brian Ley defines agroterrorism, predicts that it could become a serious problem, and proposes a multifaceted solution.

Audio

Preparing for Agroterror

The writer opens by illustrating the problem.

An Al Quaeda terrorist in Africa obtains a sample of fluid from a cow infected with foot-and-mouth disease, and he sends the fluid to an accomplice in a small, rural American town. This terrorist takes the sample around the country, stopping at several points to place small amounts of the fluid on objects that animals are likely to touch. When he is finished, he drives to the nearest airport and leaves the country unnoticed.

Cows, pigs, and sheep then come into contact with this highly contagious disease. Over the next few days, farmers see blisters on the feet and mouths of their animals. Thinking that the animals have a bacterial infection, the farmers administer antibiotics and wait for improvement. However, because antibiotics can't kill a virus, the animals get sicker. Meanwhile, the virus is spreading by means of wind and the movement of animals and humans. Within a few weeks, the virus is out of control.

While the story above is hypothetical, it is also very possible. People used to think of terrorists as men in ski masks blowing up embassies and taking hostages. But after the events of September 11, 2001, and the subsequent anthrax scares, we realize that more kinds of terrorism are possible.

He defines the problem and presents expert testimony.

One type that we rarely consider is agroterrorism, which involves using diseases as weapons to attack a country's agriculture industry in order to attack the country itself. The agroterrorist's weapons of choice are those diseases that affect plants, animals, and even humans. Professor Peter Chalk of the RAND Corporation, an expert on transnational terrorism, believes that agroterrorism should be a huge concern for Americans because it has many advantages from a terrorist's point of view (37).

He analyzes why the problem could become serious.

First of all, an attack on the agricultural sector of the United States would be quite easy. The diseases needed to kill large populations of animals can be obtained with little difficulty; the most devastating ones are ready for use in their natural form. These samples pose little risk to the terrorist because many of the diseases are harmless to humans.

In addition, doing agroterrorism is less risky in terms of getting caught and getting punished. Agroterrorism is hard to trace, especially because Americans have assumed that all animal epidemics are natural in origin and that American livestock contract such diseases only by accident. Consequences for those caught inflicting a disease on animals are also less severe than for terrorists who harm humans. In fact, because agroterrorism first affects the health of plants and animals rather than humans, terrorists using this strategy can even escape some guilt for their actions.

1

2

3

4

5

6

Using
specific
details, he
outlines the
problem's
potential
effects.

However, while agroterrorist diseases would have little direct effect on [7] people's health, they would be devastating to the agricultural economy, in part because of the many different diseases that could be used in an attack. One of the most devastating is foot-and-mouth disease. This illness hurts all infected animals by impeding their weight gain, and it hurts dairy cows in particular by decreasing their milk production. Because the disease is highly contagious, all infected animals, along with any cloven-hoofed animals within about 50 miles of the infection site, must be killed.

While foot-and-mouth disease is not dangerous to humans, other [8] animal diseases are. One of these is bovine spongiform encephalopathy, better known as mad-cow disease ("Mad Cow"). This illness is not easily spread, but a few cases in the United States would send people into a panic. Meat consumption would drop sharply, and the agricultural economy would be deeply shaken.

Another disease that could be used as a weapon is West Nile [9] encephalitis. This virus can be spread by insects and can even cross species, affecting horses, birds, pigs, and humans. It is a fatal illness without a vaccination or a cure. These diseases are likely candidates for use in an agroterrorist attack (Smith 249).

The agricultural community is particularly susceptible to a terrorist [10] attack. Unlike "typical" terrorist targets in metropolitan areas, farms do not have sophisticated security systems to protect against intruders. The average farmer's security system includes a mean dog and a shotgun: the dog for humans and the gun for animal pests. If terrorists wanted to infect a dairy, swine operation, or even a large-scale cattle-finishing operation, they would encounter few obstacles. The terrorists merely have to place a piece of infected food in an area with livestock. This single action could start an epidemic.

The writer
proposes a
multifaceted
solution.

Agroterrorism is a threat that demands our response. Several actions [11] can be taken to discourage terrorism as well as to deal with its consequences. One of the first steps is convincing all citizens—farmers and nonfarmers alike—that agroterrorism could happen, and that it could cause horrific consequences. Farmers must realize that they are susceptible to an attack even though they may live far from large metropolitan areas. Nonfarmers must realize how an attack could affect them. If nonfarmers know that an attack could create panic, drive up food prices, and possibly eliminate food sources, they will look out for suspicious activity and report it.

Preventive action on farms is needed to ensure the safety of our food [12] supply. For example, the South Dakota Animal Industry Board recently published a newsletter outlining several precautions that farmers can take. Farms should have better security, especially in areas where animals are kept. These security measures include allowing only authorized persons to have access to farm buildings and animals and keeping all key farm buildings locked ("Precautions").

Farmers also need training to detect the diseases that terrorists might use and to know what actions can contain and decontaminate an infected area. For example, if a farmer discovers that cows have blisters on their tongues and noses, and that they are behaving abnormally, the owner should immediately call a veterinarian to assess the situation. Because the disease might be foot-and-mouth, no cattle should leave the farm until a diagnosis has been made. *13*

In addition, public authorities need a plan for responding to an identified agroterrorism attack. For example, thousands of animals may have to be killed and disposed of—an action with significant environmental concerns. Moreover, public money should be used for continued research of the diseases that may be spread by agroterrorists. Vaccines and treatments may be produced that would stop diseases or limit them from becoming epidemic. *14*

The closing stresses the problem's seriousness and calls for action.

Agroterrorism has not yet been used on a large scale anywhere on the globe. However, its use seems inevitable. The United States is a prime target for terrorism of this sort because we have the largest, most efficiently raised food supply in the world. Destroying part of this supply would affect not only our own country but also all those countries with whom we trade. Because we are prime targets, we must act now to develop our defenses against agroterrorism. If we wait until an attack happens, people may become ill, our overall economy could be damaged, and our agricultural economy may never recover. ■ *15*

Note: The Works Cited page is not shown. For sample pages, see MLA (**534–535**) and APA (**564**).

Reading for Better Writing

1. This essay predicts that a problem may develop. Is the writer's prediction persuasive? Why or why not?

2. What tactics does the writer use to get readers concerned about the problem? Are these strategies successful?

3. The solution proposed is multifaceted. Briefly list who must do what. Is this solution persuasive? Is it workable? Does it get at root causes?

4. A strong proposal provides convincing evidence about both the problem and the solution. Trace the evidence used in this essay. Are the types of evidence convincing? Do any gaps need to be filled?

Proposing a Solution

Anna Quindlen's *New York Times* column "Public and Private" won the 1992 Pulitzer Prize for commentary. She now writes a regular column for *Newsweek*, where "Uncle Sam and Aunt Samantha" was originally published in 2001.

Uncle Sam and Aunt Samantha

Each of the first five paragraphs is one sentence long.

1 One out of every five new recruits in the United States military is female.

2 The Marines gave the Combat Action Ribbon for service in the Persian Gulf to 23 women.

3 Two female soldiers were killed in the bombing of the USS *Cole*.

4 The Selective Service registers for the draft all male citizens between the ages of 18 and 25.

5 What's wrong with this picture?

The writer identifies the problem that she wants solved.

6 As Americans read and realize that the lives of most women in this country are as different from those of Afghan women as a Cunard cruise is from maximum-security lockdown, there has nonetheless been little attention paid to one persistent gender inequity in U.S. public policy. An astonishing anachronism, really: while women are represented today in virtually all fields, including the armed forces, only men are required to register for the military draft that would be used in the event of a national-security crisis.

She provides background about the source and history of the problem.

7 Since the nation is as close to such a crisis as it has been in more than 60 years, it's a good moment to consider how the draft wound up in this particular time warp. It's not the time warp of the Taliban, certainly, stuck in the worst part of the 13th century, forbidding women to attend school or hold jobs or even reveal their arms, forcing them into sex and marriage. Our own time warp is several decades old. The last time the draft was considered seriously was 20 years ago, when registration with the Selective Service was restored by Jimmy Carter after the Soviet invasion of, yep, Afghanistan. The president, as well as the Army chief of staff, asked at the time for the registration of women as well as men.

8 Amid a welter of arguments—women interfere with esprit de corps, women don't have the physical strength, women prisoners could be sexually assaulted, women soldiers would distract male soldiers from their mission— Congress shot down the notion of gender-blind registration. So did the Supreme Court, ruling that since women were forbidden to serve in combat positions and the purpose of the draft was to create a combat-ready force, it made sense not to register them.

9 But that was then, and this is now. Women have indeed served in combat positions, in the Balkans and the Middle East. More than 40,000 managed to serve in the Persian Gulf without destroying unit cohesion or failing because of upper-body strength. Some are even now taking out

targets in Afghanistan from fighter jets, and apparently without any male soldier's falling prey to some predicted excess of chivalry or lust.

Talk about cognitive dissonance. All these military personnel, male and female alike, have come of age at a time when a significant level of parity was taken for granted. Yet they are supposed to accept that only males will be required to defend their country in a time of national emergency. This is insulting to men. And it is insulting to women. Caroline Forell, an expert on women's legal rights and a professor at the University of Oregon School of Law, puts it bluntly: "Failing to require this of women makes us lesser citizens."

A quotation helps to explain why the writer understands the situation to be a problem.

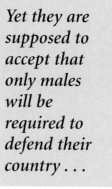

> *Yet they are supposed to accept that only males will be required to defend their country . . .*

Neither the left nor the right has been particularly inclined to consider this issue judiciously. Many feminists came from the antiwar movement and have let their distaste for the military in general and the draft in particular mute their response. In 1980 NOW [National Organization for Women] released a resolution that buried support for the registration of women beneath opposition to the draft, despite the fact that the draft had been redesigned to eliminate the vexing inequities of Vietnam, when the sons of the working class served and the sons of the Ivy League did not. Conservatives, meanwhile, used an equal-opportunity draft as the linchpin of opposition to the Equal Rights Amendment, along with the terrifying specter of unisex bathrooms. (I have seen the urinal, and it is benign.) The legislative director of the right-wing group Concerned Women for America once defended the existing regulations by saying that most women "don't want to be included in the draft." All those young men who went to Canada during Vietnam and those who today register with fear and trembling in the face of the Trade Center devastation might be amazed to discover that lack of desire is an affirmative defense.

The writer anticipates and addresses counter-arguments to her position.

She supports her position with statistics as well as personal anecdotes and comparisons to other situations.

Parents face a series of unique new challenges in this more egalitarian world, not the least of which would be sending a daughter off to war. But parents all over this country are doing that right now, with daughters who enlisted; some have even expressed surprise that young women, in this day and age, are not required to register alongside their brothers and friends. While all involved in this debate over the years have invoked the assumed opposition of the people, even ten years ago more than half of all Americans polled believed women should be made eligible for the draft. Besides, this is not about comfort but about fairness. My son has to register with the Selective Service this year, and if his sister does not when she turns 18, it makes a mockery not only of the standards of this household but of the standards of this nation.

10

11

12

The writer appeals to the reader's logic and ethics.

It is possible in Afghanistan for women to be treated like little more than fecund pack animals precisely because gender fear and ignorance and hatred have been codified and permitted to hold sway. In this country, largely because of the concerted efforts of those allied with the women's movement over a century of struggle, much of that bigotry has been beaten back, even buried. Yet in improbable places the creaky old ways surface, the ways suggesting that we women were made of finer stuff. The finer stuff was usually porcelain, decorative and on the shelf, suitable for meals and show. Happily, the finer stuff has been transmuted into the right stuff. But with rights come responsibilities, as teachers like to tell their students. This is a responsibility that should fall equally upon all, male and female alike. If the empirical evidence is considered rationally, if the decision is divested of outmoded stereotypes, that's the only possible conclusion to be reached. ■

This is a responsibility that should fall equally upon all, male and female alike.

13

Reading for Better Writing

1. What problem(s) does Quindlen identify? What solution(s) does she propose? To what extent would the proposed solution(s) solve the problem(s) Quindlen discusses?

2. Review the section in Chapter 17 about "Identifying Logical Fallacies" (see pages 255–258). Quindlen's opponents might accuse her of "either/or thinking," pointing out that instead of addressing only two options, she could also have argued to end the draft for everyone. What other logical fallacies might Quindlen's opponents accuse her of making? Would you agree with them? Why or why not?

3. What strategies does Quindlen use to try to convince readers that the situation she describes is problematic?

4. Why does the writer acknowledge that there may be opposition to her description of the problem and to her proposed solution? How does she respond to these counterarguments?

5. Why does the essay open with a series of one-sentence paragraphs? How might the effect of the essay differ if these sentences had been combined into one paragraph?

Proposing a Solution

Leigh Turner works at the Hastings Center, a nonprofit research institute in Garrison, New York. In the following essay, he explains why the current debate on cloning is a problem and he proposes a three-part solution.

The Media and the Ethics of Cloning

The writer introduces the topic with an analogy from popular culture.

If the contemporary debate on cloning has a patron saint, surely it is Andy Warhol. Not only did Warhol assert that everyone would have fifteen minutes of fame—witness the lawyers, philosophers, theologians, and bioethicists who found their expertise in hot demand on the nightly morality plays of network television following Ian Wilmut's cloning of the sheep Dolly—but he also placed "clones," multiple copies of the same phenomenon, at the heart of popular culture. Instead of multiple images of Marilyn Monroe and Campbell's soup cans, we now have cloned sheep. Regrettably, it is Warhol's capacity for hyperbole rather than his intelligence and ironic vision that permeates the current debate on cloning.

1

He identifies and outlines the problem.

It would be unfair to judge hastily written op-ed pieces, popular talk shows, and late-night radio programs by the same standards that one would apply to a sustained piece of philosophical or legal analysis. But the popular media could do more to foster thoughtful public debate on the legal, moral, political, medical, and scientific dimensions of the cloning of humans and nonhuman animals.

2

An example illustrates the problem.

As did many of my colleagues at the Hastings Center, I participated in several interviews with the media following Ian Wilmut's announcement in *Nature* that he had succeeded in cloning Dolly from a mammary cell of an adult sheep. After clearly stating to one Los Angeles radio broadcaster before our interview that I was not a theologian and did not represent a religious organization, I was rather breathlessly asked during the taping what God's view on cloning is and whether cloning is "against creation." Predictably, the broadcaster didn't want to discuss how religious ethicists are contributing to the nascent public discourse about the ethics of cloning. Instead, he wanted me to provide a dramatic response that would get the radio station's phones ringing with calls from atheists, agnostics, and religious believers of all stripes.

3

> *Instead of multiple images of Marilyn Monroe and Campbell's soup cans, we now have cloned sheep.*

In addition to inundating the public with hyperbolic sound bites and their print equivalents, the media have overwhelmingly emphasized the issues involved in cloning humans, paying almost no attention to the moral

4

implications of cloning nonhuman animals. While the ethics of cloning humans clearly need to be debated, the cloning of nonhuman animals has already taken place and deserves to be treated as a meaningful moral concern.

A transition signals a shift in focus.

Although I suspect that a compelling argument for the cloning of animals can be made, we should not ignore the difference between actually formulating such arguments and merely presuming that nonhuman cloning is altogether unproblematic. Admittedly, humans already consider non-human animals as commodities in many ways, including as a source of food. Yet perhaps cloning animals with the intent of using them as "pharmaceutical factories" to produce insulin and other substances to treat human illnesses should raise questions about how far such an attitude ought to extend. What moral obligations should extend to humans' use of other species? Do the potential medical benefits for humans outweigh the dangers of encouraging people to think of nonhuman animals as machines to be manipulated to fulfill human goals? These kinds of questions deserve to be part of the public discussion about cloning. Given some people's concerns about the use of traps to catch wild animals, the living conditions of farm animals, and the treatment of animals used in medical and pharmaceutical research, I find this gap in public discourse perplexing.

The writer identifies a key facet of the problem and gives an example.

But perhaps the most significant problem with the media hyperbole concerning cloning is the easy assumption that humans simply are a product of their genes—a view usually called "genetic essentialism." Television hosts and radio personalities have asked whether it would be possible to stock an entire basketball team with clones of Michael Jordan. In response, philosophers, theologians, and other experts have reiterated wearily that, although human behavior undeniably has a genetic component, a host of other factors—including uterine environment, family dynamics, social setting, diet, and other personal history—play important roles in an individual's development. Consequently, a clone produced from the DNA of an outstanding athlete might not even be interested in sports.

While this more sophisticated message has received some media attention, we continue to see stories emphasizing that the wealthy might some day be able to produce copies of themselves, or that couples with a dying infant might create an identical copy of the child. The popular media seem to remain transfixed by what Dorothy Nelkin, the New York University sociologist of science, refers to as "DNA as destiny."

He explains another facet of the problem.

What's more, the cloning issue reveals the way in which the mass media foster attitudes of technological and scientific determinism by implying that scientific "progress" cannot be halted. Of course, many scientists share these attitudes, and, too often, they refuse to accept moral responsibility for their participation in research that may contribute to human suffering. But scientists should not merely ply their craft, leaving moral reasoning to others. They should participate in public debates about whether certain scientific projects are harmful and should not be allowed to continue because they have unjustifiable, dehumanizing implications. A good model is the outspoken criticism of nuclear weapons by many nuclear physicists, who have helped limit research intended to produce more effective nuclear devices.

9

Scientists are not riding a juggernaut capable of crushing everything in its path simply because mass cloning of animals, and possibly eventually humans, may be technically possible. There is no reason to think that scientific research has a mandate that somehow enables it to proceed outside the web of moral concerns that govern all other human endeavors; it does not exist above the law or outside the rest of society. To think otherwise is to succumb to a technological determinism that denies the responsibilities and obligations of citizenship.

He introduces his three-part solution.

10

Despite the media's oversimplifications, citizens have an obligation to scrutinize carefully all of the issues involved and, if necessary, to regulate cloning through laws, professional codes of behavior, and institutional policies. I want to suggest three ways that scholars, policy makers, and concerned citizens can, in fact, work to improve public debate about ethical issues related to new developments in science and technology.

Recognize Moral Implications

Part one: Scientists must address the ethical issues related to their work.

11

First, scientists and ethicists need a fuller understanding of each other's work. Scientists must recognize the moral implications of their research and address those implications when they discuss the research in public. The formal education of most scientists does not encourage them to consider ethical issues. Whereas courses in bioethics are now found in most schools of medicine and nursing, graduate students in such disciplines as human genetics, biochemistry, and animal physiology are not encouraged to grapple with the ethical aspects of their research. Similarly, most ethicists have very little knowledge of science, although many of them feel perfectly entitled to comment on the moral issues of new scientific discoveries.

The writer gives examples.

12

This gap in understanding fosters an inaccurate, unrealistic conception of what the most pressing ethical issues are. For example, the real challenges for researchers today involve the cloning of nonhuman animals for use in developing pharmaceutical products. Sustained study of nonhuman clones will be needed before researchers can even begin to seriously consider research involving human subjects. Rather than encouraging the media's interest in cloning humans, ethicists more knowledgeable about the science involved might have been able to shift the public debate toward the moral questions raised by cloning sheep, pigs, and other animals, questions that need immediate public debate.

13

Thus, we need to include more courses in various scientific departments on the ethics of contemporary scientific research; offer courses for ethicists on the basics of human genetics, anatomy, and physiology; and establish continuing-education courses and forums that bring together scientists and scholars in the humanities.

Present Concerns of Ethicists

Part two: Ethicists must address ethical issues more effectively.

Second, ethicists need to do a better job of presenting their concerns in the popular media. Scientific journals written for a popular audience—such as *Scientific American, New Scientist, Discover,* and *The Sciences*—provide excellent popular accounts of scientific research and technological developments, but they rarely specifically address the moral implications of the discoveries they report. Regrettably, most of the academic journals that do address the ethical aspects of scientific topics—such as the *Hastings Center Report,* the *Journal of Medical Ethics,* and the *Cambridge Quarterly of Healthcare Ethics*—lack the broad readership of the popular-science magazines. Right now, perhaps the best "popular" source of sustained ethical analysis of science, medicine, and health care is *The New York Times Magazine.*   14

The writer gives examples.

If ethicists hope to reach larger audiences with more than trivial sound bites, they need to establish and promote appropriate outlets for their concerns. For example, Arthur Caplan, director of the Center for Bioethics at the University of Pennsylvania, wrote a regular weekly newspaper column for the *St. Paul Pioneer Press* when he directed a bioethics center at the University of Minnesota. His column addressed the ethical implications of medical and scientific research. Other scholars have yet to follow his example—perhaps, in part, because many academics feel that writing for the mass media is unworthy of their time. They are wrong.   15

One way of improving public debate on these important issues is for universities to encourage their faculty members to write for newspapers, popular magazines, and even community newsletters. Such forms of communication should be viewed as an important complement to other forms of published research. Leon Kass's writing on cloning in *The New Republic* and Michael Walzer's and Michael Sandel's writing on assisted suicide in the same publication should not be considered any less significant simply because the work appears in a magazine intended for a wide audience. After all, if universities are to retain their public support, they must consistently be seen as important players in society, and one easy way to do this is to encourage their faculty members to contribute regularly to public discussion.   16

Expand Public Debate

Part three: Scientists and ethicists must engage others in the debate.

Finally, we need to expand public debate about ethical issues in science beyond the mass media. To complement the activities of the National Bioethics Advisory Commission and the projects on ethics at universities and research centers, we should create forums at which academics and citizens from all walks of life could meet to debate the issues. Instead of   17 merely providing a gathering place for scholars pursuing research projects, institutions such as the Hastings Center, Georgetown University's Kennedy Institute of Ethics, and the University of Pennsylvania's Center for Bioethics need to foster outreach programs and community-discussion groups that include nonspecialists. My experience suggests that members of civic organizations and community-health groups, such as the New York Citizens' Committee on Health Care Decisions, are quite eager to discuss the topic of cloning.

The writer closes by summarizing his solution.

What we need are fewer commentaries by self-promoting experts on [18] network television, and more intelligent discussions by scholars and citizens in local media, including local public-television stations. We need creative alternatives to the onslaught of talking heads, all saying much the same thing (as though they themselves were clones) to docile, sheep-like audiences waiting for others to address the most pressing moral issues of the day. ■

Writing Prompt

Reading for Better Writing

1. The writer introduces the topic by using Andy Warhol as an analogy. Explain why the analogy is or is not effective.

2. Reread the first two pages, in which the writer states and explains the problem. Summarize what he says, and explain why his presentation is or is not clear.

3. Summarize the author's three-part solution, and explain why this part of the essay is or is not effective.

4. Reread the conclusion, and explain whether it effectively unifies the essay.

Guidelines
Proposing a Solution

Note: For in-depth help on developing persuasive arguments, see pages 248–261.

1. **Select and narrow a topic.** Choose a problem from "Problems to Consider" on page 302, or search for one in periodicals, on news programs, or on the Internet. Then test your topic:
   - Is the problem real, serious, and fairly complex? Does it show broken-ness, danger, or disadvantage? Does it predict future harm?
   - Do you care about this problem and believe that it must be solved?
   - Can you offer a workable solution? Should you narrow the focus to part of the problem or a local angle?

2. **Identify and analyze your audience.** Potentially, you could have three audiences: decision makers with the power to deliver change, people affected by the problem, and a public that needs to learn about the problem and get behind a solution. Once you've determined your audience, study them:
   - What do they know about the problem? What are their attitudes toward it, their likely questions, and their potential concerns?
   - Why might they accept or resist change? Would they prefer a specific solution?
   - Does the problem affect them directly or indirectly? What can and can't they do about the problem?
   - What arguments and evidence would convince them to agree that the problem exists, to care about it, and to take action?
   - What common ground do you and your readers share?

3. **Probe the problem.** If helpful, use the graphic organizer on page 47.
   Define the problem. ■ What is it, exactly? What are its parts or dimensions?
   Determine the problem's seriousness. ■ Why should it be fixed? Who is affected and how? What are its immediate, long-term, and potential effects?
   Analyze causes. ■ What are its root causes and contributing factors?
   Explore context. ■ What is the problem's background, history, and connection to other problems? What solutions have been tried in the past? Who, if anyone, benefits from the problem's existence?
   Think creatively. ■ Take a look at the problem from other perspectives— other states and countries, both genders, different races and ethnic groups, and other generations.

4. **Brainstorm possible solutions.** List all imaginable solutions—both modest and radical fixes. Then evaluate the alternatives:

- List criteria that any solution should meet. (These measurements indicate a solution's effectiveness at resolving the problem: *The solution must . . .*)
- Compare and contrast alternatives by examining strengths, weaknesses, and workability.

5. **Choose the best solution and map out support.** In a sentence, state the solution that best solves the problem—a workable plan that attacks causes and treats effects. Try this pattern for your thesis: Given [the problem—its seriousness, effects, or causes], we must [the solution]." Next, identify support for your solution. Compared with alternatives, why is it preferable? Is it more thorough, beneficial, and practical?

6. **Outline your proposal and complete a first draft.** A proposal's structure is quite simple: Describe the problem, offer a solution, and defend the solution. However, what you do in each section can become complicated. Choose strategies that fit your purpose and audience.

- **The problem:** Consider whether readers understand the problem and accept its seriousness. Inform and/or persuade them about the problem by using appropriate background information, cause/effect analysis, examples, analogies, parallel cases, visuals, and expert testimony.
- **The solution:** If necessary, first argue against alternative solutions. Then present your solution. State clearly what should happen, who should be involved, and why. For a complex solution, lay out the different stages.
- **The support:** Show how the solution solves the problem. Use facts and analysis to argue that your solution is feasible and to address objections. You may choose to accept some objections while refuting others.

7. **Get feedback and revise the draft.** Share your draft with a peer or a tutor in the writing center, getting answers to the following questions:

- Does the solution fit the problem? Is the proposal precise, well-reasoned, realistic, and complete? Does it address all possible objections?
- Is the evidence credible, compelling, clear, and well-documented?
- Does the voice fit the problem's seriousness and treat the opposition tactfully?
- Is the opening engaging? Is the closing thoughtful, forceful, and clear?

8. **Edit and proofread.** Check for accurate word choice and helpful definitions; smooth, energetic sentences; and correct grammar, spelling, and format.

9. **Prepare and share your final essay.** Submit your proposal to your instructor, but also consider posting it on the web.

Writing Checklist

Use these six traits to check your essay; then revise as needed:

_____ The **ideas** show a thorough understanding of the problem and present a workable solution. The proposal uses strong reasoning and well-researched evidence.

_____ The **organization** convincingly moves from problem to solution to support. Each part is effectively ordered using strategies such as cause/effect, compare/contrast, and process.

_____ The **voice** is positive, confident, objective, and sensitive to opposing viewpoints. The tone fits the seriousness of the problem.

_____ The **words** are precise and effectively defined.

_____ The **sentences** read and flow smoothly, with effective variations and logical transitions.

_____ The copy is **correct** and follows all the rules of grammar, format, and documentation.

Writing Activities

1. "Preparing for Agroterror" predicts that a problem may develop. Thinking about current conditions and trends, forecast a problem, and write a proposal explaining how to prepare for or prevent it.

2. Review the section in Chapter 17 about "Engaging the Opposition" (page **259**). Also review how Anna Quindlen engages her opposition in "Uncle Sam and Aunt Samantha." Then consider a persuasive piece that you are drafting or revising. How might you engage the opposition to your arguments? Revise your writing as needed.

3. Review the section in Chapter 17 about "Identifying Logical Fallacies" (pages **255–258**). Write a humorous essay in which you make an argument by relying on a number of obvious logical fallacies. A challenge: How effectively can you make serious points by combining these strategies?

4. In "The Media and the Ethics of Cloning," the writer focuses on the ethical and cultural problems related to the scientific pursuit of cloning. Select a scientific or technological advance that concerns you. Then propose ways to counter its negatives.

5. What are some challenges facing the planet Earth and the human race in the foreseeable future? Find a focused challenge and write a proposal.

Report Writing

It's tempting to suggest that the contents of reports include "just the facts." Whether they focus on observations (Chapter 21), interviews (Chapter 22), or scientific research (Chapter 23), reports at first glance seek only to share with readers the objective results of primary research. However, a more careful reading of reports shows that they do much more. For example, the reports in this section not only describe their topics, they also use analytical strategies (such as cause–effect) to interpret or explain the activities that they describe.

As you read the various types of reports in this section, note both the research methods and organizational strategies used by each writer. Then, as you write your own report, choose research methods and writing strategies that fit your rhetorical situation: your audience, purpose, and subject.

CONTENTS

Report Writing

Chapter 21
Observation Report

Observant people are insightful people. What others overlook, they notice, and they use these observations to expand and deepen their understanding of life. For such people, observing comes naturally.

Learning to observe lies at the heart of an observation report. In addition, writing such a report challenges you to effectively re-create an observed world and share it with readers. Whether the report profiles a beach or a bus terminal, it's a documentary formed in words and built upon your sensory impressions—and sometimes your thoughts and feelings, too.

Such observation is part of many college courses. An education student visiting a kindergarten classroom, a biology student observing white-tailed deer, and a theater student studying a production of *Othello* are all observing to learn. Even in the workplace, observations are shaped into reports about site inspections, incidents, and trips. This chapter will help you polish the observation skills and writing abilities needed to construct reports in college and at work.

What's Ahead

- Overview: Writing an Observation Report
  - Student Model
  - Professional Models
- Guidelines
- Writing Checklist and Activities

Overview
Writing an Observation Report

Writer's Goal

Your goal is to powerfully re-create your observations of a location and/or an event. Aim to share your sensory impressions so clearly that your reader gets an accurate, rich sense of the situation.

Keys for Success

Determine your purpose. ■ First, identify your purpose: Is it to understand the situation, discover surprises, or answer a question? Second, choose a perspective: Should you observe passively or interact? Should you observe objectively or add thoughts and feelings? Should you observe from one position or several?

Plan your observation. ■ To observe well, you must prepare. Consider these issues: permission, safety, background research, timing, transportation, clothing, and equipment.

Show rather than tell. ■ Describe what you see, hear, smell, feel, and taste. Provide concrete details, not generalities.

Develop a theme. ■ Tie together the details of your observation with an idea or mood that is stated or implied.

Sites to Consider

Use the headings below to generate a list of good observation sites.

- **Natural sites:** Select an interesting location in nature—a state park, garden, zoo, or lake.
- **People sites:** Try a location brimming with people doing interesting activities—a sports arena, a community center, a theater, or a market.
- **Unfamiliar sites:** Choose a peculiar or unfamiliar site—a different neighborhood, a work site, or an ethnic or gender-specific event.
- **Serene sites:** Try a quiet spot requiring subtle observation—a night scene, an empty building, a quiet park, or a cathedral.
- **Coursework-related sites:** If you are taking a course in early childhood education, for example, visit a day care center or kindergarten classroom.
- **Border sites:** As a margin between two worlds, a border is often a busy site. Consider lines between city and suburb, town and country, land and water, or field and forest.

Next Step Read the model essays and perform the activities that follow. As you read, think about what makes these locations good observation sites. List similar places that you could observe.

Observation Report

Laura Apol is a student who traveled to western Washington to explore a short span of shoreline on the Straits of Juan de Fuca. This essay is her report on what she observed.

Audio

The Beach

The writer opens with a contrast, a context, the location, and a theme.

Where I live in eastern Washington, water is irrigation, wildlife is rattlesnakes and coyotes, and hills are a blanket of sagebrush. But western Washington, where my grandfather lives, is different. His house sits across the road from a small beach running along the Straits of Juan de Fuca. Last March I took some friends along to visit my grandfather. I wanted to show them the Straits and its strange ocean-side world.

The focus moves from large to small.

The first day of our visit was dreary, but we crossed the road and pushed through the tall, damp weeds to the beach. The fog-filled air made the entire sky a palette of mixed grays so thick that we could barely see the distant shore of Vancouver Island. The biting breeze made my eyes water and penetrated my T-shirt and jeans. The beach itself stretched only 50 yards to either side, accepting the tame waves that every few seconds rolled up on its sand and rocks. Littered with driftwood and seaweed, the beach looked dirty and stank of dead fish.

She appeals to multiple senses: sight, sound, and touch.

The water's grayness matched the sky, and the buoys that bobbed atop the small waves marked a path for barges. As the waves came ashore, they carried with them small, smooth rocks that made clacking noises as they shuffled over the larger rocks half-buried in the sand. Each wave swirled around the rocks, disturbing the tide pools between them and pushing the driftwood a little farther up the beach. The wood—once live tree limbs—was smooth, as if rubbed with fine sandpaper that wore the branches down to nubs.

Kelp was strewn over the beach like giant worms, their hollow insides filled with debris collected from the water. When I stepped on one, it oozed black muck onto the sand. My stomach turned, and I walked away.

I flipped over a rock sticking out of the water. Where the rock had been, the water suddenly rippled, and the sand stirred with life. With a stick, I gingerly prodded the sand and neighboring rocks, trying to coax the creature out; but when it emerged, it was little more than a shell with spindly legs. One of my friends identified the creature as a hermit crab.

She uses precise nouns, vivid verbs, and strong modifiers.

Grabbing its shell and turning it upside down, he showed me the little crab stuffed inside. Repulsed, I watched the crab retreat into its shell as a turtle might have, pulling its head and legs inside.

In another tide pool, I found a bumpy, greenish-black, jelly-like lump attached to a rock. Extended a few inches from this lump were thin, cloudy-white tentacles with bright pink suckers. The tentacles swayed with the current, as if they were feeling the water for something to grab. Slowly, I extended my finger into the water toward the tentacles. When we touched, the tentacles sucked hard against my skin. Surprised, I jerked my hand out of the water and then stared down at the tentacles that waved back, unaffected. My finger didn't hurt, but it tingled. Again, I brushed my finger across hundreds of tentacles. They sucked again, but then let go when I pulled my finger away. Wondering what this creature did when its tentacles caught something edible, I spotted a shell stuck to a rock and pulled it off. I looked inside, and the shiny black thing living within hid deeper. I dropped the shell into the water beside the lump. Within seconds the lump's tentacles closed around the shell before pulling it into the creature's center, where the shell disappeared.

> **The writer shares her curiosity and describes how she became involved in the scene.**

I looked for more creatures, eventually spotting a starfish nearly hidden under a rock. Putting my fingers near the base of the arms, I pulled lightly on the starfish's body, but it didn't budge. Nor did it budge when I pulled again with all my strength. So I called a friend, and together we used a stick to pry the starfish off the rock and out of the water. Its arms didn't flop, as I had expected, but stayed stiff. Instead of being soft, the creature was as hard as the rock that it had clung to—and just as bumpy. I turned the starfish over to see thousands of tiny tentacles lining each arm like a fingerprint. Some tentacles stretched out farther than others, reaching for something to hold on to. Thinking that I could get the starfish to conform to my hand, as it had to the rock, I put it on the back of my hand and watched. But it moved so slowly that I lacked the patience to wait. So I picked it off my hand—and then yelled in pain! The creature's tiny tentacles had grabbed onto the hair on the back of my hand!

7

> **The closing contrasts a fantasy with reality and offers reflection.**

I stooped down and gently placed the starfish back onto its rock. Then I stood up again, looked over the beach, and thought. What I saw were no miles of white tropical sand, and no crashing, majestic waves—just 100 yards of kelp-covered, seaweed-littered sand and rocks. Yet this was an amazing place, and its thousands of inhabitants were amazing creatures! In fact, I thought, they and I have something in common: Just as I claim eastern Washington—a small spot on the globe—my home, so these strange creatures call this nameless beach theirs. ∎

8

Reading for Better Writing

1. In the introduction, the writer describes the location as a "strange ocean-side world." How does this phrase function as a theme for this report?

2. What sensory impressions does the writer share, and how does she do so? Select one paragraph from the body of the essay, list sensory details, and explore their effectiveness.

3. Describe the essay's tone. Is it fitting?

Observation Report

Randall VanderMey is a college professor and writer who based this report on the observations he recorded while waiting for a bus in a Greyhound station. As you will see, the report is much more than an as-it-happened record of what the writer saw and heard. It is also a brief documentary of a particular slice of American life.

"Scab!"

The opening establishes a tense context and tone.

The driver of the airport shuttle bus had to drop me off on the street so as not to cross the line of Greyhound drivers marching with their picket signs in the dusk. The picketers were angry. Had he turned in at the driveway to the terminal, they would have spat on him and yelled "Scab!" or "Strikebreaker!" Newspapers and TV had carried stories of rocks and bottles being thrown at passenger-filled buses by disgruntled Greyhound drivers whose demands for decent wages had not been heard. Most of the drivers in other unions were honoring the picket lines. Someday, they knew, they might be in the same fix.

The writer locates himself in the scene.

Inside the terminal I sat with my feet on my suitcase. I didn't want to pay four quarters for a storage box and didn't want to turn my back on my belongings. In the strange, tense atmosphere of the bus depot, I wondered if I was better off there or on a bus. Writing notes became my shield.

Switching to present tense, he describes what he senses.

A Hispanic couple behind me plays Spanish music for everyone in the terminal to hear. Men go in the men's room and stay there for a strangely long time, punching the button on the electric blow dryer over and over as if to cover up their talk. Near me an old man in a blue baseball cap and blue nylon jacket mumbles to himself as he paces the floor slowly. I hear him say, "My children is all grown up." Another man in a white yachting cap strides around the terminal making a sliding, streaking sound with a metal heel protector that's working its way loose. He seems to like the sound because he keeps walking around on the hard tile floors, over to the video-game room, over to the cafeteria, over to the bathroom, over to the ticket window, around and around in the open spaces in front of the nuns, college kids, young black girls with children, and Texas farmers waiting for their bus to Dallas. I know where the man in the yachting cap is without even looking up.

He describes the terminal and the people, including snippets of dialogue.

A tiny boy, curiosity in a red sweater, is twirling around. Everybody who sees him smiles. A while ago I saw an older man teasing him, saying "Hey, I'm gonna get you" and trying to slip a ten-gallon straw cowboy hat over his ears.

A policeman with his hair shaved off all over his round, bumpy head takes his drawn nightstick into the men's room and brings out, by the elbow, a young black man who doesn't seem to know where he is. He cradles a radio in his arm that blasts its music to everyone's discomfort. The cop says,

"Didn't I throw you out of here last night? Come on with me." The guy looks dazed and says, "Where we going?" The cop says, "We're just going to have a little talk." Turning off the blaring radio, he walks the young man toward the entrance.

He records what he sees, hears, and smells.

Something weird is in the air, as if drugs are being dealt in the bathrooms, though the place remains calm and well lit. The odor of french fries and cleaning solutions fills the air.

The Hispanic music plays much more softly now, and I hear the dyed-blond lady break out of her Spanish to say to her husband or boyfriend, "Thang you very mush."

The writer briefly reflects on the scene.

The iron screen benches are starting to lay a print in my back and rear end, so I shift and squirm. When I bought my ticket at the front counter, I asked the lady who took my money what I'd have to do for two hours and a half. She had laughed and said, "Look at the walls," and she had been right.

The man in the blue baseball cap is mumbling again. But now I see that he's reading the newspaper and seems not to be able to read unless he pronounces the words aloud. I hear him say, "That's a liquidation sale."

By comparing, he deepens the observation's meaning.

The man with the metal heel protector is back again, clicking and shrieking across the tile floor, carrying a blue nylon satchel. Out of the video-game room come noises like echoes in a long hollow pipe. A kid behind the cash register in the cafeteria has neatly combed hair and glasses. He keeps smiling all the time, looking comfortingly sane. Overhead in there, the ceiling-fan blades turn hardly faster than the second hand on a clock.

To conclude, the writer returns to the opening, putting his experience into perspective.

It has taken me some time to realize fully how I felt on that hard metal bench for two and a half hours among so many different kinds of people harboring so many different purposes. I said not a word to anyone. Only wrote and wrote. With my eyes and ears I broke into their lives while giving nothing of myself. I got in and got away without any real contact.

I hope the drivers get their money. But I'm not sure my being there helped. I felt like a scab. ■

6

7

8

9

10

11

12

Writing Prompt

Reading for Better Writing

1. This observation report is filled with tension. What is the source of this tension, and how does it create a theme for the report?

2. Locate where the writer shifts verb tenses from past to present, and then to past again. What is the effect of these shifts?

3. How does the writer make his observations vivid? Trace sights, sounds, smells, textures, and tastes. Do these details create patterns or themes?

4. The writer is both present in and separate from what he observes. Explore the strengths and limitations of the writer's uneasy position.

Report Writing

Much of Professor Deborah Tannen's linguistic research and writing is focused on gender issues in communication. In this essay, which was originally published in the *Chronicle of Higher Education* (1991) under the title "Teachers' Classroom Strategies Should Recognize that Men and Women Use Language Differently," the author reports on her observations of students' behavior.

Communication Styles

> The writer establishes her credibility by outlining her previous work on the topic.

When I researched and wrote my book, *You Just Don't Understand: Women and Men in Conversation*, the furthest thing from my mind was reevaluating my teaching strategies. But that has been one of the direct benefits of having written the book.

The primary focus of my linguistic research always has been the language of everyday conversation. One facet of this is conversational style: how different regional, ethnic, and class backgrounds, as well as age and gender, result in different ways of using language to communicate. *You Just Don't Understand* is about the conversational styles of women and men. As I gained more insight into typically male and female ways of using language, I began to suspect some of the causes of the troubling facts that women who go to single-sex schools do better in later life, and that when young women sit next to young men in classrooms, the males talk more. This is not to say that all men talk in class, nor that no women do. It is simply that a greater percentage of discussion time is taken by men's voices.

> She acknowledges and briefly outlines work that others have done on the subject.

The research of sociologists and anthropologists such as Janet Lever, Marjorie Harness Goodwin, and Donna Eder has shown that girls and boys learn to use language differently in their sex-separate peer groups. Typically, a girl has a best friend with whom she sits and talks, frequently telling secrets. It's the telling of secrets, the fact and the way that they talk to each other, that makes them best friends. For boys, activities are central: Their best friends are the ones they do things with. Boys also tend to play in larger groups that are hierarchical. High-status boys give orders and push low-status boys around. So boys are expected to use language to seize center stage: by exhibiting their skills, displaying their knowledge, and challenging and resisting challenges.

> She shows how her topic relates to the work that others have done.

These patterns have stunning implications for classroom interaction. Most faculty members assume that participating in class discussion is a necessary part of successful performance. Yet speaking in a classroom is more congenial to boys' language experience than to girls', since it entails putting oneself forward in front of a large group of people, many of whom are strangers and at least one of whom is sure to judge speakers' knowledge and intelligence by their verbal display.

Another aspect of many classrooms that makes them more hospitable to most men than to most women is the use of debate-like formats as a learning tool. Our educational system, as Walter Ong argues persuasively in his book *Fighting for Life* (Cornell University Press, 1981), is fundamentally male in that the pursuit of knowledge is believed to be achieved by ritual opposition: public display followed by argument and challenge. Father Ong demonstrates that ritual opposition—what he calls "adversativeness" or "agonism"—is fundamental to the way most males approach almost any activity. (Consider, for example, the little boy who shows he likes a little girl by pulling her braids and shoving her.) But ritual opposition is antithetical to the way most females learn and like to interact. It is not that females don't fight, but that they don't fight for fun. They don't *ritualize* opposition.

Anthropologists working in widely disparate parts of the world have found contrasting verbal rituals for women and men. Women in completely unrelated cultures (for example, Greece and Bali) engage in ritual laments: spontaneously produced rhyming couplets that express their pain, for example, over the loss of loved ones. Men do not take part in laments. They have their own, very different verbal ritual: a contest, a war of words in which they vie with each other to devise clever insults.

When discussing these phenomena with a colleague, I commented that I see these two styles in American conversation: Many women bond by talking about troubles, and many men bond by exchanging playful insults and put-downs, and other sorts of verbal sparring. He exclaimed: "I never thought of this, but that's the way I teach: I have students read an article, and then I invite them to tear it apart. After we've torn it to shreds, we talk about how to build a better model."

This contrasts sharply with the way I teach: I open the discussion of readings by asking, "What did you find useful in this? What can we use in our own theory building and our own methods?" I note what I see as weaknesses in the author's approach, but I also point out that the writer's discipline and purposes might be different from ours. Finally, I offer personal anecdotes illustrating the phenomena under discussion and praise students' anecdotes as well as their critical acumen.

These different teaching styles must make our classrooms wildly different places and hospitable to different students. Male students are more likely to be comfortable attacking the readings and might find the inclusion of personal anecdotes irrelevant and "soft." Women are more likely to resist discussion they perceive as hostile, and, indeed, it is women in my classes who are most likely to offer personal anecdotes.

A colleague who read my book commented that he had always taken for granted that the best way to deal with students' comments is to challenge them; this, he felt it was self-evident, sharpens their minds and helps them develop debating skills. But he had noticed that women were relatively silent in his classes, so he decided to try beginning discussion with relatively open-ended questions and letting comments go unchallenged. He found, to his amazement and satisfaction, that more women began to speak up.

Though some women in his class clearly liked this better, perhaps some of the men liked it less. One young man in my class wrote in a questionnaire

Examples help to show the meaning of jargon and unfamiliar terms.

The writer supports her claim using global evidence.

She also uses local evidence.

She considers the important implications of her observations.

6

7

8

9

10

11

about a history professor who gave students questions to think about and called on people to answer them: "He would then play devil's advocate . . . *i.e.,* he debated us. . . . That class *really* sharpened me intellectually. . . . We as students do need to know how to defend ourselves." This young man valued the experience of being attacked and challenged publicly. Many, if not most, women would shrink from such "challenge," experiencing it as public humiliation.

The word *many* allows for exceptions to the generalizations the author makes.

A professor at Hamilton College told me of a young man who was upset because he felt his class presentation had been a failure. The professor was puzzled because he had observed that class members had listened attentively and agreed with the student's observations. It turned out that it was this very agreement that the student interpreted as failure: Since no one had engaged his ideas by arguing with him, he felt they had found them unworthy of attention.

12

So one reason men speak in class more than women is that many of them find the "public" classroom setting more conducive to speaking, whereas most women are more comfortable speaking in private to a small group of people they know well. A second reason is that men are more likely to be comfortable with the debate-like form that discussion may take. Yet another reason is the different attitudes toward speaking in class that typify women and men.

13

The writer reviews points she has made thus far and introduces her next point.

Students who speak frequently in class, many of whom are men, assume that it is their job to think of contributions and try to get the floor to express them. But many women monitor their participation not only to get the floor but to avoid getting it. Women students in my class tell me that if they have spoken up once or twice, they hold back for the rest of the class because they don't want to dominate. If they have spoken a lot one week, they will remain silent the next. These different ethics of participation are, of course, unstated, so those who speak freely assume that those who remain silent have nothing to say, and those who are reining themselves in assume that the big talkers are selfish and hoggish.

14

The first sentence of this paragraph links key terms from the last paragraph with new ideas.

When I looked around my classes, I could see these differing ethics and habits at work. For example, my graduate class in analyzing conversation had 20 students, 11 women and 9 men. Of the men, four were foreign students: two Japanese, one Chinese, and one Syrian. With the exception of the three Asian men, all the men spoke in class at least occasionally. The biggest talker in the class was a woman, but there were also five women who never spoke at all, only one of whom was Japanese. I decided to try something different.

15

The writer describes the methods she used for creating and collecting data.

I broke the class into small groups to discuss the issues raised in the readings and to analyze their own conversational transcripts. I devised three ways of dividing the students into groups: one by the degree program they were in, one by gender, and one by conversational style, as closely as I could guess it. This meant that when the class was grouped according to

16

conversational style, I put Asian students together, fast talkers together, and quiet students together. The class split into groups six times during the semester, so they met in each grouping twice. I told students to regard the groups as examples of interactional data and to note the different ways they participated in different groups. Toward the end of the term, I gave them a questionnaire asking about their class and group participation.

She explains why her data are important.

I could see plainly from my observation of the groups at work that women who never opened their mouths in class were talking away in the small groups. In fact, the Japanese woman commented that she found it particularly hard to contribute to the all-woman group she was in because "I was overwhelmed by how talkative the female students were in the female-only group." This is particularly revealing because it highlights that the same person who can be "oppressed" into silence in one context can become the talkative "oppressor" in another. No one's conversational style is absolute; everyone's style changes in response to the context and others' styles. [17]

Some of the students (seven) said that they preferred the same-gender groups; others preferred the same-style groups. In answer to the question "Would you have liked to speak in class more than you did?" six of the seven who said Yes were women; the one man was Japanese. Most startlingly, this response did not come only from quiet women; it came from women who had indicated they had spoken in class never, rarely, sometimes, and often. Of the 11 students who said the amount they had spoken was fine, 7 were men. Of the four women who checked "fine," two added qualifications indicating it wasn't completely fine: One wrote in "maybe more," and one wrote, "I have an urge to participate but often feel I should have something more interesting/relevant/wonderful/intelligent to say!!" [18]

The writer draws conclusions, sharing what she has learned and why it is important.

I counted my experiment a success. Everyone in the class found the small groups interesting, and no one indicated he or she would have preferred that the class not break into groups. Perhaps most instructive, however, was the fact that the experience of breaking into groups, and of talking about participation in class, raised everyone's awareness about classroom participation. After we had talked about it, some of the quietest women in the class made a few voluntary contributions, though sometimes I had to insure their participation by interrupting the students who were exuberantly speaking out. [19]

Americans are often proud that they discount the significance of cultural differences: "We are all individuals," many people boast. Ignoring such issues as gender and ethnicity becomes a source of pride: "I treat everyone the same." But treating people the same is not equal treatment if they are not the same. [20]

The classroom is a different environment for those who feel comfortable putting themselves forward in a group than it is for those who find the prospect of doing so chastening, or even terrifying. When a [21] professor asks, "Are there any questions?," students who can formulate statements the fastest have the greatest opportunity to respond. Those who need significant time to do so have not really been given a chance at all, since by the time they are ready to speak, someone else has the floor.

In a class where some students speak out without raising hands, those [22] who feel they must raise their hands and wait to be recognized do not have equal opportunity to speak. Telling them to feel free to jump in will not make them feel free; one's sense of timing, of one's rights and obligations in a classroom, are automatic, learned over years of interaction. They may be changed over time, with motivation and effort, but they cannot be changed on the spot. And everyone assumes his or her own way is best. When I asked my students how the class could be changed to make it easier for them to speak more, the most talkative woman said she would prefer it if no one had to raise hands, and a foreign student said he wished people would raise their hands and wait to be recognized.

> The writer explains the limits of her findings and conclusions.

My experience in this class has convinced me that small-group [23] interaction should be part of any class that is not a small seminar. I also am convinced that having the students become observers of their own interaction is a crucial part of their education. Talking about ways of talking in class makes students aware that their ways of talking affect other students, that the motivations they impute to others may not truly reflect others' motives, and that the behaviors they assume to be self-evidently right are not universal norms.

> She makes a final case for the significance of her study.

The goal of complete equal opportunity in class may not be attainable, [24] but realizing that one monolithic classroom-participation structure is not equal opportunity is itself a powerful motivation to find more-diverse methods to serve diverse students—and every classroom is diverse. ∎

Writing Prompt

Reading for Better Writing

1. What underlying question(s) drives Tannen to make the inquiries that she does? To what extent is she able to answer the question(s)?

2. Why does Tannen acknowledge work that others have done on this subject? Why does she make an effort to demonstrate how her work relates to others' work on the topic?

3. What primary and secondary sources does Tannen use as she collects data for her observation report? How might different readers respond to the different types of sources?

4. Where does Tannen comment on the significance of her observations (either explicitly or implicitly)? Why does she do this?

Guidelines
Writing an Observation Report

1. **Select a site.** Check the list of sites you generated with "Sites to Consider" on page **320**. Choose a situation that will prove rich in sensory appeal.

2. **Consider your purpose and your readers.** What do you want to learn from your observations? Should you stand back or become involved in the situation? Who are your readers, what do they know about the event or site, and what could they gain from your observations?

3. **Prepare to observe.** Test your readiness with the checklist below:

   ____ I understand my goal for observing and have listed what to look for.

   ____ I've done necessary background research.

   ____ If the site isn't public, I've gotten permission to observe.

   ____ My timing is right: I have (1) chosen a good time to observe, (2) set aside enough time, and (3) planned multiple visits, if needed.

   ____ I have appropriate transportation and clothing, considering the site and weather.

   ____ I've gathered helpful equipment (pens, notebook, maps, measuring tools, sample containers, laptop, flashlight, camera, video recorder).

4. **Actively observe.** When on site, record the details of your visit.
   - Patiently follow your purpose and plan, but be open to surprises.
   - Identify your position. Where are you situated? What is your angle? More broadly, what is your frame of mind—are you an insider or an outsider here?
   - Focus on all five senses, recording impressions freely and thoroughly as they happen.
     - **Sights**—Record colors, shapes, and appearance; see the big picture and the little details.
     - **Sounds**—Listen for loud and subtle, harsh and pleasant, natural and mechanical sounds; if people are present, record relevant conversations.
     - **Smells**—Check out both pleasant and unpleasant odors: what's sweet, spicy, sweaty, pungent, sour, rancid, and so on.
     - **Textures**—Safely test things for temperature, smoothness, roughness, thickness, and so on.
     - **Tastes**—If your site permits (a restaurant, a ballpark), taste for sweet, sour, bitter, and so on.
   - Explore your sixth sense. Record thoughts, feelings, and associations.
   - If appropriate, collect samples, take photos, or record sounds.

5. **Organize your observations.** Soon after you observe, review your notes and other material you collected. Add details and clarify points, if necessary. Then outline your report:

- Consider a theme, perhaps an insight based on your observations. What is the site's heart, its identity? What patterns bubbled to the surface? What surprised you?

- Arrange points and supporting details to develop the theme. For example, you could move from the big picture to small details, from a wide angle to a close-up, from first impressions to second looks, from neutral observation to involvement. Alternatively, you could present observations chronologically.

6. **Write the first draft.** Consider when to use past and present verb tenses, and whether to combine reflection with observation. Follow these tips:

Opening: Offer a vivid detail, identify the site or situation, supply background, indicate your position, and establish your theme.

Middle: Present vital, well-organized details. Make observations vivid, but also make sure that all the details fit together coherently.

Conclusion: Remind readers of your theme. Stress the observation's value, along with broader insights. Perhaps explain how the observation expanded your world.

Working Title: Develop a title that identifies the site and/or hints at your theme.

7. **Get feedback and revise your draft.** Get a fresh perspective from a peer or a tutor in the writing center. Improve the draft by using his or her responses to the following questions:

- Are the place, time, and purpose of the observation clear?
- Does the report vividly appeal to multiple senses and create a strong sense of the site or situation?
- Does the report flow naturally and build to a conclusion?
- Are insights logically related to the observations themselves?
- Does the tone fit the site, the situation, and the theme?

8. **Edit and proofread.** Work through your report sentence by sentence:

- Replace vague nouns, bland verbs, and weak modifiers.
- Rewrite tired, predictable sentences. Check verb tenses for consistency.
- Proofread for typos, grammar errors, spelling mistakes, and correct format.

9. **Prepare and share the final essay.** Find ways to communicate your observations. Besides submitting the report to your instructor, turn it into a presentation, post it on the class's website, or share it with family and friends.

Writing Checklist

Use these six traits to check the quality of your writing, and then revise as needed:

_____ The **ideas** share insights derived from what you observed. The report brings the site or situation to life.

_____ The **organization** follows an effective flow, whether chronological or theme-driven.

_____ The **voice** fits the purpose. The tone is appropriately objective or subjective, relaxed or tense, matter-of-fact or surprised.

_____ The **words** are specific and powerful: precise nouns, vivid verbs, and sharp modifiers.

_____ The **sentences** are smooth and varied. Past and present verb tenses are used correctly and consistently.

_____ The copy is clean, **correct**, and attractive.

Writing Prompt

Writing Activities

1. In "The Beach," the student writer observes a natural border where land and water meet. What other natural borders exist? Select one, observe it, and write up a report.

2. Many of the moves that Deborah Tannen makes in "Communication Styles" are typical of the rhetorical moves that writers make in research reports in the social sciences. With your instructor's help, find two or three other samples of writing in this genre and identify similarities across the samples. What conclusions can you draw about what is important to readers and writers in this genre?

3. It's time to (safely) step outside your comfort zone. What places or events do you find uncomfortably strange? Select one and write an "it's-a-strange-world" report.

4. Is careful observation important in your major? Research what things get observed, what experts look for, and how they report their observations. Then perform such an observation yourself.

5. In the workplace, observation is often used in site or trip reports. Observe a site or event related to your work (or future work), and write a report for a real (or imagined) supervisor.

Chapter 22
Interview Report

The idea of an interview is simple. You talk with someone—an expert on a topic, a client, or a case-study subject—to gain insights into the topic and/or person. As a question-and-answer session, an interview can generate primary information to supplement other research, or it can provide the information and focus for an entire piece of writing such as an interview report.

The idea of an interview may be simple, but conducting a good interview and writing a good report can be tough. A good interview must be carefully planned and executed to become a productive conversation. Planning gives you background information and helps you develop questions that produce solid data, vivid details, and lively quotations. Poor interviewing leads to flat facts, irrelevant tangents, and bland generalities.

This chapter focuses on developing meaningful interview reports. The overview, guidelines, and model that follows will help you carry out your interviews and write your reports.

What's Ahead

- Overview: Writing an Interview Report
  - Student Model
- Guidelines
- Writing Checklist and Activities

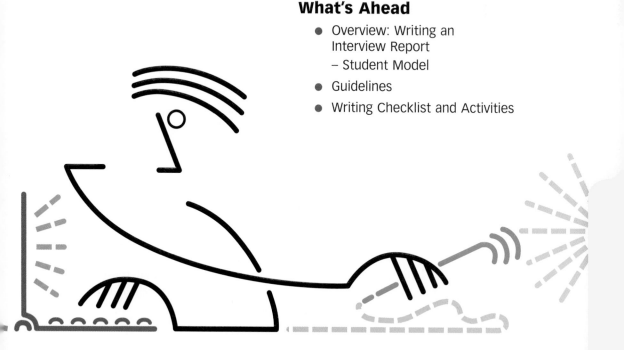

Overview
Writing an Interview Report

Writer's Goal

Your goal is to gain insights by interviewing someone and then sharing those revelations with readers. Aim to ask the right questions, record answers accurately, and report results clearly.

Keys for Success

Plan carefully. ■ An interview needs to be properly prepared, conducted, and processed. Give yourself enough time, and respect your interviewee by being on time, efficient, informed, and courteous.

Ask clear, relevant questions. ■ Clear questions yield useful information—insights into the topic or person that peek below the factual surface. Getting quality information depends on the art of interviewing—planning relevant questions, listening well, following up with sensible responses, and being open to surprises.

Respect the interviewee's voice. ■ Know the person's identity, story, and values. In the interview, listen much more than you talk. In the report, present the person's words and thoughts clearly and honestly. Consider sharing the report with the interview subject before you "go public."

Analyze and synthesize the results. ■ Analysis helps you understand pieces of information, and synthesis helps you pull together separate facts to show relationships. To write an interview report, you must both analyze and synthesize the results of your interview to discover a meaningful theme. Shape the discussion so that the report hangs together, means something, and goes somewhere.

People to Consider

Choose an interviewee from one of the following categories:

● **The expert:** Who is an authority on your topic? Could you find such an expert in your college or community, through local organizations or businesses, or on the Internet?

● **The experienced:** Who has had unique, direct experiences with the topic? Who has participated in, witnessed, or been affected by the situation?

● **The person:** If your purpose is to focus on a person rather than a topic, choose someone intriguing—someone from a particular background, generation, ethnicity, nationality, or occupation.

Next Step Read the model essay and perform the activities that follow. As you read, think about the interview subject chosen and the strategies used to report on the interview. Consider how to use similar strategies.

Interview Report

Because of a disturbing childhood experience, college student Benjamin Meyer toured a funeral home and interviewed the director. In the following essay, Benjamin reports on what he learned.

The Dead Business

The writer starts with background information that creates a personal theme.

"You're going to tour a what?" 1

"A funeral home." 2

My friends were shocked. They laughed while describing scenes from 3
Night of the Living Dead and *The Shining*.

But their stories didn't frighten me—I feared something else. When I 4
was ten, my grandmother died, and my family drove to the funeral home to
view the body. As we entered the place, I noticed the funeral director standing in the corner, looking like a too-eager-to-please salesman who'd made a
deal he didn't deserve. The guy's thin-lipped smile seemed unnatural—
almost glib. Like a ghoul in a business suit, he didn't seem to care that a
stroke had stopped my grandmother's beating heart midway through the
doxology that concluded the Sunday-evening church service. He didn't seem
to care that she and I would share no more cookies, no more coloring
books, no more Rook games, no more laughing, no more. I was ten, very
sad, and he didn't seem to care.

Freely using "I," the writer tells the story of his visit and interview.

Now a college student, I wanted to tour a different funeral home to 5
work through my earlier experience. While I no longer feared ghouls, I was
still nervous while driving to the Vander Ploeg Furniture Store/Funeral
Home. I remembered the thin-lipped smile.

I walked inside not knowing what to expect. Suddenly, a man from 6
behind a desk hopped out of his chair and said, "Hi, I'm Howard Beernink."

I looked at the tall, smiling guy, paused a moment, and glanced back at 7
the door. His partner had stepped in front of the exit while scribbling on
tags that dangled from Lazy Boy rockers. I realized that this interview was
something I had to do . . . like getting a tetanus shot.

He describes the setting.

Howard led me into a room full of furniture where he found a soft, 8
purple couch. We sat down, and he described how the business started.

He relates the early history of the business.

In 1892, pioneers established the town of Sioux Center, Iowa. Winter 9
storms and disease pummeled the tiny community, and soon residents
needed someone to bury the dead. A funeral director wasn't available, but a
furniture maker was. The furniture maker was the only person with the
tools, hardwood, and knowledge to build coffins. As a result, the Vander
Ploeg Furniture Store/Funeral Home was born.

The writer summarizes, paraphrases, and quotes from the interview.

Today, starting a funeral home isn't that easy. For example, a funeral home requires the services of an embalmer, and an embalmer must be certified by the state. To get a certificate, the person must complete two years of college, one year of embalming school, and one year of apprentice work. After that, the individual must pass a state exam every year to retain certification. *10*

"But why a funeral home director?" I was baffled. Why would anyone embalm dead bodies for a living? *11*

"Because it's a family business." Howard smiled as if he expected my question. "Vander Ploegs and Beerninks have run this place for generations. Today it's difficult to start a funeral home because there are so many of them with long histories and good reputations." *12*

After he answered the rest of my questions, Howard asked if I wanted to see the embalming room. *13*

He narrates what happened during the interview.

"Okay," I said, tentatively. *14*

He led me through doors, down hallways, up a staircase, and into a well-lighted display room containing several coffins. Finally, we entered a small, cold room containing a row of cupboards, a large ceramic table, and a small machine that resembled a bottled-water cooler. *15*

"We like to keep the room cold when we're not using it," Howard said. *16*

"What is all this stuff?" I asked. *17*

Howard described why embalming is done and what it involves. The purpose of embalming is to extend the period for viewing the body, and the process includes replacing body fluids with embalming fluid. He opened a cupboard, pulled out a bottle of fluid and said, "Here . . . smell." *18*

The writer shares surprises and what he learned.

"Smells like Pepto-Bismol," I replied. *19*

After he embalms the body, Howard applies makeup so the face appears "more natural." He gets his cosmetics (common powders and tints) from the local Avon lady. *20*

"But sometimes we also have to use this," Howard said, pulling out another bottle. *21*

"Tissue builder?" I asked, squinting at the label. *22*

"It's like silicon implants," he answered. "We inject it into sunken cheeks, like the cheeks of cancer victims." *23*

When the body is ready for burial, the funeral director must show a price list to the family of the deceased. The Funeral Rule, adopted in 1984 by the Federal Trade Commission, requires that a price list be shown to the family before they see caskets, cement boxes, and vaults. The purpose of the Funeral Rule is to prevent unethical funeral directors from manipulating customers with comments like, "But that's a pauper's casket; you don't want to bury your mother in that. Bury her in this beauty over here." *24*

Unfortunately, only a third of the country's 22,000 funeral homes abide by the Funeral Rule.

"After showing customers where the caskets are, I step away so they can talk among themselves," said Howard. "It's unethical to bother the family at this difficult time." 25

Before burying a casket, Howard and his partner place it in either a cement box or a vault. A cement box is a container that's neither sealed nor waterproofed, whereas a vault is both sealed and waterproofed. Howard explained, "Years ago, cemeteries began to sink and cave in on spots, so state authorities demanded containers. Containers make the cemetery look nicer." 26

After the tour, I asked Howard, "How has this job affected your life?" 27

He glanced at the ceiling, smiled, and said, "It's very fulfilling. My partner and I comfort people during a stressful time in their lives, and it strengthens our bond with them." 28

He ends the report with a strong quotation and personal reflection.

As I drove back to the college, I thought again about Howard's comment, and about my childhood fear. Howard was right. He doesn't exploit people. Instead, he comforts them and helps them move on. And while I still fear the pain of saying good-bye to someone I love, I don't fear funeral directors anymore. They're just people who provide services that a community needs. ■ 29

Reading for Better Writing

1. This report centers on the writer's own story, reflections, and needs. Discuss how these elements are woven into the report. Are they effective? Why or why not?

2. Examine the opening and the closing of the essay. Do they work well together? Do they effectively share a theme for the report? Explain.

3. Describe how the writer organizes the interview's results. Is the organization effective? Explain.

4. Look carefully at the writer's use of summary and paraphrase on the one hand and quotation on the other hand. Are the strategies effective? Explain.

Guidelines
Writing an Interview Report

1. **Choose a person to interview.** Review "People to Consider" on page **334** to find an interviewee. Also consider a community or campus leader.

2. **Plan the interview.** As soon as possible, take care of the details:
    - Determine your goal—what you want the interview to accomplish and what information and insights you want to gather.
    - Choose a sensible recording method (pen and paper, recorder) and a medium (face-to-face, telephone, e-mail).
    - Consider what you know about the topic and the interviewee. Then figure out what you must know to ask meaningful questions. If necessary, do some research on the interview subject.
    - Contact the interviewee and politely request an interview. Explain who you are, why you need the interview, and how you will use it. Schedule a time and place convenient for the interviewee. If you wish to record the interview, ask permission.
    - Gather and test tools and equipment: a notebook, pens, and perhaps recording equipment (tape, video, digital camera).

3. **Prepare questions.** Do the following to help you structure the interview:
    - Consider types of questions to ask—the five *W*'s and *H* (*who, what, when, where, why,* and *how*).
    - Understand open and closed questions. Closed questions ask for simple, factual answers; open questions ask for detailed explanations.
      Closed: How many months did you spend in Vietnam?
      Open: Can you describe your most vivid memory of Vietnam?
    - Avoid slanted questions pressuring readers to give a specific answer.
      Slanted: Aren't you really angry that draft dodgers didn't do their duty?
      Neutral: How do you feel about those who avoided the draft?
    - Think about specific topics to cover and write questions for each one. Start with a simple question that establishes rapport and groundwork. Plan target questions—ones that you must ask.
    - Put questions on the left side of the page with room for notes on the right. Rehearse your questions, visualizing how the interview should go.

4. **Conduct the interview.** Arrive on time and be professional:
    - Introduce yourself, reminding the interviewee why you've come.
    - If you have permission to record the interview, set up equipment off to the side so that it doesn't interfere with the conversation. However, even if you're recording, take notes on key facts and quotations.

- Listen actively by including nods and eye contact. Pay attention to the interviewee's body language.
- Be flexible. If the person looks puzzled by a question, rephrase it or ask another. Ask one of these questions if an answer needs to be amplified:

Clarifying:	"Do you mean this or that?"
Explanatory:	"What do you mean by that?"
Detailing:	"What happened exactly? Can you describe that?"
Analytical:	"Did that happen by stages? What were the causes? The outcomes?"
Probing:	"What do you think that meant?"
Comparative:	"Did that remind you of anything?"
Contextual:	"What else was going on then? Who else was involved?"
Summarizing:	"Overall, what was your response? What was the net effect?"

- Be tactful. If the person avoids a question, politely rephrase it. Don't react negatively or forcefully invade the interviewee's private territory.
- Listen "between the lines" for what the interviewee seems to want to say.
- Expect important points to come up late in the interview, and give the interviewee a chance to add any final thoughts.

5. Follow up. As soon as possible, review your notes and fill in the blanks. By phone or in writing, clarify points and thank the interviewee.

6. Organize and draft the report. Shape the opening to seize interest, the middle to sustain interest, and the closing to reward interest:

- Analyze and interpret the interview results. Locate the heart or theme of your report, and then develop an outline supporting the theme.
- Start with background, along with a point that gains readers' interest.
- Summarize and paraphrase material from the interview. (See pages **444–446**.) Use quotations selectively to share the interviewee's character or stress a point.
- If appropriate, weave your thoughts and reflections into the report.

7. Get feedback and revise the report. Ask someone to answer these questions: Does the report supply complete, satisfying insights? Is the organization effective, with an engaging opening and closing? Is the writing lively, fair, and respectful?

8. Edit and proofread. Review your report for precise word choice, smooth sentences, and correct grammar. In particular, make sure that quotations are integrated smoothly. (See page **489**.)

9. Prepare a final copy. Submit a clean copy to your instructor (and perhaps the interviewee), but also look for ways to publish your report—as a webpage with digital photos and sound clips, or as a presentation for classmates.

Writing Checklist

Use these six traits to check the quality of your writing, then revise as needed:

_____ The **ideas** share the heart of the interview—the interviewee's insights—through summary, paraphrase, and quotation.

_____ The **organization** centers on a theme and then creates, sustains, and rewards interest.

_____ The **voice** sounds genuine and interested. The interviewee's voice is understood and respected.

_____ The **words** are precise and understandable. Quotations reflect the interviewee's ideas and personality.

_____ The **sentences** are smooth, with quotations effectively integrated. Transitional words link sentences and sections.

_____ The copy is **correct** in terms of its grammar, punctuation, usage, spelling, and format.

Writing Activities

1. Generate a list of people who understand the challenges and opportunities related to the career you want to pursue. Then follow the guidelines for a personal interview on page **334** and write a report.

2. "The Dead Business" recounts the writer's exploration of a topic that caused him discomfort and sadness. What similar issues affect you? Would an interview help you work through the issue? Write your own reflective interview report.

3. Do you know someone who has led a fascinating life? someone who on the surface seems to have led an ordinary life? someone serving others in inspiring ways? Write that person's life story—an extended biography.

4. Is there a particular issue in your community that concerns you—a public debate, a college problem, a program being cut back? Who has insights into the issue? Who are people on different sides? Whose lives are affected? Who has the power to change things? Select one or more people to interview, and then write a report on the issue.

Chapter 23
Lab, Experiment, and Field Reports

Good science writing is rooted in good science—the careful study of phenomena through observation and experiment. Social scientists seek to understand human behavior and societies, whereas natural scientists investigate the physical world.

As a student, you may be asked to conduct scientific research in a range of courses. In labs and in the field, you may perform experiments, gather data, and interpret results and then share your insights with fellow students and members of the scientific community. Such experiences provide valuable preparation for a variety of careers in the sciences.

When you complete a scientific study, you share your research story. Whether you are studying the nature of hydrochloric acid or factors affecting fermentation rates in ethanol, your report shares what you did, why you did it, and what you learned. This chapter will help you put your experiments and field research into writing—and your good writing into science.

What's Ahead

- Overview: Writing Lab, Experiment, and Field Reports
  - Student Models
  - Professional Model
- Guidelines
- Writing Checklist and Activities

Web Link

Overview
Writing Lab, Experiment, and Field Reports

Writer's Goal

Your goal is to accurately record and thoughtfully interpret the results of a scientific study or experiment so clearly that others could repeat your experiment.

Keys for Success

Follow the scientific method. ■ Science focuses on measured observations aimed at understanding. Experiments are set up to test hypotheses about why things happen. However, experiments don't prove hypotheses correct: Experimental results can merely "agree with" or disprove a hypothesis. Overall, the method moves from observation to explanation as you do the following:

1. Observe something interesting (often while looking for something else).
2. Check whether other scientists have explained the same observation.
3. Summarize your observations and turn that generalization into a testable hypothesis—a working theory explaining the phenomenon.
4. Design research to test the hypothesis, paying attention to variables and controls.
5. Based on the results of your experiment, accept, reject, or modify your hypothesis.
6. Repeat steps 3 through 5 until you understand the phenomenon. Then write up your research so that others can respond to your work.

Follow the standard format. ■ To model scientific thinking, lab and field reports include an introduction establishing the problem, a methods section detailing procedures, a results section providing the data, and a discussion that interprets the data.

Distinctions to Consider

Whatever your assignment, you need to understand these distinctions:

- **Distinguish facts from possibilities.** Facts are the data you collect. Possibilities are your interpretations of the data. Don't confuse the two.
- **Distinguish experiments from studies.** Experiments test hypotheses by manipulating variables. Studies observe what's there—counting, measuring, sampling, and so on. In this chapter, the report on fermentation is an experiment; the field report on cockroaches is a study.

Next Step Read the model reports and perform the activities that follow. As you read, examine how the reports follow the scientific method so you can use that method in your own reports.

Lab Report

Student Coby Williams wrote the basic lab report below to describe a chemical compound and inform readers about its nature.

Working with Hydrochloric Acid

The writer identifies the chemical compound and states its nature.

Overview and Purpose

1

The goal in writing this report is to educate others on the dangers of using and storing hydrochloric acid in the lab (HCl) and in the home (muriatic acid). In addition, this report will provide a list of appropriate ways to protect against burns when using HCl as well as ways to dispose of it properly.

Characteristics

2

Hydrochloric acid (HCl), which is made from hydrogen gas and chlorine gas, is a clear, colorless to slightly yellow, fuming liquid with a sharp, irritating odor. HCl is a strong, highly corrosive acid, soluble in water and alcohol. Other characteristics include the following:

✔ The chemical reaction is: $H_2 + Cl_2 = 2HCl$.

✔ Its molecular weight is 36.45.

✔ Its boiling point is 85°C.

✔ Its specific gravity is 1.16.

Hydrochloric acid is commercially known as muriatic acid, a substance used to manufacture dyes and plastics or to acidize (activate) petroleum wells. It is also used in the food processing of corn, syrup, and sodium glutamate, and is an ingredient in many household and industrial cleaners.

3

Safety Procedures

4

Hydrochloric acid is highly corrosive and can severely burn skin. Whenever HCl is used, it must be handled according to the following precautions:

Storage

5

• Keep hydrochloric acid in tightly-capped bottles back from the edge of the shelf or table.

• Keep bottles away from metals. Contact will corrode metals and could release hydrogen gas, which is highly explosive.

He organizes details in distinct categories.

Protection

6

• Always wear safety glasses to protect your eyes.

• Wear latex gloves and old clothes when using concentrated HCl—not short-sleeved shirts, shorts, or sandals.

• Do not breathe the fumes, which can cause fainting.

• If acid spills on skin or splashes in someone's eyes, rinse the area with water for five minutes. Treat burns appropriately. In each case, get medical help immediately.

Usage   7

In the lab, hydrochloric acid is either diluted or titrated.

• When diluting, always pour the acid into the water. Doing the reverse can cause boiling, splashing, and burning.
• When titrating, carefully measure the HCl needed. Then react the HCl with a sample that has a base such as sodium hydroxide to get an accurate measurement of the base in the sample.

Disposal   8

• To dispose of HCl, neutralize it by mixing the acid with a sodium hydroxide solution. Flush the neutralized solution down the drain.
• If you spill HCl, cover the spill with baking soda. After the fizzing stops, sweep up the soda and flush it down the drain. ▮

> Information is accurate and terms are precise.

Reading for Better Writing

1. Who would be the main audience for this type of report? What evidence can you point to that supports your analysis?

2. List the strategies used to organize the report. Are these strategies effective? Explain.

3. How does this report demonstrate scientific thinking?

Experiment Report

In this report, student writer Andrea Pizano shares the results of a lab experiment she completed to explore how different factors affect fermentation.

The Effects of Temperature and Inhibitors on the Fermentation Process for Ethanol

Andrea Pizano
January 29, 2006

Introduction

The opening creates context and explains concepts.

Alcoholic liquids were made and used for centuries before scientists fully understood the process by which alcohol developed. An Egyptian papyrus dated 3500 B.C.E. mentions wine making, although alcoholic spirits like gin and brandy started only about a thousand years ago. From beverages such as beer and wine to fuel additives such as ethanol, alcohol has been used by people for recreation, religious rites, medical purposes, energy, and industry. Even today people are surprised to learn that it is ethanol—a by-product of yeast growth—that makes bread smell good. Studying the process by which alcohol is made can help make the process more efficient and successful. [1]

Generally, alcohol can be made by fermenting different types of sugars, including sucrose, glucose, and fructose. Fermentation is a process that creates heat and changes the properties of a substance through a leavening or fermenting agent. For the fermentation process to succeed, certain enzymes must function as catalysts. These enzymes are present in yeast, the fermenting agent. While useful as catalysts, these enzymes are sensitive to temperature changes and inhibitors. [2]

The writer describes the experiment and states her hypotheses.

In this experiment, ethanol—a specific type of alcohol—was synthesized from sucrose in the presence of yeast. The effects of extreme temperatures and of inhibitors on the rate of fermentation were tested quantitatively. The factors below were tested, and the outcomes below were anticipated. First, extremely high temperatures denature enzymes. Therefore, fermentation in the sample was expected to stop. Second, extremely cool temperatures reduce the kinetic energy of molecules. Therefore, the reaction rate in the sample was expected to drastically slow. Third, sodium fluoride can inhibit one of the enzymes needed in the fermentation process. Therefore, the presence of sodium fluoride was expected to effectively stop the reaction. Fourth, normal fermentation usually delivers a maximum of up to 15 percent ethanol. Through distillation, a 95 percent concentration of ethanol can be obtained. However, the [3] presence of concentrated ethanol kills the yeast cells and also acts as a negative feedback mechanism to the enzymes necessary for the fermentation process. Therefore, concentrated ethanol was expected to effectively stop the reaction.

Method

> She details the procedure using numbered steps and precise terms.

To test each of these hypotheses, the following procedure was followed in this experiment: 4

1. 200 mg of yeast were mixed with 1.25 ml of warm water in a 5-ml round-bottomed, long-necked flask. The mixture was shaken until the yeast was well distributed.

2. 9 mg of disodium hydrogen phosphate, 1.30 g sucrose, and 3.75 ml warm water were added to the flask. This mixture was left for 15 minutes—until the fermentation was proceeding at a vigorous rate.

3. The fermentation mixture was then divided equally into 5 reaction tubes.
   • To tube 1, 1.0 ml of water was added.
   • To tube 2, 1.0 ml of 95% ethanol was added.
   • To tube 3, 1.0 ml of 0.5 M sodium fluoride solution was added.
   • To each of tubes 4 and 5, 1.0 ml of water was added.

4. The bubbles produced in a reaction tube filled with water were counted. A septum was first fit over the neck of each reaction tube. Then some polyethylene tubing was connected from the septum to the water-filled reaction tube. In this way, the reaction rate could be quantitatively measured by counting the number of gas bubbles that were released into the water each minute for 5 minutes.

5. Test tube 4 was heated for 5 minutes in boiling water. Then it was cooled to room temperature, and the fermentation rate was measured as explained in step 4.

6. Test tube 5 was put on ice for 5 minutes, and then the fermentation rate was measured as explained in step 4, while the reaction tube was kept on ice to maintain the low temperature.

7. After the experiment was completed, the solutions were washed down the drain as waste.

Results

The reaction rates of the 5 reaction conditions are plotted on Figure 1 below.

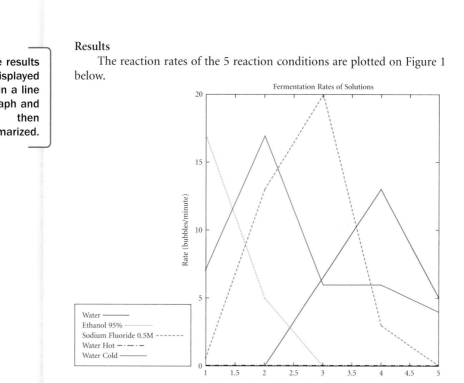

Figure 1

The results are displayed in a line graph and then summarized.

With the sample containing water at room temperature, the fermentation rate peaked at 13 bubbles/minute at minute 4. The fermentation rate of the sample with 95% ethanol started at 17 bubbles/minute, but within 2 minutes the rate quickly slowed to 5 bubbles/minute. By 3 minutes, the rate was 0 bubbles/minute. In the sample with sodium fluoride, the fermentation increased to 20 bubbles/minute after 3 minutes, but then quickly reached 0 bubbles/minute after 5 minutes. In the sample that was boiled, the fermentation rate was consistently 0 bubbles/minute. In the sample placed on ice, the fermentation rate increased to 17 bubbles/minute after 2 minutes, but then gradually slowed to 4 bubbles/minute after 5 minutes.

Discussion

Many different factors affect fermentation rates. For example, when ethanol concentration is very high, yeast usually dies. So when 95 percent ethanol is added to a fermenting sugar and yeast mixture, one would expect the fermentation rate to decline sharply. The experiment's data support this hypothesis. After 3 minutes, the fermentation had completely stopped.

In addition, sodium fluoride inhibits the action of a specific enzyme in yeast, an enzyme needed for the fermentation process. Therefore, when

The writer interprets the results for each hypothesis.

sodium fluoride is added to a fermenting mixture, one would expect a halted fermentation rate. However, the reaction rate initially increased to 20 bubbles/minute when sodium fluoride was added. This increase may have occurred because not all of the enzymes were inhibited at first. Perhaps the fermentation rate declined to 0 bubbles/minute only when the sodium fluoride became evenly distributed. This measurement occurred after 5 minutes.

She explores possible explanations for unexpected results and suggests further research.

Temperature is a third factor affecting fermentation. On the one hand, high temperatures denature many enzymes; therefore, when a fermenting mixture is placed in boiling water for 5 minutes, one would expect the fermentation rate to stop because no enzymes are present anymore to carry out the fermentation process. This hypothesis is supported by the data, as no fermentation occurred in the hot mixture. On the other hand, cold temperatures reduce the kinetic energy of molecules. As a result, the speed decreases, and the likelihood of the enzymes making contact with the substrate decreases exponentially in relation to the temperature. One would expect that the reaction rate would slow down drastically after the mixture has been cooled. This hypothesis is somewhat supported by the data. After an initial increase in the reaction rate to 17 bubbles/minute, the reaction rate slowed to 4 bubbles/minute after 5 minutes. A repeat of the experiment would be needed to clarify this result. Moreover, because the measuring method was somewhat unsophisticated (as indicated by the spikes in the line graph), perhaps a new experiment could be designed to measure fermentation-rate changes more sensitively.

9

The closing summarizes the experiment's value.

This experiment helped quantify the effects that various factors such as temperature, inhibitors, and high ethanol concentration have on fermentation rates. Even though the measuring apparatus was fairly basic, the experiment largely supported the hypotheses. Such data are helpful for determining methods of efficient and successful fermentation. Further research testing other factors and other inhibitors would add to this knowledge. ■

10

Writing Prompt Reading for Better Writing

1. Where does the writer discuss the experiment's purpose and value? Are her efforts convincing?

2. In the "Method" section, what strategies does the writer use to ensure that the experiment can be repeated?

3. In the "Results" section, what is the relationship between the line graph and the paragraph?

4. In the "Discussion" section, the writer addresses results that did and did not support the hypotheses. Are her interpretations and conclusions sound?

Field Report

In the following workplace report, a team of writers investigates the causes and effects of cockroach infestation in an apartment complex. In the study, they use their findings to recommend solutions.

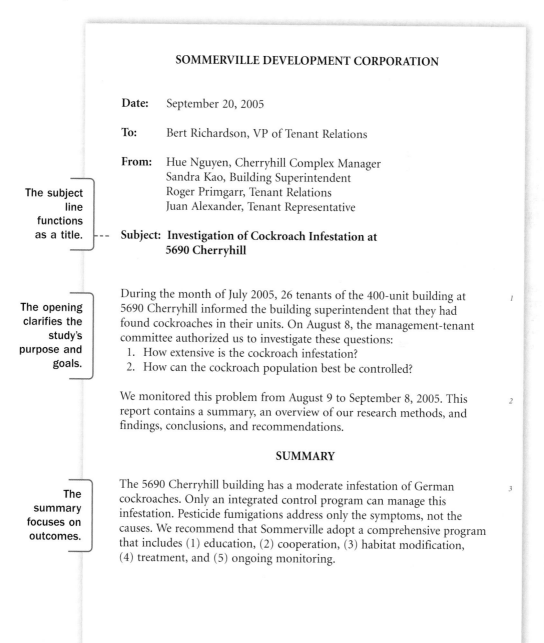

SOMMERVILLE DEVELOPMENT CORPORATION

Date: September 20, 2005

To: Bert Richardson, VP of Tenant Relations

From: Hue Nguyen, Cherryhill Complex Manager
Sandra Kao, Building Superintendent
Roger Primgarr, Tenant Relations
Juan Alexander, Tenant Representative

> The subject line functions as a title.

Subject: Investigation of Cockroach Infestation at 5690 Cherryhill

> The opening clarifies the study's purpose and goals.

During the month of July 2005, 26 tenants of the 400-unit building at 5690 Cherryhill informed the building superintendent that they had found cockroaches in their units. On August 8, the management-tenant committee authorized us to investigate these questions:
1. How extensive is the cockroach infestation?
2. How can the cockroach population best be controlled?

1

We monitored this problem from August 9 to September 8, 2005. This report contains a summary, an overview of our research methods, and findings, conclusions, and recommendations.

2

SUMMARY

> The summary focuses on outcomes.

The 5690 Cherryhill building has a moderate infestation of German cockroaches. Only an integrated control program can manage this infestation. Pesticide fumigations address only the symptoms, not the causes. We recommend that Sommerville adopt a comprehensive program that includes (1) education, (2) cooperation, (3) habitat modification, (4) treatment, and (5) ongoing monitoring.

3

RESEARCH METHODS AND FINDINGS

Overview of Research

We researched the problem in the following ways:

1. Contacted the Department of Agriculture, the Ecology Action Center, and Ecological Agriculture Projects.
2. Consulted three exterminators.
3. Inspected 5690 Cherryhill building, from ground to roof.
4. Placed pheromone traps in all units to monitor cockroach population.

Research methods are described.

4

The Cockroach Population

Pheromone traps revealed German cockroaches, a common variety. Of the 400 units, 112 units (28 percent) showed roaches. Based on the numbers, the infestation is rated moderate.

Results are categorized logically.

5

The German Cockroach

Research shows that these roaches thrive in apartment buildings.

- Populations thrive when food, water, shelter, and migration routes are available. They prefer dark, humid conditions near food sources.
- The cockroach seeks shelter in spaces that allow its back and underside to remain in constant contact with a solid surface.

6

Methods of Control

Sources we consulted stressed the need for an integrated program of cockroach control involving sanitation, habitat modification, and non-toxic treatments that attack causes. Here are the facts:

- The German cockroach is immune to many chemicals.
- Roaches detect most pesticides before direct contact.
- Spot-spraying simply causes roaches to move to unsprayed units.
- Habitat modification through (1) eliminating food and water sources, (2) caulking cracks and crevices, (3) lowering humidity, and (4) increasing light and airflow makes life difficult for cockroaches.

Findings are presented clearly and concisely.

7

CONCLUSIONS

Based on our findings, we conclude the following:

1. A single method of treatment, especially chemical, will be ineffective.
2. A comprehensive program of sanitation, habitat modification, and nontoxic treatments will eliminate the German cockroach.

Conclusions follow logically from the findings.

8

RECOMMENDATIONS

Recommend-
ations apply
what was
learned in
the study.

We recommend that Sommerville Development adopt an Integrated   *9*
Program of Cockroach Prevention and Control for its 5690 Cherryhill
building. Management would assign the following tasks to appropriate
personnel:

Education: (1) Give tenants information on sanitation, prevention, and   *10*
home remedies; and (2) hold tenant meetings to answer questions.

Habitat Modification: Revise the maintenance program and   *11*
renovation schedule to give priority to the following:
- Apply residual insecticides before sealing cracks.
- Caulk cracks and crevices (baseboards, cupboards, pipes, sinks).
  Insert steel wool in large cavities (plumbing, electrical columns).
- Repair leaking pipes and faucets. Insulate pipes to eliminate
  condensation.
- Schedule weekly cleaning of common garbage areas.

Treatment: In addition to improving sanitation and prevention through   *12*
education, attack the roach population through these methods:
- Use home remedies, traps, and hotels.
- Use borax or boric-acid powder formulations as residual, relatively
  nontoxic pesticides.
- Use chemical controls on an emergency basis.
- Ensure safety by arranging for a Health Department representative
  to make unannounced visits to the building.

Monitoring: Monitor cockroach population in the following ways: *13*
1. Every six months, use traps to check on activity in all units.
2. Keep good records on the degree of occurrence, population density,
   and control methods used.

The closing
stresses the
value and
benefits of
the study.

We believe that this comprehensive program will solve the cockroach   *14*
problem. We recommend that Sommerville adopt this program for
5690 Cherryhill and consider implementing it in all its buildings.

Writing Prompt

Reading for Better Writing

1. Examine the report's format and organizational strategies. How is this
workplace report similar to and different from the other lab and
experiment reports in this chapter?

2. Describe the tone of the report. What does this tone accomplish?

3. This report depends extensively on cause/effect thinking. Where do the
writers use cause/effect thinking, and how effective is it?

Guidelines
Writing Lab, Experiment, and Field Reports

1. **Review the lab manual and any handouts.** In most science courses, studies and experiments are assigned through textbooks, manuals, and handouts. Study those materials to understand what you must do and why. Read background information on the topic in textbooks and other sources.

2. **Use a field or lab notebook.** Accurate, complete recordkeeping is crucial to doing good scientific research. Use the notebook to plan research, record what you do, collect data, make drawings, and reflect on results. For each notebook entry, record the date and your goal.

3. **Plan and complete your study or experiment.** For a productive study, do the following:
   - Develop your key research questions. If you are conducting an experiment, not just a study, then state your hypotheses and design procedures for testing them.
   - Gather the proper tools, equipment, and materials required to conduct your study.
   - Carefully and alertly conduct your tests and perform your observations.
   - Take copious notes, being especially careful to record data accurately, clearly, and completely. If helpful, use a data collection sheet.

4. **Relying on your notebook, draft the report.** Wrestle with your data. What do they mean? Were results expected or unexpected? What factors could explain those results? What further research might be necessary? Once you have conducted this analysis, draft parts of the report in the sequence outlined below:
   - **Methods:** Start by explaining what you did to study the topic or test the hypothesis. Supply essential details, factors, and explanations. Be so clear that someone else could repeat the steps you took.
   - **Results:** Using two strategies, present the data you collected. First, share data in graphical forms—as tables, line charts, bar graphs, photographs, and so on. While the correct design of graphics and the proper presentation of statistical data are beyond the scope of this book, follow this basic rule: Make your graphic independent of the written text by giving it a descriptive title, clear headings and labels, units of measurement, and footnotes. Readers should be able to study your graphics and see the "story" of your study. Second, draw attention to the major observations and key trends available in the data. However, do not interpret the data here or give your reactions to them.

- **Discussion:** Interpret the results by relating the data to your original questions and hypotheses, offering conclusions, and supporting each conclusion with details. Essentially, answer the question, "What does it all mean?" Explain which hypotheses were supported, and why. Also explore unexpected results, and suggest possible explanations. Conclude by reemphasizing the value of what you learned.

- **Introduction:** Once you have mapped out the methods, results, and discussion, write an introduction that creates a framework for the report. Explain why you undertook the study, provide background information and any needed definitions, and raise your key questions and/or hypotheses.

- **Summary or abstract:** If required, write a summary of your study's purpose, methods, results, and conclusions. An abstract is a one-paragraph summary that allows readers to (1) get the report in a nutshell, and (2) determine whether reading the study would be worthwhile.

- **Title:** Develop a precise title that captures the "story" of your study. Worry less about the length of the title and more about its clarity.

- **Front and end matter:** If so required, add a title page, references page, and appendixes.

5. **Share and revise the draft.** Once you have roughed out the report, show it to a peer or a tutor in the writing center. Ask these questions:

   - Are the report's purpose, hypotheses, conclusions, and support clear and complete?
   - Is the traditional structure of a lab or field report followed effectively?
   - Is the voice objective, curious, and informed?

6. **Edit and proofread.** Carefully examine the style of your report, checking for these conventions of science writing:

   - **Measured use of passive voice:** Generally, use the passive voice only when needed—usually to keep the focus on the action and the receiver, not the actor. (See page 72.)
   - **Past and present tenses of verbs:** Generally, use the past tense in your report. However, present tense may be appropriate when discussing published work, established theories, and your conclusions.
   - **Objectivity:** Make sure that your writing is precise (not ambiguous), specific (not vague), concise (not wordy).
   - **Mechanics:** Follow the conventions in the discipline with respect to capitalization, abbreviations, numbers, and symbols.

7. **Prepare and share your report.** Following the format and documentation conventions of the discipline, submit a polished report to your instructor. Also find ways to share your study with the scientific community.

Writing Checklist

Use these six traits to check your report; then revise as needed:

_____ The **ideas** provide scientifically sound conclusions about accurate data.

_____ The **organization** effectively follows the standard structure: introduction, methods, results, and discussion.

_____ The **voice** demonstrates interest and curiosity, yet remains objective.

_____ The **words** are used accurately. The language of the specific discipline is used precisely.

_____ The **sentences** flow smoothly from point to point. Passive voice constructions are used only when necessary.

_____ The copy is **correct** in terms of its format, grammar, punctuation, usage, and spelling.

Writing Activities

1. The report on hydrochloric acid describes a chemical compound. In your discipline, what are the main objects of study? Write a report that introduces that topic to students new to the discipline.

2. The lab experiment on fermentation describes careful research that should be repeatable. With appropriate supervision, repeat the lab experiment and compare results.

3. The field report objectively researches the problem of cockroach infestation. What campus or community problems could you research in a similar manner? Develop a research plan, get approval from your instructor, and complete your study.

4. What issues, problems, or puzzles exist in your area of study? With help from an instructor in your major, write a proposal to conduct a lab experiment or field research.

Special Forms of Writing

Chapters 24 through 28 focus on special writing occasions—or rhetorical situations. The chapters explain how to develop a variety of writing forms: a literary analysis, an essay test, a resumé, a webpage, and an oral presentation.

As you read the model pieces, note each writer's strategies for organizing and presenting his or her message. Analyze how and why those strategies are (or are not) effective for the writer's audience, purpose, and subject. Then consider how you might address a similar writing situation.

CONTENTS
Special Forms of Writing

Chapter 24
Writing About Literature and the Arts

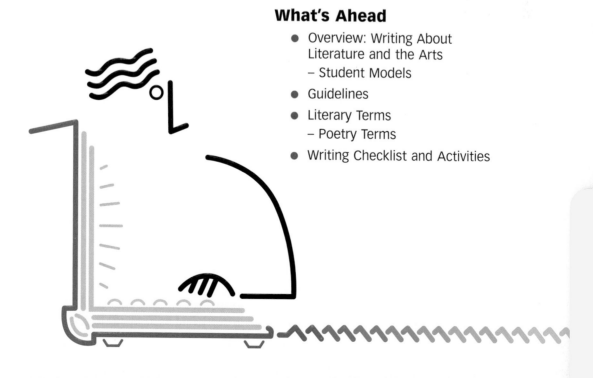

In one way or another, people respond to the arts. Audiences may applaud a dancer, gripe about a film or play, or give a standing ovation to a musician. Often writers are moved to respond even more precisely, by analyzing one actor's portrayal while criticizing another's performance, or praising a film's script but questioning camera angles or lighting.

Because the arts are complex, writing about them requires careful listening, reading, and/or viewing. For example, you may analyze a film or play in terms of the acting, the casting, or the directing. Similarly, you may analyze a poem or story by looking at its form, its diction, or the insights it provides. In other words, to write effectively about the arts, you need a good ear, a keen eye, and an open mind.

This chapter includes model essays, guidelines, literary terms, and assignments to help you evaluate a variety of art forms.

What's Ahead

- Overview: Writing About Literature and the Arts
  - Student Models
- Guidelines
- Literary Terms
  - Poetry Terms
- Writing Checklist and Activities

Overview
Writing About Literature and the Arts

Writer's Goal

Your goal is to experience an artwork or performance, understand its elements, and then write an essay analyzing and perhaps evaluating the work.

Keys for Success

Know your subject. ■ Read the poem, view the film or painting, or listen to the concert more than once, if possible. Be sure you understand what the artist/writer is trying to do, noting specific choices and their effects.

Analyze the work's key elements. ■ In works of fiction, for example, consider issues of point of view, plot, character, setting, and theme. (See the list of literary terms on pages **370–373** for other elements to think about.)

Compare it. ■ If this work of art reminds you of some other piece, review the second work and note similarities and differences.

Form your own insights and opinions. ■ If others have written about this work of art, do not read what they wrote until you have experienced the work yourself and developed your own insights and opinions.

Topics to Consider

Choose a piece of literature, a film, a concert, or a play that has meaning for you or has aroused your curiosity.

- **Poems:** You could choose one of thousands of great poems from literature or poetry anthologies. Poems from literary magazines, college classmates or relatives, or a website may also be analyzed if they merit your time and your readers' attention.
- **Short stories:** Like poems, short stories from literature anthologies, literary or popular magazines, or websites are easy to access.
- **Films:** While you could write about a current big-name film, consider analyzing a classic film or a film never shown in your area theaters. Choosing a film on video will enable you to replay the entire film or just specific scenes.
- **Concerts:** You could write about a major concert in your city or on campus, but consider analyzing the music played by lesser-known artists performing in student recitals or backstreet theaters.
- **Plays:** Any play may invite an analysis (big-name touring shows, for instance), but consider writing about campus productions or plays staged in your community. You might also analyze a play based on your reading of it.

Next Step Read the model essays and perform the activities that follow, noting strategies that help you understand an artwork and write about it.

Literary Analysis

In the essay below, student writer Anya Terekhina analyzes the characters and ideas in Flannery O'Connor's short story "Good Country People."

"Good Country People": Broken Body, Broken Soul

The writer provides background for understanding the characters in O'Connor's stories.

Flannery O'Connor's short stories are filled with characters who are *1* bizarre, freakish, devious, and sometimes even murderous. Every short story, according to O'Connor in *Mystery and Manners: Occasional Prose*, should be "long in depth" and meaning (94). To achieve this, O'Connor develops characters with heavily symbolic attributes and flaws, and "it is clearly evident that boldly outlined inner compulsions are reinforced dramatically by a mutilated exterior self" (Muller 22). In "Good Country People," Joy-Hulga is a typical O'Connor character—grotesque yet real. Her realness comes from her many flaws and, ironically, her flaws are a self-constructed set of illusions. Throughout the story, O'Connor carefully links Joy-Hulga's physical impairments with deeper handicaps of the soul; then, at the closing, she strips Hulga of these physical flaws while helping her realize that her corresponding beliefs are flawed as well.

O'Connor first introduces her character as Joy Hopewell, a name of *2* optimism. However, we soon understand that her chosen name, Hulga, is more fitting. The new name distresses her mother, Mrs. Hopewell, who is "certain that she [Joy] had thought and thought until she had hit upon the ugliest name in any language" (O'Connor 1943). Hulga has connotations of "hull = hulk = huge = ugly" (Grimshaw 51), and all of these are accurate descriptions of her. Far from having a sweet temperament, Hulga stomps and sulks around the farm, "constant outrage . . . [purging] every expression from her face" (1942).

Although Hulga's demeanor could be blamed on her physical *3* impairments, she devises her own rationalizations for behaving as she does. Ironically, each rationale is symbolized by one of her physical disabilities, yet she doesn't recognize the handicaps for what they imply.

The writer begins listing the protagonist's physical disabilities and explains how each one symbolizes a deeper problem in her soul.

One of Hulga's many ailments is her weak heart, which will likely limit *4* her life span. Hulga blames this affliction for keeping her on the Hopewell farm, making it plain that "if it had not been for this condition, she would be far from these red hills and good country people" (1944). Having a Ph.D. in philosophy, Hulga claims to want work as a university professor, lecturing to people at her intellectual level. Hulga's weak heart functions as more than a dream-crusher; it "symbolizes her emotional detachment—and inability to love anyone or anything" (Oliver 233). She exhibits no compassion or love for anything, not even "dogs or cats or birds or flowers or nature or nice young men" (1944–45).

Hulga also suffers from poor vision. Without her eyeglasses, she is helpless. Strangely though, her icy blue eyes have a "look of someone who has achieved blindness by an act of will and means to keep it" (1942). Her self-induced blindness symbolizes her blindness to reality. She is indeed intelligent, but she has packed her brain full of ideas and thoughts that only obscure common sense, let alone truth. Because of Hulga's extensive education and her focus on philosophical reasoning, she considers herself superior to everyone around her. For example, she yells at her mother, "Woman! . . . Do you ever look inside and see what you are not? God!" (1944).

Hulga's last and most noticeable physical impairment is her missing leg, which was "literally blasted off" (1944) in a hunting accident when she was ten years old. In *Mystery and Manners*, O'Connor stresses that the wooden leg operates interdependently at a literal and a symbolic level, which means "the wooden leg continues to accumulate meaning" throughout the story (99). Hulga's biggest physical handicap symbolizes her deepest affliction: her belief in nothing.

She points out the root of the protagonist's problems: her lack of belief in anything.

Hulga's philosophical studies did focus on the study of nothing, particularly on the arguments of the French philosopher Nicolas Malebranche. O'Connor describes Hulga as believing "in nothing but her own belief in nothing" (*Mystery* 99). Over time, Hulga's belief in nothing develops into more than just academic study. Her nihilism becomes her religion—suitable for a woman who considers herself superior and despises platitudes. As she explains to Manley Pointer, "We are all damned . . . but some of us have taken off our blindfolds and see that there's nothing to see. It's a kind of salvation" (1952). Hulga's religious terms suggest that she uses faith in nothingness to find the meaning that she can't find elsewhere.

> *Her nihilism becomes her religion— suitable for a woman who considers herself superior and despises platitudes.*

The writer demonstrates how the protagonist's flaws lead her to make distorted judgments.

Hulga's nihilism is symbolized by her wooden leg, which is the only thing she tends to with care: "She took care of it as someone else would his soul, in private and almost with her own eyes turned away" (1953). This limb is wooden and corresponds to Hulga's wooden soul. Whereas she believes she worships Nothing, what she actually worships is an "artificial leg and an artificial belief" (Oliver 235).

Not realizing that her false leg and false religion cripple her both physically and spiritually, Hulga considers seducing Manley Pointer, the Bible salesman. She delightfully imagines that she will have to help him deal with his subsequent remorse, and then she will instruct him into a "deeper understanding of life" (1950). Of course, her intellectual blindness keeps her from realizing that her superiority is only an illusion. Instead, she views Manley as "a vulnerable innocent, a naïve Fundamentalist, and she wishes to seduce him to prove that her sophisticated textbook nihilism is superior to his simpleminded faith" (Di Renzo 76).

In classic O'Connor fashion, the characters and situation reverse dramatically at the end of the story. Hulga and Manley are alone in a hayloft and begin embracing. At first, Hulga is pleased with her reaction to kissing as it aligns well with Malebranche's teachings: "it was an unexceptional experience and all a matter of the mind's control" (1951). Soon, however, she realizes that she is enjoying the first human connection of her life. At this point, the *innocent* Bible salesman has already stripped Hulga of her first physical impairment: her weak heart.

She revisits the protagonist's physical disabilities, showing how the Bible salesman exploits each one.

Hulga hardly notices when Manley takes advantage of her next impairment: "when her glasses got in his way, he took them off of her and slipped them into his pocket" (1952). With her heart opened and her intellectual perspective fuzzy, Hulga swiftly descends into what she despises— platitudes. Hulga and Manley exchange clichéd mumblings of love, and this leads Manley to ask if he can remove her artificial leg. After brief hesitation, Hulga agrees because she feels he has touched and understood a central truth inside her. She considers it a complete surrender, "like losing her own life and finding it again, miraculously, in his" (1953).

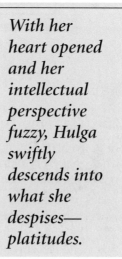

With her heart opened and her intellectual perspective fuzzy, Hulga swiftly descends into what she despises— platitudes.

As soon as the artificial leg is off, Manley whips out one of his Bibles, which is hollow. Inside are whiskey, obscene playing cards, and contraceptives. In only moments, Hulga loses control: as each of her physical handicaps is exploited, pieces of her world view crumble, leaving her confused and weak.

The writer reflects on the change in both characters.

In an ironic reversal, Hulga becomes the naïf and Manley becomes the cynic. Hulga pleads in disbelief, "Aren't you . . . just good country people?" (1954). She knows that she has reverted to her mother's platitudes: "If the language is more sophisticated than any at Mrs. Hopewell's command, it is no less trite, and the smug self-deception underlying it . . . is, if anything, greater" (Asals 105). Manley assumes a startling, haughty air, exclaiming, "'I hope you don't think . . . that I believe in that crap! I may sell Bibles but I know which end is up and I wasn't born yesterday and I know where I'm going!'" (1954). Although they exchange roles, both characters use clichés to express their immature, yet authentic, worldviews.

Manley runs off with Hulga's wooden leg, leaving her vulnerable and ¹⁴ dependent, two things she previously despised. But "Hulga's artificial self— her mental fantasy of her own perfection—has gone out the door with her artificial limb. She is stuck in the hayloft with her actual self, her body, her physical and emotional incompleteness" (Di Renzo 79).

In one brief morning of delusional seduction, Hulga learns more about ¹⁵ herself and her world than she learned in all her years of university. Forced to acknowledge her physical, emotional, and spiritual disabilities, Hulga begins to realize what she is not—neither a wise intellectual for whom there is *hope*, nor "good country people" who merely *hope well*. ■

> The closing explains how Hulga finally acknowledges the truth about herself.

Note: The Works Cited page is not shown. For sample pages, see MLA (pages **534–535**) and APA (pages **564**).

Writing Prompt

Reading for Better Writing

1. In her opening paragraph, Terekhina cites Flannery O'Connor's view that every short story should be "long in depth" and meaning. Does Terekhina adequately explore that depth and meaning? Why?

2. In her second paragraph, Terekhina analyzes Hulga Hopewell's first name; and in the last paragraph, she comments on the last name. Does Terekhina's attention to names help you understand Hulga's character and the story's themes? How?

3. A writer's thesis is a type of "contract" that he or she makes with readers, spelling out what the essay will do. Review Terekhina's thesis (last sentence, first paragraph) and assess how effectively she fulfills that contract. Cite supporting details.

4. Flannery O'Connor has received strong acclaim for her clearly developed, complex characters. Does Terekhina adequately explore that complexity? Explain.

5. Many praise O'Connor for the challenging philosophical or ethical questions raised in her fiction. What questions does Terekhina identify in "Good Country People," and does she effectively discuss them?

6. What does Terekhina say about the story's plot, symbols, and diction? Does she effectively analyze these elements? Why?

Writing About a Poem

In the essay below, student writer David Koza analyzes "The Darkling Thrush" by Thomas Hardy.

Audio

The writer introduces the poet, his poem, and its focus.	## Brooding on "The Darkling Thrush"

The close of a century often brings mixed feelings. Loud celebrations can [1] hide a deeper sadness or fear brought on by a sense of loss. Through imagery, rhythm, and rhyme, poems often capture these strong emotions. One such poem is "The Darkling Thrush," written by Thomas Hardy at the end of the nineteenth century. This poem powerfully expressed the poet's gloomy outlook as one century died and another was born. |

He focuses on the poem's imagery.

From beginning to end, "The Darkling Thrush" is filled with dismal [2] natural images and dark comparisons that create the mood of pessimism. For example, the speaker compares the world he inhabits to the dying day and the winter season. The "weakening eye of day" is upon them, and "all mankind that haunted nigh / Had sought their household fires" (7, 8). Day is dying, winter has driven everyone to seek warmth, and the speaker himself is "fervourless." Even the speaker's past successes seem buried beneath the sky:

> The land's sharp features seemed to be
> 　The Century's corpse outleant,
> His crypt the cloudy canopy,
> 　The wind his death-lament. (9–12)

Lines 5 and 6 tell us that "The tangled bine-stems scored the sky / Like strings of broken lyres" (5, 6). The music of nature is dead. But lines 9–12 above show death to be pervasive; it includes the land and even the century.

He notes a startling, unexpected contrast.

Perhaps even more striking are the lines suggesting that the very soil [3] has lost its power to give life to seeds: "The ancient pulse of germ and birth / Was shrunken hard and dry" (13, 14). If fertility is gone, what's left? Nothing that Hardy can see.

But then, surprise! Above him he sees a "darkling thrush" singing "a [4] full-hearted evensong." This bird, an "aged thrush, frail, gaunt, and small / In blast-beruffled plume," is singing joyfully in the darkness and deadness of the earth. The speaker is dumbfounded.

He reflects on the speaker's mood and emotions.

One might expect the speaker would change his mind—see that his [5] gloom was perhaps premature. But no, his gloom is too deep to be brightened by this bird's cheerful song. There is no fickle mood change. Instead the speaker concludes that the bird must know something he does not. But though he sees no cause for caroling, there may be a wistfulness in the speaker's wonder. He envies the bird's joy.

The "caroling" suggests that the bird may be aware of a long-lost God [6] that the speaker vaguely remembers but can't recover. He is not happy to have lost this God, nor free of a yearning for him. He is "free" only of what the thrush seems to know: "Some blessed Hope." Thus the poem expresses a deep loss of faith that no bird's song can cure. His gloom is not from one bad day but from one lost hope. Like his contemporary Matthew Arnold in "Dover Beach," Hardy seems to be lamenting that the "Sea of Faith" is no longer full.

Two other facts deepen our sense of the poem's gloom. First, the poem *7* was printed a couple of days before the end of the nineteenth century. Later Hardy affixed a date, December 31, 1900, to the poem. Lines 9–10 show Hardy's direct reference to the departing century: "The land's sharp features seemed to be / The Century's corpse outleant" (9, 10). Second, the meter that Hardy uses is a common meter, the meter of hymns. Writing a hymn to a dying century would seem to be a poet's duty, but a hymn is usually a song of praise. Yet the bleak landscape laid out as the corpse of the nineteenth century does not receive praise but a lament.

The closing stresses the poem's continuing power.

"The Darkling Thrush," with its dark vision of life, challenges readers *8* to understand a bleak world. The impressions, the irony, and the questioning that this poem stirs up are probably the reason that a century later—at the close of the twentieth century—readers still feel drawn to the poem. ■

Reading for Better Writing

1. Review the opening and closing paragraphs of the essay. How do they create a framework for the writer's analysis of the poem?
2. Why does the writer focus on the poem's images and comparisons?
3. Why does he devote a full paragraph to the bird's song?
4. Why does he focus on the effect of the song on the speaker?

Writing About a Performance

In the essay below, student writer Annie Moore reviews the performance of a rock music group, Sigur Ros. She praises several qualities of their experimental music.

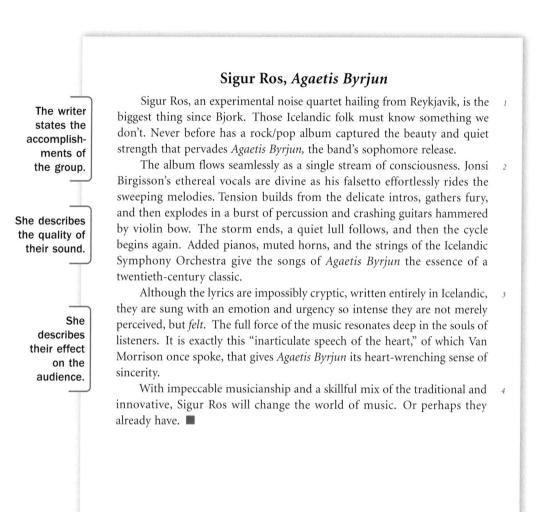

Sigur Ros, *Agaetis Byrjun*

> The writer states the accomplishments of the group.

Sigur Ros, an experimental noise quartet hailing from Reykjavik, is the biggest thing since Bjork. Those Icelandic folk must know something we don't. Never before has a rock/pop album captured the beauty and quiet strength that pervades *Agaetis Byrjun,* the band's sophomore release.

> She describes the quality of their sound.

The album flows seamlessly as a single stream of consciousness. Jonsi Birgisson's ethereal vocals are divine as his falsetto effortlessly rides the sweeping melodies. Tension builds from the delicate intros, gathers fury, and then explodes in a burst of percussion and crashing guitars hammered by violin bow. The storm ends, a quiet lull follows, and then the cycle begins again. Added pianos, muted horns, and the strings of the Icelandic Symphony Orchestra give the songs of *Agaetis Byrjun* the essence of a twentieth-century classic.

> She describes their effect on the audience.

Although the lyrics are impossibly cryptic, written entirely in Icelandic, they are sung with an emotion and urgency so intense they are not merely perceived, but *felt.* The full force of the music resonates deep in the souls of listeners. It is exactly this "inarticulate speech of the heart," of which Van Morrison once spoke, that gives *Agaetis Byrjun* its heart-wrenching sense of sincerity.

With impeccable musicianship and a skillful mix of the traditional and innovative, Sigur Ros will change the world of music. Or perhaps they already have. ■

Writing Prompt

Reading for Better Writing

1. What characteristics of the vocalists does the writer cite? Why?
2. What other instrumental sounds does she cite?
3. Why does she tell us of the effect on the audience?

Writing About a Film

In the essay below, student writer Jennifer Berkompas explains what she likes in the film *The Lord of the Rings: The Fellowship of the Ring* and what she thinks her readers might like as well.

Wonder of Wonders: *The Lord of the Rings*

I have only one problem with Peter Jackson's film *The Lord of the Rings: The Fellowship of the Ring:* His elves don't laugh.

As fans of J. R. R. Tolkien's Middle-earth know, elves (immortal creatures) live alongside men, dwarves, hobbits, and wizards. Powerful, wise, and dignified, they also laugh musically, dance passionately, tell all-night stories, and sing of their homeland. The movie elves are powerful, wise, and dignified, and have a wry sense of humor, but they don't laugh.

> *The writer cites the problem in the story.*

True, there is little to laugh about in their circumstances. An evil lord is gaining power in the South, and what he needs to plunge the world into slavery has fallen into the hands of a hobbit. Hobbits are silly and sociable and like eating, but they don't like excitement. The future looks grim.

> **Tolkien fans, be warned: the movie doesn't try to follow the book scene by scene or character by character.**

> *She notes who must solve the problem.*

But this hobbit, Frodo Baggins (played by Elijah Wood) has spirit, has common sense, and knows what he must do: Take the ring that will darken the whole earth back to the heart of the dark lord's kingdom, Mordor, to destroy the ring and the kingdom.

On his quest he is joined by eight other adventurers, including Aragorn, a mysterious wanderer who happens to be Gondor's long-lost king.

> *She alerts those who have read the book.*

Tolkien fans, be warned: The movie doesn't try to follow the book scene by scene or character by character. If you are fond of Tom Bombadil or elf lord Glorfindel, you won't find them. But the movie does stay close in spirit to the books. The director read the books often to prepare for filming, reading key scenes several times as he shot them. The martial power of Númenóreans, the rustic naivete of the Shire, the peace and beauty of Rivendell and Lothlórien, the presence of evil, the persistence of good and camaraderie, the pain, the power—it's all there.

Having read the books and seen the movie four times, I recommend that you look at the movie with an open mind. Admire the halls of Moria, the bridge of Khazad-dûm, the river of Rivendell, the towering kings, the

Argonath—all incredible scenes. Enjoy what Jackson imagines a hobbit or a Númenórean or a wizard to look like.

She assures those who have not read the book.

If you haven't read the books, you can still enjoy the movie for its scenery, gripping plot, good acting, good role models, fight scenes, compelling characters, and chivalric romance and honor rarely seen today in film or life. Peter Jackson and crew capture Tolkien well. 8

A note of caution: Evil forces in this film are portrayed powerfully. We see war, and war is violent. Some scenes you won't want kids under ten to see. 9

For more information, visit <http://www.lordoftherings.net>. ■ 10

Reading for Better Writing

1. What one drawback does the writer see in the film?

2. Reread what she says about Frodo Baggins, and explain how the comments do or do not support the main point of her review.

3. The writer describes what the director did to catch the spirit of Tolkien. How do these observations strengthen or weaken the review?

Guidelines
Writing About Literature and the Arts

1. **Select a topic.** Choose an art form or type of performance with which you are familiar or are willing to learn about. For ideas, review "Topics to Consider" on page **358**.

2. **Understand the work.** Experience it thoughtfully (two or three times, if possible), looking carefully at its content, form, and overall effect.
   - For plays and films, examine the plot, setting, characters, dialogue, lighting, costumes, sound effects, music, acting, and directing.
   - For novels and short stories, focus on point of view, plot, setting, characters, style, diction, and theme. (See **370–372**.)
   - For poems, examine diction, simile, tone, sound, figures of speech, symbolism, irony, form, and theme. (See **373**.)
   - For music, focus on harmonic and rhythmic qualities, dynamics, melodic lines, lyrics, and interpretation.

3. **Gather information.** Take notes on what you experience, using the list above to guide your thoughts. Seek to understand the whole work before you analyze the parts. Consider freewriting briefly on one or more aspects of the work to explore your response and to dig more deeply into the work. If analyzing a written text, annotate it.

4. **Organize your thoughts.** Review the notes that you took as you analyzed the work. What key insight about the work has your analysis led you to see? Make that insight or judgment your thesis, and then organize supporting points logically in a scratch or full outline.

5. **Write the first draft.**
   Opening: Use ideas like the following to gain your readers' attention, identify your topic, narrow the focus, and state your thesis:
   - Summarize your subject briefly. Include the title, the author, and the literary form or performance.
     Example: **"The Darkling Thrush," a poem written at the end of the nineteenth century, expresses Thomas Hardy's gloomy outlook.**
   - Start with a quotation from the film, story, or poem and then comment on its importance.
   - Explain the artist's purpose and how well he or she achieves it.
   - Open with a general statement about life that relates to the focus of your analysis.
     Example: **"Hardy compares the world to the dying day and winter."**

- Begin with a general statement about the literature or perforr
  (See page **366**.)

  > *Example:* **"I have only one problem with Peter Jackson's film *Th Lord of the Rings: The Fellowship of the Rings*: His elves don't laug**

- Assert your thesis. State the key insight about the work that your
  analysis has revealed—the insight your essay will seek to support.

Middle: Develop or support your focus by following this pattern:

- State the main points, relating them clearly to the focus of your essay.
- Support each main point with specific details or direct quotations.
- Explain how these details prove your point.

Conclusion: Tie key points together to focus your analysis. Assert your thesis or evaluation in a fresh way, leaving readers with a sense of the larger significance of your analysis.

6. **Review and revise**. Once you have a first draft written, relax for a time, and then reread your essay for its logic and completeness. Check whether you have supported each of your observations with evidence from the poem, story, film, or other artwork. Test your analysis with questions like these:

   - Did you fully understand the performance, the reasons for the acting or costuming, the lyrics of the song, or whatever is central to the work?
   - Did you explore the ironies, if present, or any important images, vocal nuances, dramatic action, or shift in setting, or symbolism?
   - Did you bring your analysis to a clear conclusion?

7. **Get feedback**. Ask a knowledgeable classmate, friend, or tutor to read your essay, looking for the following:

   ___ An analytical thesis statement supported by evidence (such as quotations)
   ___ Key insights into both content or meaning on the one hand and form or style on the other hand
   ___ Clear transitions between sentences and paragraphs
   ___ A tone that is respectful and honest

8. **Edit and proofread**. Once you have revised your appraisal, clarified your transitions, and checked your evidence, polish the phrasing and diction. Make certain your paper is free of awkward syntax or errors in usage, punctuation, spelling, or grammar. In particular, check that you have used the special terms of the literary genre or art form clearly and accurately.

9. **Publish your essay.**

   - Share your essay with friends and family.
   - Publish it in a journal or on a website.
   - Place a copy in your personal or professional portfolio.

ms

poems, plays, and films will be deeper and more
and the most common literary terms.

on, place, or event in history or literature.

or more similar objects, suggesting that if they are
will probably be alike in other ways, too.

.......ary of an interesting or humorous, often biographical
.....ent or event.

Antagonist is the person or thing actively working against the protagonist, or hero,
of the work.

Climax is the turning point, an intense moment characterized by a key event.

Conflict is the problem or struggle in a story that triggers the action. There are five
basic types of conflict:
  Person vs. person: One character in a story is in conflict with one or more
  of the other characters.
  Person vs. society: A character is in conflict with some element of society:
  the school, the law, the accepted way of doing things, and so on.
  Person vs. self: A character faces conflicting inner choice.
  Person vs. nature: A character is in conflict with some natural happening: a
  snowstorm, an avalanche, the bitter cold, or any other element of nature.
  Person vs. fate: A character must battle what seems to be an
  uncontrollable problem. Whenever the conflict is a strange or unbelievable
  coincidence, it can be attributed to fate.

Denouement is the outcome of a play or story. See "**Resolution.**"

Diction is an author's choice of words based on their correctness or effectiveness.
  Archaic words are old-fashioned and no longer sound natural when used, such
  as "I believe thee not" for "I don't believe you."
  Colloquialism is an expression that is usually accepted in informal situations and
  certain locations, as in "He really grinds my beans."
  Heightened language uses vocabulary and sentence constructions that produce a
  stylized effect unlike that of standard speech or writing, as in much poetry and
  poetic prose.
  Profanity is language that shows disrespect for someone or something regarded
  as holy or sacred.
  Slang is the everyday language used by group members amongst themselves.
  Trite expressions lack depth or originality, or are overworked or not worth
  mentioning in the first place.
  Vulgarity is language that is generally considered common, crude, gross, and, at
  times, offensive. It is sometimes used in fiction, plays, and films to add realism.

Exposition is the introductory section of a story or play. Typically, the setting, main characters, and themes are introduced, and the action is initiated.

Falling action is the action of a play or story that follows the climax and shows the characters dealing with the climactic event or decision.

Figure of speech is a literary device used to create a special effect or to describe something in a fresh way. The most common types are *antithesis, hyperbole, metaphor, metonymy, personification, simile,* and *understatement.*
> **Antithesis** is an opposition, or contrast, of ideas.
>> "It was the best of times, it was the worst of times, it was the age of wisdom, it was the age of foolishness . . ."
>> — Charles Dickens, *A Tale of Two Cities*
>
> **Hyperbole** (hi-pur´ ba-lee) is an extreme exaggeration or overstatement.
>> "I have seen this river so wide it had only one bank."
>> —Mark Twain, *Life on the Mississippi*
>
> **Metaphor** is a comparison of two unlike things in which no word of comparison (*as* or *like*) is used: "Life is a banquet."
>
> **Metonymy** (ma-ton´a-mee) is the substituting of one term for another that is closely related to it, but not a literal restatement.
>> "Friends, Romans, countrymen, lend me your ears." (The request is for the *attention* of those assembled, not literally their *ears.*)
>
> **Personification** is a device in which the author speaks of or describes an animal, object, or idea as if it were a person: "The rock stubbornly refused to move."
>
> **Simile** is a comparison of two unlike things in which a word of comparison (*like* or *as*) is used.
>> "She stood in front of the altar, shaking like a freshly caught trout."
>> —Maya Angelou, *I Know Why the Caged Bird Sings*
>
> **Understatement** is stating an idea with restraint, often for humorous effect. Mark Twain described Aunt Polly as being "prejudiced against snakes." Because she hated snakes, this way of saying so is *understatement.*

Genre refers to a category or type of literature based on its style, form, and content. The mystery novel is a literary *genre.*

Imagery refers to words or phrases that a writer uses to appeal to the reader's senses.
> "The sky was dark and gloomy, the air was damp and raw, the streets were wet and sloppy." —Charles Dickens, *The Pickwick Papers*

Irony is a deliberate discrepancy in meaning or in the way something is understood. There are three kinds of irony:
> **Dramatic irony,** in which the reader or the audience sees a character's mistakes or misunderstandings, but the character does not.
>
> **Verbal irony,** in which the writer says one thing and means another ("The best substitute for experience is being sixteen").
>
> **Irony of situation**, in which there is a great difference between the purpose of a particular action and the result.

Mood is the feeling that a piece of literature arouses in the reader: *happiness, sadness, peacefulness, anxiety,* and so forth.

Paradox is a statement that seems contrary to common sense yet may, in fact, be true: "The coach considered this a good loss."

Plot is the action or sequence of events in a story. It is usually a series of related incidents that build upon one another as the story develops. There are five basic elements in a plot line: *exposition, rising action, climax, falling action,* and *resolution.*

Point of view is the vantage point from which the story unfolds.

In the **first-person** point of view, the story is told by one of the characters: "I stepped into the darkened room and felt myself go cold."

In the **third-person** point of view, the story is told by someone outside the story: "He stepped into the darkened room and felt himself go cold."

Third-person narrations can be *omniscient,* meaning that the narrator has access to the thoughts of all the characters, or *limited,* meaning that the narrator focuses on the inner life of one central character.

Protagonist is the main character or hero of the story.

Resolution (or denouement) is the portion of the play or story in which the problem is solved. The resolution comes after the climax and falling action and is intended to bring the story to a satisfactory end.

Rising action is the series of conflicts or struggles that build a story or play toward a fulfilling climax.

Satire is a literary tone used to ridicule or make fun of human vice or weakness, often with the intent of correcting, or changing, the subject of the satiric attack.

Setting is the time and place in which the action of a literary work occurs.

Structure is the form or organization a writer uses for her or his literary work. A great number of possible forms are used regularly in literature: parable, fable, romance, satire, farce, slapstick, and so on.

Style refers to how the author uses words, phrases, and sentences to form his or her ideas. Style is also thought of as the qualities and characteristics that distinguish one writer's work from the work of others.

Symbol is a person, place, thing, or event used to represent something else. For example, the dove is a symbol of peace.

Theme is the statement about life that a particular work shares with readers. In stories written for children, the theme is often spelled out clearly at the end. In more complex literature, the theme will often be more complex and will be implied, not stated.

Tone is the overall feeling, or effect, created by a writer's use of words. This feeling may be serious, mock-serious, humorous, satiric, and so on.

Poetry Terms

Alliteration is the repetition of initial consonant sounds in words such as "rough and ready." An example of alliteration is underlined below:

"Our gang paces the pier like an old myth . . ."
—Anne-Marie Oomen, "Runaway Warning"

Assonance is the repetition of vowel sounds without the repetition of consonants.

"My words like silent rain drops fell . . ." —Paul Simon, "Sounds of Silence"

Blank verse is an unrhymed form of poetry. Each line normally consists of ten syllables in which every other syllable, beginning with the second, is stressed. As blank verse is often used in very long poems, it may depart from the strict pattern from time to time.

Consonance is the repetition of consonant sounds. Although it is very similar to alliteration, consonance is not limited to the first letters of words:

" . . . and high school girls with clear-skin smiles . . . "
—Janis Ian, "At Seventeen"

Foot is the smallest repeated pattern of stressed and unstressed syllables in a poetic line. (See "**Verse**.")

> **Iambic:** an unstressed followed by a stressed syllable (re-peat´)
> **Anapestic:** two unstressed followed by a stressed syllable (in-ter-rupt´)
> **Trochaic:** a stressed followed by an unstressed syllable (old´-er)
> **Dactylic:** a stressed followed by two unstressed syllables (o´-pen-ly)
> **Spondaic:** two stressed syllables (heart´-break´)
> **Pyrrhic:** two unstressed syllables (Pyrrhic seldom appears by itself.)

Onomatopoeia is the use of a word whose sound suggests its meaning, as in *clang, buzz,* and *twang.*

Refrain is the repetition of a line or phrase of a poem at regular intervals, especially at the end of each stanza. A song's refrain may be called the *chorus.*

Rhythm is the ordered or free occurrences of sound in poetry. Ordered or regular rhythm is called *meter.* Free occurrence of sound is called *free verse.*

Stanza is a division of poetry named for the number of lines it contains:

Couplet: two-line stanza	**Sestet:** six-line stanza
Triplet: three-line stanza	**Septet:** seven-line stanza
Quatrain: four-line stanza	**Octave:** eight-line stanza
Quintet: five-line stanza	

Verse is a metric line of poetry. It is named according to the kind and number of feet composing it: *iambic pentameter, anapestic tetrameter,* and so on. (See "**Foot**.")

Monometer: one foot	**Pentameter:** five feet
Dimeter: two feet	**Hexameter:** six feet
Trimeter: three feet	**Heptameter:** seven feet
Tetrameter: four feet	**Octometer:** eight feet

Writing Checklist

Use these six traits to check your writing, then revise as needed:

____ The **ideas** offer insight into what the literature or art means and how it communicates.

____ The **organization** of the essay flows logically and provides an easy-to-follow pattern.

____ The **voice** is positive, confident, objective, and sensitive to opposing viewpoints. The tone fits the literature or art being discussed.

____ The **words** are precise and effectively defined.

____ The **sentences** read and flow smoothly, with effective variations and logical transitions.

____ The copy is **correct** and follows rules of grammar, format, and documentation.

Writing Prompt

Writing Activities

1. Get a copy of "Good Country People," read the story, write your own analysis, and share the essay with your class.

2. In his essay on "The Darkling Thrush," the writer cites the mood of the poem and the images that create the mood. Find a poem in which mood or tone is essential to the overall meaning or impact. Write an essay describing how images or words work to make the poem effective for you.

3. Jennifer Berkompas reviews the film *The Lord of the Rings: The Fellowship of the Rings,* which, she notes, does "stay close in spirit to the book." Write an essay about a movie based on a book. Explain how it does or does not "stay close in spirit to the book" on which it is based.

4. Attend a concert. Respond to the style of the music, to the performance of the singer or group, and to the content of the lyrics. Note also the age of the audience, its response, and the way in which the performance is or is not affected by that response. Explain your own response as well.

5. Visit an art gallery. Find an exhibit that engages you. Explain what in this exhibit you find appealing or intriguing. Also explain what value this exhibit might have to society or to you personally, and why.

Chapter 25
Taking Essay Tests

There is nothing more disheartening than sitting down to take a test for which you're not prepared. The results are predictable—and they're not pretty. Conversely, there is nothing more exhilarating than walking out of a classroom after nailing a test. This is especially true in a college setting, where tests count for so much and second chances and extra credit are rare.

Many of the skills in writing that you've already developed should serve you well in taking essay tests. Read the instructions for an essay test carefully, and you'll find requests for describing, analyzing, classifying, persuading, and more.

This chapter will help you write better essay answers. As a bonus, it shows a variety of other helpful ways to improve your test-taking skills.

What's Ahead

- Reviewing for Tests
- Forming a Study Group
- Mnemonics and Other Memory Guides
- Taking the Essay Test
- Writing Under Pressure: The Essay Test
- Taking an Objective Test

Reviewing for Tests

Do you consider yourself a "bad" test taker? Do you know the material yet somehow perform poorly on tests? Do you feel overwhelmed by all the information you have to cover when studying for a test? Does even the thought of studying so much material make you nervous? What you need is a positive mental attitude—and good study habits. Together they can make the difference between "spacing" during a test and "acing" an exam.

Perform daily reviews.

Why Daily? Begin your reviews on the first day of class; if you miss a day, dust yourself off and keep going. Daily reviews are especially good because you tend to forget new information rapidly. Reviewing while the material is fresh in your mind helps to move it from your short-term memory into your long-term memory.

How Much Time? Even five or ten minutes before or after each class will pay big dividends. Depending on the day's class, you may read through (or talk through) your notes, look over the headings in a reading assignment, skim any summaries you have, or put information into graphic organizers.

What to Do

- Put "Daily review of . . ." on your "To Do" list, calendar, or date book.
- Use the buddy system. Make a pact with a classmate and review together.
- Put your subconscious to work by reviewing material before you go to sleep.

Perform weekly reviews.

Why Weekly? More than anything else, repetition helps anchor memory. You can cram a lot of data into your brain the night before an exam, but a day or two later you won't remember much of anything. And when final exam time comes, you'll have to learn the material all over again.

How Much Time? Plan to spend about one hour per week for each class. (This review can take place either by yourself or with a study group.) Remember that repetition is the single most important factor in learning anything.

What to Do

- Make mind maps and flash cards of important information.
- Practice answering review questions by saying them out loud and by writing out short answers.
- Test your understanding of a subject by teaching or explaining it to someone else.
- Organize a study group. (See page 377.)
- Create mnemonics. (See page 378.)

Forming a Study Group

A study group can keep you interested in a subject, force you to keep up with classwork, and increase your retention of study material. Group energy can be more powerful than individual energy. You will hear other points of view and other ways to approach a subject that you may never have thought of on your own. If you use a chat room, you can meet others via a computer. To get started, follow these guidelines.

1. Find five to six people.
- Consider people who seem highly motivated and collaborative.
- Ask your instructor to inform the class about the opportunity.

2. Consider a chat room.
- Check first with your instructor and student services about the availability of chat rooms on your campus.
- Go to any search engine (Yahoo!, Google, Excite, etc.) and enter the term "chat room." For example, Yahoo! provides both private and public chat rooms ("clubs") free of charge.
- Follow the guidelines below for forming a study group.

3. Arrange a time and place.
- Plan one session. (It may become obvious at the first meeting that your group won't work out.)
- Agree on a time limit for the initial session.
- Choose somebody in the group to keep everyone on task (or rotate this duty) and agree to accept any prodding and nudging with good humor.

4. Set realistic goals and decide on a plan of action.
- Discuss what the group needs to accomplish and what your goals are.
- Agree to practice "people skills" (listening, observing, cooperating, responding, and clarifying).
- Decide which parts of the coursework you will review (lectures? labs? texts? exam questions?).

5. Evaluate at the end of the first session.
- Honestly and tactfully discuss any problems that arose.
- Ask who wants to continue.
- Choose a time (and place) for your next session.
- Determine an agenda for the next session.
- Exchange necessary information such as phone numbers, e-mail addresses, chat room passwords, and so forth.

Mnemonics and Other Memory Guides

Mnemonics is the art of improving memory by using key words, formulas, or other aids to create "file tabs" in your brain that help you pull out hard-to-remember information.

Acronyms ■ Use the first letter in each word to form a new word. Everyone learns a few acronyms during their school years, but feel free to make up your own.

HOMES (the Great Lakes—Huron, Ontario, Michigan, Erie, Superior)

Acrostics ■ Form a phrase or silly sentence in which the first letter of each word helps you remember the items in a series.

Zoe **C**ooks **C**howder **I**n **P**ink **P**ots **I**n **M**iami. (essential minerals—**z**inc, **c**alcium, **c**hromium, **i**ron, **p**otassium, **p**hosphorus, **i**odine, **m**agnesium)

Categories ■ Organize your information into categories for easier recall.

Types of joints in body
immovable: skull sutures, teeth in sockets . . .
slightly movable: between vertebrae, junction at front of pelvis . . .
freely movable: shoulder, elbow, hip, knee, ankle . . .

Peg Words ■ Create a chain of associations with objects in a room, a sequence of events, or a pattern with which you are familiar (such as the player positions on a baseball diamond).

To remember a sequence of Civil War battles, you might "peg" them to the positions on a baseball field—for example, Shiloh to home plate (think of the "high" and "low" balls); the Battle of Bull Run to the pitcher's mound (think of the pitcher's battle for no runs); and so on.

Rhymes ■ Make up rhymes or puns.

Brown v. *Board of Education* / ended public-school segregation.

TIPS To Improve your Memory

- **Intend to remember.** Scientists say that our brains never forget anything: It's our recall that is at fault. Who forgets that they have tickets to a concert? We remember the things that are important to us.

- **Link new information** to things you already know.

- **Organize your material.** Understand the big picture and then divide the information you need to know into smaller, more manageable categories.

- **Review new material as soon as possible.** The sooner you review, the more likely you'll be to remember.

Taking the Essay Test

Your teachers expect you to include all the right information, and they expect you to organize it in a clear, well-thought-out way. In addition, they expect you to evaluate, synthesize, predict, analyze, and write a worthwhile answer.

Look for key words.

Key words help you define your task. Pay special attention to them when you read questions. Key words tell you how to present all the information you'll need to write an essay answer.

Following is a list of key terms, along with a definition and an example of how each is used. Studying these terms carefully is the first step in writing worthwhile answers to essay questions.

Analyze ■ To analyze is to break down a larger problem or situation into separate parts of relationships.

> Analyze the major difficulties found at urban housing projects.

Classify ■ To classify is to place persons or things (especially animals and plants) together in a group because they share similar characteristics. Science uses a special classification or group order: phylum, class, order, family, genus, species, and variety.

> Classify three kinds of trees found in the rainforests of Costa Rica.

Compare ■ To compare is to use examples to show how things are similar and different, placing the greater emphasis on similarities.

> Compare the vegetation in the rainforests of Puerto Rico with the vegetation in the rainforests of Costa Rica.

Contrast ■ To contrast is to use examples to show how things are different in one or more important ways.

> Contrast the views of George Washington and Harry S. Truman regarding the involvement of the United States in world affairs.

Compare and contrast ■ To compare and contrast is to use examples that show the major similarities and differences between two things (or people, events, ideas, and so forth). In other words, two things are used to clarify each other.

> Compare and contrast people-centered leadership with task-centered leadership.

Define ■ To define is to give the meaning for a term. Generally, it involves identifying the class to which a term belongs and how it differs from other things in that class.

> Define the term "emotional intelligence" as it pertains to humans.

Describe ■ To describe is to give a detailed sketch or impression of a topic.

> Describe how the Euro tunnel (the Chunnel) was built.

Diagram ■ To diagram is to explain with lines or pictures—a flowchart, map, or other graphic device. Generally, a diagram will label the important points or parts.

> Diagram the parts of a DNA molecule.

Discuss ■ To discuss is to review an issue from all sides. A discussion answer must be carefully organized to stay on track.

> Discuss how Rosa Parks's refusal to move to the back of the bus affected the civil rights movement.

Evaluate ■ To evaluate is to make a value judgment by giving the pluses and minuses along with supporting evidence.

> Evaluate the efforts of mid-sized cities to improve public transportation services.

Explain ■ To explain is to bring out into the open, to make clear, and to analyze. This term is similar to *discuss* but places more emphasis on cause/effect relationships or step-by-step sequences.

> Explain the effects of global warming on a coastal city like New Orleans.

Justify ■ To justify is to tell why a position or point of view is good or right. A justification should be mostly positive—that is, the advantages are stressed over the disadvantages.

> Justify the use of antilock brakes in automobiles.

Outline ■ To outline is to organize a set of facts or ideas by listing main points and subpoints. A good outline shows at a glance how topics or ideas fit together or relate to one another.

> Outline the events that caused the United States to enter World War II.

Prove ■ To prove is to bring out the truth by giving evidence to back up a point.

> Prove that Atticus Finch in *To Kill a Mockingbird* provided an adequate defense for his client.

Review ■ To review is to reexamine or to summarize the key characteristics or major points of the topic. Generally speaking, a review presents material in the order in which it happened or in decreasing order of importance.

> Review the events since 1976 that have led to the current hip-hop culture.

State ■ To state is to present a concise statement of a position, fact, or point of view.

> State your reasons for voting in the last national election.

Summarize ■ To summarize is to present the main points of an issue in a shortened form. Details, illustrations, and examples are usually omitted.

> Summarize the primary responsibilities of a school in a democracy.

Trace ■ To trace is to present—in a step-by-step sequence—a series of facts that are somehow related. Usually the facts are presented in chronological order.

> Trace the events that led to the fall of the Union of Soviet Socialist Republics.

Plan and write the essay-test answer.

In addition to a basic understanding of the key words, you must understand the process of writing the essay answer.

1. **Reread the question several times.** (Pay special attention to any key words used in the question.)

2. **Rephrase the question into a topic sentence/thesis statement** with a clear point.

> **Question:** Explain why public housing was built in Chicago in the 1960s.

> **Thesis statement:** Public housing was built in Chicago because of the Great Migration, the name given to the movement of African Americans from the South to the North.

3. **Outline the main points you plan to cover in your answer.** Time will probably not allow you to include all supporting details in your outline.

4. **Write your essay (or paragraph).** Begin with your thesis statement (or topic sentence). Add whatever background information may be needed, and then follow your outline, writing as clearly as possible.

One-Paragraph Answer

If you feel that only one paragraph is needed to answer the question, use the main points of your outline as supporting details for your thesis statement.

> *Question:* **Explain why public housing was built in Chicago in the 1960s.**

Topic sentence ----- Public housing was built in Chicago because of the Great Migration, the name given to the movement of African Americans from the South to the North. The mechanical cotton picker, introduced in the 1920s, replaced field hands in the cotton fields of the South. At that time Chicago's factories and stockyards were hiring workers. In addition, Jim Crow laws caused hardships and provided reasons for African Americans to move north. Finally, some African Americans had family and relatives in Chicago who had migrated earlier and who, it was thought, could provide a home base **Supporting details** for the new migrants until they could get work and housing. According to the U.S. Census Reports, there were 109,000 African Americans in Chicago in 1920. By 1960, there were more than 800,000. However, this increase in population could have been handled except that the public wanted to keep the African Americans in the Black Belt, an area in South Chicago. Reluctant lending agencies and realtors made it possible for speculators to **Conclusion** operate. Speculators increased the cost of houses by 75 percent. All of these factors led to a housing shortage for African Americans, which public housing filled.

Multiparagraph Answer

If the question is too complex to be handled in one paragraph, your opening paragraph should include your thesis statement and any essential background information. Begin your second paragraph by rephrasing one of the main points from your outline into a suitable topic sentence. Support this topic sentence with examples, reasons, or other appropriate details. Handle additional paragraphs in the same manner. If time permits, add a summary or concluding paragraph to bring all of your thoughts to a logical close.

Question: **Explain the advantages and disadvantages of wind energy.**
Thesis: **Wind energy has an equal number of advantages and disadvantages.**

Outline
    I. Advantages of wind energy
        A. Renewable
        B. Economical
        C. Nonpolluting
    II. Disadvantages of wind energy
        A. Intermittent
        B. Unsightly
        C. A danger to some wildlife

The introductory paragraph sets up the essay's organization.

Wind energy has an equal number of advantages and disadvantages. It is renewable, economical, and nonpolluting; but it is also intermittent, unsightly, and a danger to the bird population. *1*

Wind energy is renewable. No matter how much wind energy is used today, there will still be a supply tomorrow. As evidence indicates that wind energy was used to propel boats along the Nile River about 5000 B.C.E., it can be said that wind is an eternal, renewable resource. *2*

Wind energy is economical. The fuel (wind) is free, but the initial cost for wind turbines is higher than for fossil-fueled generators. However, wind energy costs do not include fuel purchases and only minimal operating expenses. Wind power reduces the amount of foreign oil the United States imports and reduces health and environmental costs caused by pollution. Is it possible to sell excess power? The Public Utilities Regulatory Policy Act of 1978 (PURPA) states that a local electric company must buy any excess power produced by a qualifying individual. This act encourages the use of wind power. *3*

Each paragraph follows a point in the outline.

Wind energy does not pollute. Whether one wind turbine is used by an individual or a wind farm supplies energy to many people, no air pollutants or greenhouse gases are emitted. California reports that 2.5 billion pounds *4* of carbon dioxide and 15 million pounds of other pollutants have *not* entered the air thanks to wind energy.

How unfortunate is it that wind energy is intermittent? If a wind does   5 not blow, there is little or no electrical power. One way to resolve this dilemma is to store the energy that wind produces in batteries. The word *intermittent* also refers to the fact that wind power is not always available at the places where it is most needed. Often the sites that offer the greatest winds are located in remote locations far from the cities that demand great electrical power.

Specific details explain the main point.

Are wind turbines unsightly? A home-sized wind machine rises about   6 30 feet with rotors between 8 and 25 feet in diameter. The largest machine in Hawaii stands about 20 stories high with rotors a little longer than the length of a football field. It supplies electricity to 1,400 homes. Does a single wind turbine upset the aesthetics of a community as much as a wind farm? The old adage "Beauty is in the eye of the beholder" holds up wherever wind turbines rotate. If ongoing electrical costs are almost nil, that wind turbine may look beautiful.

Questions help the reader understand the issue.

How serious is the issue of bird safety? The main questions are these: 7 (1) Why do birds come near wind turbines? (2) What, if any, are the effects of wind development on bird populations? (3) What can be done to lessen the problem? If even one bird of a protected species is killed, the Endangered Species Act has been violated. If wind turbines kill migratory birds, the Migratory Bird Treaty Act has been violated. As a result, many countries and agencies are studying the problem carefully.

The ending makes a final conclusion.

The advantages of wind energy seem to outweigh the disadvantages.   8 The wind energy industry has been growing steadily in the United States and around the world. The new wind turbines are reliable and efficient. People's attitudes toward wind energy are mostly positive. Many manufacturers and government agencies are now cooperating to expand wind energy, making it the fastest-growing source of electricity in the world. ■

Writing Prompt

Reading for Better Writing

1. How does the writer provide a clear focus and logical organization in the essay answer? How soon are the focus and organization provided? What advantages does this approach offer the writer? The reader?

2. How do the sentences used to introduce the advantages differ from the sentences used to introduce the disadvantages? How does this technique aid the reader?

3. Why must the paragraphs in the body contain specific facts and examples? What facts and examples does this writer use?

Writing Under Pressure: The Essay Test

QUICK GUIDE

- **Make sure you are ready for the test both mentally and physically.**

- **Carefully listen to or read the instructions.**
  - How much time do you have to complete the test?
  - Do all the essay questions count equally?
  - Can you use any aids, such as a dictionary or handbook?
  - Are there any corrections, changes, or additions to the test?

- **Begin the test immediately and watch the time.** Don't spend so much time answering one question that you run out of time before answering the others.

- **Read all the essay questions carefully,** paying special attention to the key words. (See pages 379–380.)

- **Ask the instructor for clarification** if you don't understand something.

- **Rephrase each question into a controlling idea for your essay answer.** (This idea becomes your thesis statement.)

- **Think before you write.** Jot down all the important information and work it into a brief outline. Do this on the back of the test sheet or on a piece of scrap paper.

- **Use a logical pattern of organization and a strong topic sentence for each paragraph.** Tie points together with clear, logical transitions.

- **Write concisely,** but don't use abbreviations or nonstandard language.

- **Be efficient.** Write about those areas of the subject of which you are most certain first; then work on other areas as time permits.

- **Keep your test paper neat and use reasonable margins.** Neatness is always important, and readability is a must, especially on an essay exam.

- **Revise and proofread.** Read through your essay as carefully and completely as time permits.

Note: Also see "Tips for Coping with Test Anxiety," page 386.

Taking an Objective Test

Even though objective tests are generally straightforward and clear, following some tips can help you avoid making foolish mistakes.

True/False Test

- Read the entire question before answering. Often the first half of a statement will be true or false, while the second half is just the opposite. For an answer to be true, the entire statement must be true.
- Read each word and number. Pay special attention to names, dates, and numbers that are similar and could be easily confused.
- Beware of true/false statements that contain words like *all, every, always,* and *never.* Very often these statements will be false.
- Watch for statements that contain more than one negative word. Remember: Two negatives make a positive. (*Example:* It is unlikely ice will not melt when the temperature rises above 32 degrees F.)

Matching Test

- Read through both lists quickly before you begin answering. Note any descriptions that are similar and pay special attention to the differences.
- When matching a word to a word, determine the part of speech of each word. If the word is a verb, for example, match it with another verb.
- When matching a word to a phrase, read the phrase first and look for the word it describes.
- Cross out each answer as you find it—unless you are told that the answer can be used more than once.
- Use capital letters rather than lowercase letters because they are less likely to be misread by the person correcting the test.

Multiple-Choice Test

- Read the directions to determine whether you are looking for the correct answer or the best answer. Also, check whether some questions can have two (or more) correct answers.
- Read the first part of the question, checking for negative words like *not, never, except,* and *unless.*
- Try to answer the question in your mind before looking at the choices.
- Read all the choices before selecting your answer. This step is especially important on tests in which you must select the best answer, or on tests where one of your choices is a combination of two or more answers. (*Example:* d. Both a and b / e. All of the above / f. None of the above)

TIPS FOR COPING WITH TEST ANXIETY

Consider the following advice:

- **Study smart.** Use a variety of study and memory techniques to help you see your coursework from several different angles.

- **Review with others.** Join a study group and prepare with the members. Also, ask a classmate or family member to put you to the test.

- **Prepare yourself both physically and mentally.** Get a good night's sleep and eat a healthful, light meal before the test (doughnuts and coffee are *not* a healthful, light meal).

- **Get some exercise.** Aerobic exercise (running, swimming, walking, aerobics) is a great way to relieve stress, and it has also been proven to help you think quicker and more clearly.

- **Hit the shower.** Hot water is relaxing, cold water is stimulating, and warm water is soothing. Take your pick.

- **Get to class early . . . but not too early!** Hurrying increases anxiety, but so does waiting.

- **Relax.** Take a few deep breaths, close your eyes, and think positive thoughts. The more relaxed you are, the better your memory will serve you.

- **Glance through the entire test.** Then plan your time, and pace yourself accordingly. You don't want to discover with only 5 minutes of class time left that the last question is an essay that counts for 50 percent of your grade.

- **Begin by filling in all the answers you know.** This process relieves anxiety and helps to trigger answers for other questions that you may not know immediately. Also, jot down important facts and formulas that you know you will need later on.

- **Don't panic.** If other people start handing in their papers long before you are finished, don't worry. They may have given up or rushed through the exam. The best students often finish last.

Bottom Line

The better you prepare for a test—mentally and physically—the less likely you'll be to suffer serious test anxiety.

Chapter 26
Writing for the Workplace

Audio

One thing you already know about writing in college is that you have to do a lot of it—and it has to be good. Nothing does more to help you make a good impression than writing well. You also know that college is very much like real life, in that you have to take care of business in and out of class. There are bills to pay, letters to write, memos to fax, and messages to e-mail. It's your personal responsibility to get each of these jobs done clearly, concisely, and on time.

This chapter should aid you in taking care of the business at hand. Sample letters and memos will help you communicate effectively with people ranging from the registrar to scholarship committees. The sample applications and resumés will help you make a favorable impression when you apply for a job or an internship. There's even a special set of guidelines to help you master e-mail messages so that you can "take care of business," no matter where in the world it may be.

What's Ahead

- Writing the Business Letter
- Writing Memos and E-mail
- Applying for a Job
- Preparing a Resumé

Writing the Business Letter

Business letters do many things—for example, share ideas, promote products, or ask for help. Putting a message in writing gives you time to think about, organize, and edit what you want to say. In addition, a written message serves as a record of important details for both the sender and the recipient.

Parts of the Business Letter

Heading ■ The heading gives the writer's complete address, either in the letterhead (company stationery) or typed out, followed by the date.

Inside Address ■ The inside address gives the reader's name and address.

- If you're not sure which person to address or how to spell someone's name, you could call the company for the information.
- If the person's title is a single word, place it after the name and a comma (Mary Johnson, President). A longer title goes on a separate line.

Salutation ■ The salutation begins with *Dear* and ends with a colon, not a comma.

- Use *Mr.* or *Ms.* plus the person's last name, unless you are well acquainted. Do not guess at *Miss* or *Mrs.*
- If you can't get the person's name, replace the salutation with *Dear* or *Attention* followed by the title of an appropriate reader.
  (*Examples:* Dear Dean of Students: or Attention: Personnel Manager)

  Note: See pages **94–96** for a complete list of "unbiased" ways to refer to an individual or a particular group.

Body ■ The body should consist of single-spaced paragraphs with double-spacing between paragraphs. (Do not indent the paragraphs.)

- If the body goes to a second page, put the reader's name at the top left, the number 2 in the center, and the date at the right margin.

Complimentary Closing ■ For the complimentary closing, use *Sincerely, Yours sincerely,* or *Yours truly* followed by a comma; use *Best wishes* if you know the person well.

Signature ■ The signature includes the writer's name both handwritten and typed.

Initials ■ When someone types the letter for the writer, that person's initials appear (in lowercase) after the writer's initials (in capitals) and a colon.

Enclosure ■ If a document (brochure, form, copy, or other form) is enclosed with the letter, the word *Enclosure* or *Encl.* appears below the initials.

Copies ■ If a copy of the letter is sent elsewhere, type *cc:* beneath the enclosure line, followed by the person's or department's name.

Model Letter

Heading

Box 143
Balliole College
Eugene, OR 97440-5125
August 29, 2005

Four to Seven Spaces

Inside Address

Ms. Ada Overlie
Ogg Hall, Room 222
Balliole College
Eugene, OR 97440-0222

Double Space

Salutation

Dear Ms. Overlie:

Double Space

As the president of the Earth Care Club, I welcome you to Balliole Community College. I hope the year will be a great learning experience both inside and outside the classroom.

Double Space

That learning experience is the reason I'm writing—to encourage you to join the Earth Care Club. As a member, you could participate in the educational and action-oriented mission of the club. The club has most recently been involved in the following:

Body

- Organizing a reduce, reuse, recycle program on campus
- Promoting cloth rather than plastic bag use among students
- Giving input to the college administration on landscaping, renovating, and building for energy efficiency
- Putting together the annual Earth Day celebration

Double Space

What environmental concerns and activities would you like to focus on? Bring them with you to the Earth Care Club. Simply complete the enclosed form and return it by September 8. Then watch the campus news for details on our first meeting.

Double Space

Complimentary Closing and Signature

Yours sincerely,

Four Spaces

Dave Wetland

Dave Wetland
President

Double Space

Initials Enclosure Copies

DW:kr
Encl. membership form
cc: Esther du Toit, membership committee

Writing Memos and E-mail

A memorandum is a written message sent from one person to one or more other people (usually) within the same organization. As such, it is less formal than a letter. A memo can vary in length from a sentence or two to a four- or five-page report. It can be delivered in person, dropped in a mailbox, or sent via e-mail.

Memos are written to create a flow of information within an organization—asking and answering questions, describing procedures and policies, or reminding people about appointments and meetings. Here are some guidelines:

- Write memos only when necessary, and only to those people who need them.
- Distribute them through the appropriate media—mail, fax, bulletin boards, kiosk, or e-mail.
- Make your subject line precise so that the topic is clear and the memo is easy to file.
- Get to the point: (1) state the subject, (2) give necessary details, and (3) state the response you want.

Date: September 27, 2005

To: All Users of the Bascom Hill Writing Lab

From: Kerri Kelley, Coordinator

The subject line clarifies the memo's purpose.

Subject: New Hours/New Equipment

The main point is stated immediately.

Beginning October 3, the Bascom Hill Writing Lab will expand its weekend hours as follows: Fridays, 7:00 A.M.–11:00 P.M.; Saturdays, 8:00 A.M.–11:00 P.M.

Also, six additional computers will be installed next week, making it easier to get computer time. We hope these changes will help meet the increased demand for time and assistance we've experienced this fall. Remember, it's still a good idea to sign up in advance. To reserve time, call the lab at 462-7722 or leave your request at bhill@madwis.edu.

Readers are asked to take note of a few final facts.

Finally, long-range planners, mark your calendars. The lab will be closed on Thanksgiving Day morning and open from 1:00 P.M.–11:00 P.M. We will also be closed on Christmas and New Year's Day. We will post our semester-break hours sometime next month.

Sending E-mail

With e-mail, people can correspond through computer networks around the globe. E-mail allows you to do the following:

- Send, forward, and receive many messages quickly and efficiently, making it ideal for group projects and other forms of collaboration
- Set up mailing lists (specific groups of e-mail addresses) so that you can easily send the same message to several people at the same time
- Organize messages in "folders" for later reference, and reply to messages

---

TIPS FOR E-MAIL

- **Revise and edit messages for clarity and correctness before sending them.** Confusing sentences, grammatical errors, and typos limit your ability to communicate on a computer screen just as they do on paper.

- **Use e-mail responsibly.** Sooner or later you will send e-mail to the wrong person, or a reader will forward your message to another person without your permission. Keep these possibilities in mind at all times, and never write anything that would embarrass you if the wrong party received it.

- **Make messages easy to read and understand.** (1) Provide a clear subject line so readers will scan it and decide whether to read or delete the message. (2) Type short paragraphs.

From:	"Sherry West" <SWEST@stgeorge.edu>
To:	outreach@stgeorge.edu
Date sent:	Mon, 26 Sept 2005 14:13:06 CST
Subject:	Agenda for Student Outreach Committee Meeting

Please remember that our next meeting is this Wednesday, Sept. 28, at 8:00 p.m. in SUB Room 201. We'll discuss the following agenda items:

1. The minutes of our Sept. 16 meeting
2. A proposal from SADD about Alcohol Awareness Week
3. A progress report on the Habitat for Humanity project

Before the meeting, please review the minutes and the SADD proposal attached to this message.

Applying for a Job

When you apply for some jobs, you have to do nothing more than fill out an application form. With other jobs, it's a different story. You may be required to write a letter of application, gather letters of recommendation, write an application essay, and put together a resumé. The following pages provide models to fit nearly every occasion.

The Letter of Application

Your letter of application (or cover letter) introduces you to an employer and often highlights information on an accompanying resumé. Your goal in writing this letter is to convince the employer to invite you for an interview.

Ogg Hall, Room 222
Balliole College
Eugene, OR 97440-0222
April 17, 2005

Address a specific person, if possible.

Professor Edward Mahaffy
Greenhouse Coordinator
Balliole College
Eugene, OR 97440-0316

Dear Professor Mahaffy:

State the desired position and your chief qualification.

I recently talked with Ms. Sierra Arbor in the Financial Aid Office about work-study jobs for 2005–2006. She told me about the Greenhouse Assistant position and gave me a job description. As a full-time Balliole student, I'm writing to apply for this position. I believe that my experience qualifies me for the job.

Focus on how your skills meet the reader's needs.

As you can see from my resumé, I spent two summers working in a raspberry operation, doing basic plant care and carrying out quality-control lab tests on the fruit. Also, as I was growing up, I learned a great deal by helping with a large farm garden. In high school and college, I studied botany. Because of my interest in this field, I'm enrolled in the Environmental Studies program at Balliole.

Request an interview and thank the reader.

I am available for an interview. You may phone me any time at 341-3611 (and leave a message on my machine) or e-mail me at dvrl@balliole.edu. Thank you for considering my application.

Yours sincerely,

Ada Overlie

Ada Overlie

Encl. resumé

The Recommendation Request Letter

When you apply for a job or program, it helps to present references or recommendations to show your fitness for the position. To get the support you need from people familiar with your work (instructors and employers), you need to ask for that support. You can do so in person or by phone, but a courteous and clear letter or e-mail message makes your request official and helps the person complete the recommendation effectively. Here is a suggested outline:

Situation: Remind the reader of your relationship to him or her; then ask the person to write a recommendation or to serve as a reference for you.

Explanation: Describe the work you did for the reader and the type of job, position, or program for which you are applying.

Action: Explain what form the recommendation should take, to whom it should be addressed, and where and when it needs to be sent.

2456 Charles Street
Lexington, KY 40588-8321
March 21, 2005

Dr. Rosa Perez
271 University Boulevard
University of Kentucky
Lexington, KY 40506-1440

Dear Dr. Perez:

The situation

As we discussed on the phone, I would appreciate your writing a recommendation letter for me. You know the quality of my academic work, my qualities as a person, and my potential for working in the medical field.

The explanation

As my professor for Biology 201 and 202, you are familiar with my grades and work habits. As my adviser, you know my career plans and should have a good sense of whether I have the qualities needed to succeed in the medical profession. I am asking you for your recommendation because I am applying for summer employment with the Lexington Ambulance Service. I recently received my Emergency Medical Technician (Basic) license to prepare for such work.

The action

Please send your letter to Rick Falk, EMT Coordinator, at the University Placement Office by April 8. Thank you for your help. Let me know if you need any other information (phone 231-6700; e-mail jnwllms@ukentucky.edu).

Yours sincerely,

Jon Williams

Jon Williams

The Application Essay

For some applications, you may be asked to submit an essay, a personal statement, or a response paper. For example, you might be applying for admission to an academic program (social work, engineering, optometry school) or for an internship, a scholarship, or a research grant. Whatever the situation, what you write and how well you write it will be important factors in the success of your application.

On the facing page is a model application essay. Jessy Jezowski wrote this essay as part of her application to a college social work program.

TIPS FOR AN APPLICATION ESSAY

- Understand what you are being asked to write and why. How does the essay fit into the entire application? Who will read your essay? What will they look for?

- Focus on the instructions for writing the essay. What type of question is it? What topics are you asked to write about? What hints do the directions give about possible organization, emphasis, style, length, and method of submitting the essay?

- Be honest with yourself and your readers. Don't try to write only what you think readers want to hear.

- Think about your purpose and audience:
  - What do you want to gain (internship, scholarship, job interview), and how could your writing help you gain it?
  - Who are your readers? What do they know about you? What should they know?

- Develop your essay using the following organization (if the instructions allow for it):
  - An introduction with a fresh, interesting opening statement and a clear focus or theme
  - A body that develops the focus or theme clearly and concisely—with some details and examples—in a way appropriate to the instructions
  - A conclusion that stresses a positive point and looks forward to participating in the program, internship, organization, or position

- Write in a style that is personal but professional. Use words that fit the subject and the readers. Avoid clichés, and balance generalizations with concrete examples and details.

- Refine your first draft into a polished piece. First, get feedback from another student or, if appropriate, a professor, and revise the essay. Second, edit the final version thoroughly: You don't want typos and grammar errors to derail your application.

Model Application Essay

Audio

February 28, 2005
Jessy Jezowski

Personal Statement

The opening provides a clear focus for the essay.

While growing up in Chicago, I would see people hanging out on street corners, by grocery stores, and in parks—with no home and barely any belongings. Poverty and its related problems are all around us, and yet most people walk by them with blinders on. I have found myself quick to assume that someone else will help the poor man on the corner, the woman trapped in an abusive relationship, or the teenager suffering from an eating disorder. But I know in my heart that all members of society are responsible to and for each other. Social welfare issues affect every member of society—including me.

1

The writer demonstrates knowledge of the field and explains what she hopes to learn.

Because these issues are serious and difficult to solve, I wish to major in social work and eventually become a social worker. In the major, I want to gain the knowledge, skills, and attitudes that will make me part of the solution, not part of the problem. By studying social work institutions, the practices of social work, and the theory and history behind social work, I hope to learn how to help people help themselves. When that pregnant teenager comes to me, I want to have strong, practical advice—and be part of an effective social work agency that can help implement that advice.

2

Two concrete examples help back up her general statements.

I am especially interested at this point in working with families and teenagers, in either a community counseling or school setting. Two experiences have created this interest. First, a woman in my church who works for an adoption agency, Ms. Lesage, has modeled for me what it means to care for individuals and families within a community and around the world. Second, I was involved in a peer counseling program in high school. As counselors, we received training in interpersonal relationships and the nature of helping. In a concrete way, I experienced the complex challenges of helping others.

3

The conclusion summarizes her goals for the future.

I believe strongly in the value of all people and am interested in the well-being of others. As a social worker, I would strive to make society better (for individuals, families, and communities) by serving those in need, whatever their problems.

4

Preparing a Resume

A strong resumé isn't generic—a ho-hum fill-in-the-blanker. Rather, it's a vivid word picture of your skills, knowledge, and past responsibilities. It says exactly who you are by providing the kind of information listed below.

Personal Data: name, address, phone number, e-mail address (enough for the reader to identify you and reach you easily).

Job Objective: the type of position you want and the type of organization for which you want to work.

Skills Summary: the key qualities and skills you bring to a position, listed with supporting details. Here are some skill areas that you might consider for your own resumé:

- Communication
- Organization
- Problem solving
- Computer

- Management (people, money, other resources)
- Working with people, counseling, training
- Sales, marketing, public relations
- Languages

Experience: positions you've held (where and when), and your specific duties and your accomplishments.

Education: degrees, courses, and special projects.

Other Experiences: volunteer work, awards, achievements, tutoring jobs, extra-curricular activities (related to your job objective), licenses, and certifications.

TIPS FOR RESUMÉ WRITING

- Design each resumé to fit the particular job.
- Be specific—use numbers, dates, and names.
- Present information first that is the most impressive and/or most important to the job for which you are applying. This guideline will help you determine whether to put your experience or your education first.
- Use everyday language and short, concise phrases.
- Be parallel—list similar items using similar structures.
- Use boldface type, underlining, white space, and indentations to make your resumé more readable.
- Get someone else's reaction; then revise and proofread the resumé.

Sample Resumé

Present contact information and employment objectives.

Feature skills with appropriate headings and lists.

List work and education chronologically, from most to least current.

Format for paper only: boldface, underlining, bulleted or indented lists, two columns.

Offer references.

Ada Overlie

Home
451 Wiser Lake Road
Ferndale, WA 98248-8941
(360) 354-5916

School
Ogg Hall, Room 222
Balliole College
Eugene, OR 97440-0222
Phone: (503) 341-3611
E-mail: dvrl@balliole.edu

Job Objective: Part-time assistant in a nursery or greenhouse.

Skills Summary:
Horticultural Skills: Familiar with garden planting, care, and
  harvesting practices—planning, timing, companion planting,
  fertilizing.

Lab Skills: Familiar with procedures for taking fruit
  samples, pureeing them, checking for foreign objects, and
  testing sugar content.

Experience:
Summer 2004 and 2005: Lab Technician.
  Mayberry Farms and Processing Plant, Ferndale, WA.
  Worked in Quality Control testing raspberries to make sure
  they met company standards.

Summer 2002 and 2003: Camp Counselor.
  Emerald Lake Summer Camp, Hillsboro, WA.
  Supervised 12-year-olds in many camp activities, including
  nature hikes in which we identified plants and trees.

Education:
August 2005 to present: Balliole College, Eugene, OR.
  Environmental Studies and Communication major.
  Courses completed and in progress include environmental
  studies and general botany. First semester GPA 3.7.

August 2001 to June 2005: Ferndale High School, Ferndale, WA.
  Courses included biology, agriculture, U.S. government, and
  economics.

  Special Projects: Completed research papers on
  clean-water legislation and organic farming practices.

References available upon request.

Sample Electronic Resumé

To find employees, companies often use computer programs to search electronic resumés for keywords (especially nouns) found in job descriptions or ads. Anticipating such a search, Jonathan Greenlind identified key words and inserted them into his job description and resume.

Present contact information and employment objective.

Jonathan L. Greenlind
806 5th Avenue
Waterloo, Iowa 50701
Telephone: 319.268.6955
E-mail: grnlnd@aol.com

OBJECTIVE
Position as hydraulics supervisor that calls for hydraulics expertise, technical skills, mechanical knowledge, reliability, and enthusiasm

SKILLS
Operation and repair specialist in main and auxiliary power systems, subsystems, landing gears, brakes and pneumatic systems, hydraulic motors, reservoirs, actuators, pumps and cylinders from six types of hydraulic systems

Dependable, resourceful, strong leader, team worker

List skills, experiences, and education using many keywords.

EXPERIENCE
Aviation Hydraulics Technician
United States Navy (1999–present)
* Repair, test, and maintain basic hydraulics, distribution systems, and aircraft structural hydraulics systems
* Manufacture low-, medium-, and high-pressure rubber and Teflon hydraulic hoses, and aluminum stainless-steel tubing
* Perform preflight, postflight, and other periodic aircraft inspections
* Operate ground-support equipment
* Supervise personnel
Aircraft Mechanic
Sioux Falls International Airport (1997–1999)
Sioux Falls, South Dakota
* Performed fueling, engine overhauls, minor repairs, and tire and oil changes of various aircraft

Format for e-mail:
• one column
• asterisks as bullets
• simple sans serif typeface
• flush-left margin
• no italics, boldface, or underlining
• ASCII or RTF text (readable by all computers).

EDUCATION
* United States Navy (1999–2003)
* Certificate in Hydraulic Technical School "A", GPA 3.8/4.0
* Certificate in Hydraulic, Pneumatic Test Stand School, GPA 3.9/4.0
* Courses in Corrosion Control, Hydraulic Tube Bender, Aviation Structural Mechanics
* Equivalent of 10 semester hours in Hydraulic Systems Maintenance and Structural Repair

Offer references.

References available upon request

Chapter 27
Writing and Designing for the Web

A strong website depends on well-written, well-organized, and well-designed content. Above all, web content should be concise, focused, and visually appealing. After all, people don't read websites so much as they scan them, so information should be presented in short chunks of text. Webpages should be brief, designed to minimize scrolling and maximize the use of available screen space. Moreover, because online readers can be impatient, the writing must quickly and clearly address its intended purpose, audience, and topic. The chapter addresses the rhetorical fundamentals of creating a strong website and developing strong webpages.

What's Ahead

- Webpage Elements and Functions
- Developing a Website and Webpages
  – Sample Webpages
- Writing for Different Internet Environments
- Checklist and Activities

Webpage Elements and Functions

To design an effective website and develop dynamic webpages, you need to start with a basic understanding of webpage elements and functions. Because webpages use the same elements as printed pages, many of the same design principles apply. However, unlike printed pages, webpages are fluid (flowing their contents to match screen and browser settings), and they can include both elements and functions, as shown and discussed below and on the pages that follow.

Page Elements

On the web, page elements are defined primarily by purpose—headings, body text, image, and so forth. Before designing a webpage, it helps to understand the purpose of those elements.

1. **Headings** (also called headers) come in six levels and are used to separate different sections and subsections of web documents. Heading 1 is the largest; heading 6 is the smallest. All are bold black serif font by default.

2. **Body text** is organized into chunks, called paragraphs, which are separated by white space. Unlike printed text, paragraphs on the web do not generally have a first-line indentation. By default, body text is a black serif font roughly the same size as a heading level 4 (though not bold).

3. **Preformatted text** is "monospaced"; it displays all characters at the same width, like typewriter font. It is used primarily to show mathematical formulas, computer code, and the like.

4. **Lists** can be formatted in three types: Ordered lists are numbered, unordered lists are bulleted, and definition lists present pairs of information—usually terms alongside their definitions, which are indented. Because readers can scan them quickly, lists are an efficient way to present information.

5. **Images** can include photographs, clip art, graphs, line drawings, cartoon figures, icons, and animations. These can make a page much slower to display, so use them judiciously. Always be sure you have the legal right to use any images that you include in your pages. (See "Copyright Violations," page **483**.)

6. **Background color** for a webpage is white by default (medium gray in older browsers), which makes the standard headings and text easily legible.

7. **Tables** are a common tool for webpage layout. Simply put, tables are grids made up of rows and columns. By creating a table with no visible borders, a web designer can gain some control over where elements appear on a page.

Sample Webpage

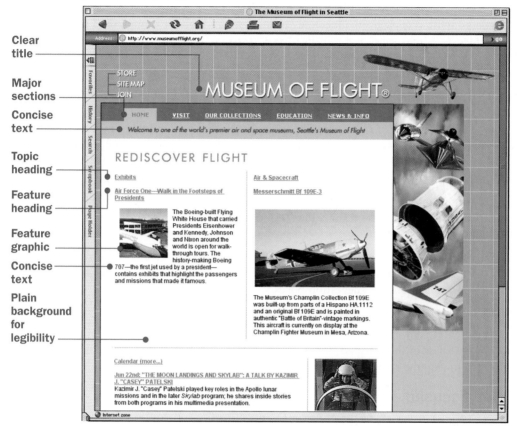

Clear title —

Major sections —

Concise text —

Topic heading —

Feature heading —

Feature graphic —

Concise text —

Plain background for legibility —

Obviously, not all webpages have black serif font on a white background. However, because web browsers are designed to flow content to suit each computer screen, changing the default styles can be problematic. It helps to keep the following tips in mind:

- **Simple is best.** Simple pages display the fastest and have the least chance of breaking. The more graphics you add, the longer a page takes to load. The more you change the default font settings, the more complicated the code becomes and the greater the chance of computer error.
- **Different computers display things differently.** Not every computer has the same font styles installed, and colors look different on different monitors. Always check your work on many different systems.
- **The user is king (or queen).** No matter what font style and size you choose, the reader can change how things display on his or her machine. So focus on useful content and clear organization instead of struggling to control graphic design.

Page Functions

Webpage functions set electronic pages apart from printed pages. On the web, readers can browse pages in almost any order, send and receive e-mail, send messages and files, post messages, and join live "chat" sessions. In short, readers can interact with webpages in ways they cannot with printed pages. Like webpage elements, webpage functions should serve your site's purpose.

1. **Hyperlinks** are strings of specially formatted text that enable readers to jump to another spot on the web. Internal hyperlinks (links for short) take you to another section of the same webpage or to another page on the same site. External links lead to pages on other websites. "Mail to" links allow readers to address e-mail to recipients, such as a professor or a classmate.

2. **Menus** offer structured lists of links that operate like a website's table of contents. Menus are typically presented in a column or row at the edge of a webpage. Good websites include a standard site menu on every page so readers don't get lost.

3. **Forms** enable the host of a website to interact with the site's readers. Web forms can be used for questionnaires, surveys, complaints and service requests, job applications, or suggestion boxes.

Developing a Website and Webpages

Regardless of the purpose, topic, and audience of your website, you can develop it by following the steps outlined on the next four pages.

Get Focused

Create an overview of the project—the purpose, the audience, and the topic. The questions below will help you get focused and develop fitting content for the site.

1. **What is the primary purpose of the website?** Am I creating a library of documents that my audience will reference? Am I going to present information and announcements about myself or my organization? Am I trying to promote a specific product or service?

2. **Who is the site's audience?** Which people will seek out this site? Why? What do they need? How often will they visit the site, and how often should it be updated? How comfortable are they using computers and websites? What level of formality is appropriate for the language? What graphics, colors, and design will appeal to them?

3. **What is the site's central topic?** What do I already know about the topic? What do I need to learn, and where can I find the information? How will I demonstrate that the information is credible and reliable? What will my audience want to know about the topic? How can I divide the information into brief segments? What visual elements would help present my message? What other websites address this topic, and should my website link to them?

Establish Your Central Message

After you've made decisions about your purpose, audience, and topic, write out the main idea you want to communicate. You might call this the theme or "mission statement" of your website.

> **The purpose of this website is to <u>inform fellow students and the general public</u> about <u>current research into hybrid-vehicle transportation.</u>**

To help you stay on target with your project, post this mission statement in plain sight. Note, too, that you might modify your goal as the site develops, or add secondary goals for the site.

Create a Site Map

As you gather content for your site, create a site map. Websites can be as simple as an elementary school bulletin board or as complex as a United States federal government site. Here are four principles to keep in mind:

1. **No one will read your entire site**. People curl up with books, not websites. If your audience is not asking for content, don't provide it.

2. **Your site will have many small audiences**—not one big audience. A site's audience may include anyone with a computer, an Internet connection, and an interest in your site's topic. Keep all potential readers in mind.

3. **Websites are not linear**. A single "home page" or "splash page" introduces the site, which branches out like tree limbs into pages with varied content. Websites "conclude" whenever the reader quits reading.

4. **You may need to build the site in phases**. You can add pages to a website after it has been published, so be careful that your site's organization does not limit future additions.

Sample Site Map

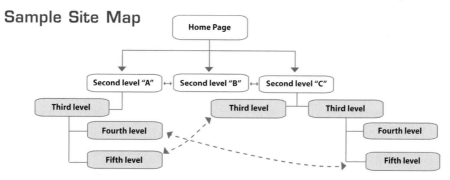

A map for a simple site might include only four items—a home page, page "A," page "B," and page "C" (as shown in white on the diagram). Users can "jump" between any of the secondary-level pages or back to the home page.

A more complex website typically needs more levels (as shown in green on the diagram). Likewise, its menu will offer more navigation choices. Related pages might be connected with links (as represented by the dotted lines).

Study Similar Sites

Learn from successful sites, especially sites that serve a similar purpose—a campus club site, a department site, a personal job-search site. How do similar sites use elements: headings, body text, preformatted text, background color, lists, images, and tables? How do the sites use functions: links, menus, and forms? The seven traits (see page 126) can also supply helpful benchmarks for evaluating sites.

1. **Ideas**: Does the site present clear ideas and information?

2. **Organization**: Is the content carefully and clearly structured?

3. **Voice**: Is the tone fitting for the audience?

4. **Words**: Is the language understandable? Is the wording concise?

5. **Sentences**: Are the sentences easy to read and generally short?

6. **Correctness**: Does the site avoid distracting errors?

7. **Design**: Are the pages user friendly? Is the site easy to navigate?

Gather and Prioritize Content

Brainstorm and research the actual content, with the goal of creating an outline for your site. How many topics will the site address? How wide will your coverage of a topic be? How deep? Your outline can also be used to create the website's table of contents. Based on your research, discussions with others, and the deadlines for the project, select the content, features, and functions your site will offer.

Think About Support Materials

List the documents (brochures, artworks, instructions, poems, reports) that will be presented on your site and note whether they will be displayed as webpages, made available for readers to download, or both. Construct a grid to keep track of how documents will be used.

List graphics that could make your pages more visual and informative and could help readers grasp the meaning of complex data or processes. Photographs may help "put a face" on your organization. Logos and icons will help brand your pages. Review the list below for electronic files that may be appropriate to your topic, audience, and purpose. (Remember: Use only graphics that are legally available. See the discussion of copyright at page 483.)

• **Images**	• **Audio**	• **Video**
charts	music	animations
drawings	sound effects	film clips
graphs	spoken text	presentations
photographs		webcasts

Design and Develop Individual Pages

When you create individual pages for your site, consider both the design and the content—specifically, how to make the two work well together.

Design Principles ■ Most webpages—and the pages of most other publications—are designed on grids. Look at any newspaper or magazine page and you should be able to draw horizontal and vertical lines denoting columns and rows of content. Some rows may span multiple columns, while some columns may overrun several rows.

Another fundamental design concept is balance. You might balance light elements with dark ones, text with images, and so forth. The balance of your page design should be driven by the purpose of your website, its audience, and its topic.

Websites may contain a variety of pages—each tailored to different purposes, audiences, and topics—to present some combination of informational and promotional content. Use each page's purpose to guide decisions about elements and functions to include.

Webpage design should follow fundamental document-design principles, including strategies for using color effectively. For more information, visit <www.thecollegewriter.com>.

Drafting Principles

1. **Identify the site.** Working from your mission statement, write an introductory sentence or brief paragraph for your site's home page. Let your visitors know immediately the site's purpose.

2. **Provide clear links.** Create links for your pages, using clear descriptors such as "Original Poetry." (Avoid phrases such as "Click here for poetry.") If necessary, add a descriptive sentence to further identify the link. Let visitors know precisely where each link will take them.

3. **Introduce each page.** Search sites may deliver some visitors to a page other than your home page. Give each page a brief introduction that clearly identifies it. Also, remember to provide a link back to your home page.

4. **Title each page.** Atop the browser window is a title bar, where the current page should be identified. This title is used in browser bookmarks, search engine listings, and the like. So be sure to give every page on your website a descriptive title.

5. **Keep pages uncluttered.** Dense text is even more difficult to read on screen than on paper, so use short paragraphs when you can. Add headings to identify sections, and include visuals to help break up the text.

6. **Save the page as HTML.** To be viewed in a web browser, your pages must be formatted in Hypertext Markup Language (HTML). Your word processor may have a "Save as HTML" or "Save as Webpage" option. Many HTML editing programs are also available on the web.

Test, Refine, and Post Your Site

Most websites are developed through the combined efforts of writers, graphic designers, and programmers. In such an environment, many content and layout ideas might be considered, rejected, and reformulated to produce and launch the site. Of course, the audience ultimately decides a website's success or failure. For that reason, test and refine your site before posting it.

1. **Check the site yourself.** Open your home page from your web browser. Does the site make sense? Can you navigate it easily?

2. **Get peer review.** Ask classmates—both experienced and inexperienced with the website's topic and with Internet searching—to use your site. Watch them navigate it, and take notes about any confusion they have.

3. **Check the text.** Reread all the text on your site. Trim wherever possible (the shorter, the better online), and check all spelling and punctuation.

4. **Check the graphics.** Do images load properly? Do they load quickly? Are menus and page headings in the same place on every page?

5. **Provide a feedback link.** Provide your e-mail address on the site, inviting visitors to contact you with any comments after the site goes "live."

6. **Post the site.** Upload the site to your hosting space. (Check your host's instructions for doing so.) Add the posting date to each page, and update it each time you change a page.

7. **Check for universality.** View the site on several different types of computers, using different browsers. Does the layout display well on all of them? Make any needed changes.

8. **Announce the site.** Advertise your site in e-mails. Submit it to search sites. Consider joining a "web ring" of similar sites to draw more traffic. Let your professors, classmates, friends, and family know about your site.

9. **Monitor the site.** After a site has been launched, its success may be measured by the amount of traffic it receives, feedback submitted by users, and any use of resources or services. (Check with your host for ways to measure traffic.)

10. **Make adjustments and updates.** A website should be a living thing. Update the content when possible to keep it fresh, and make any adjustments needed to adapt to changing technologies.

INSIGHT: Avoid using any features and functions that do not support your overall purpose for writing. If you find yourself distracted by the many bells and whistles of the web, remember that it's better to have a simple website that presents information clearly and effectively than a complex site that does not.

Sample Webpages

On the next two pages, you'll find sample pages from student and academic websites. Study each model for insights about what makes strong web content and design.

 For further analysis of webpages, including nonprofit and business sites, go to <www.thecollegewriter.com>. There you'll also find tutorials on analyzing and evaluating websites.

Student-Designed Website

The following website was developed by undergraduate students from a Southwestern U.S. university who were studying abroad. Southwest Sojourners is a multiuser site with blogs and chat rooms that allow students to keep in touch with each other and with friends and family back home.

Purpose ■ This site is a gathering place for undergraduate students studying abroad. It describes itself as a "home away from home" for such students. The tone is light, conversational, and inviting, as befitting the purpose of connecting these students to each other and to the important people in their lives.

Audience ■ The site is meant for students, friends, and family members. By providing straight news, individualized blogs, and chat rooms and e-mail options, the site allows users to be as passive or as active as they wish. Membership is required for active participation, and members must "sign" a user's agreement before posting.

Format ■ The golden background and sun icon visually convey the southwestern theme, while the minimalist format makes the site easy to navigate. A large four-item toolbar on the left of the page directs users to the linked pages, and brief text on the right of each page gives a clear indication of what lies at the end of each link.

SOUTHWEST SOJOURNERS

Welcome to Southwest Sojourners! This site is meant to be a home away from home for students from Southwestern U.S. universities who are studying abroad. If you are such a student—or a friend or family member of such a student—this is the spot for you! Lurk, if you like, or log in and join the conversation.

Sojourners News   These pages are updated regularly with information about special events on this site—and in reality.

Click here for a list of students who are blogging about their studies abroad.

Student Blogs   For members only: Join the conversation with students in England, Germany, Italy, India, Japan—and elsewhere!

Chat Rooms   Membership is free, but we do need a little information and a digital signature on our posting agreement.

Log In!   **Contact the Webmaster at:** Webmaster@southsojourn.edu.
Site design: Mikayla Evans and Griffin Jenson

site launched: 29 January 2005
last updated: 29 July 2005

Main

Academic Website

The Massachusetts Institute of Technology/Draper Technology Development Partnership Program website is an academic research site. It contains information and research about one of the Department of Aeronautics and Astronautics' surveillance projects—the Parent-Child Unmanned Aerial Vehicle (PCUAV) Project.

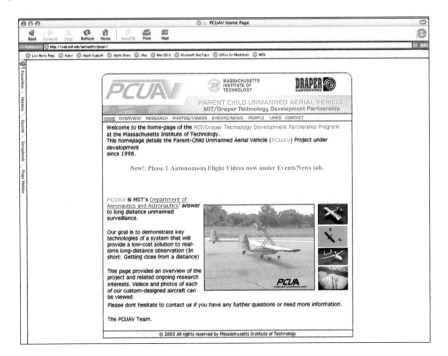

Purpose: This site aims to inform a very specific audience about an ongoing research project being conducted by MIT graduate research assistants. The entire site focuses on this one project and provides news, events, videos, photos, contact information for researchers, and an overview of the many fields being researched in conjunction with the project.

Audience: Because it shares an easy-to-understand overview rather than in-depth research stats, this site provides information for the general public, potential partners/investors, and the news media. In addition, the site provides researchers with a central place to share information and store photos and videos of test flights.

Format: The top third of the page highlights the names and logos for the project, the school, and the partner, illustrating the importance of providing credit to developers and supporters of research projects. Though a narrow gray bar provides a thorough menu of options, the large photos of the aerial vehicle are the focus of this page. In true scientific style, the site skips flashy graphics and bright colors and lets a straightforward project description and vivid photos do the storytelling.

Writing for Different Internet Environments

The Internet is a complex construct made up of much more than webpages. Other writing venues on the Net are described below, with writing tips for each.

OWLs ■ Your university or college probably has a writing lab where you can seek help with your writing assignments. It might also have a web-based OWL (online writing lab) where you can access help via an Internet connection. OWLs post answers to questions you may have about writing, and they often allow you to e-mail or send an instant message (see below) to a writing tutor. Before contacting an OWL tutor, carefully read any instructions posted on the site. *Example:* Purdue University OWL <owl.english.purdue.edu>

MUDs, MOOs, and MUSHes ■ Some instructors hold classes or deliver lectures online in a MUD (multiuser dimension), a text-based "world" that people can share. (MOOs and MUSHes are variants of MUDs.) MUDs have virtual rooms to explore and virtual objects to examine and handle. To use a MUD, you must learn the text commands for interacting with it. Most MUDs require software for a telnet connection, but some are accessible via telnet-enabled webpages. *Example:* Diversity University MOO <www.marshall.edu/commdis/moo>

Message Boards ■ Many websites have forms that allow visitors to post messages for public display. The messages and any replies are usually listed together so that readers can follow the message "thread."

Mailing Lists ■ Mailing lists allow users to send and receive text messages within a specific group of people interested in a particular subject. The software that maintains a mailing list is called a "list server." Some mailing lists are excellent resources of specialized information; others are pure frivolity. *Example:* QUANTUMTEACHING-NMC < MTEACHING-NMC@LISTS.MAINE.EDU>

Chat Servers ■ A chat server provides a place on the Net where you can type a message that other people will see instantly. They can then respond with text messages of their own. Some teachers and tutors may use a chat room to confer with students or to hold a class discussion online. Although some chat servers require special software, many are available as webpages. *Example:* Yahoo! Chat <chat.yahoo.com>

Instant Messaging Services ■ Instant messaging (IM) services allow you to send a text message instantaneously to friends and colleagues who use the same software. Most IMs also allow users to send computer files to one another. (Just be careful not to pass a computer virus this way.) *Example:* ICQ <web.icq.com>

Blogs ■ A blog (short for "weblog") is basically just an online journal posted to a webpage. In effect, it is a one-person message board (see above). For many people, blogging is more convenient than creating a webpage of their own, because it involves no design issues and requires no uploading of files.

Writing Checklist

Use this checklist to review and revise your site and its pages.

___ The purpose of the website is presented—or evident—on the homepage and elsewhere on the site.

___ The page elements—headlines, body text, preformatted text, background colors, lists, images, and tables—work together and are suited to the page's audience, topic, and purpose.

___ The page functions, including navigation menus, are logically presented and enable readers to find what they need quickly.

___ The content collected for the site (from brochures to reports) and support materials (images, audio, and video) are available, approved, accurate, and in the correct format for presentation or download.

___ The site plan allows information to be presented and cross-referenced in logical and efficient pathways.

___ The page design incorporates design principles on pages 405–406.

___ The informational and promotional aspects of the site are appropriate to the audience, topic, and purpose.

Writing Activities

1. Research and study the content, style, and design of websites related to your particular major, field, or discipline. Then develop a report on those sites, incorporating three or four screen shots for analysis.

2. Visit a familiar website. Study its home page, or another page, in terms of the site's purpose, audience, and topic. Analyze and evaluate the page's content and design. As a prewriting activity, consider diagramming the site. To conclude your analysis, explain which aspects of the page you noticed that you had not noticed before.

3. Go to the home page of your college or university and review the page elements and functions. Team up with a classmate to discuss how well the page addresses its purpose(s), audience(s), and topic(s). Then imagine you have been hired to revise and refine the page. Print out a copy and mark it up with your changes. Create a "mockup" of a new and improved home page. Draft a one-page overview that explains how your revision is better than the original.

4. Working with classmates, brainstorm a list of campus clubs and associations that currently do not have websites (or at least not quality websites). Using the guidelines from this chapter, develop a website for one of them. As another option, consider a nonprofit organization in your area. Collaborate and research as needed.

Chapter 28
Preparing Oral Presentations

Throughout your career (including your college years), you will give many oral presentations—from brief introductions to lengthy reports. In each situation, the following basic steps will help you develop a strong message.

State your purpose.
- Am I trying to persuade or inspire my audience to do something?
- Am I hoping to inform or teach my audience about something?

Identify your audience.
- What are my listeners' ages, interests, and knowledge of the topic?
- What will their attitude be toward the topic and toward me?

Select and research your topic.
- What topics fulfill my assignment and help me achieve my purpose?
- Where can I find information about the topic?
- What support materials (displays, computer projections, handouts) would help me present my message?

What's Ahead
- Organizing Your Presentation
- Writing Your Presentation
  – Student Model
- Developing Computer Presentations
- Checklist

Organizing Your Presentation

After you've gathered your information, you must organize and develop the message. How? Start by thinking about your presentation as having three distinct parts: (1) an introduction, (2) a body, and (3) a conclusion. The guidelines on this page and the following two pages will help you integrate, organize, and refine all the parts so they communicate the message and achieve your purpose.

Prepare an introduction.

For any speaking situation, you should develop an introduction that does the following things:

- greets the audience and grabs their attention
- communicates your interest in them
- introduces your topic and main idea
- shows that you have something worthwhile to say
- establishes an appropriate tone

You may greet the audience in many ways, including introducing yourself or making appropriate comments about the occasion, the individuals present, or the setting. Following these comments, introduce your topic and main idea as quickly and as clearly as you can. For example, you could open with one of these attention-grabbing strategies:

- a little-known fact or statistic
- a series of questions
- a humorous story or anecdote
- an appropriate quotation
- a description of a serious problem
- a cartoon, picture, or drawing
- a short demonstration
- a statement about the topic's importance
- an eye-catching prop or display
- a video or an audio clip

Tip: As a matter of courtesy, audiences will generally *give* you their attention—but only for about thirty seconds. After that, you must *earn* it by presenting information that they believe is worth hearing.

Develop the body.

The body of your presentation should deliver the message—and supporting points—so clearly that the audience understands the presentation after hearing it only once. The key to developing such a clear message is choosing an organizational pattern that fits your purpose.

So before you outline the body, take a moment to review what you want your presentation to do: explain a problem? promote an idea? teach a process? Be sure the organizational pattern will help you do that. For example, if you want to teach a process, the outline should list the process steps in chronological order. If your outline is clear, you may begin to write.

Organizational Patterns

Organizational patterns for explaining a process and other purposes are listed below.

- **Chronological Order**: Arrange information according to the time order in which events (or steps in a process) take place.

- **Order of Importance**: Arrange information according to its importance— greatest to least or least to greatest.

- **Comparison/Contrast**: Give information about subjects by comparing and contrasting them.

- **Cause/Effect**: Give information about a situation or problem by showing the causes and the effects.

- **Order of Location**: Arrange information about subjects according to where things are located in relation to each other.

- **Problem/Solution**: Describe a problem and then present a solution for it.

Writing an Outline or Manuscript

After deciding how to organize your message, write it out in either outline or manuscript form. For help, see the tips below and the model on pages 416–417.

Body-Building Tips

- Build your presentation around several key ideas. (Don't try to cover too much ground.)

- Write with a personal, natural voice.

- Support your main points with reliable facts and clear examples.

- Present your information in short, easy-to-follow segments.

- Use positive, respectful language. (Avoid jargon.)

- Use graphic aids and handouts.

Come to a conclusion.

A strong introduction and conclusion work like bookends supporting the body of the presentation. The introduction gets the audience's attention, sets the tone, states the main idea, and identifies the key points of the message. Almost in reverse, the conclusion reviews those points, restates the main idea, reinforces the tone, and refocuses the audience on what it should think about or do. Together, those bookends emphasize and clarify the message so that listeners will understand and remember it.

Concluding Strategies

Here are some strategies—which you can use alone or in combination—for concluding a presentation:

- Review your main idea and key points.
- Issue a personal challenge.
- Come "full circle." (State those arguments or details that back up your original point.)
- Recommend a plan of action.
- Suggest additional sources of information.
- Thank the audience and ask for questions.

Hold a Q & A session.

After your presentation, you may want to invite your audience to ask questions. Very often, a Q & A session is the real payoff for participants. They can ask for clarification of points or how your message applies to their personal situations. Audience members may even offer their own insights or solutions to problems mentioned in the presentation.

Q & A Tips

The following suggestions will help you lead a good Q & A session:

- Listen carefully and think about each part of the question.
- Repeat or paraphrase questions for the benefit of the entire group.
- Answer the questions concisely and clearly.
- Respond honestly when you don't know the answer, and offer to find one.
- Ask for a follow-up question if someone seems confused after your answer.
- Look directly at the group when you answer.
- Be prepared to pose an important question or two if no one asks a question.
- Conclude by thanking the audience for their participation.

Writing Your Presentation

How much of your presentation you actually write out depends on your topic, audience, purpose, and—of course—personal style. The three most common forms to use when making a presentation are a list, an outline, and a manuscript.

List: Use a list for a short, informal speech such as an after-dinner introduction. Think about your purpose and then list the following:

- your opening sentences (or two)
- a summary phrase for each of your main points
- your closing sentence

List

1. Opening sentence or two

2. Phrase #1
Phrase #2
Phrase #3

3. Closing sentence

Outline: Use an outline for a more complex or formal topic. You can organize your material in greater detail without tying yourself to a word-for-word presentation. Here's one way you can do it:

- opening (complete sentences)
- all main points (sentences)
- supporting points (phrases)
quotations (written out)
all supporting technical details, statistics, and sources (listed)
- closing (complete sentences)

Wherever appropriate, include notes on visual aids (in caps or boldface).

Manuscript: Use the guidelines below if you plan to write out your presentation word for word:

- Double-space and number pages (or cards).
- Use complete sentences on a page (do not run sentences from one page to another).
- Mark difficult words for pronunciation.
- Mark the script for interpretation using symbols such as boldface or italics to signal emphasis or vocal color.

Outline

I. Opening statement
   A. Point with support
   B. Point (purpose or goal)
     [VISUAL 1]

II. Body (with 3-5 main points)
   A. Main point
     1. Supporting details
     2. Supporting details
   B. Main point
     1. Supporting details
     2. Supporting details
   C. Main point
     1. Supporting details
     2. Supporting details

III. Closing statement
   A. Point, including restatement of purpose
   B. Point, possibly a call to action [VISUAL 2]

Student Model

In her formal presentation below, student Burnette Sawyer argues that college students must begin a retirement savings plan today. Notice that she uses italics to mark words needing vocal color and boldface to mark words needing emphasis. She places all visual aid cues in color.

Save Now or Pay Later

Imagine that you've finished school, gotten a job, worked hard all week, and this dollar bill represents your whole paycheck. [hold up dollar bill] As your employer, I'm about to hand you the check when I stop, tear off about 20 percent like this, give it to Uncle Sam, and say, "Here's my employee's income tax." Then I tear off another 30 percent like this, give that to Uncle Sam too, and say, "And here's her Medicare and Social Security tax." *1*

Finally, I give you this half and say, "Here, hard worker, this is what's left of your *whole paycheck.*" *2*

Does that sound like science fiction? *3*

Senator Alan Simpson doesn't think so. In the magazine *Modern Maturity*, he says that unless legislation changes the Social Security system, *our generation* will have to pay 20 percent [SLIDE 1] of our paychecks as income tax, and 30 percent [SLIDE 2] as Social Security tax. That means we can keep just **50 percent** [SLIDE 3] of what we earn. *4*

But the news gets **worse**. Remember this 30 percent that we paid to Social Security? [hold up piece of dollar bill] Well, that won't be enough money for retired people to live on in the year 2043. Remember that year, 2043—we'll come back to that soon. *5*

What's the problem? The Social Security system can't ensure our savings for retirement. *6*

What's the solution? We have to start our own savings plans, and the earlier, the better. *7*

Ever since the Social Security system started back in 1935 [SLIDE 4], it has never been secure. While the system has been "fixed" a number of times, these fix-it jobs haven't solved the problem. For example, writer Keith Carlson points out that in 1983 [SLIDE 5] Congress raised payroll taxes, extended the retirement age, and said that the system would be in good financial shape until 2056. *8*

But then, says Carlson, *just nine years later,* a report came out saying that Congress had been **wrong**. The report [SLIDE 6] said in 1992 that Social Security money wouldn't even last that long—it would run out by 2043. *Remember that year, 2043? That's before many of us are supposed to retire at age 67!* *9*

Do you think this news is bad? The AARP Bulletin reported on the Bipartisan Commission on Entitlement and Tax Reform. This commission warned that entitlement programs like Social Security [SLIDE 7] are *10*

The speaker begins with an anecdote.

She tears the dollar for emphasis.

The speaker asks questions to involve the audience.

Throughout the speech, she uses 11 slides to give her listeners a clear understanding of the main points.

growing so fast they could "bankrupt the country" by the year 2029—long before we retire!

So what should we do? This fall many of us will vote in a presidential election for the first time. Both Democrats and Republicans say they have a plan to fix Social Security. What if we all vote for the presidential candidate with the best plan? Will that save our retirement funds? **Don't count on it!** As the track record for Social Security shows, one more fix-it job won't fix the system. We have to start *our own* retirement plans—and do it early in our careers. *11*

In fact, in his book *Retirement 101*, Willard Enteman says that we should start a personal savings plan the day we get our first paychecks. In sociology class last week, Mr. Christians made the same point. He gave us this bar graph [SLIDE 8] showing that if our goal is to save $500,000 by age 67, we had better *start early* before saving gets too expensive. *12*

As you can see from the graph, if we start saving when we're 25, we can reach $500,000 by saving just $121 a month. [SLIDE 9] If we wait until we're 35, we'll have to save $282 a month. [SLIDE 10] If we wait until we're 45, we'll have to put away $698 a month. [SLIDE 11] And if we wait until we're 55, we'll need $2,079 a month. *13*

Look at the difference. To reach $500,000 by age 67 would cost $121 a month if we start at 25, and $2,079 a month if we start at 55. *14*

What's my point? The Social Security system *can't promise us* financial security when we retire in 2050. *15*

What's the solution? We have to start our own savings plans; and the *earlier* we start, the *easier* it will be to reach our goals. ∎ *16*

> The closing paragraphs help listeners reflect on the subject.

Note: Sample slides for this presentation are shown on page **418**.

Marking Your Presentation

As you rehearse your presentation, decide which words or phrases to emphasize, where to pause, and where to add visual aids. Then use the symbols and text enhancements below to mark the copy of your presentation.

Italic or boldface . . . . for additional feeling or emotion

Underlining . . . . for greater volume or emphasis

Dash, diagonal, ellipsis . . . . for a pause—or / a break in the flow

Brackets . . . . for actions or [visual aids]

Use visual aids.

While constructing your presentation, think about visual aids that would grab the audience's attention and help them understand the message. For example, in her speech, Burnette Sawyer used the computer-generated graphics below. (See pages **416–417**.)

Sample Graphics

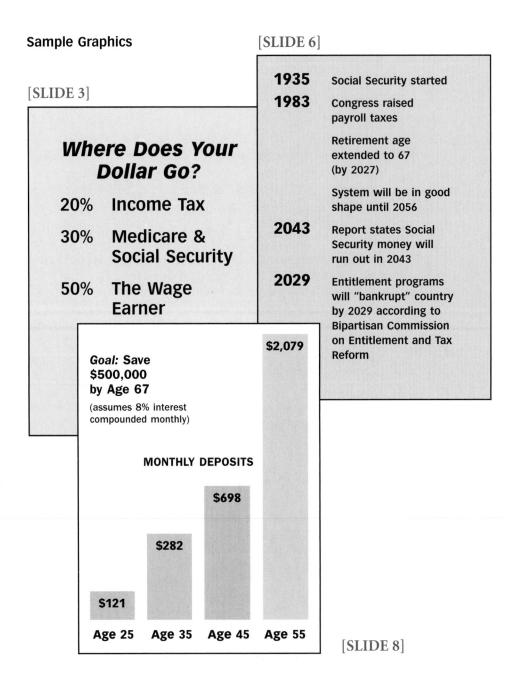

[SLIDE 6]

1935	Social Security started
1983	Congress raised payroll taxes
	Retirement age extended to 67 (by 2027)
	System will be in good shape until 2056
2043	Report states Social Security money will run out in 2043
2029	Entitlement programs will "bankrupt" country by 2029 according to Bipartisan Commission on Entitlement and Tax Reform

[SLIDE 3]

Where Does Your Dollar Go?

20% Income Tax

30% Medicare & Social Security

50% The Wage Earner

Goal: Save $500,000 by Age 67
(assumes 8% interest compounded monthly)

MONTHLY DEPOSITS

$2,079

$698

$282

$121

Age 25   Age 35   Age 45   Age 55

[SLIDE 8]

Developing Computer Presentations

To help you use presentation software effectively, follow the guidelines below.

1. **Develop a design.** Be sure your graphic design fits your topic and your audience—polished for a serious topic, casual for an informal topic.

2. **Create pages.** If a main idea has several parts, present each one on its own page. Each click of the mouse button (or computer key) should reveal a new detail.

3. **Use transitions.** Dissolves, fades, wipes, and other transitional effects refine a computer presentation and keep the audience's attention (as long as the devices don't detract from the message).

4. **Add sound.** Just as graphics and animation can enhance a presentation, so, too, can sound. Music can serve as an introduction or backdrop, and sound effects can add emphasis. Voice recording can add authority and help drive home key points.

> **Speaker's Tip:** Text can be animated to appear from off-screen at just the right moment. Graphics can be made to appear one element at a time, and illustrations can change before the viewer's eyes. Remember to use special effects—especially animation—wisely.

5. **Fine-tune your presentation.** Practice delivering your presentation while clicking through your pages. Try it with an audience of fellow students, if possible, and ask for their input.

6. **Check for word choice and style.** Make sure that the words on the screen are key words. Use these words as talking points—don't try to cover any point word for word. Also, check that transitions, animations, and sounds are smooth and not disruptive.

7. **Edit the final version.** Check spelling, punctuation, usage, and other mechanics. Remember: On-screen errors are glaringly obvious to everyone.

8. **Rehearse.** Perform your presentation for a friend or family member. Practice running the equipment until you can use it with confidence.

9. **Make a backup copy.** Protect all the effort you invested in your presentation.

> **Tip:** Choose an easy-to-read font and type-size. In most situations, 36-point heads and 24-point text work well. However, the type-size needed depends on a number of variables, including the screen size, lens type, and audience's distance from the screen.

Checklist: Overcoming Stage Fright

While it's okay to feel a little nervous before a presentation (the emotion keeps you alert), stage fright can limit your ability to communicate. The remedy for stage fright is confidence—confidence in what to say and how to say it. To develop that confidence, do the following:

Personal Preparation

_____ Know your subject well.

_____ Rehearse the presentation thoroughly, including the use of visuals.

_____ Schedule your time carefully, making sure to arrive early.

_____ Try to relax before the presentation by stretching or doing a deep-breathing exercise, remembering that your presentation can be successful without being perfect.

The Room and Equipment

_____ See that the room is clean, comfortable, and well lit.

_____ Make sure tables and chairs are set up and arranged correctly.

_____ Check that AV equipment is in place and working.

_____ Test microphone volume.

_____ Position the screen and displays for good visibility.

Personal Details

_____ Check clothing and hair.

_____ Arrange for drinking water to be available.

_____ Put your script and handouts in place.

Speaking Strategies

_____ Be confident, positive, and energetic.

_____ Maintain eye contact when speaking or listening.

_____ Use gestures naturally—don't force them.

_____ Provide for audience participation; survey the audience: "How many of you . . . ?"

_____ Maintain a comfortable, erect posture.

_____ Speak up and speak clearly—don't rush.

_____ Reword and clarify when necessary.

_____ After the presentation, ask for questions and answer them clearly.

_____ Thank the audience.

III. Research and Writing

CONTENTS
Research and Writing

Chapter 29
Getting Started: From Planning Research to Evaluating Sources

At first glance, research looks like a dry-as-dust business carried out by obsessed scholars in dim libraries and mad scientists in cluttered laboratories. Research couldn't be further from the reality of your life.

But is it? Consider car tires. Before these were mounted, scientists researched which materials would resist wear and which adhesives would keep treads on steel belts. Whereas sloppy research could cause blowouts, good research builds safe tires.

Your research projects may be your toughest college assignments. They may take weeks to complete, including hours spent on the trail of facts, figures, and ideas. These projects demand that you organize your tasks carefully and digest the thinking of others while discovering your own perspective. However, the rewards of research projects can be great—new insights into a subject that really interests you, a deepened understanding of your major or profession, reliable knowledge to share with others, and sharpened thinking skills.

What's Ahead

- Papers with Documented Research: Quick Guide
- The Research Process: A Flowchart
- Getting Started: Getting Focused
- Developing a Research Plan
- Exploring Possible Information Resources and Sites
- Conducting Effective Keyword Searches
- Engaging and Evaluating Sources
- Creating a Working Bibliography
- Developing a Note-Taking System
- Summarizing, Paraphrasing, and Quoting Source Material
- Avoiding Unintentional Plagiarism
- Writing Checklist and Activities

Papers with Documented Research:

QUICK GUIDE

When you work on a research project you ask important questions, look systematically for answers, and share your conclusions with readers. In other words, it's all about curiosity, discovery, and dialogue.

STARTING POINT: The assignment usually relates to a course concept, so consider what your instructor wants you to learn and how your project will be evaluated. Then take ownership of the project by looking for an angle that makes the writing personal.

PURPOSE: The project requires you to conduct research and share results. Your main goal is to discover the complex truth about a topic and clarify that discovery for others.

FORM: The traditional research paper is a fairly long essay (5 to 15 pages) complete with thesis, supporting paragraphs, integrated sources, and careful documentation. However, you may be asked to shape your research into a field report, a website, or a multimedia presentation.

AUDIENCE: Traditionally, research writing addresses "the academic community," a group made up mainly of instructors and students. However, your actual audience may be more specific: addicted smokers, all Floridians, fellow immigrants, and so on.

VOICE: The tone is usually semiformal, but check your instructor's expectations. In any research writing, maintain a thoughtful, confident tone. After all, your research has made you somewhat of an authority on the topic.

POINT OF VIEW: In the past, research writers avoided the pronouns "I" and "you" in order to remain properly objective and academic sounding. Unfortunately, this resulted in an overuse of both the pronoun "one" and the passive voice. Many instructors now encourage students to connect research with experience, meaning that you may use the pronouns "I" and "you" occasionally. Be careful, however, to keep the focus where it belongs—on the topic. Bottom line: Follow your instructor's requirements concerning pronoun use. For more on developing a strong academic style for your research writing, see pages 70–71.

INSIGHT: The best research writing centers on *your* ideas—ideas you develop through thoughtful engagement with sources. In poor research papers, the sources dominate, and the writer's perspective disappears.

The Research Process: A Flowchart

The research process involves getting started, planning, conducting the research, and organizing the results. This process is flexible enough to be adapted to diverse research projects. In fact, real research is typically dynamic: You might think during the planning phase that you've nailed down your topic, only to discover a surprising topical detour while conducting research. Generally, however, the research process maps out as shown below. When you get your assignment—whether to write a five-page paper on pasteurization or to develop a website on Middle Eastern political conflicts—review the process and tailor it to the task.

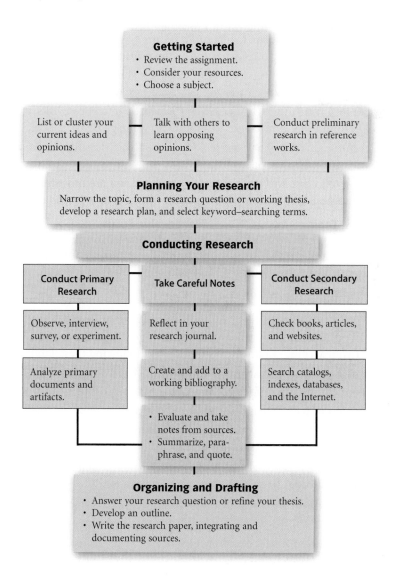

Getting Started
- Review the assignment.
- Consider your resources.
- Choose a subject.

List or cluster your current ideas and opinions.

Talk with others to learn opposing opinions.

Conduct preliminary research in reference works.

Planning Your Research
Narrow the topic, form a research question or working thesis, develop a research plan, and select keyword–searching terms.

Conducting Research

Conduct Primary Research

Take Careful Notes

Conduct Secondary Research

Observe, interview, survey, or experiment.

Reflect in your research journal.

Check books, articles, and websites.

Analyze primary documents and artifacts.

Create and add to a working bibliography.

Search catalogs, indexes, databases, and the Internet.

- Evaluate and take notes from sources.
- Summarize, paraphrase, and quote.

Organizing and Drafting
- Answer your research question or refine your thesis.
- Develop an outline.
- Write the research paper, integrating and documenting sources.

Getting Started: Getting Focused

If you have to wear glasses or contacts, you understand blurriness. Blurry research is out-of-focus research. Early in your project, get focused by narrowing your topic, brainstorming research questions, and developing a working thesis. For help understanding assignments and selecting topics, as well as other prewriting strategies, see pages 28–29.

Establish a narrow, manageable topic.

To do good research, you need an engaging, manageable topic. Once you have a broad topic, narrow your focus to a specific feature or angle that allows for in-depth research. For help, consult your instructor or the writing center. Try these strategies:

- Check your topic in the Library of Congress subject headings, available in your library. Note "narrower topics" listed (see page 432).
- Read into your topic. By consulting specialized reference works, explore background that directs you to subtopics (see page 465).
- Check the Internet. For example, follow a subject directory to see where your topic leads (see pages 471–475).
- Freewrite to discover what aspect of the topic you are most interested in: a local angle, a connection with a group of people, or a personal concern.

Broad Topic	Manageable Focus
Homelessness	Homeless Families in Los Angeles
Bacteria and Viruses	Bacterial Resistance to Antibiotics
Alternative Energy Sources	Development of Hybrid-Electric Vehicles

Brainstorm research questions.

Good research questions help you find meaningful information and ideas about your topic. These questions sharpen your research goal, and the answers will become the focus of your writing. Brainstorm questions by following these guidelines:

List both simple and substantial questions. Basic questions aim for factual answers. More complex questions get at analysis, synthesis, and evaluation.

- **Question of fact:** When did Saddam Hussein gain power in Iraq?
- **Question of interpretation:** How did Saddam Hussein maintain his power?

List main and secondary questions. Ask a primary question about your topic—the main issue that you want to get at. Then brainstorm secondary questions that you need to research in order to answer your primary question.

- **Main Question:** Should consumers embrace hybrid cars?

- **Secondary Questions** (*Who, What, When, Where, Why, How*): Who has developed hybrid cars? Who manufactures them? What is a hybrid car? What are its advantages and disadvantages? When were hybrids developed? Where are hybrids currently used? Why are hybrids being developed? How does a hybrid work? How is it related to fuel-cell technology?

Testing Your Main Research Question:

_____ Is the question so broad that I can't answer it in the project's time and page limits?

_____ Is the question so narrow that I won't be able to find sources?

_____ Is the question so simple that it will be too easy to answer?

_____ Will the question lead to significant sources and intellectual challenge?

_____ Am I committed to answering this question? Does it interest me?

_____ Will the question and answers interest my readers?

Develop a working thesis.

A working thesis offers a preliminary answer to your main research question. As your initial perspective on the topic, a good working thesis keeps you focused during research, helping you decide whether to carefully read a particular book or just skim it, fully explore a website or quickly surf through it. Make your working thesis a statement that demands "Prove it!" Don't settle for a simple statement of fact about your topic; instead, choose a working thesis that seems debatable or that requires some explanation. Try this formula:

Formula: Working Thesis = limited topic + tentative claim, statement, or hypothesis

Example: Hybrid cars are a positive step forward from the average internal-combustion car, but they don't go far enough toward cleaner air.

Working Thesis Checklist:

_____ Does my working thesis focus on a single, limited topic?

_____ Is my working thesis stated in a clear, direct sentence?

_____ Does my working thesis convey my initial perspective about the topic?

_____ Do I have access to enough good information to support this working thesis?

_____ Does my working thesis direct me to write a paper that meets all assignment requirements?

INSIGHT: Your working thesis is written in sand, not stone. It may change as you research because sources may push you in new directions. In fact, such change shows that you are engaging your sources and growing in your thinking.

Developing a Research Plan

It pays to plan your research. In fact, minutes spent planning research can save hours doing research. With your limited topic, main research question, and working thesis in front of you, plan your project more fully.

Choose research methods.

Consider these questions: What do you already know about the topic? What do you need to know? What resources will help you answer your research question? What resources does the assignment require? Based on your answers, map out a research plan that draws resources from fitting categories:

Background research ■ To find information about your topic's context, central concepts, and key terms, take these steps:

- Use the Library of Congress subject headings to find keywords for searching the library catalog, periodical databases, and the Internet (see page **432**).
- Conduct a preliminary search of the library catalog, journal databases, and the Internet to confirm that good resources on your topic exist.
- Use specialized reference works to find background information, definitions, facts, and statistics (see page **465**).

Field or primary research ■ If appropriate for your project, conduct field research:

- Use interviews (page **456**) or surveys (page **452**) to get key information from experts or others.
- Conduct observations or experiments (page **451**) to obtain hard data on your topic.
- Analyze key documents or artifacts related to your topic (pages **454–455**).

Library research ■ Select important library resources:

- Use scholarly books to get in-depth, reliable material (pages **460–461**).
- Use periodical articles (print or electronic) to get current, reliable information (pages **462–464**). Select from news sources, popular magazines, scholarly journals, and trade journals.
- Consider other library resources, such as a documentary, recorded interview, pamphlet, marketing study, or government publication.

Internet research ■ Plan effective Internet searches by considering the following:

- Search engines and subject guides: Choose tools that will lead you to quality resources (pages **474–475**).
- Expert guidance: Select reputable websites that librarians or other experts recommend (pages **470–473**).
- Evaluation: Test all web resources for reliability (pages **434–437**).
- Limitations: How many web resources are you allowed to use, if any?

Get organized to do research.

An organized approach to doing your research will save you time, help you work efficiently, and prevent frustration. Get organized by addressing these issues:

Establishing Priorities for Resources, Time, and Effort

- How much research material do you need?
- What range of resources will give you quality, reliable information?
- What types of research does the assignment specify? Are you limited, for example, in the number of Internet sources you can use?
- What are the project's priorities: What must you do? What tasks are secondary in nature?
- What weight does the project carry in the course? How should you match your time and effort with that weight?

INSIGHT: Gather more information than you could ever use in your paper. That richness gives you choices and allows you to sift for crucial information.

Selecting Research Methods and Systems

- Given the resources and technologies available, select methods that help you do research efficiently: signing out hard-copy library holdings or using interlibrary loan; photocopying book sections and journal articles; printing, saving, downloading, bookmarking, or e-mailing digital materials.
- Develop a note-taking system. Choose from the note-card, double-entry notebook, copy-and-annotate, and research-log methods (pages **440–443**), and set up a working bibliography (pages **438–439**).
- Choose and review a documentation system. It's likely that your instructor will designate a system such as MLA (pages **495–536**) or APA (pages **537–566**). If he or she doesn't do so, then use a method that suits the subject matter and discipline. Review the system's basic rules and strategies.

Establishing a Schedule

Generally, you should spend about half your time on research and half on writing. Sketch out tentative deadlines for completing each phase of your work.

Web Link: A sample schedule is provided at <www.thecollegewriter.com>.

Developing a Research Proposal

For some research projects (e.g., individual studies, field research, a senior thesis paper), you may have to formalize your plan by writing a research proposal. Such a proposal aims to show that the research is both valid (makes good scholarly sense) and valuable (will lead to significant knowledge); to communicate your enthusiasm for the project; to show that your plan is workable within the constraints of the assignment; and to gain your instructor's feedback and approval.

Web Link: A sample proposal and instructions are at <www.thecollegewriter.com>.

Exploring Possible Information Resources and Sites

To conduct thorough, creative, but efficient research, you need a sense of what types of resources are available for your project and where to find them. Check the tables that follow.

Consider different information resources.

Examine the range of resources available: Which will give you the best information for your project? While one project (for example, a sociological report on airport behaviors) might require personal, direct sources, another project (for example, the effects of the 9/11 terrorist attacks on the air transportation industry) might depend on government reports, business publications, and journal articles. Generally, a well-rounded research paper relies on a range of quality resources; in particular, it avoids relying on insubstantial web information.

Type of Resource	Examples
Personal, direct resources	Memories, diaries, journals, logs, experiments, tests, observations, interviews, surveys
Reference works (print and electronic)	Dictionaries, thesauruses, encyclopedias, almanacs, yearbooks, atlases, directories, guides, handbooks, indexes, abstracts, catalogs, bibliographies
Books (print and electronic)	Nonfiction, how-to, biographies, fiction, trade books, scholarly and scientific studies
Periodicals and news sources	Print newspapers, magazines, and journals; broadcast news and news magazines; online magazines, news sources, and discussion groups
Audiovisual, digital, and multimedia resources	Graphics (tables, graphs, charts, maps, drawings, photos), audiotapes, CDs, videos, DVDs, webpages, online databases
Government publications	Guides, programs, forms, legislation, regulations, reports, records, statistics
Business and nonprofit publications	Correspondence, reports, newsletters, pamphlets, brochures, ads, catalogs, instructions, handbooks, manuals, policies and procedures, seminar and training materials

Consider different information sites.

Where do you go to find the resources that you need? Consider the information "sites" listed below, remembering that many resources may be available in different forms in different locations. For example, a journal article may be available in library holdings or on an electronic database.

Information Location	Specific "Sites"
People	Experts (knowledge area, skill, occupation) Population segments or individuals (with representative or unusual experiences)
Libraries	General: public, college, online Specialized: legal, medical, government, business
Computer resources	Computers: software, CD-ROMs Networks: Internet and other online services (e-mail, limited-access databases, discussion groups, MUD, chat rooms, websites); Intranets
Mass media	Radio (AM and FM) Television (network, public, cable, satellite) Print (newspapers, magazines, journals)
Testing, training, meeting, and observation sites	Plants, facilities, field sites, laboratories Research centers, universities, think tanks Conventions, conferences, seminars Museums, galleries, historical sites
Municipal, state, and federal government offices	Elected officials, representatives Offices and agencies, Government Printing Office websites (GPO <www.gpoaccess.gov >)
Workplace	Computer databases, company files Desktop reference materials Bulletin boards (physical and electronic) Company and department websites Departments and offices Associations, professional organizations, consulting, training, and business information services

Web Link

Conducting Effective Keyword Searches

Keyword searching can help you find information in electronic library catalogs, online databases that index periodical articles (for example, Lexis-Nexis, EBSCOhost), print indexes to periodical publications (for example, Business Periodicals Index), Internet resources, print books, and Ebooks.

Choose keywords carefully.

Keywords give you "compass points" for navigating through a sea of information. That's why choosing the best keywords is crucial. Consider these tips:

1. **Brainstorm a list of possible keywords**—topics, titles, and names—based on your current knowledge and/or background reading.

2. **Consult the Library of Congress subject headings**. These books contain the keywords librarians use when classifying materials. For example, if you looked up *immigrants*, you would find the entry below, indicating keywords to use, along with narrower, related, and broader terms.

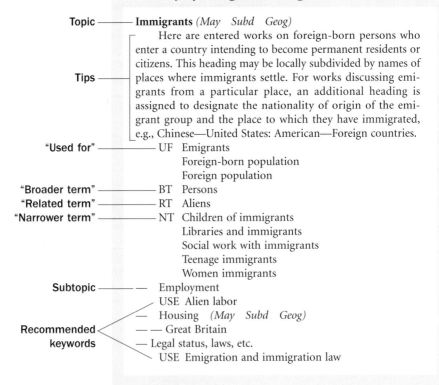

Library of Congress Excerpt

Topic —— **Immigrants** *(May Subd Geog)*

Tips —— Here are entered works on foreign-born persons who enter a country intending to become permanent residents or citizens. This heading may be locally subdivided by names of places where immigrants settle. For works discussing emigrants from a particular place, an additional heading is assigned to designate the nationality of origin of the emigrant group and the place to which they have immigrated, e.g., Chinese—United States: American—Foreign countries.

"Used for" —— UF Emigrants
　　　　　　　　　Foreign-born population
　　　　　　　　　Foreign population

"Broader term" —— BT Persons
"Related term" —— RT Aliens
"Narrower term" —— NT Children of immigrants
　　　　　　　　　　Libraries and immigrants
　　　　　　　　　　Social work with immigrants
　　　　　　　　　　Teenage immigrants
　　　　　　　　　　Women immigrants

Subtopic —— Employment
　　　　　　　　USE Alien labor
　　　— Housing *(May Subd Geog)*
Recommended —— Great Britain
keywords —— Legal status, laws, etc.
　　　　　USE Emigration and immigration law

Use keyword strategies.

The goal of a keyword search is to find quality research sources. To ensure that you identify the best resources available, follow these strategies:

Get to know the database. ■ Look for answers to these questions:

- What material does the database contain? What time frames are included?
- What are you searching—authors, titles, subjects, full text?
- What are the search rules? How can you narrow the search?

Use a shotgun approach. ■ Start with the most likely keyword. If you have no "hits," choose a related term. Once you get some hits, check the citations for clues regarding which words to use as you continue searching.

Use Boolean operators to refine your search. ■ When you combine keywords with Boolean operators—such as those below—you will obtain better results.

Boolean Operators

Narrowing a Search

And, +, not, – Use when one term gives you too many hits, especially irrelevant ones	**buffalo and bison** or **buffalo + bison**	Searches for citations containing both keywords
	buffalo not water **+buffalo –water**	Searches for "buffalo" but not "water," so that you eliminate material on water buffalo

Expanding a Search

Or Combine a term providing few hits with a related word.	**buffalo or bison**	Searches for citations containing either term

Specifying a Phrase

Quotation marks Indicate that you wish to search for the exact phrase enclosed	**"reclamation project"**	Searches for the exact phrase "reclamation project"

Sequencing Operations

Parentheses Indicate that the operation should be performed before other operations in the search string	**(buffalo or bison) and ranching**	Searches first for citations containing either "buffalo" or "bison" before checking the resulting citations for "ranching"

Finding Variations

Wild card symbols Depending on the database, symbols such as $, ?, or # can find variations of a word	**ethic#** **ethic$**	Searches for terms like *ethics* and *ethical*

Engaging and Evaluating Sources

Using reliable benchmarks, you should test all sources before you rely on them in your writing. After all, credible sources help your own credibility; sources that aren't credible destroy it. The benchmarks on the next four pages will help you test your sources' usefulness and reliability.

Engage your sources.

Engaged reading is the opposite of passive reading—treating all sources equally, swallowing whole what's in the material, or looking only for information that supports your opinion. Full engagement involves these practices:

Test each source to see if it's worth reading. When reviewing source citations and generating a working bibliography, study titles, descriptions, lengths, and publication dates, asking these questions:

- How closely related to my topic is this source?
- Is this source too basic, overly complex, or just right?
- What could this source add to my overall balance of sources?

If you were writing on NASA's space shuttle program, for example, you might find a ten-page article in *Scientific American* more valuable and insightful than a brief news article on a specific flight or a *Star Trek* fan's blog on the topic.

INSIGHT: Don't reject a source simply because it disagrees with your perspective. Good research engages rather than ignores opposition.

Skim sources before reading in-depth. Consider marking key pages or passages with sticky notes, tabs, or a digital bookmark.

- Review the author biography, preface, and/or introduction to discover the perspective, approach, scope, and research methods.
- Using your keywords, review any outline, abstract, table of contents, index, or home page to get a sense of coverage.

Read with an open but not an empty mind. Carry on a dialogue with the source, asking questions like "Why?" and "So what?"

- Note the source's purpose and audience. Was the piece written to inform or persuade? Is it aimed at the general public or specialists, at supporters or opponents?
- Read to understand the source: What's clear and what's confusing?
- Relate the source to your research question: How does the source affirm or challenge your ideas? Synthesize what you read with what you know.
- Record your reactions to it—what it makes you think, feel, believe.
- Consider how you might use this source in your writing—for background, key facts, important ideas, opposing perspectives, or examples.
- Check footnotes, references, appendices, and links for further research leads.

Rate source reliability and depth.

You should judge each source on its own merit. Generally, however, types of sources can be rated for depth and reliability, as shown in the table below, based on their authorship, length, topic treatment, documentation, publication method, review process, distance from primary sources, allegiances, stability, and so on. Use the table to

1. target sources that fit your project's goals,

2. assess the approximate quality of the sources you're gathering, and

3. build a strong bibliography that readers will respect.

Deep, Reliable, Credible Sources

Scholarly Books and Articles: largely based on careful research; written by experts for experts; address topics in depth; involve peer review and careful editing; offer stable discussion of topic

Trade Books and Journal Articles: largely based on careful research; written by experts for educated general audience. *Sample periodicals: Atlantic Monthly, Scientific American, Nature, Orion*

Government Resources: books, reports, webpages, guides, statistics developed by experts at government agencies; provided as service to citizens; relatively objective. *Sample source: Statistical Abstract of the United States*

Reviewed Official Online Documents: Internet resources posted by legitimate institutions—colleges and universities, research institutes, service organizations; although offering a particular perspective, sources tend to be balanced

Reference Works and Textbooks: provide general and specialized information; carefully researched, reviewed, and edited; lack depth for focused research (e.g., general encyclopedia entry)

News and Topical Stories from Quality Sources: provide current affairs coverage (print and online), introduction-level articles of interest to general public; may lack depth and length. *Sample sources:* the *Washington Post,* the *New York Times; Time, Psychology Today;* NPR's *All Things Considered*

Popular Magazine Stories: short, introductory articles often distant from primary sources and without documentation; heavy advertising. *Sample sources: Glamour, Seventeen, Reader's Digest*

Business and Nonprofit Publications: pamphlets, reports, news releases, brochures, manuals; range from informative to sales-focused

List Server Discussions, Usenet Postings, Blog Articles, Talk Radio Discussions: highly open, fluid, undocumented, untested exchanges and publications; unstable resource

Shallow, Unreliable, Not Credible Sources

Unregulated Web Material: personal sites, joke sites, chat rooms, special interest sites, advertising and junk e-mail (spam); no review process, little accountability, biased presentation

Tabloid Articles (print and web): contain exaggerated and untrue stories written to titillate and exploit. *Sample source:* the *National Enquirer,* the *Weekly World News*

Web Link

Evaluate print and online sources.

As you work with a source, you need to test its reliability. The benchmarks that follow apply to both print and online sources; note, however, the additional tests offered for web sources.

Credible Author ■ An expert is an authority—someone who has mastered a subject area. Is the author an expert on this topic? What are his or her credentials, and can you confirm them? For example, an automotive engineer would be an expert on hybrid vehicle technology, whereas a celebrity in a commercial would not.

Web test: Is an author indicated? If so, are the author's credentials noted and contact information offered (for example, an e-mail address)?

Reliable Publication ■ Has the source been published by a scholarly press, a peer-reviewed professional journal, a quality trade-book publisher, or a trusted news source? Did you find this resource through a reliable search tool (for example, library catalog or database)?

Web test: What individual or group posted this page? Is the site rated by a subject directory or library organization? How stable is the site—has it been around for a while and does material remain available, or is the site "fly-by-night"? Check the site's home page, and read "About Us" pages and mission statements, looking for evidence of the organization's perspective, history, and trustworthiness.

Unbiased Discussion ■ While all sources come from a specific perspective and represent specific commitments, a biased source may be pushing an agenda in an unfair, unbalanced, incomplete manner. Watch for bias toward a certain region, country, political party, industry, gender, race, ethnic group, or religion. Be alert to connections among authors, financial backers, and the points of view shared. For example, if an author has functioned as a consultant to or a lobbyist for a particular industry or group (oil, animal rights), his or her allegiances may lead to a biased presentation of an issue.

Web test: Is the online document one-sided? Is the site nonprofit (.org), government (.gov), commercial (.com), educational (.edu), business (.biz), informational (.info), network-related (.net), or military (.mil)? Is the site U.S. or international? Is this organization pushing a cause, product, service, or belief? How do advertising or special interests affect the site? You might suspect, for example, the scientific claims of a site sponsored by a pro-smoking organization.

> ***Web Link:*** Beware especially of masquerade sites—those that appear to be legitimate but are joke sites or, worse, propaganda lures. Check, for example, <www.dhmo.org>.

Current Information ■ A five-year-old book on computers may be outdated, but a forty-year-old book on Abraham Lincoln could still be the best source. Given what you need, is this source's discussion up-to-date?

Web test: When was the material originally posted and last updated? Are links live or dead?

Accurate Information ■ Bad research design, poor reporting, and sloppy documentation can lead to inaccurate information. Check the source for factual errors, statistical flaws, and conclusions that don't add up.

Web test: Is the site information-rich or -poor—filled with helpful, factual materials or fluffy with thin, unsubstantiated opinions? Can you trace and confirm sources by following links or conducting your own search?

Full, Logical Support ■ Is the discussion of the topic reasonable, balanced, and complete? Are claims backed up with quality evidence? Does the source avoid faulty assumptions, twisted statistical analysis, logical fallacies, and unfair persuasion tactics? (See "Strategies for Argument and Persuasion," pages 247–262, for help.)

Web test: Does the webpage offer well-supported claims and helpful links to additional information?

Quality Writing and Design ■ Is the source well written? Is it free of sarcasm, derogatory terms, clichés, catch phrases, mindless slogans, grammar slips, and spelling errors? Generally, poor writing correlates with sloppy thinking.

Web test: Are words neutral ("conservative perspective") or emotionally charged ("fascist agenda")? Are pages well-designed—with clear rather than flashy, distracting multimedia elements? Is the site easy to navigate?

Positive Relationship with Other Sources ■ Does the source disagree with other sources? If yes, is the disagreement about the facts themselves or about how to interpret the facts? Which source seems more credible?

Web test: Is the site's information logically consistent with print sources? Do other reputable sites offer links to this site?

INSIGHT: Engage and evaluate visual resources as thoroughly as verbal materials. For example, ask yourself what tables, graphs, and photos really "say":

- Is the graphic informative or merely decorative?
- Does the graphic create a valid or manipulative central idea? For example, does the image seek to bypass logic by appealing to sexual impulses or to crude stereotypes?
- What does the graphic include and exclude in terms of information?
- Is the graphic well-designed and easy to understand, or is it cluttered and distorted?
- Is a reliable source provided?

For more instruction on critical viewing, see pages 12–13.

Creating a Working Bibliography

A working bibliography lists sources you have used and intend to use. It helps you track your research, develop your final bibliography, and avoid plagiarism. Here's what to do:

Choose an orderly method.

Select an efficient approach for your project:

- **Paper note cards:** Use 3 × 5 inch cards, and record one source per card.
- **Paper notebook:** Use a small, spiral-bound book to record sources.
- **Computer program:** Record source information electronically, either by capturing citation details from online searches or by recording bibliographic information using word-processing software or research software such as TakeNote, EndNote Plus, or Bookends Pro.

Including Identifying Information for Sources

Start by giving each source a code number or letter: Doing so will help you when drafting and documenting your paper. Then include specific details for each kind of source listed below, shown on the facing page.

a) **Books:** author, title and subtitle, publication details (place, publisher, date)

b) **Periodicals:** author, article title, journal name, publication information (volume, number, date), page numbers

c) **Online sources:** author (if available), document title, site sponsor, database name, publication or posting date, access date, other publication information, URL

d) **Primary or field research:** date conducted, name and/or descriptive title of person interviewed, place observed, survey conducted, document analyzed

INSIGHT: Consider recording bibliographic details in the format of the documentation system you are using—MLA (pages **495–536**) or APA (pages **537–566**), for example. Doing so now will save time later. In addition, some research software allows you to record bibliographic information and then format it according to a specific system.

Adding Locating Information

Because you may need to retrace your research footsteps, include details about your research path:

a) **Books:** Include the Library of Congress or Dewey call number.

b) **Articles:** Note where and how you accessed them (stacks, current periodicals, microfilm, database)

c) **Webpages:** Record the complete URL, not just the broader site address.

d) **Field research:** Include a telephone number or e-mail address.

Annotating the Source

Add a note about the source's content, focus, reliability, and usefulness.

Sample Working Bibliography Entries

A. Book Source Note:

> #2
>
> Mackey, Sandra. *The Reckoning: Iraq and the Legacy of Saddam Hussein.* New York: W.W. Norton, 2002.
>
> 953.82
>
> Author presents case for America not to destroy Hussein. A lot of historical info on Iraq.

B. Periodical Source Note:

> #5
>
> Cortright, David, and George A. Lopez. "Are Sanctions Just? The Problematic Case of Iraq." *Journal of International Affairs* 52:2 (Spring 1999): 735–755.
>
> Bound periodicals
>
> Quality academic source with good discussion of the political and moral issues involved in the sanctions.

C. Internet Source Note:

> #3
>
> Capaccio, George. "Suffer the Little Children." *Iraq Action Coalition.* 12 March 2002.
>
> http://iraqaction.org/suffer.html
>
> Details efforts of relief workers in Iraq.

D. Interview Source Note:

> #4
>
> Capaccio, George. E-mail interview. 7 April 2002.
>
> jsmith@orc.com, 607-763-8855
>
> E-mail correspondence with author of article "Suffer the Little Children."

Developing a Note-Taking System

Accurate, thoughtful notes create a foundation for your research writing. The trick is to practice some sensible strategies and choose an efficient system.

Develop note-taking strategies.

What are you trying to do when you take notes on sources? What you are NOT doing is (a) collecting quotations to plunk in your project, (b) piling isolated grains of data into a large stack of disconnected facts, or (c) intensively reading and taking notes on every source you find. Instead, use these strategies:

Be selective ■ Guided by your research questions and working thesis, focus on sources that are central to your project. From these sources, record information clearly related to your limited topic, but also take notes on what surprises or puzzles you. Be moderate and selective, avoiding notes that are either too meager or too extensive. Suppose, for example, that you were writing a paper on the engineering problems facing NASA's space shuttle. If you were reading an article on the history and the future of this program, you might take careful notes on material describing the shuttle's technical details, but not on the experiences of astronauts in space.

Develop accurate, complete records ■ Your notes should . . .

- accurately summarize, paraphrase, and quote from sources (pages **444–446**).
- clearly show where you got your information.
- cover all the research you've done—primary research (interviews, observations, etc.), books and periodical articles, and online sources.

Engage your sources ■ Constantly evaluate what you are reading and develop your own responses and ideas. (See pages **4–11**.) For example, with an article about NASA's space shuttle, you might test the author's biases, credentials, and logic; and you might respond with knowledge you have gained about other space programs.

INSIGHT: Take good notes on graphics in sources—tables, line graphs, photographs, maps, and so on. Such graphics are typically packed with information and powerfully convey ideas. (See "Critical Thinking Through Viewing," pages **12–17**.)

Note-Taking Systems

A good note-taking system should help you do the following:

- Avoid unintentional plagiarism by developing accurate records, distinguishing among sources, and separating source material from your own ideas.
- Work efficiently at gathering what you need for the project.
- Work flexibly with a wide range of resources—primary and secondary, print and electronic, verbal and visual.
- Engage sources through creative and critical reflection.
- Record summaries, paraphrases, and quotations correctly.

- Be accurate and complete so that you need not reread sources.
- Efficiently develop your paper's outline and first draft.

INSIGHT: Different disciplines use different note-taking practices. In your major, learn these practices through courses that introduce you to the subject matter. Here are two examples:

- In literature studies, students conduct literary analyses by annotating print texts. Students may also take notes through keyword searches of Ebooks (for example, a Shakespeare play) and reviews of literary criticism.
- In environmental studies, students conduct research by (a) taking notes on published research to develop literature reviews, and (b) using a standard field notebook to collect data, make drawings, and reflect on results.

Four note-taking systems are outlined on the pages that follow. Choose the system that works best for your project, or combine elements to develop your own.

System 1: Paper or electronic note cards. Using paper note cards is the traditional method of note taking; however, note-taking software is now available with most word-processing programs and special programs like TakeNote, EndNote Plus, and Bookends Pro. Here's how a note-card system works:

1. Establish one set of cards (3 x 5 inches, if paper) for your working bibliography.

2. On a second set of cards (4 x 6 inches, if paper), take notes on sources:
   - Record one point from one source per card.
   - Clarify the source: List the author's last name, a shortened title, or a code from the matching bibliography card. Include a page number.
   - Provide a topic or heading: Called a slug, the topic helps you categorize and order information.
   - Label the note as a summary, paraphrase, or quotation of the original.
   - Distinguish between the source's information and your own thoughts.

Slug ————	① PROBLEMS WITH INTERNAL-COMBUSTION CARS
Quotation ————	"In one year, the average gas-powered car produces five tons of carbon dioxide, which as it slowly builds up in the atmosphere causes global warming." (p. 43)
Page Number ————	-helpful fact about the extent of pollution caused by the traditional i-c engine
Comments ————	-how does this number compare with what a hybrid produces?
Source ————	#7

Upside: Note cards are highly systematic, helping you categorize material and organize it for an outline and first draft.

Downside: The method can be initially tedious and time-consuming.

System 2: Copy (or save) and annotate. The copy-and-annotate method involves working with photocopies, print versions, or digital texts of sources. Here's how:

1. Selectively photocopy, print, and/or save important sources. Copy carefully, making sure you have full pages, including page number.

2. As needed, add identifying information on the copy—author, publication details, and date. Each page should be easy to identify and trace. When working with books, simply copy the title and copyright pages and keep them with the rest of your notes.

3. As you read, mark up the copy and highlight key statements. In the margins or digital file, record your ideas:
   - Ask questions. Insert a "?" in the margin, or write out the question.
   - Make connections. Draw arrows to link ideas, or make notes like "see page 36."
   - Add asides. Record what you think and feel while reading.
   - Define terms. Note important words that you need to understand.
   - Create a marginal index. Write keywords to identify themes and main parts.

Upside: Copying, printing, and/or saving helps you record sources accurately; annotating encourages careful reading and thinking.

Downside: Organizing material for drafting is inconvenient; when done poorly, annotating and highlighting involve skimming, not critical thinking.

For a sample of annotation in action, see page **7**.

System 3: The computer notebook or research log. The computer notebook or research log method involves taking notes on a computer or on sheets of paper. Here's how it works:

1. Establish a central location for your notes—a notebook, file folder, binder, or electronic folder.

2. Take notes one source at a time, making sure to identify the source fully. Number your note pages.

3. Using your initials or some other symbol, distinguish your own thoughts from source material.

4. Use codes in your notes to identify which information in the notes relates to which topic in your outline. Then, under each topic in the outline, write the page number in your notes where that information is recorded. With a notebook or log, you may be able to rearrange your notes into an outline by using copy and paste—but don't lose source information in the process!

Upside: Taking notes feels natural without being overly systematic.

Downside: Outlining and drafting may require time-consuming paper shuffling.

System 4: The double-entry notebook. The double-entry notebook involves parallel note taking—notes from sources beside your own brainstorming, reaction, and reflection. Using a notebook or the columns feature of your word-processing program, do the following:

1. Divide pages in half vertically.

2. In the left column, record bibliographic information and take notes on sources.

3. In the right column, write your responses. Think about what the source is saying, why the point is important, whether you agree with it, and how the point relates to other ideas and other sources.

Upside: This method creates accurate source records while encouraging thoughtful responses; also, it can be done on a computer.

Downside: Organizing material for drafting may be a challenge.

Cortright, David, and George A. Lopez. "Are Sanctions Just? The Problematic Case of Iraq." *Journal of International Affairs* 52.2 (1999): 735–755.	*Cortright and Lopez really get to the heart of the problem, which is a terrible irony in a way. The sanctions are an effective way to pressure a nation into stopping terrible behavior.*
Sanctions have become a common UN policy tool for resolving disputes. (735)	
"Although often intended to protect human rights, sanctions may contribute to the further deterioration of the human rights situation in a target nation." (735)	*The problem is that these sanctions often end up hurting some of the people they're meant to help—the average people suffering under unjust governments.*
The sanctions often affect the average person, not the political leaders causing the problem. (735–736)	*That's the challenge—how to make sanctions work without making the situation worse.*
Sanctions work as a "middle ground between mere diplomatic protest and ultimate military force." (736)	*Question: How do sanctions relate to diplomacy and military action?*
The sanctions situation is complicated by the way the UN implements them. Sanctions are largely in the hands of the members of the Security Council because they can block changes or push their own agenda. (736–737)	*I didn't realize that the Security Council (including America) had so much power. In what ways is power a central issue both in the UN and in Iraq? What are the motives behind the power?*

Summarizing, Paraphrasing, and Quoting Source Material

As you work with sources, you must decide what to put in your notes and how to record it—as a summary, a paraphrase, or a quotation. Use these guidelines:

- How relevant is the passage to your research question or working thesis?
- How strong and important is the information offered?
- How unique or memorable is the thinking or phrasing?

The more relevant, the stronger, and the more memorable the material is, the more likely you should note it.

The passage below comes from an article on GM's development of fuel-cell technology. Review the passage; study how the researcher summarizes, paraphrases, and quotes from the source; and then practice these same strategies as you take notes on sources.

INSIGHT: Whenever possible, include a page number, paragraph number, or other locating detail with your paraphrase, summary, or quotation. Such identification at this stage is crucial to avoiding plagiarism down the road (see pages **488–491**).

From Burns, L.D., McCormick, J.B., and Borroni-Bird, C.E. "Vehicle of Change." *Scientific American* **287:4 (October 2002): 10 pp.**

When Karl Benz rolled his Patent Motorcar out of the barn in 1886, he literally set the wheels of change in motion. The advent of the automobile led to dramatic alterations in people's way of life as well as the global economy—transformations that no one expected at the time. The ever increasing availability of economical personal transportation remade the world into a more accessible place while spawning a complex industrial infrastructure that shaped modern society.

Now another revolution could be sparked by automotive technology: one fueled by hydrogen rather than petroleum. Fuel cells—which cleave hydrogen atoms into protons and electrons that drive electric motors while emitting nothing worse than water vapor—could make the automobile much more environmentally friendly. Not only could cars become cleaner, they could also become safer, more comfortable, more personalized—and even perhaps less expensive. Further, these fuel-cell vehicles could be instrumental in motivating a shift toward a "greener" energy economy based on hydrogen. As that occurs, energy use and production could change significantly. Thus, hydrogen fuel-cell cars and trucks could help ensure a future in which personal mobility—the freedom to travel independently—could be sustained indefinitely, without compromising the environment or depleting the earth's natural resources.

A confluence of factors makes the big change seem increasingly likely. For one, the petroleum-fueled internal-combustion engine (ICE), as highly refined, reliable and economical as it is, is finally reaching its limits. Despite steady improvements, today's ICE vehicles are only 20 to 25 percent efficient in converting the energy content of fuels into drive-wheel power. And although the U.S. auto industry has cut exhaust emissions substantially since the unregulated 1960s—hydrocarbons dropped by 99 percent, carbon monoxide by 96 percent and nitrogen oxides by 95 percent—the continued production of carbon dioxide causes concern because of its potential to change the planet's climate.

Summarize useful passages.

Summarizing condenses in your own words the main points in a passage. Summarize when the source provides relevant ideas and information on your topic.

1. Reread the passage, jotting down a few keywords.

2. State the main point in your own words. Add key supporting points, leaving out examples, details, and long explanations. Be objective: Don't mix your reactions with the summary.

3. Check your summary against the original, making sure that you use quotation marks around any exact phrases you borrow.

Sample Summary:

While the introduction of the car in the late nineteenth century has led to dramatic changes in society and world economics, another dramatic change is now taking place in the shift from gas engines to hydrogen technologies. Fuel cells may make the car "greener," and perhaps even safer, cheaper, and more comfortable. These automotive changes will affect the energy industry by making it more environmentally friendly; as a result, people will continue to enjoy mobility while transportation moves to renewable energy. One factor leading to this technological shift is that the internal-combustion engine has reached the limits of its efficiency, potential, and development—while remaining problematic with respect to emissions, climate change, and health.

Paraphrase key passages.

Paraphrasing puts a whole passage in your own words. Paraphrase passages that present important points, explanations, or arguments but that don't contain memorable or straightforward wording. Follow these steps:

1. Quickly review the passage to get a sense of the whole, and then go through the passage carefully, sentence by sentence.
   - State the ideas in your own words, defining words as needed.
   - If necessary, edit for clarity, but don't change the meaning.
   - If you borrow phrases directly, put them in quotation marks.

2. Check your paraphrase against the original for accurate tone and meaning.

Sample Paraphrase of the Second Paragraph in the Passage:

Automobile technology may lead to another radical economic and social change through the shift from gasoline to hydrogen fuel. By breaking hydrogen into protons and electrons so that the electrons run an electric motor with only the by-product of water vapor, fuel cells could make the car a "green" machine. But this technology could also increase the automobile's safety, comfort, personal tailoring, and affordability. Moreover, this shift to fuel-cell engines in automobiles could lead to drastic, environmentally friendly changes in the broader energy industry, one that will be now tied to hydrogen rather than fossil fuels. The result from this shift will be radical changes in the way we use and produce energy. In other words, the shift to hydrogen-powered vehicles could promise to maintain society's valued mobility, while the clean technology would preserve the environment and its natural resources.

Quote crucial phrases, sentences, and passages.

Quoting records statements or phrases in the original source word for word. Quote nuggets only—statements that are well phrased or authoritative:

1. Note the quotation's context—how it fits in the author's discussion.

2. Copy the passage word for word, enclosing it in quotation marks and checking its accuracy.

3. If you omit words, note that omission with an ellipsis. If you change any word for grammatical reasons, put changes in brackets. (See page **491**).

Sample Quotations:

"[H]ydrogen fuel-cell cars and trucks could help ensure a future in which personal mobility . . . could be sustained indefinitely, without compromising the environment or depleting the earth's natural resources."

Note: This sentence captures the authors' main claim about the benefits and future of fuel-cell technology.

"[T]he petroleum-fueled internal-combustion engine (ICE), as highly refined, reliable and economical as it is, is finally reaching its limits."

Note: This quotation offers a well-phrased statement about the essential problem.

INSIGHT: Whether you are summarizing, paraphrasing, or quoting, aim to be true to the source by respecting the context and spirit of the original. Avoid shifting the focus or ripping material out of its context and forcing it into your own. For example, in the sample passage the authors discuss the limits of the internal-combustion engine. If you were to claim that these authors are arguing that the internal-combustion engine was an enormous engineering and environmental mistake, you would be twisting their comments to serve your own writing agenda.

For instruction on effectively integrating quotations, paraphrases, and summaries into your writing, see pages **488–491**.

Avoiding Unintentional Plagiarism

Careful note taking helps prevent unintentional plagiarism. Plagiarism—using source material without giving credit—is treated more fully elsewhere (pages 478–481); essentially, however, unintentional plagiarism happens when you accidentally use a source's ideas, phrases, or information without documenting that material. At the planning stage of your project, you can prevent this problem from happening by adhering to principles of ethical research and following some practical guidelines.

Practice the principles of ethical research.

Because of the nature of information and the many challenges of working with it, conducting ethical research can be very complex and involved. To start with, however, commit to these principles of ethical research:

- Do the research and write the paper yourself.
- Adhere to the research practices approved in your discipline.
- Follow school- and discipline-related guidelines for working with people, resources, and technology.
- Avoid one-sided research that ignores or conceals opposition.
- Present real, accurate data and results—not "fudged" or twisted facts.
- Treat source material fairly in your writing.

Practices That Prevent Unintentional Plagiarism

The principles of ethical research above find expression when you prevent unintentional plagiarism. Do so by following these practices:

- Maintain an accurate working bibliography (pages 438–439).
- When taking notes, distinguish source material from your own reflection by using quotation marks, codes, and/or separate columns or note cards.
- When you draft your paper, transfer source material carefully by coding material that you integrate into your discussion, using quotation marks, double-checking your typing, or using copy and paste to ensure accuracy.
- Take time to do the project right—both research and writing. Avoid pulling an all-nighter during which you can't properly work with sources.

Practices That Prevent Internet Plagiarism

An especially thorny area related to unintentional plagiarism centers on the Internet. As with traditional print sources, Internet sources must be properly credited; in other words, web material cannot simply be transferred to your paper without acknowledgement. So treat web sources like print sources. And if you copy and paste digital material while taking notes and drafting, always track the origins with codes, abbreviations, or separate columns.

Writing Checklist

Use the checklist below to test how well you have gotten started on any given research project.

_____ I have clarified my assignment: the purpose, readers, and resources.

_____ I have selected an appropriate topic, conducted preliminary research, narrowed my focus, and developed a key research question or a clear working thesis.

_____ I have chosen research methods and gotten organized to do my research effectively.

_____ I have considered the range of resources and possible research sites available for my project.

_____ I have established and used a note-taking system that effectively keeps track of research resources, helps me gather key ideas and information from these sources, and encourages me to do my own thinking.

_____ I have carefully engaged and evaluated all my sources.

_____ I have sensibly summarized, paraphrased, and quoted useful sources in my notes.

_____ I have taken careful notes in order to prevent unintentional plagiarism.

Writing Activities

1. Write a research report about your major area of study. Discuss the types of knowledge the major explores and the professions to which it leads. Address the paper to students considering this major.

2. For a current research project, find and list 15 to 20 available sources on your topic. Visit libraries to locate books, articles, and so forth. Use a search engine and locate sources on the web. Finally, list any interviews, observations, surveys, and questionnaires that you might set up.

3. Test the reliability of one of your Internet sources for a current research project. Refer to the "web test" questions on pages **436–437**, and see if you can answer all of them. Based on your answers, decide whether the source is credible enough to strengthen your paper.

4. Choose a short article or passage from one of your sources. Restate (paraphrase) what you have read using your own words. Put quotation marks around keywords and phrases that you take directly from the text. Next, use the same materials to create a summary. Reduce what you just read to a few clear and important points using your own words.

Chapter 30
Conducting Primary and Library Research

Today, conducting research is both easy and difficult. It's easy because research technology is powerful and many research methods are available. It's difficult because that technology and those methods provide access to so much information—the good, the bad, and the ugly.

How do you meet this challenge and conduct quality research? First, consider whether your project would benefit from primary research. When you engage in primary research, you gather information firsthand by observing sites, interviewing people, and analyzing documents. Second, learn how to use an expert resource—your college library. The library is your gateway to print and electronic materials.

What's Ahead

- Primary and Secondary Sources
- Conducting Primary Research
- Using the Library
- Using Books in Research
- Finding Periodical Articles
- Checklist and Writing Activities

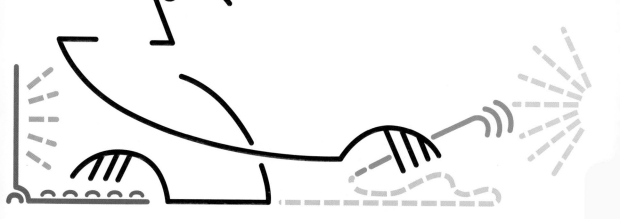

Primary and Secondary Sources

Information sources for your research project can be either primary or secondary. Depending on your assignment, you may be expected to use one or both kinds of sources.

Consider primary sources.

A primary source is an original source, which gives firsthand information on a topic. This source (such as a diary, a person, or an event) informs you directly about the topic, rather than through another person's explanation or interpretation. The most common forms of primary research are observations, interviews, surveys, experiments, and analyses of original documents and artifacts.

Consider secondary sources.

Secondary sources present secondhand information on your topic—information at least once removed from the original. This information has been compiled, summarized, analyzed, synthesized, interpreted, or evaluated by someone studying primary sources. Journal articles, encyclopedia entries, documentaries, and nonfiction books are typical examples of such secondary sources.

Example: Below are possible primary and secondary sources for a research project exploring hybrid car technology and its viability.

Primary Sources	Secondary Sources
E-mail interview with automotive engineer	Journal article discussing the development of hybrid car technology
Fuel-efficiency legislation	Newspaper editorial on fossil fuels
Visit and test-drive a car at a dealership	TV news roundtable discussion of hybrid car advantages and disadvantages
Published statistics about hybrid car sales	Automobile manufacturer promotional literature for a specific hybrid car

Whether a source is primary or secondary depends on what you are studying. For example, if you were studying U.S. attitudes toward hybrid cars (and not hybrid car technology itself), the newspaper editorial and TV roundtable would be primary sources.

Conducting Primary Research

When published sources can't give you the information that you need, consider conducting primary research. However, you must first weigh all its advantages and disadvantages.

Upside of Primary Research

- It produces information precisely tailored to your research needs.
- It gives you direct, hands-on access to your topic.

Downside of Primary Research

- It can take a lot of time and many resources to complete.
- It can require special skills, such as designing surveys and analyzing statistics and original documents.

Conduct primary research.

You need to choose the method of primary research that best suits your project. For help, review the following descriptions:

1. **Surveys and questionnaires** gather written responses you can review, tabulate, and analyze. These research tools pull together varied information—from simple facts to personal opinions and attitudes. See "Conduct Surveys" on the following page.

2. **Interviews** involve consulting two types of people. First, you can interview experts for their insights on your topic. Second, you can interview people whose direct experiences with the topic give you their personal insights. See "Conduct Interviews," page **456**, and "Interview Reports," pages **333–340**.

3. **Observations, inspections, and field research** require you to examine and analyze people, places, events, and so on. Whether you rely simply on your five senses or use scientific techniques, observing provides insights into the present state of your subject. See "Observation Reports," pages **319–332**.

4. **Experiments** test hypotheses—predictions about why things do what they do—to arrive at conclusions that can be accepted and acted upon. Such testing often explores cause/effect relationships. See "Experiment, Lab, and Field Reports," pages **341–354**.

5. **Analysis of documents and artifacts** involves studying original reports, statistics, legislation, literature, artwork, and historical records. Such analysis provides unique, close-up interpretations of your topic. See "Analyze Texts, Documents, Records, and Artifacts" on pages **454–455**, as well as "Writing About Literature and the Arts," pages **357–374**.

Conduct surveys.

One source of primary information that you can use for research projects is a survey or questionnaire. Surveys can collect facts and opinions from a wide range of people about virtually any topic. To get valid information, follow these guidelines:

1. Find a focus.
- Limit the purpose of your survey.
- Target a specific audience.

2. Ask clear questions.
- Phrase questions so they can be easily understood.
- Use words that are objective (not biased or slanted).

3. Match your questions to your purpose.
- Closed questions give respondents easy-answer options, and the answers are easy to tabulate. Closed questions can provide two choices (*yes* or *no*, *true* or *false*), multiple choices, a rating scale (*poor 1 2 3 excellent*), or a blank to fill.
- Open-ended questions bring in a wide variety of responses and more complex information, but they take time to complete, and the answers can be difficult to summarize.

4. Organize your survey so that it's easy to complete.
- In the introduction, state who you are and why you need the information. Explain how to complete the survey and when and where to return it.
- Guide readers by providing numbers, instructions, and headings.
- Begin with basic questions and end with any complex, open-ended questions that are necessary. Move in a logical order from one topic to the next.

5. Test your survey before using it.
- Ask a friend or classmate to read your survey and help you revise it, if necessary, before printing it.
- Try out your survey with a small test group.

6. Conduct your survey.
- Distribute the survey to a clearly defined group that won't prejudice the sampling (random or cross section).
- Get responses from a good sample of your target group (10 percent if at all possible).
- Tabulate responses carefully and objectively.
  Note: To develop statistically valid results, you may need expert help. Check with your instructor.

Sample Survey

Confidential Survey

The introduction includes the essential information about the survey.

My name is Cho Lang, and I'm conducting research about the use of training supplements. I'd like to hear from you, Alfred University's athletes. Please answer the questions below by circling or writing out your responses. Return your survey to me, care of the Dept. of Psychology, through campus mail by Friday, April 5. Your responses will remain confidential.

The survey begins with clear, basic questions.

1. Circle your gender. **Male**   **Female**

2. Circle your year.
   Freshman   **Sophomore**   **Junior**   **Senior**

3. List the sports that you play.

4. Are you presently using a training supplement?
   Yes   **No**
   Note: If you circled "no," you may turn in your survey at this point.

The survey asks an open-ended question.

5. Describe your supplement use (type, amount, and frequency).

6. Who supervises your use of this training supplement?
   Coach   **Trainer**   **Self**   **Others**

7. How long have you used it?
   Less than 1 month   **1–12 months**
   12+ months

The survey covers the topic thoroughly.

8. How many pounds have you gained while using this supplement?

9. How much has your athletic performance improved?
   None   1   2   3   4   5   **Greatly**

10. Circle any side effects you've experienced.
    Dehydration   **Nausea**   **Diarrhea**

Analyze texts, documents, records, and artifacts.

An original document or record is one that relates directly to the event, issue, object, or phenomenon you are researching. Examining original documents and artifacts can involve studying letters, e-mail exchanges, case notes, literary texts, sales records, legislation, and material objects such as tools, sculptures, buildings, and tombs. As you analyze such documents and records, you examine evidence in order to understand a topic, arrive at a coherent conclusion about it, and support that judgment. How do you work with such diverse documents, records, and artifacts? Here are guidelines:

Choose evidence close to your topic. What texts, documents, records, and artifacts originated from or grew out of the topic you are researching? The closer to the topic, the more primary the source. Select materials that are directly related to your research questions and/or working thesis.

Example: If you were studying English labor riots of the 1830s, you could investigate these primary sources:

- to understand what rioters were demanding, copies of speeches given at demonstrations
- to know who the rioters were, names from police reports or union membership lists
- to learn the political response to the riots, political speeches or legislation
- to get at the attitudes of people from that time, newspaper reports, works of art, or novels from the period
- to find people's personal stories and private opinions related to the riots, personal letters, diaries, family albums, gravestones, and funeral eulogies

Frame your examination with questions. To make sense of the text, document, record, or artifact, understand what you are looking for and why. List the secondary questions that you want to answer in relation to the main question behind your research project.

Example: To study the legislative background behind the development of cleaner cars, such as the hybrid-fuel vehicle, you could access various documents on the Clean Air Act of 1990 (for example, *The Plain English Guide to the Clean Air Act*, an EPA publication). As you study this legislation, you could frame your reading with these additional questions:

- What are the requirements of the Clean Air Act?
- Specifically, how do those requirements affect automotive technology?
- What private and public research projects will likely impact these requirements?
- Are schedules for change or deadlines written into the Act?

Put the document or artifact in context. So that the material takes on meaning, clarify its external and internal natures. First, consider its external context—the five W's and H: What exactly is it? Who made it, when, where, why, and how? Second, consider its internal nature—what the document means, based on what it can and cannot show you: What does the language mean or refer to? What is the document's structure? What are the artifact's composition and style?

Example: If you were examining Mary Wollstonecraft's *A Vindication of the Rights of Woman* in a history or women's studies course, you would consider the following:

- **External Context:** who Mary Wollstonecraft was; when and why she wrote *A Vindication*, and under what conditions; for whom she wrote it and their response; the type of document it is

- **Internal Context:** Wollstonecraft's essential argument and evidence; the nature of her views, their relationship to her times, and their relevance today

Draw coherent conclusions about meaning. Make sense of the source in relation to your research questions. What connections does the source reveal? What important changes or developments? What cause and effect relationships? What themes?

Example: A study of the Clean Air Act might lead you to a variety of conclusions regarding how environmental legislation relates to the development of hybrid technology—for example, that the United States must produce cleaner cars in order to gain improved air quality.

INSIGHT: Studying primary documents and artifacts is central to many disciplines: history, literature, theology, philosophy, political studies, and archaeology, for example. Good analysis depends on asking research questions appropriate for the discipline. With the English labor riots of the 1830s again as an example, here's what two disciplines might ask:

- **Political science:** What role did political theories, structures, and processes play in the riots—both in causing and in responding to them?

- **Art:** How were the concerns of the rioters embodied in the new "realist" style of the mid-1800s? Did artists sympathize with and address an alienated working-class audience? How did art comment on the social structures of the time?

- **Sociology:** What type and quality of education did most workers have in the 1830s? How did that education impact their economic status and employment opportunities? Did issues related to the riots prompt changes in the English educational system? What changes and why?

With these examples in mind, consider your own major: What questions would this discipline ask of the English labor riots, of Mary Wollstonecraft's *A Vindication of the Rights of Woman*, or of the Clean Air Act of 1990?

Conduct interviews.

The purpose of an interview is simple. To get information, you talk with some-one who has significant experience or someone who is an expert on your topic. Use the guidelines below whenever you conduct an interview. (See also pages 333–340.)

1. **Before the interview,** do your homework about the topic and the person you are planning to interview.

   - Arrange the interview in a thoughtful way. Explain to the interviewee your purpose and the topics to be covered.
   - Think about the specific ideas you want to cover in the interview and write questions for each. Addressing the 5 W's and H (*Who? What? Where? When? Why?* and *How?*) is important for good coverage.
   - Organize your questions in a logical order so the interview moves smoothly from one subject to the next.
   - Write the questions on the left side of a page. Leave room for quotations, information, and impressions on the right side.

2. **During the interview,** try to relax so that your conversation is natural and sincere.

   - Provide some background information about yourself, your project, and your plans for using the interview information.
   - Use recording equipment only with the interviewee's permission.
   - Jot down key facts and quotations.
   - Listen actively. Show that you're listening through your body language—eye contact, nods, smiles. Pay attention not only to what the person says, but also to how he or she says it.

   > *Based on the interviewee's responses, ask follow-up questions, and don't limit yourself to your planned questions only.*

   - Be flexible. If the person looks puzzled by a question, rephrase it. If the discussion gets off track, redirect it. Based on the interviewee's responses, ask follow-up questions, and don't limit yourself to your planned questions only.

3. **After the interview,** do the appropriate follow-up work.

   - As soon as possible, review your notes. Fill in responses you remember but couldn't record at the time.
   - Thank the interviewee with a note, an e-mail, or a phone call.
   - If necessary, ask the interviewee to check whether your information and quotations are accurate.
   - Offer to send the interviewee a copy of your writing.

Using the Library

The library door is your gateway to information. Inside, the college library holds a wide range of research resources, from books to periodicals, from reference librarians to electronic databases.

Become familiar with the library.

To improve your ability to succeed at all your research assignments, become familiar with your college library system. Take advantage of tours and orientation sessions to learn its physical layout, resources, and services. Check your library's website for policies, tutorials, and research tools. The college library offers a variety of resources for your research projects.

Librarians ■ Librarians are information experts:

- Librarians manage the library's materials and guide you to resources.
- They help you perform online searches.

Collections ■ The library collects and houses a variety of materials:

- **Books and electronic materials**—videotapes, CD-ROMs, CDs, and DVDs
- **Periodicals**—journals, magazines, and newspapers (in print or microform)
- **Reference materials**—directories, indexes, handbooks, encyclopedias, and almanacs
- **Special collections**—government publications, historical documents, and original artifacts

Research Tools ■ The library contains many tools that direct you to materials:

- The online catalog allows you to search everything in the library.
- Print indexes and subscription databases (Lexis-Nexis, EBSCOhost, ProQuest Direct) point you to abstracts and full-text articles.
- Internet access connects you with other library catalogs and online reference.

Special Services ■ Special services may also help you to complete research projects:

- Interlibrary loan allows you to obtain books and articles not available in your library.
- "Hold" allows you to request a book that is currently signed out.
- Photocopiers, CD burners, scanners, and presentation software help you perform and share your research.

Search the catalog.

Library materials are catalogued so they are easy to find. In most college libraries, books, videos, and other holdings are catalogued in an electronic database. To find material, use book titles, author names, and related keyword searching. (See related pages **432–433**.)

Sample Electronic Catalog

◉ Keyword ○ Browse ○ Exact

```
┌─────────────────────────────────────────────┐
│                                             │
└─────────────────────────────────────────────┘
```

SEARCH EVERYTHING   AUTHOR   TITLE   SUBJECT   SERIES   PERIODICAL TITLE

1. Enter the word(s) you want to find.
   Keyword returns records *containing* the word(s) entered.
   Browse returns catalog headings *beginning* with the first word entered.
   Exact returns records that *exactly* match the word(s) entered.
2. Choose a target search field.
   Search everything targets all indexed fields within a record.
   All other choices target specified fields within a record.

When you find a citation for a book or other resource, the result will provide some or all of the following information. Use that information to determine whether the resource is worth exploring further and to figure out other avenues of research.

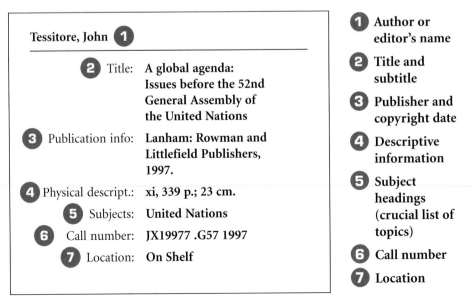

Tessitore, John **1**		
2 Title:	A global agenda: Issues before the 52nd General Assembly of the United Nations	
3 Publication info:	Lanham: Rowman and Littlefield Publishers, 1997.	
4 Physical descript.:	xi, 339 p.; 23 cm.	
5 Subjects:	United Nations	
6 Call number:	JX19977 .G57 1997	
7 Location:	On Shelf	

1 Author or editor's name

2 Title and subtitle

3 Publisher and copyright date

4 Descriptive information

5 Subject headings (crucial list of topics)

6 Call number

7 Location

Locating Resources by Call Numbers

Library of Congress (LC) call numbers combine letters and numbers to specify a resource's broad subject area, topic, and authorship or title. Finding a book, DVD, or other item involves combining both the alphabetical and the numerical order. Here is a sample call number for *Arctic Refuge: A Vanishing Wilderness?*:

VIDEO QH84.1.A72 1990

subject area (**QH**) topic number (**84**) subtopic number (**1**) cutter number (**A72**)

To find this resource in the library, first note the tab VIDEO. Although not part of the call number, this locator may send you to a specific area of the library. Once there, follow the parts of the call number one at a time:

1. Find the library section on natural history containing videos with the "QH" designation.

2. Follow the numbers until you reach "84."

3. Within the "84" items, find those with the subtopic "1."

4. Use the cutter "A72" to locate the resource alphabetically with "A," and numerically with "72."

Note: In the LC system, pay careful attention to the arrangement of subject area letters, topic numbers, and subtopic numbers: Q98 comes before QH84; QH84 before QH8245; QH84.A72 before QH84.1.A72.

Classification Systems

The LC classification system combines letters and numbers. The Dewey decimal system, used in some libraries, uses numbers only. Here is a list of the subject classes for both the LC and Dewey systems.

The Library of Congress and Dewey Decimal Systems

LC Category		Dewey Decimal	LC Category		Dewey Decimal
A	General Works	000–999	K	Law	340–349
B	Philosophy	100–199	L	Education	370–379
	Psychology	150–159	M	Music	780–789
	Religion	200–299	N	Fine Arts	700–799
C	History: Auxiliary Sciences	910–929	P	Language	800–899
D	History: General and			Literature	400–499
	Old World	930–999	Q	Science	500–599
E–F	History: American	970–979	R	Medicine	610–619
G	Geography	910–919	S	Agriculture	630–639
	Anthropology	571–573	T	Technology	600–699
	Recreation	700–799	U	Military Science	355–359, 623
H	Social Sciences	300–399	V	Naval Science	359, 623
J	Political Science	320–329	Z	Bibliography and	010–0199
				Library Science	020–029

Using Books in Research

Your college library contains a whole range of reference books for you to use. Unfortunately, for most research projects you simply don't have time to read an entire book, and rarely do the entire contents relate to your topic. Instead, use the strategy outlined below to refine your research effort.

Use a research strategy.

1. **Check out front and back information.**
   The title and copyright pages give the book's full title and subtitle; the author's name; and publication information, including publication date and Library of Congress subject headings. The back may contain a note on the author's credentials and other publications.

2. **Scan the table of contents.**
   Examine the contents page to see what the book covers and how it is organized. Ask yourself which chapters are relevant to your project.

3. **Using key words, search the index.**
   Check the index for coverage and page locations of the topics most closely related to your project. Are there plenty of pages, or just a few? Are these pages concentrated or scattered throughout the book?

4. **Skim the preface, foreword, or introduction.**
   Skimming the opening materials will often indicate the book's perspective, explain its origin, and preview its contents.

5. **Check appendices, glossaries, or bibliographies.**
   These special sections may be a good source of tables, graphics, definitions, statistics, and clues for further research.

6. **Carefully read appropriate chapters and sections.**
   Think through the material you've read and take good notes. (See pages 440–443.) Follow references to authors and other works to do further research on the topic. Study footnotes and endnotes for insights and leads.

Consider these options for working productively with books:
- When you find a helpful book, browse nearby shelves for more books.
- To confirm a book's quality, check *Book Review Digest* for a review.
- If your library subscribes to an Ebook service such as NetLibrary, you have access to thousands of books in electronic form. You can conduct electronic searches, browse or check out promising books, and read them online.

Reference Works That Supply Information

Encyclopedias supply facts and overviews for topics arranged alphabetically.

- General encyclopedias cover many fields of knowledge: *Encyclopedia Britannica, Collier's Encyclopedia.*
- Specialized encyclopedias focus on a single topic: *McGraw-Hill Encyclopedia of Science and Technology, Encyclopedia of American Film Comedy.*

Almanacs, yearbooks, and statistical resources, normally published annually, contain diverse facts.

- *The World Almanac and Book of Facts* presents information on politics, history, religion, business, social programs, education, and sports.
- *Statistical Abstract of the United States* provides data on population, geography, politics, employment, business, science, and industry.

Vocabulary resources supply information on languages.

- General dictionaries, such as *The American Heritage College Dictionary,* supply definitions and histories for a whole range of words.
- Specialized dictionaries define words common to a field, topic, or group of people: *Dictionary of Engineering, The New Harvard Dictionary of Music.*
- Bilingual dictionaries translate words from one language to another.

Biographical resources supply information about people. General biographies cover a broad range of people. Other biographies focus on people from a specific group. *Examples: Who's Who in America, Dictionary of Scientific Biography, World Artists 1980–1990.*

Directories supply contact information for people, groups, and organizations. *Examples: The National Directory of Addresses and Telephone Numbers, USPS ZIP Code Lookup and Address Information* (online), *Official Congressional Directory.*

Reference Works That Are Research Tools

Guides and handbooks help readers explore specific topics. *Examples: The Handbook of North American Indians, A Guide to Prairie Fauna.*

Indexes point you to useful resources. Some indexes are general, such as *Readers' Guide to Periodical Literature;* others are specific, such as *Environment Index* or *Business Periodicals Index.* (Many are now available online.)

Bibliographies list resources on a specific topic. A good, current bibliography can be used as an example when you compile your own bibliography on a topic.

Abstracts, like indexes, direct you to articles on a particular topic. But abstracts also summarize those materials so you learn whether a resource is relevant before you invest time in locating and reading it. Abstracts are usually organized into subject areas: Computer Abstracts, Environmental Abstracts, Social Work Abstracts. They are incorporated in many online databases.

Web Link

Finding Periodical Articles

Periodicals are publications or broadcasts produced at regular intervals (daily, weekly, monthly, quarterly). Although some periodicals are broad in their subject matter and audience, as a rule, they focus on a narrow range of topics geared toward a particular audience.

- **Daily newspapers and newscasts** provide up-to-date information on current events, opinions, and trends—from politics to natural disasters (*Wall Street Journal, USA Today, The NewsHour*).

- **Weekly and monthly magazines** generally provide more in-depth information on a wide range of topics (*Time, Newsweek, 60 Minutes*).

- **Journals,** generally published quarterly, provide specialized scholarly information for a narrowly focused audience (*English Journal, Journal of Labor Economics*).

With thousands of periodicals available, how do you find helpful articles? Learn (a) what search tools your library offers, (b) what periodicals it has available in what forms, and (c) how to gain access to those periodicals.

Search online databases.

If your library subscribes to EBSCOhost, LexisNexis, or another database service, use keyword searching (see pages **432–433**) to find citations on your topic. You might start with the general version of such databases, such as EBSCOhost's Academic Search Premier, which provides access to more than 4,100 scholarly publications covering all disciplines, or LexisNexis' News resource, which offers access to a range of articles and transcripts.

Basic Search: The example below shows an EBSCOhost search screen using Academic Search Premier for a search on hybrid electric cars. Notice how limiters, expanders, and other advanced features help you find the highest-quality materials.

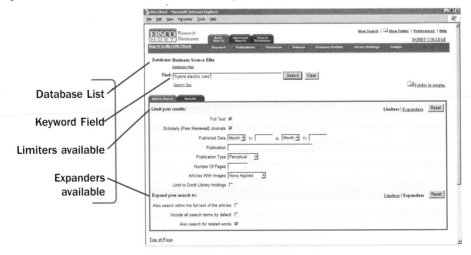

Database List

Keyword Field

Limiters available

Expanders available

Advanced Search: A more focused research strategy would involve turning to specialized databases, available for virtually every discipline and often an option within search services such as EBSCOhost (for example, Business Source Elite, PsycINFO, ERIC) and LexisNexis (for example, Legal, Medical, and Business databases). If a basic search turns up little, turn to specialized databases, seeking help from a librarian if necessary. For a list of specialized databases, see page **465**.

 Particularly if you need articles published before 1985, you may need to go to the *Readers' Guide to Periodical Literature* or another print index. While databases are beginning to convert pre-1985 articles to digital (for example, the JSTOR database), many excellent periodical articles are available only in print. To use the *Readers' Guide*, consult a librarian.

Generate citation lists of promising articles.

Your database search should generate lists of citations, brief descriptions of articles that were flagged through keywords in titles, subject terms, abstracts, and so on. For example, a search focused on hybrid electric cars leads to the results shown below. At this point, study the results and do the following:

- Refine the search by narrowing or expanding.
- Mark specific citations for "capture" or further study.
- Re-sort the results.
- Follow links in a specific citation to further information.

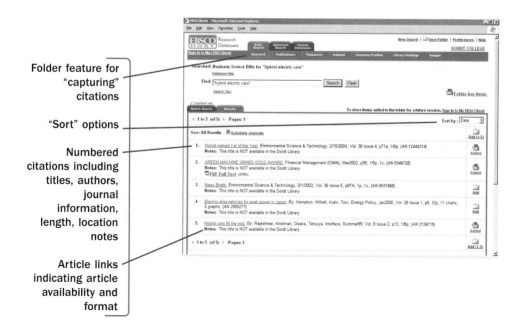

Folder feature for "capturing" citations

"Sort" options

Numbered citations including titles, authors, journal information, length, location notes

Article links indicating article availability and format

Study citations and capture identifying information.

By studying citations, especially abstracts, you can determine three things:

- Is this article relevant to your research?
- Is an electronic, full-text version available?
- If not, does the library have this periodical?

To develop your working bibliography (see pages **438–439**), you should also "capture" the article's identifying details by using the save, print, or e-mail function, or by recording the periodical's title, the issue and date, and the article's title and page numbers. These functions are shown in the EBSCOhost citation below.

Save options →

Source link for more details or full text →

Subject links for further research →

Summary with keywords highlighted →

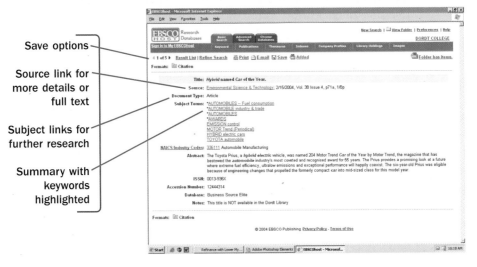

Find and retrieve the full text of the article.

When citations indicate that you have promising articles, access those articles efficiently, preferably through a direct link in the citation to an electronic copy. From there you can print, save, or e-mail the article. If the article is not available electronically, track down a print version:

- Check the online citation to see if your library has the article. If necessary, check your library's inventory of periodicals held, a list available online and/or in print. Examine especially the issues and dates available, the form (print or microfilm), and the location (bound or current shelves).

- To get the article, follow your library's procedure. You may have to submit a request slip so that a librarian can get the periodical, or you may be able to get it yourself in the current, bound, or microfilm collection. If the article is not available online or in your library, use interlibrary loan.

Databases for Disciplines

Most libraries offer you access to databases from a wide range of disciplines. Check your library's website for access to databases like these:

- **Agricola** offers citations from the National Agricultural Library group—with materials focused on issues from animal science to food and nutrition.
- **ARTbibliographies Modern** abstracts articles, books, catalogs, and other resources on modern and contemporary art.
- **CAIRSS for Music** offers bibliographic citations for articles on music-related topics, from music education to music therapy.
- **Communication & Mass Media Complete** offers access to resources on topics like public speaking and TV broadcasting.
- **Engineering E-journal Search Engine** offers free, full-text access to more than 150 online engineering journals.
- **ERIC** offers citations, abstracts, and digests for more than 980 journals in the education field.
- **First Search,** a fee-based information service, offers access to more than 30 scholarly databases in a range of disciplines.
- **GPO,** the Government Printing Office, offers access to records for U.S. government documents (reports, hearings, judicial rules, addresses, etc.).
- **Health Source** offers access to abstracts, indexing, and full-text material on health-related topics, from nutrition to sports medicine.
- **Ingenta** offers citations for over 25,000 journals, particularly in the sciences.
- **JSTOR** offers full-text access to scholarly articles in a full range of disciplines, articles once available only in print.
- **Math Database** offers access to article citations for international mathematics research.
- **Medline** offers access to journals in medicine and medicine-related disciplines through references, citations, and abstracts.
- **MLA Bibliography** provides bibliographic citations for articles addressing a range of modern-language and literature-related topics.
- **National Environmental Publications Internet Site (NEPIS)** offers access to more than 6,000 EPA documents (full text, online).
- **PsycINFO** offers access to materials in psychology and psychology-related fields (for example, social work, criminology, organizational behavior).
- **Scirus** indexes science resources, citing article titles and authors, source publication information, and lines of text indicating the article's content.
- **Vocation and Career Collection** offers full-text access to more than 400 trade- and industry-related periodicals.
- **Worldwide Political Science Abstracts** offers bibliographic citations in politics-related fields, from public policy to international law.

Checklist for Research

Use the following checklist to monitor how well you are conducting primary and library research for your project.

___ I have chosen methods of primary research that fit the assignment.

___ I have effectively prepared to do the research.

___ I have systematically and carefully gathered primary information.

___ I have followed up in fitting ways to make sense of the research results.

___ I have conducted primary research according to ethical standards.

___ I have become thoroughly familiar with my library's resources and services.

___ Using solid keyword searching strategies, I have effectively searched the library's holdings for items relevant to my topic.

___ I have tapped print and electronic reference works for information.

___ I have used my library's print and electronic periodical search tools and holdings to find relevant articles on my topic.

Writing Activities

1. For the subject "Gender Differences in Toy Preferences," indicate whether the following sources would be considered primary or secondary (P or S):

   ___ a. Observing children in a day-care setting

   ___ b. Journal article about gender-based differences in the brain

   ___ c. Magazine article about a hot new toy

   ___ d. Survey of day-care workers

   ___ e. *Boys' Toys of the Fifties and Sixties* (a book)

   ___ f. Interviews with parents

2. Indicate which section of the library would house each of the following items:

   _____ a. *JAMA (Journal of the American Medical Association)*

   _____ b. *Places Rated Almanac*

   _____ c. *Principles of Corporate Finance* (book)

   _____ d. *Merck Index: An Encyclopedia of Chemicals, Drugs, and Biologicals*

3. Obtain a map of your college library. Highlight the following areas:

- Computer card catalog(s)
- Reference books
- Nonfiction books
- Journals and magazines

Chapter 31
Conducting Research on the Internet

If you're young enough, it's probably hard for you to imagine a pre-web world, but trust us when we say that the digital revolution has radically transformed research—for good and ill. In other words, the Internet can be a great resource or a great waste of time. For researchers both young and old, the trick is developing positive e-search skills. To start with, consider the Internet's benefits and drawbacks:

Benefits

- The Internet, which is always "open," contains a wealth of current information in text, sound, and visual formats.
- Because the information is digital, it can be searched quickly and conveniently, and it can be copied, saved, and sent.

Drawbacks

- Because of the large amount and relative disorganization of material, finding relevant in-depth information requires careful digging and thoughtful evaluation of sources.
- The Internet lacks quality control: Virtually anybody can post anything.
- Surfing can encourage shallow research practices.
- The Net changes rapidly—what's here today may be gone, changed, or outdated tomorrow.
- Information access makes plagiarism—unintentional and deliberate—easy.

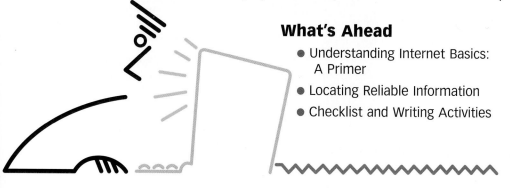

What's Ahead

- Understanding Internet Basics: A Primer
- Locating Reliable Information
- Checklist and Writing Activities

Understanding Internet Basics:
A Primer

If you're familiar with the Internet, you already understand the basics of searching this medium. However, the following questions and answers may help you do quality research on the Net.

What is the Internet?

The Internet is a worldwide network of connected local computers and computer networks that allows computers to share information with one another. For example, your college's network likely gives you access to the library, local resources, and the Internet.

What is the World Wide Web?

The **web** provides access to much of the material on the Internet. Millions of webpages are available because of **hypertext links** that connect them. These links appear as clickable icons or highlighted web addresses. A **website** is a group of related webpages posted by the same sponsor or organization. A **home page** is a website's "entry" page. A **web browser** such as Netscape, Internet Explorer, or Firefox gives you access to web resources through a variety of tools, such as directories and search engines. (**Directories** and **search engines** are special websites that provide a searchable listing of many services on the web.)

Sample Webpage:

Navigation buttons

Address bar

Title bar

Graphic link

Text links

Status bar

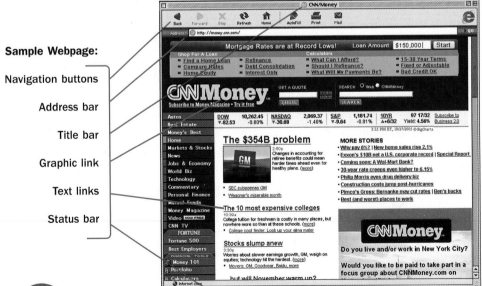

For instructions on writing for the web, see pages 399–410.

What does an Internet address mean?

An Internet address is called a URL, or Uniform Resource Locator. The address includes the protocol indicating how the computer file should be accessed—often *http:* or *ftp:* (followed by a double slash); a domain name—often beginning with *www*; and additional path information (following a single slash) to access other pages within a site.

http://www.nrcs.usda.gov/news/index.html#csp_watershed2

The domain name is a key part of the address because it indicates what type of organization created the site and gives you clues about its goal or purpose. Does the site aim to educate, inform, persuade, sell, and/or entertain? Most sites combine a primary purpose with secondary ones.

.com	**a commercial organization or business**
.gov	**a government organization—federal, state, or local**
.edu	**an educational institution**
.org	**a nonprofit organization**
.net	**an organization that is part of the Internet's infrastructure**
.mil	**a military site**
.biz	**a business site**
.info	**any site primarily providing information**

INSIGHT: International addresses generally include national abbreviations (for example, Canada = .ca). This clue helps you determine the origin of the information and communicate more sensitively on the Internet.

How can you save Internet information?

Accurately saving Internet addresses and material is an essential part of good research. Moreover, you may want to revisit sites and embed URLs in your research writing. Save Internet information through these methods:

Bookmark ▪ Your browser can save a site's address through a "bookmark" or "favorites" function on your menu bar.

Printout ▪ If a document looks promising, print a hard copy of it. Remember to write down all details needed for citing the source. (Although many details will automatically print with the document, some could be missing.)

Save or Download ▪ To keep an electronic copy of material, save the document to a specific drive on your computer. Beware of large files with many graphics: They take up a lot of space. To save just the text, highlight it, copy it, and then paste it into a word-processing program.

E-mail ▪ If you're not at your own computer, you can e-mail the document's URL to your e-mail address through copy and paste.

Locating Reliable Information

Because the Internet contains so much information of varying reliability, you need to become familiar with search tools that locate information you can trust. The key is knowing which search tool to use in which research situation.

Proceed with caution.

When it comes to doing Internet research, proceed with caution:

- Adhere to your assignment's restrictions on using websites (number and type). In fact, some instructors may not allow web resources for specific projects, limiting you to print sources and scholarly articles available in subscription databases.

- When you are using web resources, make sure the sites are sponsored by legitimate, recognizable organizations: government agencies, nonprofit groups, and educational institutions. For most projects, avoid relying on personal, commercial, and special-interest sites, as well as chat rooms and news groups. Test the quality and reliability of online information by using the benchmarks outlined on pages **434–437**.

- Avoid developing your paper based on copying and pasting together chunks of webpages. By doing so, you not only fail to engage your sources meaningfully, you also commit plagiarism. For more on plagiarism, see pages **478–481**.

Use your library's website.

Your library may sponsor a website that gives you access to quality Internet resources. For example, it may provide the following assistance:

- Tutorials on using the Internet
- Guides to Internet resources in different disciplines
- Links to online document collections (Project Gutenberg, Etext Archives, New Bartleby Digital Library, and so on)
- Connections to virtual libraries, subscription databases, search engines, directories, government documents, and online reference works

Example: Your library may give you access to WorldCat, a global catalog. If you click on the "Internet" limiter, you'll be able to search specifically for websites and other Internet information recommended by librarians.

> **Tip:** If you need help doing electronic research, consider these options:
> - Ask a librarian for instructions.
> - Attend one of the library's training sessions on using library resources and conducting research.
> - Request instructions or a tutorial from your college writing center.

Work with URLs.

Finding useful Internet resources can be as easy as typing in a URL. If you don't have the exact URL, sometimes you can guess it, especially for an organization (company, government agency, or nonprofit group). Try the organization's name or a logical abbreviation to get the home page.

Follow helpful links.

Locating information on the Net can involve "surfing" leads:

- If you come across a helpful link (often highlighted in blue), click on the link to visit that new page. Note that the link may take you to another site.
- Your browser keeps a record of the pages you visit. Click the back arrow to go back one page or the forward arrow to move ahead again. Clicking the right mouse button on these arrows shows a list of recently visited pages.

INSIGHT: Note that "sponsored links" listed at a website are a form of advertising. Their purpose is primarily commercial, though they may contain useful information.

Follow the branches of a "subject tree."

A *subject tree*, sometimes called a *subject guide* or *directory*, lists websites that have been organized into categories by experts who have reviewed those sites. Use subject trees or directories for the following reasons:

- You need to narrow down a broad topic.
- You want sites that have been evaluated, or you desire quality over quantity.

How does a subject tree work? Essentially, it allows you to select from a broad range of subjects or "branches." With each topic choice, you narrow down your selection until you arrive at a list of websites, or you can keyword-search a limited number of websites.

Check whether your library subscribes to a service such as NetFirst, a database in which subject experts have catalogued Internet resources by topic. Here are some other common subject directories that you can likely access at your library:

WWW Virtual Library	**<http://vlib.org/Overview.html>**
Argus	**<http://www.clearinghouse.net>**
Librarians' Index to the Internet	**<http://www.lii.org>**
Google Directory	**<http://www.google.com/dirhp>**
LookSmart	**<http://looksmart.com>**

A sample subject tree search is outlined on the pages that follow. Study the search, and then try one yourself with the subject trees available through your library.

> **Tip:** To get the best results from your search, avoid these problems: misspelling keywords; using vague or broad keywords (*education* or *business*); incorrectly combining Boolean operators; or shortening keywords too much.

Step 1: Select an appropriate broad category. Study the subject tree below provided by the Librarians' Index to the Internet (Lii). To find reviewed websites containing information on hybrid electric cars, you could select from this start page a range of categories, depending on the angle you want to explore: Arts & Humanities, Business, Computers, and so on. Each of these starting points will lead to a different listing of relevant sites. Another option would be to use the keyword search feature shown. Hybrid cars would likely appear under Science.

Step 2: Choose a fitting subcategory. If you chose Science, the subcategories shown below would appear. At this point, you would again have several choices: (1) to select Environment, (2) to follow Transportation, or (3) to do a keyword search of this now more limited grouping of websites. Each choice might lead to a distinct set of websites. In fact, your research may benefit by trying all three options.

Step 3: Work toward a listing of websites. As you work down through narrower branches of the tree, you will arrive at a listing of relevant websites. For example, the site below is one of those listed under the topic "electric vehicles." Such sites, remember, have all been reviewed in terms of quality, though you still need to evaluate what you find. In the citation for a site, study the site title, the description of information available, site sponsorship, and the web address (particularly the domain name). Use that information to determine the site's relevance to your research. At this point, you can save the results (see page 469) and/or click on the site's web address and proceed to research the site.

Site title

Site description, types of content, members and sponsors

Web address (link)

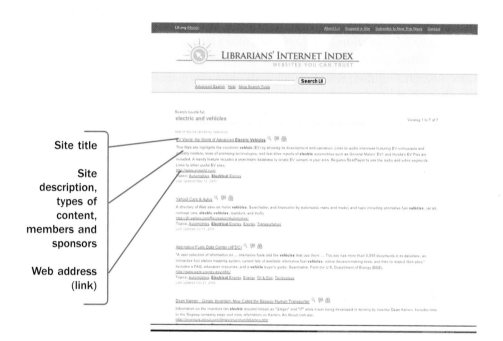

Web Link

Use search engines and metasearch tools.

Unlike a subject directory, which is constructed with human input, a search engine is a program that automatically scours a large amount of Internet material for keywords that you submit. A search engine is useful in the following circumstances:

- You have a very narrow topic in mind.
- You have a specific word or phrase to use in your search.
- You want a large number of results.
- You are looking for a specific type of Internet file.
- You have the time to sort through the material for reliability.

Be aware that not all search engines are the same. Some search citations of Internet materials, whereas others conduct full-text searches. Choose a search engine that covers a large portion of the Internet, offers quality indexing, and provides high-powered search capabilities. Here's an overview of some popular search engines.

Basic Search Engines: Search millions of webpages gathered automatically.

Alta Vista	<http://www.altavista.com>
AllTheWeb	<http://www.alltheweb.com>
Google	<http://www.google.com>
HotBot	<http://www.hotbot.com>
Vivísimo	<http://www.vivisimo.com>

Metasearch Tools: Search several basic search engines at once, saving you the time and effort of checking more than one search engine.

Ask Jeeves	<http://www.ask.com>
Dog Pile	<http://www.dogpile.com>
Ixquick	<http://www.ixquick.com>
Northern Light	<http://www.northernlight.com>

"Deep Web" Tools: Check Internet databases and other sources not accessible to basic search engines.

Complete Planet	<http://www.completeplanet.com>
The Invisible Web	<http://www.invisibleweb.com>

INSIGHT: One key to successfully using search engines lies in effective keyword searching (see pages **432–433**). To ensure successful searches, it's best to become familiar with a few search engines—what areas of the Internet they search, whether they can access full text, and what rules you must follow.

A sample search. What would a search look like? If you were interested in information specifically on the Toyota hybrid electric vehicles (a fairly narrow search term), you could conduct a search using the metasearch engine Ask Jeeves, following these steps:

Step 1: Begin your search with precise, narrow terms. Using Boolean operators and quotation marks, you might begin with the search terms "Toyota" and "hybrid electric vehicles." The more precise and narrow your terms are, the better your results will be.

Step 2: Study the results and refine your search as needed. The results of the initial search are shown below. At this point, you have several choices:

- Narrowing or broadening your search by using the drop-down menus in the box.
- Following the links (on the right) to related topics.
- Searching the "Sponsored Web Results"—essentially advertising sites, such as Toyota's own website for the Prius.
- Searching "Web Results"—sites that generally go beyond advertising into more in-depth information, although the site sponsorship is still important.
- Exploring a related search of other topics and of other Internet resources.

For example, you might choose to check Toyota's pages on the Prius, to view Toyota's North America Environmental Report at its website, or to examine the "Honda Insight / Toyota Prius" comparison, which comes from an educational site (.edu). The key is to use sound judgment about where the information comes from, which sites provide the most reliable information, how the information relates to your research question, and what web graphics offer as potential resources for your research writing.

Refinement through search questions with drop-down lists

Results: sponsored sites (primarily advertising)

Results: other webpages

Revising search and advanced search option

Narrow Your Search links

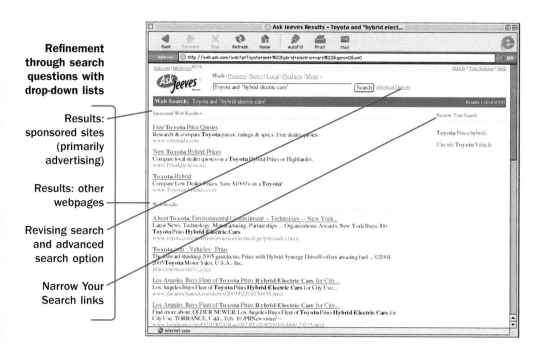

Checklist for Internet Research

As you conduct Internet research, use the following checklist to remind yourself of key principles to follow.

_____ I have avoided an over-reliance on web resources at the expense of more traditional scholarly sources.

_____ By studying sites and their URLs, I understand where the information is coming from.

_____ I have used Internet search tools intelligently—from URL addresses to subject trees to search engines—to find quality, reliable information.

_____ I have carefully saved Internet information through bookmarking, printing, saving, or e-mailing.

_____ When copying and pasting material from Internet sources, I have carefully tracked that material so as to avoid plagiarism.

_____ I have carefully evaluated each Internet source for credible authorship, reliable sponsorship, lack of bias, currency, accuracy, logical support, and quality design. (See page **470** for more details on evaluating web resources.)

Writing Prompt

Writing Activities

1. Explore your library's handouts and website for information about Internet research. What services, support, and access does the library provide? Explore the various resources with your own major in mind, and draft an informal report to share with your instructor and classmates about web resources available in your discipline.

2. With a current research project in one of your classes as the focus, use one of the subject trees on page **471** to investigate and evaluate potential websites. After saving useful information in an appropriate fashion, conduct a search for this project using a search engine listed on page **474**. Compare and contrast these two processes for finding Internet information.

3. Using the variety of methods outlined in this chapter, conduct an Internet search for information on a controversial topic, event, person, or place (for example, a civil rights leader such as Martin Luther King, Jr.; debates surrounding smoking; the human tragedy of hurricane Katrina's effect on New Orleans; the softwood lumber disagreement between the United States and Canada). Carefully analyze and evaluate the range of web information you find—the quality, perspective, depth, and reliability. Bring your results to class, including printouts of specific webpages.

Chapter 32
Drafting a Paper with Documented Research

"That's incredible!" is normally a positive exclamation of amazement. But maybe it's an exclamation you DON'T want to hear about your writing, if incredible means unbelievable. Think about it:

- **A poor paper** reads like a recitation of unconnected facts, a set of unsupported opinions, or a string of undigested quotations. Sources are absent, or sources dominate and the writer disappears. At its worst, it's plagiarism.
- **A strong paper** centers on the writer's ideas, ideas advanced through thoughtful engagement with and crediting of sources.

Obviously, you want to draft a strongly documented paper—a credible discussion of your carefully researched topic. This chapter will help you achieve that goal.

What's Ahead

- Avoiding Plagiarism
- Avoiding Other Source Abuses
- Organizing and Synthesizing Your Findings
- Developing Your First Draft
- Using Source Material in Your Writing
- Checklist and Writing Activities

Web Link

Avoiding Plagiarism

The road to plagiarism may be paved with the best intentions—or the worst. Either way, the result is still a serious academic offense. As you write your research paper, do everything you can to stay off that road! Start by studying your school's and your instructor's guidelines on plagiarism and other academic offenses. Then study the following pages.

What is plagiarism?

Plagiarism is using someone else's words, ideas, or images (what's called intellectual property) so they appear to be your own. When you plagiarize, you use source material—whether published in print or online—without acknowledging the source. In this sense, plagiarism refers to a range of thefts:

- Submitting a paper you didn't write yourself.
- Pasting large chunks of a source into your paper and passing it off as your own work.
- Using summaries, paraphrases, or quotations without documentation.
- Using the exact phrasing of a source without quotation marks.
- Mixing up source material and your own ideas—failing to distinguish between the two.

Plagiarism refers to more than "word theft." Because plagiarism is really about failing to credit ideas and information, the rules also apply to visual images, tables, graphs, charts, maps, music, and so on.

In other words, plagiarism refers to a range of source abuses. What exactly do these violations look like? Read the passage below, which comes from a scholarly article about the 1990s United Nations economic sanctions against Iraq. Then review the five types of plagiarism that follow, noting how each misuses the source.

Original Article

The paragraph below is from pages 748–749 of "Are Sanctions Just? The Problematic Case of Iraq," by David Cortright and George A. Lopez, published in the *Journal of International Affairs* (Spring 1999, Volume 52:2): 735–755.

As noted earlier, sanctions can help to encourage a process of dialogue and negotiation, but they cannot by themselves remove a targeted regime or force a drastic change in policy. Sanctions should not be used in a purely punitive manner to starve an opponent into submission. Sanctions work best in combination with incentives and other forms of external influence as part of a carrot-and-stick diplomacy designed to resolve a conflict through negotiation.

Submitting Another Writer's Paper

The most blatant plagiarism is taking an entire piece of writing and claiming it as your own work. Examples:

- Downloading, reformatting, and submitting an article as your own work.
- Buying a paper from a "paper mill" or taking a "free" paper off the Internet.
- Turning in another student's work as your own (see "Falstaffing" on page 483).

 Just as it's easy to plagiarize using the Internet, it's easy for your professors to recognize and track down plagiarism using Internet tools.

Using Copy and Paste

It is unethical to take chunks of material from another source and splice them into your paper without acknowledgment. In the example below, the writer pastes in a sentence from the original article (boldfaced) without using quotation marks or a citation. Even if the writer changed some words, it would still be plagiarism.

> **For sanctions to work, we need to understand their value and their limits. Sanctions can help to encourage a process of dialogue and negotiation, but they cannot by themselves remove a targeted regime or force a drastic change in policy.**

Failing to Cite a Source

Borrowed material must be documented. Even if you use information accurately and fairly, don't neglect to cite the source. Below, the writer correctly summarizes the passage's idea but offers no citation.

> **Sanctions alone do not force unjust governments to change. Instead, sanctions should be combined with other tactics rooted in carrot-and-stick negotiation.**

Neglecting Necessary Quotation Marks

Whether it's a paragraph or a phrase, if you use the exact wording of a source, that material must be enclosed in quotation marks. In the example below, the writer cites the source but doesn't use quotation marks around a phrase taken from the original (boldfaced).

> **Sanctions fail when they are used in a purely punitive manner** (Cortright and Lopez 749).

Confusing Borrowed Material with Your Own Ideas

Through carelessness (often in note taking), you may confuse source material with your own thinking. Below, the writer indicates that he borrowed material in the first sentence, but fails to indicate that he also borrowed the next sentence.

> **Sanctions work best "to encourage a process of dialogue and negotiation" (Cortright and Lopez 748). By themselves, they cannot remove a targeted regime or force a drastic change in policy.**

Why is plagiarism serious?

Perhaps the answer is obvious. But some people operate with the notion that material on the Internet (whether text, graphics, or sound) is "free" and therefore fair game for research writing. After all, a lot of stuff on the web doesn't even list an author, so what's the harm? Here's some food for thought:

Academic Dishonesty

At its heart, plagiarism is cheating—stealing intellectual property and passing it off as one's own work. Colleges take such dishonesty seriously. Plagiarism, whether intentional or unintentional, will likely be punished in one or more ways:

- Failing grade for the assignment
- Failing grade for the course
- A note on your academic transcript (often seen by potential employers) that failure resulted from academic dishonesty
- Expulsion from college

Theft from the Academic Community

The research paper represents your dialogue with other members of the academic community—classmates, the instructor, others in your major, and so on. When you plagiarize, you short-circuit the dialogue:

- You gain an unfair advantage over your classmates who follow the rules and earn their grades.
- You disrespect other writers, researchers, and scholars.
- You disrespect your readers by passing off others' ideas as your own.
- You insult your instructor, a person whose respect you need.
- You harm your college by risking its reputation and its academic integrity.

Now and in the Future

Because research projects help you master course-related concepts and writing skills, plagiarism robs you of an opportunity to learn either. Moreover, you rob yourself of your integrity and reputation. After all, as a student you are seeking to build your credibility within the broader academic community, your major, and your future profession.

In addition, research projects often train you for your future work in terms of research, thinking, and writing skills, skills that you will need to succeed in the workplace. If you do not learn the skills now, you will enter the workplace without them—a situation that your employer will, at some point, find out.

How do I avoid plagiarism?

Preventing plagiarism begins the moment you get an assignment. Essentially, prevention requires your commitment and diligence throughout the project.

Resist temptation. With the Internet, plagiarism is a mouse click away. Avoid last-minute all-nighters that make you desperate; start research projects early. **Note:** It's better to ask for an extension or accept a penalty for lateness than to plagiarize.

Play by the rules. Become familiar with your college's definition, guidelines, and policies regarding plagiarism so that you don't unknowingly violate them. When in doubt, ask your instructor for clarification.

Take orderly, accurate notes. From the start, carefully keep track of source material and distinguish it from your own thinking. Specifically, do the following:

- Maintain an accurate working bibliography (pages **438–439**).
- Adopt a decent note-taking system (pages **440–443**).
- Accurately summarize, paraphrase, and quote sources in your notes (pages **444–446**).

Document borrowed material. Credit information that you have summarized, paraphrased, or quoted from any source, whether that information is statistics, facts, graphics, phrases, or ideas. Readers can then see what's borrowed and what's yours, understand your support, and do their own follow-up research.

Common Knowledge Exception: Common knowledge is information—a basic fact, for instance—that is generally known to readers or easily found in several sources, particularly reference works. Such knowledge need *NOT* be cited. However, when you go beyond common knowledge into research findings, interpretations of the facts, theories, explanations, claims, arguments, and graphics, you *MUST* document the source. Study the examples below, but whenever you are in doubt, document.

Examples:

- The fact that automakers are developing hybrid electric cars is common knowledge, whereas the precise details of GM's AUTOnomy project are not.
- The fact that Shakespeare wrote *Hamlet* is common knowledge, whereas the details of his sources are not.

Work carefully with source material in your paper. See pages **488–491** for more on integrating and documenting sources, but here, briefly, are your responsibilities:

- Distinguish borrowed material from your own thinking by signaling where source material begins and ends.
- Indicate the source's origin with an attributive phrase and a citation (parenthetical reference or footnote).
- Provide full source information in a works-cited or references page.

Avoiding Other Source Abuses

Plagiarism, though the most serious offense, is not the only source abuse to avoid when writing a paper with documented research. Consider these pitfalls, which refer again to the sample passage on page 478.

Using Sources Inaccurately

When you get a quotation wrong, botch a summary, paraphrase poorly, or misstate a statistic, you misrepresent the original. *Example:* In this quotation, the writer carelessly drops the important word "not" and replaces "starve" with "bully."

> According to Cortright and Lopez, "sanctions **should be** used in a purely punitive fashion to **bully** an opponent into submission" (749).

Using Source Material Out of Context

By ripping a statement out of its context and forcing it into yours, you can make a source seem to say something that it didn't really say. *Example:* This writer uses part of a statement to say the opposite of the original.

> The example of Iraq proves the failure of "carrot-and-stick diplomacy designed to resolve a conflict through negotiation" (Cortright and Lopez 749).

Overusing Source Material

When your paper reads like a string of references, especially quotations, your own thinking disappears. *Example:* The writer takes the source passage, chops it up, and splices it together.

> It is important to understand that "sanctions can help to encourage a process of dialogue and negotiation, but they cannot by themselves remove a targeted regime or force a drastic change in policy." Moreover, "Sanctions should not be used in a purely punitive manner to starve an opponent into submission." Instead, say the authors, "Sanctions work best in combination with incentives and other forms of external influence as part of a carrot-and-stick diplomacy" (Cortright and Lopez 748-749).

"Plunking" Quotations

When you "plunk" quotations into your paper by failing to prepare the reader for them and follow them up, the discussion becomes choppy and disconnected. *Example:* The writer interrupts the flow of ideas with a quotation "out of the blue." In addition, the quotation hangs at the end of a paragraph with no follow-up or transition.

> In Iraq, the UN sanctions failed to bring results. "As noted earlier, sanctions can help to encourage a process of dialogue and negotiation" (Cortright and Lopez 748).
>
> Saddam Hussein continued to seek ways to rebuild his military. . . .

Using "Blanket" Citations

Your reader shouldn't have to guess where borrowed material begins and ends. For example, if you place a parenthetical citation at the end of a paragraph, does that citation cover the whole paragraph or just the final sentence?

Relying Heavily on One Source

If your writing is dominated by one source, readers may doubt the depth and integrity of your research.

Failing to Match In-Text Citations to Bibliographic Entries

All in-text citations must clearly refer to accurate entries in the works-cited, references, or endnotes page. Mismatching occurs when

- an in-text citation refers to a source that is not listed in the bibliography.
- a bibliographic resource is never actually referenced anywhere in the paper.

Related Academic Offenses

Beyond plagiarism and related source abuses, steer clear of these academic offenses:

Double-Dipping ■ When you submit one paper in two different classes without permission from both instructors, you take double credit for one project.

Falstaffing ■ This practice refers to a particular type of plagiarism where one student submits another student's work. Know that you are guilty of Falstaffing if you let another student submit your paper.

Copyright Violations ■ When you copy, distribute, and/or post in whole or in part any intellectual property without permission from or payment to the copyright holder, you commit a copyright infringement, especially when you profit from this use. To avoid copyright violations in your research projects, do the following:

- **Observe *fair use* guidelines:** Quote small portions of a document for limited purposes, such as education or research. Avoid copying large portions for your own gain.

- **Understand what's in the *public domain:*** You need not obtain permission to copy and use public domain materials—primarily documents created by the government.

- **Observe *intellectual property and copyright laws:*** First, know your college's policies on copying documents. Second, realize that copyright protects the expression of ideas in a range of materials—writings, videos, songs, photographs, drawings, computer software, and so on. Always obtain permission to copy and distribute copyrighted materials.

- **Avoid changing a source** (a photo) without permission of the creator or copyright holder.

Organizing and Synthesizing Your Findings

Your research may generate a mass of notes, printouts, photocopies, electronic files, and more. The challenge is to move from this mass to a coherent structure for the paper you need to write. If you have systematically taken good notes (see pages 440–443), you are well on the way. In addition, the tips below and on the next page will help you move toward order.

Develop your ideas.

Good thinking is foundational to good research writing. To develop ideas for your research project, follow these steps:

Refocus on your research questions and working thesis. Has research changed your perspective and position?

Study the evidence. Review your materials once, twice, or more—as long as it takes for ideas to percolate and information to make sense. Consider these questions:

- Is the information complete or at least sufficient for the project?
- Does the information seem reliable and accurate?
- How does the information relate to the topic?
- What connections exist among different pieces of evidence?
- Does the information gathered fall naturally into patterns?

Develop sound conclusions through analysis and synthesis. Practice these strategies (and check pages 18–25 for more on sound thinking):

- Work against personal biases that create blind spots to what the evidence is saying. Be open to different angles provided by *all* the evidence. Think through both pros and cons.
- Practice logic in your analysis, but also tap into your intuition, creativity, and imagination.
- Interpret statistical data carefully and correctly.
- Logically distinguish between causes and effects; carefully link them.
- If you are comparing, make sure that the items can logically be compared, and make sure that you think through both similarities and differences.
- Avoid either/or and black-and-white thinking, as well as circular arguments, slippery slope claims, and sweeping generalizations. (See logical fallacies at pages 255–258.)
- Check your conclusions against counterarguments, your experience, and common sense. For example, what are the limits of hybrid vehicle technology? What does your experience with cars and with culture tell you about how technological changes happen and get accepted?

Develop a structure for delivering research results.

Using your research questions and conclusions as guides, sift through and order your information. Consider these strategies:

Follow assignment recommendations: A pattern for your paper may be built into the assignment. For example, you may be asked to write a comparison/contrast paper. Shape your outline within that framework.

Clump and split: Using key ideas as main headings, arrange support and evidence under the most fitting heading. Depending on the note-taking system you used, separate and pile note cards, sketch out the structure on paper, use a graphic organizer (see pages **46–47**), use a code system, copy and paste material electronically, or cut up your note pages. After categorizing information, decide how best to sequence the key ideas.

Rely on tested patterns: The patterns below offer sound methods for developing your thinking. Each choice offers a basic structure for your paper, but several patterns may be useful within your paper's body.

- *Argumentation* asserts and supports a claim, counters any opposition, and then reasserts the claim (perhaps in a modified form). See pages **247–300**.
- *Cause/effect* can (1) explore the factors that led to an event, or (2) explore the consequences of a specific event. See pages **175–186**.
- *Chronological order* puts items in a sequence (order of events, steps in a process). See pages **217–230**.
- *Classification* groups details based on their common traits or qualities. See pages **203–216**.
- *Comparison/contrast* shows similarities and/or differences between specific elements of a topic. See pages **187–202**.
- *Description* orders details in terms of spatial relationships, color, form, texture, etc. See pages **131–172**.
- *Explanation* clarifies how something works by breaking the object or phenomenon into parts or phases and then showing how they work together. See pages **217–230**.
- *Order of importance* arranges items from most to least important, or least to most.
- *Partitioning* breaks down an object, space, or location into ordered parts; or a process into steps or phases.
- *Problem/solution* states a problem, explores its causes and effects, and presents solutions. See pages **301–316**.
- *Question/answer* moves back and forth from questions to answers in a sequence that logically clarifies a topic

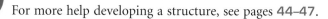

fyi For more help developing a structure, see pages **44–47**.

Video

Developing Your First Draft

As you write your paper, your first goal is to develop and support your ideas—referring to sources, not being dominated by them. The discussion that follows will help you achieve this goal. Your second goal is to respect sources by integrating them naturally and providing correct documentation; that goal is addressed on pages **488–491**.

Choose a drafting method.

Before starting your draft, choose a drafting method that makes sense for your project and your writing style. Consider these two options or something in between:

Writing Systematically

1. Develop a detailed outline, including supporting evidence.

2. Arrange your notes in precise order.

3. Write methodically, following your thesis, outline, and notes.

4. Cite your sources as you write.

Writing Freely

1. Review your working thesis and notes. Then set them aside.

2. If you need to, jot down a brief outline.

3. Write away—get all your research-based thinking down on paper.

4. Going back to your research notes, develop your draft further and integrate your citations.

Shape your first draft.

To successfully complete your paper's first draft, develop the following parts. Note that you can draft the parts in any order. For more on drafting, see pages **49–62**.

Draft an introduction. The introduction should do two things. The first part should say something interesting, surprising, or personal about your subject to gain your readers' attention. The second part should identify the specific focus, or thesis, of your research. Consider these options:

- Begin with a revealing story or quotation.
- Give important background information.
- Offer a series of interesting or surprising facts.
- Cite details showing the topic's relevance.
- Provide important definitions.
- Identify your focus or thesis.

Draft the body. How do you develop a complete and insightful research paper? How do you add dimension and depth to your writing? For starters, you make sure that you have carefully explored and reflected on your specific topic. You also make sure that you have gathered plenty of compelling evidence to support your thesis.

It's in the main part of your paper—in the body—that you develop your thesis. The process usually works in this way: You present each main point, expand on it by including supporting facts or examples, and offer additional analysis or documentation as needed.

Another way to approach your writing is to envision it as a series of paragraph clusters—one cluster of paragraphs for each main point. As you write, you imagine yourself conversing with your readers, telling them what they need to know, and communicating it as clearly and interestingly as you can.

Draft a conclusion. An effective closing adds to the reader's understanding of a research paper. The first part of the closing usually reviews (or ties together) important points in the paper, reinforces or reasserts the thesis, and/or draws a conclusion. The closing's final lines may expand the scope of the text by making a connection between the paper and the reader's experience, or between the paper and life in general.

Create a working title. At any point in the writing process, jot down possible titles that capture your paper's focused topic, research discoveries, and spirit. Consider key words and phrases that hint at your paper's thesis. For some papers, you may want to create a main title and a subtitle, separated by a colon.

TIPS FOR RESEARCH WRITING

- As you draft your paper, keep the focus on your own thoughts. You don't want your paper to read like a strung-together series of references to other sources.

- Present your own ideas honestly and clearly. Although you will be considering the research of others, be sure to analyze this information yourself and relate your sources to one another. Work at offering your personal perspective on the topic.

- Your instructor may want your thesis in a specific location (perhaps in the last sentence of your first paragraph). Follow his or her wishes.

- Don't try to cram everything you've learned into your draft. Select material that is truly needed to develop your thesis.

- Avoid overusing one particular source; also avoid using too many direct quotations.

- To avoid accidental plagiarism, indicate the sources of all borrowed facts as you write your draft. (See "Avoiding Plagiarism," pages 478–481.)

Using Source Material in Your Writing

After you've found good sources and taken good notes on them, you want to use that research effectively in your writing. Specifically, you want to show (1) what information you are borrowing, and (2) where you got it. By doing so, you create credibility. This section shows you how to develop credibility by integrating and documenting sources so as to avoid plagiarism and other abuses. *Note:* For a full treatment of documentation, see Chapter 33 (MLA) and Chapter 34 (APA).

Integrate source material carefully.

Source material—whether a summary, a paraphrase, or a quotation—should be integrated smoothly into your discussion. Follow these strategies:

The Right Reasons

Focus on what you want to say, not on all the source material you've collected. Use sources to do the following:

- Support your point with facts, statistics, and details.
- Give credibility to your point with an expert's supporting statement.
- Bring your point to life with an example, observation, or illustration.
- Address a counterargument or an alternative.

Quotation Restraint

In most research documents, restrict your quoting to nuggets:

- Key statements by authorities (the main point that a respected Shakespeare scholar makes about the role of Ophelia in *Hamlet*)
- Well-phrased claims and conclusions (a powerful conclusion by an ethicist about the problem with the media's coverage of cloning debates and technological developments)
- Passages where careful word-by-word analysis and interpretation are important to your argument (an excerpt from a speech made by a politician about the future of the NASA space shuttle program—a passage that requires a careful analysis for the between-the-lines message)

Quotations, especially long ones, must pull their weight, so generally paraphrase or summarize source material instead.

Primary Document Exception: When a primary text (a novel, a piece of legislation, a speech) is a key piece of evidence or the actual focus of your project, careful analysis of quoted excerpts is required. See pages 454–455 for more.

Smooth Integration

When you use quotations, work them into your writing as smoothly as possible. To do so, you need to pay attention to style, punctuation, and syntax. (See pages 490–491.)

Use enough of the quotation to make your point without changing the meaning of the original. Use quotation marks around key phrases taken from the source.

> *Example:* Ogden, Williams, and Larson also conclude that the hydrogen fuel-cell vehicle is "a strong candidate for becoming the Car of the Future," given the trend toward "tighter environmental constraints" and the "intense efforts underway" by automakers to develop commercially viable versions of such vehicles (25).

Integrate all sources thoughtfully. Fold source material into your discussion by relating it to your own thinking. Let your ideas guide the way, not your sources, by using this pattern:

1. State and explain your idea, creating a context for the source.

2. Identify and introduce the source, linking it to your discussion.

3. Summarize, paraphrase, or quote the source, providing a citation in an appropriate spot.

4. Use the source by explaining, expanding, or refuting it.

5. When appropriate, refer back to a source to further develop the ideas it contains.

Sample Passage: Note the integration of sources in the paragraph below.

writer's ideas	The motivation and urgency to create and improve hybrid-electric technology comes from a range of complex forces. Some of these forces are
attributive phrase	economic, others environmental, and still others social. In "Societal lifestyle costs of cars with alternative fuels/engines," Joan Ogden, Robert Williams,
paraphrase, quotation, or summary	and Eric Larson argue that "[c]ontinued reliance on current transportation fuels and technologies poses serious oil supply insecurity, climate change,
citation	and urban air pollution risks" (7). Because of the nonrenewable nature of fossil fuels as well as their negative side effects, the transportation industry
commentary	is confronted with making the most radical changes since the introduction
conclusion	of the internal-combustion automobile more than 100 years ago. Hybrid-electric vehicles are one response to this pressure.

Effectively document your sources.

Just as you need to integrate source material carefully into your writing, you must also carefully document where that source material comes from. From your first word to your last, readers should be able to recognize what material is yours and what facts and ideas come from other sources.

Identify clearly where source material begins. Your discussion must offer a smooth transition to source material. To achieve such a transition, follow these guidelines below:

For first references to a specific source, use an attributive statement that indicates some of the following information: the author's name and credentials, the title of the source, the nature of the study or research, and helpful background.

> *Example: Joan Ogden, Robert Williams, and Eric Larson, members of the Princeton Environmental Institute, explain* that modest improvements in energy efficiency and emissions reductions will not be enough over the next century because of anticipated transportation increases (7).

For subsequent references to a source, use a simplified attributive phrase, such as the author's last name(s) or a shortened version of the title.

> *Example: Ogden, Williams, and Larson go on to argue* that "[e]ffectively addressing environmental and oil supply concerns will probably require radical changes in automotive engine/fuel technologies" (7).

In some situations, such as quoting straightforward facts, simply skip the attributive phrase. The parenthetical citation supplies sufficient attribution.

> *Example:* Various types of transportation are by far the main consumers of oil (3/4 of world oil imports); moreover, these same technologies are responsible for 1/4 of all greenhouse gas sources (Ogden, Williams, and Larson 7).

The verb you use to introduce source material is a key part of the attribution. Use fitting verbs, such as those in the table below. Normally, use the present tense. Use the past tense only when you want to stress the "pastness" of a source.

> *Example:* In their 2004 study, "Societal Lifecycle Costs of Cars with Alternative Fuels/Engines," Ogden, Williams, and Larson *present* a method for comparing and contrasting alternatives to the traditional internal-combustion engine. In an earlier study, these authors *had made* preliminary steps toward this analysis. . . .

accepts	considers	explains	rejects	acknowledges
contradicts	highlights	reminds	adds	contrasts
identifies	responds	affirms	criticizes	insists
shares	argues	declares	interprets	shows
asserts	defends	lists	states	believes
denies	maintains	stresses	cautions	describes
outlines	suggests	claims	disagrees	points out

Indicate where source material ends. Closing quotation marks and a citation, as shown below, indicate the end of a source quotation. Generally, place the citation immediately after any quotation, paraphrase, or summary. However, you may also place the citation early in the sentence or at the end if the parenthetical note is obviously obtrusive. When you discuss several details from a page in a source, use an attributive phrase at the beginning of your discussion and a single citation at the end.

> *Example:* As the "Lifestyle Costs" study concludes, when greenhouse gases, air pollution, and oil insecurity are factored into the analysis, alternative-fuel vehicles "offer lower LCCs than typical new cars" (Ogden, Williams, and Larson 25).

Set off longer quotations. If a quotation is longer than four typed lines, set it off from the main text. Generally, introduce the quotation with a complete sentence and a colon. Indent the quotation one inch (10 spaces) and double-space it, but don't put quotation marks around it. Put the citation outside the final punctuation mark.

> *Example:* Toward the end of the study, Ogden, Williams, and Larson argue that changes to the fuel delivery and filling system must be factored into planning:
>
>> In charting a course to the Car of the Future, societal LCC comparisons should be complemented by considerations of fuel infrastructure requirements. Because fuel infrastructure changes are costly, the number of major changes made over time should be minimized. The bifurcated strategy advanced here—of focusing on the H2 FCV for the long term and advanced liquid hydrocarbon-fueled ICEVs and ICE/HEVs for the near term—would reduce the number of such infrastructure change to one (an eventual shift to H2). (25)

Marking Changes to Quotations

You may shorten or change a quotation so that it fits more smoothly into your sentence—but don't alter the original meaning. Use an ellipsis within square brackets to indicate that you have omitted words from the original. An ellipsis is three periods with a space before and after each period.

> *Example:* In their projections of where fuel-cell vehicles are heading, Ogden, Williams, and Larson discuss GM's AUTOnomy vehicle, with its "radical redesign of the entire car. [. . .] In these cars, steering, braking, and other vehicle systems are controlled electronically rather than mechanically" (24).

Use square brackets to indicate a clarification or to change a pronoun or verb tense or to switch around uppercase and lowercase.

> *Example:* As Ogden, Williams, and Larson explain, "[e]ven if such barriers [the high cost of fuel cells and the lack of an H2 fuel infrastructure] can be overcome, decades would be required before this embryonic technology could make major contributions in reducing the major externalities that characterize today's cars" (25).

Writing Checklist

Use the seven-traits checklist below to review any paper that contains documented research.

Ideas:
- The thesis is clear, sharp, and thoughtful; the support strong and balanced.
- Researched data are accurate, complete, and properly credited.

Organization:
- Information is delivered in a structured chain of ideas.
- The opening presents the purpose and scope of the research, the middle provides complete discussion, and the closing focuses on conclusions.

Voice:
- The tone is confident but also sincere, measured, and objective.
- "I" and "you" are avoided unless directed by the instructor.

Words:
- Precise, clear phrasing is used throughout the paper.
- Terms are defined as needed.

Sentences:
- The prose contains a good blend of sentence lengths and patterns.
- Source material is carefully integrated.

Copy:
- Grammar, punctuation, mechanics, usage, and spelling are correct.
- Documentation is complete, correct, and consistent.

Design:
- The format, page layout, and typography are all reader friendly.
- Data are effectively presented in discussion, lists, tables, graphs, etc.

Writing Prompt

Writing Activities

1. Good research papers grow out of a writer's "burning questions." In a 10- to 15-minute brainstorming session, list your burning questions.

2. Choose a short article or passage from one of your sources. Restate (paraphrase) what you have read using your own words, but put quotation marks around anything taken directly from the text.

Documentation and Format Styles

CONTENTS

Documentation and Format Styles

Chapter 33
MLA Documentation Format

In research papers, it is commonly said, "you are commanded to borrow but forbidden to steal." To borrow ideas while avoiding plagiarism (see pages **478–481**), you must not only mention the sources you borrow from but also document them completely and accurately. You must follow to the last dot the documentation conventions for papers written in your general subject area.

If you are composing a research paper in the humanities, your instructor will most likely require you to follow the conventions established in the style manual of the Modern Language Association (MLA). This chapter provides you with explanations and examples for citing sources in MLA format. An excellent way to learn MLA documentation is to see it in use, so turn to the sample paper demonstrating MLA form on pages **524–535**. Additional information and MLA updates can be found on the website for this book: <**www.thecollegewriter.com**>.

What's Ahead

- MLA Research Paper Guidelines
- Guidelines for In-Text Citations
- Sample In-Text Citations
- MLA Works-Cited: Quick Guide
- Works-Cited Entries:
  Books and Other Documents
- Works-Cited Entries:
  Print Periodical Articles
- Works-Cited Entries:
  Online Sources
- Works-Cited Entries: Other
  Sources (Primary, Personal,
  and Multimedia)
- Sample MLA Paper
- Checklist and Writing Activities

MLAMLAMLAMLAMLAMLAM

MLA Research Paper Guidelines

Video

Questions & Answers

Is a separate title page required?	*No* (unless your instructor requires one, in which case you would format it according to his or her instructions). On the first page of a research paper, type your name, your instructor's name, the course name and number, and the date, one below the other. The title comes next, centered. Then simply begin the text on the next line.
Is the research paper double-spaced?	*Yes.* Do not single-space anywhere, even in tables, captions, or long quotations.
What about longer quotations?	Verse quotations of more than three lines should be indented one inch (ten spaces) and double-spaced. Do not add quotation marks. Each line of a poem or play begins a new line of the quotation; do not run the lines together. When you are quoting prose that needs more than four typed lines, indent each line of the quotation one inch (ten spaces) from the left margin and double-space it; do not add quotation marks. To quote two or more paragraphs—in addition to the one inch that you are already indenting for the lengthy quotation—you should indent the first line of each paragraph an extra quarter-inch (three spaces). However, if the first sentence quoted does not begin a paragraph in the source, do not make the additional indent. Indent only the first lines of the successive paragraphs.
Are page numbers required?	*Yes.* Pages should be numbered consecutively in the upper-right corner, one-half inch from the top and flush with the right margin (one inch). Your last name should precede the page number, and no abbreviations or other symbols should be included.
Is an appendix required?	*No.* In MLA style, tables and illustrations are placed as close as possible to the related text.

Is an abstract required?	*No.* An abstract, or summary of your research paper, is not an MLA requirement.
How wide should the margins be?	Top, bottom, left, and right margins should be one inch (except for page numbering). The first word in a paragraph should be indented one-half inch (five spaces). Longer quotations should be set off one inch (ten spaces) from the left margin (see page **491**).
Are references placed in the text?	*Yes.* Indicate only page numbers parenthetically if you identify the author in your text. Give the author's last name in a parenthetical reference if it is not mentioned in the text.
Is a list of sources used in the paper required?	*Yes.* Full citations for all sources used (books, periodicals, etc.) are placed in an alphabetized list labeled "Works Cited" at the end of the paper. Whereas in-text parenthetical references generally indicate just the author's last name and a page number for the source material, the works-cited entry provides full publication details.
What about headings?	MLA style does not specify a particular format for headings within the text; normally, headings are used only for separate sections of the paper ("Works Cited" or "Notes," for example).
How do I incorporate reference markers if I submit my paper electronically?	Numbering paragraphs is common in electronic publications. Place the paragraph number in brackets. Follow with a space and begin the paragraph. (For other electronic formatting guidelines, check with your instructor.)
Any other special instructions?	Always ask whether your school, department, or instructor has special requirements that may take precedence over those listed here.

Web Link: For additional questions and answers about MLA format, see the MLA Q&A page at <http://www.mla.org/style_faq>.

Guidelines for In-Text Citations

The *MLA Handbook for Writers of Research Papers* suggests giving credit for your sources of information in the body of your research paper. One way to do so is by indicating the author and/or title in the text of your essay, and then putting a page reference in parentheses after the summary, paraphrase, or quotation, as needed. The simplest way to do so is to insert the appropriate information (usually the author and page number) in parentheses after the words or ideas taken from the source. To avoid disrupting your writing, place citations where a pause would naturally occur (usually at the end of a sentence but sometimes within a sentence, before internal punctuation such as a comma or semicolon). These in-text citations (often called "parenthetical references") refer to sources listed on the "Works Cited" page at the end of your paper. (See pages 534–535.)

General Guidelines for In-Text Citations

As you integrate citations into your paper, follow the guidelines below, referring to the sample citation as needed.

Sample In-Text Citation

Linda Bren of <u>FDA Consumer</u> explains that doctors often inappropriately prescribe antibiotics for viral infections because of uncertainty about the type of infection present, limits on time for further testing, and pressure from patients demanding prescriptions (30).

- Make sure each in-text citation clearly points to an entry in your list of works cited. The identifying information provided (usually the author's last name) must be the word or words by which the entry is alphabetized in that list.
- Keep citations brief, and integrate them smoothly into your writing.
- When paraphrasing or summarizing rather than quoting, make it clear where your borrowing begins and ends. Use stylistic cues to distinguish the source's thoughts ("Kalmbach points out . . . ," "Some critics argue . . .") from your own ("I believe . . . ," "It seems obvious," "however"). See pages 488–489 for more on integrating sources.
- When using a shortened title of a work, begin with the word by which the work is alphabetized in your list of works cited (e.g., "Antibiotic Overuse," not "Overuse Campaign," for "Antibiotic Overuse Campaign Gets Underway").
- For inclusive page numbers larger than ninety-nine, give only the two digits of the second number (113–14, not 113–114).
- When including a parenthetical citation at the end of a sentence, place it before the end punctuation. (Citations for long, indented quotations are an exception. See pages 491, 496.)

Special Guidelines for Sources Without Traditional Authorship and/or Pagination

Today many sources, especially electronic ones, have no stated authors and/or no pagination. For such sources, use these in-text citation strategies:

Source Without a Stated Author: In a signal phrase or in the parenthetical reference, identify the source as precisely as possible by indicating the sponsoring agency, the type of document, or the title (shortened in the parenthetical reference). See page 502.

> **The National Institute of Allergy and Infectious Diseases reports that antibiotic resistance has caused common diseases like tuberculosis, gonorrhea, pneumonia, and ear and urinary tract infections to become increasingly difficult to treat ("Fact Sheet").**

Source with No Pagination: If no pagination exists within the document, use paragraph numbers (with the abbreviation *par.*), if the document provides them. If the document includes neither page nor paragraph numbers, cite the entire work. Do not create your own numbering system.

> **Antibiotics become ineffective against such organisms through two natural processes: first, genetic mutation; and second, the subsequent transfer of this mutated genetic material to other organisms, which appears to be the main way that bacteria attain a state of resistance (Davies par. 5).**

Note: Because parenthetical notations are used to signal the end of an attribution, sources with no pagination or paragraph numbers offer a special challenge. When no parenthetical notation is possible, signal a shift back to your own discussion with a source-reflective statement indicating your thinking about the source.

> **. . . the main effects of antibiotic resistance. Bren's description of these effects helps us understand the seriousness of the problem. . . .**

INSIGHT:

- Stable pagination for many electronic resources is available when you use the ".pdf" rather than the ".html" version of the source.

- For instruction on smoothly integrating source material into your paper, see pages 488–489.

- For cautions about sources without identified authors, see pages 502, 508, and 514.

Sample In-Text Citations

The following entries illustrate the most common in-text citations.

Video

One Author: A Complete Work

You do not need an in-text citation if you identify the author in your text. (See the first entry below.) However, you must give the author's last name in an in-text citation if it is not mentioned in the text. (See the second entry.) When a source is listed in your works-cited page with an editor, a translator, a speaker, or an artist instead of the author, use that person's name in your citation.

WITH AUTHOR IN TEXT (This is the preferred way of citing a complete work.)

> In <u>No Need for Hunger</u>, Robert Spitzer recommends that the U.S. government develop a new foreign policy to help Third World countries overcome poverty and hunger.

WITHOUT AUTHOR IN TEXT

> <u>No Need for Hunger</u> recommends that the U.S. government develop a new foreign policy to help Third World countries overcome poverty and hunger (Spitzer).

Note: Do not offer page numbers when citing complete works, articles in alphabetized encyclopedias, one-page articles, and unpaginated sources.

One Author: Part of a Work

List the necessary page numbers in parentheses if you borrow words or ideas from a particular source. Leave a space between the author's last name and the page reference. No abbreviation or punctuation is needed.

WITH AUTHOR IN TEXT

> Bullough writes that genetic engineering was dubbed "eugenics" by a cousin of Darwin's, Sir Francis Galton, in 1885 (5).

WITHOUT AUTHOR IN TEXT

> Genetic engineering was dubbed "eugenics" by a cousin of Darwin's, Sir Francis Galton, in 1885 (Bullough 5).

A Work by Two or Three Authors

Give the last names of every author in the same order that they appear in the works-cited section. (The correct order of the authors' names can be found on the title page of the book.)

> Students learned more than a full year's Spanish in ten days using the complete supermemory method (Ostrander and Schroeder 51).

A Work by Four or More Authors

Give the first author's last name as it appears in the works-cited section followed by *et al.* (meaning "and others").

> **Communication on the job is more than talking; it is "inseparable from your total behavior" (Culligan et al. 111).**

Note: You may instead choose to list all of the authors' last names.

Two or More Works by the Same Author(s)

In addition to the author's last name(s) and page number(s), include a shortened version of the work's title when you cite two or more works by the same author(s).

WITH AUTHOR IN TEXT

> **Wallerstein and Blakeslee claim that divorce creates an enduring identity for children of the marriage (<u>Unexpected Legacy</u> 62).**

WITHOUT AUTHOR IN TEXT

> **They are intensely lonely despite active social lives (Wallerstein and Blakeslee, <u>Second Chances</u> 51).**

Note: When including both author(s) and title in a parenthetical reference, separate them with a comma, as shown above.

Works by Authors with the Same Last Name

When citing different sources by authors with the same last name, it is best to use the authors' full names in the text in order to avoid confusion. However, if circumstances call for parenthetical references, add each author's first initial. If first initials are the same, use each author's full name.

> **Some critics think <u>Titus Andronicus</u> too abysmally melodramatic to be a work of Shakespeare (A. Parker 73). Others suggest that Shakespeare meant it as black comedy (D. Parker 486).**

A Work Authored by Agency, Committee, or Organization

If a book or other work was written by an organization such as an agency, a committee, or a task force, it is said to have a corporate author. (See also page 508.) If the corporate name is long, include it in the text (rather than in parentheses) to avoid disrupting the flow of your writing. After the full name has been used at least once, use a shortened form of the name (common abbreviations are acceptable) in subsequent references. For example, *Task Force* may be used for *Task Force on Education for Economic Growth*.

> **The thesis of the Task Force's report is that economic success depends on our ability to improve large-scale education and training as quickly as possible (113–14).**

An Anonymous Work

When there is no author listed, give the title or a shortened version of the title as it appears in the works-cited section. (See page 508.)

> **Statistics indicate that drinking water can make up 20 percent of a person's total exposure to lead (Information 572).**

Two or More Works Included in One Citation

To cite multiple works within a single parenthetical reference, separate the references with a semicolon.

> **In Medieval Europe, Latin translations of the works of Rhazes, a Persian scholar, were a primary source of medical knowledge (Albala 22; Lewis 266).**

A Series of Citations from a Single Work

If no confusion is possible, it is not necessary to name a source repeatedly when making multiple parenthetical references to that source in a single paragraph. If all references are to the same page, identify that page in a parenthetical note after the last reference. If the references are to different pages within the same work, you need identify the work only once, and then use a parenthetical note with page number alone for the subsequent references.

> **Domesticating science meant not only spreading scientific knowledge, but also promoting it as a topic of public conversation (Heilbron 2). One way to enhance its charm was by depicting cherubic putti as "angelic research assistants" in book illustrations (5).**

A Work Referred to in Another Work

If you must cite an indirect source—that is, information from a source that is quoted from another source—use the abbreviation *qtd. in* (quoted in) before the indirect source in your reference.

> **Paton improved the conditions in Diepkloof (a prison) by "removing all the more obvious aids to detention. The dormitories [were] open at night: the great barred gate [was] gone" (qtd. in Callan xviii).**

A Work Without Page Numbers

If a work has no page numbers or paragraph numbers, treat it as you would a complete work. (See page 500.) This is commonly the case with electronic resources, for example. Do not count pages to create reference numbers of your own.

> **Antibiotics become ineffective against such organisms through two natural processes: first, genetic mutation; and second, the subsequent transfer of this mutated genetic material to other organisms (Davies par. 5).**

A Work in an Anthology or Collection

When citing the entirety of a work that is part of an anthology or collection, if it is identified by author in your list of works cited, treat the citation as you would for any other complete work. (See page 500.)

> **In "The Canadian Postmodern," Linda Hutcheon offers a clear analysis of the self-reflexive nature of contemporary Canadian fiction.**

Similarly, if you are citing particular pages of such a work, follow the directions for citing part of a work. (See page 500.)

> **According to Hutcheon, "postmodernism seems to designate cultural practices that are fundamentally self-reflexive, in other words, art that is self-consciously artifice" (18).**

(To format this sort of entry in your list of works cited, see pages 508–509.)

An Item from a Reference Work

An entry from a reference work such as an encyclopedia or dictionary should be cited similarly to a work from an anthology or collection (see above). For a dictionary definition, include the abbreviation *def.* followed by the particular entry designation.

> **This message becomes a juggernaut in the truest sense, a belief that "elicits blind devotion or sacrifice" ("Juggernaut," def. 1).**

Note that while many such entries are identified only by title (as above), some reference works include an author's name for each entry (as below). Others may identify the entry author by initials, with a list of full names elsewhere in the work.

> **The decisions of the International Court of Justice are "based on principles of international law and cannot be appealed" (Pranger).**

(See page 510 for guidelines to formatting these entries in your works-cited list.)

A Part of a Multivolume Work

When citing only one volume of a multivolume work, if you identify the volume number in the works-cited list, there is no need to include it in your in-text citation. However, if you cite more than one volume of a work, each in-text reference must identify the appropriate volume. Give the volume number followed by page number, separated by a colon and a space.

> **"A human being asleep," says Spengler, ". . . is leading only a plantlike existence" (2: 4).**

When citing a whole volume, however, either identify the volume number in parentheses with the abbreviation *vol.* (using a comma to separate it from the author's name) or use the full word *volume* in your text.

> **The land of Wisconsin has shaped its many inhabitants more significantly than they ever shaped that land (Stephens, vol. 1).**

A One-Page Work

Cite a one-page work just as you would a complete work. (See page 500.)

> **As Samantha Adams argues in her editorial, it is time for NASA "to fully reevaluate the Space Shuttle's long-term viability for sending humans into space."**

A Sacred Text or Famous Literary Work

Sacred texts and famous literary works are published in many different editions. For that reason, it is helpful to identify sections, parts, chapters, and such instead of or in addition to page numbers. If using page numbers, list them first, followed by an abbreviation for the type of division and the division number.

> **The more important a person's role in society—the more apparent power an individual has—the more that person is a slave to the forces of history (Tolstoy 690; bk. 9, ch. 1).**

Books of the Bible and other well-known literary works may be abbreviated, if no confusion is possible.

> **"A generation goes, and a generation comes, but the earth remains forever" (The New Oxford Annotated Bible, Eccles. 1.4)**

> **As Shakespeare's famous Danish prince observes, "One may smile, and smile, and be a villain" (Ham. 1.5.104).**

Quoting Prose

To cite prose from fiction (novels, short stories), list more than the page number if the work is available in several editions. Give the page reference first, and then add a chapter, section, or book number in abbreviated form after a semicolon.

> **In The House of the Spirits, Isabel Allende describes Marcos, "dressed in mechanic's overalls, with huge racer's goggles" (13; ch. 1).**

When you are quoting any sort of prose that takes more than four typed lines, indent each line of the quotation one inch (ten spaces) and double-space it; do not add quotation marks. In this case, you put the parenthetical citation (the pages and chapter numbers) outside the end punctuation mark of the quotation itself.

> **Allende describes the flying machine that Marcos has assembled:**

> > **The contraption lay with its stomach on terra firma, heavy and sluggish and looking more like a wounded duck than like one of those newfangled airplanes they were starting to produce in the United States. There was nothing in its appearance to suggest that it could move, much less take flight across the snowy peaks. (12; ch. 1)**

Quoting Verse

Do not use page numbers when referencing classic verse plays and poems. Instead, cite them by division (act, scene, canto, book, part) and line, using Arabic numerals for the various divisions unless your instructor prefers Roman numerals. Use periods to separate the various numbers.

> **In the first act of the play named after him, Hamlet comments, "How weary, stale, flat and unprofitable, / Seem to me all the uses of this world" (1.2.133-134).**

Note: A slash, with a space on each side, shows where each new line of verse begins. If you are citing lines only, use the word line or lines in your first reference and numbers only in additional references.

> **In book five of Homer's <u>Iliad</u>, the Trojans' fear is evident: "The Trojans were scared when they saw the two sons of Dares, one of them in fright and the other lying dead by his chariot" (lines 22-24)**

Verse quotations of more than three lines should be indented one inch (ten spaces) and double-spaced. Do not add quotation marks. Each line of the poem or play begins a new line of the quotation; do not run the lines together. If a line or lines of poetry are dropped from the quotation, ellipses that extend the width of the stanza should be used to indicate the omission.

> **Bin Ramke's poem "A Little Ovid Late in the Day" tells of reading by the last light of a summer day:**
>> **[T]ales of incest, corruption,**
>> **any big, mythic vice**
>> **against the color of the sun,**
>> **the sweetness of the time of day—**
>> **I know the story,**
>> **it is the light I care about. (3-8)**

Listing an Internet Address

In printed documents, Internet addresses and e-mail addresses should always be enclosed in angle brackets. Without these brackets, these addresses might otherwise be confusing because of their internal punctuation.

> **<http://college.hmco.com/english/vandermey/college_writer/2e/ student_home.html>**

Unfortunately, many modern word processors automatically convert such addresses to live hyperlinks, removing the angle brackets and adding an underline. To avoid this in your printed documents, either turn off the auto-formatting option in your word processor or cancel such formatting immediately after it occurs. If your instructor allows, you may use live links in electronic versions of your text.

Web Link

MLA Works Cited

QUICK GUIDE

The works-cited section lists all of the sources you have cited (referred to) in your text. It does not include any sources you may have read or studied but did not refer to in your paper (that's a bibliography). Begin your list of works cited on a new page (the next page after the text), and number each page, continuing from the number of the last page of the text. A sample works-cited page is shown on pages 534–535; the guidelines here describe the form of the works-cited section.

1. Type the page number in the upper-right corner, one-half inch from the top of the page, with your last name before it.

2. Center the title *Works Cited* (not in italics or underlined) one inch from the top; then double-space before the first entry.

3. Begin each entry flush with the left margin. If the entry runs more than one line, indent additional lines one-half inch (five spaces) or use the hanging indent function on your computer.

4. End each element of the entry with a period. (Elements are separated by periods in most cases unless only a space is sufficient.) Use a single space after all punctuation.

5. Double-space lines within each entry and between entries.

6. List each entry alphabetically by the author's last name. If there is no author, use the first word of the title (disregard *A, An, The* as the first word). If there are multiple authors, alphabetize according to which author is listed first in the publication.

7. A basic entry for a book would be as follows:

   Opie, John. Ogallala: Water for a Dry Land. Lincoln: U of Nebraska P, 1993.

8. A basic entry for a periodical (a magazine) would be as follows:

   Stearns, Denise Heffernan. "Testing by Design." Middle Ground Oct. 2000: 21-25.

9. A basic entry for an online source would be as follows. (Note the URL in angle brackets followed by a period.)

   Tenenbaum, David. "Dust Never Sleeps." The Why Files. 28 July 1999. U of Wisconsin, Board of Regents. 26 April 2005 <http://whyfiles.org/shorties/air.dust.html>.

Works-Cited Entries: Books and Other Documents

Components

The entries that follow illustrate the information needed to cite books, sections of a book, pamphlets, and government publications. The possible components of these entries are listed in order below:

1. Author's name

2. Title of a part of the book (an article in the book or a foreword)

3. Title of the book

4. Name of editor or translator

5. Edition

6. Number of volume

7. Name of series

8. Place of publication, publisher, year of publication

9. Page numbers, if citation is to only a part (For page spans, use a hyphen; if clarity is maintained, you may also drop a digit from the second number—for example, 141–43, 201–334.)

Note: In general, if any of these components do not apply, they are not included in the works-cited entry. However, in the rare instance that a book does not state publication information, use the following abbreviations in place of information you cannot supply:

n.p.	**No place of publication given**
n.p.	**No publisher given**
n.d.	**No date of publication given**
n. pag.	**No pagination given**

Additional Guidelines

- List only the city for the place of publication if the city is in the United States. For cities outside the United States, add an abbreviation for the country if necessary for clarity. If several cities are listed, give only the first.

- Publishers' names should be shortened by omitting articles (a, an, the), business abbreviations (Co., Inc.), and descriptive words (Books, Press). For publishing houses that consist of the names of more than one person, cite only the first of the surnames. Abbreviate *University Press* as *UP*. Also use standard abbreviations whenever possible. See page 566 for more details.

A Book by One Author

Baghwati, Jagdish. <u>In Defense of Globalization</u>. New York: Oxford UP, 2004.

Two or More Books by the Same Author

List the books alphabetically according to title. After the first entry, substitute three hyphens for the author's name.

Dershowitz, Alan M. <u>Rights from Wrongs</u>. New York: Basic Books, 2005.

- - - . <u>Supreme Injustice: How the High Court Hijacked Election 2000</u>. Oxford: Oxford UP, 2001.

A Work by Two or Three Authors

Bystydzienski, Jill M., and Estelle P. Resnik. <u>Women in Cross-Cultural Transitions</u>. Bloomington: Phi Delta Kappa Educational Foundation, 1994.

Note: List the authors in the same order as they appear on the title page. Reverse only the name of the first author.

A Work by Four or More Authors

Schulte-Peevers, Andrea, et al. <u>Germany</u>. Victoria, Austral.: Lonely Planet, 2000.

Note: You may also choose to give all names in full in the order used on the title page.

A Work Authored by Agency, Committee, or Organization

Exxon Mobil Corporation. <u>Great Plains 2000</u>. Lincolnwood: Publications Intl., 2001.

An Anonymous Book

<u>Chase's Calendar of Events 2002</u>. Chicago: Contemporary, 2002.

A Single Work from an Anthology

Mitchell, Joseph. "The Bottom of the Harbor." <u>American Sea Writing</u>. Ed. Peter Neill. New York: Library of America, 2000. 584–608.

A Complete Anthology

If you cite a complete anthology, begin the entry with the editor(s).

Neill, Peter, ed. <u>American Sea Writing</u>. New York: Library of America, 2000.

Smith, Rochelle, and Sharon L. Jones, eds. <u>The Prentice Hall Anthology of African American Literature</u>. Upper Saddle River: Prentice Hall, 2000.

Two or More Works from an Anthology or Collection

To avoid unnecessary repetition when citing two or more entries from a larger collection, you may cite the collection once with complete publication information (see Forbes, below). The individual entries (see Joseph and MacNeice, below) can then be cross-referenced by listing the author, title of the piece, editor of the collection, and page numbers.

Forbes, Peter, ed. <u>Scanning the Century</u>. London: Penguin, 2000.

Joseph, Jenny. "Warning." Forbes 335–36.

MacNeice, Louis. "Star-Gazer." Forbes 504.

One Volume of a Multivolume Work

Cooke, Jacob Ernest, and Milton M. Klein, eds. <u>North America in Colonial Times</u>. Vol. 2. New York: Scribner's, 1998.

Note: If you cite two or more volumes in a multivolume work, give the total number of volumes after each title. Offer specific references to volume and page numbers in the parenthetical reference in your text, like this: (8:112–114).

Salzman, Jack, David Lionel Smith, and Cornel West. <u>Encyclopedia of African-American Culture and History</u>. 5 vols. New York: Simon, 1996.

An Introduction, a Preface, a Foreword, or an Afterword

To cite the introduction, preface, foreword, or afterword of a book, list the author of the part first. Then identify the part by type, with no quotation marks or underlining, followed by the title of the book. Next, identify the author of the work, using the word *by*. (If the book's author and the part's author are the same person, give just the last name after *by*.) For a book that gives cover credit to an editor instead of an author, identify the editor as usual. Finally, list any page numbers for the part cited.

Barry, Anne. Afterword. <u>Making Room for Students</u>. By Celia Oyler. New York: Teachers College, 1996.

Lefebvre, Mark. Foreword. <u>The Journey Home</u>. Vol. 1. Ed. Jim Stephens. Madison: North Country, 1989. ix.

A Republished Book (Reprint)

Give the original publication date after the title.

Atwood, Margaret. <u>Surfacing</u>. 1972. New York: Doubleday, 1998.

Note: New material added to the reprint, such as an introduction, should be cited after the original publication facts: Introd. C. Becker.

A Book with Multiple Publishers

When a book lists more than one publisher (not just different offices of the same publisher), include all of them in the order given on the book's title page, separated by a semicolon.

> Wells, H. G. The Complete Short Stories of H. G. Wells. New York: St.
> Martin's; London: A. & C. Black, 1987.

Second and Subsequent Editions

An edition refers to the particular publication you are citing, as in the third (3rd) edition.

> Joss, Molly W. Looking Good in Presentations. 3rd ed. Scottsdale:
> Coriolis, 1999.

An Edition with Author and Editor

The term *edition* also refers to the work of one person that is prepared by another person, an editor.

> Shakespeare, William. A Midsummer Night's Dream. Ed. Jane
> Bachman. Lincolnwood: NTC, 1994.

A Translation

> Lebert, Stephan, and Norbert Lebert. My Father's Keeper. Trans. Julian
> Evans. Boston: Little, 2001.

An Article in a Familiar Reference Book

It is not necessary to give full publication information for familiar reference works (encyclopedias and dictionaries). For these titles, list only the edition (if available) and the publication year. If an article is initialed, check the index of authors (in the opening section of each volume) for the author's full name.

> "Technical Education." Encyclopedia Americana. 2001 ed.

> Lum, P. Andrea. "Computed Tomography." World Book. 2000 ed.

When citing a single definition of several listed, add the abbreviation *Def.* and the particular number or letter for that definition.

> "Macaroni." Def. 2b. The American Heritage College Dictionary. 4th
> ed. 2002.

An Article in an Unfamiliar Reference Book

For citations of lesser-known reference works, give full publication information, as for any other sort of book.

> "S Corporation." The Portable MBA Desk Reference. Ed. Paul A.
> Argenti. New York: Wiley, 1994.

A Government Publication

State the name of the government (country, state, and so on) followed by the name of the agency. Most federal publications are published by the Government Printing Office (GPO).

United States. Dept. of Labor. Bureau of Labor Statistics. Occupational

Outlook Handbook 2000–2001. Washington: GPO, 2000.

When citing the Congressional Record, the date and page numbers are all that is required for that source.

Cong. Rec. 5 Feb. 2002: S311–15.

A Book in a Series

Give the series name and number (if any) before the publication information.

Paradis, Adrian A. Opportunities in Military Careers. VGM

Opportunities Series. Lincolnwood: VGM Career Horizons, 1999.

A Book with a Title Within Its Title

If the title contains a title normally in quotation marks, keep the quotation marks and underline the entire title.

Stuckey-French, Elizabeth. "The First Paper Girl in Red Oak, Iowa" and

Other Stories. New York: Doubleday, 2000.

Note: If the title contains a title that is normally underlined, do not underline that title in your entry:

Beckwith, Charles E. Twentieth Century Interpretations of A Tale of

Two Cities: A Collection of Critical Essays. Upper Saddle River:

Prentice Hall, 1972.

A Sacred Text

The Bible and other such sacred texts are treated as anonymous books. Documentation should read exactly as it is printed on the title page.

The Jerusalem Bible. Garden City: Doubleday, 1966.

The Published Proceedings of a Conference

The published proceedings of a conference should be treated as a book. However, if the title of the publication does not identify the conference by title, date, and location, add the appropriate information immediately after the title.

McIlwaine, Ia C., ed. Advances in Knowledge Organization. Vol. 9.

Proc. of Eighth Intl. ISKO Conf., 13–16 July 2004, London.

Wurzburg, Ger.: Ergon-Verlag, 2004.

To cite a particular presentation from the published proceedings of a conference, treat it as a work in an anthology.

> Vizine-Goetz, Diane, and Julianne Bea. "Using Literary Warrant to Define a Version of the DDC for Automated Classification Services." <u>Advances in Knowledge Organization</u>. Ed. Ia C. McIlwaine. Vol. 9. Proc. of Eighth Intl. ISKO Conf., 13-16 July 2004, London. Wurzburg, Ger.: Ergon-Verlag, 2004.

A Published Dissertation

An entry for a published dissertation contains the same information as a book entry, with a few added details. Add the abbreviation *Diss.* and the degree-granting institution before the publication facts. You may also add the order number at the end of the entry, if the work was published by University Microfilms International.

> Jansen, James Richard. <u>Images of Dostoevsky in German Literary Expressionism</u>. Diss. U of Utah, 2003. Ann Arbor: UMI, 2003. AAT 3084161.

An Unpublished Dissertation

The entry for an unpublished dissertation lists author, title in quotation marks, degree-granting institution, and year of acceptance. (For a master's thesis, use *MA thesis* or *MS thesis* rather than *Diss.*)

> Vaidhyanathan, Siva. "Unoriginal Sins: Copyright and American Culture." Diss. U Texas, 1999.

An Unpublished Essay

For an unpublished essay, list the author, the title of the work in quotation marks, the description *Unpublished essay*, and the year it was produced.

> Carmichael, F. "Bukowski's Faith." Unpublished essay, 2004.

A Pamphlet, Manual, or Other Workplace Document

Treat any such publication as you would a book.

> Grayson, George W. <u>The North American Free Trade Agreement</u>. New York: Foreign Policy Assn., 1993.

If publication information is missing, list the country of publication in brackets if known. Use n.p. (no place) if the country or the publisher is unknown and n.d. if the date is unknown, just as you would for a book.

> <u>Pedestrian Safety</u>. [United States]: n.p., n.d.

Works-Cited Entries: Print Periodical Articles

Possible Components, in Order

1. Author's name, last name first
2. Title of article, in quotation marks and headline style
3. Name of periodical, underlined
4. Series number or name, if relevant (not preceded by period or comma)
5. Volume number (for a scholarly journal)
6. Issue number, separated from volume with a period but no space
7. Date of publication (abbreviate all months but May, June, July)
8. Page numbers, preceded by a colon, without "p." or "pp." (For articles continued nonconsecutively, add a plus sign after the first page number.)

If any of these components do not apply, they are not listed. The entries that follow illustrate the information and arrangement needed to cite periodicals.

An Article in a Weekly or Biweekly Magazine

List the author (if identified), article title (in quotation marks), publication title (underlined), full date of publication, and page numbers for the article. Do not include volume and issue numbers.

> Goodell, Jeff. "The Uneasy Assimilation." <u>Rolling Stone</u> 6–13 Dec. 2001: 63–66.

An Article in a Monthly or Bimonthly Magazine

As for a weekly or biweekly magazine, list the author (if identified), article title (in quotation marks), and publication title (underlined). Then identify the month(s) and year of the issue, followed by page numbers for the article. Do not give volume and issue numbers.

> "Patent Pamphleteer." <u>Scientific American</u> Dec. 2001: 33.

An Article in a Scholarly Journal Paginated by Issue

Rather than month or full date of publication, scholarly journals are identified by volume number. If each issue is numbered from page 1, your works-cited entry should identify the issue number as well. List the volume number immediately after the journal title, followed by a period and the issue number, and then the year of publication (in parentheses). End with the page numbers of the article, as usual.

> Chu, Wujin. "Costs and Benefits of Hard-Sell." <u>Journal of Marketing Research</u> 32.2 (1995): 97–102.

An Article in a Scholarly Journal with Continuous Pagination

For scholarly journals that continue pagination from issue to issue, no issue number is needed in the works-cited entry.

> Tebble, Nicola J., David W. Thomas, and Patricia Price. "Anxiety and
>> Self-Consciousness in Patients with Minor Facial Lacerations."
>> <u>Journal of Advanced Nursing</u> 47 (2004): 417–26.

An Unsigned Article in a Periodical

If no author is identified for an article, list the entry alphabetically by title among your works cited (ignoring any initial *A*, *An*, or *The*).

> "Feeding the Hungry." <u>Economist</u>. 371.8374 (2004): 74.

A Printed Interview

Begin with the name of the person interviewed if that's who you are quoting.

> Cantwell, Maria. "The New Technocrat." By Erika Rasmusson. <u>Working
>> Woman</u> Apr. 2001: 20–21.

Note: If the interview is untitled, the word *Interview* (no italics) and a period follow the interviewee's name.

A Newspaper Article

> Bleakley, Fred R. "Companies' Profits Grew 48% Despite Economy."
>> <u>Wall Street Journal</u> 1 May 1995, Midwest ed.: 1.

Note: Cite the edition of a major daily newspaper (if given) after the date (1 May 1995, Midwest ed.: 1). If a local paper's name does not include the city of publication, add it in brackets (not underlined) after the name.

To cite an article in a lettered section of the newspaper, list the section and the page number. (For example, A4 would refer to page 4 in section A of the newspaper.) If the sections are numbered, however, use a comma after the year (or the edition); then indicate the section and follow with a colon and the page number (sec. 1:20).

An unsigned newspaper article follows the same format:

> "Bombs—Real and Threatened—Keep Northern Ireland Edgy." <u>Chicago
>> Tribune</u> 6 Dec. 2001, sec. 1: 20.

A Newspaper Editorial or Letter to the Editor

If an article is an editorial, put *Editorial* (no italics) and a period after the title.

> "Hospital Power." Editorial. <u>Bangor Daily News</u> 14 Sept. 2004: A6.

To identify a letter to the editor, put *Letter* (no italics) and a period after the author's name.

> Sory, Forrest. Letter. <u>Discover</u> July 2001: 10.

A Review

Begin with the author (if identified) and title of the review. Use the notation *Rev. of* (no italics) between the title of the review and that of the original work. Identify the author of the original work with the word *by* (not italics). Then follow with publication data for the review.

> Olsen, Jack. "Brains and Industry." Rev. of <u>Land of Opportunity</u> by
>
> Sarah Marr. <u>New York Times</u> 23 Apr. 1995, sec. 3: 28.

Note: If you cite the review of a work by an editor or a translator, use *ed.* or *trans.* instead of *by.*

An Abstract

An abstract is a summary of a work. To cite an abstract, first give the publication information for the original work (if any); then list the publication information for the abstract itself. Add the term *Abstract* and a period between these if the journal title does not include that word. If the journal identifies abstracts by item number, include the word *item* (no italics) followed by the number. (Add the section identifier [A, B, or C] for those volumes of *Dissertation Abstracts [DA]* and *Dissertation Abstracts International [DAI]* that have one.) If no item number exists, list the page number(s).

> Faber, A.J. "Examining Remarried Couples Through a Bowenian Family
>
> System Lens." <u>Journal of Divorce and Remarriage</u> 40.3/4 (2004):
>
> 121–33. <u>Social Work Abstracts</u> 40 (2004): item 1298.

An Article with a Title or Quotation Within Its Title

> Morgenstern, Joe. "Sleeper of the Year: <u>In the Bedroom</u> Is Rich Tale
>
> of Tragic Love." <u>Wall Street Journal</u> 23 Nov. 2001: W1.

Note: Use single quotation marks around the shorter title if it is a title normally punctuated with quotation marks.

An Article Reprinted in a Loose-Leaf Collection

The entry begins with original publication information and ends with the name of the loose-leaf volume (<u>Youth</u>), editor, volume number, publication information including name of the information service (SIRS), and the article number. (In the example below, the plus sign indicates continuing but nonconsecutive pages.

> O'Connell, Loraine. "Busy Teens Feel the Beep." <u>Orlando Sentinel</u> 7
>
> Jan. 1993: E1+. <u>Youth</u>. Ed. Eleanor Goldstein. Vol. 4. Boca Raton:
>
> SIRS, 1993. Art. 41.

Video

Works-Cited Entries: Online Sources

Components

Citations for online sources follow the strategies used for print sources, with a few additions to reflect the changeable nature of the Internet. After the author's name and title of the document, include any print publication information (using the guidelines elsewhere in this chapter), then the electronic publication details and access information.

1. Author's name

2. Title of article or webpage

3. Print publication information

4. Title of Internet site

5. Site editor's name

6. Version (volume or issue) number

7. Date of electronic publication

8. Name of subscription service

9. Name of list or forum

10. Number range or total number of pages (or other sections)

11. Site sponsor's name

12. Date of access (most recent date on which you viewed the document)

13. URL in angle brackets (including access-mode identifiers such as http, ftp, etc.)

If any of these components do not apply, they are not listed. For documents with no listed date of electronic publication, use the site's posting date, date of update, or copyright date if available. MLA asks for page, paragraph, or section numbers if the document includes them.

A Personal Site

After the author's name, list the site title (underlined) or the words *Home page* (without italics), whichever is appropriate, followed by a period. Add the date of publication or most recent update (if available), your date of visit, and the URL.

> **Mehuron, Kate. Home page. 30 Sept. 2004 <http://www.emich.edu/**
> **public/history/faculty/mehuron.html>.**

A Professional Site

Generally, no author is identified for a professional site, so the entry begins with the site title. Use the copyright date if no date of update is given. A site sponsor can nearly always be found. Conclude with your date of access and the URL for the site's home page.

> Latimes.com. 1 Oct. 2004. Los Angeles Times. 1 Oct. 2004 <http://
> www.latimes.com/>.

A Site for a Department of a College or University

Begin with the name of the department, followed by a description such as *Dept. home page* (without italics), followed by a period. Then list the name of the institution, your date of access, and the URL. No date of publication or latest update is necessary.

> Department of Foreign Languages and Literatures. Dept. home page.
> Marquette U College of Arts & Sciences. 6 Nov. 2004 <http://
> www.marquette.edu/fola/>.

A Site for a Study Course

Start with the instructor's name, reversed as for an author. Then give the course title, without quotation marks, underlining, or italics. Follow with the phrase *Course home page* (without italics), followed by a period, the course dates, and the department and institution. End with your date of access and the URL, as usual.

> Strickland, Ron. Shakespeare on Stage. Course home page. 14 June
> 2004 - 4 Aug. 2004. Dept. of English. Illinois State U. 4 Oct.
> 2004 <http://www.english.ilstu.edu/strickland/378/>.

A Site with a Long URL

If you must include a line break in a URL, do so only after a slash, and do not add a hyphen to indicate the break. For a URL that is long and complicated enough to invite errors in transcription, give the URL of the site's search page instead.

> MacLeod, Donald. "Shake-Up for Academic Publishing." Guardian
> Unlimited. 10 Nov. 2004 <http://www.guardian.co.uk/Archive/>.

If no search page is available, give the home page URL and path of links to the specific document.

> "Frederica: An 18th-Century Planned Community." National Register of
> Historic Places. National Parks Service. 27 Feb. 2004.
> <http://www.cr.nps.gov/nr/>. Path: Education; Hispanic Heritage
> Month; Frederica.

An Online Book

In general, follow the format for printed books. Include publication information for the original print version if available. Follow the date of publication with the access date and web address.

> Simon, Julian L. **The Ultimate Resource II: People, Materials, and Environment**. College Park: U of Maryland, 1996. 9 Apr. 2001 <http://www.inform.umd.edu/EdRes/Colleges/BMGT/Faculty/JSimon/Ultimate_Resource/>.

When citing part of an online book, the title (or name of the part, such as Foreword) follows the author's name; the title of the book (underlined) is followed by its author's name if different from the first name listed.

> Untermeyer, Louis. "Author's Apology." **The Donkey of God**. 1999. iUniverse. 7 March 2003 <http://books.iuniverse.com/>.

An Article in an Online Periodical

The format for printed periodical matter applies here, with modifications. Begin with the author's name; the article title in quotation marks; and the underlined name of the periodical, its volume or issue number, and date of publication. Include page numbers (or other sections) if numbered. Close with the date of access and URL.

> Dickerson, John. "Nailing Jello." **Time.com** 5 Nov. 2001. 9 Dec. 2001 <http://www.time.com/time/columnist/dickerson/>.

An Article in an Online Reference Work

Unless the author of the entry is identified, begin with the entry name in quotation marks. Follow with the usual online publication information.

> "Eakins, Thomas." **Britannica Concise Encyclopedia** 2004. Encyclopedia Britannica. 26 Sept. 2004 <http://concise.britannica.com/ebc/article?tocId=9363299>.

An Article in an Online Service

When you use a library to access a subscription service, add the name of the database if known (underlined), the service, and the library. Then give the date of access followed by the Internet address for the home page of the service (if known). If no Internet address is given for an entry, add a keyword or path statement in its place, if appropriate ("Keyword: Kiev" or "Path: World Events; Conflicts; Kiev").

> Davis, Jerome. "Massacre in Kiev." **Washington Post** 29 Nov. 1999, final ed.: C12. **National Newspapers**. ProQuest. Gateway Technical College Elkhorn Campus Library. 30 Nov. 1999 <http://proquest.umi.com/pqdweb>.

A Scholarly Project or Information Database

The title of the site is listed first, then the name of the editor (if given). Follow this with the version number (if relevant), the date of publication or update, name of the sponsor, date of access, and URL.

> Wired Style: Principles of English Usage in the Digital Age. 1994. Wired
>
> Digital Inc. 5 Nov. 2001 <http://hotwired.lycos.com/
>
> hardwired/wiredstyle/>.

If you are citing a book that is part of an online scholarly project, first list information about the printed book, followed by publication information for the project. End with the URL of the book and a period.

> Astell, Mary. Reflections on Marriage. London: Wilkin, 1706. Women
>
> Writers Project. Providence: Brown UP, 1999. 7 Feb. 2002
>
> <http://www.wwp.brown.edu/texts/astell/marriage.html>.

An Online Government Publication

As with a governmental publication in print, begin with the name of the government (country, state, and so on) followed by the name of the agency. After the publication title, add the electronic publication information.

> United States. Dept. of Labor. Office of Disability Employment Policy.
>
> Emergency Preparedness for People with Disabilities. Apr. 2004.
>
> 12 Sept. 2004. <http://www.dol.gov/odep/ep/eps.pdf>.

An Online Posting in a List Server

Begin the citation with author name and document title (from the subject line). Follow this with the description *Online posting* (without italics) and a period, the date of posting, the name of the group, your date of access, and the URL of the list's Internet site (if any) or the e-mail address of the list's moderator. Whenever possible, cite an archived version of the posting so that your readers can easily find the source.

> Moody, Ellen. "Alternate Persuasions." Online posting. 25 April 1998.
>
> The Austen-L Mailing List. 12 Jan. 2005. <http://lists.mcgill.ca>.

An Online Posting in a Web Forum

List the author's name and the title of the posting (in quotation marks), followed by *Online posting* (without italics) and a period. Then give the posting date, the forum name, your date of access, and the URL of the posting.

> Cubby, J. "Re: Connecting Playwrights & Theatre Companies." Online
>
> posting. 27 May 2004. AACT Online Forums: Playwriting &
>
> Playwrights. 12 Jan. 2005. <http://www.aact.org/cgi-bin/yabb/
>
> YaBB.cgi>. Path: Public Boards; Playwriting & Playwrights;
>
> Connecting Playwrights & Theatre Companies.

An Online Posting in a Newsgroup

Start a newsgroup message as you would a posting to a list server or web forum, with author's name, posting title, the description *Online posting* (without italics), and a period. Then give the date of posting and your date of access, followed by the name and address of the group in angle brackets, with the prefix *news*: (no italics).

> Silverman, Neal. "Re: Perimeter of a Triangle." Online posting. 1 Oct.
> 2004. 12 Dec. 2004 <news:geometry.college>.

An Online Posting in a MUD, a MOO, an IRC, or Other Real-time (Synchronous) Communication Forum

If you are citing a particular speaker, identify that person. Follow with the event description, the date of the event, the communication forum, the date of access, and the telnet URL.

> Del Rey, Juan Roberto. Online defense of dissertation "Chaos, Cadence,
> Tonality, Dissonance, and Meaning in the Music of Leonard Bernstein."
> 18 July 2005. Connections. 18 July 2005
> <telnet://connections.moo.mud.org:3333>.

If possible, provide readers with a link to an archived version of the posting.

> Del Rey, Juan Roberto. Online defense of dissertation "Chaos,
> Cadence, Tonality, Dissonance, and Meaning in the Music of
> Leonard Bernstein." 18 July 2005. Connections. 3 Aug. 2005
> <http://web.nwe.ufl.edu/~tari/connections/archives/
> delrey_phd_defense.txt>.

An Online Poem

List the poet's name, the title of the poem, and any print publication information before the electronic publication details.

> Nemerov, Howard. "Found Poem." <u>War Stories</u>. By Nemerov. U. of Chicago
> Press: 1987. Poets.org. 5 Oct. 2004 <http://www.poets.org/poems/
> poems.cfm?45442B7C000C040D0170>.

An Online Multimedia Resource: Painting, Photograph, Musical Composition, Film, or Film Clip

After the usual information for the type of work being cited, add electronic publication information.

> Goya, Francisco de. <u>Saturn Devouring His Children</u>. 1819–1823.
>
> Museo del Prado, Madrid. 13 Dec. 2003 <http://www.usc.edu/
>
> schools/annenberg/asc/projects/comm544/library/>.

A Publication in More than One Medium

For a work that consists of more than one type of medium, either list all the media that make up the work or cite only the medium that contains the specific material cited in your paper.

> <u>CultureGrams</u>. Book, CD-ROM. Lindon: Axiom, 2002.

An Online Transcript of a Broadcast

Give the original publication information for the broadcast. Then add the description *Transcript* (without italics), followed by a period, and the electronic publication information for that document.

> Lehrer, Jim. "Character Above All." <u>Online NewsHour</u> 29 May 1996.
>
> Transcript. 23 Apr. 2004 <http://www.pbs.org/newshour/
>
> character/transcript/trans1.html>.

A Document Accessed by FTP

Cite a document accessed by ftp as you would one accessed by http, but with "ftp://" in the URL.

> Lewis, Winfred. "Three Translations of Rainer Rilke's 'Along the
>
> sun-drenched roadside, from the great.'" 19 Feb. 2005 <ftp://
>
> english.saku.edu/writingprograms/documents/rilke_trans.rtf>.

An E-mail Communication

Identify the author of the e-mail, then list the "Subject" line of the e-mail as a title, in quotation marks. Next, include a description of the entry, including the recipient—usually *E-mail to the author* (no italics), meaning you, the author of the paper. Finally, give the date of the message.

> Barzinji, Atman. "Re: Frog Populations in Wisconsin Wetlands." E-mail
>
> to the author. 1 Jan. 2002.

Video

Works-Cited Entries: Other Sources (Primary, Personal, and Multimedia)

The following examples of works-cited entries illustrate how to cite sources such as television or radio programs, films, live performances, works of art, and other miscellaneous nonprint sources.

A Periodically Published Electronic Database

Citations for materials published on CD-ROM, diskette, or magnetic tape are similar to those for print sources, with these added considerations: (1) The contents of a work may vary from one medium to another; therefore, the citation should always identify the medium. (2) The publisher and vendor of the publication may be different, in which case both must be identified. (3) Because of periodic updates, multiple versions of the same database may exist, which calls for citation if possible of both the date of the document cited and the date of the database itself.

> Ackley, Patricia. "Jobs of the Twenty-First Century." <u>New Rochelle
> Informer</u> 15 (Apr. 1994): A4. <u>New Rochelle Informer Ondisc</u>. CD-
> ROM. Info-Line. Oct. 1994.

> Baker, Anthony. <u>The New Earth Science</u>. Diskette. Cincinnati:
> Freeman's P, 1991.

Reference Work on CD-ROM

If you use an encyclopedia or other reference book recorded on CD-ROM, use the form below. If available, include publication information for the printed source.

> <u>The American Heritage Dictionary of the English Language</u>. 3rd ed.
> Boston: Houghton-Mifflin, 1992. CD-ROM. Cambridge, MA: Softkey
> Intl., 1994.

A Television or Radio Program

> "The Ultimate Road Trip: Traveling in Cyberspace." <u>48 Hours</u>. CBS.
> WBBM, Chicago. 13 Apr. 1995.

A Film

The director, distributor, and year of release follow the title. Other information may be included if pertinent.

> <u>Titanic</u>. Dir. James Cameron. Perf. Leonardo DiCaprio, Kate Winslet.
> Paramount Pictures, 1997.

A Video Recording or an Audio Recording

Cite a filmstrip, slide program, videocassette, or DVD as you do a film, but include the medium before the name of the distributor.

Monet: Shadow & Light. Videocassette. Devine Productions, 1999.

If you are not citing a CD, indicate LP, Audiocassette, or Audiotape, followed by a period. If you are citing a specific song on a musical recording, place its title in quotation marks before the title of the recording.

O'Higgins, Michael B. Beating the Dow with Bonds. Audiocassette.
Harper Audio, 1999.

A Performance

Treat this similarly to a film, adding the location and date of the performance.

Chanticleer. Young Auditorium, Whitewater, Wisconsin. 23 Feb. 2003.

An Artwork on Display

Titian. The Entombment. The Louvre, Paris.

A Letter or Memo Received by the Author (You)

Thomas, Bob. Letter to the author. 10 Jan. 1999.

An Interview by the Author (You)

Brooks, Sarah. Personal interview. 15 Oct. 2002.

A Cartoon or Comic Strip (in Print)

Luckovich, Mike. "The Drawing Board." Cartoon. Time 17 Sept. 2001:
18.

An Advertisement (In Print)

List the subject of the advertisement (product, company, organization, or such), followed by *Advertisement* (without italics) and a period. Then give the usual publication information.

Vaio Professional Notebooks. Advertisement. Campus Technology Oct.
2004: 45.

A Lecture, a Speech, an Address, or a Reading

If there is a title, use it instead of the descriptive label (for example, *Lecture*).

Annan, Kofi. Lecture. Acceptance of Nobel Peace Prize. Oslo City Hall,
Oslo, Norway. 10 Dec. 2001.

A Legal or Historical Document

Familiar historical documents such as the U.S. Constitution and the United States code are typically not included in a works-cited list because they can so easily be abbreviated in a parenthetical note within the text of your paper: "(US Const., art. 4, sec. 1,)" and "(7 USC 308a, 1928)," for example. (Note that such documents are not underlined when referenced in this way.)

To list an act in your works cited, begin with the name of the act, then give its public law number (abbreviation *Pub. L.*), its date of enactment, and its Statutes at Large (abbreviation *Stat.*) cataloging number.

> **Do-Not-Call Implementation Act. Pub. L. 108–010. 11 Mar. 2003.**
>
> **Stat. 117–557.**

Abbreviate the names of law cases (spelling out the first important word of each party's name). Do not underline the name in your works cited (although it should be underlined within the body of your paper). Follow with the case number, the name of the court, and the date of the decision.

> **Missouri v. Seibert. No. 02–1371. Supreme Ct. of the US. 28 June**
>
> **2004.**

A Map or Chart

Follow the format for an anonymous book, adding *Map* or *Chart* (without italics), followed by a period.

> <u>**Wisconsin Territory**</u>. **Map. Madison: Wisconsin Trails, 1988.**

Sample MLA Paper

Student writer Kyle Van Arendonk wrote the following research paper on the growing problem of antibiotic resistance. Although the paper is on a science topic, Kyle wrote for a general audience, seeking to educate them about this public health challenge. Also, the paper was written for an undergraduate expository writing class. For these reasons, Kyle formatted the paper in MLA. (For a traditional literary-analysis essay formatted in MLA style, see pages **359–362**.) You can use Kyle's paper in three ways:

1. To study how a well-written research paper builds a discussion from start to finish.

2. To examine how sources are carefully integrated into research writing—a full-length example of the strategies addressed on pages **488–491**.

3. To see in detail the format and documentation practices of MLA style.

Sample Title Page (Optional)

The title page and outline are not required for MLA papers, but if your instructor asks for one or both, use these guidelines.

Use standard typeface, type size, and type styles—no flashy scripts, large print, or features like bold and all caps.

Center the title one-third down the page.

The Threat of Antibiotic Resistance

Center identifying information— student, instructor, course, date— two-thirds of the way down. Double-space between lines.

Kyle Van Arendonk

Professor D. Schelhaas

English 302

17 April 2005

Sample Outline (Optional)

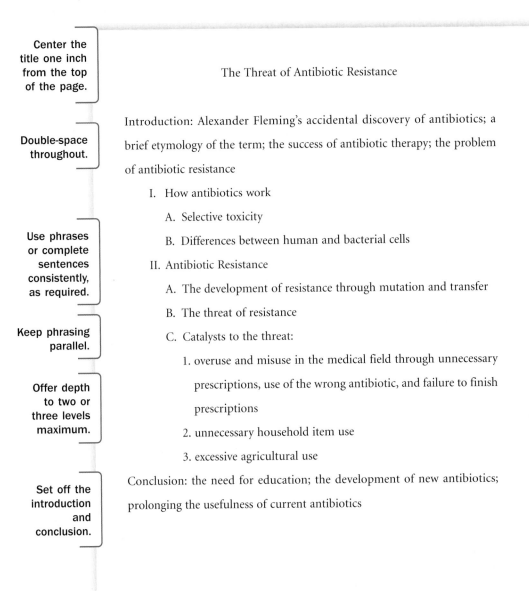

Center the title one inch from the top of the page.

Double-space throughout.

Use phrases or complete sentences consistently, as required.

Keep phrasing parallel.

Offer depth to two or three levels maximum.

Set off the introduction and conclusion.

The Threat of Antibiotic Resistance

Introduction: Alexander Fleming's accidental discovery of antibiotics; a brief etymology of the term; the success of antibiotic therapy; the problem of antibiotic resistance

I. How antibiotics work

  A. Selective toxicity

  B. Differences between human and bacterial cells

II. Antibiotic Resistance

  A. The development of resistance through mutation and transfer

  B. The threat of resistance

  C. Catalysts to the threat:

    1. overuse and misuse in the medical field through unnecessary prescriptions, use of the wrong antibiotic, and failure to finish prescriptions

    2. unnecessary household item use

    3. excessive agricultural use

Conclusion: the need for education; the development of new antibiotics; prolonging the usefulness of current antibiotics

For more on principles of outlining, see pages **44–45**.

Sample Paper

Normally, an MLA research paper begins with a page like the one below—with the header (the writer's last name and page number), the heading, and the title as key identifying information.

The heading supplies identifying details.

The title indicates the topic and the theme.

The opening uses an anecdote to create context and background.

Authors' names, titles of works, and page references create clear, accurate citations for borrowed material.

The writer offers basic definitions and explanations.

Van Arendonk 1

Kyle Van Arendonk
Professor D. Schelhaas
English 302
17 April 2005

The Threat of Antibiotic Resistance

Antibiotics are one of modern medicine's proudest achievements. The accidental discovery that led to this achievement, as told by Gerard Tortora, Berdelle Funke, and Christine Case, occurred in 1928. A scientist named Alexander Fleming noticed an unusual occurrence on a Petri plate of growing bacteria. The Petri plate had been contaminated by a small amount of mold, and the bacteria in the region around this mold were not growing normally. Fleming saw a clearly defined area around the mold in which the bacteria were inhibited. He determined that the mold was a species of Penicillium and found a way to extract the organism's chemical that inhibited the bacteria's growth. He named the chemical penicillin, the first antibiotic, and doctors were soon using it to treat a wide variety of bacterial infections (13).

Since Fleming's great discovery, scientists have discovered many other antibiotics. The word <u>antibiotic</u>, at first glance, may seem like a misnomer considering its use in the medical field. According to <u>Stedman's Medical Dictionary</u>, the Greek word from which antibiotic is derived actually translates as <u>against</u> [anti] <u>life</u> [bios] (96). However, while antibiotics work for the lives of human patients, they work against the lives of the microorganisms that cause infections.

According to Tortora, Funke, and Case, antibiotics can be broadly defined as any microorganism-produced substances that can inhibit the growth of other microorganisms (549). Most antibiotics, like erythromycin and bacitracin for example, now come from certain strains of bacteria, but antibiotics can also be found in fungi like the Penicillium mold and made synthetically (549–550). Antibiotics have greatly enhanced

1

2

3

Van Arendonk 2

the treatment of many human sicknesses caused by bacterial infections. Strep throat, sinus infection, urinary tract infection, and ear infection are all less serious now than in the past because antibiotic therapies are available. For example, while tuberculosis, pneumonia, and gastrointestinal infections, all caused by bacteria, were the three major causes of death near the beginning of the twentieth century, respiratory tract infections were the only bacterial infection remaining in the top ten causes of death by the end of the twentieth century (Wenzel and Edmond 1961). The availability and use of antibiotics was in most part responsible for this impressive change. However, after all of this success with antibiotic use, a phenomenon called antibiotic resistance is now seriously threatening the effectiveness of antibiotic use in medicine.

To understand antibiotic resistance, one first needs to understand how antibiotics work. Although the distinction is not always clear, antibiotics can be divided into two groups: agents that kill bacteria (bactericidal), and agents that only inhibit the growth of bacteria (bacteriostatic) while giving the body's immune system the time it needs to fight off the invader on its own (Mims et al. 487). Antibiotics typically achieve their restraining effects in one of several ways. The key to these methods lies in selective toxicity, defined by Medical Microbiology and Immunology as "selective inhibition of the growth of the microorganism [a bacterium] without damage to the host [the human patient]" (Levinson and Jawetz 48). To accomplish this discriminatory damage, antibiotics exploit one of the main differences between human cells and bacterial cells. Bacteria differ from human cells in certain steps of their metabolic pathways; in the structure of their ribosomes, nucleic acids, and cell membrane; and in the presence of a cell wall, which human cells lack (48–49). By using these differences, antibiotics are able to selectively inhibit bacterial growth. For example, aminogylcoside antibiotics like gentamicin and streptomycin take advantage of bacteria's slightly different ribosomes to selectively halt the production of proteins within the bacteria (Mims et al. 487).

Antibiotic resistance, then, refers to the ability of some microorganisms to avoid these inhibitory effects of antibiotics. Antibiotics become ineffective against such organisms through two natural processes:

Facts and statistics are carefully documented.

The writer states his thesis.

"Mims et al." refers to a source with more than three authors.

The writer uses a quotation from an authoritative source to provide a precise definition; brackets indicate changes and clarifications made by the writer.

Van Arendonk 3

For a source
without
pagination,
the writer
uses
paragraph
numbers to
indicate the
location of the
information.

first, genetic mutation; and second, the subsequent transfer of this
mutated genetic material to other organisms, which appears to be the
main way that bacteria attain a state of resistance (Davies par. 5). First,
the genetic material of bacteria, DNA, can spontaneously mutate.
Sometimes, albeit very rarely, these mutations can be advantageous to
the bacteria, specifically when the mutation allows the bacteria to survive
the presence of antibiotics.

Indicating the
author and his
credentials,
the writer
effectively
summarizes
the source.

In an article in <u>Review of Optometry</u>, David Kairys, an optometrist
and instructor at Pennsylvania State University, explains three main types
of genetic mutations that can provide bacteria with a means of antibiotic
resistance. First, mutations can produce "plugs" that block an antibiotic
from entering the bacterial cell. Second, mutations can enable the
production of new enzymes that break down the antibiotic after it has
entered the bacteria. And third, genetic mutations can offer bacteria the
ability to make proteins that effectively block the antibiotic from attaching
to its target site, often the bacteria's ribosomes where proteins are
produced (42-44). From these mutations that Kairys describes, bacteria
find a way to survive the presence of normally lethal antibiotics. Bacteria
without these mutations are inhibited normally, and in a type of natural
selection, antibiotic–resistant bacteria become prevalent as the others
die out.

Strong topic
sentences
offer
transitions
between
paragraphs
and move the
discussion
forward.

Once bacteria have gained antibiotic–resistant abilities through
genetic mutations, they often pass the mutations on to other cells.
This occurrence is the second process involved in developing antibiotic
resistance. The transfer of mutated genetic material from antibiotic–
resistant bacteria to normal bacteria occurs by any of the three bacterial
mechanisms of conjugation, transduction, and transformation (Kairys 44).
Regardless of the specific transfer mechanism, bacteria normally sensitive
to an antibiotic are transformed into the resistant form that is unaffected
by the antibiotic. This process is shown in more detail in Figure 1, where
antibiotic–resistant genes are shown creating efflux "pumps" that get rid
of antibiotics (a), creating enzymes that break down antibiotics (b), or
changing the antibiotic chemically in order to make it ineffective (c). As
a result of this process, these exchanges of genetic mutations between
bacteria, along with spontaneous mutations, rapidly increase the

The writer
refers to and
discusses a
visual used to
explain a
complex
concept.

Van Arendonk 4

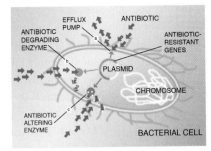

Figure 1. Strategies of Antibiotic-Resistant Genes. Ilustration by Sol Ivanski in S. S. Davidson, "Perils of Antibiotic Overuse," <u>Genetic Frontiers</u> July 2005.

The visual is placed after the first reference to it and is labeled with a number, a title, and source information.

proportion of bacteria that are resistant to an antibiotic. While the normal bacteria decrease in number as the antibiotic inhibits their growth, the resistant forms of the bacteria thrive and reproduce to quickly increase in number.

The writer shifts his discussion from explaining the process to arguing its seriousness.

Clearly, the development of antibiotic-resistant organisms poses a huge threat to the present system of health care, a system that relies heavily on antibiotic therapies. Antibiotics normally used to treat bacterial infections are becoming increasingly ineffective as the number of antibiotic-resistant organisms increases. According to Linda Bren, a staff writer for <u>FDA Consumer</u>, the threat is large and is getting worse:

8

A quotation longer than four lines is introduced with a complete sentence and a colon, and is indented 10 spaces. The in-text reference is placed one space after the period at the end of the quotation.

> For some of us, bacterial resistance could mean more visits to the doctor, a lengthier illness, and possibly more toxic drugs. For others, it could mean death. The CDC [Centers for Disease Control and Prevention] estimates that each year, nearly 2 million people in the United States acquire an infection while in a hospital, resulting in 90,000 deaths. More than 70 percent of the bacteria that cause these infections are resistant to at least one of the antibiotics commonly used to treat them. (28)

9

The results of antibiotic resistance can range from minor inconveniences, to higher health-care costs, and even to death. This widespread resistance to antibiotics affects doctors' abilities to treat many human infections. The National Institute of Allergy and Infectious Diseases reports that antibiotic resistance has caused common diseases like tuberculosis, gonorrhea, pneumonia, and ear and urinary tract infections to become increasingly difficult to treat ("Fact Sheet").

10

In order to maintain the efficacy of antibiotics for the future, health-care workers and the general public must cooperate to limit any further

11

Van Arendonk 5

A source's authority is emphasized through its links to government agencies.

increase in antibiotic-resistant organisms. While a certain level of antibiotic resistance develops naturally, several controllable factors have greatly accelerated the increase in antibiotic-resistant organisms. First of all, a widespread overuse and misuse of antibiotics within the medical field has greatly contributed to this problem. The <u>Medical Letter on the CDC and FDA</u> suggests that the unnecessary use of antibiotics, the use of the wrong antibiotic, and patients' failure to finish an antibiotic prescription are all causing an increase in the level of antibiotic resistance (25).

An analogy clarifies a concept.

Antibiotics are effective only against infections caused by bacteria and should never be used against infections caused by viruses. Using an antibiotic against a viral infection is like throwing water on a grease fire—water may normally put out fires but will only worsen the situation for a grease fire. In the same way, antibiotics fight infections, but they only cause the body harm when used to fight infections that are caused by viruses. Viruses cause the common cold, the flu, and most sore throats, sinus infections, coughs, and bronchitis. Yet antibiotics are commonly prescribed for these viral infections. The <u>New England Journal of Medicine</u> reports that 22.7 million kilograms (25,000 tons) of antibiotics are prescribed each year in the U.S. alone (Wenzel and Edmond 1962). Meanwhile, the CDC reports that approximately 50 percent of those prescriptions are completely unnecessary ("Antibiotic Overuse" 25). "Every year, tens of millions of prescriptions for antibiotics are written to treat viral illnesses for which these antibiotics offer no benefits," says the CDC's antimicrobial resistance director David Bell, M.D. (qtd. in Bren 30).

A source without an author is referenced by the sponsoring agency using a shortened version of the title.

A lack of knowledge is certainly one cause of this misuse. According to the <u>Medical Letter on the CDC and FDA</u>, a study by the Council for Affordable and Quality Health Care, an alliance of health-care providers, found that one out of three U.S. citizens thinks that antibiotics are effective against the viruses that cause colds and flu and uses them in those situations ("Antibiotic Overuse" 9). Poor decision-making by physicians also causes antibiotic misuse. Linda Bren of <u>FDA Consumer</u> explains that doctors often inappropriately prescribe antibiotics for viral infections because of uncertainty about the type of infection present, limits on time for further testing, and pressure from patients demanding

12

13

Van Arendonk 6

prescriptions (30). The problem is worsened by the fact that in many underdeveloped countries, antibiotics are available without any prescription (Tortora, Funke, and Case 569). Without extensive medical education, the lay people of these countries use antibiotics in hopes of treating many sicknesses that aren't caused by bacteria, even common ailments like headaches (569).

Similarly, even when antibiotics are properly prescribed for bacterial infections, the wrong antibiotic is often used. To save money, people often use a friend's or family member's leftover antibiotic prescription. But antibiotics are tailored to inhibit the growth of specific bacteria, so a friend's prescription is not guaranteed to attack the bacteria actually causing an infection. Patients' failure to complete antibiotic prescriptions causes further misuse of antibiotics. One survey even found that 59 percent of patients in a general-practice setting did not finish the prescribed course of antibiotic treatment (Davies par. 7). When symptoms go away, people are tempted to discontinue the antibiotic prescription for an infection. But premature termination of an antibiotic therapy encourages the survival of some bacteria, specifically those bacteria that have developed antibiotic resistance.

All of this misuse and overuse of antibiotics creates unnecessary problems. The antibiotics kill off susceptible bacteria, while antibiotic-resistant bacteria, the "fittest" organisms, survive and multiply to increase the population of resistant organisms and decrease the antibiotic's future usefulness. In addition, unnecessary antibiotics can destroy the valuable bacteria that live in the human body. These bacteria are helpful and necessary for the body's proper functioning. For example, intestinal bacteria have a vital nutritional function, producing several B vitamins and vitamin K (Levinson and Jawetz 22). The removal of these bacteria not only is dangerous to a patient's health but also allows antibiotic resistant bacteria to thrive. In the absence of these useful, nonpathogenic bacteria, the antibiotic-resistant organisms are no longer held in check by the competition for nutrients and the inhibition provided by the bacteria normally residing in the body.

Several other situations have also contributed to the problem of antibiotic resistance. The use of antibacterial soaps, detergents, lotions, and other household items is becoming increasingly common. Stuart Levy,

---

Margin notes:

A source with three authors lists all three last names in the citation. A citation to the same source that follows closely simply lists the page reference, not the authors' names.

A quotation by an authoritative source is integrated using an attributive phrase.

14

15

16

Van Arendonk 7

M.D., president of the Alliance for the Prudent Use of Antibiotics, says that "there has never been evidence that they [antibacterial products] have a public health benefit. Good soap and water is sufficient in most cases" (qtd. in Bren 31). People buy into the idea that antibacterial products are of great benefit to public health, that these products are dutifully protecting them from pathogens lurking all around them. Usually, however, these products just kill off harmless bacteria on the surface of the skin while encouraging the development and proliferation of resistant strains of bacteria.

The citation indicates that the source was quoted in another source.

Finally, the extensive use of antibiotics in agriculture also contributes to this problem. Of the 160 million prescriptions written for antibiotics each year in the U.S., approximately 50 percent of those antibiotics are used in animals, agriculture, and aquaculture (Wenzel and Edmond 1962). Plants used for food are often sprayed with antibiotic fertilizers, and food-producing animals are often given antibiotics in their food. These measures help to control diseases and improve growth rates, but they also increase the unnecessary exposure of bacteria to antibiotics (Tortora, Funke, and Case 562). This exposure encourages the growth of antibiotic-resistant bacteria, and these bacteria can then be passed to humans where their infections can no longer be treated with past antibiotic therapies.

The writer summarizes his discussion and deepens it with a related point backed up with a documented example.

17

As antibiotic resistance reaches a threatening level, several organizations have started educational campaigns that seek to teach health-care workers and the public about the proper use of antibiotics. Programs like the CDC's National Campaign for Appropriate Antibiotic Use are trying to raise awareness of antibiotic resistance and its threat to health care. Many more educational efforts are needed to limit the overuse and misuse of antibiotics that are causing the threatening rise of antibiotic resistance. In addition to these efforts, researchers are also working to develop new antibiotics that can target the organisms that have grown resistant to the present arsenal of antibiotics. Until these new antibiotics are found, however, we must do everything possible to extend the effectiveness of the antibiotics that we already have. The proper use of antibiotics can limit the development of antibiotic resistance and prolong our ability to use the current antibiotics to successfully treat a wide array of human diseases. As we face the challenge of antibiotic resistance, we must not allow indiscriminate use and a lack of knowledge to destroy the great medical benefits of antibiotic therapies.

18

Sample Paper: Works-Cited List

The list of works cited begins on a separate page and includes the title, header, and page number.

Van Arendonk 8

Works Cited

"Antibiotic Overuse Campaign Gets Underway." <u>Medical Letter on the
CDC and FDA</u> 23 Feb. 2003: 24–25. <u>Academic Search Elite</u>.
EBSCOhost. U of Iowa Library. 4 Apr. 2005 <http://
www.ebscohost.com>.

"Antibiotic Resistance." <u>Postgraduate Medicine</u> Aug. 2002. <u>Academic
Search Elite</u>. EBSCOhost. U of Iowa Library. 8 Apr. 2005
<http://www.ebscohost.com>.

Bren, Linda. "Battle of the Bugs: Fighting Antibiotic Resistance." <u>FDA
Consumer</u> July/Aug. 2002: 28–34. <u>Academic Search Elite</u>.
EBSCOhost. U of Iowa Library. 8 Apr. 2005
<http://www.ebscohost.com>.

Sources are listed in alphabetical order by author (or by title if no author is given).

Davies, Peter D. "Does Increased Use of Antibiotics Result in Increased
Antibiotic Resistance?" <u>Clinical Infectious Diseases</u> 39.1
(2004). <u>PubMed</u>. U of Iowa Library. 3 Apr. 2005
<http://www.ncbi.nlm.nih.gov/entrez/query.fcgi>.

"Fact Sheet: The Problem of Antibiotic Resistance." <u>National Institute of
Allergy and Infectious Diseases.</u> Apr. 2004. U.S. Department
of Health and Human Services. 31 Mar. 2005.
<http://www.niaid.nih.gov/factsheets/antimicro.htm>.

Titles are properly underlined (not italicized) or placed in quotation marks.

Kairys, David J. "The Science Behind Antibiotic Resistance." <u>Review of
Optometry</u> 15 Oct. 2002: 39–44. <u>Academic Search Elite</u>. EBSCOhost.
U of Iowa Library. 5 Apr. 2005 <http://www.ebscohost.com>.

Levinson, Warren, and Ernest Jawetz. <u>Medical Microbiology and
Immunology</u>. Stamford, CT: Appleton and Lange, 1996.

Van Arendonk 9

Items are double-spaced throughout. Second and subsequent lines are indented (hanging indent).

Mims, Cedric, Hazel M. Dockrell, Richard V. Goering, Ivan Roitt, Derek Wakelin, and Mark Zuckerman. <u>Medical Microbiology</u>. Edinburgh: Mosby, 2004.

Pugh, Maureen B., and Barbara Werner, eds. "Antibiotic." <u>Stedman's Medical Dictionary</u>. 27th ed. Philadelphia: Lippincott Williams & Wilkins, 2000.

"Survey: One-Third of Americans Use Antibiotics Inappropriately." <u>Medical Letter on the CDC and FDA</u> 19 Jan. 2003: 9–10. <u>Academic Search Elite</u>. EBSCOhost. U of Iowa Library. 8 Apr. 2005 <http://www.ebscohost.com>.

Tortora, Gerard J., Berdell R. Funke, and Christine L. Case. <u>Microbiology: An Introduction</u>. San Francisco: Benjamin Cummings, 2002.

Wenzel, Richard P., and Michael B. Edmond. "Managing Antibiotic Resistance." <u>New England Journal of Medicine</u> 343.26 (2000): 1961–63.

Correct abbreviations are used throughout.

Writing Prompt

Reading for Better Writing

1. What do you know about antibiotics and bacterial infections? How did Kyle's paper affect your understanding?

2. Did you find the essay engaging? Why or why not?

3. What types of evidence does Kyle provide in his writing? Where does he get his evidence?

4. How does Kyle distinguish his own ideas from source material? Why are these strategies necessary?

5. Kyle's topic is related to the broader subject of illness and medication. How is his discussion related to other issues, such as global health, the U.S. health system, and the pharmaceutical industry?

Checklist for MLA Format

As you format your paper and document your research according to MLA guidelines, use the checklist below to review your work.

_____ All borrowed material is acknowledged with an appropriate attributive phrase and/or in-text citation indicating author and page number, as appropriate.

_____ The works-cited list includes entries for all works referred to in the body of the paper: No sources are missing from the list; no extra sources are listed that have no reference within the paper.

_____ The entire works-cited list is properly alphabetized by authors' last names (or by the first main word in the title for anonymous works).

_____ Each works-cited entry contains the maximum amount of identifying and publication information, in the proper order, using all of the expected abbreviations.

_____ The entire paper is properly formatted from the first page heading and title to the final works-cited page entry.

_____ Placement, spacing, and margins are correct for the paper's header, the heading, the title, and "Works Cited."

_____ Pagination is correct and consistent.

_____ First lines of paragraphs and inset quotations are properly indented; works-cited entries are properly formatted with hanging indent.

_____ The paper is cleanly printed single-sided on quality paper.

_____ The paper is properly bound with a paper clip in the upper left corner.

Writing Prompt

Writing Activities

1. Create MLA works-cited entries for the following publications:

a. An article in the May 27, 2002, issue (vol. 145, no. 11) of *Fortune* magazine by Joseph Nocera titled "Return of the Raider" (pages 97–114)

b. Ernest Hemingway's novel *A Farewell to Arms*, published in 1986 by Collier Books, located in New York City

c. A webpage called "Aruba," part of *The World Factbook 2001* site, sponsored by the Central Intelligence Agency. No author or publication date is listed on the site; it was last accessed on March 8, 2002, at <http://www.cia.gov/cia/publications/ factbook/ index.html>.

2. Using the MLA documentation style, create works-cited entries for three possible sources (one book, one magazine or journal article, and one online source) for a research paper.

Chapter 34
APA Documentation Format

Those who write papers in the social sciences—psychology, sociology, political science, education, journalism, or public health—usually refer to the style guidelines found in the *Publication Manual of the American Psychological Association* (APA). The questions and answers on the next two pages should help you set up a research paper using this style.

APA documentation format is similar to MLA format in two ways: Both require (1) parenthetical citations within the text and (2) a final listing of all references cited in the paper. But in the social sciences, the date of publication is often much more crucial than it is in the humanities, so the date is highlighted in in-text citations. APA format also requires a cover page and an abstract. For exact instructions in proper APA documentation style, consult this chapter and the model APA-style research paper on pages 556–564.

What's Ahead

- APA Research Paper Guidelines
- APA Paper Format
- Guidelines for In-Text Citations
- Sample In-Text Citations
- APA References: Quick Guide
- Reference Entries: Books and Other Documents
- Reference Entries: Print Periodical Articles
- Reference Entries: Online Sources
- Reference Entries: Other Sources (Primary, Personal, and Multimedia)
- Sample APA Paper
- Checklist and Writing Activities
- Research Paper Abbreviations

APAAPAAPAAPAAPAAPAAPA

APA Research Paper Guidelines

Questions & Answers

Is a separate title page required?	*Yes.* Include your paper's title, your name, and the name of your school on three separate lines, double-spaced, centered, and beginning approximately one-third of the way down from the top of the page. Place a shortened title and page number 1 in the top right corner. (See "What about paging?" on the next page.)
What is an abstract and where does it go?	An abstract is required in APA format. An abstract is a 100- to 150-word paragraph summarizing your research paper. (See page **557**.) Place your abstract on a new page and label it "Abstract" (centered); type your short title and page number 2 flush right one-half inch from the top.
Are references placed in the text?	*Yes.* Include the author and year, separated by a comma; for quotations, add the page number after a comma and "p."
Do you need a bibliography of sources used in the paper?	*Yes.* Full citations for all sources used (books, periodicals, and so on) are placed in an alphabetized list labeled "References" at the end of the paper.
How are the reference lists to be indented?	Confusion sometimes arises over how the reference lists of APA manuscripts should be indented. Normal paragraph indentation has been called for by APA in the past. However, hanging indentation as shown in this chapter is currently the preferred manuscript form for APA documents, including student papers. As always, ask your instructor if you are in doubt.
Do you need an appendix?	*Maybe.* Ask your instructor. In student papers, charts, tables, and graphs may sometimes be incorporated at appropriate points in the text, making appendices unnecessary.

What about longer quotations?	Type quotations of 40 or more words in block style (all lines flush left) five spaces in from the left margin. Indent the first lines of any additional paragraphs in the long quotation five spaces in from the margin set for the quotation.
What about margins?	Leave a margin of at least one inch on all four sides (if you are binding your paper, leave one and one-half inches at the left margin); computer users may use a justified right margin, and end-of-line hyphens are acceptable in this format.
What about paging?	Page numbers appear at the top right margin, above the first line of text. Instead of your name, place the short title (first two or three words) either above, or five spaces to the left of, each page number.
What about headings?	Headings, like an outline, show the organization of your paper and the importance of each topic. All topics of equal importance should have headings of the same level, or style. Below are the various levels of headings used in APA papers. (In most research papers, only levels 1, 3, and 4 are used.)

LEVEL 1:   Centered Uppercase and Lowercase Heading

LEVEL 2:   *Centered, Italicized, Uppercase and Lowercase Heading*

LEVEL 3:   *Flush Left, Italicized, Uppercase and Lowercase Side Heading*

LEVEL 4:   *Indented, italicized, lowercase paragraph heading ending with a period.*

Any other special instructions?	Always ask whether your school or department has special requirements that may take precedence over these guidelines.

Web Link

APA Paper Format

This overview gives formatting guidelines for an APA research paper. Ask your instructor for any special requirements that he or she may have.

Title Page On the first page, include your paper's title, your name, and your institution's name on three separate lines. Double-space and center the lines beginning approximately one-third of the way down from the top of the page.

Abstract On the second page, include an abstract—a 100- to 150-word paragraph summarizing your paper. Place the title *Abstract* approximately one inch from the top of the page and center it.

Body Format the body (which begins on the third page) of your paper as follows:

> **Margins:** Leave a one-inch margin on all four sides of each page (one and one-half inches on the left for paper to be bound). A justified right margin and end-of-line hyphens are acceptable.

> **Line Spacing:** Double-space your entire paper, unless your instructor allows single spacing for tables, titles, captions, and so on, for the sake of readability.

> **Headings:** Main headings should be centered, using standard upper-case and lowercase text.

> **Page Numbers:** Place your short title (the first two or three words) and the page number at the upper-right margin of all pages beginning with the title page. The title should be either just above or five spaces to the left of the page number.

Citations Within your paper, give credit for others' ideas by including the author and year in a citation. For quotations, add the page number(s) to the citation. (See page **541**.) If a quotation runs 40 words or more, type it in block style, five spaces in from the left margin, with all lines flush left along that new margin. If it is more than one paragraph, indent the first line of the second and later paragraphs another five spaces.

References Place full citations from all sources in an alphabetized list at the end of your paper. Place the title *References* approximately one inch from the top of the page and center it. (See page **564**.)

Appendix If your instructor requires it, place your charts, tables, and graphs in an appendix. Otherwise, include them within the body of your paper.

Guidelines for In-Text Citations

The Form of an Entry

The APA documentation style is sometimes called the "author-date" system because both the author and the date of the publication must be mentioned in the text when citing a source. Both might appear in the flow of the sentence, like this:

> **Only South Africa has more people infected with AIDS than India, according to a 2001 article by Mike Specter.**

If either name or date does not appear in the text, it must be mentioned within parentheses at the most convenient place, like this:

> **According to an article by Mike Specter (2001), only South Africa . . .**
>
> **According to a recent article (Specter, 2001), only South Africa . . .**

Points to Remember

1. When paraphrasing rather than quoting, make it clear where your borrowing begins and ends. Use stylistic cues to distinguish the source's thoughts ("Kalmbach points out . . . ," "Some critics argue . . .") from your own ("I believe . . . ," "It seems obvious, however . . .").

2. When using a shortened title of a work, begin with the word by which the work is alphabetized in your references list (for example, for "Measurement of Stress in Fasting Man," use "Measurement of Stress," not "Fasting Man").

3. When including a parenthetical citation at the end of a sentence, place it before the end punctuation: *(Sacks, 1964).*

Sample In-Text Citations

One Author: A Complete Work

The correct form for a parenthetical reference to a single source by a single author is parenthesis, last name, comma, space, year of publication, parenthesis. Also note that final punctuation should be placed outside the parentheses.

> **. . . and the great majority of Venezuelans live near the Caribbean coast (Anderson, 2001).**

One Author: Part of a Work

When you cite a specific part of a source, give the page number, chapter, or section, using the appropriate abbreviations (*p.* or *pp., chap.,* or *sec.*—for other abbreviations, see pages 545, 566). Always give the page number for a direct quotation.

> **. . . Bush's 2002 budget was based on revenue estimates that "now appear to have been far too optimistic" (Lemann, 2001, p. 48).**

One Author: Several Publications in the Same Year

If the same author has published two or more articles in the same year, avoid confusion by placing a small letter *a* after the first work listed in the references list, *b* after the next one, and so on. The order of such works is determined alphabetically by title.

PARENTHETICAL CITATION

Reefs harbor life forms heretofore unknown (Milius, 2001a, 2001b).

REFERENCES

Milius, D. (2001a). Another world hides inside coral reefs. *Science News, 160*(16), 244.

Milius, D. (2001b). Unknown squids—with elbows—tease science. *Science News, 160*(24), 390.

Works by Authors with the Same Last Name

When citing different sources by authors with the same last name, add the authors' initials in order to avoid confusion, even if the publication dates are different.

While J. D. Wallace (2005) argued that privatizing social security would benefit only the wealthiest citizens, others such as E. S. Wallace (2006) supported greater control for individuals.

Two to Five Authors

In APA style, all authors—up to as many as five—must be mentioned in the text citation, like this:

Love changes not just who we are, but who we can become, as well (Lewis, Amini, & Lannon, 2000).

Note: The last two authors' names are always separated by a comma and an ampersand (&) when enclosed in parentheses.

For works with more than two but less than six authors, list all the authors the first time; after that, use only the name of the first author followed by "et al." (the Latin abbreviation for *et alii,* meaning "and others"), like this:

These discoveries lead to the hypothesis that love actually alters the brain's structure (Lewis et al., 2000).

Six or More Authors

If your source has six or more authors, refer to the work by the first author's name followed by "et al.," both for the first reference in the text and all references after that. However, be sure to list all the authors (up to six) in your references list.

According to a recent study, posttraumatic stress disorder (PTSD) continues to dominate the lives of Vietnam veterans, though in modified forms (Trembley et al, 2005).

A Work Authored by Agency, Committee, or Other Organization

Treat the name of the group as if it were the last name of the author. If the name is long and easily abbreviated, provide the abbreviation in square brackets. Use the abbreviation without brackets in subsequent references, as follows:

First Text Citation:

A problem for many veterans continues to be heightened sensitivity to noise (National Institute of Mental Health [NIMH], 2005).

Subsequent Citations:

In addition, veterans suffering from PTSD continue to have difficulty discussing their experiences (NIMH, 2005).

A Work with No Author Indicated

If your source lists no author, treat the first two or three words of the title (capitalized normally) as you would an author's last name. A title of an article or a chapter belongs in quotation marks; the titles of books or reports should be italicized:

. . . including a guide to low-stress postures ("How to Do It," 2001).

A Work Referred to in Another Work

If you need to cite a source that you have found referred to in another source (a "secondary" source), mention the original source in your text. Then, in your parenthetical citation, cite the secondary source, using the words "as cited in."

. . . theorem given by Ullman (as cited in Hoffman, 1998).

Note: In your references list at the end of the paper, you would write out a full citation for Hoffman (not Ullman).

A Work in an Anthology

When citing an article or a chapter in an anthology or collection, use the authors' names for the specific article, not the names of the anthology's editors. (Similarly, the article should be listed by its authors' names in the references section. See page 546.)

Phonological changes can be understood from a variationist perspective (Guy, 2005).

An Electronic or Other Internet Source

As with print sources, cite an electronic source by the author (or by shortened title if the author is unknown) and the publication date (not the date you accessed the source). If citing a specific part of the source, use an appropriate abbreviation: p. for page, ¶ (paragraph symbol) or para. for paragraph, and chap. for chapter.

One study compared and contrasted the use of web and touch screen transaction log files in a hospital setting (Nicholas, Huntington, & Williams, 2001).

A Website

Whenever possible, cite a website by its author and posting date. In addition, refer to a specific page or document rather than to a home page or a menu page. If you are referring to a specific part of a webpage that does not have page numbers, direct your reader, if possible, with a section heading and a paragraph number.

> **According to the National Multiple Sclerosis Society (2003,**
> **"Complexities" section, para. 2), understanding of MS could not begin**
> **until scientists began to research nerve transmission in the 1920s.**

Two or More Works in a Parenthetical Reference

Sometimes it is necessary to lump several citations into one parenthetical reference. In that case, cite the sources as you usually would, separating the citations with semicolons. Place the citations in alphabetical order, just as they would be ordered in the references list:

> **These near-death experiences are reported with conviction (Rommer,**
> **2000; Sabom, 1998).**

A Sacred Text or Famous Literary Work

Sacred texts and famous literary works are published in many different editions. For that reason, the original date of publication may be unavailable or not pertinent. In these cases, use your edition's year of translation (for example, trans. 2003) or indicate your edition's year of publication (2003 version). When you are referring to specific sections of the work, it is best to identify parts, chapters, or other divisions instead of your version's page numbers.

> **An interesting literary case of such dysfunctional family behavior can**
> **be found in Franz Kafka's *The Metamorphosis*, where it becomes the**
> **commandment of family duty for Gregor's parents and sister to swallow**
> **their disgust and endure him (trans. 1972, part 3).**

Books of the Bible and other well-known literary works may be abbreviated, if no confusion is possible.

> **"Generations come and generations go, but the earth remains forever"**
> **(*The New International Version Study Bible*, 1985 version, Eccles. 1.4)**

Personal Communications

If you do the kind of personal research recommended elsewhere in *The College Writer*, you may have to cite personal communications that have provided you with some of your knowledge. Personal communications may include personal letters, phone calls, memos, and so forth. Because they are not published in a permanent form, APA style does not place them among the citations in your references list. Instead, cite them only in the text of your paper in parentheses, like this:

> **. . . according to M. T. Cann (personal communication, April 1, 1999).**
> **. . . by today (M. T. Cann, personal communication, April 1, 1999).**

APA References

The references section lists all the sources you have cited in your text (with the exception of personal communications such as phone calls and e-mails). Begin your reference list on a new page after the last page of your paper. Number each references page, continuing the numbering from the text. Then format your references list by following the guidelines below.

1. Type the short title and page number in the upper-right corner, approximately one-half inch from the top of the page.

2. Center the title, *References*, approximately one inch from the top; then double-space before the first entry.

3. Begin each entry flush with the left margin. If the entry runs more than one line, indent additional lines approximately one-half inch (five to seven spaces) using a hanging indent.

4. Adhere to the following conventions about spacing, capitalization, and italics:

- Double-space between all lines on the references page.
- Use one space following each word and punctuation mark in an entry.
- With book and article titles, capitalize only the first letter of the title (and subtitle) and proper nouns. (Note that this practice differs from the presentation of titles in the body of the essay.) ***Example:*** The impact of the cold war on Asia.
- Use italics for titles of books and periodicals, not underlining.

5. List each entry alphabetically by the last name of the author, or, if no author is given, by the title (disregarding *A, An,* or *The*). For works with multiple authors, use the name of the first author listed in the publication.

6. Follow these conventions with respect to abbreviations:

- With authors' names, generally shorten first and middle names to initials, leaving a space after the period. For a work with more than one author, use an ampersand (&) before the last author's name.
- For publisher locations, use the full city name plus the two-letter U.S. Postal Service abbreviation for the state. For international publishers, include a province and country name; for well-known publishing cities such as Boston and Amsterdam, whether U.S. or international, you may name the city only.
- Spell out "Press" in full, but for other publishing information, use the abbreviations below. Also see page 566.

Second edition	. . . . . . .2nd ed.	Technical Report	. . . . . .Tech. Rep.
Part	. . . . .Pt.	Supplement	. . . . .Suppl.

Video

Reference Entries: Books and Other Documents

The general form for a book or brochure entry is this:
Author, A. (year). *Title*. Location: Publisher.

The entries that follow illustrate the information needed to cite books, sections of a book, brochures, and government publications.

A Book by One Author

Guttman, J. (1999). *The gift wrapped in sorrow: A mother's quest for healing*. Palm Springs, CA: JMJ Publishing.

A Book by Two or More Authors

Lynn, J., & Harrold, J. (1999). *Handbook for mortals: Guidance for people facing serious illness*. New York: Oxford University Press.

An Anonymous Book

If an author is listed as "Anonymous," treat it as the author's name. Otherwise, follow this format:

Publication manual of the American Psychological Association (5th ed.). (2001). Washington, DC: American Psychological Association.

A Chapter from a Book

List the chapter title after the date of publication, followed by a period or appropriate end punctuation. Use *In* before the book title, and follow the book title with the inclusive page numbers of the chapter.

Tattersall, I. (2002). How did we achieve humanity? In *The monkey in the mirror* (pp. 138–168). New York: Harcourt.

A Single Work from an Anthology

Start with information about the individual work, followed by details about the collection in which it appears, including the page span. When editors' names come in the middle of an entry, follow the usual order: initial first, surname last. Note the placement of *Eds.* in parentheses.

Guy, G. R. (2005). Variationist approaches to phonological change. In B. D. Joseph & R. D. Janda (Eds.), *The handbook of historical linguistics* (pp. 369–400). Malden, MA: Blackwell.

One Volume of a Multivolume Edited Work

Indicate the volume in parentheses after the work's title.

Salzman, J., Smith, D. L., & West, C. (Eds.). (1996). *Encyclopedia of African-American culture and history* **(Vol. 4). New York: Simon & Schuster Macmillan.**

A Separately Titled Volume in a Multivolume Work

The Associated Press. (1995). *Twentieth-Century America: Vol. 8. The crisis of national confidence: 1974–1980.* **Danbury, CT: Grolier Educational Corp.**

Note: When a work is part of a larger series or collection, as with this example, make a two-part title of the series and the particular volume you are citing.

An Edited Work, One in a Series

Start the entry with the work's author, publication date, and title. Then follow with publication details about the series.

Marshall, P. G. (2002). The impact of the cold war on Asia. In T. O'Neill (Ed.), *World history by era: Vol. 9. The nuclear age* **(pp. 162-166). San Diego: Greenhaven Press.**

A Group Author as Publisher

When the author is also the publisher, simply put *Author* in the spot where you would list the publisher's name.

Amnesty International. (2000). *Hidden scandal, secret shame: Torture and ill-treatment of children.* **New York: Author.**

Note: If the publication is a brochure, identify it as such in brackets after the title.

An Edition Other Than the First

Trimmer, J. (2001). *Writing with a purpose* **(13th ed.). Boston: Houghton Mifflin.**

Two or More Books by the Same Author

When you are listing multiple works by the same author, arrange them by the year of publication, earliest first.

Dershowitz, A. (2000). *The Genesis of justice: Ten stories of biblical injustice that led to the Ten Commandments and modern law.* **New York: Warner Books.**

Dershowitz, A. (2002). *Shouting fire: Civil liberties—past, present, and future.* **Boston: Little, Brown.**

An English Translation

Setha, R. (1998). *Unarmed* (R. Narasimhan, Trans.). Chennai, India: Macmillan. (Original work published 1995)

Note: If you use the original work, cite the original version; the non-English title is followed by its English translation, not italicized, in square brackets.

An Article in a Reference Book

Start the entry with the author of the article, if identified. If no author is listed, begin the entry with the title of the article.

Lewer, N. (1999). Non-lethal weapons. In *World encyclopedia of peace* (pp. 279–280). Oxford: Pergamon Press.

A Reprint, Different Form

Albanov, V. (2000). *In the land of white death: An epic story of survival in the Siberian Arctic.* New York: Modern Library. (Original work published 1917)

Note: This work was originally published in Russia in 1917; the 2000 reprint is the first English version. If you are citing a reprint from another source, the parentheses would contain "Reprinted from *Title*, pp. xx–xx, by A. Author, year, Location: Publisher."

A Technical or Research Report

Taylor, B. G., Fitzgerald, N., Hunt, D., Reardon, J. A., & Brownstein, H. H. (2001). *ADAM preliminary 2000 findings on drug use and drug markets: Adult male arrestees.* Washington, DC: National Institute of Justice.

A Government Publication

Generally, refer to the government agency as the author. When possible, provide an identification number for the document after the title in parentheses.

National Institute on Drug Abuse. (2000). *Inhalant abuse* (NIH Publication No. 00–3818). Rockville, MD: National Clearinghouse on Alcohol and Drug Information.

Note: If the document is not available from the Government Printing Office (GPO), the publisher would be either "Author" or the separate government department that published it.

Video

Reference Entries: Print Periodical Articles

The general form for a periodical entry is this:
Author, A. (year). Article title. *Periodical Title, volume number*, page numbers.

Include some other designation with the year (such as a month or a season) if a periodical does not use volume numbers. The entries that follow illustrate the information and arrangement needed to cite periodicals.

An Article in a Scholarly Journal, Consecutively Paginated

Epstein, R., & Hundert, E. (2002). Defining and assessing professional competence. *JAMA, 287*, 226–235.

Note: Pay attention to the features of this basic reference to a scholarly journal: (1) last name and initial(s) as for a book reference, (2) year of publication, (3) title of article in lowercase, except for the first word; title not italicized or in quotations, (4) title and volume number of journal italicized, and (5) inclusive page numbers.

An Abstract of a Scholarly Article (from a Secondary Source)

When referencing an abstract published separately from an article, provide publication details of the article followed by information about where the abstract was published.

Shlipak, M. G., Simon, J. A., Grady, O., Lin, F., Wenger, N. K., & Furberg, C. D. (2001, September). Renal insufficiency and cardiovascular events in postmenopausal women with coronary heart disease. *Journal of the American College of Cardiology, 38*, 705–711. Abstract obtained from *Geriatrics*, 2001, 56(12), Abstract No. 5645351.

A Journal Article, Paginated by Issue

Lewer, N. (1999, summer). Nonlethal weapons. *Forum, 14*(2), 39–45.

Note: When the page numbering of the issue starts with page 1, the issue number (not italicized) is placed in parentheses after the volume number. (Some journals number pages consecutively, from issue to issue, through their whole volume year.)

A Journal Article, More Than Six Authors

> Wang, X., Zuckerman, B., Pearson, C., Kaufman, G., Chen, C., Wang, G., et al. (2002, January 9). Maternal cigarette smoking, metabolic gene polymorphism, and infant birth weight. *JAMA, 287,* 195–202.

Note: In the text, abbreviate the parenthetical citation as follows: (Wang et al., 2002).

A Review

To reference a book review or a review of another medium (film, exhibit, and so on), indicate the review and the medium in brackets, along with the title of the work being reviewed by the author listed.

> Updike, J. (2001, December 24). Survivor/believer [Review of the book *New and Collected Poems 1931–2001*]. *The New Yorker,* 118–122.

A Magazine Article

> Silberman, S. (2001, December). The geek syndrome. *Wired, 9*(12), 174–183.

Note: If the article is unsigned, begin the entry with the title of the article.

> Tomatoes target toughest cancer. (2002, February). *Prevention, 54*(2), 53.

A Newspaper Article

For newspaper articles, include the full publication date, year first followed by a comma, the month (spelled out) and the day. Identify the article's location in the newspaper using page numbers and section letters, as appropriate. If the article is a letter to the editor, identify it as such in brackets following the title. For newspapers, use *p.* or *pp.* before the page numbers; if the article is not on continuous pages, give all the page numbers, separated by commas.

> Stolberg, S. C. (2002, January 4). Breakthrough in pig cloning could aid organ transplants. *The New York Times,* pp. 1A, 17A.

> AOL to take up to $60 billion charge. (2002, January 8). *Chicago Tribune,* sec. 3, p. 3.

A Newsletter Article

Newsletter article entries are similar to newspaper article entries; only a volume number is added.

> Teaching mainstreamed special education students. (2002, February). *The Council Chronicle, 11,* 6–8.

Reference Entries: Online Sources

APA style prefers a reference to the print form of a source, even if the source is available online. If you have read *only* the electronic form of an article's print version, add "Electronic version" in brackets after the title of the article. In other words, the electronic address (URL) is not required if a print version exists. If an online article has been changed from the print version or has additional information, follow the same general format for the author, date, and title elements of print sources, but follow it with a "retrieved from" statement, citing the date of retrieval and the URL. When offering a URL, make sure that the address is correct; in addition, if the URL ends the reference entry, do not follow the address with a punctuation mark such as a period. Here are basic forms:

Online Periodical:
Author, A. A. (year). Title of article. *Title of Periodical, xx*, xxx–xxx.
      Retrieved month day, year, from source.

Online Document:
Author, A. A. (year). *Title of work*. Retrieved month day, year, from
      source.

Periodical, Identical to Print Version

Author, A., & Author, B. (year, month day). Title of article, chapter, or webpage [Electronic version]. *Title of Periodical, volume number or other designation,* inclusive page numbers (if available).

> **Ashley, S. (2001, May). Warp drive underwater [Electronic version].**
> ***Scientific American* (2001, May).**

Periodical, Different from Print Version or Online Only

Author, A., & Author, B. (year, month day). Title of article, chapter, or webpage. *Title of Periodical, volume number,* inclusive page numbers if available. Retrieved Month day, year, from electronic address

> **Nicholas, D., Huntington, P., & Williams, P. (2001, May 23). Comparing**
> **web and touch screen transaction log files. *Journal of Medical***
> ***Internet Research*, 3. Retrieved Nov. 15, 2001, from**
> **http://www.jmir.org/2001/2/e18/index.htm**

Note: Include an issue number in parentheses following the volume number if each issue of a journal begins on page 1. Use *pp.* (page numbers) for newspapers. Page numbers are often not relevant for online sources. End the citation with a period unless it ends with the electronic address.

A Multipage Document Created by a Private Organization

> National Multiple Sclerosis Society. (n.d.) *About MS: For the newly diagnosed.* Retrieved May 20, 2002, from http://www.nationalmssociety.org

Note: Use *n.d.* (no date) when a publication date is not available. Provide the URL of the home page for an Internet document when its pages have different URLs.

A Document from an Online Database

Author, A., & Author, B. (year). Title of article or webpage. *Title of Periodical, volume number,* inclusive page numbers. Retrieved Month day, year, from name of database.

> Belsie, Laurent. (1999). Progress or peril? *Christian Science Monitor,* 91(85), 15. Retrieved September 15, 1999, from DIALOG online database (#97, IAC Business A.R.T.S., Item 07254533).

Note: If the document cited is an abstract, include *Abstract* before the "retrieved" statement. The item or access numbers may be included but are not required.

Other Nonperiodical Online Document

> Boyles, S. (2001, Nov. 14). World diabetes day. Retrieved Nov. 16, 2001, from http://my.webmd.com/content/article/1667.51328

Note: To cite only a chapter or section of an online document, follow the title of the chapter with "In *Title of document* (chap. number)." If the author is not identified, begin with the title of the document. If a date is not identified, put "n.d." in parentheses after the title.

> Catholic Near East Welfare Association. (2002). Threats to personal security. In *Report on Christian emigration: Palestine* (sect. 5). Retrieved May 20, 2002, from http://www.cnewa.org/news-christemigrat-part1.htm

A Document or Abstract Available on University Program or Department Website

> Magill, G. (2001). *Ethics of stem cell research.* Retrieved Nov. 23, 2001, from St. Louis University, Center for Health Care Ethics website: http://www.slu.edu/centers/chce/drummond/magill.html

Note: Name the university or government agency (and the department or division, if it is named), followed by a colon and the URL. The host organization and the relevant program or department are listed before the URL when a document is contained within a large, complex website. If the document or abstract has no author indicated, begin the entry with the work's title.

A Report from a University, Available on Private Organization's Website

University, Institute. (Year, month). *Title of work*. Retrieved Month day, year, from electronic address

> **Kaiser Family Foundation and University of Wisconsin, Sonderegger Research Center. (2000, July).** *Prescription drug trends—a chartbook.* **Retrieved Nov. 19, 2001, from http://www.kff.org/ content/2000/3019/**

Note: If the private organization is not listed as an author, identify it in the "retrieved from" statement.

A U.S. Government Report Available on Government Agency Website

Name of government agency. (Year, month day). *Title of report*. Retrieved Month day, year, from electronic address

> **United States Department of Commerce, Office of the Inspector General. (2001, March).** *Internal controls over bankcard program need improvement.* **Retrieved July 23, 2001, from http://www.oig.doc.gov/e-library/reports/recent/recent.html**

Note: If no publication date is given, use *n.d.* in parentheses after the agency name.

A Paper Presented at a Symposium or Other Event, Abstract Retrieved from University Website

Author, A. (Year, month day). *Title of paper*. Paper presented at name of event. Abstract retrieved Month day, year, from electronic address

> **Smale, S. (2001, Nov. 7).** *Learning and the evolution of language.* **Paper presented at Brains and Machines Seminar Series. Abstract retrieved Nov. 23, 2001, from http://www.ai.mit.edu/ events/talks/brainsMachines/abstracts/F2001/ 200111071700_StephenSmale.shtml**

Note: To cite a virtual conference, do not use *Abstract* before the "retrieved from" statement.

An E-mail Message

E-mail is cited only in the text of the paper, not in the references list. See "Personal Communications," on page 544.

Video

Reference Entries: Other Sources (Primary, Personal, and Multimedia)

The following citation entries are examples of audiovisual media sources and sources available electronically.

Specialized Computer Software with Limited Distribution

Standard nonspecialized computer software does not require a reference entry. Treat software as an unauthored work unless an individual has property rights to it.

> Carreau, Stéphane. (2001). Champfoot (Version 3.3) [Computer software]. Saint Mandé, France: Author.

Show the software version in parentheses after the title and the medium in brackets.

An Electronic Abstract of a Journal Article Retrieved from a Database

The following format applies whether the database is on CD, a website, or a university server. The item or accession number is not required, but may be included in parentheses at the end of the retrieval statement.

> Seyler, T. (1994). College-level studies: New memory techniques. *New Century Learners, 30*, 814–822. Abstract retrieved Feb. 1, 1995, from Platinum File: EduPLUS database (40–18421).

A Television or Radio Broadcast

List a broadcast by the show's producer or executive producer, and identify the type of broadcast in brackets after the show's title.

> Crystal, L. (Executive Producer). (2002, February 11). *The NewsHour with Jim Lehrer* [Television broadcast]. New York and Washington, DC: Public Broadcasting Service.

A Television or Radio Series or Episode

When referencing an entire series, identify the series producer and indicate the type of series in brackets after the title.

> Bloch, A. (Producer). (2002). *Thinking allowed* [Television series]. Berkeley: Public Broadcasting Service.

When identifying a specific episode in a television or radio series, indicate the episode by writers, if possible. Then follow with the airing date, the episode title, and the type of series in brackets. Complete the entry with details about the series itself.

> Berger, Cynthia. (Writer). (2001, December 19). Feederwatch [Radio series program]. In D. Byrd & J. Block (Producers), *Earth & Sky*. Austin, TX: The Production Block.

An Audio Recording

Begin the entry with the speaker's or writer's name, not the producer. Indicate the type of recording in brackets.

> **Kim, E. (Author, speaker). (2000).** *Ten thousand sorrows* **[CD]. New York: Random House.**

A Music Recording

Give the name and function of the originators or primary contributors. Indicate the recording medium in brackets immediately following the title.

> **ARS Femina Ensemble. (Performers). (1998).** *Musica de la puebla de los angeles: Music by women of baroque Mexico, Cuba, & Europe* **[CD]. Louisville, KY: Nannerl Recordings.**

A Motion Picture

Give the name and function of the director, producer, or both.

> **Jackson, P. (Director). (2001).** *The lord of the rings: The fellowship of the ring* **[Motion picture]. United States: New Line Productions, Inc.**

A Published Interview, Titled, No Author

Start the entry with the interview's title, followed by publication details.

> **Stephen Harper: The Report interview. (2002, January 7).** *The Report* **(Alberta, BC), 29, 10–11.**

A Published Interview, Titled, Single Author

Start the entry with the interviewee's name, followed by the date and the title. Place the interviewer's name in brackets before other publication details.

> **Fussman, C. (2002, January). What I've learned [Interview with Robert McNamara].** *Esquire, 137(1),* **85.**

An Unpublished Paper Presented at a Meeting

Indicate when the paper was presented, at what meeting, in what location.

> **Lycan, W. (2002, June).** *The plurality of consciousness.* **Paper presented at the meeting of the Society for Philosophy and Psychology, New York, NY.**

An Unpublished Doctoral Dissertation

Place the dissertation's title in italics, even though the work is unpublished. Indicate the school at which the writer completed the dissertation.

> **Roberts, W. (2001).** *Youth crime amidst suburban wealth.* **Unpublished doctoral dissertation, Bowling Green State University, Bowling Green, OH.**

Sample APA Paper

Student writers Thomas Delancy and Adam Solberg wrote the following research paper based on an experiment they conducted in a psychology course. You can use this model paper in three ways:

1. To study how a well-written research paper based in experimentation structures and builds a discussion from start to finish. (See pages **341–354** for more on experimentation and experiment reports.)

2. To examine how sources are used and integrated into social-science research writing—a full-length example of the strategies addressed on pages **488–491**.

3. To see in detail the format and documentation practices of APA style.

Sample Title Page

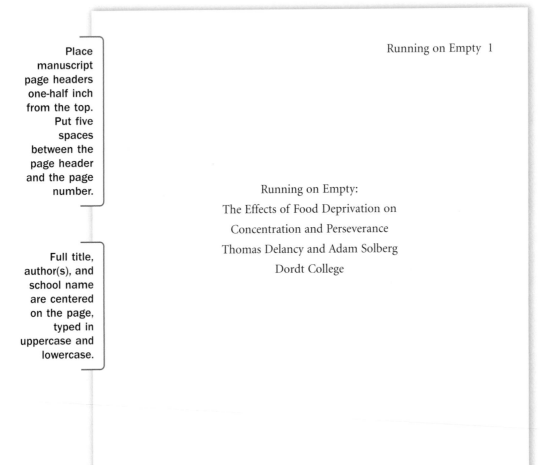

Running on Empty 1

Place manuscript page headers one-half inch from the top. Put five spaces between the page header and the page number.

Running on Empty:
The Effects of Food Deprivation on
Concentration and Perseverance
Thomas Delancy and Adam Solberg
Dordt College

Full title, author(s), and school name are centered on the page, typed in uppercase and lowercase.

Sample Abstract

The abstract summarizes the problem, participants, hypotheses, methods used, results, and conclusions.

Abstract

This study examined the effects of short-term food deprivation on two cognitive abilities—concentration and perseverance. Undergraduate students (N-51) were tested on both a concentration task and a perseverance task after one of three levels of food deprivation: none, 12 hours, or 24 hours. We predicted that food deprivation would impair both concentration scores and perseverance time. Food deprivation had no significant effect on concentration scores, which is consistent with recent research on the effects of food deprivation (Green et al., 1995; Green et al., 1997). However, participants in the 12-hour deprivation group spent significantly less time on the perseverance task than those in both the control and 24-hour deprivation groups, suggesting that short-term deprivation may affect some aspects of cognition and not others.

An APA Research Paper Model

As you review this paper, read the side notes and examine the following:

- The writers' use and documentation of numerous sources.
- The background they provide before getting into their own study results.
- The scientific language they use in reporting their results.

Running on Empty 3

Running on Empty: The Effects of Food Deprivation
on Concentration and Perseverance

Many things interrupt people's ability to focus on a task. To some
extent, people can control the environmental factors that make it difficult
to focus. However, what about internal factors, such as an empty stomach?
Can people increase their ability to focus simply by eating regularly?

One theory that prompted research on how food intake affects the
average person was the glucostatic theory, which suggested that the brain
regulates food intake (and hunger) in order to maintain a blood-glucose
set point. This theory seemed logical because glucose is the brain's primary
fuel (Pinel, 2000). The earliest investigation of the general effects of food
deprivation found that long-term food deprivation (36 hours or more)
was associated with sluggishness, depression, irritability, reduced heart
rate, and inability to concentrate (Keys, Brozek, Henschel, Mickelsen, &
Taylor, 1950). Since then, research has focused mainly on how nutrition
affects cognition. However, as Green, Elliman, and Rogers (1995) point
out, the effects of food deprivation on cognition have received
comparatively less attention in recent years, leaving room for further
research.

According to some researchers, most of the results so far indicate that
cognitive function is not affected significantly by short-term fasting
(Green et al., 1995, p. 246). However, this conclusion seems premature: No
study has tested perseverance, despite its importance in cognitive
functioning. Perseverance may be a better indicator than achievement tests
in assessing growth in learning and thinking abilities, as it helps in solving
complex problems (Costa, 1984). Testing as many aspects of cognition as

Side notes:

Center the title one inch from the top. Double-space throughout.

The introduction states the topic and the main questions to be explored.

The researchers supply background information by discussing past research on the topic.

The researchers support their decision to focus on concentration and perseverance.

Paragraph markers: 1, 2, 3

Running on Empty 4

possible is key because the nature of the task is important when interpreting the link between deprivation and cognitive performance (Smith & Kendrick, 1992).

The researchers state their initial hypotheses.

Therefore, the current study helps us understand how short-term food deprivation affects concentration on and perseverance with a difficult task. Specifically, participants deprived of food for 24 hours were expected to perform worse on a concentration test and a perseverance task than those deprived for 12 hours, who in turn were predicted to perform worse than those who were not deprived of food.

Method

Headings and subheadings show the paper's organization.

Participants

Participants included 51 undergraduate-student volunteers. The mean college grade point average (GPA) was 3.19. Potential participants were excluded if they were dieting, menstruating, or taking special medication. Those who had ever struggled with an eating disorder were excluded, as were potential participants addicted to nicotine or caffeine.

The experiment's method is described, using the terms and acronyms of the discipline.

Materials

Concentration speed and accuracy were measured using a numbers-matching test that consisted of 26 lines of 25 numbers each. Scores were calculated as the percentage of correctly identified pairs out of a possible 120. Perseverance was measured with a puzzle that contained five octagons, which were to be placed on top of each other in a specific way to make the silhouette of a rabbit. However, three of the shapes were slightly altered so that the task was impossible. Perseverance scores were calculated as the number of minutes that a participant spent on the puzzle task before giving up.

Passive voice is used to emphasize the experiment, not the researchers; otherwise, active voice is used.

Procedure

At an initial meeting, participants gave informed consent and supplied their GPAs. Students were informed that they would be notified about their assignment to one of the three groups and were given instructions.

The experiment is laid out step by step, with time transitions like "then" and "next."

Participants were then randomly assigned to one of the experimental conditions using a design based on the GPAs (to control individual differences in cognitive ability). Next, participants were informed of their group assignment and reminded of their instructions. Participants from the control group were tested at 7:30 p.m. on the day the deprivation started. Those in the 12-hour group were tested at 10 p.m. on that same day. Those in the 24-hour group were tested at 10:40 a.m. on the following day.

Attention is shown to the control features.

At their assigned time, participants arrived at a computer lab for testing. After all participants had completed the concentration test and their scores were recorded, participants were each given the silhouette puzzle. They were told that (1) they would have an unlimited amount of time to complete the task, and (2) they were not to tell any other participant whether they had completed the puzzle or simply given up. This procedure prevented group influence. Any participant still working on the puzzle after 40 minutes was stopped.

9

The writers summarize their findings, including problems encountered.

Results

Perseverance data from one control-group participant were eliminated, and concentration data from another control-group participant were dropped. The average concentration score was 77.78 (SD = 14.21), which was very good considering that anything over 50 percent is labeled "good" or "above average." The average time spent on the puzzle was 24.00 minutes (SD = 10.16).

10

The researchers restate their hypotheses and the results, and go on to interpret those results.

We predicted that participants in the 24-hour deprivation group would perform worse on the concentration test and the perseverance task than those in the 12-hour group, who in turn would perform worse than those in the control group. A one-way analysis of variance (ANOVA) showed no significant effect of deprivation condition on concentration, $F(2,46) = 1.06$, $p = .36$ (see Figure 1). Another one-way ANOVA indicated a significant effect of deprivation condition on perseverance time, $F(2,47) = 7.41$, $p < .05$. Post-hoc Tukey tests indicated that the 12-hour deprivation group (M = 17.79, SD = 7.84) spent significantly less time on the perseverance task than either the control group (M = 26.80, SD = 6.20) or the 24-hour group (M = 28.75, SD = 12.11), with no significant

11

"See Figure 1" sends readers to a figure (graph, photograph, chart, or drawing) contained in the paper.

Running on Empty 6

All figures
are
numbered in
the order in
which they
are first
mentioned in
the paper.

Figure 1.

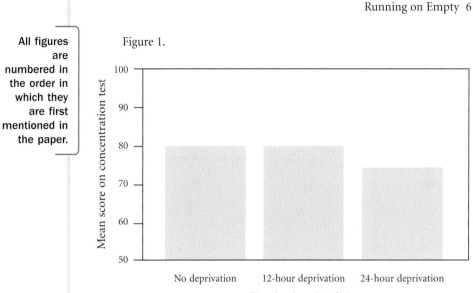

difference between the latter two groups (see Figure 2). Unexpectedly, food deprivation had no significant effect on concentration scores. Overall, we found support for our hypothesis that 12 hours of food deprivation would significantly impair perseverance when compared to no deprivation. Unexpectedly, 24 hours of food deprivation did not significantly affect perseverance relative to the control group.

Discussion

The purpose of this study was to test how different levels of food deprivation affect concentration on and perseverance with difficult tasks. We predicted that the longer people had been deprived of food, the lower they would score on the concentration task, and the less time they would spend on the perseverance task. In this study, those deprived of food did give up more quickly on the puzzle, but only in the 12-hour group. Thus, the hypothesis was partially supported for the perseverance task. However, concentration was found to be unaffected by food deprivation, and thus the hypothesis was not supported for that task.

The writers
speculate on
possible
explanations
for the
unexpected
results.

¹²

Figure 2.

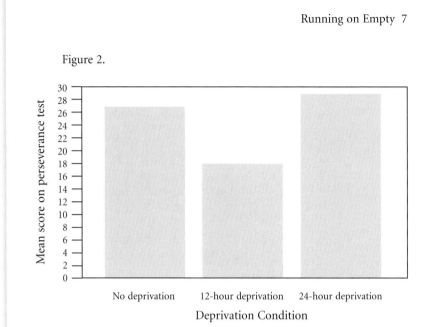

In terms of concentration, the findings of this study are consistent [13] with those of Green et al. (1995), where short-term food deprivation did not affect some aspects of cognition, including attentional focus. The findings on perseverance, however, are not as easily explained. We surmise that the participants in the 12-hour group gave up more quickly on the perseverance task because of their hunger. But those in the 24-hour group failed to yield the same effect. We postulate that this result can be explained by the concept of "learned industriousness," wherein participants who perform one difficult task do better on a subsequent task than participants who never did the initial task (Eisenberger & Leonard, 1980; Hickman, Stromme, & Lippman, 1998). Another possible explanation is that the motivational state of a participant may be a significant determinant of behavior under testing (Saugstad, 1967).

Research on food deprivation and cognition could continue in several [14] directions. First, other aspects of cognition may be affected by short-term food deprivation, such as reading comprehension or motivation. Perhaps, then, the motivation level of food-deprived participants could be

Running on Empty 8

effectively tested. Second, longer-term food deprivation periods, such as those experienced by people fasting for religious reasons, could be explored. It is possible that cognitive function fluctuates over the duration of deprivation. Third, and perhaps most fascinating, studies could explore how food deprivation affects learned industriousness.

In conclusion, the results of this study provide some fascinating insights into the cognitive and physiological effects of skipping meals. Contrary to what we predicted, a person may indeed be very capable of concentrating after not eating for many hours. On the other hand, performing a tedious task that requires perseverance, one may be hindered by not eating for a short time, as shown by the 12-hour group's performance on the perseverance task. Many people have to deal with short-term food deprivation, intentional or unintentional. This research and other research to follow will contribute to knowledge of the disadvantages—and possible advantages—of skipping meals. The mixed results of this study suggest that we have much more to learn about short-term food deprivation.

15

The conclusion summarizes the outcomes, stresses the experiment's value, and anticipates further advances on the topic.

Writing Prompt

Reading for Better Writing

1. Before you read Thomas and Adam's paper, what were your expectations about food deprivation's effects on concentration and perseverance? Did the paper confirm or confound your expectations?

2. Did you find the report interesting? Why or why not?

3. What types of evidence did Thomas and Adam use in their paper? Where did they obtain their evidence?

4. How did Thomas and Adam distinguish their own ideas from their sources' ideas? Was it necessary for them to do, and if so, why?

5. Could the results of Thomas and Adam's research be applied to other situations? How might particular groups interpret these findings?

References

Costa, A. L. (1984). Thinking: How do we know students are getting better at it? *Roeper Review, 6,* 197–199.

Eisenberger, R., & Leonard, J. M. (1980). Effects of conceptual task difficulty on generalized persistence. *American Journal of Psychology, 93,* 285–298.

Green, M. W., Elliman, N. A., & Rogers, P. J. (1995). Lack of effect of short-term fasting on cognitive function. *Journal of Psychiatric Research, 29,* 245–253.

Green, M. W., Elliman, N. A., & Rogers, P. J. (1997). The study effects of food deprivation and incentive motivation on blood glucose levels and cognitive function. *Psychopharmacology, 134,* 88–94.

Hickman, K. L., Stromme, C., & Lippman, L. G. (1998). Learned industriousness: Replication in principle. *Journal of General Psychology, 125,* 213–217.

Keys, A., Brozek, J., Henschel, A., Mickelsen, O., & Taylor, H. L. (1950). *The biology of human starvation* (Vol. 2). Minneapolis: University of Minnesota Press.

Pinel, J. P. (2000). *Biopsychology* (4th ed.). Boston: Allyn and Bacon.

Saugstad, P. (1967). Effect of food deprivation on perception-cognition: A comment [Comment on the article by David L. Wolitzky]. *Psychological Bulletin, 68,* 345–346.

Smith, A. P., & Kendrick, A. M. (1992). Meals and performance. In A. P. Smith & D. M. Jones (Eds.), *Handbook of human performance: Vol. 2, Health and performance* (pp. 1–23). San Diego: Academic Press.

All works referred to in the paper appear on the reference page, listed alphabetically by author (or title).

Each entry follows APA guidelines for listing authors, dates, titles, and publishing information.

Capitalization, punctuation, and hanging indentation are consistent with APA format.

Checklist for APA Format

When you are completing a paper in APA format, use the checklist below to ensure that you are following the format correctly.

_____ All borrowed material is acknowledged with an appropriate attributive phrase and/or in-text citation indicating author(s), publication date, and page number, as appropriate.

_____ All in-text citations effectively point readers to resources in the references list or to personal communication not listed.

_____ The references list includes entries for all works referred to in the body of the paper: No sources are missing from the list; no extra sources are listed that have no reference within the paper. Exception: personal communications are identified in in-text citations but not in the references list.

_____ The entire references list is properly alphabetized by authors' last names (or by the first main word in the title for anonymous works).

_____ Each references entry (whether for an article, a book, an online document, or other source) contains the maximum amount of identifying and publication information, in the proper order, using the expected abbreviations.

_____ The paper is properly formatted from the title page to any appendix.

Writing Activities

1. Create references list entries in correct APA style for the following sources:

a. An article in the October 2001 issue (vol. 29, no. 2) of *Learning & Leading with Technology* magazine by Bob Albrecht and Paul Davis titled "The Metric Backpack" (pages 29–31, 55)

b. The book *The Playful World: How Technology Is Transforming Our Imagination,* by Mark Pesce, published in 2000 by Ballantine Books, located in New York City

c. A webpage by Roger Fouts called "Frequently Asked Questions," part of the *Chimpanzee and Human Communication Institute* site, sponsored by Central Washington University. No publication date is listed on the site; it was accessed on May 8, 2002, at <http://www.cwu.edu/~cwuchci/quanda.html>.

2. Using the APA documentation style, format references list entries for three different sources (one book, one magazine or journal article, and one online source) you might use for a research paper. Have a classmate review your entries for correctness—spacing, italics, indenting, and so on.

Research Paper Abbreviations

anon.	anonymous
bk.	book(s)
©	copyright
chap., ch.	chapter(s)
comp.	compiler, compiled, compiled by
ed.	editor(s), edition(s), edited by
e.g.	for example; *exempli gratia*
et al.	and others; *et alii, et aliae*
ex.	example
fig.	figure(s)
GPO	Government Printing Office, Washington, DC
ibid.	in the same place; *ibidem*
i.e.	that is; *id est*
illus.	illustration, illustrated by
introd.	introduction, introduced by
loc. cit.	in the place cited; *loco citato*
ms., mss.	manuscript(s)
narr.	narrated by, narrator(s)
n.d.	no date given
no.	number(s)
n.p.	no place of publication, no publisher given
n. pag.	no pagination
op. cit.	in the work cited; *opere citato*
p., pp.	page(s) (if necessary for clarity)
+	plus the pages that follow
pub. (or publ.)	published by, publication(s), publisher
rev.	revised by, revision, review, reviewed by
rpt.	reprinted by, reprint
sc.	scene
sec. (sect.)	section(s)
sic	thus in the source (used within brackets to indicate an error is that way in the original)
trans. (tr.)	translator, translation
viz.	namely; *videlicet*
vol	volume(s): capitalize when used with Roman numerals
vs. (v.)	versus (*v.* preferred in legal case titles)

IV. Handbook

CONTENTS

Punctuation, Mechanics, Usage, and Grammar

Sentence Issues

Addressing Multilingual/ESL Issues

Chapter 35
Marking Punctuation

Period

After Sentences

569.1

Use a **period** to end a sentence that makes a statement, requests something, or gives a mild command.

- **(Statement)** By 1997 almost 22 percent of females in the United States had received four or more years of college education**.**
- **(Request)** Please read the instructions carefully**.**
- **(Mild command)** If your topic sentence isn't clear, rewrite it**.**

Note: It is *not* necessary to place a period after a statement that has parentheses around it and is part of another sentence.

- Think about joining a club **(the student affairs office has a list of organizations)** for fun and for leadership experience.

After Initials and Abbreviations

569.2

Use a period after an initial and some abbreviations.

Mr.	**Mrs.**	**B.C.E.**	**Ph.D.**	**Sen. Daniel K. Inouye**
Jr.	**Sr.**	**D.D.S.**	**U.S.**	**Booker T. Washington**
Dr.	**M.A.**	**p.m.**	**B.A.**	**A. A. Milne**

When an abbreviation is the last word in a sentence, use only one period at the end of the sentence.

- Mikhail eyed each door until he found the name Rosa Lopez, **Ph.D.**

As Decimal Points

569.3

Use a period as a decimal point.

- The government spends approximately **$15.5** million each year just to process student loan forms.

Ellipsis

To Show Omitted Words

570.1

Use an **ellipsis** (three periods) to show that one or more words have been omitted in a quotation. When typing, leave one space before and after each period.

■ **(Original)** We the people of the United States, in order to form a more perfect Union, establish justice, insure domestic tranquility, provide for the common defense, promote the general welfare, and secure the blessings of liberty to ourselves and our posterity, do ordain and establish this Constitution for the United States of America.

—Preamble, U.S. Constitution

■ **(Quotation)** "We the people ... in order to form a more perfect Union ... establish this Constitution for the United States of America."

Note: Omit internal punctuation (a comma, a semicolon, a colon, or a dash) on either side of the ellipsis marks unless it is needed for clarity.

To Use After Sentences

570.2

If words from a quotation are omitted at the end of a sentence, place the ellipsis after the period or other end punctuation.

■ **(Quotation)** "Five score years ago, a great American, in whose symbolic shadow we stand, signed the Emancipation Proclamation. . . . But one hundred years later, we must face the tragic fact that the Negro is still not free."

—Martin Luther King, Jr., "I Have a Dream"

The first word of a sentence following a period and an ellipsis may be capitalized, even though it was not capitalized in the original.

■ **(Quotation)** "Five score years ago, a great American ... signed the Emancipation Proclamation. . . . One hundred years later, . . . the Negro is still not free."

Note: If the quoted material is a complete sentence (even if it was not in the original), use a period, then an ellipsis.

■ **(Original)** I am tired; my heart is sick and sad. From where the sun now stands I will fight no more forever.

—Chief Joseph of the Nez Percé

■ **(Quotation)** "I am tired. . . . I will fight no more forever."

To Show Pauses

570.3

Use an ellipsis to indicate a pause or to show unfinished thoughts.

■ Listen ... did you hear that?

I can't figure out ... this number doesn't ... just how do I apply the equation in this case?

Comma

Between Independent Clauses

Use a **comma** between independent clauses that are joined by a coordinating conjunction (*and, but, or, nor, for, yet, so*).

- The most expensive film ever made was *Titanic*, **but** the largest makeup budget for any film was $1 million for *Planet of the Apes*.

Note: Do not confuse a compound verb with a compound sentence.

- The $1 million makeup budget for *Planet of the Apes* shocked Hollywood **and** made producers uneasy. (compound verb)

 The $1 million makeup budget was 17 percent of the film's total production cost, **but** the film became a box-office hit and financial success. (compound sentence)

Between Items in a Series

Use commas to separate individual words, phrases, or clauses in a series. (A series contains at least three items.)

- Many college students must balance studying with **taking care of a family, working a job, getting exercise, and finding time to relax.**

Note: Do *not* use commas when all the items in a series are connected with *or, nor,* or *and.*

- Hmm . . . should I study **or** do laundry **or** go out?

To Separate Adjectives

Use commas to separate adjectives that *equally* modify the same noun. Notice in the examples below that no comma separates the last adjective from the noun.

- You should exercise regularly and follow a **sensible, healthful** diet.
 A good diet is one that includes lots of **high-protein, low-fat** foods.

To Determine Equal Modifiers

To determine whether the adjectives in a sentence modify a noun *equally*, use these two tests.

1 Reverse the order of the adjectives; if the sentence is clear, the adjectives modify equally. (In the example below, *hot* and *crowded* can be reversed, and the sentence is still clear; *short* and *coffee* cannot.)

- Matt was tired of working in the **hot, crowded** lab and decided to take a **short coffee** break.

2 Insert *and* between the adjectives; if the sentence reads well, use a comma when *and* is omitted. (The word *and* can be inserted between *hot* and *crowded*, but *and* does not make sense between *short* and *coffee*.)

572.1 To Set Off Appositives

A specific kind of explanatory word or phrase called an **appositive** identifies or renames a preceding noun or pronoun.

- Albert Einstein, **the famous mathematician and physicist,** developed the theory of relativity.

Note: Do *not* use commas with *restrictive appositives.* A restrictive appositive is essential to the basic meaning of the sentence.

- The famous mathematician and physicist **Albert Einstein** developed the theory of relativity.

572.2 To Set Off Clauses

Use a comma after most introductory clauses functioning as adverbs.

- **Although Charlemagne was a great patron of learning,** he never learned to write properly. (adverb clause)

Use a comma if the adverb clause following the main clause is not essential. Clauses beginning with *even though, although, while,* or another conjunction expressing a contrast are usually not needed to complete the meaning of a sentence.

- Charlemagne never learned to write properly, **even though he continued to practice.**

Note: A comma is *not* used if the clause following the main clause is needed to complete the meaning of the sentence.

- Maybe Charlemagne didn't learn **because he had an empire to run.**

572.3 After Introductory Phrases

Use a comma after introductory phrases.

- **In spite of his practicing,** Charlemagne's handwriting remained poor.

Note: A comma is usually omitted if the phrase follows the independent clause.

- Charlemagne's handwriting remained poor **in spite of his practicing.**

Also Note: You may omit the comma after a short (four or fewer words) introductory phrase unless it is needed to ensure clarity.

- **At 6:00 a.m.** he would rise and practice his penmanship.

572.4 To Set Off Transitional Expressions

Use a comma to set off conjunctive adverbs and transitional phrases. (See **576.2–576.3.**)

- Handwriting is not, **as a matter of fact,** easy to improve upon later in life; **however,** it can be done if you are determined enough.

Note: If a transitional expression blends smoothly with the rest of the sentence, it does not need to be set off. *Example:* If you are in fact coming, I'll see you there.

A Closer Look
at Nonrestrictive and Restrictive Clauses and Phrases

Use Commas with
Nonrestrictive Clauses and Phrases

573.1

Use commas to enclose **nonrestrictive** (unnecessary) clauses and phrases. A non-restrictive clause or phrase adds information that is not necessary to the basic meaning of the sentence. For example, if the clause or phrase (in **boldface**) were left out of the two examples below, the meaning of the sentences would remain clear. Therefore, commas are used to set off the nonrestrictive information.

- The locker rooms in Swain Hall**, which were painted and updated last summer,** give professors a place to shower. (nonrestrictive clause)

  Work-study programs**, offered on many campuses,** give students the opportunity to earn tuition money. (nonrestrictive phrase)

Don't Use Commas with
Restrictive Clauses and Phrases

573.2

Do *not* use commas to set off **restrictive** (necessary) clauses and phrases. A restrictive clause or phrase adds information that the reader needs in order to understand the sentence. For example, if the clause and phrase (in **boldface**) were dropped from the examples below, the meaning would be unclear.

- Only the professors **who run at noon** use the locker rooms in Swain Hall to shower. (restrictive clause)

  Tuition money **earned through work-study programs** is the only way some students can afford to go to college. (restrictive phrase)

Using "That" or "Which"

573.3

Use *that* to introduce restrictive (necessary) clauses; use *which* to introduce non-restrictive (unnecessary) clauses. When the two words are used in this way, the reader can quickly distinguish the necessary information from the unnecessary.

- Campus jobs **that are funded by the university** are awarded to students only. (restrictive)

  The cafeteria**, which is run by an independent contractor,** can hire nonstudents. (nonrestrictive)

Note: Clauses beginning with *who* can be either restrictive or nonrestrictive.

- Students **who pay for their own education** are highly motivated. (restrictive)

  The admissions counselor**, who has studied student records,** said that many returning students earn high GPAs in spite of demanding family obligations. (nonrestrictive)

574.1

To Set Off Items in Addresses and Dates

Use commas to set off items in an address and the year in a date.

- Send your letter to **1600 Pennsylvania Avenue, Washington, DC 20006, before January 1, 2006,** or send e-mail to president@whitehouse.gov.

Note: *No* comma is placed between the state and ZIP code. Also, *no* comma separates the items if only the month and year are given: January 2007.

574.2

To Set Off Dialogue

Use commas to set off the words of the speaker from the rest of the sentence.

- **"Never be afraid to ask for help,"** advised Ms. Kane.

  "With the evidence that we now have," Professor Thom said**, "many scientists believe there is life on Mars."**

574.3

To Separate Nouns of Direct Address

Use a comma to separate a noun of direct address from the rest of the sentence.

- **Jamie,** would you please stop whistling while I'm trying to work?

574.4

To Separate Interjections

Use a comma to separate a mild interjection from the rest of the sentence.

- **Okay,** so now what do I do?

Note: Exclamation points are used after strong interjections: Wow! You're kidding!

574.5

To Set Off Interruptions

Use commas to set off a word, phrase, or clause that interrupts the movement of a sentence. Such expressions usually can be identified through the following tests: (1) They may be omitted without changing the meaning of a sentence; and (2) they may be placed nearly anywhere in the sentence without changing its meaning.

- For me**, well,** it was just a good job gone!

  —Langston Hughes, "A Good Job Gone"

  Lela**, as a general rule,** always comes to class ready for a pop quiz.

574.6

To Separate Numbers

Use commas to separate a series of numbers to distinguish hundreds, thousands, millions, and so on.

- Do you know how to write the amount **$2,025** on a check?

  25,000   **973,240**   **18,620,197**

To Enclose Explanatory Words

575.1

Use commas to enclose an explanatory word or phrase.

- Time management, **according to many professionals,** is such an important skill that it should be taught in college.

To Separate Contrasted Elements

575.2

Use commas to separate contrasted elements within a sentence.

- We work to become, **not to acquire.**   —Eugene Delacroix
- Where all think alike, **no one thinks very much.**   —Walter Lippmann

Before Tags

575.3

Use a comma before tags, which are short statements or questions at the ends of sentences.

- You studied for the test, **right?**

To Enclose Titles or Initials

575.4

Use commas to enclose a title or initials and given names that follow a surname.

- Until Martin, **Sr.,** was 15, he never had more than three months of schooling in any one year.

    —Ed Clayton, *Martin Luther King: The Peaceful Warrior*

    The genealogical files included the names Sanders, **L. H.,** and Sanders, **Lucy Hale.**

For Clarity or Emphasis

575.5

Use a comma for clarity or for emphasis. There will be times when none of the traditional rules call for a comma, but one will be needed to prevent confusion or to emphasize an important idea.

- What she does, does matter to us. (clarity)
  It may be those who do most, dream most. (emphasis)   —Stephen Leacock

---

Avoid Overusing Commas

The commas (in **red**) below are used incorrectly. Do *not* use a comma between the subject and its verb or the verb and its object.

- Current periodicals on the subject of psychology, are available at nearly all bookstores.
  I think she should read, *Psychology Today*.

Do *not* use a comma before an indirect quotation.

- My roommate said, that she doesn't understand the notes I took.

Exercise

576.1

Semicolon

To Join Two Independent Clauses

Use a **semicolon** to join two or more closely related independent clauses that are not connected with a coordinating conjunction. In other words, each of the clauses could stand alone as a separate sentence.

■ I was thrown out of college for cheating on the metaphysics exam; I looked into the soul of the boy next to me.

—Woody Allen

576.2

With Conjunctive Adverbs

Use a semicolon before a conjunctive adverb when the word clarifies the relationship between two independent clauses in a compound sentence. A comma often follows the conjunctive adverb. Common conjunctive adverbs include *also, besides, however, instead, meanwhile, then*, and *therefore.*

■ Many college freshmen are on their own for the first time; **however,** others are already independent and even have families.

576.3

With Transitional Phrases

Use a semicolon before a transitional phrase when the phrase clarifies the relationship between two independent clauses in a compound sentence. A comma usually follows the transitional phrase.

■ Pablo was born in the Andes; **as a result,** he loves mountains.

Transitional Phrases			
after all	at the same time	in addition	in the first place
as a matter of fact	even so	in conclusion	on the contrary
as a result	for example	in fact	on the other hand
at any rate	for instance	in other words	

576.4

To Separate Independent Clauses

Use a semicolon to separate independent clauses that contain internal commas, even when they are connected by a coordinating conjunction.

■ Make sure your CD player, computer, bike, and other valuables are covered by a homeowner's insurance policy; and be sure to use the locks on your door, bike, and storage area.

576.5

To Separate Items in a Series That Contain Commas

Use a semicolon to separate items in a series that already contain commas.

■ My favorite foods are pizza with pepperoni, onions, and olives; peanut butter and banana sandwiches; and liver with bacon, peppers, and onions.

Colon

✓ Exercise

After Salutations

577.1

Use a **colon** after the salutation of a business letter.

- Dear Mr. Spielberg: Dear Professor Higgins: Dear Members:

Between Numbers Indicating Time or Ratios

577.2

Use a colon between the hours, minutes, and seconds of a number indicating time.

- 8:30 p.m.   9:45 a.m.   10:24:55

Use a colon between two numbers in a ratio.

- The ratio of computers to students is 1:20. (one to twenty)

For Emphasis

577.3

Use a colon to emphasize a word, a phrase, a clause, or a sentence that explains or adds impact to the main clause.

- **I have one goal for myself:** to become the first person in my family to graduate from college.

To Distinguish Parts of Publications

577.4

Use a colon between a title and a subtitle, volume and page, and chapter and verse.

- *Ron Brown: An Uncommon Life*   *Britannica* 4: 211   Psalm 23:1–6

To Introduce Quotations

577.5

Use a colon to introduce a quotation following a complete sentence.

- **John Locke is credited with this prescription for a good life:** "A sound mind in a sound body."

  Lou Gottlieb, however, offered this version: "A sound mind or a sound body—take your pick."

To Introduce a List

577.6

Use a colon to introduce a list following a complete sentence.

- **A college student needs a number of things to succeed:** basic skills, creativity, and determination.

Avoid Colon Errors

Do *not* use a colon between a verb and its object or complement.

- Dave likes: comfortable space and time to think. **(Incorrect)**

  Dave likes two things: comfortable space and time to think. **(Correct)**

Hyphen

In Compound Words

Use a **hyphen** to make some compound words.

- great-great-grandfather (noun)   starry-eyed (adjective)
  mother-in-law (noun)   three-year-old (adjective)

Writers sometimes combine words in a new and unexpected way. Such combinations are usually hyphenated.

- And they pried pieces of **baked-too-fast** sunshine cake from the roofs of their mouths and looked once more into the boy's eyes.

—Toni Morrison, *Song of Solomon*

Note: Consult a dictionary to find how it lists a particular compound word. Some compound words (*living room*) do not use a hyphen and are written separately. Some are written solid (*bedroom*). Some do not use a hyphen when the word is a noun (*ice cream*) but do use a hyphen when it is a verb or an adjective (*ice-cream sundae*).

To Join Letters and Words

Use a hyphen to join a capital letter or a lowercase letter to a noun or a participle.

- T-shirt   U-turn   V-shaped   x-axis

To Join Words in Compound Numbers

Use a hyphen to join the words in compound numbers from *twenty-one* to *ninety-nine* when it is necessary to write them out. (See **595.1**.)

- **Forty-two** people found seats in the cramped classroom.

Between Numbers in Fractions

Use a hyphen between the numerator and the denominator of a fraction, but not when one or both of these elements are already hyphenated.

- four-tenths   five-sixteenths   seven thirty-seconds (7/32)

In a Special Series

Use a hyphen when two or more words have a common element that is omitted in all but the last term.

- We have cedar posts in **four-**, **six-**, and **eight-**inch widths.

To Create New Words

Use a hyphen to form new words beginning with the prefixes *self, ex, all,* and *half.* Also use a hyphen to join any prefix to a proper noun, a proper adjective, or the official name of an office.

- post-Depression   mid-May   ex-mayor

To Prevent Confusion

Use a hyphen with prefixes or suffixes to avoid confusion or awkward spelling.

■ **re-cover** (not *recover*) the sofa   **shell-like** (not *shelllike*) shape

To Join Numbers

Use a hyphen to join numbers indicating a range, a score, or a vote.

■ Students study **30–40** hours a week.   The final score was **84–82.**

To Divide Words

Use a hyphen to divide a word between syllables at the end of a line of print.

Guidelines for Word Division

1. Leave enough of the word at the end of the line to identify the word.
2. Never divide a one-syllable word: **rained, skills, through.**
3. Avoid dividing a word of five or fewer letters: **paper, study, July.**
4. Never divide a one-letter syllable from the rest of the word: **omit-ted,** not **o-mitted.**
5. Always divide a compound word between its basic units: **sister-in-law,** not **sis-ter-in-law.**
6. Never divide abbreviations or contractions: **shouldn't,** not **should-n't.**
7. When a vowel is a syllable by itself, divide the word after the vowel: **epi-sode,** not **ep-isode.**
8. Avoid dividing a numeral: **1,000,000;** not **1,000,-000.**
9. Avoid dividing the last word in a paragraph.
10. Never divide the last word in more than two lines in a row.
11. Check a dictionary.

To Form Adjectives

Use a hyphen to join two or more words that serve as a single-thought adjective before a noun.

■ In real life I am a large, **big-boned** woman with rough, **man-working** hands.
                                                    —Alice Walker, "Everyday Use"

Most single-thought adjectives are not hyphenated when they come after the noun.

■ In real life, I am large and **big boned.**

Note: When the first of these words is an adverb ending in *ly,* do *not* use a hyphen. Also, do *not* use a hyphen when a number or a letter is the final element in a single-thought adjective.

■ fresh**ly** painted barn   grade **A** milk (letter is the final element)

✓
Exercise

Dash

580.1

To Set Off Nonessential Elements

Use a **dash** to set off nonessential elements—explanations, examples, or definitions—when you want to emphasize them.

- Near the semester's end—**and this is not always due to poor planning**—some students may find themselves in academic trouble.

  The term *caveat emptor*—**let the buyer beware**—is especially appropriate to Internet shopping.

Note: A dash is indicated by two hyphens--with no spacing before or after--in typewriter-generated material. Don't use a single hyphen when a dash (two hyphens) is required.

580.2

To Set Off an Introductory Series

Use a dash to set off an introductory series from the clause that explains the series.

- **Cereal, coffee, and a newspaper**—without these I can't get going in the morning.

580.3

To Show Missing Text

Use a dash to show that words or letters are missing.

- **Mr. —** won't let us marry.

  —Alice Walker, *The Color Purple*

580.4

To Show Interrupted Speech

Use a dash (or ellipsis) to show interrupted or faltering speech in dialogue.

- Well, **I—ah—had** this terrible case of the flu, **and—then—ah—the** library closed because of that flash flood, **and—well—the** high humidity jammed my printer. —Excuse No. 101

  "You told me to tell her about the—"
  "Oh, just stop."

  —Joyce Carol Oates,
  "Why Don't You Come Live With Me It's Time"

580.5

For Emphasis

Use a dash in place of a colon to introduce or to emphasize a word, a series, a phrase, or a clause.

- **Jogging**—that's what he lives for.

  Life is like a grindstone—whether it grinds you down or polishes you up depends on what you're made of.

  This is how the world moves—not like an arrow, but a boomerang.

  —Ralph Ellison

Question Mark

After Direct Questions

Use a **question mark** at the end of a direct question.

■ What can I know**?** What ought I to do**?** What may I hope**?**

—Immanuel Kant

Since when do you have to agree with people to defend them from injustice**?**

—Lillian Hellman

Not After Indirect Questions

No question mark is used after an indirect question.

■ After listening to Edgar sing, Mr. Noteworthy asked him if he had ever had formal voice training.

Note: When a single-word question like *how, when,* or *why* is woven into the flow of a sentence, capitalization and special punctuation are not usually required.

■ The questions we need to address at our next board meeting are not *why* or *whether,* but *how* and *when.*

After Quotations That Are Questions

When a question ends with a quotation that is also a question, use only one question mark, and place it within the quotation marks.

■ Do you often ask yourself, "What should I be**?**"

To Show Uncertainty

Use a question mark within parentheses to show uncertainty about a word or phrase within a sentence.

■ This July will be the 34th **(?)** anniversary of the first moon walk.

Note: Do *not* use a question mark in this manner for formal writing.

For Questions in Parentheses or Dashes

A question within parentheses—or a question set off by dashes—is punctuated with a question mark unless the sentence ends with a question mark.

■ You must consult your handbook **(what choice do you have?)** when you need to know a punctuation rule.

Should I use your charge card (you have one, don't you), or should I pay cash?

Maybe somewhere in the pasts of these humbled people, there were cases of bad mothering or absent fathering or emotional neglect—**what family surviving the '50s was exempt?**—but I couldn't believe these human errors brought the physical changes in Frank.

—Mary Kay Blakely, *Wake Me When It's Over*

Quotation Marks

To Punctuate Titles of Works Within Other Works

Use **quotation marks** to punctuate some titles. (Also see **584.2**.)

- "Two Friends" (short story)
  "New Car Designs" (newspaper article)
  "Desperado" (song)
  "Multiculturalism and the Language Battle" (lecture title)
  "The New Admissions Game" (magazine article)
  "Reflections on Advertising" (chapter in a book)
  "Force of Nature" (television episode from *Star Trek*: *The Next Generation*)
  "Annabel Lee" (short poem)

For Special Words

Use quotation marks (1) to show that a word is being discussed as a word, (2) to indicate that a word is slang, or (3) to point out that a word is being used in a humorous or ironic way.

1. A commentary on the times is that the word **"honesty"** is now preceded by **"old-fashioned."**
   —Larry Wolters

2. I drank a Dixie and ate bar peanuts and asked the bartender where I could hear **"chanky-chank,"** as Cajuns call their music.
   —William Least Heat-Moon, *Blue Highways*

3. In order to be popular, he works very hard at being **"cute."**

Placement of Periods or Commas

Always place periods and commas inside quotation marks.

- "Dr. Slaughter wants you to have liquids, Will," Mama said anxiously. "He said not to give you any solid food tonight." —Olive Ann Burns, *Cold Sassy Tree*

Placement of Exclamation Points or Question Marks

Place an exclamation point or a question mark inside quotation marks when it punctuates both the main sentence and the quotation *or* just the quotation; place it outside when it punctuates the main sentence.

- Do you often ask yourself, "What should I be?"
  I almost croaked when he asked, "That won't be a problem, will it?"
  Did he really say, "Finish this by tomorrow"?

Placement of Semicolons or Colons

Always place semicolons or colons outside quotation marks.

- I just read "Computers and Creativity"; I now have some different ideas about the role of computers in the arts.

A Closer Look at Marking Quoted Material

For Direct Quotations

583.1

Use quotation marks before and after a direct quotation—a person's exact words.

- ■ Sitting in my one-room apartment, I remember Mom saying, **"Don't go to the party with him."**

Note: Do *not* use quotation marks for *indirect* quotations.

- ■ I remember Mom saying **that I should not date him.** (These are not the speaker's exact words.)

For Quoted Passages

583.2

Use quotation marks before and after a quoted passage. Any word that is not part of the original quotation must be placed inside brackets.

- ■ **(Original)** First of all, it must accept responsibility for providing shelter for the homeless.
- ■ **(Quotation)** "First of all, it **[the federal government]** must accept responsibility for providing shelter for the homeless."

Note: If you quote only part of the original passage, be sure to construct a sentence that is both accurate and grammatically correct.

- ■ The report goes on to say that the federal government **"must accept responsibility for providing shelter for the homeless."**

For Long Quotations

583.3

If more than one paragraph is quoted, quotation marks are placed before each paragraph and at the end of the last paragraph **(Example A)**. Quotations that are five or more lines (MLA style) or forty words or more (APA style) are usually set off from the text by indenting ten spaces from the left margin (a style called "block form"). Do not use quotation marks before or after a block-form quotation **(Example B)**, except in cases where quotation marks appear in the original passage **(Example C)**.

Example A	Example B	Example C

For Quoting Quotations

583.4

Use single quotation marks to punctuate quoted material within a quotation.

- ■ "I was lucky," said Jane. "The proctor announced, **'Put your pencils down,'** just as I was filling in the last answer."

Italics (Underlining)

In Handwritten and Printed Material

584.1

Italics is a printer's term for a style of type that is slightly slanted. In this sentence, the word *happiness* is printed in italics. In material that is handwritten or typed on a machine that cannot print in italics, underline each word or letter that should be in italics.

- In **The Road to Memphis,** racism is a contagious disease.
  (typed or handwritten)
  Mildred Taylor's ***The Road to Memphis*** exposes racism. (printed)

In Titles

584.2

Use italics to indicate the titles of magazines, newspapers, books, pamphlets, full-length plays, films, videos, radio and television programs, book-length poems, ballets, operas, lengthy musical compositions, cassettes, CDs, paintings and sculptures, legal cases, websites, and the names of ships and aircraft. (Also see **582.1**)

- *Newsweek* (magazine)
  New York Times (newspaper)
  Sister Carrie (book)
  Othello (play)
  Enola Gay (airplane)
  The Joshua Tree (CD)
  ACLU **v.** *State of Ohio* (legal case)
- *The Nutcracker* (ballet)
  Babe (film)
  The Thinker (sculpture)
  Nightline (television program)
  GeoCities (website)
  College Loans (pamphlet)

When one title appears within another title, punctuate as follows:

- "**The *Fresh Prince of Bel-Air* Rings True**" is an article I read.
  (title of TV program in an article title)
  He wants to watch ***Inside the "New York Times"*** on PBS tonight.
  (title of newspaper in title of TV program)

For Key Terms

584.3

Italics are often used for a key term in a discussion or for a technical term, especially when it is accompanied by its definition. Italicize the term the first time it is used. Thereafter, put the term in Roman type.

- This flower has a ***zygomorphic*** (bilateral symmetry) structure.

For Foreign Words and Scientific Names

584.4

Use italics for foreign words that have not been adopted into the English language; italics are also used to denote scientific names.

- Say ***arrivederci*** to your fears and try new activities. (foreign word)
  The voyageurs discovered the shy ***Castor canadensis,*** or North American beaver. (scientific name)

Parentheses

To Enclose Explanatory or Supplementary Material

585.1

Use **parentheses** to enclose explanatory or supplementary material that interrupts the normal sentence structure.

■ The RA **(resident assistant)** became my best friend.

To Set Off Numbers in a List

585.2

Use parentheses to set off numbers used with a series of words or phrases.

■ Dr. Beck told us **(1)** plan ahead, **(2)** stay flexible, and **(3)** follow through.

For Parenthetical Sentences

585.3

When using a full "sentence" within another sentence, do not capitalize it or use a period inside the parentheses.

■ Your friend doesn't have the assignment **(he was just thinking about calling you),** so you'll have to make a couple more calls.

When the parenthetical sentence comes after the main sentence, capitalize and punctuate it the same way you would any other complete sentence.

■ But Mom doesn't say boo to Dad; she's always sweet to him. **(Actually she's sort of sweet to everybody.)**   —Norma Fox Mazer, *Up on Fong Mountain*

To Set Off References

585.4

Use parentheses to set off references to authors, titles, pages, and years.

■ The statistics are alarming **(see page 9)** and demand action.

Note: For unavoidable parentheses within parentheses (... [...] ...), use brackets. Avoid overuse of parentheses by using commas instead.

Diagonal

To Form Fractions or Show Choices

585.5

Use a **diagonal** (also called a *slash*) to form a fraction. Also place a diagonal between two words to indicate that either is acceptable.

■ My **walking/running** shoe size is **5 1/2**; my dress shoes are **6 1/2.**

When Quoting Poetry

585.6

When quoting poetry, use a diagonal (with one space before and after) to show where each line ends in the actual poem.

■ A dryness is upon the house / My father loved and tended. / Beyond his firm and sculptured door / His light and lease have ended.

                —Gwendolyn Brooks, "In Honor of David Anderson Brooks, My Father"

Brackets

586.1

With Words That Clarify

Use **brackets** before and after words that are added to clarify what another person has said or written.

■ "They'd **[the sweat bees]** get into your mouth, ears, eyes, nose. You'd feel them all over you."

—Marilyn Johnson and Sasha Nyary, "Roosevelts in the Amazon"

Note: The brackets indicate that the words *the sweat bees* are not part of the original quotation but were added for clarification. (See **583.2**.)

586.2

Around Comments by Someone Other Than the Author

Place brackets around comments that have been added by someone other than the author or speaker.

■ "In conclusion, *docendo discimus*. Let the school year begin!" **[Huh?]**

586.3

Around Editorial Corrections

Place brackets around an editorial correction.

■ "Brooklyn alone has 8 percent of lead poisoning **[victims]** nationwide," said Marjorie Moore.
—Donna Actie, student writer

586.4

Around the Word *Sic*

Brackets should be placed around the word *sic* (Latin for "so" or "thus") in quoted material; the word indicates that an error appearing in the quoted material was made by the original speaker or writer.

■ "There is a higher principal *[sic]* at stake here: Is the school administration aware of the situation?"

Exclamation Point

586.5

To Express Strong Feeling

Use an **exclamation point** to express strong feeling. It may be placed at the end of a sentence (or an elliptical expression that stands for a sentence). Use exclamation points sparingly.

■ "That's not the point," said Wangero. "These are all pieces of dresses Grandma used to wear. She did all this stitching by hand. **Imagine!**"
—Alice Walker, "Everyday Use"

Su-su-something's crawling up the back of my neck**!**
—Mark Twain, *Roughing It*

She was on tiptoe, stretching for an orange, when they heard, "**HEY YOU!**"
—Beverley Naidoo, *Journey to Jo'burg*

Apostrophe

In Contractions

587.1

Use an **apostrophe** to show that one or more letters have been left out of two words joined to form a contraction.

■ **don't** → **o** is left out   **she'd** → **woul** is left out   **it's** → **i** is left out

Note: An apostrophe is also used to show that one or more numerals or letters have been left out of numbers or words.

■ class of **'02** → **20** is left out   good **mornin'** → **g** is left out

To Form Plurals

587.2

Use an apostrophe and an *s* to form the plural of a letter, a number, a sign, or a word discussed as a word.

■ A → **A's**   8 → **8's**   + → **+'s**
  You use too many **and's** in your writing.

Note: If two apostrophes are called for in the same word, omit the second one.

■ Follow closely the do's and **don'ts** (not **don't's**) on the checklist.

To Form Singular Possessives

587.3

The possessive form of singular nouns is usually made by adding an apostrophe and an *s*.

■ **Spock's** ears   my **computer's** memory

Note: When a singular noun of more than one syllable ends with an *s* or a *z* sound, the possessive may be formed by adding just an apostrophe—or an apostrophe and an *s*. When the singular noun is a one-syllable word, however, the possessive is usually formed by adding both an apostrophe and an *s*.

■ **Dallas'** sports teams (or) **Dallas's** sports teams (two-syllable word)
  Kiss's last concert   my **boss's** generosity (one-syllable words)

To Form Plural Possessives

587.4

The possessive form of plural nouns ending in *s* is made by adding just an apostrophe.

■ the **Joneses'** great-grandfather   **bosses'** offices

Note: For plural nouns not ending in *s*, add an apostrophe and *s*.

  women's health issues   **children's** program

To Determine Ownership

You will punctuate possessives correctly if you remember that the word that comes immediately before the apostrophe is the owner.

girl's guitar *(girl is the owner)*   **girls'** guitar *(girls are the owners)*
boss's office *(boss is the owner)*   **bosses'** office *(bosses are the owners)*

588.1

To Show Shared Possession

When possession is shared by more than one noun, use the possessive form for the last noun in the series.

■ Jason, Kamil, and **Elana's** sound system
(All three own the same system.)

Jason's, Kamil's, and Elana's sound systems
(Each owns a separate system.)

588.2

In Compound Nouns

The possessive of a compound noun is formed by placing the possessive ending after the last word.

■ his **mother-in-law's** name (singular)
the **secretary of state's** career (singular)

their **mothers-in-law's** names (plural)
the **secretaries of state's** careers (plural)

588.3

With Indefinite Pronouns

The possessive form of an indefinite pronoun is made by adding an apostrophe and an *s* to the pronoun. (See **623.4**.)

■ **everybody's** grades   **no one's** mistake   **one's** choice

In expressions using *else,* add the apostrophe and *s* after the last word.

■ **anyone else's**   **somebody else's**

588.4

To Show Time or Amount

Use an apostrophe and an *s* with an adjective that is part of an expression indicating time or amount.

■ **yesterday's** news   a **day's** wage   a **month's** pay

588.5

Punctuation Marks

´ (é)	**Accent, acute**	:	**Colon**	¶	**Paragraph**
` (è)	**Accent, grave**	,	**Comma**	( )	**Parentheses**
< >	**Angle brackets**	†	**Dagger**	.	**Period**
'	**Apostrophe**	—	**Dash**	?	**Question mark**
*	**Asterisk**	¨ (ä)	**Dieresis**	" "	**Quotation marks**
{ }	**Braces**	/	**Diagonal/slash**	§	**Section**
[ ]	**Brackets**	...	**Ellipsis**	;	**Semicolon**
^	**Caret**	!	**Exclamation point**	˜ (ñ)	**Tilde**
ç	**Cedilla**	-	**Hyphen**	___	**Underscore**
^ (â)	**Circumflex**	.....	**Leaders**		

Chapter 36
Checking Mechanics

Capitalization

Proper Nouns and Adjectives

Capitalize all proper nouns and all proper adjectives (adjectives derived from proper nouns). The chart below provides a quick overview of capitalization rules. The pages following explain specific or special uses of capitalization.

Capitalization at a Glance

Days of the week............................	**Sunday, Monday, Tuesday**
Months...	**June, July, August**
Holidays, holy days	**Thanksgiving, Easter, Hanukkah**
Periods, events in history......................	**Middle Ages, World War I**
Special events	**Tate Memorial Dedication Ceremony**
Political parties........................	**Republican Party, Socialist Party**
Official documents	**the Declaration of Independence**
Trade names....................	**Oscar Mayer hot dogs, Pontiac Firebird**
Formal epithets..	**Alexander the Great**
Official titles	**Mayor John Spitzer, Senator Feinstein**
Official state nicknames	**the Badger State, the Aloha State**
Geographical names	
Planets, heavenly bodies.................	**Earth, Jupiter, the Milky Way**
Continents.................................	**Australia, South America**
Countries...............................	**Ireland, Grenada, Sri Lanka**
States, provinces...........................	**Ohio, Utah, Nova Scotia**
Cities, towns, villages	**El Paso, Burlington, Wonewoc**
Streets, roads, highways	**Park Avenue, Route 66, Interstate 90**
Sections of the U.S. and the world...........	**the Southwest, the Far East**
Landforms	**the Rocky Mountains, the Kalahari Desert**
Bodies of water.........	**Nile and Ural rivers, Lake Superior, Bee Creek**
Public areas	**Central Park, Yellowstone National Park**

First Words

Capitalize the first word in every sentence and the first word in a full-sentence direct quotation.

- **Attending** the orientation for new students is a good idea.
  Max suggested, "**Let's** take the guided tour of the campus first."

Sentences in Parentheses

Capitalize the first word in a sentence that is enclosed in parentheses if that sentence is not contained within another complete sentence.

- The bookstore has the software. (**Now** all I need is the computer.)

Note: Do *not* capitalize a sentence that is enclosed in parentheses and is located in the middle of another sentence.

- Your college will probably offer everything (**this** includes general access to a computer) that you'll need for a successful year.

Sentences Following Colons

Capitalize a complete sentence that follows a colon when that sentence is a formal statement, a quotation, or a sentence that you want to emphasize.

- Sydney Harris had this to say about computers: "**The** real danger is not that computers will begin to think like people, but that people will begin to think like computers."

Salutation and Complimentary Closing

In a letter, capitalize the first and all major words of the salutation. Capitalize only the first word of the complimentary closing.

- **Dear Personnel Director:**   **Sincerely** yours,

Sections of the Country

Words that indicate sections of the country are proper nouns and should be capitalized; words that simply indicate direction are not proper nouns.

- Many businesses move to the **South.** (section of the country)
  They move **south** to cut fuel costs and other expenses. (direction)

Languages, Ethnic Groups, Nationalities, and Religions

Capitalize languages, ethnic groups, nationalities, and religions.

African American   **Latino**   **Navajo**   **French**   **Islam**

Nouns that refer to the Supreme Being and holy books are capitalized.

God   **Allah**   **Jehovah**   **the Koran**   **Exodus**   **the Bible**

Titles

591.1

Capitalize the first word of a title, the last word, and every word in between except articles (*a, an, the*), short prepositions, and coordinating conjunctions. Follow this rule for titles of books, newspapers, magazines, poems, plays, songs, articles, films, works of art, and stories.

■ ***Going to Meet the Man***   ***Chicago Tribune***
    "Nothing Gold Can Stay"   **"Jobs in the Cyber Arena"**
    A Midsummer Night's Dream   ***The War of the Roses***

Note: When citing titles in a bibliography, check the style manual you've been asked to follow. For example, in APA style, only the first word of a title is capitalized.

Organizations

591.2

Capitalize the name of an organization, or a team and its members.

■ **American Indian Movement**   **Republican Party**
    Tampa Bay Buccaneers   **Tucson Drama Club**

Abbreviations

591.3

Capitalize abbreviations of titles and organizations. (Some other abbreviations are also capitalized. See pages **597-598**.)

■ **M.D.** **Ph.D.** **NAACP** **C.E.** **B.C.E.** **GPA**

Letters

591.4

Capitalize letters used to indicate a form or shape.

■ **U**-turn **I**-beam **S**-curve **V**-shaped **T**-shirt

Words Used as Names

591.5

Capitalize words like *father, mother, uncle, senator,* and *professor* when they are parts of titles that include a personal name, or when they are substituted for proper nouns (especially in direct address).

■ Hello, **Senator** Feingold. (*Senator* is part of the name.)
    Our **senator** is an environmentalist.
    Who was your chemistry **professor** last quarter?
    I had **Professor** Williams for Chemistry 101.

Note: To test whether a word is being substituted for a proper noun, simply read the sentence with a proper noun in place of the word. If the proper noun fits in the sentence, the word being tested should be capitalized. Usually the word is not capitalized if it follows a possessive—*my, his, our, your,* and so on.

■ Did **Dad (Brad)** pack the stereo in the trailer? (*Brad* works in this sentence.)
    Did your **dad (Brad)** pack the stereo in the trailer? (*Brad* does not work in this sentence; the word *dad* follows the possessive *your.*)

592.1

Titles of Courses

Words such as *technology, history,* and *science* are proper nouns when they are included in the titles of specific courses; they are common nouns when they name a field of study.

■ Who teaches **Art History 202?** (title of a specific course)
Professor Bunker loves teaching **history.** (a field of study)

Note: The words *freshman, sophomore, junior,* and *senior* are not capitalized unless they are part of an official title.

■ The **seniors** who maintained high GPAs were honored at the **Mount Mary Senior Honors Banquet.**

592.2

Internet and E-mail

The words *Internet* and *World Wide Web* are always capitalized because they are considered proper nouns. When your writing includes a web address (URL), capitalize any letters that the site's owner does (on printed materials or on the site itself). Not only is it respectful to reprint it exactly as it appears elsewhere, but, in fact, some web addresses are case-sensitive and must be entered into a browser's address bar exactly as presented.

■ When doing research on the **Internet**, be sure to record each site's **web** address (**URL**) and each contact's **e-mail** address.

Note: Some people include capital letters in their e-mail addresses to make certain features evident. Although e-mail addresses are not case-sensitive, repeat each letter in print just as its owner uses it.

592.3

Avoid Capitalization Errors

Do *not* capitalize any of the following:

- A prefix attached to a proper noun
- Seasons of the year
- Words used to indicate direction or position
- Common nouns and titles that appear near, but are not part of, a proper noun

Capitalize	Do Not Capitalize
American	un-American
January, February	winter, spring
The South is quite conservative.	Turn south at the stop sign.
Duluth City College	a Duluth college
Chancellor John Bohm	John Bohm, our chancellor
President Bush	the president of the United States
Earth (the planet)	earthmover
Internet	e-mail

Plurals

Exercise

Nouns Ending in a Consonant

593.1

Some nouns remain unchanged when used as plurals (*species, moose, halibut,* and so on), but the plurals of most nouns are formed by adding an *s* to the singular form.

- dorm—**dorms**   credit—**credits**   midterm—**midterms**

The plurals of nouns ending in *sh, ch, x, s,* and *z* are made by adding *es* to the singular form.

- lunch—**lunches**   wish—**wishes**   class—**classes**

Nouns Ending in *y*

593.2

The plurals of common nouns that end in *y*—preceded by a consonant—are formed by changing the *y* to *i* and adding *es.*

- dormitory—**dormitories**   sorority—**sororities**   duty—**duties**

The plurals of common nouns that end in *y* (preceded by a vowel) are formed by adding only an *s.*

- attorney—**attorneys**   monkey—**monkeys**   toy—**toys**

The plurals of all proper nouns ending in *y* (whether preceded by a consonant or a vowel) are formed by adding an *s.*

- the three **Kathys**   the five **Faheys**

Nouns Ending in *o*

593.3

The plurals of words ending in *o* (preceded by a vowel) are formed by adding an *s.*

- radio—**radios**   cameo—**cameos**   studio—**studios**

The plurals of most nouns ending in *o* (preceded by a consonant) are formed by adding *es.*

- echo—**echoes**   hero—**heroes**   tomato—**tomatoes**

Musical terms always form plurals by adding an *s*; check a dictionary for other words of this type.

- alto—**altos**   banjo—**banjos**   solo—**solos**   piano—**pianos**

Nouns Ending in *f* or *fe*

593.4

The plurals of nouns that end in *f* or *fe* are formed in one of two ways: If the final *f* sound is still heard in the plural form of the word, simply add *s*; if the final sound is a *v* sound, change the *f* to *ve* and add an *s.*

- **Plural ends with *f* sound:** roof—**roofs**   chief—**chiefs**
- **Plural ends with *v* sound:** wife—**wives**   loaf—**loaves**

Note: The plurals of some nouns that end in *f* or *fe* can be formed by either adding *s* or changing the *f* to *ve* and adding an *s.*

- **Plural ends with either sound:** hoof—**hoofs, hooves**

594.1

Irregular Spelling

Many foreign words (as well as some of English origin) form a plural by taking on an irregular spelling; others are now acceptable with the commonly used *s* or *es* ending. Take time to check a dictionary.

- child—**children**   alumnus—**alumni**   syllabus—**syllabi, syllabuses**
  goose—**geese**   datum—**data**   radius—**radii, radiuses**

594.2

Words Discussed as Words

The plurals of symbols, letters, figures, and words discussed as words are formed by adding an apostrophe and an *s*.

- Many colleges have now added **A/B's** and **B/C's** as standard grades.

Note: You can choose to omit the apostrophe when the omission does not cause confusion.

  YMCA's or YMCAs   CD's or CDs

594.3

Nouns Ending in *ful*

The plurals of nouns that end with *ful* are formed by adding an *s* at the end of the word.

- three **teaspoonfuls**   two **tankfuls**   four **bagfuls**

594.4

Compound Nouns

The plurals of compound nouns are usually formed by adding an *s* or an *es* to the important word in the compound.

- **brothers**-in-law   **maids** of honor   **secretaries** of state

594.5

Collective Nouns

Collective nouns do not change in form when they are used as plurals.

- **class** (a unit—singular form)
  class (individual members—plural form)

Because the spelling of the collective noun does not change, it is often the pronoun used in place of the collective noun that indicates whether the noun is singular or plural. Use a singular pronoun (**its**) to show that the collective noun is singular. Use a plural pronoun (**their**) to show that the collective noun is plural.

- The class needs to change **its** motto.
  (The writer is thinking of the group as a unit.)
- The class brainstormed with **their** professor.
  (The writer is thinking of the group as individuals.)

esl **Note:** To determine whether a plural requires the article *the*, you must first determine whether it is definite or indefinite. Definite plurals use *the*, whereas indefinite plurals do not require any article. (See **658.3–659.1**.)

Numbers

Numerals or Words

Numbers from one to one hundred are usually written as words; numbers 101 and greater are usually written as numerals. Hyphenate numbers written as two words if less than one hundred.

■ **two   seven   ten   twenty-five   106   1,079**

The same rule applies to the use of ordinal numbers.

■ **second   tenth   twenty-fifth   ninety-eighth   106th   333rd**

If numbers greater than 101 are used infrequently in a piece of writing, you may spell out those that can be written in one or two words.

■ **two hundred   fifty thousand   six billion**

You may use a combination of numerals and words for very large numbers.

■ **1.5 million   3 billion to 3.2 billion   6 trillion**

Numbers being compared or contrasted should be kept in the same style.

■ **8** to **11** years old *or* **eight** to **eleven** years old

Particular decades may be spelled out or written as numerals.

■ the **'80s** and **'90s** *or* the **eighties** and **nineties**

Numerals Only

Use numerals for the following forms: decimals, percentages, pages, chapters (and other parts of a book), addresses, dates, telephone numbers, identification numbers, and statistics.

■ **26.2**   **8** percent   Chapter **7**
  pages **287–289**   Highway **36**   **(212) 555–1234**
  398-55-0000   a vote of **23** to **4** May **8, 2007**

Note: Abbreviations and symbols are often used in charts, graphs, footnotes, and so forth, but typically are not used in texts.

■ He is **five feet one inch** tall and **ten years old.**
  She walked **three and one-half miles** to work through **twelve inches** of snow.

However, abbreviations and symbols may be used in scientific, mathematical, statistical, and technical texts.

■ Between **20%** and **23%** of the cultures yielded positive results.
  Your **245B** model requires **220V.**

Always use numerals with abbreviations and symbols.

■ **5'4"**   **8**%   **10** in.   **3** tbsp.   **6** lb. **8** oz.   **90**°F

Use numerals after the name of local branches of labor unions.

■ The Office and Professional Employees International Union, Local **8**

596.1

Hyphenated Numbers

Hyphens are used to form compound modifiers indicating measurement. They are also used for inclusive numbers and written-out fractions.

- a **three-mile** trip
- a **2,500-mile** road trip
- a **thirteen-foot** clearance

- the **2001–2005** presidential term
- **one-sixth** of the pie
- **three-eighths** of the book

596.2

Time and Money

If time is expressed with an abbreviation, use numerals; if it is expressed in words, spell out the number.

- **4:00** a.m. or **four** o'clock (not 4 o'clock)
- the **5:15** p.m. train
- a **seven o'clock** wake-up call

If money is expressed with a symbol, use numerals; if the currency is expressed in words, spell out the number.

- **$20** or **twenty** dollars (not 20 dollars)

Abbreviations of time and of money may be used in text.

- The concert begins at **7:00** p.m., and tickets cost $**30.**

596.3

Words Only

Use words to express numbers that begin a sentence.

- **Fourteen** students "forgot" their assignments.
  Three hundred contest entries were received.

Note: Change the sentence structure if this rule creates a clumsy construction.

- **Six hundred thirty-nine** students are new to the campus this fall. (Clumsy)
  This fall, **639** students are new to the campus. (Better)

Use words for numbers that precede a compound modifier that includes a numeral. (If the compound modifier uses a spelled-out number, use numerals in front of it.)

- She sold **twenty 35-millimeter** cameras in one day.
  The chef prepared **24 eight-ounce** filets.

Use words for the names of numbered streets of one hundred or less.

- **Ninth** Avenue
  123 Forty-fourth Street

Use words for the names of buildings if that name is also its address.

- **One Thousand State Street**   **Two Fifty Park Avenue**

Use words for references to particular centuries.

- the **twenty-first century**   the **fourth century B.C.E.**

Abbreviations

An **abbreviation** is the shortened form of a word or a phrase. These abbreviations are always acceptable in both formal and informal writing:

■ **Mr. Mrs. Ms. Dr. Jr. a.m. (A.M.) p.m. (P.M.)**

Note: In formal writing, do not abbreviate the names of states, countries, months, days, units of measure, or courses of study. Do not abbreviate the words *Street, Road, Avenue, Company,* and similar words when they are part of a proper name. Also, do not use signs or symbols (%, &, #, @) in place of words. (The dollar sign, however, is appropriate when numerals are used to express an amount of money.)

Also Note: When abbreviations are called for (in charts, lists, bibliographies, notes, and indexes, for example), standard abbreviations are preferred. Reserve the postal abbreviations for ZIP code addresses.

597.1

Exercise

597.2

Correspondence Abbreviations

States/Territories

	Standard	Postal
Alabama	Ala.	AL
Alaska	Alaska	AK
Arizona	Ariz.	AZ
Arkansas	Ark.	AR
California	Cal.	CA
Colorado	Colo.	CO
Connecticut	Conn.	CT
Delaware	Del.	DE
District of Columbia	D.C.	DC
Florida	Fla.	FL
Georgia	Ga.	GA
Guam	Guam	GU
Hawaii	Hawaii	HI
Idaho	Idaho	ID
Illinois	Ill.	IL
Indiana	Ind.	IN
Iowa	Ia.	IA
Kansas	Kans.	KS
Kentucky	Ky.	KY
Louisiana	La.	LA
Maine	Me.	ME
Maryland	Md.	MD
Massachusetts	Mass.	MA
Michigan	Mich.	MI
Minnesota	Minn.	MN
Mississippi	Miss.	MS
Missouri	Mo.	MO
Montana	Mont.	MT
Nebraska	Neb.	NE
Nevada	Nev.	NV
New Hampshire	N.H.	NH
New Jersey	N.J.	NJ
New Mexico	N. Mex.	NM
New York	N.Y.	NY
North Carolina	N.C.	NC
North Dakota	N. Dak.	ND
Ohio	Ohio	OH

	Standard	Postal
Oklahoma	Okla.	OK
Oregon	Ore.	OR
Pennsylvania	Pa.	PA
Puerto Rico	P.R.	PR
Rhode Island	R.I.	RI
South Carolina	S.C.	SC
South Dakota	S. Dak.	SD
Tennessee	Tenn.	TN
Texas	Tex.	TX
Utah	Utah	UT
Vermont	Vt.	VT
Virginia	Va.	VA
Virgin Islands	V.I.	VI
Washington	Wash.	WA
West Virginia	W. Va.	WV
Wisconsin	Wis.	WI
Wyoming	Wyo.	WY

Canadian Provinces

	Standard	Postal
Alberta	Alta.	AB
British Columbia	B.C.	BC
Labrador	Lab.	LB
Manitoba	Man.	MB
New Brunswick	N.B.	NB
Newfoundland	N.F.	NF
Northwest Territories	N.W.T.	NT
Nova Scotia	N.S.	NS
Nunavut		NU
Ontario	Ont.	ON
Prince Edward Island	P.E.I.	PE
Quebec	Que.	PQ
Saskatchewan	Sask.	SK
Yukon Territory	Y.T.	YT

Address Abbreviations

	Standard	Postal
Apartment	Apt.	APT
Avenue	Ave.	AVE
Boulevard	Blvd.	BLVD
Circle	Cir.	CIR
Court	Ct.	CT
Drive	Dr.	DR
East	E.	E
Expressway	Expy.	EXPY
Freeway	Frwy.	FWY
Heights	Hts.	HTS
Highway	Hwy.	HWY
Hospital	Hosp.	HOSP
Junction	Junc.	JCT
Lake	L.	LK
Lakes	Ls.	LKS
Lane	Ln.	LN
Meadows	Mdws.	MDWS
North	N.	N
Palms	Palms	PLMS
Park	Pk.	PK
Parkway	Pky.	PKY
Place	Pl.	PL
Plaza	Plaza	PLZ
Post Office Box	P.O. Box	PO BOX
Ridge	Rdg.	RDG
River	R.	RV
Road	Rd.	RD
Room	Rm.	RM
Rural	R.	R
Rural Route	R.R.	RR
Shore	Sh.	SH
South	S.	S
Square	Sq.	SQ
Station	Sta.	STA
Street	St.	ST
Suite	Ste.	STE
Terrace	Ter.	TER
Turnpike	Tpke.	TPKE
Union	Un.	UN
View	View	VW
Village	Vil.	VLG
West	W.	W

Common Abbreviations

abr. abridged, abridgment
AC, ac alternating current, air-conditioning
ack. acknowledgment
AM amplitude modulation
A.M., a.m. before noon (Latin *ante meridiem*)
AP advanced placement
ASAP as soon as possible
avg., av. average
B.A. bachelor of arts degree
BBB Better Business Bureau
B.C.E. before common era
bibliog. bibliography
biog. biographer, biographical, biography
B.S. bachelor of science degree
C 1. Celsius 2. centigrade 3. coulomb
c. 1. *circa* (about) 2. cup(s)
cc 1. cubic centimeter 2. carbon copy 3. community college
CDT, C.D.T. central daylight time
C.E. common era
CEEB College Entrance Examination Board
chap. chapter(s)
cm centimeter(s)
c/o care of
COD, c.o.d. 1. cash on delivery 2. collect on delivery
co-op cooperative
CST, C.S.T. central standard time
cu 1. cubic 2. cumulative
D.A. district attorney
d.b.a., d/b/a doing business as
DC, dc direct current
dec. deceased
dept. department
disc. discount
DST, D.S.T. daylight saving time
dup. duplicate
ed. edition, editor
e.g. for example (Latin *exempli gratia*)
EST, E.S.T. eastern standard time
etc. and so forth (Latin *et cetera*)
F Fahrenheit, French, Friday
FM frequency modulation
F.O.B., f.o.b. free on board
FYI for your information
g 1. gravity 2. gram(s)
gal. gallon(s)
gds. goods
gloss. glossary
GNP gross national product
GPA grade point average
hdqrs. headquarters

HIV human immunodeficiency virus
hp horsepower
Hz hertz
ibid. in the same place (Latin *ibidem*)
id. the same (Latin *idem*)
i.e. that is (Latin *id est*)
illus. illustration
inc. incorporated
IQ, I.Q. intelligence quotient
IRS Internal Revenue Service
ISBN International Standard Book Number
JP, J.P. justice of the peace
K 1. kelvin (temperature unit) 2. Kelvin (temperature scale)
kc kilocycle(s)
kg kilogram(s)
km kilometer(s)
kn knot(s)
kw kilowatt(s)
l liter(s), lake
lat. latitude
l.c. lowercase
lit. literary; literature
log logarithm, logic
long. longitude
Ltd., ltd. limited
m meter(s)
M.A. master of arts degree
man. manual
Mc, mc megacycle
MC master of ceremonies
M.D. doctor of medicine (Latin *medicinae doctor*)
mdse. merchandise
mfg. manufacture, manufacturing
mg milligram(s)
mi. 1. mile(s) 2. mill(s) (monetary unit)
misc. miscellaneous
ml milliliter(s)
mm millimeter(s)
mpg, m.p.g. miles per gallon
mph, m.p.h. miles per hour
MS 1. manuscript 2. multiple sclerosis
Ms. title of courtesy for a woman
M.S. master of science degree
MST, M.S.T. mountain standard time
NE northeast
neg. negative
N.S.F., n.s.f. not sufficient funds
NW northwest
oz, oz. ounce(s)
PA public-address system
pct. percent
pd. paid

PDT, P.D.T. Pacific daylight time
PFC, Pfc. private first class
pg., p. page
Ph.D. doctor of philosophy
P.M., p.m. after noon (Latin *post meridiem*)
POW, P.O.W. prisoner of war
pp. pages
ppd. 1. postpaid 2. prepaid
PR, P.R. public relations
PSAT Preliminary Scholastic Aptitude Test
psi, p.s.i. pounds per square inch
PST, P.S.T. Pacific standard time
PTA, P.T.A. Parent-Teacher Association
R.A. residence assistant
RF radio frequency
R.P.M., rpm revolutions per minute
R.S.V.P., r.s.v.p. please reply (French *répondez s'il vous plaît*)
SAT Scholastic Aptitude Test
SE southeast
SOS 1. international distress signal 2. any call for help
Sr. 1. senior (after surname) 2. sister (religious)
SRO, S.R.O. standing room only
std. standard
SW southwest
syn. synonymous, synonym
tbs., tbsp. tablespoon(s)
TM trademark
UHF, uhf ultrahigh frequency
v 1. physics: velocity 2. volume
V electricity: volt
VA Veterans Administration
VHF, vhf very high frequency
VIP informal: very important person
vol. 1. volume 2. volunteer
vs. versus, verse
W 1. electricity: watt(s) 2. physics: (also **w**) work 3. west
whse., whs. warehouse
whsle. wholesale
wkly. weekly
w/o without
wt. weight
www World Wide Web

Acronyms and Initialisms

Acronyms

An **acronym** is a word formed from the first (or first few) letters of words in a set phrase. Even though acronyms are abbreviations, they require no periods.

- **radar**   radio detecting and ranging
  CARE   Cooperative for Assistance and Relief Everywhere
  NASA   National Aeronautics and Space Administration
  VISTA   Volunteers in Service to America
  FICA   Federal Insurance Contributions Act

Initialisms

An **initialism** is similar to an acronym except that the initials used to form this abbreviation are pronounced individually.

- **CIA**   Central Intelligence Agency
  FBI   Federal Bureau of Investigation
  FHA   Federal Housing Administration

Common Acronyms and Initialisms

AIDS	acquired immunodeficiency syndrome	**OSHA**	Occupational Safety and Health Administration
APR	annual percentage rate		
CAD	computer-aided design	**PAC**	political action committee
CAM	computer-aided manufacturing	**PIN**	personal identification number
CETA	Comprehensive Employment and Training Act	**POP**	point of purchase
		PSA	public service announcement
FAA	Federal Aviation Administration	**REA**	Rural Electrification Administration
FCC	Federal Communications Commission		
		RICO	Racketeer Influenced and Corrupt Organizations (Act)
FDA	Food and Drug Administration		
FDIC	Federal Deposit Insurance Corporation	**ROTC**	Reserve Officers' Training Corps
		SADD	Students Against Destructive Decisions
FEMA	Federal Emergency Management Agency	**SASE**	self-addressed stamped envelope
		SPOT	satellite positioning and tracking
FHA	Federal Housing Administration	**SSA**	Social Security Administration
FTC	Federal Trade Commission	**SUV**	sport-utility vehicle
IRS	Internal Revenue Service	**SWAT**	Special Weapons and Tactics
MADD	Mothers Against Drunk Driving	**TDD**	telecommunications device for the deaf
NAFTA	North American Free Trade Agreement	**TMJ**	temporomandibular joint
		TVA	Tennessee Valley Authority
NATO	North Atlantic Treaty Organization	**VA**	Veterans Administration
OEO	Office of Economic Opportunity		
ORV	off-road vehicle	**WHO**	World Health Organization

Exercise

Basic Spelling Rules

600.1
Write *i* Before *e*

Write *i* before *e* except after *c*, or when sounded like *a* as in *neighbor* and *weigh*.

- **believe**   **relief**   **receive**   **eight**

Note: This sentence contains eight exceptions:

- **Neither sheik** dared **leisurely seize either weird species** of **financiers.**

600.2
Words with Consonant Endings

When a one-syllable word (*bat*) ends in a consonant (*t*) preceded by one vowel (*a*), double the final consonant before adding a suffix that begins with a vowel (*batting*).

- sum—**summary**   god—**goddess**

Note: When a multisyllable word (*control*) ends in a consonant (*l*) preceded by one vowel (*o*), the accent is on the last syllable (*con trol´*), and the suffix begins with a vowel (*ing*)—the same rule holds true: double the final consonant (*controlling*).

- prefer—**preferred**   begin—**beginning**
  forget—**forgettable**   admit—**admittance**

600.3
Words with a Final Silent *e*

If a word ends with a silent *e*, drop the *e* before adding a suffix that begins with a vowel. Do *not* drop the *e* when the suffix begins with a consonant.

- state—**stating**—**statement**   like—**liking**—**likeness**
  use—**using**—**useful**   nine—**ninety**—**nineteen**

Note: Exceptions are **judgment, truly, argument, ninth**.

600.4
Words Ending in *y*

When *y* is the last letter in a word and the *y* is preceded by a consonant, change the *y* to *i* before adding any suffix except those beginning with *i*.

- fry—**fries, frying**   hurry—**hurried, hurrying**
  lady—**ladies**   ply—**pliable**
  happy—**happiness**   beauty—**beautiful**

Note: When forming the plural of a word that ends with a *y* that is preceded by a vowel, add *s*.

- toy—**toys**   play—**plays**   monkey—**monkeys**

TIP: Never trust your spelling to even the best spell checker. Carefully proofread and use a dictionary for words you know your spell checker does not cover.

Commonly Misspelled Words

The commonly misspelled words that follow are hyphenated to show where they would logically be broken at the end of a line.

A

ab-bre-vi-ate
a-brupt
ab-scess
ab-sence
ab-so-lute (-ly)
ab-sorb-ent
ab-surd
a-bun-dance
ac-a-dem-ic
ac-cede
ac-cel-er-ate
ac-cept (-ance)
ac-ces-si-ble
ac-ces-so-ry
ac-ci-den-tal-ly
ac-com-mo-date
ac-com-pa-ny
ac-com-plice
ac-com-plish
ac-cor-dance
ac-cord-ing
ac-count
ac-crued
ac-cu-mu-late
ac-cu-rate
ac-cus-tom (-ed)
ache
a-chieve (-ment)
ac-knowl-edge
ac-quaint-ance
ac-qui-esce
ac-quired
ac-tu-al
a-dapt
ad-di-tion (-al)
ad-dress
ad-e-quate
ad-journed
ad-just-ment
ad-mi-ra-ble
ad-mis-si-ble
ad-mit-tance
ad-van-ta-geous
ad-ver-tise-ment

ad-ver-tis-ing
ad-vice (n.)
ad-vis-able
ad-vise (v.)
ad-vis-er
ae-ri-al
af-fect
af-fi-da-vit
a-gainst
ag-gra-vate
ag-gres-sion
a-gree-able
a-gree-ment
aisle
al-co-hol
a-lign-ment
al-ley
al-lot-ted
al-low-ance
all right
al-most
al-ready
al-though
al-to-geth-er
a-lu-mi-num
al-um-nus
al-ways
am-a-teur
a-mend-ment
a-mong
a-mount
a-nal-y-sis
an-a-lyze
an-cient
an-ec-dote
an-es-thet-ic
an-gle
an-ni-hi-late
an-ni-ver-sa-ry
an-nounce
an-noy-ance
an-nu-al
a-noint
a-non-y-mous
an-swer
ant-arc-tic

an-tic-i-pate
anx-i-ety
anx-ious
a-part-ment
a-pol-o-gize
ap-pa-ra-tus
ap-par-ent (-ly)
ap-peal
ap-pear-ance
ap-pe-tite
ap-pli-ance
ap-pli-ca-ble
ap-pli-ca-tion
ap-point-ment
ap-prais-al
ap-pre-ci-ate
ap-proach
ap-pro-pri-ate
ap-prov-al
ap-prox-i-mate-ly
ap-ti-tude
ar-chi-tect
arc-tic
ar-gu-ment
a-rith-me-tic
a-rouse
ar-range-ment
ar-riv-al
ar-ti-cle
ar-ti-fi-cial
as-cend
as-cer-tain
as-i-nine
as-sas-sin
as-sess (-ment)
as-sign-ment
as-sist-ance
as-so-ci-ate
as-so-ci-a-tion
as-sume
as-sur-ance
as-ter-isk
ath-lete
ath-let-ic
at-tach
at-tack (-ed)

at-tempt
at-tend-ance
at-ten-tion
at-ti-tude
at-tor-ney
at-trac-tive
au-di-ble
au-di-ence
au-dit
au-thor-i-ty
au-to-mo-bile
au-tumn
aux-il-ia-ry
a-vail-a-ble
av-er-age
aw-ful
aw-ful-ly
awk-ward

B

bac-ca-lau-re-ate
bach-e-lor
bag-gage
bal-ance
bal-loon
bal-lot
ba-nan-a
ban-dage
bank-rupt
bar-gain
bar-rel
base-ment
ba-sis
bat-tery
beau-ti-ful
beau-ty
be-com-ing
beg-gar
be-gin-ning
be-hav-ior
be-ing
be-lief
be-lieve
ben-e-fi-cial
ben-e-fit (-ed)
be-tween

bi-cy-cle
bis-cuit
bliz-zard
book-keep-er
bought
bouil-lon
bound-a-ry
break-fast
breath (n.)
breathe (v.)
brief
bril-liant
Brit-ain
bro-chure
brought
bruise
bud-get
bul-le-tin
buoy-ant
bu-reau
bur-glar
bury
busi-ness
busy

C

caf-e-te-ria
caf-feine
cal-en-dar
cam-paign
can-celed
can-di-date
can-is-ter
ca-noe
ca-pac-i-ty
cap-i-tal
cap-i-tol
cap-tain
car-bu-ret-or
ca-reer
car-i-ca-ture
car-riage
cash-ier
cas-se-role
cas-u-al-ty
cat-a-log

ca-tas-tro-phe
caught
cav-al-ry
cel-e-bra-tion
cem-e-ter-y
cen-sus
cen-tu-ry
cer-tain
cer-tif-i-cate
ces-sa-tion
chal-lenge
chan-cel-lor
change-a-ble
char-ac-ter (-is-tic)
chauf-feur
chief
chim-ney
choc-o-late
choice
choose
Chris-tian
cir-cuit
cir-cu-lar
cir-cum-stance
civ-i-li-za-tion
cli-en-tele
cli-mate
climb
clothes
coach
co-coa
co-er-cion
col-lar
col-lat-er-al
col-lege
col-le-giate
col-lo-qui-al
colo-nel
col-or
co-los-sal
col-umn
com-e-dy
com-ing
com-mence
com-mer-cial
com-mis-sion
com-mit
com-mit-ment
com-mit-ted
com-mit-tee
com-mu-ni-cate

com-mu-ni-ty
com-par-a-tive
com-par-i-son
com-pel
com-pe-tent
com-pe-ti-tion
com-pet-i-tive-ly
com-plain
com-ple-ment
com-plete-ly
com-plex-ion
com-pli-ment
com-pro-mise
con-cede
con-ceive
con-cern-ing
con-cert
con-ces-sion
con-clude
con-crete
con-curred
con-cur-rence
con-demn
con-de-scend
con-di-tion
con-fer-ence
con-ferred
con-fi-dence
con-fi-den-tial
con-grat-u-late
con-science
con-sci-en-tious
con-scious
con-sen-sus
con-se-quence
con-ser-va-tive
con-sid-er-ably
con-sign-ment
con-sis-tent
con-sti-tu-tion
con-tempt-ible
con-tin-u-al-ly
con-tin-ue
con-tin-u-ous
con-trol
con-tro-ver-sy
con-ven-ience
con-vince
cool-ly
co-op-er-ate
cor-dial

cor-po-ra-tion
cor-re-late
cor-re-spond
cor-re-spond-
  ence
cor-rob-o-rate
cough
coun-cil
coun-sel
coun-ter-feit
coun-try
cour-age
cou-ra-geous
cour-te-ous
cour-te-sy
cous-in
cov-er-age
cred-i-tor
cri-sis
crit-i-cism
crit-i-cize
cru-el
cu-ri-os-i-ty
cu-ri-ous
cur-rent
cur-ric-u-lum
cus-tom
cus-tom-ary
cus-tom-er
cyl-in-der

D

dai-ly
dair-y
dealt
debt-or
de-ceased
de-ceit-ful
de-ceive
de-cid-ed
de-ci-sion
dec-la-ra-tion
dec-o-rate
de-duct-i-ble
de-fend-ant
de-fense
de-ferred
def-i-cit
def-i-nite (-ly)
def-i-ni-tion

del-e-gate
de-li-cious
de-pend-ent
de-pos-i-tor
de-pot
de-scend
de-scribe
de-scrip-tion
de-sert
de-serve
de-sign
de-sir-able
de-sir-ous
de-spair
des-per-ate
de-spise
des-sert
de-te-ri-o-rate
de-ter-mine
de-vel-op
de-vel-op-ment
de-vice
de-vise
di-a-mond
di-a-phragm
di-ar-rhe-a
dic-tio-nary
dif-fer-ence
dif-fer-ent
dif-fi-cul-ty
di-lap-i-dat-ed
di-lem-ma
din-ing
di-plo-ma
di-rec-tor
dis-agree-able
dis-ap-pear
dis-ap-point
dis-ap-prove
dis-as-trous
dis-ci-pline
dis-cov-er
dis-crep-an-cy
dis-cuss
dis-cus-sion
dis-ease
dis-sat-is-fied
dis-si-pate
dis-tin-guish
dis-trib-ute
di-vide

di-vis-i-ble
di-vi-sion
doc-tor
doesn't
dom-i-nant
dor-mi-to-ry
doubt
drudg-ery
du-pli-cate
dye-ing
dy-ing

E

ea-ger-ly
ear-nest
eco-nom-i-cal
econ-o-my
ec-sta-sy
e-di-tion
ef-fer-ves-cent
ef-fi-ca-cy
ef-fi-cien-cy
eighth
ei-ther
e-lab-o-rate
e-lec-tric-i-ty
el-e-phant
el-i-gi-ble
e-lim-i-nate
el-lipse
em-bar-rass
e-mer-gen-cy
em-i-nent
em-pha-size
em-ploy-ee
em-ploy-ment
e-mul-sion
en-close
en-cour-age
en-deav-or
en-dorse-ment
en-gi-neer
En-glish
e-nor-mous
e-nough
en-ter-prise
en-ter-tain
en-thu-si-as-tic
en-tire-ly
en-trance

en-vel-op (v.)
en-ve-lope (n.)
en-vi-ron-ment
equip-ment
equipped
e-quiv-a-lent
es-pe-cial-ly
es-sen-tial
es-tab-lish
es-teemed
et-i-quette
ev-i-dence
ex-ag-ger-ate
ex-ceed
ex-cel-lent
ex-cept
ex-cep-tion-al-ly
ex-ces-sive
ex-cite
ex-ec-u-tive
ex-er-cise
ex-haust (-ed)
ex-hi-bi-tion
ex-hil-a-ra-tion
ex-is-tence
ex-or-bi-tant
ex-pect
ex-pe-di-tion
ex-pend-i-ture
ex-pen-sive
ex-pe-ri-ence
ex-plain
ex-pla-na-tion
ex-pres-sion
ex-qui-site
ex-ten-sion
ex-tinct
ex-traor-di-nar-y
ex-treme-ly

F

fa-cil-i-ties
fal-la-cy
fa-mil-iar
fa-mous
fas-ci-nate
fash-ion
fa-tigue (-d)
fau-cet
fa-vor-ite

fea-si-ble
fea-ture
Feb-ru-ar-y
fed-er-al
fem-i-nine
fer-tile
fic-ti-tious
field
fierce
fi-ery
fi-nal-ly
fi-nan-cial-ly
fo-li-age
for-ci-ble
for-eign
for-feit
for-go
for-mal-ly
for-mer-ly
for-tu-nate
for-ty
for-ward
foun-tain
fourth
frag-ile
fran-ti-cal-ly
freight
friend
ful-fill
fun-da-men-tal
fur-ther-more
fu-tile

G

gad-get
gan-grene
ga-rage
gas-o-line
gauge
ge-ne-al-o-gy
gen-er-al-ly
gen-er-ous
ge-nius
gen-u-ine
ge-og-ra-phy
ghet-to
ghost
glo-ri-ous
gnaw
go-ril-la

gov-ern-ment
gov-er-nor
gra-cious
grad-u-a-tion
gram-mar
grate-ful
grat-i-tude
grease
grief
griev-ous
gro-cery
grudge
grue-some
guar-an-tee
guard
guard-i-an
guer-ril-la
guess
guid-ance
guide
guilty
gym-na-si-um
gyp-sy
gy-ro-scope

H

hab-i-tat
ham-mer
hand-ker-chief
han-dle (-d)
hand-some
hap-haz-ard
hap-pen
hap-pi-ness
ha-rass
har-bor
hast-i-ly
hav-ing
haz-ard-ous
height
hem-or-rhage
hes-i-tate
hin-drance
his-to-ry
hoarse
hol-i-day
hon-or
hop-ing
hop-ping
horde

hor-ri-ble
hos-pi-tal
hu-mor-ous
hur-ried-ly
hy-drau-lic
hy-giene

I

i-am-bic
i-ci-cle
i-den-ti-cal
id-io-syn-cra-sy
il-leg-i-ble
il-lit-er-ate
il-lus-trate
im-ag-i-nary
im-ag-i-na-tive
im-ag-ine
im-i-ta-tion
im-me-di-ate-ly
im-mense
im-mi-grant
im-mor-tal
im-pa-tient
im-per-a-tive
im-por-tance
im-pos-si-ble
im-promp-tu
im-prove-ment
in-al-ien-able
in-ci-den-tal-ly
in-con-ve-nience
in-cred-i-ble
in-curred
in-def-i-nite-ly
in-del-ible
in-de-pend-ence
in-de-pend-ent
in-dict-ment
in-dis-pens-able
in-di-vid-u-al
in-duce-ment
in-dus-tri-al
in-dus-tri-ous
in-ev-i-ta-ble
in-fe-ri-or
in-ferred
in-fi-nite
in-flam-ma-ble
in-flu-en-tial

in-ge-nious
in-gen-u-ous
in-im-i-ta-ble
in-i-tial
ini-ti-a-tion
in-no-cence
in-no-cent
in-oc-u-la-tion
in-quir-y
in-stal-la-tion
in-stance
in-stead
in-sti-tute
in-struc-tor
in-sur-ance
in-tel-lec-tu-al
in-tel-li-gence
in-ten-tion
in-ter-cede
in-ter-est-ing
in-ter-fere
in-ter-mit-tent
in-ter-pret (-ed)
in-ter-rupt
in-ter-view
in-ti-mate
in-va-lid
in-ves-ti-gate
in-ves-tor
in-vi-ta-tion
ir-i-des-cent
ir-rel-e-vant
ir-re-sis-ti-ble
ir-rev-er-ent
ir-ri-gate
is-land
is-sue
i-tem-ized
i-tin-er-ar-y

J

jan-i-tor
jeal-ous (-y)
jeop-ar-dize
jew-el-ry
jour-nal
jour-ney
judg-ment
jus-tice
jus-ti-fi-able

K

kitch-en
knowl-edge
knuck-le

L

la-bel
lab-o-ra-to-ry
lac-quer
lan-guage
laugh
laun-dry
law-yer
league
lec-ture
le-gal
leg-i-ble
leg-is-la-ture
le-git-i-mate
lei-sure
length
let-ter-head
li-a-bil-i-ty
li-a-ble
li-ai-son
lib-er-al
li-brar-y
li-cense
lieu-ten-ant
light-ning
lik-able
like-ly
lin-eage
liq-ue-fy
liq-uid
lis-ten
lit-er-ary
lit-er-a-ture
live-li-hood
log-a-rithm
lone-li-ness
loose
lose
los-ing
lov-able
love-ly
lun-cheon
lux-u-ry

M

ma-chine
mag-a-zine
mag-nif-i-cent
main-tain
main-te-nance
ma-jor-i-ty
mak-ing
man-age-ment
ma-neu-ver
man-u-al
man-u-fac-ture
man-u-script
mar-riage
mar-shal
ma-te-ri-al
math-e-mat-ics
max-i-mum
may-or
mean-ness
meant
mea-sure
med-i-cine
me-di-eval
me-di-o-cre
me-di-um
mem-o-ran-dum
men-us
mer-chan-dise
mer-it
mes-sage
mile-age
mil-lion-aire
min-i-a-ture
min-i-mum
min-ute
mir-ror
mis-cel-la-neous
mis-chief
mis-chie-vous
mis-er-a-ble
mis-ery
mis-sile
mis-sion-ary
mis-spell
mois-ture
mol-e-cule
mo-men-tous
mo-not-o-nous

mon-u-ment
mort-gage
mu-nic-i-pal
mus-cle
mu-si-cian
mus-tache
mys-te-ri-ous

N

na-ive
nat-u-ral-ly
nec-es-sary
ne-ces-si-ty
neg-li-gi-ble
ne-go-ti-ate
neigh-bor-hood
nev-er-the-less
nick-el
niece
nine-teenth
nine-ty
no-tice-able
no-to-ri-ety
nu-cle-ar
nui-sance

O

o-be-di-ence
o-bey
o-blige
ob-sta-cle
oc-ca-sion
oc-ca-sion-al-ly
oc-cu-pant
oc-cur
oc-curred
oc-cur-rence
of-fense
of-fi-cial
of-ten
o-mis-sion
o-mit-ted
op-er-ate
o-pin-ion
op-po-nent
op-por-tu-ni-ty
op-po-site
op-ti-mism
or-di-nance
or-di-nar-i-ly

orig-i-nal
out-ra-geous

P

pag-eant
pam-phlet
par-a-dise
para-graph
par-al-lel
par-a-lyze
pa-ren-the-ses
pa-ren-the-sis
par-lia-ment
par-tial
par-tic-i-pant
par-tic-i-pate
par-tic-u-lar-ly
pas-time
pa-tience
pa-tron-age
pe-cu-liar
per-ceive
per-haps
per-il
per-ma-nent
per-mis-si-ble
per-pen-dic-u-lar
per-se-ver-ance
per-sis-tent
per-son-al (-ly)
per-son-nel
per-spi-ra-tion
per-suade
phase
phe-nom-e-non
phi-los-o-phy
phy-si-cian
piece
planned
pla-teau
plau-si-ble
play-wright
pleas-ant
plea-sure
pneu-mo-nia
pol-i-ti-cian
pos-sess
pos-ses-sion
pos-si-ble
prac-ti-cal-ly

prai-rie
pre-cede
pre-ce-dence
pre-ced-ing
pre-cious
pre-cise-ly
pre-ci-sion
pre-de-ces-sor
pref-er-a-ble
pref-er-ence
pre-ferred
prej-u-dice
pre-lim-i-nar-y
pre-mi-um
prep-a-ra-tion
pres-ence
prev-a-lent
pre-vi-ous
prim-i-tive
prin-ci-pal
prin-ci-ple
pri-or-i-ty
pris-on-er
priv-i-lege
prob-a-bly
pro-ce-dure
pro-ceed
pro-fes-sor
prom-i-nent
pro-nounce
pro-nun-ci-a-tion
pro-pa-gan-da
pros-e-cute
pro-tein
psy-chol-o-gy
pub-lic-ly
pump-kin
pur-chase
pur-sue
pur-su-ing
pur-suit

Q

qual-i-fied
qual-i-ty
quan-ti-ty
quar-ter
ques-tion-naire
quite
quo-tient

R

raise
rap-port
re-al-ize
re-al-ly
re-cede
re-ceipt
re-ceive
re-ceived
rec-i-pe
re-cip-i-ent
rec-og-ni-tion
rec-og-nize
rec-om-mend
re-cur-rence
ref-er-ence
re-ferred
reg-is-tra-tion
re-hearse
reign
re-im-burse
rel-e-vant
re-lieve
re-li-gious
re-mem-ber
re-mem-brance
rem-i-nisce
ren-dez-vous
re-new-al
rep-e-ti-tion
rep-re-sen-ta-tive
req-ui-si-tion
res-er-voir
re-sis-tance
re-spect-a-bly
re-spect-ful-ly
re-spec-tive-ly
re-spon-si-bil-i-ty
res-tau-rant
rheu-ma-tism
rhyme
rhythm
ri-dic-u-lous
route

S

sac-ri-le-gious
safe-ty
sal-a-ry

sand-wich
sat-is-fac-to-ry
Sat-ur-day
scarce-ly
scene
scen-er-y
sched-ule
schol-ar-ship
sci-ence
scis-sors
sec-re-tary
seize
sen-si-ble
sen-tence
sen-ti-nel
sep-a-rate
ser-geant
sev-er-al
se-vere-ly
shep-herd
sher-iff
shin-ing
siege
sig-nif-i-cance
sim-i-lar
si-mul-ta-ne-ous
since
sin-cere-ly
ski-ing
sol-dier
sol-emn
so-phis-ti-cat-ed
soph-o-more
so-ror-i-ty
source
sou-ve-nir
spa-ghet-ti
spe-cif-ic
spec-i-men
speech
sphere
spon-sor
spon-ta-ne-ous
sta-tion-ary
sta-tion-ery
sta-tis-tic
stat-ue
stat-ure
stat-ute
stom-ach
stopped

straight
strat-e-gy
strength
stretched
study-ing
sub-si-dize
sub-stan-tial
sub-sti-tute
sub-tle
suc-ceed
suc-cess
suf-fi-cient
sum-ma-rize
su-per-fi-cial
su-per-in-tend-ent
su-pe-ri-or-i-ty
su-per-sede
sup-ple-ment
sup-pose
sure-ly
sur-prise
sur-veil-lance
sur-vey
sus-cep-ti-ble
sus-pi-cious
sus-te-nance
syl-la-ble
sym-met-ri-cal
sym-pa-thy
sym-pho-ny
symp-tom
syn-chro-nous

T

tar-iff
tech-nique
tele-gram
tem-per-a-ment
tem-per-a-ture
tem-po-rary
ten-den-cy
ten-ta-tive
ter-res-tri-al
ter-ri-ble
ter-ri-to-ry
the-ater
their
there-fore
thief
thor-ough (-ly)

though
through-out
tired
to-bac-co
to-geth-er
to-mor-row
tongue
to-night
touch
tour-na-ment
tour-ni-quet
to-ward
trag-e-dy
trai-tor
tran-quil-iz-er
trans-ferred
trea-sur-er
tru-ly
Tues-day
tu-i-tion
typ-i-cal
typ-ing

U

unan-i-mous
un-con-scious
un-doubt-ed-ly
un-for-tu-nate-ly
unique
u-ni-son
uni-ver-si-ty
un-nec-es-sary
un-prec-e-dent-ed
un-til
up-per
ur-gent
us-able
use-ful
using
usu-al-ly
u-ten-sil
u-til-ize

V

va-can-cies
va-ca-tion
vac-u-um
vague
valu-able
va-ri-ety

var-i-ous
veg-e-ta-ble
ve-hi-cle
veil
ve-loc-i-ty
ven-geance
vi-cin-i-ty
view
vig-i-lance
vil-lain
vi-o-lence
vis-i-bil-i-ty
vis-i-ble
vis-i-tor
voice
vol-ume
vol-un-tary
vol-un-teer

W

wan-der
war-rant
weath-er
Wednes-day
weird
wel-come
wel-fare
where
wheth-er
which
whole
whol-ly
whose
width
wom-en
worth-while
wor-thy
wreck-age
wres-tler
writ-ing
writ-ten
wrought

Y

yel-low
yes-ter-day
yield

Steps to Becoming a Better Speller

1. Be patient. Becoming a good speller takes time.

2. Check the correct pronunciation of each word you are attempting to spell.

Knowing the correct pronunciation of each word can help you to remember its spelling.

3. Note the meaning and history of each word as you are checking the dictionary for the pronunciation.

Knowing the meaning and history of a word provides you with a better notion of how the word is properly used, and it can help you remember the word's spelling.

4. Before you close the dictionary, practice spelling the word.

You can do so by looking away from the page and trying to "see" the word in your "mind's eye." Write the word on a piece of paper. Check the spelling in the dictionary and repeat the process until you are able to spell the word correctly.

5. Learn some spelling rules.

The four rules in this handbook (page **600**) are four of the most useful—although there are others.

6. Make a list of the words that you misspell.

Select the first ten words and practice spelling them.

First: Read each word carefully; then write it on a piece of paper. Look at the written word to see that it's spelled correctly. Repeat the process for those words that you misspelled.

Then: Ask someone to read the words to you so you can write them again. Then check for misspellings. Repeat both steps with your next ten words.

7. Write often.

As noted educator Frank Smith said,

> " *There is little point in learning to spell*
> *if you have little intention of writing."*

Chapter 37
Using the Right Word

a, an Use *a* as the article before words that begin with consonant sounds and before words that begin with the long vowel sound *u* (yü). Use *an* before words that begin with other vowel sounds.

■ **An** older student showed Kris **an** easier way to get to class.
  A uniform is required attire for **a** cafeteria worker.

607.1

a lot, alot, allot *Alot* is not a word; *a lot* (two words) is a vague descriptive phrase that should be used sparingly, especially in formal writing. *Allot* means to give someone a share.

■ Prof Dubi **allots** each of us five spelling errors per semester and he thinks that's **a lot**.

607.2

accept, except The verb *accept* means "to receive or believe"; the preposition *except* means "other than."

■ The instructor **accepted** the student's story about being late, but she wondered why no one **except** him had forgotten about the change to daylight saving time.

607.3

adapt, adopt, adept *Adapt* means "to adjust or change to fit"; *adopt* means "to choose and treat as your own" (a child, an idea). *Adept* is an adjective meaning "proficient or well trained."

■ After much thought and deliberation, we agreed to **adopt** the black Lab from the shelter. Now we have to agree on how to **adapt** our lifestyle to fit our new roommate.

607.4

adverse, averse *Adverse* means "hostile, unfavorable, or harmful." *Averse* means "to have a definite feeling of distaste—disinclined."

■ Groans and other **adverse** reactions were noted as the new students, **averse** to strenuous exercise, were ushered past the X-5000 pump-and-crunch machine.

607.5

advice, advise *Advice* is a noun meaning "information or recommendation"; *advise* is a verb meaning "to recommend."

■ Successful people will often give you sound **advice**, so I **advise** you to listen.

607.6

affect, effect *Affect* means "to influence"; the noun *effect* means "the result."

■ The employment growth in a field will **affect** your chances of getting a job. The **effect** may be a new career choice.

607.7

608.1 **aid, aide** As a verb, *aid* means "to help"; as a noun, *aid* means "the help given." An *aide* is a person who acts as an assistant.

608.2 **all of** *Of* is seldom needed after *all*.

☑ **All** the reports had an error in them.
All the speakers spoke English.
All of us voted to reshedule the meeting.
(Here *of* is needed for the sentence to make sense.)

Exercise

608.3 **all right, alright** *Alright* is the incorrect form of *all right*. (**Note:** The following are spelled correctly: *always, altogether, already, almost*.)

608.4 **allude, elude** *Allude* means "to indirectly refer to or hint at something"; *elude* means "to escape attention or understanding altogether."

■ Ravi often **alluded** to wanting a supper invitation by mentioning the "awful good" smells from the kitchen. These hints never **eluded** Ma's good heart.

608.5 **allusion, illusion** *Allusion* is an indirect reference to something or someone, especially in literature; *illusion* is a false picture or idea.

■ Did you recognize the **allusion** to David in the reading assignment? Until I read that part, I was under the **illusion** that the young boy would run away from the bully.

608.6 **already, all ready** *Already* is an adverb meaning "before this time" or "by this time." *All ready* is an adjective form meaning "fully prepared." (**Note:** Use *all ready* if you can substitute *ready* alone in the sentence.)

■ By the time I was a junior in high school, I had **already** taken my SATs. That way, I was **all ready** to apply early to college.

608.7 **altogether, all together** *Altogether* means "entirely." *All together* means "in a group" or "all at once." (**Note:** Use *all together* if you can substitute *together* alone in the sentence.)

■ **All together** there are 35,000 job titles to choose from. That's **altogether** too many to even think about.

608.8 **among, between** *Among* is typically used when emphasizing distribution throughout a body or a group of three or more; *between* is used when emphasizing distribution to individuals.

■ There was discontent **among** the relatives after learning that their aunt had divided her entire fortune **between** a canary and a favorite waitress at the local cafe.

608.9 **amoral, immoral** *Amoral* means "neither moral (right) nor immoral (wrong)"; *immoral* means "wrong, or in conflict with traditional values."

■ Carnivores are **amoral** in their hunt; poachers are **immoral** in theirs.

608.10 **amount, number** *Amount* is used for bulk measurement. *Number* is used to count separate units. (See also "fewer.")

■ The **number** of new instructors hired next year will depend on the **amount** of revenue raised by the new sales tax.

and etc. Don't use *and* before *etc.*

- Did you remember your textbook, notebook, handout, **etc.**?

609.1

annual, biannual, semiannual, biennial, perennial An *annual* event happens once every year. A *biannual* event happens twice a year (*semiannual* is the same as *biannual*). A *biennial* event happens every two years. A *perennial* event happens throughout the year, every year.

609.2

anxious, eager Both words mean "looking forward to," but *anxious* also connotes fear or concern.

- The professor is **eager** to move into the new building, but she's a little **anxious** that students won't be able to find her new office.

609.3

anymore, any more *Anymore* means "any longer"; *any more* means "any additional."

- We won't use that textbook **anymore**; please call if you have **any more** questions.

609.4

any one (of), anyone *Any one* means "any one of a number of people, places, or things"; *anyone* is a pronoun meaning "any person."

- Choose **any one** of the proposed weekend schedules. **Anyone** wishing to work on Saturday instead of Sunday may do so.

609.5

appraise, apprise *Appraise* means "to determine value." *Apprise* means "to inform."

- Because of the tax assessor's recent **appraisal** of our home, we were **apprised** of an increase in our property tax.

609.6

as Don't use *as* in place of *whether* or *if*.

- I don't know **as** I'll accept the offer. (Incorrect)
  I don't know **whether** I'll accept the offer. (Correct)

  Don't use *as* when it is unclear whether it means *because* or *when*.

- We rowed toward shore **as** it started raining. (Unclear)
  We rowed toward shore **because** it started raining. (Correct)

609.7

assure, ensure, insure (See "insure.")

bad, badly *Bad* is an adjective, used both before nouns and after linking verbs. *Badly* is an adverb.

- Christina felt **bad** about serving us **bad** food.
  Larisa played **badly** today.

609.8

beside, besides *Beside* means "by the side of." *Besides* means "in addition to."

- **Besides** the two suitcases you've already loaded into the trunk, remember the smaller one **beside** the van.

609.9

between, among (See "among.")

bring, take *Bring* suggests the action is directed toward the speaker; *take* suggests the action is directed away from the speaker.

- If you're not going to **bring** the video to class, **take** it back to the resource center.

609.10

610.1   **can, may**   In formal contexts, *can* is used to mean "being able to do"; *may* is used to mean "having permission to do."

- **May** I borrow your bicycle to get to the library? Then I **can** start working on our group project.

610.2   **capital, capitol**   The noun *capital* refers to a city or to money. The adjective *capital* means "major or important" or "seat of government." *Capitol* refers to a building.

- The **capitol** is in the **capital** city for a **capital** reason. The city government contributed **capital** for the building expense.

610.3   **cent, sent, scent**   *Cent* is a coin; *sent* is the past tense of the verb "send"; *scent* is an odor or a smell.

- For thirty-seven **cents**, I **sent** my friend a love poem in a perfumed envelope. She adored the **scent** but hated the poem.

610.4   **chord, cord**   *Chord* may mean "an emotion or a feeling," but it also may mean "the combination of three or more tones sounded at the same time," as with a guitar *chord*. A *cord* is a string or a rope.

- The guitar player strummed the opening **chord**, which struck a responsive **chord** with the audience.

610.5   **chose, choose**   *Chose* (chōz) is the past tense of the verb *choose* (chüz).

- For generations, people **chose** their careers based on their parents' careers; now people **choose** their careers based on the job market.

610.6   **climactic, climatic**   *Climactic* refers to the climax, or high point, of an event; *climatic* refers to the climate, or weather conditions.

☑ Exercise

- Because we are using the open-air amphitheater, **climatic** conditions in these foothills will just about guarantee the wind gusts we need for the **climactic** third act.

610.7   **coarse, course**   *Coarse* means "of inferior quality, rough, or crude"; *course* means "a direction or a path taken." *Course* also means "a class or a series of studies."

- A basic writing **course** is required of all students.
  Due to years of woodworking, the instructor's hands are rather **coarse**.

610.8   **compare with, compare to**   Things in the same category are *compared with* each other; things in different categories are *compared to* each other.

- **Compare** Christopher Marlowe's plays **with** William Shakespeare's plays.
  My brother **compared** reading *The Tempest* **to** visiting another country.

610.9   **complement, compliment**   *Complement* means "to complete or go well with." *Compliment* means "to offer an expression of admiration or praise."

- We wanted to **compliment** Zach on his decorating efforts; the bright yellow walls **complement** the purple carpet.

610.10   **comprehensible, comprehensive**   *Comprehensible* means "capable of being understood"; *comprehensive* means "covering a broad range, or inclusive."

- The theory is **comprehensible** only to those who have a **comprehensive** knowledge of physics.

comprise, compose *Comprise* means "to contain or consist of"; *compose* means "to create or form by bringing parts together." 611.1
- Fruitcake **comprises** a variety of nuts, candied fruit, and spice.
  Fruitcake is **composed** of (not *comprised of*) a variety of ingredients.

conscience, conscious A *conscience* gives one the capacity to know right from wrong. *Conscious* means "awake or alert, not sleeping or comatose." 611.2
- Your **conscience** will guide you, but you have to be **conscious** to hear what it's "saying."

continual, continuous *Continual* often implies that something is happening often, recurring; *continuous* usually implies that something keeps happening, uninterrupted. 611.3
- The **continuous** loud music during the night gave the building manager not only a headache, but also **continual** phone calls.

counsel, council, consul When used as a noun, *counsel* means "advice"; when used as a verb, *counsel* means "to advise." *Council* refers to a group that advises. A *consul* is a government official appointed to reside in a foreign country. 611.4
- The city **council** was asked to **counsel** our student **council** on running an efficient meeting. Their **counsel** was very helpful.

decent, descent, dissent *Decent* means "good." *Descent* is the process of going or stepping downward. *Dissent* means "disagreement." 611.5
- The food was **decent**.
  The elevator's fast **descent** clogged my ears.
  Their **dissent** over the decisions was obvious in their sullen expressions.

desert, dessert *Desert* is barren wilderness. *Dessert* is food served at the end of a meal. The verb *desert* means "to abandon." 611.6

different from, different than Use *different from* in formal writing; use either form in informal or colloquial settings. 611.7
- Rafael's interpretation was **different from** Andrea's.

discreet, discrete *Discreet* means "showing good judgment, unobtrusive, modest"; *discrete* means "distinct, separate." 611.8
- The essay question had three **discrete** parts.
  Her roommate had apparently never heard of quiet, **discreet** conversation.

disinterested, uninterested Both words mean "not interested." However, *disinterested* is also used to mean "unbiased or impartial." 611.9
- A person chosen as an arbitrator must be a **disinterested** party.
  Professor Eldridge was **uninterested** in our complaints about the assignment.

effect, affect (See "affect.")

elicit, illicit *Elicit* is a verb meaning "to bring out." *Illicit* is an adjective meaning "unlawful." 611.10
- It took two quick hand signals from the lookout at the corner to **elicit** the **illicit** exchange of cash for drugs.

612.1   **eminent, imminent**   *Eminent* means "prominent, conspicuous, or famous"; *imminent* means "ready or threatening to happen."

- With the island's government about to collapse, assassination attempts on several **eminent** officials seemed **imminent**.

ensure, insure, assure   (See "insure.")

except, accept   (See "accept.")

612.2   **explicit, implicit**   *Explicit* means "expressed directly or clearly defined"; *implicit* means "implied or unstated."

- The professor **explicitly** asked that the experiment be wrapped up on Monday, **implicitly** demanding that her lab assistants work on the weekend.

612.3   **farther, further**   *Farther* refers to a physical distance; *further* refers to additional time, quantity, or degree.

- **Further** research showed that walking **farther** rather than faster would improve his health.

612.4   **fewer, less**   *Fewer* refers to the number of separate units; *less* refers to bulk quantity.

- Because of spell checkers, students can produce papers containing **fewer** errors in **less** time.

612.5   **figuratively, literally**   *Figuratively* means "in a metaphorical or analogous way—describing something by comparing it to something else"; *literally* means "actually."

- The lab was **literally** filled with sulfurous gases—**figuratively** speaking, dragon's breath.

612.6   **first, firstly**   Both words are adverbs meaning "before another in time" or "in the first place." However, do not use *firstly*, which is stiff and unnatural sounding.

- **Firstly** I want to see the manager. (Incorrect)
  First I want to see the manager. (Correct)

Note: When enumerating, use the forms *first, second, third, next, last*—without the *ly.*

612.7   **fiscal, physical**   *Fiscal* means "related to financial matters"; *physical* means "related to material things."

- The school's **fiscal** work is handled by its accounting staff.
  The **physical** work is handled by its maintenance staff.

612.8   **for, fore, four**   *For* is a conjunction meaning "because," or a preposition used to indicate the object or recipient of something; *fore* means "earlier" or "the front"; *four* is the word for the number 4.

- The crew brought treats **for** the barge's **four** dogs, who always enjoy the breeze at the **fore** of the vessel.

612.9   **former, latter**   When two things are being discussed, *former* refers to the first thing, and *latter* to the second.

- Our choices are going to a movie or eating at the Pizza Palace: The **former** is too expensive, and the **latter** too fattening.

good, well *Good* is an adjective; *well* is nearly always an adverb. (When used to indicate state of health, *well* is an adjective.)

■ A **good** job offers opportunities for advancement, especially for those who do their jobs **well.**

613.1

heal, heel *Heal* means "to mend or restore to health"; a *heel* is the back part of a human foot.

613.2

healthful, healthy *Healthful* means "causing or improving health"; *healthy* means "possessing health."

■ **Healthful** foods and regular exercise build **healthy** bodies.

613.3

I, me *I* is a subject pronoun; *me* is used as an object of a preposition, a direct object, or an indirect object. (A good way to know if *I* or *me* should be used in a compound subject is to eliminate the other subject; the sentence should make sense with the pronoun—*I* or *me*—alone.)

■ My roommate and **me** went to the library last night. (Incorrect)
My roommate and **I** went to the library last night. (Correct: Eliminate "my roommate and"; the sentence still makes sense.)

■ Rasheed gave the concert tickets to Erick and **I.** (Incorrect)
Rasheed gave the concert tickets to Erick and **me.** (Correct: Eliminate "Erick and"; the sentence still makes sense.)

613.4

illusion, allusion (See "allusion.")

immigrate (to), emigrate (from) *Immigrate* means "to come into a new country or environment." *Emigrate* means "to go out of one country to live in another."

■ **Immigrating** to a new country is a challenging experience.
People **emigrating** from their homelands face unknown challenges.

613.5

imminent, eminent (See "eminent.")

imply, infer *Imply* means "to suggest without saying outright"; *infer* means "to draw a conclusion from facts." (A writer or a speaker *implies*; a reader or a listener *infers*.)

■ Dr. Rufus **implied** I should study more; I **inferred** he meant my grades had to improve or I'd be repeating the class.

613.6

ingenious, ingenuous *Ingenious* means "intelligent, discerning, clever"; *ingenuous* means "unassuming, natural, showing childlike innocence and candidness."

■ Gretchen devised an **ingenious** plan to work and receive college credit for it.
Ramón displays an **ingenuous** quality that attracts others.

613.7

insure, ensure, assure *Insure* means "to secure from financial harm or loss," *ensure* means "to make certain of something," and *assure* means "to put someone's mind at rest."

■ Plenty of studying generally **ensures** academic success.
Nicole **assured** her father that she had **insured** her new car.

613.8

interstate, intrastate *Interstate* means "existing between two or more states"; *intrastate* means "existing within a state."

613.9

614.1 **irregardless, regardless** *Irregardless* is the substandard synonym for *regardless*.

- **Irregardless** of his circumstance, José is cheerful. (Incorrect)
  Regardless of his circumstance, José is cheerful. (Correct)

614.2 **it's, its** *It's* is the contraction of "it is." *Its* is the possessive form of "it."

- **It's** not hard to see why my husband feeds that alley cat; **its** pitiful limp and mournful mewing would melt any heart.

614.3 **later, latter** *Later* means "after a period of time." *Latter* refers to the second of two things mentioned.

- The **latter** of the two restaurants you mentioned sounds good. Let's meet there **later**.

614.4 **lay, lie** *Lay* means "to place." *Lay* is a transitive verb. (See **626.2**.) Its principal parts are *lay, laid, laid*.

- If you **lay** another book on my table, I won't have room for anything else. Yesterday, you **laid** two books on the table. Over the last few days, you must have **laid** at least 20 books there.

Exercise

Lie means "to recline." *Lie* is an intransitive verb. (See **626.2**.) Its principal parts are *lie, lay, lain*.

- The cat **lies** down anywhere it pleases. It **lay** down yesterday on my tax forms. It has **lain** down many times on the kitchen table.

614.5 **learn, teach** *Learn* means "to acquire information"; *teach* means "to give information."

- Sometimes it's easier to **teach** someone else a lesson than it is to **learn** one yourself.

614.6 **leave, let** *Leave* means "to allow something to remain behind." *Let* means "to permit."

- Please **let** me help you carry that chair; otherwise, **leave** it for the movers to pick up.

614.7 **lend, borrow** *Lend* means "to give for temporary use"; *borrow* means "to receive for temporary use."

- I asked Haddad to **lend** me $15 for a CD, but he said I'd have to find someone else to **borrow** from.

less, fewer (See "fewer.")

614.8 **liable, libel** *Liable* is an adjective meaning "responsible according to the law" or "exposed to an adverse action"; the noun *libel* is a written defamatory statement about someone, and the verb *libel* means "to publish or make such a statement."

- Supermarket tabloids, **liable** for ruining many a reputation, make a practice of **libeling** the rich and the famous.

614.9 **liable, likely** *Liable* means "responsible according to the law" or "exposed to an adverse action"; *likely* means "in all probability."

- Rain seems **likely** today, but if we cancel the game, we are still **liable** for paying the referees.

like, as *Like* should not be used in place of *as*. *Like* is a preposition, which is followed by a noun, a pronoun, or a noun phrase. *As* is a subordinating conjunction, which introduces a clause. Avoid using *like* as a subordinating conjunction. Use *as* instead.

- ▪ You don't know her **like** I do. (Incorrect)

  You don't know her **as** I do. (Correct)

  Like the others in my study group, I do my work **as** any serious student would—carefully and thoroughly. (Correct)

615.1

literally, figuratively (See " figuratively.")

loose, lose, loss The adjective *loose* (lüs) means "free, untied, unrestricted"; the verb *lose* (lüz) means "to misplace or fail to find or control"; the noun *loss* (lòs) means "something that is misplaced and cannot be found."

- ▪ Her sadness at the **loss** of her longtime companion caused her to **lose** weight, and her clothes felt uncomfortably **loose**.

615.2

may, can (See "can.")

maybe, may be Use *maybe* as an adverb; use *may be* as a verb phrase.

- ▪ She **may be** the computer technician we've been looking for. **Maybe** she will upgrade the software and memory.

615.3

miner, minor A *miner* digs in the ground for ore. A *minor* is a person who is not legally an adult. The adjective *minor* means "of no great importance."

- ▪ The use of **minors** as coal **miners** is no **minor** problem.

615.4

number, amount (See "amount.")

oral, verbal *Oral* means "uttered with the mouth"; *verbal* means "relating to or consisting of words and the comprehension of words."

- ▪ The actor's **oral** abilities were outstanding, her pronunciation and intonation impeccable, but I doubted the playwright's **verbal** skills after trying to decipher the play's meaning.

615.5

OK, okay This expression, spelled either way, is appropriate in informal writing; however, avoid using it in papers, reports, or formal correspondence of any kind.

- ▪ Your proposal is satisfactory [not *okay*] on most levels.

615.6

passed, past *Passed* is a verb. *Past* can be used as a noun, an adjective, or a preposition.

- ▪ That little pickup truck **passed** my 'Vette! (verb)

  My stepchildren hold on dearly to the **past**. (noun)

  I'm sorry, but my **past** life is not your business. (adjective)

  The officer drove **past** us, not noticing our flat tire. (preposition)

615.7

peace, piece *Peace* means "tranquility or freedom from war." A *piece* is a part or fragment.

- ▪ Someone once observed that **peace** is not a condition, but a process—a process of building goodwill one **piece** at a time.

615.8

616.1 **people, person** Use *people* to refer to human populations, races, or groups; use *person* to refer to an individual or the physical body.

■ What the American **people** need is a good insect repellent.

The forest ranger recommends that we check our **persons** for wood ticks when we leave the woods.

616.2 **percent, percentage** *Percent* means "per hundred"; for example, 60 percent of 100 jelly beans would be 60 jelly beans. *Percentage* refers to a portion of the whole. Generally, use the word *percent* when it is preceded by a number. Use *percentage* when no number is used.

■ Each person's **percentage** of the reward amounted to $125—25 **percent** of the $500 offered by Crime Stoppers.

616.3 **personal, personnel** *Personal* means "private." *Personnel* are people working at a particular job.

■ Although choosing a major is a **personal** decision, it can be helpful to consult with guidance **personnel**.

616.4 **perspective, prospective** *Perspective* is a person's point of view or the capacity to view things realistically; *prospective* is an adjective meaning "expected in or related to the future."

■ From my immigrant neighbor's **perspective**, any job is a good job.

Prospective students wandered the campus on visitors' day.

616.5 **pore, pour, poor** The noun *pore* is an opening in the skin; the verb *pore* means "to gaze intently." *Pour* means "to move with a continuous flow." *Poor* means "needy or pitiable."

■ **Pour** hot water into a bowl, put your face over it, and let the steam open your **pores**. Your **poor** skin will thank you.

616.6 **precede, proceed** To *precede* means "to go or come before;" *proceed* means "to move on after having stopped" or "go ahead."

■ Our biology instructor often **preceded** his lecture with these words:

"OK, sponges, **proceed** to soak up more fascinating facts!"

616.7 **principal, principle** As an adjective, *principal* means "primary." As a noun, it can mean "a school administrator" or "a sum of money." A *principle* is an idea or a doctrine.

■ His **principal** gripe is lack of freedom. (adjective)

My son's **principal** expressed his concerns to the teachers. (noun)

After 20 years, the amount of interest was higher than the **principal**. (noun)

The **principle** of *caveat emptor* guides most consumer groups.

616.8 **quiet, quit, quite** *Quiet* is the opposite of noisy. *Quit* means "to stop or give up." *Quite* means "completely" or "to a considerable extent."

■ The meeting remained **quite quiet** when the boss told us he'd **quit**.

616.9 **quote, quotation** *Quote* is a verb; *quotation* is a noun.

■ The **quotation** I used was from Woody Allen. You may **quote** me on that.

616.10 **real, very, really** Do not use the adjective *real* in place of the adverbs *very* or *really*.

■ My friend's cake is usually **very** [not *real*] fresh, but this cake is **really** stale.

right, write, wright, rite *Right* means "correct or proper"; it also refers to that which a person has a legal claim to, as in *copyright*. *Write* means "to inscribe or record." A *wright* is a person who makes or builds something. *Rite* is a ritual or ceremonial act.

617.1

■ Did you **write** that it is the **right** of the **shipwright** to perform the **rite** of christening—breaking a bottle of champagne on the bow of the ship?

scene, seen *Scene* refers to the setting or location where something happens; it also may mean "sight or spectacle." *Seen* is the past participle of the verb "see."

617.2

■ An exhibitionist likes to be **seen** making a **scene**.

set, sit *Set* means "to place." *Sit* means "to put the body in a seated position." *Set* is a transitive verb; *sit* is an intransitive verb (See **626.2**.).

617.3

■ How can you just **sit** there and watch as I **set** the table?

sight, cite, site *Sight* means "the act of seeing" or "something that is seen." *Cite* means "to quote" or "to summon to court." *Site* means "a place or location" or "to place on a site."

617.4

■ After **sighting** the faulty wiring, the inspector **cited** the building contractor for breaking two city codes at a downtown work **site**.

some, sum *Some* refers to an unknown thing, an unspecified number, or a part of something. *Sum* is a certain amount of money or the result of adding numbers together.

617.5

■ **Some** of the students answered too quickly and came up with the wrong **sum**.

stationary, stationery *Stationary* means "not movable"; *stationery* refers to the paper and envelopes used to write letters.

617.6

■ Odina uses **stationery** that she can feed through her portable printer. Then she drops the mail into a **stationary** mail receptacle at the mall.

take, bring (See "bring.")

teach, learn (See "learn.")

than, then *Than* is used in a comparison; *then* tells when.

617.7

■ Study more **than** you think you need to. **Then** you will probably be satisfied with your grades.

their, there, they're *Their* is a possessive personal pronoun. *There* is a pronoun used as a function word to introduce a clause or an adverb used to point out location. *They're* is the contraction for "they are."

617.8

■ Look over **there**. **There** is a comfortable place for students to study for **their** exams, so **they're** more likely to do a good job.

threw, through *Threw* is the past tense of "throw." *Through* means "from one side of something to the other."

617.9

■ In a fit of frustration, Sachiko **threw** his cell phone right **through** the window.

to, too, two *To* is a preposition that can mean "in the direction of." *To* is also used to form an infinitive. *Too* means "also" or "very." *Two* is the number 2.

617.10

■ **Two** causes of eye problems among students are lights that fail **to** illuminate properly and computer screens with **too** much glare.

618.1 **vain, vane, vein** *Vain* means "valueless or fruitless"; it may also mean "holding a high regard for one's self." *Vane* is a flat piece of material set up to show which way the wind blows. *Vein* refers to a blood vessel or a mineral deposit.

■ The weather **vane** indicates the direction of the wind; the blood **vein** determines the direction of flowing blood; and the **vain** mind moves in no particular direction, content to think only about itself.

618.2 **vary, very** *Vary* means "to change"; *very* means "to a high degree."

■ To ensure the **very** best employee relations, the workloads should not **vary** greatly from worker to worker.

verbal, oral (See "oral.")

618.3 **waist, waste** *Waist* is the part of the body just above the hips. The verb *waste* means "to squander" or "to wear away, decay"; the noun *waste* refers to material that is unused or useless.

■ His **waist** is small because he **wastes** no opportunity to exercise.

618.4 **wait, weight** *Wait* means "to stay somewhere expecting something." *Weight* refers to a degree or unit of heaviness.

■ The **weight** of sadness eventually lessens; one must simply **wait** for the pain to dissipate.

618.5 **ware, wear, where** *Ware* refers to a product that is sold; *wear* means "to have on or to carry on one's body"; *where* asks the question "In what place?" or "In what situation?"

■ The designer boasted, "**Where** can one **wear** my **wares**? Anywhere."

618.6 **weather, whether** *Weather* refers to the condition of the atmosphere. *Whether* refers to a possibility.

■ **Weather** conditions affect nearly all of us, **whether** we are farmers, pilots, or plumbers.

well, good (See "good.")

which, that (See 573.3.)

618.7 **who, which, that** *Who* refers to people. *Which* refers to nonliving objects or to animals. (*Which* should never refer to people.) *That* may refer to animals, people, or nonliving objects. (See also 573.3.)

618.8 **who, whom** *Who* is used as the subject of a verb; *whom* is used as the object of a preposition or as a direct object.

■ Captain Mather, to **whom** the survivors owe their lives, is the man **who** is being honored today.

618.9 **who's, whose** *Who's* is the contraction for "who is." *Whose* is a possessive pronoun.

■ **Whose** car are we using, and **who's** going to pay for the gas?

618.10 **your, you're** *Your* is a possessive pronoun. *You're* is the contraction for "you are."

■ If **you're** like most Americans, you will have held eight jobs by **your** 40th birthday.

Chapter 38
Understanding Grammar

Grammar is the study of the structure and features of the language, consisting of rules and standards that are to be followed to produce acceptable writing and speaking. **Parts of speech** refers to the eight different ways words are used in the English language—as *nouns, pronouns, verbs, adjectives, adverbs, prepositions, conjunctions,* or *interjections.*

Noun

A **noun** is a word that names something: a person, a place, a thing, or an idea.

619.1

- **Toni Morrison/author**   *Lone Star*/**film**   **Renaissance/era**
   UC-Davis/university   *A Congress of Wonders*/**book**

esl *Note:* See 657.1–658.2 for information on count and noncount nouns.

Classes of Nouns

All nouns are either *proper nouns* or *common nouns.* Nouns may also be classified as *individual* or *collective,* or *concrete* or *abstract.*

Proper Nouns

619.2

A **proper noun**, which is always capitalized, names a specific person, place, thing, or idea.

- **Rembrandt, Bertrand Russell** (people)
   Stratford-upon-Avon, Tower of London (places)
   The Night Watch, **Rosetta stone** (things)
   New Deal, Christianity (ideas)

Common Nouns

619.3

A **common noun** is a general name for a person, a place, a thing, or an idea. Common nouns are not capitalized.

- **optimist, instructor** (people)   **cafeteria, park** (places)
   computer, chair (things)   **freedom, love** (ideas)

620.1

Collective Nouns

A **collective noun** names a group or a unit.

■ family   audience   crowd   committee   team   class

620.2

Concrete Nouns

A **concrete noun** names a thing that is tangible (can be seen, touched, heard, smelled, or tasted).

■ child   Pearl Jam   gymnasium   village   microwave oven   pizza

620.3

Abstract Nouns

An **abstract noun** names an idea, a condition, or a feeling—in other words, something that cannot be seen, touched, heard, smelled, or tasted.

■ beauty   Jungian psychology   anxiety   agoraphobia   trust

Forms of Nouns

Nouns are grouped according to their *number, gender,* and *case.*

620.4

Number of Nouns

Number indicates whether a noun is singular or plural.

A singular noun refers to one person, place, thing, or idea.

■ student   laboratory   lecture   note   grade   result

A plural noun refers to more than one person, place, thing, or idea.

■ students   laboratories   lectures   notes   grades   results

620.5

Gender of Nouns

Gender indicates whether a noun is masculine, feminine, neuter, or indefinite.
Masculine:

■ father   king   brother   men   colt   rooster

Feminine:

■ mother   queen   sister   women   filly   hen

Neuter (without sex):

■ notebook   monitor   car   printer

Indefinite or **common** (masculine or feminine):

■ professor   customer   children   doctor   people

Case of Nouns

621.1

The **case** of a noun tells how it is related to other words within a sentence. There are three cases: *nominative, possessive,* and *objective.*

Nominative case describes a noun used as a subject. The subject of a sentence tells who or what the sentence is about.

■ **Dean Henning** manages the College of Arts and Communication.

Note: A noun is also in the nominative case when it is used as a predicate noun (or predicate nominative). A predicate noun follows a form of the *be* verb (such as *am, is, are, was, were, be, being, been*) and repeats or renames the subject.

■ Either Mr. Cassett or Ms. Yokum is the **person** to talk to about the college's impact in our community.

Possessive case describes a noun that shows possession or ownership.

■ Our **president's** willingness to discuss concerns with students has boosted campus morale.

Objective case describes a noun used as an object of the preposition, a direct object, or an indirect object.

■ To survive, institutions of higher **learning** sometimes cut **budgets** in spite of **protests** from **students** and **instructors**.
(*Learning* is the object of the preposition *of, protests* is the object of the preposition *in spite of, budgets* is the direct object of the verb *cut,* and *students* and *instructors* are the objects of the preposition *from.*)

A Closer Look
at Direct and Indirect Objects

621.2

A **direct object** is a noun (or pronoun) that identifies what or who receives the action of the verb.

● Budget cutbacks reduced class **choices**.
(*Choices* is the direct object of *reduced.*)

An **indirect object** is a noun (or pronoun) that identifies the person *to whom* or *for whom* something is done, or the thing *to which* or *for which* something is done. An indirect object is always accompanied by a direct object.

● Recent budget cuts have given **students** fewer class choices.
(*Choices* is the direct object of *have given; students* is the indirect object.)

esl **Note:** Not every verb can be followed by *both* a direct object and an indirect object. Both can, however, follow *give, send, show, tell, teach, find, sell, ask, offer, pay, pass,* and *hand.*

622.1

Pronoun

A **pronoun** is a word that is used in place of a noun.

■ Roger was the most interesting 10-year-old **I** ever taught. **He** was a good thinker and thus a good writer. **I** remember **his** paragraph about the cowboy hat **he** received from **his** grandparents. **It** was "too new looking." The brim was not rolled properly. But the hat's imperfections were not the main idea in Roger's writing. No, the main idea was about how **he** was fixing the hat **himself** by wearing **it** when **he** showered.

622.2

Antecedents

An **antecedent** is the noun that the pronoun refers to or replaces. Most pronouns have antecedents, but not all do. (See **623.4**.)

■ As the wellness **counselor** checked *her* chart, several **students** *who* were waiting *their* turns shifted uncomfortably. (*Counselor* is the antecedent of *her*; *students* is the antecedent of *who* and *their*.)

Note: Each pronoun must agree with its antecedent in number, person, and gender. (See pages **624–625** and **649**.)

622.3

Classes of Pronouns

Personal
I, me, my, mine / we, us, our, ours / you, your, yours
they, them, their, theirs / he, him, his, she, her, hers, it, its

Reflexive and Intensive
myself, yourself, himself, herself, itself, ourselves, yourselves, themselves

Relative
who, whose, whom, which, that

Indefinite

all	anything	everybody	most	no one	some
another	both	everyone	much	nothing	somebody
any	each	everything	neither	one	someone
anybody	each one	few	nobody	other	something
anyone	either	many	none	several	such

Interrogative
who, whose, whom, which, what

Demonstrative
this, that, these, those

Reciprocal
each other, one another

Classes of Pronouns

There are several classes of pronouns: *personal, reflexive and intensive, relative, indefinite, interrogative,* and *demonstrative.*

Personal Pronouns

623.1

A **personal pronoun** refers to a specific person or thing.

- *Marge* started **her** car; **she** drove the antique *convertible* to Monterey where **she** hoped to sell **it** at an auction.

Reflexive and Intensive Pronouns

623.2

A **reflexive pronoun** is formed by adding *-self* or *-selves* to a personal pronoun. A reflexive pronoun can act as a direct object or an indirect object of a verb, an object of a preposition, or a predicate nominative.

- Charles loves **himself.** (direct object of *loves*)
  Charles gives **himself** A's for fashion sense. (indirect object of *gives*)
  Charles smiles at **himself** in store windows. (object of preposition *at*)
  Charles can be **himself** anywhere. (predicate nominative)

An **intensive pronoun** intensifies, or emphasizes, the noun or pronoun it refers to.

- Leo **himself** taught his children to invest their lives in others.
  The lesson was sometimes painful—but they learned it **themselves**.

Relative Pronouns

623.3

A **relative pronoun** relates an adjective clause to the noun or pronoun it modifies. (The noun is italicized in each example below; the relative pronoun is in bold.)

- *Freshmen* **who** believe they have a lot to learn are absolutely right.
  Just navigating this *campus,* **which** is huge, can be challenging.

esl **Note:** Make sure you know when to use the relative pronouns *who* or *whom* and *that* or *which.* (See **573.3, 618.7,** and **618.8.**)

Indefinite Pronouns

623.4

An **indefinite pronoun** refers to unnamed or unknown people, places, or things.

- **Everyone** seemed amused when I was searching for my classroom in the student center. (The antecedent of *everyone* is unnamed.)

- **Nothing** is more unnerving than rushing last minute into the wrong room for the wrong class. (The antecedent of *nothing* is unknown.)

esl **Note:** Most indefinite pronouns are singular, so when they are used as subjects, they should have singular verbs.

624.1
Interrogative Pronouns

An **interrogative pronoun** asks a question.

- So **which** will it be—highlighting and attaching a campus map to the inside of your backpack, or being lost and late for the first two weeks?

624.2
Demonstrative Pronouns

A **demonstrative pronoun** points out people, places, or things.

- We advise **this:** Bring along as many maps and schedules as you need. **Those** are useful tools. **That** is the solution.

Note: When a demonstrative pronoun *modifies* a noun (instead of replacing it), it functions as an adjective: *this* teacher, *that* test.

Forms of Personal Pronouns

The **form** of a personal pronoun indicates its *number* (singular or plural), its *person* (first, second, or third), its *case* (nominative, possessive, or objective), and its *gender* (masculine, feminine, neuter, or indefinite).

624.3
Number of Pronouns

A **personal pronoun** is either singular (*I, you, he, she, it*) or plural (*we, you, they*) in number.

- **He** should have a budget and stick to it. (singular)
  We can help new students learn about budgeting. (plural)

624.4
Person of Pronouns

The **person** of a pronoun indicates whether the person is speaking (first person), is spoken to (second person), or is spoken about (third person).

First person is used to name the speaker(s).

- **I** know **I** need to handle **my** stress in a healthful way, especially during exam week; **my** usual chips-and-donuts binge isn't helping. (singular)
  We all decided to bike to the tennis court. (plural)

Second person is used to name the person(s) spoken to.

- Maria, **you** grab the rackets, okay? (singular)
  John and Tanya, can **you** find the water bottles? (plural)

Third person is used to name the person(s) or thing(s) spoken about.

- Today's students are interested in wellness issues. **They** are concerned about **their** health, fitness, and nutrition. (plural)
  Maria practices yoga and feels **she** is calmer for **her** choice. (singular)
  One of the advantages of regular exercise is that **it** raises one's energy level. (singular)

Case of Pronouns

The **case** of each pronoun tells how it is related to the other words within a sentence. There are three cases: *nominative, possessive,* and *objective.*

Nominative case describes a pronoun used as a subject. The following are nominative forms: *I, you, he, she, it, we, they.*

- **He** found an old map in the trunk.

  My friend and **I** went biking. (not *me*)

A pronoun is in the nominative case when it is used as a predicate noun (predicate nominative) following a form of the *be* verb (*am, is, are, was, were, be, being, been*).

- It was **he** who discovered electricity. (not *him*)

Possessive case describes a pronoun that shows possession or ownership: *my, mine, our, ours, his, her, hers, their, theirs, its, your, yours.*

- That coat is **hers**.   This coat is **mine**.   **Your** coat is lost.

Objective case describes a pronoun used as the direct object, indirect object, or object of a preposition: *me, you, him, her, it, us, them.*

- Professor Adler hired **her**.
  (*Her* is the direct object of the verb *hired.*)

  He showed Mary and **me** the language lab.
  (*Me* is the indirect object of the verb *showed.*)

  He introduced the three of **us**—Mary, Shavonn, and **me**—to the faculty.
  (*Us* is the object of the preposition *of; me* is part of the appositive of the object *us.*)

Gender of Pronouns

The **gender** of a pronoun indicates whether the pronoun is masculine, feminine, neuter, or indefinite. (See page **96**.)

Masculine:
- he, him, his

Feminine:
- she, her, hers

Neuter (without sex):
- it, its

Indefinite (masculine or feminine):
- they, them, their

Number, Person, and Case of Personal Pronouns

	Nominative Case	Possessive Case	Objective Case
First Person Singular	I	my, mine	me
Second Person Singular	you	your, yours	you
Third Person Singular	he, she, it	his, her, hers, its	him, her, it
First Person Plural	we	our, ours	us
Second Person Plural	you	your, yours	you
Third Person Plural	they	their, theirs	them

626.1 Verb

Exercise

A **verb** shows action (*pondered, grins*), links words (*is, seemed*), or accompanies another action verb as an auxiliary or helping verb (*can, does*).

- Harry **honked** the horn. (shows action)
  Harry **is** impatient. (links words)
  Harry **was** honking the truck's horn. (accompanies the verb *honking*)

Classes of Verbs

Verbs are classified as action, auxiliary (helping), or linking (state of being).

626.2 Action Verbs: Transitive and Intransitive

As its name implies, an **action verb** shows action. Some action verbs are *transitive*; others are *intransitive*. (The term *action* does not always refer to a physical activity.)

- Rain **splashed** the windshield. (transitive verb)
  Josie **drove** off the road. (intransitive verb)

Transitive verbs have direct objects that receive the action (**621.2, 639.5**).

- The health care industry **employs** more than 7 million **workers** in the United States. (*Workers* is the direct object of the action verb *employs*.)

Intransitive verbs communicate action that is complete in itself. They do not need an object to receive the action.

- My new college roommate **smiles** and **laughs** a lot.

Note: Some verbs can be either transitive or intransitive.

- Ms. Hull **teaches** physiology and microbiology. (transitive)
  She **teaches** well. (intransitive)

626.3 Auxiliary (Helping) Verbs

Auxiliary verbs (helping verbs) help to form some of the *tenses* (**628.1**), the *mood* (**629.2**), and the *voice* (**629.1**) of the main verb. In the following example, the auxiliary verbs are in **bold**, and the main verbs are in *italics*.

- I *believe*, I **have** always *believed*, and I **will** always *believe* in private enterprise as the backbone of economic well-being in America.

  —Franklin D. Roosevelt

Common Auxiliary Verbs

am	been	could	does	have	might	should	will
are	being	did	had	is	must	was	would
be	can	do	has	may	shall	were	

esl *Note:* "Be" auxiliary verbs are always followed by either a verb ending in *ing* or a past participle. Also see "Common Modal Auxiliary Verbs" (**662.2**).

Linking (State of Being) Verbs

627.1

A **linking verb** is a special form of intransitive verb that links the subject of a sentence to a noun, a pronoun, or an adjective in the predicate. (See the chart below.)

- The streets **are** flooded. (adjective)   The streets **are** rivers! (noun)

> ## Common Linking Verbs
> am   are   be   become   been   being   is   was   were
>
> ## Additional Linking Verbs
> appear   feel   look   seem   sound   grow   remain   smell   taste

Note: The verbs listed as "additional linking verbs" above function as linking verbs when they do not show actual action. An adjective usually follows these linking verbs.

- The thunder **sounded** ominous. (adjective)
  My little brother **grew** frightened. (adjective)

Note: When these same words are used as action verbs, an adverb or a direct object may follow them.

- I **looked** carefully at him. (adverb)
  My little brother **grew** corn for a science project. (direct object)

Forms of Verbs

A verb's **form** differs depending on its *number* (singular, plural), *person* (first, second, third), *tense* (present, past, future, present perfect, past perfect, future perfect), *voice* (active, passive), and *mood* (indicative, imperative, subjunctive).

Number of a Verb

627.2

Number indicates whether a verb is singular or plural. The verb and its subject both must be singular, or they both must be plural. (See "Subject-Verb Agreement," pages **645–648**.)

- My college **enrolls** high schoolers in summer programs. (singular)
  Many colleges **enroll** high schoolers in summer courses. (plural)

Person of a Verb

627.3

Person indicates whether the subject of the verb is *first, second,* or *third person.* The verb and its subject must be in the same person. Verbs usually have a different form only in **third person singular of the present tense.**

	First Person	**Second Person**	**Third Person**
Singular	I think	you think	he/ she/it thinks
Plural	we think	you think	they think

628.1 ## Tense of a Verb

Tense indicates the time of an action or state of being. There are three basic tenses (*past*, *present*, and *future*) and three verbal aspects (*progressive*, *perfect*, and *perfect progressive*).

628.2 ## Present Tense

Present tense expresses action that is happening at the present time or action that happens continually, regularly.

- In the United States, more than 75 percent of workers **hold** service jobs.

Present progressive tense also expresses action that is happening at the present time, but it is always formed by combining *am*, *are*, or *is* and the present participle (ending in *ing*) of the main verb.

- More women than ever before **are working** outside the home.

Present perfect tense expresses action that began in the past and has recently been completed or is continuing up to the present time.

- My sister **has taken** four years of swimming lessons.

Present perfect progressive tense also expresses an action that began in the past but stresses the continuing nature of the action. Like the present progressive tense, it is formed by combining auxiliary verbs (*have been* or *has been*) and present participles.

- She **has been taking** them since she was six years old.

628.3 ## Past Tense

Past tense expresses action that is completed at a particular time in the past.

- A hundred years ago, more than 75 percent **worked** in agriculture.

Past progressive tense expresses past action that continued over an interval of time. It is formed by combining *was* or *were* with the present participle of the main verb.

- A century ago, my great-grandparents **were farming**.

Past perfect tense expresses an action in the past that occurs before another past action or an action that was completed by some specific past time.

- By dinnertime my cousins **had eaten** all the olives.

Past perfect progressive tense expresses a past action but stresses the continuing nature of the action. It is formed by using *had been* along with the present participle.

- They **had been eating** the olives since they arrived two hours earlier.

628.4 ## Future Tense

Future tense expresses action that will take place in the future.

- Next summer I **will work** as a lifeguard.

Future progressive tense expresses a continuous or repeating future action.

- I **will be working** for the park district at North Beach.

Future perfect tense expresses action that will begin in the future and be completed by a specific time in the future.

- By 10:00 p.m., I **will have completed** my research project.

Future perfect progressive tense also expresses future action that will be completed by a specific time, but (as with other perfect progressive tenses) stresses the action's continuous nature. It is formed using *will have been* along with the present participle.

- I **will have been researching** the project for three weeks by the time it's due.

Voice of a Verb

629.1

Voice indicates whether the subject is acting or being acted upon.

Active voice indicates that the subject of the verb is doing something.

- People **update** their resumés on a regular basis.
  (The subject, *People*, is acting; *resumés* is the direct object.)

Passive voice indicates that the subject of the verb is being acted upon or is receiving the action. A passive verb combines a *be* verb with a past participle.

- Your resumé **should be updated** on a regular basis.
  (The subject, *resumé*, is receiving the action.)

Using Active Voice

Generally, use active voice rather than passive voice for more direct, energetic writing. To change your passive sentences to active ones, do the following: First, find the noun that is doing the action and make it the subject. Then find the word that had been the subject and use it as either a direct object or an indirect object.

Passive: The winning goal **was scored** by Eva. (The subject, *goal*, is not acting.)

Active: Eva **scored** the winning goal. (The subject, *Eva*, is acting.)

Note: When you want to emphasize the receiver more than the doer—or when the doer is unknown—use the passive voice. (Much technical and scientific writing regularly uses the passive voice.)

Mood of a Verb

629.2

The **mood** of a verb indicates the tone or attitude with which a statement is made.

Indicative mood, the most common, is used to state a fact or to ask a question.

- **Can** any theme **capture** the essence of the complex 1960s culture? President John F. Kennedy's directive [stated below] **represents** one ideal popular during that decade.

Imperative mood is used to give a command. (The subject of an imperative sentence is *you*, which is usually understood and not stated in the sentence.)

- **Ask** not what your country can do for you—**ask** what you can do for your country.
  —John F. Kennedy

Subjunctive mood is used to express a wish, an impossibility or unlikely condition, or a necessity. The subjunctive mood is often used with *if* or *that*. The verb forms below create an atypical subject-verb agreement, forming the subjunctive mood.

- If I **were** rich, I would travel for the rest of my life. (a wish)

  If each of your brain cells **were** one person, there would be enough people to populate 25 planets. (an impossibility)

  The English Department requires that every student **pass** a proficiency test. (a necessity)

630.1   Verbals

A **verbal** is a word that is made from a verb, but it functions as a noun, an adjective, or an adverb. There are three types of verbals: *gerunds, infinitives,* and *participles.*

630.2   Gerunds

A **gerund** ends in *ing* and is used as a noun.

- **Waking** each morning is the first challenge. (subject)
  I start **moving** at about seven o'clock. (direct object)
  I work at **jump-starting** my weary system. (object of the preposition)
  As Woody Allen once said, "Eighty percent of life is **showing up**." (predicate noun)

630.3   Infinitives

An **infinitive** is usually introduced by *to*; the infinitive may be used as a noun, an adjective, or an adverb.

- **To succeed** is not easy. (noun)
  That is the most important thing **to remember**. (adjective)
  Students are wise **to work** hard. (adverb)

esl **Note:** It can be difficult to know whether a gerund or an infinitive should follow a verb. It's helpful to become familiar with lists of specific verbs that can be followed by one but not the other. (See **661.2–662.1.**)

630.4   Participles

A **present participle** ends in *ing* and functions as an adjective. A **past participle** ends in *ed* (or another past tense form) and also functions as an adjective.

- The students **reading** those study-skill handouts are definitely **interested**.
  The prospect of **aced** tests and assignments must be **appealing**.
  (These participles function as adjectives: *reading* students, *interested* students, *aced* tests and assignments, and *appealing* prospect. Notice, however, that *reading* has a direct object: *handouts*. Verbals may have direct objects.)

Using Verbals

Make sure that you use verbals correctly; look carefully at the examples below.

Verbal: **Diving** is a popular Olympic sport.
(*Diving* is a gerund used as a subject.)

Diving gracefully, the Olympian hoped to get high marks.
(*Diving* is a participle modifying *Olympian.*)

Verb: The next competitor was **diving** in the practice pool.
(Here, *diving* is a verb, not a verbal.)

Irregular Verbs

Irregular verbs can often be confusing. That's because the past tense and past participle of irregular verbs are formed by changing the word itself, not merely by adding *d* or *ed*. The following list contains the most troublesome irregular verbs.

Common Irregular Verbs and Their Principal Parts

Present Tense	Past Tense	Past Participle	Present Tense	Past Tense	Past Participle	Present Tense	Past Tense	Past Participle
am, be	was, were	been	fly	flew	flown	see	saw	seen
arise	arose	arisen	forget	forgot	forgotten, forgot	set	set	set
awake	awoke, awaked	awoken, awaked	freeze	froze	frozen	shake	shook	shaken
						shine (light)	shone	shone
beat	beat	beaten	get	got	gotten	shine (polish)	shined	shined
become	became	become	give	gave	given	show	showed	shown
begin	began	begun	go	went	gone	shrink	shrank	shrunk
bite	bit	bitten, bit	grow	grew	grown	sing	sang	sung
blow	blew	blown	hang (execute)	hanged	hanged	sink	sank	sunk
break	broke	broken	hang (suspend)	hung	hung	sit	sat	sat
bring	brought	brought	have	had	had	sleep	slept	slept
build	built	built	hear	heard	heard	speak	spoke	spoken
burn	burnt, burned	burnt, burned	hide	hid	hidden	spend	spent	spent
			hit	hit	hit	spring	sprang	sprung
burst	burst	burst	keep	kept	kept	stand	stood	stood
buy	bought	bought	know	knew	known	steal	stole	stolen
catch	caught	caught	lay	laid	laid	strike	struck	struck, stricken
choose	chose	chosen	lead	led	led			
come	came	come	leave	left	left	strive	strove	striven
cost	cost	cost	lend	lent	lent	swear	swore	sworn
cut	cut	cut	let	let	let	swim	swam	swum
dig	dug	dug	lie (deceive)	lied	lied	swing	swung	swung
dive	dived, dove	dived	lie (recline)	lay	lain	take	took	taken
do	did	done	make	made	made	teach	taught	taught
draw	drew	drawn	mean	meant	meant	tear	tore	torn
dream	dreamed, dreamt	dreamed, dreamt	meet	met	met	tell	told	told
			pay	paid	paid	think	thought	thought
drink	drank	drunk	prove	proved	proved, proven	throw	threw	thrown
drive	drove	driven				wake	woke, waked	woken, waked
eat	ate	eaten	put	put	put			
fall	fell	fallen	read	read	read			
feel	felt	felt	ride	rode	ridden	wear	wore	worn
fight	fought	fought	ring	rang	rung	weave	wove	woven
find	found	found	rise	rose	risen	wind	wound	wound
flee	fled	fled	run	ran	run	wring	wrung	wrung
						write	wrote	written

Exercise

Adjective

632.1 An **adjective** describes or modifies a noun or pronoun. The articles *a, an,* and *the* are adjectives.

- Advertising is **a big** and **powerful** industry.
  (*A, big,* and *powerful* modify industry.)

Numbers are also adjectives.

- **Fifty-three** relatives came to my party.

632.2 *Note:* Many demonstrative, indefinite, and interrogative forms may be used as either adjectives or pronouns (*that, these, many, some, whose,* and so on). These words are adjectives if they come before a noun and modify it; they are pronouns if they stand alone.

- **Some** advertisements are less than truthful.
  (*Some* modifies *advertisements* and is an adjective.)
  Many cause us to chuckle at their outrageous claims.
  (*Many* stands alone; it is a pronoun and replaces the noun *advertisements.*)

632.3 ## Proper Adjectives

Proper adjectives are created from proper nouns and are capitalized.

- **English** has been influenced by advertising slogans. (proper noun)
  The **English** language is constantly changing. (proper adjective)

632.4 ## Predicate Adjectives

A **predicate adjective** follows a form of the *be* verb (or other linking verb) and describes the subject.

- At its best, advertising is **useful**; at its worst, **deceptive**.
  (*Useful* and *deceptive* modify the noun *advertising.*)

632.5 ## Forms of Adjectives

Adjectives have three forms: *positive, comparative,* and *superlative.*

The **positive form** is the adjective in its regular form. It describes a noun or a pronoun without comparing it to anyone or anything else.

- Joysport walking shoes are **strong** and **comfortable**.

The **comparative form** (*er, more,* or *less*) compares two things. (*More* and *less* are used generally with adjectives of two or more syllables.)

- Air soles make Mile Eaters **stronger** and **more comfortable** than Joysports.

The **superlative form** (*est, most,* or *least*) compares three or more things. (*Most* and *least* are used most often with adjectives of two or more syllables.)

- My old Canvas Wonders are the **strongest, most comfortable** shoes of all!

esl **Note:** Two or more adjectives before a noun should have a certain order when they do not modify the noun equally. (See **666.1**.)

Adverb

633.1

An **adverb** describes or modifies a verb, an adjective, another adverb, or a whole sentence. An adverb answers questions such as *how, when, where, why, how often,* or *how much.*

- The temperature fell **sharply**. (*Sharply* modifies the verb *fell*.)
  The temperature was **quite** low. (*Quite* modifies the adjective *low*.)
  The temperature dropped **very quickly**.
  (*Very* modifies the adverb *quickly*, which modifies the verb *dropped*.)
  Unfortunately, the temperature stayed cool.
  (*Unfortunately* modifies the whole sentence.)

Types of Adverbs

633.2

Adverbs can be grouped in four ways: *time, place, manner,* and *degree.*

Time (These adverbs tell *when, how often,* and *how long.*)
- **today, yesterday   daily, weekly   briefly, eternally**

Place (These adverbs tell *where, to where,* and *from where.*)
- **here, there   nearby, beyond   backward, forward**

Manner (These adverbs often end in *ly* and tell *how* something is done.)
- **precisely   regularly   regally   smoothly   well**

Degree (These adverbs tell *how much* or *how little.*)
- **substantially   greatly   entirely   partly   too**

Forms of Adverbs

633.3

Adverbs have three forms: *positive, comparative,* and *superlative.*

The **positive form** is the adverb in its regular form. It describes a verb, an adjective, or another adverb without comparing it to anyone or anything else.
- With Joysport shoes, you'll walk **fast**. They support your feet **well**.

The **comparative form** (*er, more,* or *less*) compares two things. (*More* and *less* are used generally with adverbs of two or more syllables.)
- Wear Jockos instead of Joysports, and you'll walk **faster**. Jockos' special soles support your feet **better** than the Roksports do.

The **superlative form** (*est, most,* or *least*) compares three or more things. (*Most* and *least* are used most often with adverbs of two or more syllables.)
- Really, I walk **fastest** wearing my old Canvas Wonders. They seem to support my feet, my knees, and my pocketbook **best** of all.

Regular Adverbs			Irregular Adverbs		
positive	comparative	superlative	positive	comparative	superlative
fast	faster	fastest	well	better	best
effectively	more effectively	most effectively	badly	worse	worst

634.1

Exercise

Preposition

A **preposition** is a word (or group of words) that shows the relationship between its object (a noun or pronoun following the preposition) and another word in the sentence.

■ **Regarding** your reasons **for** going **to** college, do they all hinge **on** getting a good job **after** graduation?
(In this sentence, *reasons, going, college, getting,* and *graduation* are objects of their preceding prepositions *regarding, for, to, on,* and *after.*)

634.2

Prepositional Phrases

A **prepositional phrase** includes the preposition, the object of the preposition, and the modifiers of the object. A prepositional phrase may function as an adverb or adjective.

■ A broader knowledge **of the world** is one benefit **of higher education**.
(The two phrases function as adjectives modifying the nouns *knowledge* and *benefit* respectively.)
Exercising your brain may safeguard **against atrophy**. (The phrase functions as an adverb modifying the verb *safeguard*.)

634.3

Prepositions

aboard	back of	except for	near to	round
about	because of	excepting	notwithstanding	save
above	before	for	of	since
according to	behind	from	off	subsequent to
across	below	from among	on	through
across from	beneath	from between	on account of	throughout
after	beside	from under	on behalf of	till
against	besides	in	onto	to
along	between	in addition to	on top of	together with
alongside	beyond	in behalf of	opposite	toward
alongside of	but	in front of	out	under
along with	by	in place of	out of	underneath
amid	by means of	in regard to	outside	until
among	concerning	inside	outside of	unto
apart from	considering	inside of	over	up
around	despite	in spite of	over to	upon
as far as	down	instead of	owing to	up to
aside from	down from	into	past	with
at	during	like	prior to	within
away from	except	near	regarding	without

esl Note: Prepositions often pair up with a verb and become part of an idiom, a slang expression, or a two-word verb. (See pages **663** and **674–676**.)

Conjunction

635.1

A **conjunction** connects individual words or groups of words.

- When we came back to Paris, it was clear **and** cold **and** lovely.

—Ernest Hemingway

Coordinating Conjunctions

635.2

Coordinating conjunctions usually connect a word to a word, a phrase to a phrase, or a clause to a clause. The words, phrases, or clauses joined by a coordinating conjunction are equal in importance or are of the same type.

- Civilization is a race between education **and** catastrophe.

—H. G. Wells

Correlative Conjunctions

635.3

Correlative conjunctions are a type of coordinating conjunction used in pairs.

- There are two inadvisable ways to think: **either** believe everything **or** doubt everything.

Subordinating Conjunctions

635.4

Subordinating conjunctions connect two clauses that are not equally important. A subordinating conjunction connects a dependent clause to an independent clause.

- Experience is the worst teacher; it gives the test **before** it presents the lesson. (The clause *before it presents the lesson* is dependent. It connects to the independent clause *it gives the test*.)

Conjunctions

635.5

Coordinating: and, but, or, nor, for, so, yet

Correlative: either, or; neither, nor; not only, but (but also); both, and; whether, or

Subordinating: after, although, as, as if, as long as, because, before, even though, if, in order that, provided that, since, so that, than, that, though, unless, until, when, whenever, where, while

---

Note: Relative pronouns and conjunctive adverbs (**576.2**) can also connect clauses.

Interjection

635.6

An **interjection** communicates strong emotion or surprise (*oh, ouch, hey,* and so on). Punctuation (often a comma or an exclamation point) is used to set off an interjection.

- **Hey! Wait! Well,** so much for catching the bus.

A Closer Look
at the Parts of Speech

Noun

A **noun** is a word that names something: a person, a place, a thing, or an idea.

- ■ **Toni Morrison/author**   *Lone Star*/**film**
  UC-Davis/university   **Renaissance/era**
  A Congress of Wonders/**book**

Pronoun

A **pronoun** is a word used in place of a noun.

- ■ **I**   **my**   **that**   **themselves**   **which**
  it   **ours**   **they**   **everybody**   **you**

Verb

A **verb** is a word that expresses action, links words, or acts as an auxiliary verb to the main verb.

- ■ **are**   **break**   **drag**   **fly**   **run**   **sit**   **was**
  bite   **catch**   **eat**   **is**   **see**   **tear**   **were**

Adjective

An **adjective** describes or modifies a noun or pronoun. (The articles *a, an,* and *the* are adjectives.)

- ■ **The carbonated** drink went down easy on **that hot, dry** day. (*The* and *carbonated* modify *drink*; *that, hot,* and *dry* modify *day*.)

Adverb

An **adverb** describes or modifies a verb, an adjective, another adverb, or a whole sentence. An adverb generally answers questions such as *how, when, where, how often,* or *how much.*

- ■ **greatly**   **precisely**   **regularly**   **there**
  here   **today**   **partly**   **quickly**
  slowly   **yesterday**   **nearly**   **loudly**

Preposition

A **preposition** is a word (or group of words) that shows the relationship between its object (a noun or pronoun that follows the preposition) and another word in the sentence. Prepositions introduce prepositional phrases.

- ■ **across   for   with   out   to   of**

Conjunction

A **conjunction** connects individual words or groups of words.

- ■ **and   because   but   for   or   since   so   yet**

Interjection

An **interjection** is a word that communicates strong emotion or surprise. Punctuation (often a comma or an exclamation point) is used to set off an interjection from the rest of the sentence.

- ■ **Stop! No! What,** am I invisible?

Chapter 39
Constructing Sentences

A **sentence** is made up of one or more words that express a complete thought. Sentences are groups of words that make statements, ask questions, or express feelings.

■ The web delivers the universe in a box.

Using Subjects and Predicates

637.1

Sentences have two main parts: a **subject** and a **predicate**.

■ Technology frustrates many people.

Note: In the sentence above, *technology* is the subject—the sentence talks about technology. *Frustrates many people* is the complete predicate—it says something about the subject.

The Subject

637.2

The **subject** names the person or thing either doing the action in a sentence or being talked about. The subject is most often a noun or a pronoun.

■ **Technology** is an integral part of almost every business.
Manufacturers need technology to compete in the world market.
They could not go far without it.

A phrase or a clause may also function as a subject.

■ **To survive without technology** is difficult. (infinitive phrase)
Downloading information from the web is easy. (gerund phrase)
That the information age would arrive was inevitable. (noun clause)

Note: To determine the subject of a sentence, ask yourself a question that begins with *who* or *what* and ends with the predicate.

In most sentences, the subject comes before the verb; however, in many questions and some exclamations, that order is reversed. (See **643.2**, **643.4**, **646.1**, and **669**.)

esl *Note:* Some languages permit the omission of a subject in a sentence; English does not. A subject must be included in every sentence. (The only exception is an "understood subject," which is discussed at **638.4**.)

638.1

Simple Subject

A **simple subject** is the subject without the words that modify it.

- Thirty years ago, reasonably well-trained **mechanics** could fix any car on the road.

638.2

Complete Subject

A **complete subject** is the simple subject and the words that modify it.

- Thirty years ago, **reasonably well-trained mechanics** could fix any car on the road.

638.3

Compound Subject

A **compound subject** is composed of two or more simple subjects joined by a conjunction and sharing the same predicate(s).

- Today, **mechanics** and **technicians** would need to master a half million manual pages to fix every car on the road.
  Dealerships and their service **departments** must sometimes explain that to the customers.

638.4

Understood Subject

Sometimes a subject is **understood**. This means it is missing in the sentence, but a reader clearly understands what the subject is. An understood subject is most likely in an imperative sentence. (See **643.3**.)

- **(You)** Park on this side of the street. (The subject *you* is understood.)
  Put the CD player in the trunk.

638.5

Delayed Subject

In sentences that begin with *There is, It is, There was,* or *It was,* the subject usually follows the verb.

- There were 70,000 **fans** in the stadium. (The subject is *fans; were* is the verb. *There* is an expletive, an empty word.)
  It was a **problem** for stadium security. (*Problem* is the subject.)

The subject is also delayed in questions.

- Where was the **event**? (*Event* is the subject.)
  Was **Dave Matthews** playing? (*Dave Matthews* is the subject.)

Note: In sentences that begin with *It is* or *It was* and describe the weather, distance, time, and some other conditions, the word *it* serves as the subject.

- **It** was raining.
  It is 90 miles from Chicago to Milwaukee.
  It is three o'clock.

The Predicate (Verb)

639.1

The **predicate**, which contains the verb, is the sentence part that either tells what the subject is doing or says something about the subject.

- Students **need technical skills as well as basic academic skills.**

Simple Predicate

639.2

A **simple predicate** is the verb without the words that describe or modify it.

- Today's workplace **requires** employees to have a range of skills.

Complete Predicate

639.3

A **complete predicate** is the verb and all the words that modify or explain it.

- Today's workplace **requires employees to have a range of skills.**

Compound Predicate

639.4

A **compound predicate** is composed of two or more verbs and all the words that modify or explain them.

- Engineers **analyze problems and calculate solutions.**

Direct Object

639.5

A **direct object** is the part of the predicate that receives the action of the verb. A direct object makes the meaning of the verb complete.

- Marcos visited several **campuses.**
  (The direct object *campuses* receives the action of the verb *visited* by answering the question "Marcos visited what?")

Note: A direct object may be compound.

- An admissions counselor explained the academic **programs** and the application **process.**

Indirect Object

639.6

An **indirect object** is the word(s) that tells *to whom/to what* or *for whom/for what* something is done. A sentence must have a direct object before it can have an indirect object.

- I showed our **children** my new school.

  Use these questions to find an indirect object:

What is the verb?	*showed*
Showed what?	*school* (direct object)
Showed *school* to whom?	*children* (indirect object)

- I wrote **them** a note.

Note: An indirect object may be compound.

- I gave the **instructor** and a few **classmates** my e-mail address.

Using Phrases

640.1

A **phrase** is a group of related words that functions as a single part of speech. A phrase lacks a subject, a predicate, or both. There are three phrases in the following sentence.

■ Examples of technology can be found in ancient civilizations.

of technology
(prepositional phrase that functions as an adjective; no subject or predicate)
can be found
(verb phrase; no subject)
in ancient civilizations
(prepositional phrase that functions as an adverb; no subject or predicate)

Types of Phrases

There are several types of phrases: *verb, verbal, prepositional, appositive,* and *absolute.*

Verb Phrase

640.2

A **verb phrase** consists of a main verb and its helping verbs.

■ Students, worried about exams, **have camped** at the library all week.

Verbal Phrase

640.3

A **verbal phrase** is a phrase based on one of the three types of verbals: *gerund, infinitive,* or *participle.* (See **630.1–630.4.**)

A **gerund phrase** consists of a gerund and its modifiers. The whole phrase functions as a noun. (See **630.2.**)

■ **Becoming a marine biologist** is Rashanda's dream.
(The gerund phrase is used as the subject of the sentence.)
She has acquainted herself with the various methods for **collecting sea-life samples.** (The gerund phrase is the object of the preposition *for.*)

An **infinitive phrase** consists of the introductory word *to,* the fundamental form of a verb, and its modifiers. The whole phrase functions as a noun, an adjective, or an adverb.

■ **To dream** is the first step in any endeavor.
(The infinitive phrase functions as a noun used as the subject.)
Remember **to make a plan to realize your dream.**
(The infinitive phrase *to make a plan* functions as a noun used as a direct object; *to realize your dream* functions as an adjective modifying *plan.*)
Finally, apply all of your talents and skills **to achieve your goals.**
(The infinitive phrase functions as an adverb modifying *apply.*)

A **participial phrase** consists of a present or past participle (a verb form ending in *ing* or *ed*) and its modifiers. The phrase functions as an adjective.

■ **Doing poorly in biology,** Theo signed up for a tutor.
(The participial phrase modifies the noun *Theo.*)
Some students **frustrated by difficult course work** don't seek help.
(The participial phrase modifies the noun *students.*)

Functions of Verbal Phrases

641.1

	Noun	**Adjective**	**Adverb**
Gerund	■		
Infinitive	■	■	■
Participial		■	

Prepositional Phrase

641.2

A **prepositional phrase** is a group of words beginning with a preposition and ending with a noun or a pronoun. Prepositional phrases are used mainly as adjectives and adverbs. See **634.3** for a list of prepositions.

■ Denying the existence **of exam week** hasn't worked **for anyone** yet.
   (The prepositional phrase *of exam week* is used as an adjective modifying the noun *existence; for anyone* is used as an adverb modifying the verb *has worked.*)
   Test days still dawn and GPAs still plummet **for the unprepared student**.
   (The prepositional phrase *for the unprepared student* is used as an adverb modifying the verbs *dawn* and *plummet.*)

esl **Note:**   A prepositional phrase may contain adjectives, but not adverbs. Do not mistake the following adverbs for nouns and incorrectly use them with a preposition: *here, there, everywhere, inside, outside, uptown, downtown.*

Appositive Phrase

641.3

An **appositive phrase,** which follows a noun or a pronoun and renames it, consists of a noun and its modifiers. An appositive adds new information about the noun or pronoun it follows.

■ The Olympic-size pool, **a prized addition to the physical education building,** gets plenty of use. (The appositive phrase renames *pool.*)

Absolute Phrase

641.4

An **absolute phrase** consists of a noun and a participle (plus the participle's object, if there is one, and any modifiers). Because the noun acts like a subject and is followed by a verbal, an absolute phrase resembles a clause.

■ **Their enthusiasm sometimes waning,** the students who cannot swim are required to take lessons. (The noun *enthusiasm* is modified by the present participle *waning;* the entire phrase modifies *students.*)

Phrases can add valuable information to sentences, but some phrases add nothing but "fat" to your writing. For a list of phrases to avoid, see page **93**.

Using Clauses

A **clause** is a group of related words that has both a subject and a predicate.

Independent/Dependent Clauses

642.1

An **independent clause** presents a complete thought and can stand alone as a sentence; a **dependent clause** (also called a subordinate clause) does not present a complete thought and cannot stand alone as a sentence.

■ Though airplanes are twentieth-century inventions (dependent clause), people have always dreamed of flying (independent clause).

Types of Clauses

There are three basic types of dependent, or subordinate, clauses: *adverb, adjective,* and *noun.*

Adverb Clause

642.2

An **adverb clause** is used like an adverb to modify a verb, an adjective, or an adverb. All adverb clauses begin with subordinating conjunctions. (See **635.4**.)

■ **Because Orville won a coin toss,** he got to fly the power-driven air machine first. (The adverb clause modifies the verb *got.*)

Adjective Clause

642.3

An **adjective clause** is used like an adjective to modify a noun or a pronoun. Adjective clauses begin with relative pronouns (*which, that, who*). (See **623.3**.)

■ The men **who invented the first airplane** were brothers, Orville and Wilbur Wright. (The adjective clause modifies the noun *men. Who* is the subject of the adjective clause.)

The first flight, **which took place December 17, 1903,** was made by Orville. (The adjective clause modifies the noun *flight. Which* is the subject of the adjective clause.)

Noun Clause

642.4

A **noun clause** is used in place of a noun. Noun clauses can appear as subjects, as direct or indirect objects, as predicate nominatives, or as objects of prepositions. They are introduced by subordinating words such as *what, that, when, why, how, whatever, who, whom, whoever,* and *whomever.*

■ He wants to know **what made modern aviation possible**.
(The noun clause functions as a direct object.)

Whoever invents an airplane with vertical takeoff ability will be a hero. (The noun clause functions as the subject.)

TEST IT! If you can replace a whole clause with the pronoun *something* or *someone*, it is a noun clause.

Using Sentence Variety

A sentence can be classified according to the kind of statement it makes and according to the way it is constructed.

Kinds of Sentences

Sentences can make five basic kinds of statements: *declarative, interrogative, imperative, exclamatory,* or *conditional.*

Declarative Sentence

643.1

Declarative sentences make statements. They tell us something about a person, a place, a thing, or an idea.

- **In 1955, Rosa Parks refused to follow segregation rules on a bus in Montgomery, Alabama.**

Interrogative Sentence

643.2

Interrogative sentences ask questions.

- **Do you think Ms. Parks knew she was making history?**
  Would you have had the courage to do what she did?

Imperative Sentence

643.3

Imperative sentences give commands. They often contain an understood subject (you). (See **638.4.**)

- **Read Chapters 6 through 10 for tomorrow.**

esl **Note:** Imperative sentences with an understood subject are the only sentences in which it is acceptable to have no subjects stated.

Exclamatory Sentence

643.4

Exclamatory sentences communicate strong emotion or surprise.

- **I simply can't keep up with these long reading assignments!**
  Oh my gosh, you scared me!

Conditional Sentence

643.5

Conditional sentences express two circumstances. One of the circumstances depends on the other circumstance. The words *if, when,* or *unless* are often used in conditional statements.

- **If** you practice a few study-reading techniques, college reading loads will be manageable.
  When I manage my time, it seems I have more of it.
  Don't ask me to help you, **unless** you are willing to do the reading first.

Exercise

Structure of Sentences

A sentence may be *simple, compound, complex,* or *compound-complex,* depending on the relationship between the independent and dependent clauses in it.

Simple Sentence

644.1

A **simple sentence** contains one independent clause. The independent clause may have compound subjects and predicates, and it may also contain phrases.

■ My **back aches**.
(single subject: *back;* single predicate: *aches*)

My **teeth** and my **eyes hurt**.
(compound subject: *teeth* and *eyes;* single predicate: *hurt*)

My **memory** and my **logic come** and **go**.
(compound subject: *memory* and *logic;* compound predicate: *come* and *go*)

I must be in need of a vacation.
(single subject: *I;* single predicate: *must be;* phrases: *in need, of a vacation*)

Compound Sentence

644.2

A **compound sentence** consists of two independent clauses. The clauses must be joined by a semicolon, by a comma and a coordinating conjunction (*and, but, or, nor, so, for, yet*), or by a semicolon and a conjunctive adverb (*besides, however, instead, meanwhile, then, therefore*).

■ I had eight hours of sleep**, so** why am I so exhausted?
I take good care of myself; I get enough sleep.
I still feel fatigued**; therefore,** I must need more exercise.

Complex Sentence

644.3

A **complex sentence** contains one independent clause (in bold) and one or more dependent clauses (underlined).

■ When I can, **I get eight hours of sleep**. (dependent clause; independent clause)

When I get up on time, and if someone hasn't used up all the milk,
I eat breakfast. (two dependent clauses; independent clause)

Compound-Complex Sentence

644.4

A **compound-complex sentence** contains two or more independent clauses (in bold type) and one or more dependent clauses (underlined).

■ If I'm not in a hurry, **I take leisurely walks, and I try to spot some wildlife**.
(dependent clause; two independent clauses)

I saw a hawk when I was walking, **and other smaller birds were chasing it**.
(independent clause, dependent clause; independent clause)

Chapter 40
Avoiding Sentence Errors

Subject-Verb Agreement

645.1

The subject and verb of any clause must agree in both *person* and *number*. *Person* indicates whether the subject of the verb is *first, second,* or *third person. Number* indicates whether the subject and verb are *singular* or *plural*.

	Singular	Plural
First Person	I think	we think
Second Person	you think	you think
Third Person	he/she/it thinks	they think

Agreement in Number

645.2

A verb must agree in number (singular or plural) with its subject.

- The **student was** rewarded for her hard work. (Both the subject *student* and the verb *was* are singular; they agree in number.)

Note: Do not be confused by phrases that come between the subject and the verb. Such phrases may begin with words like *in addition to, as well as,* or *together with.*

- The **instructor,** as well as the students, **is** expected to attend the orientation. (*Instructor,* not *students,* is the subject.)

Compound Subjects

645.3

Compound subjects connected with *and* usually require a plural verb.

- **Dedication and creativity are** trademarks of successful students.

Note: If a compound subject joined by *and* is thought of as a unit, use a singular verb.

- **Macaroni and cheese is** always available in the cafeteria.

Delayed Subjects

Delayed subjects occur when the verb comes *before* the subject in a sentence. In these inverted sentences, the true (delayed) subject must be made to agree with the verb.

- There **are** many nontraditional **students** on our campus.
  Here **is** the **syllabus** you need.
  (*Students* and *syllabus* are the true subjects of these sentences, not *there* and *here*.)

Note: Using an inverted sentence, on occasion, will lend variety to your writing style. Simply remember to make the delayed subjects agree with the verbs.

- However, included among the list's topmost items **was "revise research paper."**
  (Because the true subject here is singular—one item—the singular verb *was* is correct.)

Titles as Subjects

When the subject of a sentence is the title of a work of art, literature, or music, the verb should be singular. This is also true of a word (or phrase) being used as a word (or phrase).

- ***Lyrical Ballads* was** published in 1798 by two of England's greatest poets, Wordsworth and Coleridge. (Even though the title of the book, *Lyrical Ballads,* is plural in form, it is still a single title being used as the subject, correctly taking the singular verb *was.*)
  "Over-the-counter drugs" is a phrase that means nonprescription medications. (Even though the phrase is plural in form, it is still a single phrase being used as the subject, correctly taking the singular verb *is.*)

Singular Subjects with *Or* or *Nor*

Singular subjects joined by *or* or *nor* take a singular verb.

- Neither a **textbook** nor a **notebook is required** for this class.

Note: When the subject nearer a present-tense verb is the singular pronoun *I* or *you,* the correct singular verb does not end in *s.* (See the chart on page **645.**)

- Neither **Marcus** nor **I feel** (not *feels*) right about this.
  Either **Rosa** or **you have** (not *has*) to take notes for me.
  Either **you** or **Rosa has** to take notes for me.

Singular/Plural Subjects

When one of the subjects joined by *or* or *nor* is singular and one is plural, the verb must agree with the subject nearer the verb.

- Neither the **professor** nor her **students were** in the lab. (The plural subject *students* is nearer the verb; therefore, the plural verb *were* agrees with *students.*)
  Neither the **students** nor the **professor was** in the lab. (The singular subject *professor* is nearer the verb; therefore, the singular verb *is* is used to agree with *professor.*)

Collective Nouns

Generally, **collective nouns** (*faculty, pair, crew, assembly, congress, species, crowd, army, team, committee,* and so on) take a singular verb. However, if you want to emphasize differences among individuals in the group or are referring to the group as individuals, you can use a plural verb.

- My lab **team takes** its work very seriously. (*Team* refers to the group as a unit; it requires a singular verb, *takes.*)

  The **team assume** separate responsibilities for each study they undertake. (In this example, *team* refers to individuals within the group; it requires a plural verb, *assume.*)

Note: Collective nouns such as *police, poor, elderly,* and *young* use plural verbs.

- The **police direct** traffic here between 7:00 and 9:00 a.m.

Plural Noun with Singular Meaning

Some nouns that are plural in form but singular in meaning take a singular verb: *mumps, measles, news, mathematics, economics, robotics,* and so on.

- **Economics is** sometimes called "the dismal science."

  The economic **news is** not very good.

Note: The most common exceptions are *scissors, trousers, tidings,* and *pliers.*

- The **scissors are** missing again.

  Are these **trousers** prewashed?

Be Verbs (*am, is, are, was, were*)

When a sentence contains a form of the *be* verb—and a noun comes before and after that verb—the verb must agree with the subject, not the *complement* (the noun coming after the verb).

- The cause of his problem **was** poor study habits. (*Cause* requires a singular verb, even though the subject's complement, *habits,* is plural.)

  His poor study habits **were** the cause of his problem. (*Habits* requires a plural verb, even though the subject's complement, *cause,* is singular.)

Nouns Showing Measurement, Time, and Money

Mathematical phrases and phrases that name a period of time, a unit of measurement, or an amount of money take a singular verb.

- Three and three **is** six.

  Eight pages **is** a long paper on this topic.

  In my opinion, two dollars **is** a high price for a cup of coffee.

Relative Pronouns

648.1

When a **relative pronoun** (*who, which, that*) is used as the subject of a clause, the number of the verb is determined by that pronoun's antecedent. (The antecedent is the word to which the pronoun refers.)

- This is one of the **books that are** required for English class.
  (The relative pronoun *that* requires the plural verb *are* because its antecedent is *books*, not the word *one*. To test this type of sentence for agreement, read the *of* phrase first: *Of the books that are . . .*)

Note: Generally, the antecedent is the nearest noun or pronoun and is often the object of a preposition. Sometimes, however, the antecedent is not the nearest noun or pronoun, especially in sentences containing the phrase "the only one of."

- Dr. Graciosa wondered why Claire was the only **one** of her students **who was** not attending lectures regularly. (In this case, the addition of the modifiers *the only* changes the sense of the sentence. The antecedent of *who* is *one*, not *students*. Only one student was not attending.)

Indefinite Pronoun with Singular Verb

648.2

Many indefinite pronouns (*someone, somebody, something; anyone, anybody, anything; no one, nobody, nothing; everyone, everybody, everything; each, either, neither, one, this*) require a singular verb.

- **Everybody is** welcome to attend the chancellor's reception.
  No one was sent an invitation.

Note: Although it may seem to indicate more than one, *each* is a singular pronoun and requires a singular verb. Do not be confused by words or phrases that come between the indefinite pronoun and the verb.

- **Each** of the new students **is** (not *are*) encouraged to attend the reception.

Indefinite Pronoun with Plural Verb

648.3

Some indefinite pronouns (*both, few, many, most,* and *several*) are plural; they require a plural verb.

- **Few are** offered the opportunity to study abroad.
  Most take advantage of opportunities closer to home.

Indefinite Pronoun with Singular or Plural Verb

648.4

Some indefinite pronouns (*all, any, most, none,* and *some*) may be either singular or plural, depending on the nouns they refer to.

- **Some** of the students **were** missing. (*Students*, the noun that *some* refers to, is plural; therefore, the pronoun *some* is considered plural, and the plural verb *were* is used to agree with it.)
  Most of the lecture **was** over by the time we arrived. (Because *lecture* is singular, *most* is also singular, requiring the singular verb *was*.)

Pronoun-Antecedent Agreement

649.1

A pronoun must agree in number, person, and gender (sex) with its *antecedent*. The antecedent is the word to which the pronoun refers.

- **Yoshi** brought **his** laptop computer and e-book to school.
  (The pronoun *his* refers to the antecedent *Yoshi*. Both the pronoun and its antecedent are singular, third person, and masculine; therefore, the pronoun is said to agree with its antecedent.)

Singular Pronoun

649.2

Use a singular pronoun to refer to such antecedents as *each, either, neither, one, anyone, anybody, everyone, everybody, somebody, another, nobody,* and *a person.*

- **Each** of the maintenance vehicles has **their** doors locked at night. (Incorrect)
  Each of the maintenance vehicles has **its** doors locked at night.
  (Correct: Both *Each* and *its* are singular.)
  Somebody left **his or her** (not *their*) vehicle unlocked. (Correct)

Plural Pronoun

649.3

When a plural pronoun (*they, their*) is mistakenly used with a singular indefinite pronoun (such as *everyone* or *everybody*), you may correct the sentence by replacing *their* or *they* with optional pronouns (*his or her* or *he or she*), or you may make the antecedent plural.

- **Everyone** must learn to wait **their** turn. (Incorrect)
  Everyone must learn to wait **his or her** turn.
  (Correct: Optional pronouns *his or her* are used.)
  People must learn to wait **their** turn.
  (Correct: The singular antecedent, *Everyone*, is changed to the plural antecedent, *People*.)

Two or More Antecedents

649.4

When two or more antecedents are joined by *and*, they are considered plural.

- **Tomas** and **Jamal** are finishing **their** assignments.

When two or more singular antecedents are joined by *or* or *nor*, they are considered singular.

- Either **Connie** or **Shavonn** left **her** headset in the library.

Note: If one of the antecedents is masculine and one feminine, the pronouns should likewise be masculine and feminine.

- Is either **Ahmad** or **Phyllis** bringing **his or her** laptop computer?

Note: If one of the antecedents joined by *or* or *nor* is singular and one is plural, the pronoun is made to agree with the nearer antecedent.

- Neither **Ravi** nor **his friends** want to spend **their** time studying.
  Neither **his friends** nor **Ravi** wants to spend **his** time studying.

Shifts in Sentence Construction

A shift is an improper change in structure midway through a sentence. The following examples will help you identify and fix several different kinds of shifts.

650.1

Shift in Person

Shift in person is mixing first, second, or third person within a sentence.

Shift	**One** may get spring fever unless **you** live in California or Florida. (The sentence shifts from third person, *one*, to second person, *you*.)
Corrected	**You may get spring fever unless you live in California or Florida.** (Stays in second person)
Corrected	**People may get spring fever unless they live in California or Florida.** (*People*, a third person plural noun, requires a third person plural pronoun, *they*.)

650.2

Shift in Tense

Shift in tense is using more than one tense in a sentence when it is unnecessary.

Shift	Sheila **looked** at nine apartments in one weekend before she **had chosen** one. (Tense shifts from past to past perfect for no reason.)
Corrected	**Sheila looked at nine apartments in one weekend before she chose one.** (Tense stays in past.)

650.3

Shift in Voice

Shift in voice is mixing active with passive voice. Usually, a sentence beginning in active voice should remain so to the end.

Shift	As you look (active voice) for just the right place, many interesting apartments will probably be seen. (passive voice)
Corrected	**As you look** (active voice) **for just the right place, you will probably see** (active voice) **many interesting apartments.**

650.4

Unparallel Construction

Unparallel construction occurs when the kind of words or phrases being used shifts or changes in the middle of a sentence.

Shift	In my hometown, people pass the time shooting pool, pitching horseshoes, and at softball games. (Sentence shifts from *ing* words, *shooting* and *pitching*, to the phrase *at softball games*.)
Parallel	**In my hometown, people pass the time shooting pool, pitching horseshoes, and playing softball.** (Now all three activities are *ing* words—they are consistent, or parallel.)

Fragments, Comma Splices, and Run-Ons

Except in a few special situations, you should use complete sentences when you write. By definition, a complete sentence expresses a complete thought. However, a sentence may actually contain several ideas, not just one. The trick is getting those ideas to work together to form a clear, interesting sentence that expresses your exact meaning. Among the most common sentence errors that writers make are fragments, comma splices, and run-ons.

Fragment

651.1

A **fragment** is a group of words used as a sentence. It is not a sentence, however, because it lacks a subject, a verb, or some other essential part. That missing part results in an incomplete thought.

Fragment	Pete gunned the engine. Forgetting that the boat was hooked to the truck. (This is a sentence followed by a fragment. This error can be corrected by combining the fragment with the sentence.)
Corrected	**Pete gunned the engine, forgetting that the boat was hooked to the truck.**
Fragment	Even though my best friend had a little boy last year. (This clause does not convey a complete thought. We need to know what is happening despite the birth of the little boy.)
Corrected	**Even though my best friend had a little boy last year, I do not comprehend the full meaning of "motherhood."**

Comma Splice

651.2

A **comma splice** is a mistake made when two independent clauses are connected ("spliced") with only a comma. The comma is not enough: A period, semicolon, or conjunction is needed.

Splice	People say that being a stay-at-home mom or dad is an important job, their actions tell a different story.
Corrected	**People say that being a stay-at-home mom or dad is an important job, but their actions tell a different story.** (The coordinating conjunction *but*, added after the comma, corrects the splice.)
Corrected	**People say that being a stay-at-home mom or dad is an important job; their actions tell a different story.** (A semicolon—rather than just a comma—makes the sentence correct.)
Corrected	**People say that being a stay-at-home mom or dad is an important job. Their actions tell a different story.** (A period creates two sentences and corrects the splice.)

Run-Ons

Exercise

A **run-on sentence** is actually two sentences joined without adequate punctuation or a connecting word.

Run-on   The Alamo holds a special place in American history it was
           the site of an important battle between the United States and
           Mexico.

Corrected **The Alamo holds a special place in American history because it
           was the site of an important battle between the United States
           and Mexico.** (A subordinating conjunction is added to fix the
           run-on.)

Run-ons   Antonio de Santa Anna, the president of Mexico who once held a
           funeral for his amputated leg, is the same Santa Anna who stormed
           the Alamo he led his troops to victory over the Texan rebels
           defending that fort. Two famous American frontiersmen died they
           were James Bowie and Davy Crockett. Santa Anna enjoyed fame,
           power, and respect among his followers. He died in 1876 he was
           poor, blind, and ignored.

Corrected **Antonio de Santa Anna, the president of Mexico who once held
           a funeral for his amputated leg, is the same Santa Anna who
           stormed the Alamo. He led his troops to victory over Texan
           rebels defending that fort. Two famous American frontiersmen
           were killed in the battle; they were James Bowie and Davy
           Crockett. Santa Anna enjoyed fame, power, and respect
           among his followers. When he died in 1876, he was poor,
           blind, and ignored.**

The writer corrected the run-on sentences in the paragraph above by adding punctuation. While doing so, the writer also made a few changes to improve the ideas. The writer makes further improvements in the paragraph below by revising one sentence and by combining two sets of short sentences into one stronger sentence.

Improved   **Antonio de Santa Anna, the president of Mexico who once held
           a funeral for his amputated leg, is the same Santa Anna who
           stormed the Alamo. He led his troops to victory over Texan
           rebels defending that fort. Two famous American frontiersmen,
           James Bowie and Davy Crockett, were killed in the battle. Santa
           Anna enjoyed fame, power, and respect among his followers;
           but when he died in 1876, he was poor, blind, and ignored.**

fyi   Once you make a correction, you may see an opportunity to add, cut,
           or improve something else. Correcting and editing sentences is
           frustrating at times, but with practice, it can become one of the more
           enjoyable parts of the writing process.

Misplaced and Dangling Modifiers

Writing is thinking. Before you can write clearly, you must think clearly. Nothing is more frustrating for the reader than having to reread writing just to understand its basic meaning. Look carefully at the common errors that follow. Then use this section as a checklist when you revise. Always avoid leaving misplaced or dangling modifiers in your finished work.

Misplaced Modifiers

653.1

Misplaced modifiers are descriptive words or phrases so separated from what they are describing that the reader is confused.

Misplaced	The neighbor's dog has nearly been barking nonstop for two hours. (*Nearly* been barking?)
Corrected	**The neighbor's dog has been barking nonstop for nearly two hours.** (Watch your placement of *only, just, nearly, barely,* and so on.)
Misplaced	The commercial advertised an assortment of combs for active people with unbreakable teeth. (*People* with unbreakable teeth?)
Corrected	**The commercial advertised an assortment of combs with unbreakable teeth for active people.** (*Combs* with unbreakable teeth)
Misplaced	The pool staff gave large beach towels to the students marked with chlorine-resistant ID numbers. (*Students* marked with chlorine-resistant ID numbers?)
Corrected	**The pool staff gave large beach towels marked with chlorine-resistant ID numbers to the students.** (*Towels* marked with chlorine-resistant ID numbers)

Dangling Modifiers

653.2

Dangling modifiers are descriptive words that modify a subject that isn't stated in the sentence. These often occur as phrases containing *ing* words.

Dangling	After standing in line all afternoon, the manager informed us that all the tickets had been sold. (It sounds as if the manager has been *standing in line all afternoon.*)
Corrected	**After we stood in line all afternoon, the manager informed us that all the tickets had been sold.**
Dangling	After living in the house for one month, the electrician recommended we update all the wiring. (It sounds as if the electrician has been *living in the house.*)
Corrected	**After living in the house for one month, we hired an electrician, who recommended we update all the wiring.**

Exercise

Ambiguous Wording

Sloppy sentences confuse readers. No one should have to wonder, "What does this writer mean?" When you revise and edit, check for indefinite pronoun references, incomplete comparisons, and unclear wording.

654.1 Indefinite Pronoun References

An **indefinite reference** is a problem caused by careless use of pronouns. There must always be a word or phrase nearby that a pronoun clearly replaces.

Indefinite	When Tonya attempted to put her dictionary on the shelf, it fell to the floor. (The pronoun *it* could refer to either the dictionary or the shelf.)
Corrected	**When Tonya attempted to put her dictionary on the shelf, the shelf fell to the floor.**
Indefinite	Juanita reminded Kerri that she needed to photocopy her resumé before going to her interview. (Who *needed to photocopy her resumé*—Juanita or Kerri?)
Corrected	**Juanita reminded Kerri to photocopy her resumé before going to her interview.**

654.2 Incomplete Comparisons

Incomplete comparisons—leaving out words that show exactly what is being compared to what—can confuse readers.

Incomplete	After completing our lab experiment, we concluded that helium is lighter. (*Lighter* than what?)
Corrected	**After completing our lab experiment, we concluded that helium is lighter than oxygen.**

654.3 Unclear Wording

One type of ambiguous writing is wording that has two or more possible meanings due to an unclear reference to something elsewhere in the sentence. (See **654.1**.)

Unclear	I couldn't believe my sister bought a cat with all those allergy problems. (Who has the *allergy problems*—the cat or the sister?)
Corrected	**I couldn't believe my sister, who is very allergic, bought a cat.**
Unclear	Dao intended to wash the car when he finished his homework, but he never did. (It is unclear which he *never did*—wash the car or finish his homework.)
Corrected	**Dao intended to wash the car when he finished his homework, but he never did get around to washing the car.**

Nonstandard Language

Nonstandard language is language that does not conform to the standards set by schools, media, and public institutions. It is often acceptable in everyday conversation and in fictional writing, but seldom in formal speech or other forms of writing.

Exercise

Colloquial Language

655.1

Colloquial language is wording used in informal conversation that is unacceptable in formal writing.

Colloquial	Hey, wait up! Cal wants to go with.
Standard	**Hey, wait! Cal wants to go with us.**

Double Preposition

655.2

The use of certain **double prepositions**—*off of, off to, from off*—is unacceptable.

Double Preposition	Pick up the dirty clothes from off the floor.
Standard	**Pick up the dirty clothes from the floor.**

Substitution

655.3

Avoid substituting *and* for *to*.

Substitution	Try and get to class on time.
Standard	**Try to get to class on time.**

Avoid substituting *of* for *have* when combining with *could, would, should,* or *might*.

Substitution	I should of studied for that exam.
Standard	**I should have studied for that exam.**

Double Negative

655.4

A **double negative** is a sentence that contains two negative words used to express a single negative idea. Double negatives are unacceptable in academic writing.

Double Negative	After paying for essentials, I haven't got no money left.
Standard	**I haven't got any money left. / I have no money left.**

Slang

655.5

Avoid the use of **slang** or any "in" words in formal writing.

Slang	The way the stadium roof opened was way cool.
Standard	**The way the stadium roof opened was remarkable.**

Avoiding Sentence Problems

QUICK GUIDE

Does every subject agree with its verb? (See pages 645–648.)

- In person and number?
- When a word or phrase comes between the subject and verb?
- When the subject is delayed?
- When the subject is a title?
- When a compound subject is connected with *or*?
- When the subject is a collective noun (*faculty, team,* or *crowd*)?
- When the subject is a relative pronoun (*who, which, that*)?
- When the subject is an indefinite pronoun (*everyone, anybody,* or *many*)?

Does every pronoun agree with its antecedent? (See page 649.)

- When the pronoun is a singular indefinite pronoun such as *each, either,* or *another*?
- When two antecedents are joined with *and*?
- When two antecedents are joined with *or*?

Did you unintentionally create inappropriate shifts? (See page 650.)

- In person?
- In tense?
- From active to passive voice?
- Other unparallel construction?

Are all your sentences complete? (See pages 651–652.)

- Have you used sentence fragments?
- Are some sentences "spliced" or run together?

Did you use any misplaced modifiers or ambiguous wording? (See pages 653–654.)

- Have you used misplaced or dangling modifiers?
- Have you used incomplete comparisons or indefinite references?

Did you use any nonstandard language? (See page 655.)

- Have you used slang or colloquial language?
- Have you used double negatives or double prepositions?

Chapter 41
Multilingual and ESL Guidelines

English may be your second, third, or fifth language. As a multilingual learner, you bring to your writing the culture and knowledge of the languages you use. This broader perspective enables you to draw on many experiences and greater knowledge as you write and speak. Whether you are an international student or someone who has lived here a long time and is now learning more about English, this chapter provides you with important information about writing in English.

Five Parts of Speech

Noun

Count Nouns

657.1

Count nouns refer to things that can be counted. They can have *a, an, the,* or *one* in front of them. One or more adjectives can come between the articles *a, an, the,* or *one* and the singular count noun.

■ **an apple, one orange, a plum, a purple plum**

Count nouns can be singular, as in the examples above, or plural, as in the examples below.

■ **plums, apples, oranges**

Note: When count nouns are plural, they can have the article *the*, a number, or a demonstrative adjective in front of them. (See **659.1** and **659.3**.)

■ I used **the** plums to make a pie.
He placed **five** apples on my desk.
These oranges are so juicy!

The *number* of a noun refers to whether it names a single thing (book), in which case its number is *singular*, or whether it names more than one thing (books), in which case the number of the noun is *plural*.

Note: There are different ways in which the plural form of nouns is created. For more information, see pages **593–594**.

Noncount Nouns

Noncount nouns refer to things that cannot be counted. Do not use *a, an,* or *one* in front of them. They have no plural form, so they always take a singular verb. Some nouns that end in *s* are not plural; they are noncount nouns.

■ **fruit, furniture, rain, thunder, advice, mathematics, news**

Abstract nouns name ideas or conditions rather than people, places, or objects. Many abstract nouns are noncount nouns.

■ The students had **fun** at the party. Good **health** is a wonderful gift.

Collective nouns name a whole category or group and are often noncount nouns.

■ **homework, furniture, money, faculty, committee, flock**

Note: The parts or components of a group or category named by a noncount noun are often count nouns. For example, *report* and *assignment* are count nouns that are parts of the collective, noncount noun *homework*.

Two-Way Nouns

Some nouns can be used as either count or noncount nouns, depending on what they refer to.

■ I would like a **glass** of water. (count noun)
Glass is used to make windows. (noncount noun)

Articles and Other Noun Markers

Specific Articles

Use articles and other noun markers or modifiers to give more information about nouns. The **specific** (or **definite**) **article** *the* is used to refer to a specific noun.

■ I found **the** book I misplaced yesterday.

Indefinite Articles

Exercise

Use the **indefinite article** *a* or *an* to refer to a nonspecific noun. Use *an* before singular nouns beginning with the vowels *a, e, i, o,* and *u.* Use *a* before nouns beginning with all other letters of the alphabet, the consonants. Exceptions do occur: *a* unit; *a* university.

■ I always take **an** apple to work.
It is good to have **a** book with you when you travel.

Indefinite pronouns can also mark nonspecific nouns—*all, any, each, either, every, few, many, more, most, neither, several, some* (for singular and plural count nouns); *all, any, more, most, much, some* (for noncount nouns).

■ **Every** student is encouraged to register early.
Most classes fill quickly.

Determining Whether to Use Articles

659.1

Listed below are a number of guidelines to help you determine whether to use an article and which one to use.

Use *a* or *an* with singular count nouns that do not refer to one specific item.
- **A zebra** has black and white stripes. **An apple** is good for you.

Do not use *a* or *an* with plural count nouns.
- **Zebras** have black and white stripes. **Apples** are good for you.

Do not use *a* or *an* with noncount nouns.
- **Homework** needs to be done promptly.

Use *the* with singular count nouns that refer to one specific item.
- **The apple** you gave me was delicious.

Use *the* with plural count nouns.
- **The zebras** at Brookfield Zoo were healthy.

Use *the* with noncount nouns.
- **The money** from my uncle is a gift.

Do not use *the* with most singular proper nouns.
- **Mother Theresa** loved the poor and downcast.

    Note: There are many exceptions: the Sahara Desert, the University of Minnesota, the Fourth of July

Use *the* with plural nouns.
- **the Joneses** (both Mr. and Mrs. Jones), **the Rocky Mountains, the United States**

Possessive Adjectives

659.2

Possessive nouns and pronouns can be used as adjectives to mark nouns.

possessive nouns: *Tanya's, father's, store's*
- The car is **Tanya's**, not her **father's**.

possessive pronouns: *my, your, his, her, its, our*
- **My** hat is purple.

Demonstrative Adjectives

659.3

Demonstrative pronouns can be used as adjectives to mark nouns.

demonstrative pronouns: *this, that, these, those* (for singular and plural count nouns); *this, that* (for noncount nouns)
- **Those** chairs are lovely. Where did you buy **that** furniture?

660.1

Quantifiers

Expressions of quantity and measure are often used with nouns. Below are some of these expressions and guidelines for using them.

The following expressions of quantity can be used with count nouns: *each, every, both, a couple of, a few, several, many, a number of.*

- We enjoyed **both** concerts we attended. **A couple of** songs performed were familiar to us.

Use a number to indicate a specific quantity of a continuum.

- I saw **fifteen** cardinals in the park.

To indicate a specific quantity of a noncount noun, use *a* + quantity (such as *bag, bottle, bowl, carton, glass,* or *piece*) + *of* + noun.

- I bought **a carton of milk**, **a head of lettuce**, **a piece of cheese**, and **a bag of flour** at the grocery store.

The following expressions can be used with noncount nouns: *a little, much, a great deal of.*

- We had **much** wind and **a little** rain as the storm passed through yesterday.

The following expressions of quantity can be used with both count and noncount nouns: *no/not any, some, a lot of, lots of, plenty of, most, all, this, that.*

- I would like **some** apples *(count noun)* and **some** rice *(noncount noun)*, please.

Verb

Exercise

As the central part of the predicate, a verb conveys much of a sentence's meaning. Using verb tenses and forms correctly ensures that your readers will understand your sentences as you intend them to. For a more thorough review of verbs, see pages **626–631**.

660.2

Progressive (Continuous) Tenses

Progressive or continuous tense verbs express action that is in progress (see page **628**).

To form the **present continuous** tense, use the helping verb *am, is,* or *are* with the *ing* form of the main verb.

- He **is washing** the car right now.
  Kent and Chen **are studying** for a test.

To form the **past continuous** tense, use the helping verb *was* or *were* with the *ing* form of the main verb.

- Yesterday he **was working** in the garden all day.
  Julia and Juan **were watching** a movie.

To form the **future continuous** tense, use *will* or a phrase that indicates the future, the helping verb *be*, and the *ing* form of the main verb.

- Next week he **will be painting** the house.
  He **plans to be painting** the house soon.

Note that some verbs are generally not used in the continuous tenses, such as the following groups of frequently used verbs:

661.1

Exercise

- Verbs that express thoughts, attitudes, and desires: *know, understand, want, prefer*
- Verbs that describe appearances: *seem, resemble*
- Verbs that indicate possession: *belong, have, own, possess*
- Verbs that signify inclusion: *contain, hold*
  - ■ Kala **knows** how to ride a motorcycle.
    NOT THIS: Kala **is knowing** how to ride a motorcycle.

Verb Complements

661.2

Verb complements are words used to complete the meaning of transitive verbs. A verb complement can be a direct object (sometimes with an indirect object), an object complement, or a subject complement in the case of a linking verb.

Verb complements include verb forms called verbals. There are three kinds of verbals: infinitives, gerunds, and participles (see **630.4**). There are no grammar rules describing which verbs accompany which complements, so take note of the following information.

Infinitives as Complements

661.3

Infinitives can follow many verbs, including these: *agree, appear, attempt, consent, decide, demand, deserve, endeavor, fail, hesitate, hope, intend, need, offer, plan, prepare, promise, refuse, seem, tend, volunteer, wish.* (See **630.3** for more on infinitives.)

■ He **promised to bring** some samples.

The following verbs are among those that can be followed by a noun or pronoun plus the infinitive: *ask, beg, choose, expect, intend, need, prepare, promise, want.*

■ I **expect you to be** there on time.

Note: Except in the passive voice, the following verbs must have a noun or pronoun before the infinitive: *advise, allow, appoint, authorize, cause, challenge, command, convince, encourage, forbid, force, hire, instruct, invite, order, permit, remind, require, select, teach, tell, tempt, trust.*

■ I will **authorize Emily to use** my credit card.

Unmarked infinitives (no *to*) can follow these verbs: *have, help, let, make.*

■ These glasses **help me see** the board.

Gerunds as Complements

661.4

Gerunds can follow these verbs: *admit, avoid, consider, deny, discuss, dislike, enjoy, finish, imagine, miss, postpone, quit, recall, recommend, regret.* (Also see **630.2**.)

■ I **recommended hiring** Ian for the job.

662.1
Infinitives or Gerunds as Complements

Either gerunds or infinitives can follow these verbs: *begin, continue, hate, like, love, prefer, remember, start, stop, try.*

■ I **hate having** cold feet. I **hate to have** cold feet.

Note: Sometimes the meaning of a sentence will change depending on whether you use a gerund or an infinitive.

■ I **stopped to smoke**. (I *stopped* weeding the garden *to smoke* a cigarette.)
I **stopped smoking**. (I no longer smoke.)

662.2
Common Modal Auxiliary Verbs

Modal auxiliary verbs are a kind of auxiliary verb. (See **626.3**.) They help the main verb express meaning. Modals are sometimes grouped with other helping or auxiliary verbs.

Modal verbs must be followed by the base form of a verb without *to* (not by a gerund or an infinitive). Also, modal verbs do not change form; they are always used as they appear in the following chart.

Modal	Expresses	Sample Sentence
can	ability	I **can** program a VCR.
could	ability	I **could** babysit Tuesday.
	possibility	He **could** be sick.
might	possibility	I **might** be early.
may, might	possibility	I **may** sleep late Saturday.
	request	**May** I be excused?
must	strong need	I **must** study more.
have to	strong need	I **have to** (have got to) exercise.
ought to	feeling of duty	I **ought to** (should) help Dad.
should	advisabillity	She **should** retire.
	expectation	I **should** have caught that train.
shall	intent	**Shall** I stay longer?
will	intent	I **will** visit my grandma soon.
would	intent	I **would** live to regret my offer.
	repeated action	He **would** walk in the meadow.
would + you	polite request	**Would you** help me?
could + you	polite request	**Could you** type this letter?
will + you	polite request	**Will you** give me a ride?
can + you	polite request	**Can you** make supper tonight?

Common Two-Word Verbs

This chart lists some common verbs in which two words—a verb and a preposition—work together to express a specific action. A noun or pronoun is often inserted between the parts of the two-word verb when it is used in a sentence: break *it* down, call *it* off.

break down	to take apart or fall apart
call off	cancel
call up	make a phone call
clear out	leave a place quickly
cross out	draw a line through
do over	repeat
figure out	find a solution
fill in/out	complete a form or an application
fill up	fill a container or tank
* **find out**	discover
* **get in**	enter a vehicle or building
* **get out of**	leave a car, a house, or a situation
* **get over**	recover from a sickness or a problem
give back	return something
give in/up	surrender or quit
hand in	give homework to a teacher
hand out	give someone something
hang up	put down a phone receiver
leave out	omit or don't use
let in/out	allow someone or something to enter or go out
look up	find information
mix up	confuse
pay back	return money or a favor
pick out	choose
point out	call attention to
put away	return something to its proper place
put down	place something on a table, the floor, etc.
put off	delay doing something
shut off	turn off a machine or light
* **take part**	participate
talk over	discuss
think over	consider carefully
try on	put on clothing to see if it fits
turn down	lower the volume
turn up	raise the volume
write down	write on a piece of paper

* These two-word verbs should not have a noun or pronoun inserted between their parts.

Spelling Guidelines for Verb Forms

The same spelling rules that apply when adding a suffix to other words apply to verbs as well. Most verbs need a suffix to indicate tense or form. The third-person singular form of a verb, for example, usually ends in *s*, but it can also end in *es*. Formation of *ing* and *ed* forms of verbs and verbals needs careful attention, too. Consult the rules below to determine which spelling is correct for each verb. (For general spelling guidelines, see page **600**.)

There may be exceptions to these rules when forming the past tense of irregular verbs because the verbs are formed by changing the word itself, not merely by adding *d* or *ed*. (See the chart of irregular verbs on page **631**.)

664.1 | ## Past Tense: Adding *ed*

Add *ed* . . .
- When a verb ends with two consonants:
  - touch—**touched** ask—**asked** pass—**passed**
- When a verb ends with a consonant preceded by two vowels:
  - heal—**healed** gain—**gained**
- When a verb ends in *y* preceded by a vowel:
  - annoy—**annoyed** flay—**flayed**
- When a multisyllable verb's last syllable is not stressed (even when the last syllable ends with a consonant preceded by a vowel):
  - budget—**budgeted** enter—**entered** interpret—**interpreted**

Change *y* to *i* and add *ed* when a verb ends in a consonant followed by *y*:
  - liquefy—**liquefied** worry—**worried**

Double the final consonant and add *ed* . . .
- When a verb has one syllable and ends with a consonant preceded by a vowel:
  - wrap—**wrapped** drop—**dropped**
- When a multisyllable verb's last syllable (ending in a consonant preceded by a vowel) is stressed:
  - admit—**admitted** confer—**conferred** abut—**abutted**

664.2 | ## Past Tense: Adding *d*

Add *d* . . .
- When a verb ends with *e*:
  - chime—**chimed** tape—**taped**
- When a verb ends with *ie*:
  - tie—**tied** die—**died** lie—**lied**

Present Tense: Adding *s* or *es*

Add *es* . . .

- When a verb ends in *ch, sh, s, x,* or *z:*
  - ◼ watch—**watches** fix—**fixes**
- To *do* and *go:*
  - ◼ do—**does** go—**goes**

Change *y* to *i* and add *es* when the verb ends in a consonant followed by *y:*
  - ◼ liquefy—**liquefies** quantify—**quantifies**

Add *s* to most other verbs, including those already ending in *e* and those that end in a vowel followed by *y:*
  - ◼ write—**writes** buy—**buys**

Present Tense: Adding *ing*

Drop the *e* and add *ing* when the verb ends in *e:*
  - ◼ drive—**driving** rise—**rising**

Double the final consonant and add *ing* . . .

- When a verb has one syllable and ends with a consonant preceded by a vowel:
  - ◼ wrap—**wrapping** sit—**sitting**
- When a multisyllable verb's last syllable (ending in a consonant preceded by a vowel) is stressed:
  - ◼ forget—**forgetting** begin—**beginning** abut—**abutting**

Change *ie* to *y* and add *ing* when a verb ends with *ie:*
  - ◼ tie—**tying** die—**dying** lie—**lying**

Add *ing* . . .

- When a verb ends with two consonants:
  - ◼ touch—**touching** ask—**asking** pass—**passing**
- When a verb ends with a consonant preceded by two vowels:
  - ◼ heal—**healing** gain—**gaining**
- When a verb ends in *y:*
  - ◼ buy—**buying** study—**studying** cry—**crying**
- When a multisyllable verb's last syllable is not stressed (even when the last syllable ends with a consonant preceded by a vowel):
  - ◼ budget—**budgeting** enter—**entering** interpret—**interpreting**

Note: Never trust your spelling to even the best computer spell checker. Carefully proofread. Use a dictionary for questionable words your spell checker may miss.

Adjective

Placing Adjectives

You probably know that an adjective often comes before the noun it modifies. When several adjectives are used in a row to modify a single noun, it is important to arrange the adjectives in the well-established sequence used in English writing and speaking. The following list shows the usual order of adjectives when you use more than one.

First, place . . .

1. articles . . . . **a, an, the**
   demonstrative adjectives. . . . . **that, those**
   possessives . . . . **my, her, Misha's**

Then, place words that . . .

2. indicate time . . . . **first, next, final**
3. tell how many . . . . **one, few, some**
4. evaluate. . . . . **beautiful, dignified, graceful**
5. tell what size . . . . **big, small, short, tall**
6. tell what shape . . . . **round, square**
7. describe a condition. . . . . **messy, clean, dark**
8. tell what age . . . . **old, young, new, antique**
9. tell what color. . . . . **blue, red, yellow**
10. tell what nationality . . . . **English, Chinese, Mexican**
11. tell what religion . . . . **Buddhist, Jewish, Protestant**
12. tell what material . . . . **satin, velvet, wooden**

Finally, place nouns . . .

13. used as adjectives. . . . . **computer [monitor], spice [rack]**

   ■ **my second try** (1 + 2 + noun)
   gorgeous young white swans (4 + 8 + 9 + noun)

Present and Past Participles as Adjectives

Both the **present participle**, which always ends in *ing*, and the **past participle** can be used as adjectives. Exercise care in choosing whether to use the present or the past participle. A participle can come either before a noun or after a linking verb.

A **present participle** used as an adjective should describe a person or thing that is causing a feeling or situation.

   ■ His **annoying** comments made me angry.

A **past participle** should describe a person or thing that experiences a feeling or situation.

   ■ He was **annoyed** because he had to wait so long.

Note: Within each of the following pairs, the present (*ing* form) and past participles (*ed* form) have different meanings.

   ■ **annoying/annoyed**   **depressing/depressed**   **fascinating/fascinated**
   boring/bored   **exciting/excited**   **surprising/surprised**
   confusing/confused   **exhausting/exhausted**

Nouns as Adjectives

667.1

Nouns sometimes function as adjectives by modifying another noun. When a noun is used as an adjective, it is always singular.

- Many European cities have **rose** gardens.
  Marta recently joined a **book** club.

TIP: Try to avoid using more than two nouns as adjectives for another noun. These "noun compounds" can get confusing. Prepositional phrases may get the meaning across better than long noun strings.

- Omar is a **crew** member in the **restaurant** kitchen during **second** shift.
  NOT THIS: Omar is a **second-shift restaurant kitchen crew** member.

Adverb

Exercise

Placing Adverbs

667.2

Consider the following guidelines for placing adverbs correctly. See page **633** for more information about adverbs.

Place adverbs that tell how often (*frequently, seldom, never, always, sometimes*) after a helping verb and before the main verb. In a sentence without a helping verb, adverbs that tell *how often* are placed before an action verb but after a "be" verb.

- The salesclerk will **usually** help me.

Place adverbs that tell when (*yesterday, now, at five o'clock*) at the end of a sentence.

- Auntie El came home **yesterday**.

Adverbs that tell where (*upside-down, around, downstairs*) usually follow the verb they modify. Many prepositional phrases (*at the beach, under the stairs, below the water*) are used as adverbs that tell *where*.

- We waited **on the porch**.

Adverbs that tell how (*quickly, slowly, loudly*) can be placed either at the beginning, in the middle, or at the end of a sentence—but not between a verb and its direct object.

- **Softly** he called my name. He **softly** called my name. He called my name **softly**.

Place adverbs that modify adjectives directly before the adjective.

- That is a **most** unusual dress.

Adverbs that modify clauses are most often placed in front of the clause, but they can also go inside or at the end of the clause.

- **Fortunately**, we were not involved in the accident.
  We were not involved, **fortunately**, in the accident.
  We were not involved in the accident, **fortunately**.

Note: Adverbs that are used with verbs that have objects must *not* be placed between the verb and its object.

- Luis **usually** catches the most fish. **Usually**, Luis catches the most fish.
  NOT THIS: Luis catches **usually** the most fish.

Preposition

Exercise

A **preposition** combines with a noun to form a prepositional phrase, which usually acts as an adverb or adjective. See pages **634** and **636** for a list of common prepositions and for more information about prepositions.

668.1

Using *in, on, at,* and *by*

In, on, at, and *by* are four common prepositions that refer to time and place. Here are some examples of how these prepositions are used in each case.

To show time

- **on** a specific day or date: *on* June 7, *on* Wednesday

  in part of a day: *in* the afternoon

  in a year or month: *in* 2008, *in* April

  in a period of time: completed *in* an hour

  by a specific time or date: *by* noon, *by* the fifth of May

  at a specific time of day or night: *at* 3:30 this afternoon

To show place

- **at** a meeting place or location: *at* school, *at* the park

  at the edge of something: standing *at* the bar

  at the corner of something: turning *at* the intersection

  at a target: throwing a dart *at* the target

  on a surface: left *on* the floor

  on an electronic medium: *on* the Internet, *on* television

  in an enclosed space: *in* the box, *in* the room

  in a geographic location: *in* New York City, *in* Germany

  in a print medium: *in* a journal

  by a landmark: *by* the fountain

TIP: Do not insert a preposition between a transitive verb and its direct object. Intransitive verbs, however, are often followed by a prepositional phrase (a phrase that begins with a preposition).

- I **cooked** hot dogs on the grill. (transitive verb)

  I **ate** in the park. (intransitive verb)

668.2

Phrasal Prepositions

Some prepositional phrases begin with more than one preposition. These **phrasal prepositions** are commonly used in both written and spoken communication. A list of common phrasal prepositions follows:

according to	**because of**	**in case of**	**on the side of**
across from	**by way of**	**in spite of**	**up to**
along with	**except for**	**instead of**	**with respect to**

Exercise

Understanding Sentence Basics

Simple sentences in the English language follow the five basic patterns shown below. (See pages **637–644** for more information.)

Subject + Verb

┌─ S ─┐┌─V─┐
Naomie winked.

Some verbs like *winked* are intransitive. Intransitive verbs *do not* need a direct object to express a complete thought. (See **626.2**.)

Subject + Verb + Direct Object

┌─ S ─┐┌─ V ─┐┌─ DO ─┐
Harris grinds his teeth.

Some verbs like *grinds* are transitive. Transitive verbs *do* need a direct object to express a complete thought. (See **626.2**.)

Subject + Verb + Indirect Object + Direct Object

┌─ S ─┐┌─V─┐┌─ IO ─┐┌─ DO ─┐
Elena offered her friend an anchovy.

The direct object names who or what receives the action; the indirect object names to whom or for whom the action was done.

Subject + Verb + Direct Object + Object Complement

┌───── S ─────┐┌─V─┐ DO ┌────── OC ──────┐
The chancellor named Ravi the outstanding student of 2007.

The object complement renames or describes the direct object.

Subject + Linking Verb + Predicate Noun (or Predicate Adjective)

┌─S─┐ LV ┌──── PN ────┐   ┌─S─┐ LV ┌─ PA ─┐
Paula is a computer programmer.   Paula is very intelligent.

A linking verb connects the subject to the predicate noun or predicate adjective. The predicate noun renames the subject; the predicate adjective describes the subject.

Inverted Order

In the sentence patterns above, the subject comes before the verb. In a few types of sentences, such as those below, the subject comes *after* the verb.

LV ┌─S─┐ ┌ PN ┐
Is Larisa a poet? (A question)

LV ┌── S ──┐
There was a meeting. (A sentence beginning with "there")

Exercise

Sentence Problems

This section looks at potential trouble spots and sentence problems. For more information about English sentences, their parts, and how to construct them see pages **637** through **644** in the handbook. Pages **645** through **656** cover the types of problems and errors found in English writing. The guide to avoiding sentence problems found on page **656** is an excellent editing tool.

670.1

Double Negatives

When making a sentence negative, use *not* or another negative adverb (*never, rarely, hardly, seldom,* and so on), but not both. Using both results in a double negative (see **655.4**).

670.2

Subject-Verb Agreement

Be sure the subject and verb in every clause agree in person and number.

- The **student was** rewarded for her hard work.
  The **students were** rewarded for their hard work.
  The **instructor**, as well as the students, **is** expected to attend the orientation.
  The **students**, as well as the instructor, **are** expected to attend the orientation.

670.3

Omitted Words

Do not omit subjects or the expletives *there* or *it*. In all English clauses and sentences (except imperatives, where the subject *you* is understood), there must be a subject.

- Your mother was very quiet; **she** seemed to be upset.
  NOT THIS: Your mother was very quiet; seemed to be upset.

  There is not much time left.
  NOT THIS: Not much time left.

  It is well known that fruits and grains are good for you.
  NOT THIS: Well known that fruits and grains are good for you.

670.4

Repeated Words

Do not repeat the subject of a clause or sentence.

- The doctor prescribed an antibiotic.
  NOT THIS: The doctor, **she** prescribed an antibiotic.

Do not repeat an object in an adjective clause.

- I forgot the flowers that I intended to give to my hosts.
  NOT THIS: I forgot the flowers that I intended to give **them** to my hosts.

Note: Sometimes the beginning relative pronoun is omitted but understood.

- I forgot the flowers I intended to give to my hosts.
  (The relative pronoun *that* is omitted.)

Conditional Sentences

671.1

Conditional sentences express a situation requiring that a condition be met in order to be true. Selecting the correct verb tense for use in the two clauses of a conditional sentence can be problematic. Below you will find an explanation of the three types of conditional sentences and the verb tenses that are needed to form them.

1. **Factual conditionals:** The conditional clause begins with *if, when, whenever,* or a similar expression. Furthermore, the verbs in the conditional clause and the main clause should be in the same tense.
   - **Whenever** we **had** time, we **took** a break and **went** for a swim.

2. **Predictive conditionals** express future conditions and possible results. The conditional clause begins with *if* or *unless* and has a present tense verb. The main clause uses a modal (*will, can, should, may, might*) plus the base form of the verb.
   - **Unless** we **find** a better deal, we **will buy** this sound system.

3. **Hypothetical past conditionals** describe a situation that is unlikely to happen or that is contrary to fact. To describe situations in the past, the verb in the conditional clause is in the past perfect tense, and the verb in the main clause is formed from *would have, could have,* or *might have* plus the past participle.
   - **If** we **had started out** earlier, we **would have arrived** on time.

Note: If the hypothetical situation is a present or future one, the verb in the conditional clause is in the past tense, and the verb in the main clause is formed from *would, could,* or *might* plus the base form of the verb.
   - **If** we **bought** groceries once a week, we **would** not **have** to go to the store so often.

Quoted and Reported Speech

671.2

Quoted speech is the use of exact words from another source in your own writing; you must enclose these words in quotation marks. It is also possible to report nearly exact words without quotation marks. This is called **reported speech**, or indirect quotation. (See pages **582–583** for a review of the use of quotation marks.)
- **Direct quotation:** Felicia said, "Don't worry about tomorrow."
- **Indirect quotation:** Felicia said that you don't have to worry about tomorrow.

In the case of a question, when a direct quotation is changed to an indirect quotation, the question mark is not needed.
- **Direct quotation:** Ahmad asked, "Which of you will give me a hand?"
- **Indirect quotation:** Ahmad asked which of us would give him a hand.

Notice how pronouns are often changed in indirect quotations.
- **Direct quotation:** My friends said, "**You**'re crazy."
- **Indirect quotation:** My friends said that **I** was crazy.

Note: In academic writing, the use of another source's spoken or written words in one's own writing without proper acknowledgment is called *plagiarism.* Plagiarism is severely penalized in academic situations. (See pages **478–481**.)

Numbers, Word Parts, and Idioms

Numbers

Exercise

As a multilingual/ESL learner, you may be accustomed to a way of writing numbers that is different than the way it is done in North America. Become familiar with the North American conventions for writing numbers. Pages **595** and **596** show you how numbers are written and punctuated in both word and numeral form.

672.1
Using Punctuation with Numerals

Note that the **period** is used to express percentages (5.5%, 75.9%) and the **comma** is used to organize large numbers into units (7,000; 23,100; 231,990,000). Commas are not used, however, in writing the year (2002).

672.2
Cardinal Numbers

Cardinal numbers are used when counting a number of parts or objects. Cardinal numbers can be used as nouns (she counted to **ten**), pronouns (I invited many guests, but only **three** came), or adjectives (there are **ten** boys here).

Write out in words the numbers one through one hundred. Numbers 101 and greater are often written as numerals. (See **595.1**.)

672.3
Ordinal Numbers

Ordinal numbers show place or succession in a series: the fourth row, the twenty-first century, the tenth time, and so on. Ordinal numbers are used to talk about the parts into which a whole can be divided, such as a fourth or a tenth, and as the denominator in fractions, such as one-fourth or three-fifths. Written fractions can also be used as nouns (I gave him **four-fifths**) or as adjectives (a **four-fifths** majority).

Note: See the list below for names and symbols of the first twenty-five ordinal numbers. Consult a college dictionary for a complete list of cardinal and ordinal numbers.

First	1st	Tenth	10th	Nineteenth	19th
Second	2nd	Eleventh	11th	Twentieth	20th
Third	3rd	Twelfth	12th	Twenty-first	21st
Fourth	4th	Thirteenth	13th	Twenty-second	22nd
Fifth	5th	Fourteenth	14th	Twenty-third	23rd
Sixth	6th	Fifteenth	15th	Twenty-fourth	24th
Seventh	7th	Sixteenth	16th	Twenty-fifth	25th
Eighth	8th	Seventeenth	17th		
Ninth	9th	Eighteenth	18th		

Prefixes, Suffixes, and Roots

Following is a list of many common word parts and their meanings. Learning them can help you determine the meaning of unfamiliar words as you come across them in your reading. For instance, if you know that "hemi" means "half," you can conclude that "hemisphere" means "half of a sphere."

Prefixes	Meaning
a, an	not, without
anti, ant	against
co, con, com	together, with
di	two, twice
dis, dif	apart, away
ex, e, ec, ef	out
hemi, semi	half
il, ir, in, im	not
inter	between
intra	within
multi	many
non	not
ob, of, op, oc	toward, against
per	throughout
post	after
super, supr	above, more
trans, tra	across, beyond
tri	three
uni	one

Suffixes	Meaning
able, ible	able, can do
age	act of, state of
al	relating to
ate	cause, make
en	made of
ence, ency	action, quality
esis, osis	action, process
ice	condition, quality
ile	relating to
sion, tion	act of, state of
ish	resembling
ment	act of, state of
ology	study, theory
ous	full of, having
some	like, tending to
tude	state of
ward	in the direction of

Roots	Meaning	Roots	Meaning
acu	sharp	ject	throw
am, amor	love, liking	log, ology	word, study, speech
anthrop	man	man	hand
aster, astr	star	micro	small
auto	self	mit, miss	send
biblio	book	nom	law, order
bio	life	onym	name
capit, capt	head	path, pathy	feeling, suffering
chron	time	rupt	break
cit	to call, start	scrib, script	write
cred	believe	spec, spect, spic	look
dem	people	tele	far
dict	say, speak	tempo	time
erg	work	tox	poison
fid, feder	faith, trust	vac	empty
fract, frag	break	ver, veri	true
graph, gram	write, written	zo	animal

☑ Exercise

👆 Web Link

Idioms

Idioms are phrases that are used in a special way. An idiom can't be understood just by knowing the meaning of each word in the phrase. It must be learned as a whole. For example, the idiom *to bury the hatchet* means "to settle an argument," even though the individual words in the phrase mean something much different. These pages list some of the common idioms in American English.

a bad apple	■ One troublemaker on a team may be called **a bad apple**. (*a bad influence*)
an axe to grind	■ Mom has **an axe to grind** with the owners of the dog that dug up her flower garden. (*a problem to settle*)
as the crow flies	■ She lives only two miles from here **as the crow flies**. (*in a straight line*)
beat around the bush	■ Dad said, "Where were you? Don't **beat around the bush**." (*avoid getting to the point*)
benefit of the doubt	■ Ms. Hy gave Henri the **benefit of the doubt** when he explained why he fell asleep in class. (*another chance*)
beyond the shadow of a doubt	■ Salvatore won the 50-yard dash **beyond the shadow of a doubt**. (*for certain*)
blew my top	■ When my money got stolen, I **blew my top**. (*showed great anger*)
bone to pick	■ Nick had a **bone to pick** with Adrian when he learned they both liked the same girl. (*problem to settle*)
break the ice	■ Shanta was the first to **break the ice** in the room full of new students. (*start a conversation*)
burn the midnight oil	■ Carmen had to **burn the midnight oil** the day before the big test. (*work late into the night*)
chomping at the bit	■ Dwayne was **chomping at the bit** when it was his turn to bat. (*eager, excited*)
cold shoulder	■ Alicia always gives me the **cold shoulder** after our disagreements. (*ignores me*)
cry wolf	■ If you **cry wolf** too often, no one will come when you really need help. (*say you are in trouble when you aren't*)
drop in the bucket	■ My donation was a **drop in the bucket**. (*a small amount compared to what's needed*)
face the music	■ José had to **face the music** when he got caught cheating on the test. (*deal with the punishment*)
flew off the handle	■ Tramayne **flew off the handle** when he saw his little brother playing with matches. (*became very angry*)

floating on air	■ Teresa was **floating on air** when she read the letter. *(feeling very happy)*
food for thought	■ The coach gave us some **food for thought** when she said that winning isn't everything. *(something to think about)*
get down to business	■ In five minutes you need to **get down to business** on this assignment. *(start working)*
get the upper hand	■ The other team will **get the upper hand** if we don't play better in the second half. *(probably win)*
hit the ceiling	■ Rosa **hit the ceiling** when she saw her sister painting the television. *(was very angry)*
hit the hay	■ Patrice **hit the hay** early because she was tired. *(went to bed)*
in a nutshell	■ **In a nutshell**, Coach Roby told us to play our best. *(to summarize)*
in the nick of time	■ Zong grabbed his little brother's hand **in the nick of time** before he touched the hot pan. *(just in time)*
in the same boat	■ My friend and I are **in the same boat** when it comes to doing Saturday chores. *(have the same problem)*
iron out	■ Jamil and his brother were told to **iron out** their differences about cleaning their room. *(solve, work out)*
it stands to reason	■ **It stands to reason** that if you keep lifting weights, you will get stronger. *(it makes sense)*
knuckle down	■ Grandpa told me to **knuckle down** at school if I want to be a doctor. *(work hard)*
learn the ropes	■ Being new in school, I knew it would take some time to **learn the ropes**. *(get to know how things are done)*
let's face it	■ "**Let's face it!**" said Mr. Sills. "You're a better long distance runner than you are a sprinter." *(let's admit it)*
let the cat out of the bag	■ Tia **let the cat out of the bag** and got her sister in trouble. *(told a secret)*
lose face	■ If I strike out again, I will **lose face**. *(be embarrassed)*
nose to the grindstone	■ If I keep my **nose to the grindstone**, I will finish my homework in one hour. *(working hard)*
on cloud nine	■ Walking home from the party, I was **on cloud nine**. *(feeling very happy)*
on pins and needles	■ I was **on pins and needles** as I waited to see the doctor. *(feeling nervous)*

over and above	■ **Over and above** the assigned reading, I read two library books. *(in addition to)*
put his foot in his mouth	■ Chivas **put his foot in his mouth** when he called his teacher by the wrong name. *(said something embarrassing)*
put your best foot forward	■ Grandpa said that whenever you do something, you should **put your best foot forward**. *(do the best that you can do)*
rock the boat	■ The coach said, "Don't **rock the boat** if you want to stay on the team." *(cause trouble)*
rude awakening	■ I had a **rude awakening** when I saw the letter *F* at the top of my Spanish quiz. *(sudden, unpleasant surprise)*
save face	■ Grant tried to **save face** when he said he was sorry for making fun of me in class. *(fix an embarrassing situation)*
see eye to eye	■ My sister and I finally **see eye to eye** about who gets to use the phone first after school. *(are in agreement)*
sight unseen	■ Grandma bought the television **sight unseen**. *(without seeing it first)*
take a dim view	■ My brother will **take a dim view** if I don't help him at the store. *(disapprove)*
take it with a grain of salt	■ If my sister tells you she has no homework, **take it with a grain of salt**. *(don't believe everything you're told)*
take the bull by the horns	■ This team needs to **take the bull by the horns** to win the game. *(take control)*
through thick and thin	■ Max and I will be friends **through thick and thin**. *(in good times and in bad times)*
time flies	■ When you're having fun, **time flies**. *(time passes quickly)*
time to kill	■ We had **time to kill** before the ballpark gates would open. *(extra time)*
to go overboard	■ The teacher told us not **to go overboard** with fancy lettering on our posters. *(to do too much)*
under the weather	■ I was feeling **under the weather**, so I didn't go to school. *(sick)*
word of mouth	■ We found out who the new teacher was by **word of mouth**. *(talking to other people)*

Note: Like idioms, **collocations** are groups of words that often appear together. They may help you identify different senses of a word; for example, "old" means slightly different things in these collocations: *old* man, *old* friends. You will find sentence construction easier if you check for collocations.

Web Link

Targeting Trouble Spots

A sentence that is perfectly acceptable in one language may be unacceptable when directly translated into English. For example, many East Asian languages do not use articles, so these words can be a challenge to learners of English. The following pages will help you target trouble spots for your general language group.

Help for Speakers of Latin American Languages

Advice	DO NOT Write . . .	DO Write . . .
Study the use of count and noncount nouns (**657.1–658.2**).	I have three homeworks.	I have three homework assignments. (**or**) I have three types of homework.
Do not omit the subject, or *it* or *there* with delayed subjects (**638.5, 670.3**).	Is hot sitting here. Are going to the theater.	It is hot sitting here. We are going to the theater.
Place most subjects before the verb (**669**).	Gave I the tutor my thanks.	I gave the tutor my thanks.
Avoid using *the* with certain generalizations (**659.1**).	The business is a difficult major.	Business is a difficult major.
Avoid using *the* with singular proper nouns (**659.1**).	The April is the cruelest month.	April is the cruelest month.
Avoid double subjects (**670.4**).	My mother she is a nurse.	My mother is a nurse.
Learn whether to use a gerund or an infinitive after a verb (**661.2–662.1**).	The professor wants finishing the paperwork. She regrets to wait till the last minute.	The professor wants to finish the paperwork. She regrets waiting till the last minute.
Do not use *which* to refer to people (**618.7**).	The professors which teach English are here.	The professors who teach English are here. (**or**) The professors that teach English are here.
Avoid double negatives (**655.4**).	I never got no assignment.	I never got the assignment. (**or**) I got no assignment.

Help for Speakers of European Languages

Advice	DO NOT Write . . .	DO Write . . .
Do not omit the subject or *there* or *it* with delayed subjects (**638.5, 670.3**).	Are thousands of books in the library. Is okay to talk.	There are thousands of books in the library. It is okay to talk.
Avoid using *the* with certain generalizations and singular proper nouns (**659.1**).	I excel at the physics. The Professor Smith marks grammar errors.	I excel at physics. Professor Smith marks grammar errors.
Learn to use progressive verb forms (**660.2**).	I still work on my term paper.	I am working on my term paper.
Learn whether to use a gerund or an infinitive after a verb (**661.2–662.1**).	The students need finishing their projects. The professors finished to grade the papers.	The students need to finish their projects. The professors finished grading the papers.
Avoid placing adverbs between verbs and objects (**667.2**).	I wrote very quickly the first draft.	I wrote the first draft very quickly.
Do not use *which* to refer to people (**618.7**).	I am one of the students which sing in the choir.	I am one of the students who sing in the choir.

Help for Speakers of African and Caribbean Languages

Advice	DO NOT Write . . .	DO Write . . .
Avoid double subjects (**670.4**).	The professor she gave us an assignment.	The professor gave us an assignment.
Use plural nouns after plural numbers (**660.1**).	The class has two professor.	The class has two professors.
Use the correct form of the *be* verb (**627.1**).	The union be having a blood drive. We be going.	The union is having a blood drive. We are going.
Make subjects and verbs agree in number (**645.2**).	She have her own notes. They finishes on time.	She has her own notes. They finish on time.
Use past tense verbs correctly (**628.1–628.4**).	When the semester began, I study hard.	When the semester began, I studied hard.
Study the rules for article use (**658.3–659.1**).	I need to buy computer. Entrance exam is required.	I need to buy a computer. An entrance exam is required.

Help for Speakers of East Asian Languages

Advice	DO NOT Write . . .	DO Write . . .
Use plural forms of nouns (**657.1–658.2**).	I have three difficult class.	I have three difficult classes.
Learn to use adjectival forms (**666.1–667.1**).	He is a very intelligence professor.	He is a very intelligent professor.
Use the objective case of pronouns (**625.1**).	The tutor helps I with homework.	The tutor helps me with homework.
Include a subject (or *it* or *there*) (**646.1, 670.2**).	Is good to be here. Are many parts.	It is good to be here. There are many parts.
Study subject-verb agreement (**670.3**).	The course have a long reading list.	The course has a long reading list.
Study past tenses (**628.1–628.4**).	We study yesterday. At first, I don't get it.	We studied yesterday. At first, I didn't get it.
Use articles—*a, an,* and *the* (**658.3–659.1**).	I want to be nurse. Go to lab.	I want to be a nurse. Go to the lab.
Study conjunction use (**635.1–635.5**).	Though she studies, but she struggles.	Though she studies, she struggles.
Learn whether to use a gerund or an infinitive (**661.2–662.1**).	The students need helping each other study.	The students need to help each other study.

Help for Speakers of Middle-Eastern Languages

Advice	DO NOT Write . . .	DO Write . . .
Study pronoun gender and case (**625.1–625.3**).	My mother works hard at his job. Give she credit.	My mother works hard at her job. Give her credit.
Don't include a pronoun after a relative clause (**642.3, 670.4**).	The study space that I share with two others it is too small.	The study space that I share with two others is too small.
Place most subjects before the verb (**669**).	Received the freshmen the assignment.	The freshmen received the assignment.
Don't overuse progressive verb forms (**660.2**).	I am needing a nap. I am wanting food.	I need a nap. I want food.
Use the definite article "the" correctly (**659.1**).	Union is closed during the July.	The union is closed during July.

Credits

Page 15: "Seedy Beauty Shop" Copyright © 2006 David Perry/Getty Images.

Page 138: "That Morning on the Prairie," by James Schaap. Reprinted by permission of the author.

Page 140: "A Hanging" from SHOOTING AN ELEPHANT AND OTHER ESSAYS by George Orwell, copyright 1950 by the Estate of Sonia B. Orwell and renewed 1978 by Sonia Pitt-Rivers. Reprinted by permission of Harcourt, Inc.

Page 144: Bel Kaufman, "Sunday in the Park." Bel Kaufman is the author of the best-selling novel *Up the Down Staircase.* Reprinted by permission of the author.

Page 148: II from "Northing" [pp. 252-6] from *Pilgrim at Tinker Creek* by Annie Dillard. Copyright © 1974 by Annie Dillard. Reprinted by permission of HarperCollins Publishers.

Page 159: From *Newsweek*, July 29, 2002. © 2002 Newsweek, Inc. All rights reserved. Reprinted by permission.

Page 161: "None of This is Fair" from HUNGER OF MEMORY by Richard Rodriguez. Reprinted by permission of David R. Godine, Publisher, Inc. Copyright © 1982 by Richard Rodriguez.

Page 165: Debra Dickerson, "Who Shot Johnny?" First appeared in THE NEW REPUBLIC. Copyright 1996 by Debra Dickerson. Reprinted by permission of the Wylie Agency Inc.

Page 179: From *Newsweek*, July 12, 1999. © 1999 Newsweek, Inc. All rights reserved. Reprinted by permission.

Page 181: Anna Quindlen, "Our Tired, Our Poor, Our Kids." Reprinted by permission of International Creative Management, Inc. Copyright © 2001 by Anna Quindlen.

Page 191: "Two Views of the River," by Mark Twain, excerpted from Life on the Mississippi, 1883.

Page 193: Gelareh Asayesh, "Shrouded in Contradiction," Copyright 2001 Gelarah Asayesh. First appeared in *The New York Times Magazine*, November 2, 2001. Reprinted by permission of the author.

Page 196: "Like Mexicans" from *The Effects of Knut Hamsun on a Fresno Boy: Recollections and Short Essays* by Gary Soto. Copyright © 1983, 2000 by Gary Soto. Reprinted by permission of Persea Books, Inc. (New York).

Page 208: "Four Ways to Talk About Literature," by John Van Rys. Reprinted by permission of the author.

Page 210: Ann Hodgman, "No Wonder They Call Me a Bitch." First published in *Spy*. Copyright 1989 by Ann Hodgman. Reprinted by permission of the author.

Page 221: "Downloading Photographs from the MC-150 Digital Camera," from Van Rys/Meyer/Sebranek, *The Business Writer*, 1st edition. Copyright © 2006 by Houghton Mifflin Company. Reprinted with permission.

Page 222: "Hair Today, Gone Tomorrow," by Verne Meyer. Reprinted by permission of the author.

Page 224: "Campus Racism 101" from *Racism 101* by Nikki Giovanni. Copyright © 1994 by Nikki Giovanni. Reprinted by permission of HarperCollins Publishers.

Page 238: "Deft or Daft," by David Schelhaas. Reprinted by permission of the author.

Page 239: "On *Excellence*" from METAPHOR AND MEMORY by Cynthia Ozick, copyright © 1989 by Cynthia Ozick. Used by permission of Alfred A. Knopf, a division of Random House, Inc.

Page 267: From Meg Greenfield, "In Defense of the Animals," as appeared in *Newsweek*, April 17, 1989. Copyright © 1989. Reprinted with permission.

Page 269: Leonard Pitts, "Apostles of Hatred Find It Easy to Spread Their Message," *The Miami Herald*, March 28, 2005, Page 1B. Reprinted by permission of Knight Ridder/Tribune, represented by TMS Reprints.

Page 271: "Pornography" by Margaret Atwood, copyright ©1983 by O.W. Toad, Ltd. First appeared in *Chatelaine Magazine*. Reprinted by permission of the author.

Page 277: "Demystifying Multiculturalism," by Linda Chavez. Copyright © 1994. Reprinted by permission of the author.

Page 288: From SOUL OF A CITIZEN by Paul Rogat Loeb. Copyright © 1999 by the author and reprinted by permission of St. Martin's Press, LLC.

Page 291: "I Have a Dream," by Martin Luther King, Jr. Reprinted by arrangement with the Estate of Martin Luther King, Jr., c/o Writer's House as agent for the proprietor, New York, NY. Copyright © 1963 Martin Luther King., Jr., copyright renewed 1991 Coretta Scott King.

Page 295: Jack G. Shaheen, "The Media's Image of Arabs." *Newsweek*, February 29, 1988. Reprinted by permission of the author, Professor of Mass Communications Emeritus at SIU Edwardsville.

Page 306: Anna Quindlen, "Uncle Sam and Aunt Samantha." from *Newsweek*, November 5, 2001. Reprinted by permission of International Creative Management, Inc. Copyright © 2001 by Anna Quindlen.

Page 309: "The Media and the Ethics of Cloning," by Leigh Turner, as appeared in *The Chronicle of Higher Education*, September 26, 1997. Reprinted by permission of Dr. Leigh Turner, Assistant Professor, Biomedical Ethics Unit and Department of Social Studies of Medicine at McGill University.

Page 323: "'Scab!'" by Randall VanderMey. Reprinted by permission of the author.

Page 325: "Teachers' Classroom Strategies Should Recognize that Men and Women Use Language Differently," by Deborah Tannen, *The Chronicle of Higher Education*, June 19, 1991. Copyright Deborah Tannen. Reprinted by permission.

Page 401: Museum of Flight ®, Seattle. Reprinted with permission.

Page 408: As appeared on web.mit.edu/aeroastro/pcuav

Pages 462, 463, and 464: © 2005 EBSCO Publishing. All rights reserved.

Page 468: Reprinted by permission of CNN ImageSource.

Pages 472 and 473: © LII.ORG. Reprinted with permission.

Page 487: © 2005 Ask Jeeves, Inc.

Index